The Cost of Counterterrorism

Power, Politics, and Liberty

LAURA K. DONOHUE
Stanford University

CAMBRIDGE
UNIVERSITY PRESS

CAMBRIDGE UNIVERSITY PRESS
Cambridge, New York, Melbourne, Madrid, Cape Town, Singapore, São Paulo, Delhi

Cambridge University Press
32 Avenue of the Americas, New York, NY 10013-2473, USA

www.cambridge.org
Information on this title: www.cambridge.org/9780521605878

First published 2008

Printed in the United States of America

A catalog record for this publication is available from the British Library.

Library of Congress Cataloging in Publication Data

Donohue, Laura K., 1969–
The cost of counterterrorism: power, politics, and liberty / Laura K. Donohue.
    p.   cm.
Includes bibliographical references and index.
ISBN 978-0-521-84444-4 (hardback) – ISBN 978-0-521-60587-8 (pbk.)
1. National security – Law and legislation – United States. 2. Civil rights – United States.
3. Terrorism – United States – Prevention.   4. National security – Law and legislation –
Great Britain.   5. Terrorism – Great Britain – Prevention.   6. Terrorism – Prevention –
International cooperation.   I. Title.
KF4850.D66   2008
343.73′.01–dc22   2007041286

ISBN   978-0-521-84444-4 hardback
ISBN   978-0-521-60587-8 paperback

Dedicated to
Tansel
Jasmine and
Ayla Rose

Contents

Acknowledgments

This research began six years ago with a grant from the Carnegie Corporation of New York. I am grateful to Dorothy Zinberg for her nomination to the Carnegie Scholars program, to Vartan Gregorian for funding *Security and Freedom in the Face of Terrorism*, and to Patricia Rosenfield for her encouragement throughout the project.

Christopher Chyba and Scott Sagan, the Co-Directors at Stanford University's Center for International Security and Cooperation, provided me with the opportunity to take up the Carnegie project at Stanford. I appreciate the support they have given my work from that time forward. At the Institute for International Studies (later the Freeman-Spogli Institute), my colleagues – particularly Fiona Adamson, Coit Blacker, George Bunn, Lynn Eden, Jim Fearon, Deborah Gordon, Ron Hassner, Sig Hecker, David Holloway, Gail Lapidus, Michael May, Michael McFaul, Khalid Medani, Norman Naimark, Charles Perrow, William Perry, Jake Shapiro, Helen Stacy, Stephen Stedman, and Dean Wilkening – challenged and encouraged me. I have learned a tremendous amount from them and FSI's vibrant intellectual community. I also am grateful to Byron Bland and the Stanford Center on International Conflict and Negotiation for providing me with a fellowship in 2005–06, during which I further developed my ideas.

In the course of writing this book, I worked out various portions of the legal history and arguments in a handful of shorter articles. Barbara Babcock, Mariano-Florentino Cuéllar, George Fisher, Barbara Fried, Conor Gearty, Jennifer Granick, Tom Grey, Anthony Kennedy, David Luban, Eugene Volokh, Clive Walker, and Allen Weiner provided thoughtful critique on these pieces. The editors of the *Cardozo Law Review*, the *Journal of Criminal Law and Criminology*, *Michigan Journal of International Law*, *Stanford Law Review*, and *Terrorism and Political Violence*, as well as the edited volumes *Democratic Responses to Terrorism* and *Terrorism and Counterterrorism*, provided permission for me to revisit some of my earlier work in the ensuing text.

Paul Lomio, the Director of the Robert Crown Law Library at Stanford Law School, and the law librarians – particularly Sonia Moss, Erika Wayne, Kate Wilko, and Naheed Zaheer – have, for the past five years, provided research space, helped locate important documents, and alerted me to new sources of information. Christine Su, my research assistant, helped obtain materials used in the text. Diana Jansons-Quihuis, Joyce Jiawan, and Mary Ann Rundell kindly provided administrative assistance. In addition, I thank my editors – John Haslam at Cambridge University Press, and Phoebe Hoss – for their suggestions and patience throughout this process.

In October 2006 a number of friends and colleagues held my feet to the fire in a final manuscript review. David Ball, Farah Brelvi, Martha Crenshaw, Lynn Eden, Tom Grey, Ron Hassner, David Holloway, Matt Kramer, Richard Rhodes, Derek Shaffer, Peter Stansky, Kathleen Sullivan, Eugene Volokh, and Clive Walker offered sound critique. Robert Weisberg not only participated in the review, but provided advice throughout the book project. I am grateful to him and to Barbara Fried and Larry Kramer, who helped me to secure summer funding to complete the first draft. Additionally, Gerhard Casper and Lord Lloyd of Berwick kindly read the manuscript and provided valuable suggestions.

It was as a Fellow at Stanford Law School's Constitutional Law Center that I completed the book. Kathleen Sullivan has been unfailingly supportive, challenging my ideas and giving me the opportunity to delve into new areas. It is because of Peter Bing's generosity that I was able to take up the fellowship and finish this volume. I sincerely thank him for his advice, guidance, and friendship.

Finally, I could neither have done the research nor written this book without Tansel Ozyar's support. Jasmine Aileen and Ayla Rose give meaning to life, and it is to them, and to Tansel, that I dedicate this work.

Laura K. Donohue
Stanford, California
December 10, 2007

The Perilous Dichotomy

"In times of danger, the weight of concerns for public safety increases relative to that of liberty concerns, and civil liberties are narrowed. In safer times, the balance shifts the other way and civil liberties are broadened."

Judge Richard Posner, US Seventh Circuit Court of Appeals, 2006

"Civil liberties are a vital part of our country, and of our world. But the most basic liberty of all is the right of the ordinary citizen to go about their business free from fear or terror."

Prime Minister Tony Blair, 2001

"I think that the [1974] Terrorism Act helped to both steady opinion and to provide some additional protection. I do not regret having introduced it. But I would have been horrified to have been told at the time that it would still be law nearly two decades later . . . It should teach one to be careful about justifying something on the ground that it is only for a short time."

Baron Jenkins of Hillhead, former UK Home Secretary, 1991

Six days after the attacks on the World Trade Center and the Pentagon, Representative James Sensenbrenner, Chair of the House Judiciary Committee, stepped out of the shower in his home in Wisconsin and overheard a familiar voice on television: Attorney General John Ashcroft was calling on Congress to pass the administration's antiterrorism legislation within a week. Sensenbrenner, for whom this bill came as something of a surprise, immediately got on the telephone to demand a copy of it. The draft, which arrived by fax, numbered hundreds of pages and included, *inter alia*, the indefinite suspension of the writ of habeas corpus in the United States. Sensenbrenner sat down on his porch and put a red line through the measure.[1]

The next six weeks became an exercise in high politics.[2] The executive branch sought significantly broader powers and insisted on haste. In the Senate, the administration's bill bypassed committee markup and went straight behind closed doors. The House held only one hearing, at which Attorney General

Ashcroft served as the sole witness.[3] At 3:45 a.m. on October 12, the morning of the vote, the final bill reached print. The 342-page document amended fifteen federal statutes.[4] Legislators, many of whom were unable even to read the text, were given only the opportunity to vote thumbs up or thumbs down – with no chance of further amendment.[5] Dennis Hastert, the Speaker of the House, ruled out of order the one legislator who tried to debate parts of the act.[6]

Nevertheless, the legislation commanded nearly 80 percent of the vote: 337 Representatives voted for the measure, and only 79 objected. The numbers in the Senate were even more extreme: 96 cast their vote in favor, whereas only 1 – Russ Feingold, a Democrat from Wisconsin – objected. Ashcroft later announced to the Senate Judiciary Committee, "[T]o those who scare peace-loving people with phantoms of lost liberty, my message is this: your tactics only aid terrorists, for they erode our national unity and diminish our resolve. They give ammunition to America's enemies, and pause to America's friends. They encourage people of good will to remain silent in the face of evil."[7]

Despite Ashcroft's admonition, the 2001 USA PATRIOT Act did have an immediate and far-reaching erosive effect on civil liberties.[8] To make the statute more palatable, Congress placed sunset provisions on some of the most intrusive powers, setting them to expire December 31, 2005. But in July 2005, the House of Representatives voted not just to renew them but also to make permanent fourteen of the sixteen temporary powers – narrowly defeating an effort to limit the provisions to another four years.[9] Although the 2006 USA PATRIOT Improvement Act incorporated some protections for individual rights, it also expanded counterterrorist powers – and attached antidrug measures unrelated to the terrorist threat.[10]

This pattern is a common one. In the aftermath of a terrorist attack, the immediate assumption is that the incident occurred because the state lacked the information and authority necessary to avert it. The executive branch therefore seeks broader powers. And the political stakes are high: legislators are loath to be seen as indifferent to the latest atrocity or, worse, as soft on terror. Accordingly, the legislature grants the executive broader authorities, often under abbreviated procedures and without careful inquiry into what went wrong. Government officials claim that the new powers will be applied only to terrorists. To make the most extreme provisions more palatable, the legislature appends sunset clauses. But in the rush to pass new measures, legislators rarely incorporate sufficient oversight authorities. New powers end up being applied to nonterrorists – often becoming part of ordinary criminal law. And temporary provisions rarely remain so – instead, they become a baseline on which future measures are built. At each point at which the legislature would otherwise be expected to push back – at the introduction of the measures, at the renewal of the temporary provisions, and in the exercise of oversight – its ability to do so is limited. The judiciary's role, too, is restricted: constitutional structure and cultural norms narrow the courts' ability to check the executive at all but the margins.

This pattern is lost in the dominant paradigm that shapes how we think about counterterrorist law. "What is the tradeoff between security and freedom?" is the question that is posed most often. The assumption is that security and freedom align on a fulcrum, so that elevating one sends the other plummeting toward the ground. The dichotomy assumes that, when threatened, a state may deprive individuals of certain rights. And it implicitly limits the range of choices to only two: security, on the one hand; on the other, the freedom traded away.

These assumptions are troubling. Some rights are fundamental to liberal democracy and cannot be relinquished. Setting such rights to one side, the security or freedom framework fails to capture the most important characteristic of counterterrorist law: it increases executive power, both in absolute and relative terms, and, in so doing, alters the relationships among the branches of government with implications well beyond the state's ability to respond to terrorism. But this is not the framework's only omission. Missing, too, are the broad social, political, and economic effects of counterterrorism. The dichotomy also glosses over the complex nature of both security and freedom. The resulting danger is that the true cost of the new powers goes uncalculated – to the detriment of the state.

Focusing on these costs does not mean that no benefits accrue from counterterrorist law. Indeed, it is important to recognize where security is gained. In the six years following 9/11, no major al Qaeda attack has occurred on American soil, and in Britain, intelligence agencies and law enforcement have successfully broken up a number of terrorist cells.[11] This does not mean that every counterterrorist measure introduced has been responsible for these gains, but calculating such benefits is essential to instituting a strong counterterrorist regime. Sometimes this information is in the public domain; other times it is not. Statistics on the number of terrorist operations interrupted as a result of wiretapping operations are not provided in open source documents; nor is information gleaned from interrogation made widely available. Although this data may be visible to intelligence analysts at the National Security Agency or at Government Communications Headquarters and to interrogators at the US Department of Defense or the UK Ministry of Defence, it may not be available even to those with high-level security clearances.

This book, however, is not about the security benefits of counterterrorist law. Instead, it focuses on its costs, which the assumptions in the security or freedom dichotomy ignore. Here it suggests that the damage caused to the United States and the United Kingdom by antiterror legislation is significantly greater than it first appears. These two countries, moreover, are setting global counterterrorist norms and risk the transfer of these detrimental effects to other liberal, democratic states. Furthermore, it is in response to conventional attacks that both states' counterterrorist regimes have developed. The proliferation of biological and nuclear materials and their impact on the calculus behind the security side of the equation – together with a growing willingness on the part of extremists to sacrifice themselves – may drive the two countries to take increasingly drastic measures. The result could be a shift in the basic structure of both states.

SECURITY AND FREEDOM WITHIN CONSTITUTIONAL CONSTRAINTS

The constitutional structures of the United States and the United Kingdom shape what each country means by "security or freedom." In America, security and freedom tend to be treated as separate and distinct: policy considerations set against preexisting political rights. Thus, Judge Richard Posner, an eminent scholar and member of the federal judiciary, argues that, in dangerous times, concern about security grows and civil liberties narrow.[12] Constitutional rights must be adjusted to meet the demands of security. For Posner, it is a zero-sum game: "[O]ne would like to locate the point at which a slight expansion in the scope of the right would subtract more from public safety than it would add to personal liberty and a slight contraction would subtract more from personal liberty.... [T]hat is the point of balance ... [which] shifts continuously as threats to liberty and safety wax and wane."[13]

Professors Adrian Vermeule and Eric Posner also posit "a basic tradeoff between security and liberty. Both are valuable goods that contribute to social welfare, so neither good can simply be maximized without regard to the other."[14] They write that "in some situations, rational policymakers can increase security at no cost to liberty, or increase liberty at no cost to security. But it is plausible to assume that advanced liberal democracies are typically at or near the frontier already. In these circumstances," they suggest, "an appreciable increase in security will require some decrease in liberty, and vice-versa."[15] In other words, terrorism, one type of security threat, forces choices to be made that may restrict civil liberties.

This security-freedom framework marks not just the academic realm, but the public discourse as well. Former Attorney General Alberto Gonzales, for example, directed the US Attorneys to focus on "how we as a government achieve the balance between individual rights and national security."[16] The legislature routinely couches the issue in similar terms.[17] And although this dichotomy tends to be used to justify incursions into individual rights, it also serves as the dominant framework for opponents of expanded executive authority. Thus Professor David Cole argues, "[W]hen we balance liberty and security, we should do so in ways that respect the equal dignity and basic human rights of all persons and not succumb to the temptation of purchasing security at the expense of noncitizens' basic rights."[18]

In the United Kingdom, scholars and policymakers tend to consider security versus freedom not as a policy matter set against previously established constitutional rights, but as a case of competing rights. On the day of the World Trade Center attack, Prime Minister Tony Blair told the press, "[W]e have got to exercise the power and vigilance to ensure that [mass terrorism is] restrained and defeated. Now, I don't believe that is to act in contradiction of our civil liberties. I believe it is in part pursuing the basic civil liberty that people have to go about their business free from terror."[19] The Attorney General, Lord Peter Goldsmith, later explained, "[M]any ... rights ... are qualified and require a balance to be struck against the rights of others or the rights of society as a whole."[20] He continued, "I would suggest that the greatest challenge which free and democratic states face today is how to balance the need to protect individual rights with the imperative of protecting the lives of the rest of the community."[21]

This framework – of competing rights – is not unique to the post-9/11 world. In the early 1970s, when Westminster assumed direct control of the province of Northern Ireland, William Whitelaw, the Secretary of State for Northern Ireland, defended the 1974 Prevention of Terrorism Act by saying that, although it infringed parliamentarians' "shared concept of civil liberties. . . . [,] that is the price which the House has always accepted must be paid for protecting the most fundamental liberty of all – the liberty not to be killed or maimed when going about one's lawful business."[22] The Reverend Ian Paisley, the leader of Northern Ireland's Democratic Unionist Party, explained, "Where there is a terrorist situation in any country, the rights of the individual in the community have to be surrendered to a degree in order that his real rights may be defended and eventually maintained."[23]

To some extent, this framing of the issue – as one of competing rights – reflects the constitutional structure of the United Kingdom, where, in contrast to the United States, measures introduced by the legislative body do not have to comport with a written constitution. As Professor Albert Dicey, the British jurist and constitutional scholar, famously explained, Westminster has "the right to make or unmake any law whatever; and . . . no person or body is recognized by the law of England as having a right to override or set aside the legislation of Parliament."[24] Parliamentary supremacy means that Westminster can change any of its laws at will. Some statutes do carry special significance (such as the 1215 Magna Carta, the 1628 Petition of Right, and the 1689 Bill of Rights), but the statutes work together with case law and nonlegal rules to form the British constitution.[25] Throughout English history, rights have been woven through this constitution, creating a complex system of implicit legal protections.

Further complicating rights in English law is Britain's relationship with the continent, the European Community, and European jurisprudence. In the 1970s, English courts began to refer to the European Convention on Human Rights (ECHR) as an aid to statutory interpretation in English cases – particularly where the statute being considered by the court was intended to implement the Convention.[26] Judges were required to prefer an interpretation that rendered English law compliant with the Convention – rather than one that resulted in an apparent breach of it. But there were limits: where English law clearly departed from the ECHR, the courts did not defer. Instead, they simply applied the statute in question.[27] Where a statute was clear, the courts did not need to consider the Convention.[28] And although this requirement applied at the level of statutory interpretation, no commensurate requirement at the administrative level demanded that officials consider the Convention in exercise of their discretion.[29]

In regard to common law, the connection between English law and the ECHR was more attenuated. There were no clear rules requiring the courts to interpret common law in a manner consistent with the ECHR. Nevertheless, a number of judges have considered the ECHR to be consistent with – indeed, influenced by – English common law and so have drawn on European jurisprudence in their interpretation of the common law – a practice, however, by no means consistent among judges.[30]

European Communities (EC) law also connected Britain to European jurisprudence. The 1972 European Communities Act expressly incorporated EC law into the domestic realm.[31] Two years later, the European Court of Justice found that, because all members of the EC had ratified the ECHR, it was applicable to interpretations of EC law.[32] This precedent has been applied broadly – even where the ECHR has had only a secondary relationship to the issue in question.[33] Then, under the 1992 Maastricht Treaty, member states became required to act in accordance with the ECHR.[34]

Finally, in 1998, British law made reference to the ECHR even more explicit, incorporating it directly into domestic law. The Human Rights Act (HRA), which came into force in October 2000, carries the same status as any other act of Parliament. Yet it influences statutory interpretation: "So far as it is possible," all British legislation must be read or given effect by the courts in a manner compatible with the ECHR.[35] This binds English law even more closely to the Convention, but it is English courts, not Strasbourg, that make this determination.[36] In the event that Parliament does pass a contradictory measure, the courts cannot strike it down. Instead, the judiciary declares the legislation incompatible with the 1998 statute.[37]

As a constitutional matter, then, English law provides a variety of ways whereby the state protects a broad range of individual rights. The social-democratic tradition in Britain, for instance, celebrates – along with the right to free speech and freedom of religion – the right to welfare and the right to employment. Like the British common law and the ECHR, it also embraces the right to security – making the debate over security and freedom, as I have said, a contest over *which* rights should prevail.

The United States and United Kingdom thus interpret security or freedom in a manner that reflects their constitutional differences. Yet in both states, the dichotomy prevails. And in both countries, because this dichotomy ignores in its narrow terms of reference the fundamental and far-reaching effects of counterterrorism, it stifles the counterterrorist debate.

THE SHIFT IN POWER AMONG THE BRANCHES OF GOVERNMENT

The single most defining feature of counterterrorist law is hypertrophic executive power – power sought with increasing urgency when the terrorist threat is viewed through the lens of war. Much of the debate about whether certain powers can be granted, in fact, often turns on whether the struggle against terrorism is seen as war, as law enforcement, as some sort of Hegelian synthesis between the two – or as *sui generis*.[38] As a practical matter, though, states tend to use both national security and law enforcement structures to respond to the terrorist challenge. And regardless of which approach dominates, the structure is almost a constant: the executive gains strength while the relative authority of the legislative and the judicial branches diminishes.

The War Model Versus Criminal Law

On September 11, 2001, the United Kingdom's defense forces moved into high alert. Air traffic control halted all civil flights over central London. Security increased at government buildings, and police forces were placed on full alert. Prime Minister Tony Blair "offered President Bush and the American people our solidarity, our profound sympathy, and our prayers."[39] This was "not a battle between the United States of America and terrorism, but between the free and democratic world and terrorism." Blair continued, "We, therefore, here in Britain stand shoulder to shoulder with our American friends in this hour of tragedy, and we, like them, will not rest until this evil is driven from our world."[40] Nine days later, he flew to Washington, D.C., to meet with Bush. Blair explained to the press en route, "This has been the work of allies from the very beginning, united in these two objectives... Firstly to find and bring to account those responsible for the particular terrorist atrocity in the United States and secondly to devise the right agenda for action at an international level."[41] On September 20, 2001, Blair sat in the House of Representatives as President Bush addressed a joint session of Congress.

Like Blair, President Bush called for an end to terrorism. "[T]he only way to defeat terrorism as a threat to our way of life," Bush pronounced, "is to stop it, eliminate it, and destroy it where it grows."[42] It would be an international struggle: "This is not... just America's fight. And what is at stake is not just America's freedom. This is the world's fight. This is civilization's fight. This is the fight of all who believe in progress and pluralism, tolerance and freedom." He turned to acknowledge the British prime minister: "America has no truer friend than Great Britain."[43] His words echoed Sir Winston Churchill, who 55 years before had stood on US soil and sanctioned the "special relationship" between the two countries.[44] "Once again," Bush said, "we are joined together in a great cause – so honored the British Prime Minister has crossed an ocean to show his unity of purpose with America." He nodded at Blair, "Thank you for coming, friend."[45]

As the United Kingdom subsequently participated in military action in Afghanistan and Iraq, it appeared to be taking the same line as the United States in the global war on terror. When asked on September 12 whether he considered there to be a state of war, Prime Minister Blair declined to answer.[46] Four days later, after President Bush referred to it as war, Blair concurred: "Yes, whatever the technical or legal issues about the declaration of war, the fact is that we are at war with terrorism. What happened on Tuesday was an attack not just upon the United States but upon the civilized world." He estimated that two to three hundred Britons had died, making it "the worst terrorist attack on British citizens that there has been since the Second World

War."[47] The United Kingdom subsequently offered military support to the coalition forces in Afghanistan and, more controversially for the British public, Iraq.[48]

But these foreign policy decisions obscured important differences between the two nations, foremost of which was the primary lens through which the two countries viewed the terrorist threat. In the United States, a war model dominated. President Bush announced on September 15, 2001, that the United States was at war.[49] Three days later, Congress authorized the president "to use all necessary and appropriate force against those nations, organizations, or persons he determines planned, authorized, committed, or aided the terrorist attacks that occurred on September 11, 2001, or harbored such organizations or persons, in order to prevent any future acts of international terrorism against the United States."[50] The country subsequently attacked Afghanistan and Iraq. The executive instituted a wide range of wartime measures: categorizing "enemy combatants"; transferring terrorist suspects to a newly built military prison in Guantánamo Bay, Cuba; forming military tribunals in lieu of domestic criminal courts; and using the military to carry out a wide range of surveillance programs on US soil. In the security or freedom balance, the Department of Defense (DoD) placed exceedingly heavy emphasis on the former. Preexisting political rights, like al Qaeda, were the enemy – prompting DoD later to assert in its National Security Strategy, "Our strength as a nation state will continue to be challenged by those who employ a strategy of the weak using international fora, judicial processes, and terrorism."[51] This troika was to be guarded against, as even peaceful institutions were transformed into national security threats. Outside of DoD, massive bureaucratic shifts occurred: the formation of the Department of Homeland Security proved to be the largest domestic reorganization since World War II, bringing under one umbrella 22 agencies and more than 170,000 government employees.[52] Much of the subsequent debate about whether certain measures were acceptable centered on whether this war model was appropriate.

In contrast, outside of engaging in direct military action in Afghanistan and Iraq, as a domestic matter Britain answered the attacks of 9/11 – and, indeed, of July 7, 2005 – in a more restrained fashion, placing law enforcement above defense force capabilities. The British Government framed the issue as a "struggle" or "fight" against terrorism.[53] The Ministry of Defence would not suddenly begin collecting information on British subjects, nor would widespread detention follow. Not that extraordinary powers were not adopted – indeed, as I discuss in Chapter 2, the government introduced the indefinite detention of noncitizens and, later, control orders. But the new powers stopped short of drastic wartime measures. Sir Ken Macdonald, the Director of Public Prosecutions, explained, "London is not a battlefield. Those innocents who were murdered on July 7, 2005 were not victims of war." He emphasized, "We need to be very clear about this. On the streets of London, there is no such thing as a war on terror."[54] Although Britain did develop new bureaucratic structures to respond to the Islamist threat, the scale was more limited than the one adopted across the Atlantic. As discussed in subsequent chapters, the state largely continued or intensified counterterrorist policies already in place.

To the extent that the language used by the two countries' political leadership is more than just rhetoric, the distinction between the two approaches matters in at least two ways. First, the language used reflects the source of the authority sought by the executive branch. The British Government, for instance, did not claim royal prerogative in defense of its subsequent counterterrorist agenda. In contrast, the US president cited his authority as commander in chief and the powers conferred in Article II of the US Constitution as a basis for domestic and international action. (Section 2 of Article II states: "The President shall be Commander in Chief of the Army and Navy of the United States, and of the Militia of the several States, when called into the actual Service of the United States.") As validation, the president pointed to Congress's 2001 Authorization for the Use of Military Force.

Second, depending on the approach, the range of powers sought may expand or contract – the former where war dominates, the latter where crime takes precedence. For the war model sees terrorism as a curse on liberal democracy, a threat to "civilization." It emphasizes that acts of terrorism are more than criminality: they are an attack on the very institution of government.[55] Terrorists are enemies of the state. *Raison d'etat* dictates that, to defend itself, the government can adopt a wide range of measures, which may include missile strikes either in response or as a preemptive measure.[56] The military, not law enforcement, takes the lead. Waiting for reasonable suspicion and hard evidence risks making the state vulnerable, and so broader powers to detain, search, and interrogate suspects; place citizens under surveillance; and restrict speech prevail.[57]

Despite these broad distinctions, it would be a mistake to put too much emphasis on the war v. crime approach. Neither the war nor the crime model holds wholly true. The former incorporates a range of criminal law responses. And a state may treat some terrorist organizations as national security threats – and others as criminal organizations. Thus, US State Department Legal Adviser, John Bellinger, explained in February 2007, "The United States does not believe that it is engaged in a legal state of armed conflict at all times with every terrorist group in the world ... Nor is military force the appropriate response in every situation across the globe. When we state that there is a 'global war on terror,' we primarily mean that the scourge of terrorism is a global problem that the international community must recognize and work together to eliminate. Having said that," he added, "the United States does believe that it is in an armed conflict with al Qaida, the Taliban, and associated forces."[58]

Countries also change their approach over time. To some extent, the Clinton administration could be said to have followed a law enforcement model: the executive responded to the 1993 World Trade Center bombing and the 1998 East African bombings by pursuing terrorist suspects through the courts. When asked on Jim Lehrer's *Newshour* in 1998 whether this was "an ongoing war" or "a new war," Sandy Berger, President Clinton's National Security Adviser, replied that it was "a multifaceted effort." He explained that "part of that is law enforcement. Part of it is beefing up our intelligence. Part of it is stronger laws."[59] By the time 9/11 occurred, some 26 individuals had been found guilty by regular judges, in ordinary criminal courts, of complicity in these attacks.

In similar fashion, the United Kingdom has not always taken a measured approach to terrorism: from 1922 to 1972, the Northern Ireland government viewed Republican violence as an attack on the state itself, and in 1971, the Home Secretary declared that Britain was "at war with the IRA" – language echoed by Brian Faulkner, the Northern Ireland Prime Minister.[60] But in 1976 British policy shifted back to one predominantly of law enforcement. Northern Ireland's Secretary of State William Whitelaw instituted a policy of "Ulsterization" and criminalization: it returned control to security forces in the province and began to treat terrorists as criminals, not as political activists. Calling the violence "war" and the terrorists "enemies" elevated their status. In dropping the Special Category status for Republican and Loyalist prison inmates, Prime Minister Margaret Thatcher's government stripped them of their prisoner of war designation. Although over the next three decades British soldiers and special forces remained active in Northern Ireland – as of 9/11, there were still approximately 15,000 troops in the province, a number that had dropped by March 2007 to 8,500 – as a political matter a law enforcement approach dominated.[61] The state emphasized that terrorism is a violent, criminal act, a form of private power – not unlike organized crime.[62]

Neither model is exclusive. It would be more accurate to say that, although a broad framing may influence the source of authority claimed and the extremity of measures sought, as a purely descriptive measure, the United Kingdom and the United States tend to use military or criminal authorities as each state finds most useful.[63] Thus, Prime Minister Blair's Official Spokesman explained in April 2007 that Blair had always made it clear that, where necessary, military responses to terrorism were appropriate – as well as were political means.[64] The reason neither model fits is because terrorism is neither war nor crime. It is something different.[65] Yet its general effect on the state is remarkably constant.

The Expansion of Executive Authority

Surveillance measures in the United States enacted following September 11 offer a powerful example of the tendency of counterterrorist law to expand executive power (see also Chapter 4). For the DoD was not the only executive entity to engage in counterterrorism. The 2001 USA PATRIOT Act also increased the powers available to the Federal Bureau of Investigation (FBI) and the Department of Justice. It eliminated the wall between intelligence gathering and prosecution and expanded the state's ability to make use of the Foreign Intelligence Surveillance Act. Special administrative warrants, with fewer requirements than for ordinary criminal law investigations, could be obtained and used to collect information on Americans or non-US citizens. The USA PATRIOT Act also gave the government the authority to enter and search premises without notice.

This expanded executive authority has serious implications. The state may use the information it acquires not just for counterterrorism, but to prevent popular dissent, to manipulate the other branches of government, or to exert social control. Many examples in American history suggest that, to some extent, the drive to increase power is a function of the office, not of the political affiliation of those in power. For instance, President Harry Truman, a Democrat, bugged Speaker of the House Thomas Corcoran's telephone and recorded his conversations with Supreme Court justices Hugo Black, William O. Douglas, and Stanley Reed. After hearing the justices' views on nominees for chief justice, Truman went outside the Court to nominate his secretary of the treasury, Fred Vinson.[66] Attorney General Robert Kennedy, also a Democrat, authorized the FBI to wiretap opponents of the Kennedy administration's Sugar Bill.[67] The Republican Nixon administration attempted to use its powers to obtain Defense Department analyst Daniel Ellsberg's psychiatric records to use as leverage in legal proceedings after he leaked the Pentagon Papers.[68] President Johnson, a Democrat, wiretapped Martin Luther King, Jr., and Vice President Hubert H. Humphrey.[69] And the FBI files of 408 Republicans reportedly found their way to the Clinton White House.[70]

The tendency of the executive branch to acquire power was not lost on the American founders, who used the separation of powers doctrine to check executive strength. The problem is that in the face of terrorism the legislature's and the judiciary's ability to offset the executive is severely diminished. In a parliamentary system, which does not rely on separation of powers, in some ways the structures are more effective; in others, they present even weaker restraints on government initiatives in the wake of terrorist attack.

Legislative Failure: The Counterterrorist Spiral

One might well assume that the most effective check on executive strength would be the legislative branch, which does, after all, pass the laws whereby the executive exerts its authority. This assumption is unfortunately wrong, specifically in regard to counterterrorism. The power of the legislature may be severely limited at each of the three points where one might expect it to limit the executive: when the measures are enacted, when temporary provisions are up for statutory renewal, and in the exercise of its oversight functions.

Counterterrorist laws are, almost without exception, introduced in the wake of a major terrorist attack. Legislators must be seen to respond to protect the life and property of the citizens. Despite the United Kingdom's lengthy, thoughtful review of all counterterrorist law, and the passage of permanent counterterrorist provisions just seven months previously, the September 11, 2001, attacks spurred the introduction of Britain's Anti-Terrorism, Crime, and Security Act (ATCSA).[71] On the American side of the Atlantic, between September 11, 2001, and January 11, 2002, 98 percent of all bills, resolutions, and amendments proposed by the House of Representatives and 97 percent of those by the Senate related to terrorism. Congress introduced more than 450 such measures (compared with approximately 1,300 total in the course of US history). Within four months of the attacks, more than two dozen of these bills became law.

New initiatives tend to be broad and frequently have a sort of omnibus security character. For instance, between 1920 and 1922 in Northern Ireland – long before passage of the USA PATRIOT Act – political violence claimed 428 lives. In response, the 1922 Civil Authorities (Special Powers) Act, introduced to quell violence, empowered the Civil Authority to do the following: impose curfew; close premises, roads, and transportation routes; detain and intern individuals; proscribe organizations; censor newspapers and radio broadcasts; ban meetings, processions, and gatherings; alter the court system; and ban uniforms, weapons, and the use of cars. It granted extensive powers of entry, search, and seizure and, in a draconian catch-all phrase, gave the state the power "to take all such steps and issue all such orders as may be necessary for preserving the peace and maintaining order."[72] This clause led to more than one hundred new regulations, whose substance ranged from preventing gatherings and processions to outlawing the wearing of an Easter lily.

Not only do new laws incorporate a range of responses but they also tend to be extreme: no politician wants to be seen as responsible for the next, possibly more lethal attack. Part of the problem stems from the secretive nature of terrorism. Enemies are hidden.* Security forces operate with incomplete information. Unable to calculate the risk to the state, legislators err on the side of caution. As technology steadily progresses, possible harm increases, pushing political leaders further in the direction of the worst-case scenario – which tends to view security concerns as more important than individual rights.

Public sentiment also plays a crucial role. Moral outrage and emotional fervor reach a crescendo in the aftermath of an attack. The newsworthiness of the types of events considered terrorist – bombings, shootings, and maiming civilians – ensures wide publicity. Simultaneously, political leaders initiate media campaigns to demonstrate that they *are* doing something. But these campaigns may exacerbate the sense of public crisis linked to the attack and lead to broad popular support for ever more stringent measures, again privileging security over individual rights.

In this heated atmosphere, measures previously rejected, or considered unnecessary, often pass – as they did in respect to Britain's financial counterterrorist laws (see Chapter 3). In the United States, as I discuss in Chapter 5,

---

* This is the conscious aim of terrorist organizations. In the *Minimanual of the Urban Guerrilla*, for instance, a basic text for numerous terrorist movements, Carlos Marighella writes, "The urban guerrilla must know how to live among the people and must be careful not to appear strange and separated from ordinary city life. He should not wear clothes that are different from those that other people wear." CARLOS MARIGHELLA, MINIMANUAL OF THE URBAN GUERRILLA, available at www.baader-meinhof.com. The 1956 *Handbook for Volunteers of the Irish Republican Army* also emphasizes the importance of being able to move among the population, as does the al Qaeda *Training Manual*, recovered from a house in Manchester, England. The latter notes the importance of blending in by avoiding Muslim appearance and living in a manner consistent with the operative's undercover identity. *Al Qaeda Manual*, UK-BM-26, available at www.usdoj.gov.

efforts after the Oklahoma City bombing in 1995 to expand the FBI's investigative powers died – only to be successfully revived after 9/11; roving wiretaps, rejected in the 1996 Antiterrorism and Effective Death Penalty Act, were incorporated into the 2001 USA PATRIOT Act. Financial operations were subject to similar alteration, as I discuss in Chapter 3.

Not only are measures that were previously rejected then adopted, but new provisions may well go one step further. Thus, in 1972, Westminster refused to give the state the authority to seize private property used in the commission of a terrorist offense. After the 1998 Omagh bombing, new legislation provided for the state to seize any property used by a terrorist organization – regardless of whether the owner had known that the property was being so used. On September 10, 2001, U.S. Attorney General Ashcroft rejected a funding increase of $58 million that the FBI requested for counterterrorism. Following the attacks he called for $2 billion in new funding.[73]

In essence, at the point of attack, a recalculation occurs: terrorism's (limited) impact on rights is held constant, while the perceived security risk posed by terrorism dramatically increases – and eclipses other types of security concerns. In this context, pressure increases on legislators to support the new measures. Couched in terms of patriotism, failure to back the government becomes seen as support for terrorist entities – a dynamic notable in successive debates in the United Kingdom on the Prevention of Terrorism (Temporary Provisions) Act.[74] In 1983, Roy Hattersley, Deputy Leader of the Opposition, actually went out of his way to preempt the accusation: "I hope that our debate today will be conducted on the understanding that, whatever our disagreements, we all occupy ... common ground. Certainly I do not propose ... to accuse the Home Secretary of being negligent in the cause of civil liberties, and I suspect that neither he nor his Minister will want to accuse us of being irresponsible in the face of terrorism." President George Bush's post-9/11 warning to Congress echoed these sentiments: "Either you are with us, or you are with the terrorists."[75] Representative Sensenbrenner followed his redlining of the USA PATRIOT Act by carefully crafting a new, compromise bill with his Democratic counterpart in the House Judiciary Committee. But when the Republican leadership brought pressure to bear, Sensenbrenner abandoned the compromise bill and embraced the administration's version – later explaining, "The Speaker said to me that we had to do this for the sake of the country, so I reluctantly agreed."[76]

With security concerns foremost in elected officials' minds, new laws fly through legislatures under extraordinary procedures. In Britain, the 1974 Prevention of Terrorism Act was introduced on November 25, 1974 – four days after the Birmingham bombings – and received Royal Assent three days later, on November 28, 1974.[77] On August 15, 1998, Omagh sustained the worst bombing in the Troubles; just two weeks later, the Criminal Justice (Terrorism and Conspiracy) Bill lay before Westminster. Less than 48 hours later, it received Royal Assent.

In the abbreviated timelines and the heated atmosphere that accompany a terrorist attack, formal inquiry into what has gone wrong – and into which measures would actually be most likely to strengthen state security – becomes untenable. From 1972 to 2000, calls for a formal report on the state's use of the powers in the Northern Ireland (Emergency Provisions) Act or Prevention of Terrorism (Temporary Provisions) Act were seen as a retreat from the fight against terrorism. In 1981 the Opposition couched in careful terms even the mere suggestion that the government institute a review.

The irony, of course, is that by the time an inquiry does occur, new legislation, which privileges security concerns, has already been introduced and used. Yet, there may be many explanations for the success of a terrorist attack. In the United States, for example, al Qaeda may have benefited from a lack of information at the top of the FBI. Although Director Robert Mueller thrice denied any knowledge that terrorists might be training in flight schools, FBI Agent Colleen Rowley's letter and the leaked memo from the Bureau's Phoenix, Arizona, office later showed that at some level the organization was well aware of the threat. Or the problem may have been a failure to connect the dots: in addition to domestic information, British, French, and German foreign intelligence received by the United States warned of impending attacks. Or it might have been bureaucratic, linked to the divisions between the CIA and the FBI or to either organization's reporting procedures. Or it may have been resource-dependent – not enough money spent on training Arabic-language specialists – or related to political considerations. It might have arisen from the risk-averse culture, developed through past catastrophes, such as Ruby Ridge, the heavy-handed investigation of Wen Ho Lee, or the Robert P. Hanssen debacle.[78] Or it may have stemmed from the Bureau's orientation toward criminal law, not toward intelligence gathering: that is, the FBI may be particularly efficient where a crime has already been committed and agents can initiate a criminal investigation, but it may lack the right mindset where the aim is to look for a needle in the terrorist haystack.[79] In short, the hijackers may have succeeded for one or several reasons – none of which did the USA PATRIOT Act address.

For all these reasons, the introduction of a new statute therefore turns out to be *not* the point where legislators are in the strongest position to limit the growth of executive power. Instead, legislators hedge: to the provisions that have the greatest impact on individual rights and depart the most from criminal law norms, lawmakers attach conditions. New powers are accompanied by sunset provisions, which make them temporary. The basic idea is that the legislature will not hamstring the executive branch in a time of crisis – but will provide temporary flexibility until the executive proves that it needs the powers and can use them responsibly. The provisions will return to the legislative chambers for more full discussion when the country is not in the middle of an emergency.

Unfortunately, this approach turns out, more often than not, to be wishful thinking. It is very difficult to repeal temporary counterterrorist powers – an effort requiring the conclusion either that a level of violence commensurate with the last attack is acceptable or that terrorism no longer presents a threat. The former is unfathomable; the second, impossible to prove. Terrorism, in a liberal state, is always possible.

And so the temporary provisions become a baseline on which future measures are built, and laws are steadily ratcheted up that promise to ensure more security, but at the expense of civil liberties. The history of counterterrorist law in the United Kingdom clearly follows this pattern. For nearly one hundred years – despite long periods of almost no political violence – the state continued "temporary" authorities to deal with Ireland: the 1914–15 Defence of the Realm Acts became the 1920 Restoration of Order in Ireland Acts – which morphed into the 1922–43 Civil Authorities (Special Powers) Acts (SPAs).[80] Although violence ceased within six months of their introduction, and the first SPA was limited to one year, it was repeatedly extended and then made indefinite. The 1973 Northern Ireland (Emergency Powers) Act, which added further extraordinary authorities, was originally limited to two years but remained in force for twenty-seven before being made permanent.

To this pattern, the United States has proved no exception: in 2001, Congress made temporary sixteen of the most intrusive provisions of the USA PATRIOT Act. Five years later, as previously mentioned, the legislature made fourteen of them permanent – and continued the remaining two.

Thus, a spiral – not a pendulum – best characterizes counterterrorist law.[81] And in this spiral, special interests take hold. A state may use terrorist incidents to pursue agendas that reach far beyond the immediate threat. Furthermore, once enacted, counterterrorist measures create an institutional interest: intelligence agencies and law enforcement are reluctant to relinquish powers once secured – particularly if they can be used in other areas to diminish crime or other threats to national security. Administrative structures established to deal with a specific threat come to need to reinforce their own existence – or face extinction.

Passed in an emotional atmosphere, new counterterrorist measures tend to be written broadly and incorporate a range of interests. And these measures often creep into the criminal realm – by way of two mechanisms. In the first, legislation may limit the new powers to fight terrorism. The rationale is that because the powers are extraordinary, they can be justified only in reference to particular and significant types of threat. But once such measures are implemented, the idea of using them is no longer extraordinary – an effect apparent in the renewal debates of even highly contentious measures. In 2005, for instance, the House of Lords dug in its heels and forced the British government into the fight of its life to get control orders through Parliament (see Chapter 2). The Lords acquiesced on the condition that a longer debate would be held the following year. The debate never transpired.

Not only does the exceptional nature of the powers diminish, but they may turn out to be very useful – after all, they are not limited by the protections otherwise provided to defendants. Subsequent laws may thus explicitly transfer counterterrorist authorities to ordinary criminal law. In Northern Ireland, the 1954 Flags and Emblems Act derived from statutory instruments issued under the 1922–43 Civil Authorities (Special Powers) Act.[82] In 1973, at Lord Diplock's recommendation, the British government instituted juryless courts to try terrorist offenses in Northern Ireland; in 2003, the British government extended juryless trials to complex fraud and organized crime cases throughout the United Kingdom. The control orders in the 2005 Prevention of Terrorism Act soon were echoed in proposals to restrict individuals who were associated with drug-related criminal activity – but had not been convicted of criminal offenses. In both countries, finance provisions initially used for antiterrorism became applied to criminal networks.

A second mechanism allowing counterterrorist law to seep into the criminal realm derives from a lack of specificity in the original power granted: in other words, the counterterrorist law is written so broadly that it can be applied to nonterrorist crime. The emphasis here lies on the implementation of the statute, although the lack of controls in the original provision proves equally important. Again, many examples exist. The habeas corpus provisions of the US Antiterrorism and Effective Death Penalty Act of 1996 now figure largely in criminal law cases (see Chapter 2). A congressional report found hundreds of cases in which the USA PATRIOT Act had been applied to nonterrorist crimes.[83] In the United Kingdom, by the mid-1980s, 40 percent of the cases coming before Diplock judges had nothing to do with terrorism.

Along with primary legislation, secondary and tertiary instruments may be implemented in a manner that departs from the original intent. FBI guidelines issued in May 2002 allowed the Bureau to monitor Internet sites, libraries, and religious institutions – without any evidence of potential criminal activity (see Chapter 5).[84] Even when efforts are made to limit the broad use of powers intended as part of the state's counterterrorist arsenal – but not, as a statutory matter, specifically limited to terrorist cases – memoranda and other devices appear ill suited to the task. After passage of the USA PATRIOT Act, the FBI, for instance, issued a memo specifically limiting the use of National Security Letters (NSLs) to national security cases. But within a year NSLs became a routine tool of investigation in ordinary criminal cases. By 2004, the FBI was issuing some 56,000 of these per year.[85]

Where counterterrorist provisions seep into other areas, their impact on rights is troubling. Often, the reason why counterterrorist measures are allowed is, precisely, because of the extraordinary challenge. But what are the grounds for allowing the erosion of protections, such as probable cause as an antecedent for arrest, the presumption of innocence, and the right to a fair trial, when the extraordinary challenge is absent? As the Privy Review committee looking into the ATCSA recognized, "Counter-terrorist powers are . . . more likely to interfere with the rights of the individual than conventional police powers because they seek to preempt terrorism, that is to allow intervention before a specific crime has taken place, as well as to punish crimes after the event."[86] Yet, as the measures move to criminal law, the state's policy toward ordinary crime correspondingly changes.

Even if the legislature does not effectively limit the executive either at the introduction of counterterrorist laws or at their renewal, it could still push back through its oversight function. Here the United Kingdom and the United States differ substantially.

The British parliamentary system is not built on strict separation of powers. Because the Government generally holds a majority in the House of Commons, the executive and legislative functions are, in a sense, fused. Thus, although cabinet ministers are answerable to Parliament, the system gives the ruling party almost all power. Particularly between 1986 and 2005, a strong system of whips further ensured that the Government was able to advance its agenda. The Lords of Appeal in Ordinary – the final court of appeal (excepting, for example, criminal appeals in Scotland, for whom Scotland's High Court of Justiciary is the highest court) – also sit in the House of Lords, a parliamentary body. While custom dictates that the Law Lords recuse themselves on politically sensitive matters, it has historically allowed them to speak to a wide range of legislative concerns before the House. With this said, it is important to recognize that since the times of Lord Richard Wilberforce (Lord of Appeal in Ordinary 1964–83), Lord Simon of Glaisdale (Lord of Appeal in Ordinary 1971–77), and Lord Desmond Ackner (Lord of Appeal in Ordinary 1986–92), the Law Lords have not played a particularly active role in legislative debates.[87] (In some measure this can be attributed to scheduling: the Law Lords currently hear appeals during the same time that the House of Lords sits.) The permeability of the judicial-legislative divide additionally can be seen upon the conclusion of the Law Lords' judicial service: they face mandatory retirement at age seventy (or following special government extension at age seventy-five), but by virtue of their judicial appointment, they are life peers and thus able to shape legislation after their tenure on the bench ends. Executive, legislative, and judicial functions combine further in the position of lord chancellor. Until 2005, by convention, this position was filled by a peer, who served as a member of the cabinet and as both presiding officer of the House of Lords and head of the judiciary.

Despite the lack of a strict separation of powers, Britain does have a complex system that provides some check on the executive branch. In the House of Commons, the official Opposition forms a shadow government, ready to take power should the opportunity arise. The members of the shadow cabinet sit in the front bench of the House, directly opposite (and two sword lengths apart from) their counterparts in the ruling party. They criticize the cabinet's policies and offer alternatives to them. Although the Opposition cannot set the formal agenda, it can bring political pressure to bear, through the question-and-answer period and through legislative activity, to force the government to address specific issues, for ministers must publicly defend their policies and answer questions put by Members of Parliament. In at least some cases, there is cross-party support for Opposition party members to chair parliamentary committees as a further check on the government.*

In addition to the Opposition party structure, in the House of Lords a considerable number of cross-benchers affiliate with neither the government nor the

---

* Prime Minister Tony Blair, for instance, initially appointed a prominent Conservative Party member, the Rt. Hon. Tom King, to chair the Intelligence and Security Committee. The subsequent two chairs of the committee, however, the Rt. Hon. Ann Taylor, and the Rt. Hon. Paul Murphy, were both drawn from the Prime Minister's party. *See* www.cabinetoffice.gov.uk/intelligence/.

Opposition and take an active role in the debates. The Lords' legislative power, although less than that of the House of Commons, is not inconsequential: the ability to delay legislation even one year buys time for more considered treatment of a law.* As the constitution of the House of Lords changes to make it more accountable, its strength in relation to the government may increase.†

Added to the constitutional protections are a set of legal and institutional checks unique to the exercise of terrorist powers. For instance, the United Kingdom routinely uses independent reviewers – who are senior members of the judiciary, chosen for their stature within the legal community and appointed outside of political concerns – to issue reports on the operation of specific laws. Occasionally, formal, independent inquiries supplement these annual reviews. In addition, a Parliamentary Select Committee oversees particularly the expenditures of the executive branch – which includes the manner in which monies "below the line" are used by intelligence-gathering agencies; and special auditors examine all agencies that gather information on private citizens: that is, everyone from intelligence agencies and law enforcement to local boards and egg inspectors. Finally, an ombudsperson oversees complaints.

This complex web of oversight authorities allows legislators – and, to the extent that the reports are made public, citizens – to look at how the government exercises the powers it has been given. Although a certain amount of political jockeying may accompany select committee reports, the committees do draw attention to the government's exercise of its powers and serve as an institutional check on the abuse of counterterrorist authority.

Legally and structurally, the complex web of oversight mechanisms present in the United Kingdom is missing in the United States. In the latter, as a constitutional matter, the Framers sought to provide checks on the independent exercise of authority not by embedding government ministers in the legislature – or

---

* The House of Lords is weaker than the House of Commons: it can delay for only twelve months public legislation that originates in and is approved by the lower chamber; for "money bills" – legislation concerning government appropriations – it can delay passage for only one month. Parliament Act 1911 (1 & 2 Geo. 5, c. 13); Parliament Act 1949 (12, 13, & 14 Geo. 6, c. 103).

† In 1997, the Labour government began introducing a series of constitutional reforms. First among these was the aforementioned insertion of the European Convention of Human Rights into domestic law through the 1998 Human Rights Act. Labour also undertook reforms in the House of Lords, eliminating the automatic hereditary right of peers to sit in it. House of Lords Act 1999, c. 34. (An interim compromise retained ninety-two hereditary positions, elected, for the most part, by the hereditary peerage. There are now 751 members in the upper chamber.) In 2005, the Constitutional Reform Act provided for a supreme court to assume the responsibilities of the Law Lords and some areas previously reserved for the Judicial Committee of the Privy Council. Constitutional Reform Act 2005, c. 4. This act also stripped the lord chancellor of his responsibilities as Speaker of the House of Lords and head of the judiciary. There are proposals to further reform the manner in which lords are chosen: although general agreement has been reached on retaining the twenty-six "Lords Spiritual" (two archbishops and the twenty-four most senior bishops from the Church of England), it has not been decided whether the remaining members of the House of Lords ought to be appointed, elected, or a combination of the two. If the House of Lords does turn into an elective body, though, then one issue that would have to be addressed is its strength in relation to the House of Commons.

the judiciary in the upper chamber – but by dividing power among the different branches and offsetting them against each other. In James Madison's renowned words, "Ambition must be made to counteract ambition."[88] Individual interests had to align with the constitutional rights of the office; in this manner, government would be obliged to control itself.

This system did not envision, however, either a party system or a situation in which one political party controls two or more branches.[89] In such circumstances – particularly, where the executive and legislature are controlled by the same party – it can be extremely difficult, if not impossible, for Congress to perform effective oversight. In contrast to the Senate, where unanimous consent is required to change procedural rules, the majority party in the House determines how it will conduct business. For decades, the majority has chaired every committee and had the final word on what hearings will be held. So, too, has it controlled who will testify, whether subpoenas will be issued, and what information will be made available. Thus, not only are there no formal, independent reviews of counterterrorist law, but as I discuss in Chapter 4, even direct congressional oversight is limited.

This is not a new concern: Justice Robert H. Jackson understood that party power unifying the branches could trump the separation of powers doctrine. As Professors Daryl Levinson and Richard Pildes point out, in the 1952 decision containing his famous exposition of executive authority, Jackson also wrote a passage that failed to attract as much attention[90]:

[The] rise of the party system has made a significant extraconstitutional supplement to real executive power. No appraisal of [the executive's] necessities is realistic which overlooks that he heads a political system as well as a legal system. Party loyalties and interests, sometimes more binding than law, extend his effective control into branches of government other than his own and he often may win, as a political leader, what he cannot command under the Constitution.[91]

As an empirical matter, when the government is divided – that is, different parties control the different branches – Congress does tend to delegate less authority to the executive branch and to institute stronger procedural controls on that branch's exercise of discretion.[92] Levinson and Pildes suggest that, in addition to unified government, cohesive and polarized political parties also play a role: under such circumstances, "[T]he degree and kind of competition between the legislative and executive branches will vary significantly and may all but disappear."[93]

There was an attempt, in the wake of the 9/11 Commission Report, to establish a special body to consider the civil liberties implications of new counterterrorist provisions. After Vice President Dick Cheney vigorously opposed the initiative, the White House tried to head off Congress by setting up its own panel – entirely composed of senior officials in the administration drawn from intelligence and law enforcement bodies.[94] The legislature persevered and, in December 2004, established the Privacy and Civil Liberties Oversight Board, but political wrangling almost stripped this body of any meaningful role. It lacks subpoena power and acts in a purely advisory capacity, reporting directly to the president. The White House delayed nominations, allowing only one Democrat to participate. Fifteen months after being signed into law, the board had yet to hire staff or hold a single meeting. In neither of the formal budgets for fiscal year 2006 and 2007 did the White House allocate separate funding for the board.

The relatively undeveloped oversight mechanisms in the United States may stem in part from the absence of an ongoing domestic terrorist campaign. The United Kingdom has had nearly forty years in the current round of Troubles to develop bureaucratic structures to help it address the exercise of extraordinary power. However, the United States' oversight failure may also stem from its federal structure, which was established to create a balance of power among the branches of government – a structure that loses its effectiveness when a single political party controls multiple branches.

Limits on the Judiciary

With the legislature extremely limited in its ability to check and monitor the executive, it falls to the judiciary to push back on both branches. Sometimes it does. In June 2006, the US Supreme Court issued a 5-3 decision that established the Court's jurisdiction over the military tribunals established to try terrorist suspects held at Guantánamo Bay, finding that the special military commissions violated the Uniform Code of Military Justice and the Geneva Conventions.[95] At stake was not just the judicial branch's strength vis-à-vis the executive. Four justices averred that Congress holds the keys to establish such tribunals. Justice Stephen Breyer wrote, "Where, as here, no emergency prevents consultation with Congress, judicial insistence upon that consultation does not weaken our Nation's ability to deal with danger. To the contrary, that insistence strengthens the Nation's ability to determine – through democratic means – how best to do so."[96] In the United Kingdom, too, the courts recently exerted authority over issues related to life and liberty. In 2004, the Law Lords found the post-9/11 authority to detain indefinitely noncitizens to be incompatible with the 1998 Human Rights Act.[97] An extraordinary nine Law Lords sat, underscoring the importance of the case. The legal proceedings became a battleground for the distribution of political legitimacy – and authority – among the branches, as I discuss in Chapter 2.[98]

Only relatively recently, however, has the House of Lords begun to push back on the government in cases of national security; where it has done so, it has used the incorporation of the ECHR to strengthen its position. But even here there are limits: the Convention allows states to derogate from many obligations in response to the demands of national security, and the European Courts have exhibited considerable deference to the executive arm of member states when such claims are made. Although the 1998 HRA has special status, it does not amount to a written constitution for the United Kingdom, and the Law Lords cannot "strike down" a law as forcefully as their American counterparts can.

Traditionally, moreover, the absence of a limited, written constitution, in concert with parliamentary supremacy, has meant that judicial review focuses not on statutory validity, but on questions such as whether subsidiary measures fall within the remit granted by Westminster (the procedural doctrine of *ultra vires*).[99] The courts consider whether officials have abused their discretion under the law, and they also oversee the application of remedial guarantees.[100] The onus lies on Parliament and a rich common law history to prevent the law from infringing too far on individual rights; yet, as illustrated by the *Spycatcher* case in 1987, the judiciary often demonstrates great deference to the executive when issues of national security are on the line (see Chapter 5).* Similarly, in response to the 1988 broadcast ban placed by the Home Secretary – to prevent the transmission of support for terrorist organizations – the Court of Appeal noted, "The Home Secretary's decision... involved him in a delicate and difficult political judgment. It was a judgment for him and not the courts, who should intervene only if he took account of irrelevant matters, failed to take account of relevant matters or made a decision which was manifestly outside the wide spectrum of reasonable decisions."[101]

In the United States, since *Marbury* v. *Madison* (1803) it has fallen to the judicial branch to determine the constitutionality of federal law – a situation so ingrained in political culture that members of the other branches at times agree to laws that they rely on the courts to strike down.† In 2006, Senator Arlen Specter, the chair of the Judiciary Committee, told reporters that he would oppose the Military Commissions Act (MCA) because it was "patently unconstitutional on its face."[102] His chief complaint was that the legislation denied habeas proceedings to detainees.[103] He admonished the Senate, "Surely as we are standing here, if this bill is passed and habeas corpus is stricken, we'll be back on this floor again."[104] But when it came time to vote, Specter supported the legislation on the grounds that "the court will clean it up."[105] Specter was not alone: 13 of the legislators supporting him in his initial opposition to the bill similarly voted for the legislation.[106] The court's ability to "clean it up," though, was limited, as legislative constraints temporarily prevailed. Six months after Congress passed the statute, the Supreme Court declined to hear two habeas applications – on the grounds that the Detainee Treatment Act and the MCA

---

* In this case, the Law Lords found a general, long-term prejudice to the reputation of the security services to be a sufficient concern to meet a national security claim. It was not that Sara Tisdall's memo carried any value, but the mere possibility that such leaks *might* undermine allies' future confidence in the United Kingdom proved sufficient. [1985] A.C. at 357 (Lord Fraser) *See Attorney-General* v. *Newspapers Publishing Plc.* [1987] 3 W.L.R. 942, 946 (Ch. D); *A-G* v. *Guardian Newspapers Ltd.* (No. 2) [1988] 2 W.L.R. 805, 815 (Ch. D); and *A-G* v. *Observer, Ltd.* (C.A. July 25, 1986) (LEXIS, Enggen library, Cases file).

† In 2002, for instance, President Bush issued a statement announcing that although he had signed the Campaign Finance Reform Act, he doubted whether the legislation was constitutional, and expected "that the courts [would] resolve" the issue. *President Signs Campaign Finance Reform Act, Statement by the President,* March 27, 2002, available at www.whitehouse.gov/news/releases/.

restricted their ability to do so.[107] Although three justices dissented, and two others – Justice Stevens and Justice Kennedy – wrote separately that the applicants should return if the executive branch unreasonably delayed proceedings or imposed other injury, the Court's ability to act was weaker than Specter and other senators had anticipated.

The courts are limited as well as in the remedies available to them. Under Article III of the Constitution, the courts' authority is restricted to cases and controversies – meaning "the legal rights of litigants in actual controversies"[108]– which has come to include the requirement that an individual have standing: that is, be locked in dispute with the other party.[109] Although the richness of this doctrine is well beyond my immediate subject, of relevance here is the fact that the standing requirement may be difficult to meet in at least some portion of the counterterrorist authorities I address.* Consider surveillance. How does a person demonstrate that he or she is under surveillance when the very existence of the program is classified? Even when programs are known – like Total Information Awareness or the National Security Agency wiretapping operation, discussed in Chapter 4 – it may be extremely unclear exactly who is under surveillance, who has access to information about that target, and how those data are being used. Efforts to obtain this information through the Freedom of Information Act, as discussed in Chapter 5, can be blocked under the national security exception. Congress may be able to write into a statute the right to bring a case, but this right, too, must be tied to direct injury.[110] The Supreme Court, moreover, operates under the principle of self-restraint: that is, it avoids "unnecessary and inappropriate constitutional adjudications."[111] These include "generalized grievances" that may be of considerable and broad public importance – precisely the type of harm that comes from counterterrorist law.

The remedies available to the courts in terrorism cases – although marginally stronger in criminal law than in tort law – are still limited.† In the former area,

---

* The justiciability doctrine includes advisory opinions, feigned and collusive cases, standing, ripeness, mootness, and abatement. Political and administrative issues also come into play in determining whether cases ever even reach the Supreme Court. ROBERT L. STERN, EUGENE GRESSMAN, STEPHEN M. SHAPIRO, & KENNETH S. GELLER, SUPREME COURT PRACTICE, 8TH ED., (2002), at 809, citing C. WRIGHT, A. MILLER, AND E. COOPER, FEDERAL PRACTICE AND PROCEDURE, secs. 2539–35, (2d ed. 1984).

† In regard to torts, counterterrorism law affects not just individuals but groups – particularly minority groups with marginal political power. Although statutes like the 1964 Civil Rights Act 42 U.S.C. §1983 seek to protect such classes, they are not particularly effective for the types of injury sustained in counterterrorism. Such statutes assume that the harms are known and that victims know they have been hurt. And they follow the contours of private law, suggesting that damages may provide a way to obtain redress. Even the strongest case for reducing the harms sustained by counterterrorist law to financial terms – antiterrorist finance – presents problems. Compensatory damages would not address the social and economic costs borne by being labeled a terrorist. Yet even when the state is wrong – a difficult showing in the case of secret evidence – stigma persists. Neither are punitive damages a realistic option. *See Anti-Fascist Committee v. McGrath*, 341 U.S. 123, 162 (1951) (Frankfurter, J. concurring); *Ciraolo v. City of New York*,

some fundamental rights can be litigated. Individuals, for instance, may seek relief for violations of due process or file habeas applications. Since these rights are the ones judges will be more likely to protect, it is here that the courts may be at their strongest. At some level, though, these decisions may be symbolic: that is, a substantial practical protection may not be generated for a broad number of individuals. Nevertheless, the declaratory nature of such decisions – announcing, as it were, the constitutionality of certain acts – can be important: they may act as a deterrent to future executive and legislative actions. And, indeed, the more that counterterrorist cases bleed over into the criminal law realm, the more likely it may be that the courts will take on this deterrent role. But set against the vast amount of counterterrorist law (the USA PATRIOT Act runs to hundreds of pages and has generated tens of thousands of pages in the Federal Register), limited time and resources mean that only a minute fraction of the cases dealing with the exercise of executive discretion ever makes it to the courts' docket.[112]

In addition, like courts in the United Kingdom, the American judiciary tends to be reluctant to play too strong a role in cases involving national security.[113] The 1798 Alien and Sedition Acts made it unlawful "to write, print, utter, or publish . . . any false, scandalous and malicious writing . . . against" the US government, the Congress, or the president with the intent "to bring them . . . into contempt or disrepute" (see Chapter 5). Several lower court judges – including three Supreme Court justices sitting on circuit – deferred to the executive. The 1917 Espionage Act, amended in 1918, made it illegal willfully "to utter, print, write, or publish any disloyal, profane, scurrilous, or abusive language about" the American government, the Constitution, or the flag; it also banned "any language intended to bring the [same] into contempt, scorn, contumely, or disrepute."[114] None of the thousands of prosecutions under the act reached the Supreme Court until after World War I, at which time the judiciary upheld the convictions.[115]

Even when liberty rights are implicated, in an emergency or in wartime, the courts may prove loath to intervene. In both *Hirayabashi* v. *U.S.* (1943) and *Korematsu* v. *U.S.* (1944), the Supreme Court deferred to the executive: "The war power of the national government is 'the power to wage war successfully.' It extends to every matter and activity so related to war as substantially to affect its conduct and progress."[116] The Court would bow to the executive on issues concerning not just the movement of soldiers and repelling enemy forces but also "every phase of the national defense, including the protection of war materials and the members of the armed forces from injury and from the dangers which attend the rise, prosecution and progress of war."[117] The Court felt that it was up to the executive, in concert with the legislature, to determine "the nature and extent of the threatened injury or danger and in the selection of the means for resisting it,"[118] and it concluded, "[I]t is not for any court

---

216 F.3d 236 (2d Cir. 2000); *Joan W.* v. *City of Chicago*, 771 F.2d 1020 (7th Cir. 1985); *Hudson* v. *Reno*, 130 F.3d 1193, 1207 & n.11 (6th Cir. 1997).

to sit in review of the wisdom of their action or substitute its judgment for theirs."[119]

Although we should not discount the times the judiciary has pushed back, an important point is that in both countries, where the judiciary has shrunk from intervening, claims of institutional competence underlie the established deference. Britain's Law Lords repeatedly underscore this point. In 2004, Lord Nicholls wrote,

All courts are very much aware of the heavy burden, resting on the elected government and not the judiciary, to protect the security of this country and all who live here. All courts are acutely conscious that the government alone is able to evaluate and decide what counter-terrorism steps are needed and what steps will suffice. Courts are not equipped to make such decisions, nor are they charged with that responsibility.[120]

Thus, the government's access to classified information and intelligence assessments puts it in a better position than the courts to determine the appropriate steps to take to safeguard national security.[121]

Similarly, in 1936, the US Supreme Court recognized the president as the "sole organ of the federal government in the field of foreign relations,"[122] with jurisdiction over national defense and war[123] – areas closely related to terrorism. Early in the 1990s, Justice William J. Brennan, Jr., speculated that the judiciary's reluctance to interfere in the use of national security measures had to do with the episodic nature of emergencies. Peacetime jurisprudence does not include a tradition for defending civil liberties against particular security concerns and so fails to adjust until long after an emergency has passed. Lack of experience means that decision makers do not question the claims being presented; when they do, they lack the expertise necessary to determine whether the executive has overstated the threat. Judge Richard Posner draws attention to the absence of the courts' "machinery for systematic study of a problem. Its staffs are small. It has to wait until it has a case to begin its inquiry into the facts and policy ramifications, and the pressure of its caseload requires it to decide the case without being able to take the time to study background and circumstances and likely consequences."[124] He suggests that judges are generalists – whose "knowledge deficit" in relation to national security diminishes their willingness to question the executive branch.[125] "Judges," he writes, "aren't *supposed* to know much about national security; at least they don't think they are supposed to know much about it."[126]

Indeed, courts do frequently note their lack of expertise – even as secrecy, which increases after an act of terrorism, firmly falls within the legitimate exercise of executive power.[127] Judges routinely decline requests to review, for instance, the classification of documents.[128] And although judges have the authority to examine information in chambers, they rarely choose to do so.[129] Intelligence bodies consciously reinforce the barrier between the courts and national security concerns; in 1985, for instance, the CIA secured a blanket exception, exempting its files from classification review.[130] The USA PATRIOT Act extended this to include information held by the National Security Agency.

The central idea is that courts should not be in the middle of the intelligence-gathering business: "Even a small chance that some court will order disclosure of a source's identity could well impair intelligence gathering and cause sources to 'close up like a clam.'"[131]

Not only are the courts reluctant to intervene, but counterterrorist law often directly targets judicial mechanisms and reduces their role in the state's counterterrorist efforts. Special courts – such as the Diplock Courts in the United Kingdom, the Special Criminal Courts in Ireland, and military tribunals in the United States – may be instituted to address a terrorist threat. Certain powers, such as executive detention, internment, exclusion, and restriction (discussed in Chapter 2), reduce the judiciary's role, limiting the courts to simply reviewing executive decisions – a function with weaker standards than where the judiciary acts in a primary decision-making capacity. Even when terrorist cases are left in the ordinary criminal system, new rules regarding evidence, habeas corpus, and client-attorney privilege for terrorist suspects may further restrict the judiciary's role.

Some American constitutional law scholars see little that is problematic about this situation. Eric Posner, for instance, argues that the executive ought to be given wide latitude to restrict rights and adjust policies when national security demands it. Writing with Adrian Vermeule, Posner suggests that courts and legislators are institutionally incapable of second-guessing security policy and that trying to enforce ordinary law during times of emergency shackles government when it most needs flexibility.[132] For Posner and Vermeule, the judiciary should interfere only when particularly controversial measures are adopted.[133] If, however, the courts are allowed access to information, the argument that they are ill suited to considering national security cases becomes weaker, as I discuss in Chapter 6.

One final consideration in relation to the role of the judiciary underscores another important difference between the two countries: although neither judiciary – British or American – is in a particularly strong position to curb the executive, senior judges in the United Kingdom, as previously discussed, do act in their individual capacity in the exercise of oversight authorities. The annual reviews of counterterrorist law, annual audits of surveillance authorities, and specific inquiries established by the government offer concrete ways in which senior and respected members of the judiciary play a key role.

THE POLITICAL, SOCIAL, AND ECONOMIC COSTS OF COUNTERTERRORIST LAW

In respect to a state's political, social, and economic life – concerns masqued by the security or freedom dichotomy – counterterrorist law may bring to the surface latent tensions between the population and the state, or it may disenfranchise minority groups. It may play into the aims of terrorist organizations – while alienating important domestic and foreign allies. It may create bureaucratic inefficiencies and interrupt commercial activity.

The issue of privacy in the United States provides a good example of how counterterrorist powers may heighten tension in the state, undermining security in ways unrelated to an immediate terrorist threat. The USA PATRIOT Act aggravated privacy concerns, as I discuss in Chapter 4. By June 2005, 377 cities and counties in 43 different states had passed resolutions, and 5 states had passed condemnatory declarations, against the legislation. Even the targets of the 9/11 attacks – New York City and Washington, D.C. – condemned it. Forced on the offensive, Attorney General John Ashcroft instituted a speaking tour and launched a new Web site, "Preserving Life and Liberty" (www.lifeandliberty.gov), to defend the government's use of the legislation.

The privacy concern is not just academic. The United States has a long history of militias dedicated to preventing undue government interference in the daily lives of citizens. From 1650 to 1750, dozens of political riots and rebellions occurred.[134] Shays' Rebellion in the eighteenth century, for instance, stemmed from grievances against heavy-handed state initiatives. Increasing government presence may create a more explosive danger than the immediate terrorist threat such measures are meant to counter. Although some private militias operated in the 1970s and 1980s, it was in the early 1990s that the so-called Patriot Movement grew in importance. Spurred by the FBI's confrontation with white separatist Randy Weaver at Ruby Ridge in 1992 and with cult leader David Koresh and the Branch Davidians at Waco, Texas, in 1993, the militia movement subsequently seized on the 1995 Oklahoma City bombing as an effort by the government to force through draconian measures.[135] Congress did subsequently pass new counterterrorist law – the 1996 Antiterrorism and Effective Death Penalty Act – and the number of militia groups rapidly increased, peaking at 858 in 1996.[136] The number of domestic terrorist plots correspondingly exploded: from an average of approximately 100 domestic terrorism cases open per year prior to the bombing, the number increased tenfold in the following years.[137] The plans ranged from blowing up buildings, banks, refineries, and bridges to assassinating politicians and judges.[138]

Counterterrorist measures also may alienate important ethnic or religious minority groups that the state needs to counter the terrorist threat. Here, the supposed trade-off between collective security and society's rights grossly ignores the fact that the liberties of only some groups tend to be restricted and that the minority group that shares particular characteristics with those guilty of the latest offense bears the brunt of executive power. Napoleon, the pig in George Orwell's *Animal Farm*, puts it most succinctly: "All animals are equal, but some animals are more equal than others."[139]

There is a straightforward reason for this effect. If a measure is justified on the grounds that it applies only to terrorists, how is the state to identify the terrorist? Individuals involved in clandestine violence make a concerted effort to remain hidden. To try to ferret out those guilty of complicity in acts of violence, the state must use patterns and individual characteristics, which involve, at the crudest level, ethnicity, religion, gender, and age. For this reason, measures frequently infringe on the rights of individuals who have nothing to do with terrorism – as happened in the United Kingdom in 1971 in respect to executive detention in Operation Demetrius, which swept up many more men than had actually been involved in paramilitary activity (see Chapter 2).* Between 2001 and 2004, in turn, the number of Asians annually targeted in the United Kingdom by the police, exercising counterterrorist stop and search powers, increased 300 percent.[140] In 2003 alone, 12.1% percent of the searches targeted Asians – although they comprised only 4 percent of the population.[141]† Despite the concern of high-level law enforcement officers that racial profiling was taking the place of more valuable investigatory work, Hazel Blears, the Home Office minister, defended the disproportionate impact of the extraordinary powers: Muslims simply needed to accept the "reality" that, in the fight against extremism, they were more likely to be stopped and searched.[142] Prime Minister Tony Blair remarked, "[I]t is right to protect the civil liberties of the vast majority of people in this country."[143]

Such treatment makes the integration of minority groups into society more difficult and attenuates the minority's experience of the rule of law, for the procedural protections in counterterrorism often substantially depart from those of ordinary criminal law. Single-judge tribunals in Northern Ireland, for instance, shifted the presumption of innocence, lowered the standards of proof, allowed for secret evidence, weakened evidentiary rules, and tolerated abuses during interrogation. These measures alienated the Catholic community and undermined the political legitimacy of the courts. Even as such standards are relaxed, the redress available to those wrongly targeted often is minimal.‡

Under these circumstances, prominent miscarriages of justice – made more likely by the watered-down judicial standards – breed further resentment. As

---

* What makes such provisions ineffective is that not only do they demonstrate the state's ignorance of clandestine groups, but because terrorists frequently "go to ground" immediately before and after operations, most people picked up by the state in such broad sweeps have nothing to do with the central movement. Operation Demetrius aside, in the United States, following 9/11, not a single terrorist conviction resulted from the indefinite detention of more than 1,200 noncitizens within domestic bounds. Detention is not alone in ensnaring the wrong people. Illegal substance provisions in the USA PATRIOT Act, for instance, caught scientists and artists – not members of terrorist cells seeking to develop weapons. Tomas Foral, a University of Connecticut graduate student, made the mistake of cleaning out a broken laboratory freezer, and, finding anthrax samples collected nearly four decades previously, moved them to a new freezer. He promptly forgot about it – until the FBI placed him on a watch list and charged him with a violation of the USA PATRIOT Act. *See Bioterrorism: Student Charged with Possessing Anthrax*, May 25, 2007, available at www.sciencemag.org.

† The classification of "Asian" in the United Kingdom refers to individuals from South Asia – particularly Bangladesh, India, and Kashmir. A different designation is given to those of East Asian descent. British Sociological Association, *Equality and Diversity: Language and the BSA: Ethnicity and Race*, Oct. 26, 2005. Available at www.britsoc.co.uk.

‡ As the Privy Counsellor Review Committee commented, "Giving the authorities untrammeled powers to exercise against suspected terrorists may seem reasonable in the heat of the moment, until they are exercised against the wrong people ... and those at the wrong end of them find that the procedures for redress are inadequate." Privy Counsellor Review Committee, *Anti-terrorism, Crime and Security Act 2001 Review*, Dec. 18, 2003, p. 25.

David Davis, the shadow Home Secretary, observed, "In anti-terrorist law every miscarriage of justice is a seed from which anger and resentment grow."[144] Perceived miscarriages of justice – both in practice and in official acquiescence – may isolate individuals and persuade younger members of society to choose an ethnic or religious identity in opposition to the state. Such decisions may reduce the willingness of individuals to pass information on to the state while encouraging paramilitary organizations to increase their recruitment activities. Accidents, too, may take on significance beyond the event itself: on July 22, 2005, the London metropolitan police shot Jean Charles de Menezes in the head seven times[145] – an incident that became a lightning rod for the anger felt by Britain's minority Islamic community.[146]

Beyond the domestic social and political concerns, counterterrorism can affect a state's ability to pursue its foreign policy goals. Thus, the United Kingdom found that its response to terrorism in Northern Ireland – using some of the same techniques the United States later used at Guantánamo Bay (hooding, wall standing, noise, food and water deprivation, and sleep deprivation) – crippled its efforts to convince the Republic of Ireland to sign an extradition agreement. American use of coercive interrogation and rendition after 9/11 meant that other nations – including close allies, such as Germany – refused to extradite suspects to the United States. Likewise, the US decision not to apply the Geneva Conventions alienated countries and diminished their ability to openly support US foreign policy in a range of areas. It also undermined the rule of law – at a time when the state was trying to win other countries over to liberal democracy (see Chapter 3). International enmity took the form of legal challenge: US agents who participated in rendition now find themselves the object of legal indictments in several European countries.

Counterterrorism may retard the administrative efficiency of a state. The creation of the US Department of Homeland Security, as I have mentioned, required massive institutional changes at the federal level. Professors Mariano-Florentino Cuéllar, Charles Perrow, and Richard Posner have drawn attention to the result of layering so many levels of bureaucracy: delays, loss and distortion of information, turf fights, and demoralization.[147] From the Federal Emergency Management Agency (FEMA) to the Coast Guard, a range of agencies were hurt by the reorganization – raising concerns well outside the counterterrorist realm.[148]

Counterterrorist provisions may also adversely affect commercial growth. Laws meant to monitor border traffic to prevent the movement of weapons or illicit materials may severely hamper the transfer of commercial goods. Limits on the publication of basic scientific research may hurt a country's ability to pursue research central to the development of the pharmaceuticals and plastics industries. The withholding of patents on everything from cryptography to vacuum technology may hinder development in a range of industries. In the meantime, other countries, with fewer strictures, may leap ahead.

This is not to say that counterterrorist provisions with political, social, or economic effects ought never to be adopted. To the contrary, most counterterrorist laws have broader consequences, but by narrowing the terms of reference, the ability of the state to identify, and mitigate, the costs is limited. Consider, for example, a relatively minor concern: tourism. The United States followed 9/11 with a range of measures particularly hostile to noncitizens. And tourism plummeted. From $82 billion in US international tourism receipts in 2000, by 2003 the amount had dropped to $64 billion. A slow recovery increased that amount in the following years, but the country has not yet returned to its 2000 level. The difference in receipts from 2000 through 2005 – had the country simply maintained its 2000 level throughout that period – is more than $50 billion. The US pattern of tourism during this time is remarkably different from that of its allies and many of the top tourist countries worldwide. France, Germany, Spain, the United Kingdom, Turkey, and China show steady increases in tourism – some having more than doubled their international tourist receipts during the same period.[149]*

In focusing exclusively on security or freedom, the attendant effects on tourism went largely ignored. Yet, what would it have taken to acknowledge the impact of new provisions on this area and to try to develop security policies cognizant of the potential effect? With all 19 hijackers drawn from overseas, the state would still want to track foreign visitors to the country. However, it could go about it in a different way – for instance, running a simultaneous public relations campaign to make the United States attractive to visitors, perhaps establishing a fast pass system early on – and instituting special training for customs agents in dealing with foreign visitors. Identifying the costs allows for the possibility of ameliorating them through other, less harmful provisions.

THE COMPLEXITY OF RIGHTS AND SECURITY

Rights and security are far more complex than the customary trade-off implies. Restrictions that affect one right, for instance, resonate in others. Consider free speech and due process. On the surface, they appear to be two distinct rights, with different counterterrorist measures affecting each. Censorship affects free speech; indefinite detention, due process. But if a state were to continue to protect free speech while restricting due process, a person might be detained arbitrarily because of a suspicious public communication – detention that would

---

* Of the many possible explanations for the difference in pattern, some are more plausible than others. There is, for instance, a finite pool of international travelers, and increased infrastructure investments may attract tourists to new regions. Alternatively, travelers may fear that the United States will be the target of another attack. (If this is the case, however, then it is at least odd that the greatest dip in tourist dollars to the United States took place in 2003 – two years after 9/11 and with no intervening incident on domestic soil; while Turkey, Spain, and the United Kingdom, all of whom suffered al Qaeda attacks, did not see a corresponding decrease in tourist dollars.) But whatever the explanation, the fact that the United States's adoption of particularly aggressive anti-foreigner policies was followed by a notable drop in its tourist industry bears out my point that counterterrorism provisions may reverberate well beyond the security or freedom dichotomy.

render meaningless his or her right to free speech. Similarly, if due process were to remain unchanged and free speech, instead, limited, then lapses in due process might go unreported. Thus, changes to one right may have a snowball effect on the freedom of citizens to claim – and to act upon – other rights. Policies, initially treated as one liberty concern, thus end up affecting other entitlements: whereas extended detention may be considered a restriction of the right to life or liberty, it also – as I discuss in Chapters 2 and 5 – constricts free speech, freedom of association, and freedom of religion. And outright bans on political speech – prevalent in the United Kingdom, but largely absent now in the United States – have many unfortunate consequences for freedom of religion and association.

As for the security side of the equation, physical security from nonstate violence is just one type of protection. Other kinds of security may be equally important, such as environmental security or security against state aggression. Even within the arena of physical security, terrorist groups are not the only threat facing the state. Initiatives introduced to help the government respond to terrorism, like suspicious activity reports, may end up – as I discuss in Chapter 6 – hurting the state's ability to respond to other threats, such as money laundering related to illicit drugs. And attempts to mitigate the threat posed by one organization may change the threat from others. Terrorist groups themselves are not monolithic. Although they may try to use weapons of mass destruction, whether they could actually obtain and use them is impossible to determine with any certainty. Levels of security are constantly in flux – in some part because of circumstances completely beyond a state's control.

Security, moreover, may be undermined by inroads into rights, making it not a choice between security or freedom, but rather a decision to safeguard security *through* freedom. In Northern Ireland, the use of coercive questioning heightened support for republican paramilitaries. Aggressive questioning techniques in Guantánamo Bay, Abu Ghraib, and elsewhere increased support for Islamist movements and alienated important allied and nonallied countries that the United States needed to respond to a global threat. Antiterrorist finance initiatives drove remittances away from countries like Yemen, where the United States wanted a strong civil society to counter efforts by al Qaeda to gain ground.

Perhaps the best example comes from the free speech realm. Efforts to stifle microbiologists from publishing or transferring knowledge may hurt both countries' ability to respond to natural disease outbreaks – as well as to biological attack. In Chapter 5, I highlight the Bush administration's reaction to the publication of research conducted by scientists in Australia, who discovered that a simple genetic alteration to the mousepox virus yielded a 100 percent lethality rate. Although prior restraints may have been an appropriate response to developments in nuclear weapon design, biology is different: approximately 11 million people die worldwide, each year, from infectious disease.[150] In contrast, there have been only a handful of biological attacks by terrorists.[151] Protecting scientists' freedom to publish may make a state more, not less, secure.

Likewise, it is entirely conceivable that measures that seemingly violate individual rights may simultaneously preserve them more effectively. Thus, identity cards and biometric tracking may, by clearly establishing that a suspect was or was not present in the course of a robbery, make more efficient and fair the operation of the criminal justice system. In this way, security can advance liberty. Benefits from liberty-restricting provisions may include regulatory mechanisms to increase bureaucratic efficiency or the use of radio-frequency identification tags to ensure the more efficient shipment of containers or distribution of goods. Other counterterrorist provisions may not directly affect rights and may be effective: for example, initiatives such as Nunn-Lugar-Domenici, which address the proliferation of nuclear material and expertise, may be particularly helpful in reducing the threat.

The United States and the United Kingdom, prominent partners in the struggle against terrorism, confront many of the same policy decisions – not all of which are unique to the post-9/11 world. In 1971, for instance, the United Kingdom questioned whether Common Articles 2 and 3 of the Geneva Conventions applied to the conflict in Northern Ireland. The Parker Committee, which examined interrogation in Northern Ireland, decided that, whether or not they applied, the state was bound by them because a domestic Army Directive incorporated the Geneva Conventions. Three decades later, the US executive confronted the exact same question – and determined, to the contrary, that the Geneva Conventions applied neither to al Qaeda nor to the Taliban. The resulting vacuum created by the sudden withdrawal of traditional interrogation standards, as addressed in Chapter 2, contributed significantly to the subsequent coercive interrogation of prisoners.

There is much to be gained by looking at where the two countries converge – and where their approaches to terrorist challenge sharply differ. For despite constitutional and historical differences, the two countries share a common past and continue to face common challenges. They also both fall victim to the vicissitudes of the security or freedom dichotomy.

In this book I thus step outside the traditional framework to recalculate the price the United States and the United Kingdom have paid for their counterterrorist regimes. I focus on laws that have been promoted as increasing the security of each nation at the expense of five rights central to liberal democracy – life, liberty, property, privacy, and free speech. What, I ask, has been the true cost of these measures, for citizens on both sides of the Atlantic, over the past forty years? In Chapter 2, I focus on the provisions that most directly affect a person's life and liberty. I compare Britain's methods of interrogation, as well as policies related to internment, detention, and control orders, to the US's use of coercive interrogation and indefinite detention. Antiterrorist finance initiatives on both sides of the Atlantic that alter property rights ground the discussion in Chapter 3. In Chapter 4, I turn to privacy and surveillance. Free expression and restrictions on speech – such as treason, treason-felony, bans on political speech, and limits on knowledge-based speech – provide the nexus for Chapter 5. I conclude in Chapter 6 by suggesting ways to offset some of the most deleterious effects of counterterrorist law.

In the mid-twentieth century, Justice Felix Frankfurter warned, "The accretion of dangerous power does not come in a day. It does come, however, slowly, from the generative force of unchecked disregard of the restrictions that fence in even the most disinterested assertion of authority."[152] Frankfurter's premonitory passage resonates still, more than 50 years later. And it is not unique to the American context. Lord Lloyd of Berwick, a British Law Lord, recently admonished, "The safety of the state has always been used as a justification for undermining civil liberties. That does not happen overnight, but it will happen in the end, unless we are very careful."[153] It is my aim in this book to step back and consider how counterterrorist law has affected the two countries and to propose a way to counteract the perils of the dichotomy that currently shapes our counterterrorist discourse.

Indefinite Detention and Coercive Interrogation

"No exceptional circumstances whatsoever, whether a state of war or a threat of war, internal political instability or any other public emergency, may be invoked as a justification of torture."

CONVENTION AGAINST TORTURE, 1984

"The use of force, mental torture, threats, insults, or exposure to unpleasant and inhumane treatment of any kind is prohibited by law and is neither authorized nor condoned by the US Government. Experience indicates that the use of force is not necessary to gain the cooperation of sources for interrogation. Therefore, the use of force is a poor technique, as it yields unreliable results, may damage subsequent collection efforts, and can induce the source to say whatever he thinks the interrogator wants to hear."

US ARMY FIELD MANUAL, May 8, 1987

"[Al Qaeda members attacked] purely civilian targets of no military value; they refused to wear uniform or insignia or carry arms openly, but instead hijacked civilian airliners, took hostages, and killed them; they have deliberately targeted and killed thousands of civilians; and they themselves do not obey the laws of war concerning the protection of the lives of civilians or the means of legitimate combat."

John Yoo, Deputy Assistant Attorney General, and Robert J. Delahunty, Special Counsel, US Department of Justice Office of Legal Counsel, January 9, 2002

"Some argue that since our actions are not as horrifying as Al Qaeda's we should not be concerned. When did Al Qaeda become any type of standard by which we measure the morality of the United States? We are America, and our actions should be held to a higher standard, the ideals expressed in documents such as the Declaration of Independence and the Constitution."

Captain Ian Fishback, 82nd Airborne, US Army, September 16, 2005

"The U.S. is doing what the British did in the nineteen seventies, detaining people and violating their civil liberties. It did nothing but exacerbate the situation.... You'll end up radicalizing the entire population."

Tom Parker, former MI5 officer who now teaches at Yale University, February 2005

Indefinite detention and coercive interrogation are anathema to the British constitution. The United States similarly embraces the right to a speedy and public trial, eschews cruel and unusual punishment, and considers the inhuman treatment of prisoners to be a violation of due process. The two countries have long condemned other nations' use of detention without trial and physical coercion – and have signed international instruments binding themselves to this principle. Yet both states have used precisely these techniques as part of their own counterterrorist regimes.

For the United Kingdom, in the twentieth century Northern Ireland provided the focus of this regime. The state imposed internment and restriction orders primarily against the minority, Catholic population. In the late 1960s, question arose as to whether the Geneva Conventions applied to the conflict. As prominent members of the judiciary examined the five "deep interrogation" techniques imported from Britain's overseas campaigns, the government decided that the Geneva Conventions did apply and abrogated coercive interrogation – but not before the techniques had been used and had backfired, contributing to decades of violence. These techniques ran afoul of the European Convention of Human Rights (ECHR) and hurt the United Kingdom's ability to negotiate international instruments.

Sixty-seven Britons died on September 11, and in the weeks that followed, al Qaeda named the United Kingdom as a target.[1] The government reintroduced detention, this time using it exclusively against the foreign Muslim minority. The struggle between controlling terrorism and maintaining citizens' liberty rights ignited power struggles at the highest levels of government – particularly between the government and the Law Lords. The judiciary used the European Convention to push back against the executive, finding detention discriminate and disproportionate to the threat. The Labour government responded by resurrecting control orders – and extending their reach to citizens and noncitizens alike.

These measures all represent attempts to address the apparent inability of the ordinary criminal system to meet the terrorist challenge. Violence, a significant and clandestine threat, and the potential of witness and juror intimidation convinced successive governments that special rules were necessary. But the measures had serious and adverse consequences – just as American initiatives did in the wake of September 11.

Questions about whether the Geneva Conventions applied to terrorism also accompanied the Bush administration's decision to detain individuals indefinitely. But, unlike the United Kingdom, the United States decided that the Conventions did *not* apply to "enemy combatants." Efforts by detainees to obtain habeas relief through the courts led to massive power struggles between the branches of government. And the international fallout was considerable. In the vacuum created by departing from the Geneva standards, the use of new and cruel methods of questioning began seeping into the detention centers. Some prisoners were deliberately hidden and moved to black sites run by the Central Intelligence Agency; others were deported to third countries that the United

States had previously condemned precisely for their treatment of prisoners, and where they were subsequently tortured.

However important the moral issues involved in these policies, in this chapter I examine their enormous costs. As in the United Kingdom, many of the people subjected to these powers were innocent. Their use alienated minority communities – in both states the primary target of the provisions. They undermined both countries' international relationships – at a time when both needed international cooperation to respond to the terrorist threat. In the American context, they led to a series of formal legal actions against the United States and helped radicalize individuals around the world, thus playing into al Qaeda's strategy. They worked against American efforts to win countries over to a democratic design. And they undermined other important domestic and foreign policy objectives.

CONTROLLING VIOLENCE IN NORTHERN IRELAND

The right to life and liberty is embedded in English legal history. It was the 1215 Magna Carta – the "Great Charter" and forerunner of constitutional democracy – that guaranteed that no freeman would be imprisoned, exiled, "or in any way destroyed...except by the lawful judgment of his peers or by the law of the land."[2] Justice would be swift.[3] And punishment would be proportionate to the degree of the offense.[4] This document helped cement the rule of law, binding even the will of the monarch.

As early as 1305 the English writ of *habeas corpus ad subjiciendum* gave effect to this bodily freedom.[5] Referred to as "the great and efficacious writ in all manner of illegal confinement,"[6] the 1628 Petition of Right affirmed this entitlement.[7] Subsequent judicial decisions upheld the writ through its codification in the 1679 Habeas Corpus Act.[8] Nearly one hundred years later, the great English jurist, Sir William Blackstone, concluded that liberty is a "natural inherent right, which could not be surrendered or forfeited unless by the commission of some great and atrocious crime."[9] Its abridgement could only occur with "the special permission of law."[10] Blackstone explained,

The glory of the English law consists in clearly defining the times, the causes, and the extent, when, wherefore, and to what degree, the imprisonment of the subject may be lawful. This induces an absolute necessity of expressing upon every commitment the reason for which it is made; that the court upon an *habeas corpus* may examine into its validity; and according to the circumstances of the case may discharge, admit to bail, or remand the prisoner.[11]

This framework – the guarantee of liberty and safeguards when it is abridged – has broadly governed the United Kingdom's approach to counterterrorism. Indeed, in 2003, Lord Falconer of Thoroton observed in the House of Lords, "[O]ur society is based on the liberty of the individual. It is what we fight to protect."[12] It is not that liberty rights are never infringed. But, as Falconer continued, "[a]ny limitations on individual freedom must be proportionate to the threat; they must be sanctioned by law and cannot take place on an ad hoc basis."[13] Moreover, "they must be implemented in a way which ensures that there are safeguards and that the activities of the executive are subject to monitoring, scrutiny and accountability."[14] In other words, such protections must be effective.[15]

But how effective have the protections been? At the start of the Troubles, the answer would be "not very." In stark contrast to English law's traditional embrace of liberty rights, the Northern Ireland government, and later the British government, made extensive use of indefinite detention and coercive interrogation.

The context mattered: as in the colonies, a different set of rules held for Ireland. For centuries, English politicians had viewed extraordinary powers as a necessary, albeit regrettable, part of governing the island, and the twentieth century proved no exception. After World War I, Sir Winston Churchill lamented the reemergence of the "dreary steeples of Fermanagh and Tyrone."[16] "The integrity of their quarrel," he said, "is one of the few institutions that has been unaltered in the cataclysm which has swept the world."[17] Decades later, one Member of Parliament commented, "[I]nternment has been one of the facts of Irish history and one of the means for securing the State in Ireland, north or south."[18] Another asserted, "We have never been able to maintain a Northern Ireland State, since its very inception, without some kind of repressive law."[19] In 1979, Humphrey Atkins, the Secretary of State for Northern Ireland, explained, "Northern Ireland, for reasons that cannot be undone, is not like any other part of the United Kingdom."[20] It was a place with "special problems," requiring special solutions.[21] Tom Litterick observed, "Ulster is a foreign country. I have been there and it is, in every sense, unmistakably a foreign country."[22] Defending the 1974 Prevention of Terrorism (Emergency Provisions) Act that he had driven through Parliament, Roy Jenkins wrote, "I always believed in keeping as much as possible of the contagion of Northern Irish terrorism out of Great Britain. I thought we had responsibilities in Northern Ireland, both to uphold security and to assuage the conflict, but I did not think they extended to absorbing any more than we had to of the results of many generations of mutual intolerance."[23]

The problem is that by introducing extraordinary provisions to address the special problems of Northern Ireland, the state breathed life into a paramilitary movement that was to last for decades. And it damaged Britain's ability to achieve its domestic and foreign policy goals.

Indefinite Detention

In 1922, the Civil Authorities (Special Powers) Act (SPA) gave the Minister of Home Affairs for Northern Ireland the power "to take all such steps and issue all such orders as may be necessary for preserving the peace and maintaining order."[24] Under this statute, the government subsequently issued more than 100 regulations, one of which – Regulation 23 – allowed the state to indefinitely imprison anyone suspected of acting, having acted, or "being about to act in a manner prejudicial to the preservation of the peace and the maintenance of order."[25] Within six weeks of its enactment, Richard Dawson Bates, the first Minister of Home Affairs for Northern Ireland, amended this regulation to allow for the detention of individuals wherever and under whatever conditions the civil authority deemed appropriate.[26] Regulations also authorized the civil authority to restrict the movement of individuals not otherwise detained – the legal forerunners of the control orders currently in force in the United Kingdom. Although in 1949 the civil authority revoked Regulations 23 and 23B, seven years later a renewed Irish Republican Army (IRA) campaign spurred the state to reintroduce powers of exclusion and restriction.[27] A series of conditions, such as the imposition of curfew and the requirement that a suspect regularly report to the police, accompanied orders issued under these regulations, which were used with some frequency until the late 1940s.[28]

The 1922 SPA, intended to operate just for one year, was, as I noted in Chapter 1, repeatedly extended until it was made permanent in 1933.[29] Under its authority, on three occasions – 1921–24, 1938–46, and 1956–62 – the Northern Ireland government exercised extended detention.[30] It was used for the fourth and final time in 1971.[31]

On August 5, Brian Faulkner, the Northern Ireland Prime Minister, authorized internment.[32] Two days later, Graham Shillington, the Chief Constable of the Royal Ulster Constabulary (RUC), directed the security forces to arrest and interrogate individuals identified by the RUC special branch.[33] On August 9, 1971, at four o'clock in the morning, Northern Ireland security forces, with the assistance of the British military, arrested 342 men. This was only the beginning; by February 14, 1972, the state had arrested 2,447 people.[34] The British Home Secretary explained in Parliament that the aim was "to hold in safety, where they can do no further harm, active members of the I.R.A."

The whole operation proved a disaster. Among those picked up in the initial sweep were trade unionists, civil rights activists, and the elderly.[35] A number of people were held on mistaken identity – and several individuals on the initial list were dead.[36] The government, nevertheless, insisted that at least 160 of the initial 342 people interned were hardened members of the IRA.[37]

These numbers were misleading: the RUC Special Branch, which supplied the intelligence, failed to distinguish between republican sympathizers and active paramilitaries. Some internees *had* been involved in a 1956–62 IRA campaign – an isolated resurgence of paramilitary violence. But in 1969, the IRA had split into two organizations: the Official IRA objected to taking up arms against the British state, whereas the Provisional IRA pushed for violence as a way to achieve a united Ireland. The state's information related almost exclusively to members of the Official IRA.*

---

* Lord Diplock later acknowledged that inadequate information, coupled with the sheer scale of the enterprise, had undermined the operation. REPORT OF THE COMMISSION TO CONSIDER LEGAL PROCEDURES TO DEAL WITH TERRORIST ACTIVITIES IN NORTHERN IRELAND. Dec. 1972, Cmnd. 5185.

Tensions in the province, already near their boiling point, overflowed. By the end of the first day of internment, 100 houses had been set on fire, as Catholic and Protestant families were forced from their homes. Bus services were suspended, vehicles were burned, and crowds attacked the security forces. Ten people were killed. The following day, 13 more people died and hundreds more homes were burned to the ground. The Community Relations Commission later estimated that, over the next month, around 10,000 people were forced to move because of intimidation.[38] The violence was much greater than that before internment: in the four months preceding the sweep, eight people had died from Troubles-related violence; in the four months following, 114 individuals were killed.[39] From 78 explosions in July, there were 131 in August and 196 in September.[40] Efforts to control the violence by rearming the local police force failed. By the end of the year, there had been more than three times as many deaths as in the previous year.[41] Tension continued to build. On January 30, 1972, British paratroopers, believing themselves under attack, opened fire on unarmed demonstrators. Thirteen civilians died on what came to be known as "Bloody Sunday."

It was notable that internment and its aftermath not only increased the violence but also enhanced sympathy for those opposed to the state. When the British Army first arrived in the province in 1969, the soldiers saw scrawled on the walls: "I.R.A. = I Ran Away," and disorder stemmed not from terrorist campaigns, but from civil rights agitation. After internment, however, support for the Provisional Irish Republican Army steadily grew. The organization used the state's policies to increase the number of recruits and to jump-start a violent campaign that was to last for decades.

Habeas Corpus Relief

In the handful of cases that came before the courts questioning the legality of the detentions and seeking relief under a writ of habeas corpus, the judiciary offered some resistance to the exercise of executive power.

Among the first to be interned were James McElduff and Sean Keenan. At 4:30 a.m. on August 9, 1971, Corporal Rowbottom knocked on McElduff's door in Merchantstown, Co. Tyrone, and arrested him.[42] Acting under the 1922–43 SPAs, Rowbottom took McElduff first to Lisanelly Camp, Omagh, and then transferred him to the RUC camp at Magilligan.[43] There, McElduff was brought before Sergeant Sharpe, who checked his name against Shillington's list and told him that he was being arrested under the Special Powers Act – without informing him either of the grounds of suspicion or the power of arrest being exercised. Special Branch officers then interrogated McElduff.[44] On August 10, 1971, Brian Faulkner issued a detention order under Regulation 11(2).*

---

* The order read, "To: The officer in charge of the place of detention in the Maidstone I, the Right
  Honourable Brian Faulkner, Minister of Home Affairs for Northern Ireland, by virtue of the

The same day, the police transferred McElduff to the *HMS Maidstone*, a ship being used as a detention center, and the next day served him with a copy of the August 10th order. McElduff and Sean Keenan, similarly arrested, applied for a writ of habeas corpus to the High Court of England.[45]

The first judge to hear the case dismissed the application on the merits: the courts in England had jurisdiction, but the legislation was not *ultra vires* – the 1922 Special Powers Act fell within the authorities delegated by Westminster to the Northern Ireland parliament. The applicants appealed.[46]

Like the American courts more than three decades later (see page 87), the question addressed by the English Court of Appeal in the habeas application centered on jurisdiction. The applicants cited Blackstone (who wrote that the writ extends "into all parts of the King's dominions") in arguing that, wherever Her Majesty's subjects found themselves deprived of liberty, the courts in London had the authority to inquire into the matter.[47] Although the 1862 Habeas Corpus Act had subsequently restricted the writ to "any colony or foreign dominion of the Crown where Her Majesty has a lawfully established court or courts of justice,"[48] Ireland did not then qualify either as a colony or as a foreign dominion of the Crown. And although Southern Ireland did later become an independent and thus "foreign" state, the North remained part of the United Kingdom.

The court rejected this argument and held that English courts lacked jurisdiction to hear habeas claims in Ireland. Throughout unionist control of Northern Ireland – indeed, for two hundred years – despite the regular use of internment and detention, not a single habeas application had been filed from Ireland to an English court.[49] The reason was structural: a series of statutes in the late eighteenth century had given Ireland legislative and judicial independence.[†] And the 1862 Habeas Corpus Act specifically addressed, on the one hand, the courts of

---

powers vested in me by the Civil Authorities (Special Powers) Acts (Northern Ireland) 1922–1943, do hereby order and require you to receive James Anthony McElduff, Merchantstown, Omagh, County Tyrone, who has been arrested under the provisions of the said Civil Authorities (Special Powers) Acts as a person who is suspected of acting, or having acted or being about to act in a manner prejudicial to the preservation of peace or the maintenance of order, at the place of detention in the Maidstone and therein to detain him until he has been discharged by direction of the Attorney-General or brought before a magistrates' court." In re Keenan and another [1971] 3 W.L.R., at 538 (Lord Denning, M.R.)

[†] In 1782, Parliament repealed the 1719 Act that stated "the Kingdom of Ireland has been, is, and of right ought to be subordinate unto and dependent upon the Imperial Crown of Great Britain, as being inseparably united and annexed thereunto." Dependency of Ireland on Great Britain Act of 1719, 6 Geo. 1, c. 5; and Repeal of Act for Security Dependence of Ireland Act of 1782, 22 Geo. 3, c. 53. The following year, Westminster passed another statute expressly removing the authority of English courts to hear any writ of error or appeal or any other proceeding relating to cases in Ireland. Irish Appeals Act of 1783, 23 Geo. 3, c. 28. *See also* In re Keenan and another [1971] 3 W.L.R., at 541 (Lord Denning, M.R.). Lord Denning said of this body of laws, "It is plain to my mind that it carried the implication that the English courts should not issue writs of habeas corpus to Ireland." *Id.*

England and Wales and, on the other, those of Ireland. The later 1920 Government of Ireland Act did not give English courts in London jurisdiction over either the North or the South of Ireland.[50]

Accordingly, McElduff and Keenan applied to the Queen's Bench Division in Northern Ireland for relief. Although Keenan later withdrew, McElduff's case went forward, arguing that the exercise of arrest powers under the Special Powers Act violated the common law in that the only requirement was that the arresting officer entertain suspicion.*

The subsequent decision shows that the court had an important role to play in monitoring the exercise of executive powers. Yet, it also shows how incredibly narrow that role was. Judge McGonigal, who heard the case, drew attention to the extraordinary nature of the provisions: "A person arrested under this regulation has . . . no right of appeal against his arrest, nor any right to apply to the courts for release on bail. The only right is to apply to the civil authority for release on bail." The decision as to whether any particular individual should be detained lay entirely in the executive realm: "The courts have no jurisdiction to entertain the application for release by the arrested man himself and can only act if so directed by the civil authority."[51] The legislation set no limit on the length of time the civil authority could hold the person.[52] The only relief that could be sought through the courts was an application for habeas corpus: "[E]ven then, as the regulations stand, the court is only concerned with the question of whether the powers conferred by the regulations have been validly exercised. If the powers have been validly exercised and the arrest properly made, the courts cannot act as a court of appeal as to the ground of arrest, nor as to the time the arrested man can be held under this power of arrest."[53]

Even though the inquiry was thus extremely narrow, the court carefully considered whether the state had acted outside its authority – and found that it had. For an arrest to be valid under the act, the officer carrying it out had to take reasonable steps to inform the target both that he was under compulsion and the true grounds of his arrest.[54] The common law standard applied: "[I]f the citizen is not so informed but is nevertheless seized, the policeman, apart from certain exceptions, is liable for false imprisonment."[55] McGonigal rejected the government's argument that this principle did not apply to the 1922–43 SPAs. The fact of an emergency, or emergency powers, mattered naught: it was "a fundamental

* Regulation 11(1). The court also rejected the government's contention that emergency legislation is unfettered and that the suspicion required by Regulation 11 could be any type of suspicion, whether or not it passed any objective or subjective test of reasonableness. "If this view is correct, it follows that a person empowered by the regulation to arrest on suspicion could arrest a person because he considered that the way that person looked at him in passing made him suspect him, because he had the cast of features or the intonation that one associated with one area rather than another, or merely because the arrestor himself for one reason or another was in a state when he was suspicious of many of his fellow citizens and this person became at that point of time the focal point of his suspicions." In Re McElduff, p. 16, lines 17–25. (McGonigal, J.) A completely innocent person could thus be arrested and held indefinitely, with no right of appeal to any but the entity imprisoning him.

right of any man" to know the powers under which he was being detained: "To deny him that right – and the fact that it is so limited in certain cases only makes it all the more important – to deny him that right would, in my opinion, be a negation of justice."[56] McElduff, and hundreds of other men processed at Magillian, had been arrested under Regulation 10 and, later, detained under Regulation 11(2). In the middle of the process, Sergeant Sharpe had initiated a new arrest under Regulation 11(1) without specific direction from the civil authority to do so – and without informing the prisoners the grounds of suspicion and the new authority under which they were being detained. Resultantly, Sergeant Sharpe had failed to arrest them lawfully – making the subsequent detention order, based on the arrest, invalid.

Several other such habeas cases came before the courts. In 1972, an Armagh County Court ruled that the detention of William John Moore – who had also been picked up in the initial sweep and held for 17 days at Ballykinler without being informed either of the charges against him or that he would be held for questioning for 48 hours – was "deliberate, unlawful and harsh."[57] He was awarded £300 in damages.[58]

In *Kelly* v. *Faulkner*, the courts again ruled in favor of a detainee. On August 9, 1971, Captain Tighe, an intelligence officer in the army, had raided the defendant's home looking for one of Oliver Kelly's brothers. He found Oliver home instead. Tighe's commanding officer directed him to arrest Oliver, which he did, saying, "I arrest you under the Special Powers Act."[59]* When Kelly's sister asked the reason for the arrest, Tighe told her that he was not obliged to make any further statement.

Like the court in *In re McElduff*, Judge Gibson rejected the government's contention that the Special Powers Act, designed to meet an emergency, must be evaluated outside of common law restrictions.[60] There did not appear to be any practical reason, under even emergency conditions, for the arresting officer not to indicate the grounds for the arrest.[61] Like McElduff, moreover, Kelly was not informed of the nature of his arrest, making his detention unlawful. (The court in *Kelly*, however, did find lawful the subsequent internment order, as it did not depend upon the validity of the earlier arrest and detention powers). The court took "into account the fact of arrest in the middle of the night, the vexation and perhaps humiliation of the circumstances of his arrest in the presence of his recently reunited family, the interrogation and the frustration and deprivation necessarily involved in prison life, not knowing when or how its term would expire," and awarded Oliver Kelly £400 in damages.[62]

These narrowly drawn cases countered the use of executive powers – and threatened to bring a deluge of claims against the government for the manner in which it had conducted the internment operation. This danger was enhanced when, on February 23, 1972, the courts further held, in *Regina (Hume and*

---

* Even though Kelly was not on the list of individuals to be detained, the court found that, because Tighe also genuinely suspected him of involvement in paramilitary activity, Tighe had grounds for effecting the arrest.

others) v. *Londonderry Justices*, that the basis for the army operations in Northern Ireland – a 1957 regulation issued under the 1922–43 Special Powers Acts – violated a section of the 1920 Government of Ireland Act that did not include action by Her Majesty's forces.[63] The army could thus only exercise whatever powers it held under common law: the duty of citizens to assist the civil authorities in suppressing disorder. But the army was conducting searches, arresting citizens, enforcing curfew, stopping vehicles, and interrogating suspects – powers well beyond those exercised by ordinary citizens.[64]

In an effort to head off future challenges, the Government immediately introduced a bill into Parliament to legalize all actions taken by the military in Northern Ireland. Reginald Maudling, the Home Secretary, emphasized the need for its swift implementation.[65] Within hours of the Belfast High Court ruling, the Northern Ireland Bill obtained Royal Assent. Not only did the statute establish a legal framework for British forces in the province, but it retroactively legalized all security force actions since the army had been deployed in 1969.[66] Decades later, the American executive would similarly force a statute through the legislature to head off future judicial challenges to detention (see page 116).

In November 1972, the Detention of Terrorists Order, issued under the Northern Ireland Act, replaced the Special Powers Act regulations.[67] Under the old process, the civil authority simply issued an Internment or Detention Order, which was then referred to an Advisory Committee. The civil authority could either accept or reject the committee's recommendations.[68] The new Detention of Terrorists Order (DTO) gave the Northern Ireland Secretary the authority to sign an Interim Custody Order, which allowed a target to be detained for up to 28 days. Where the Chief Constable referred the case to a Commissioner, a hearing would be held to determine whether the detention should be extended. In this event, the Commissioner issued a Detention Order. If the Commissioner did not recommend an extension, the individual would be released.[69] In 1973, the DTO became incorporated into the 1973 Emergency Provisions Act.[70]

The government went to great lengths to try, by emphasizing the independence of the commissioners, to distinguish detention from the previous internment policy.[71] This independence, the argument went, provided a check on the system similar to that introduced by judicial review. In reality, though, the system looked nothing like judicial review and took place entirely within the executive branch. Its objective, moreover, was the same: to detain people indefinitely, on the basis of secret information.[72]

The Diplock Courts. In March 1972, Westminster assumed direct rule of Northern Ireland. It was clear that internment had failed. Since its introduction, there had been 1,130 bomb explosions and more than 2,000 shooting incidents. Nearly 3,000 people had been injured, and 233 had lost their lives as a result of political violence.[73] Although the British government announced its intent to move away from internment, it reserved the right to continue to use this power.[74] Nevertheless, William Whitelaw, the new Northern Ireland Secretary, refused to issue new internment orders.[75] He also began a series of phased releases that, within five months, dropped the number of individuals still interned or detained from 940 to 239.

Of concern at the time was not just whether those released would take up arms, but how the majority of the population would respond to the phased release program. As Whitelaw explained: "[O]ne had to move very carefully. The place was in an uproar when I went there. It was in an uproar in the whole of the summer in 1972. It is easy to sit here now and forget that if you didn't keep at least enough of the Protestant community believing that you meant to deal with the I.R.A. they would have, in their turn, went [sic] berserk."[76] To avoid such trouble, the government turned to Lord Diplock.

Described upon his death in 1985 as "a formidable intellect and one of the greatest judicial craftsmen of his generation,"[77] Lord Diplock was "a powerful, if not always a sympathetic, judge." He was "tensely analytical, and – although never discourteous to counsel who appeared before him – he never left them in any doubt about his intellectual superiority."[78] Diplock took the central chair in the House of Lords, instituting the practice of issuing only one leading judgment where there were no dissents – often writing them himself.[79] It was thus entirely consistent with his character for him, commissioned by the government to find an alternative to internment, to recommend suspending jury trial in Northern Ireland and replacing it with a single-judge tribunal.

The problems he sought to address were many: internment had not only allowed for coercive interrogation (see page 53) but had also undermined the legal system. Furthermore, the judicial system was skewed against Catholics, both in popular perception and according to statistics. A study by Tom Hadden and Paddy Hillyard in 1973, for instance, found that in political cases, the court denied bail to 79 percent of Catholics who came before it, but to only 54 percent of Protestants.[80] Juries, in turn, acquitted approximately 15 percent of Protestant defendants, in contrast to only 5 percent of Catholics.[81] And the judiciary itself derived almost entirely from the Protestant majority. Even as late as 1976, Protestants held 68 of the 74 senior court appointments.[82] Father Dennis Faul, a Catholic priest and civil rights leader, explained that the minority community was "afraid of the Courts: they believe the judicial system as it operates in the blatantly sectarian conditions of life here is loaded against them."[83]

Lord Diplock, however, discounted the minority community's concerns. In his final report, published in December 1972, he suggested that the courts "held the respect and the trust of all except the extremists."[84] His view might have stemmed in part from the limited nature of information provided to the Diplock commission, which lasted just seven weeks, received only three written submissions, and heard the evidence – almost all of it oral – in London. Lord Diplock himself made just two trips to the province, in the course of which he only met with the security forces and those administering the judicial system; almost all the witnesses were Protestants.[85]

Nevertheless, Lord Diplock had other reasons for considering the court system an inadequate alternative to internment. For one thing, jurors could be intimidated by the paramilitaries who wielded considerable social control throughout the province. This concern was borne out by perverse verdicts, where juries allowed seemingly guilty individuals to go free.

To solve the problem, Diplock proposed seven recommendations: that the army be allowed to hold a suspect without charge for up to 28 days; that decisions for bail be transferred to high court judges, insulating magistrates from possible retaliation; that the burden of proof be shifted for firearms and explosives discovery (if found, the defense would have to prove ignorance of the weapon's presence); that standards for confessions be lowered to make them consistent with Article 3 jurisprudence of the European Convention of Human Rights*; that the 1922–43 Civil Authorities (Special Powers) Acts be suspended and capital punishment ended; that written affidavits be accepted from witnesses later murdered, to protect against paramilitaries covering their tracks by killing those who might testify against them; and, finally, that a single high or country court judge, without a jury, hear cases involving political offenses.[86]

Reaction to Lord Diplock's report, especially to the suspension of jury trials, fell largely along party lines. Catholics roundly denounced it. The nationalist Social, Democratic, and Labour Party expressed dismay. Bernadette Devlin, a fiery republican, observed, "We have not heard from the government, and certainly not from Lord Diplock, one concrete point of evidence to show that it is necessary" to suspend jury trial.[87] She challenged, "We have heard of packed juries. But where is the statistical evidence? How many packed juries have there been? What is the percentage of juries that have been packed one way or the other? If there have been perverse judgments, convictions, or acquittals, what is the percentage?"[88] Ian Paisley, the Democratic Unionist Party autarch, welcomed the findings but expressed his outrage at the implication that a Protestant jury could be anything *but* fair minded.[89] The *Economist* and the London *Times* ran editorials supporting the recommendations, whereas a *Criminal Law Review* article by Professor William Twining accused the report of being written in haste, poorly researched, and generating widespread panic.[90] The government, however, accepted Lord Diplock's conclusions – while remaining "firmly committed to the restoration of law in Northern Ireland."[91] William Whitelaw vowed to "continue to bring suspected persons before the courts whenever possible."[92] The 1973 Northern Ireland (Emergency Provisions) Act channeled the recommendations into law.

The Diplock courts in Northern Ireland brought with them both advantages and disadvantages in combating terrorism.[93] First and foremost among the former, in contrast to internment, they emphasized the rule of law and the role

* The English Judges' Rules currently in operation provided a higher bar: under them, any admission made in the course of a situation meant to induce confessions was considered involuntary and could not be admitted into court as evidence. See *Reg.* v. *Flynn and Leonard* (Belfast City Commission 24 May 1972); *Queen* v. *Gargan* (Belfast city Commission, 10 May 1972), digested at 23 Northern Ireland Legal Quarterly 343 (1972) and quoted in Joseph W. Bishop, Jr., *Law in the control of Terrorism and Insurrection: The British Laboratory Experience*, Law & Contemporary Problems, 42 (1978), 140–201, at 172.

of the judiciary in stemming violence. By helping prevent known terrorists from walking free and thus diminishing the violence in the province, they bolstered citizens' belief in the state's ability to protect them. Indeed, after the courts' introduction, violence plummeted.[94] And, as intended, convictions increased: in the first five years, murder convictions rose from 9 to 77, wounding convictions from 142 to 499, and robbery convictions from 791 to 1,836.[95] Through the new courts, the government was able to take affirmative and visible steps to enhance security.

As a structural matter, the shift from internment to the Diplock court system meant that individuals did not lose their freedom at the say-so of the executive branch, but as a result of a deliberative, judicial process. Most of the minority community found this an improvement: a survey taken a year into the courts' operation found that 55 percent of Catholics thought that the new system was better than internment.[96]

The reforms also neutralized the risk that jury trials had posed to ordinary citizens. Northern Ireland was, and remains, an extremely close-knit society. The paramilitaries held a strong grip on many local areas, making highly doubtful the effectiveness of many of the alternative solutions – such as masking the identity of jurors. Jurors would have to make the journey to and from court, where they would be seen. As soon as one juror became known to a paramilitary organization, it could threaten that juror or his or her family members to get the juror to identify others. The sudden shift signaled a break with the past and suggested a fresh start – while removing juror bias from consideration.

The system carried other important benefits as well. To retain the adversarial nature of the proceedings, Diplock judges were required to spell out both the factual and the legal basis of their decisions. Defendants, in addition, were granted an automatic right of appeal. Matters of either fact or law could be reviewed. These changes subjected decisions to greater scrutiny and allowed counsel to challenge their basis. The written findings required a high level of discipline in the fact-finding phase of the trial: appellate courts tended to reverse Diplock convictions more frequently than jury convictions – most likely because the requirement that the judges write out their findings made it easier to challenge their conclusions.[97] Judges, in turn, keen to avoid a reversal of their opinion, went to some lengths to ensure the strength of their information.[98] Their judgments offered defendants more protection than jury verdicts would have – the latter being returned without explanation and in relation to which there was no automatic right of appeal.*

Despite the advantages of the Diplock courts over internment, a crucial weakness of the new system was that it eliminated the defendant's peers from the

---

* Another advantage of the single-judge courts may have been that they lowered the cost of prosecution: now that the state did not have to provide security measures for 12 more people, it could focus its resources on the judiciary itself. A contrary argument could be made that other characteristics of the system, such as the automatic right to appeal, increased costs. But in the absence of more concrete data, speculation remains just that.

courtroom. Perhaps most dramatically, the new system clashed with Britain's long tradition of the jury trial, which had come to symbolize the nation's embrace of liberty rights. Although Lord Diplock squarely addressed this issue, stating that jury trial was *not* a fundamental right, giving up juries did weaken state legitimacy at a time when it was under attack, and implied that a different standard existed for Northern Ireland than for Great Britain – thus playing into an old grievance in the province.

While jury suspension protected the Catholic minority, it also restricted them from having a significant role in the administration of justice, except as its object. Social and economic obstacles continued to play a role in limiting the number of Catholics who could become solicitors, and after 50 years of systematic discrimination against the minority, attempts to overcome the barriers to participation in the legal system may have seemed futile. The dearth of Catholic judges was exacerbated by republican insistence that nationalists not "buy in" to the British government. Jury service thus could have created an opportunity for the minority community to take part in the system.

The simultaneous weakening of *voir dire* (referring, in the British context, to the admissibility of confessions as opposed to the US context, where it means empaneling a jury) and the relaxed rules of evidence bolstered dissidents' claims against the government. The state began to allow inferences to be drawn from silence, and police testimony became sufficient to find membership in proscribed organizations.[99] The combination of these changes may have contributed to miscarriages of justice, further eroding public confidence in the system and making it seem as though the state was trying to "stack the deck" against (primarily minority community) defendants.

The single-judge courts also hurt the state's international standing – and its ability to conduct foreign affairs. In the mid-1980s, for instance, the Diplock tribunals and the continued refusal of the British government to restore jury trial nearly prevented the Republic of Ireland from signing an extradition treaty.[100] Such effects can be serious: in the case of extradition, the state's inability to obtain suspects, particularly from a neighboring territory, potentially increases violence.

The new single-judge courts did not remain isolated from ordinary criminal law. Owing to the broad range of scheduled offenses that automatically fell under the Diplock system, many nonterrorist cases, where no risk of juror intimidation existed, came before the courts. By the mid-1980s, some 40 percent of Diplock cases bore no relationship to paramilitary activity. Eventually, this problem of jurisdiction did abate: in 1986, Westminster responded to calls to end the system by expanding the number of scheduled crimes that could be certified out – that is, sent to non-Diplock courts. The Director of Public Prosecutions, accordingly, began increasing the number of cases that went to jury trial. (The Attorney General would only deschedule a case where he was "satisfied that it is not connected with the emergency in Northern Ireland.")[101] By October 2006, some 85 to 90 percent of the cases were being descheduled.[102]

Another way in which the tribunals were brought into the criminal law realm was even more direct. Although efforts were made to restore juries in Northern Ireland in the early twenty-first century, the government began calling for the suspension of jury trial for ordinary criminal law, where particularly complex information or long trials existed.[103] In 2003, the Criminal Justice Bill provided for the creation of single-judge tribunals throughout England and Wales for cases involving complex fraud or where a significantly high danger of jury tampering exists.[104] The House of Lords balked. Among others in protest, the Labour peer Baroness Kennedy of the Shaws QC suggested that the jury "protects the judiciary. It is what maintains the esteem of the British judiciary." Trial by a single judge, she continued, "catapults judges into a position which makes them very vulnerable."[105] She tackled class concerns: "white collared professionals" would be "tried by other white collared professionals. How will ordinary citizens, excluded from the process, feel about acquittals in those circumstances?"[106] Other objections surfaced.

To secure the Lords' agreement, Home Secretary David Blunkett negotiated a compromise: section 43 would only come into force through affirmative procedure.[107] The Lords agreed and passed the Criminal Justice Bill. But the battle between the House of Lords and the government was not over: Two years later, the government brought forward a draft commencement order to implement section 43. Although the House of Commons Standing Committee approved it, the House of Lords resisted. The government withdrew the order – and introduced new legislation that would remove any role for the House of Lords.[108] Instead, section 43 could be brought into force solely at the say-so of the Secretary of State. This bill was in committee as of spring 2007.

The End of Indefinite Detention. In 1974, the government appointed Lord Gardiner to head his own inquiry into what powers ought to be used to deal with terrorism while preserving civil liberties and protecting human rights in Northern Ireland. The Gardiner Committee concluded:

After long and anxious consideration, we are of the opinion that detention cannot remain as a long-term policy. In the short term, it may be an effective means of containing violence, but the prolonged effects of the use of detention are ultimately inimical to community life, fan a widespread sense of grievance and injustice, and obstruct those elements in Northern Ireland society which could lead to reconciliation.

Despite the committee's stand against detention ("Detention can only be tolerated in a democratic society in the most extreme circumstances; it must be used with the utmost restraint and retained only as long as it is strictly necessary"), the time was not quite right to abolish it: "We think that this grave decision can only be made by the Government."[109]

In the February 1974 election, Labour upset the Conservative Party. That July, Merlyn Rees, who had, when in Opposition, spoken against detention, now as Secretary of State for Northern Ireland began a policy of phased releases. Although he also issued some new interim custody orders, he continued with the release program until, by December 1975, no detainees were left. The powers remained, unused, on the statute book, until their formal repeal in 1996. Although many troops in Northern Ireland supported the end of the practice, not all participants in the conflict were so well disposed toward it. Many Loyalists, for instance, saw it as capitulation. The Conservative party, now in Opposition, lambasted Labour for being soft on terror.

Coercive Interrogation

For centuries Britain's treatment of insurrection in its far-flung colonies had differed from what it would allow on domestic soil. Indeed, from the Middle Ages on, the structure and substance of English law had severely restricted the use of torture. In 1949, the United Kingdom was one of the first states to be party to the Geneva Conventions, which banned the use of coercive questioning during times of war. Nevertheless, military interrogation techniques adopted at the start of the Troubles brought Britain into violation of both its domestic and international obligations.

Torture in English Law. Legal principles given traction by the Magna Carta obviated the necessity of hurting people to obtain information.[110] The jury acted as fact-finder, and an accused's culpability was determined by its verdict – not by a painful examination of the prisoner.[111] The use of jurors meant, in addition, that an accused would be judged by his or her peers. And inflicting pain in their presence risked alienating them; while inflicting it elsewhere and introducing the information so obtained as evidence could result in recantation and claims of duress – and strongly prejudice the jury in favor of the defendant.[112] So, too, did the presumption of innocence carry important protections. Because of it – in contrast, for instance, to Roman law – the English system did not require a confession to corroborate proof of guilt.[113]

Outside of judicial structures, the common law banned the use of torture.[114] Henry of Bracton, writing in the thirteenth century, and Sir Edward Coke, in the seventeenth, both recognized that, under the common law, prisoners could not be subjected to pain prior to judicial sentence.[115] The terms of a sentence strictly prescribed the contours of any subsequent punishment.[116] If a jailer caused the death of a prisoner, the killing was considered a felony.[117] If the prisoner was unlawfully and forcibly mistreated, he or she would be entitled to a remedy by writ.[118] A jailer engaging in such actions could lose his job.

Legal treatises from the Middle Ages to the early modern period applauded English law for eschewing torture. In the sixteenth century, for instance, Sir John Fortescue condemned the Continent's civil law for allowing such techniques where enough evidence could not otherwise be obtained:

[W]hat man is there so stout or resolute, who has once gone through this horrid trial by torture, be he never so innocent, who will not rather confess himself guilty of all kinds of wickedness, than undergo the likes of tortures a second time? Who would not rather die once, since death would put an end to all his fears, than to be killed so many times, and suffer so many hellish tortures, more terrible than death itself?[119]

Torture bordered on evil: "[H]ow inhuman," Fortesque wrote, "must that law be, which does its utmost to condemn the innocent, and convict the judge of cruelty? A practice so inhuman, deserves not indeed to be called a law, but the high road to hell."[120] Sir Thomas Smith opined that no amends could be made to an innocent person who had been forced to bear such torment. And if death were the goal, "what crueltie is it so to torment him before?" It was not in "[t]he nature of English men" to withstand such suffering: "[T]herefore he will confesse rather to have done any thing, yea, to have killed his own father, than to suffer torment, for death our nation doth not so much esteem as a mean torment. In no place shal you see malefactors go more constantly, more assuredly, and with lesse lamentation to their death than in England."[121]

Nonetheless, where the Crown saw a serious danger to the state, it circumvented common law and issued torture warrants – "for the Queen's safety, to know the manner of the treason and the accomplices."[122] Thus, by the fifteenth century, parallel systems had emerged: where defendants would be brought to trial, torture did not serve the state interest,[123] but where the purpose was to protect the security of the state, such methods were condoned.[124] In the latter case, coercive interrogation techniques were increasingly exercised by the Star Chamber – the device through which successive monarchs ever more cruelly suppressed the population. Under the Stuart monarchs into the seventeenth century, the power of this chamber grew along with its ability to sidestep the common law restrictions.[125] Under Cromwell, however, more humane methods began to come to the fore. In 1769, Blackstone observed that "trial by rack is utterly unknown to the law of England,"[126] and he scorned civil law, which accepted the use of torture as a protection against miscarriage of justice – "Thus rating a man's virtue by the hardiness of his constitution, and his guilt by the sensibility of his nerves!"[127]

Yet, while the ban against using torture to extract information was thus, by the early twentieth century, well established in England, a different rule held for the colonies. Recent scholarship shows that a range of coercive interrogation techniques were used by the British military in Aden, Kenya, Malaysia, and elsewhere.[128] Northern Ireland fell between these standards: not quite England and not quite Empire. As Kevin McNamara, the British Labour MP, pointed out, "no one in Britain will undergo the [counterterrorist] procedures that apply in Northern Ireland."[129] There, in the early 1970s, the rules were unclear. Violence in the province was growing. And the military was given the lead.

Coercive Interrogation in Northern Ireland. By July 1971, some 11,800 British troops had been moved to the province. It quickly became clear that domestic intelligence agencies did not have sufficient information. The military took it upon itself to obtain it. To get detainees to talk, the security forces used five "deep interrogation" techniques: wall-standing, hooding, noise, a bread and water diet, and sleep deprivation[130] – some or all of which had been used in Palestine, Malaya, Kenya, Cyprus, the British Cameroons, Brunei, British Guiana, Aden, Borneo/Malaysia, and the Persian Gulf.[131] Allegations began to circulate that men also had been forced to run barefoot over barbed wire and broken glass, had had their scrotums slammed in drawers, and had been severely beaten.[132] Father Dennis Faul, the Catholic priest and civil rights activist (see page 47), placed his phone number in an advertisement in the *Irish News* and declared himself available for advice.[133] He subsequently documented 25 methods of physical abuse used in Holywood and Girdwood Barracks (which included physical beatings, injections, electric shocks, burns, and security forces urinating on prisoners), as well as psychological torture (such as interrogators wearing surgical dress, playing Russian roulette with the detainees, and threatening their family members.)[134] Although violent attacks were also being carried out by members of the Protestant majority, most of those people interned and interrogated by the government came from the Catholic minority.[135]

As complaints of mistreatment grew more frequent, the British government commissioned, first, an inquiry in November 1971, which reported that "physical ill-treatment took place"[136]; then, in early 1972, a committee of three Privy Counsellors, headed by Lord Parker and including Lord Gardiner and John Archibald Boyd-Carpenter, to consider "whether, and if so in what respects, the procedures currently authorised for the interrogation of persons suspected of terrorism and for their custody while subject to interrogation require amendment."

The military's authorized interrogation procedures at that point stemmed from a *Joint Directive on Military Interrogation in Internal Security Operations Overseas*, issued February 17, 1965, and amended in 1967. The title itself – indicating that the procedures applied only to "Internal Security Operations Overseas" – underscored the fact that special rules had been developed for British operations abroad. Applied to Northern Ireland, it also indicated that to some extent the province was being treated under the colonial standard.

This directive stated, "Persons arrested or detained during Internal Security operations or in near emergency situations are likely to be valuable sources of intelligence." Adding, "They may be the only sources of intelligence at a time when it is urgently required," it called for "a psychological attack." Coercive techniques, though, had to stop short of torture and physical cruelty: "Apart from legal and moral considerations, torture and physical cruelty of all kinds are professionally unrewarding since a suspect so treated may be persuaded to talk, but not to tell the truth." Thus, "[s]uccessful interrogation may be a lengthy process." The directive required that the military follow Article 3 of Geneva Convention III, which relates to the treatment of prisoners of war (see page 76).

In contrast to the directive, however, the Parker Committee's majority report, signed by Lord Parker of Waddington and John Archibald Boyd-Carpenter, questioned whether the Geneva Conventions applied to the terrorist conflict in Northern Ireland. Foreshadowing the same debate that took place in the United

States three decades later, the committee suggested that Geneva Convention III applied only to international warfare; thus, "the more apt Convention is Convention No. IV, dealing with internal civilian disturbances in which Article 3 is in the same terms."[137] Yet, the report continued, "Even so, it is arguable that Convention No. IV itself does not apply in the emergencies which we are considering and the same can be argued in respect of our other international obligations under the European Convention for the Protection of Human Rights and Fundamental Freedoms (Article 3) and under the Universal Declaration of Human Rights (Article 5)."[138]

Because the applicability of the United Kingdom's international obligations was the subject of a dispute at the European Commission, the Parker Committee refrained from expressing a view. However, because the joint directive itself noted the state's obligations under the Geneva Conventions, and the current interrogations in the province were taking place under that authority, the Parker Committee determined that the security forces were obliged to comply with the Conventions.

The majority report raised difficult questions: a distinction could be drawn between what was technically allowed by the directive and what would be "morally permissible." Even if the techniques being used complied with the directive, it was not clear whether "their application by a civilized and humane society can be morally justified."[139] For the Parker Committee, there was "a wide spectrum between discomfort and hardship at the one end and physical or mental torture at the other end."[140] "Where," the committee asked, "does hardship and discomfort end and for instance humiliating treatment begin, and where does the latter end and torture begin?"[141]

The problem, the committee suggested, was that *"no rules or guidelines had been laid down to restrict the degree to which these techniques can properly be applied.* Indeed, it cannot be assumed that any UK Minister has ever had the full nature of these particular techniques brought to his attention, and, consequently, that he has ever specifically authorised their use."[142]

Abuse linked to the absence of clear guidelines and specific authorization returned decades later in the American context. As in the United Kingdom, interrogation techniques taught to soldiers to train them how to resist questioning became the tools they then used to interrogate detainees. And on both sides of the Atlantic the length of time such measures were used, and their combination, mattered: what might not initially be considered cruel treatment became different in kind when extended and combined.

Even as the Parker Committee highlighted areas of concern, it drew attention to the potential benefits of coercive interrogation.[143] Interrogators had obtained details of the safe houses, supply routes, and communication strategies; information related to paramilitary morale; and explanations for incidents recorded in police files. The number of arms, ammunition, and explosives finds had suddenly increased: between January 1971 and August 8, 1971, 1 machine gun was uncovered; between internment and the end of the year, another 25. From 66 rifles found, the number increased to 178, and from 86 pistols or revolvers to

158.[144] The Parker Committee wrote "There is no doubt that the information obtained by these two operations directly and indirectly was responsible for the saving of lives of innocent citizens."[145]

The committee concluded that the application of the five techniques, "subject to proper safeguards, limiting the occasion on which and the degree to which they can be applied, would be in conformity with the Directive"[146]: that is, only where it was "considered vitally necessary to obtain information" should coercion be used.[147] Authority would have to be given expressly by a UK minister, with full knowledge of particular techniques and the individual to whom they would be applied.[148] The report recommended that information be kept secret, with the minister advised by a committee and appointed by the prime minister after consulting with the leader of the Opposition.[149] In addition to a clear chain of command between the senior officer and the minister authorizing the interrogation techniques,[150] there should be as well a highly trained interrogation panel drawn from the military, a psychiatric doctor present at all interrogations to ensure that the questioning was not carried too far,[151] and a complaints body.[152]

Lord Gardiner, writing the minority report, strongly disagreed with the majority's conclusions. He noted that the procedures for deep interrogation had not been written down in any document.[153] Indeed, he suggested, they could not be – nor could any minister authorize them – as such authorization would have violated domestic law and possibly international law as well.[154] Forcibly hooding a man against his will and handcuffing him for trying to remove the hood would be an assault – both a tort and a crime – so, too, with the other techniques.[155] Because the measures were illegal under domestic law, he did not need to reach a conclusion on whether they also violated Common Article III of the Geneva Convention; or Article 5 of the Universal Declaration of Human Rights, which declared, "No one shall be subjected to torture or to cruel, inhuman or degrading treatment or punishment"; or Articles 7 and 10 of the International Covenant on Civil and Political Rights (which the United Kingdom had signed but not yet ratified). These articles provided the following:

7. No one shall be subjected to torture or to cruel, inhuman, or degrading treatment or punishment. In particular, no one shall be subjected without his free consent to medical or scientific experimentation.
10. (i) All persons deprived of their liberty shall be treated with humanity and with respect for the inherent dignity of the human person.

Lord Gardiner recognized that, although the IRA was conducting in Northern Ireland a brutal campaign that was "virtually a war,"[156] this situation did not make it morally permissible to use deep interrogation. He pointed to the particularly unsavory aspects of deep interrogation. Sensory isolation leading to mental disorientation, which had been invented in Soviet Russia by the KGB, was described by medical specialists as one method of inducing an artificial psychosis or episode of insanity. We know that people who have been through such an experience do not forget it quickly and may experience symptoms of mental distress for months or years. We know that some artificially induced psychoses... have in fact proved permanent; and there is no reason to suppose that this may not be a danger with psychoses produced by sensory deprivation. Even if such psychotic symptoms as delusions and hallucinations do not persist, a proportion of persons who have been subjected to these procedures are likely to continue to exhibit anxiety attacks, tremors, insomnia, nightmares, and other symptoms of neurosis with which psychiatrists are familiar from their experience of treating ex-prisoners of war and others who have been confined and ill-treated.[157]

Lord Gardiner reported the results of "Lancet," a 1959 experiment conducted in England, in which 20 volunteers at a hospital were placed in a silent room, with translucent goggles and padded fur gloves. They could walk around, or sleep or rest, and were given four meals a day, during which time the goggles and gloves would be removed and other hospital staff would visit with them. They were told that they would have paid time off equal to however long they stayed in the room. Fourteen of the 20 volunteers gave up after fewer than 48 hours – some after only 5 hours. The usual causes were unbearable anxiety, tension, and panic attacks. One-quarter of the 20 had nightmares that included drowning, suffocating, and killing people.[158] What was remarkable about the experiment is that it was conducted in a hospital, where the volunteers had no reason for panic. And they had been neither subjected to wall-standing nor deprived of food, water, or sleep.

As for the information obtained from the deep interrogations, Gardiner noted that some targets were cooperative from the start – making use of the procedures unnecessary. The sudden arrest of so many people was bound to increase the amount of information available. Nor was Gardiner convinced by the argument that the need for pressing information was unusual: always, in times of war, information was necessary and circumstances pressing. Nevertheless, the state had signed the Third Geneva Convention, whose Article 17 provided the following:

No physical or mental torture, nor any other form of coercion, may be inflicted on prisoners of war to secure from them information of any kind whatever. Prisoners of war who refuse to answer may not be threatened, insulted, or exposed to any unpleasant or disadvantageous treatment of any kind.[159]

During World War II, prisoners had been treated with kindness and courtesy; questioning, cross-referencing information, and placing "stool pigeons" in cells obtained the necessary information – even within hours.[160]

Lord Gardiner also pointed to the importance of winning over the population in a guerrilla war type of situation, and considered the extent to which such techniques affected the United Kingdom's reputation: "If, by a new Act of Parliament, we now depart from world standards which we have helped to create, I believe that we should both gravely damage our own reputation and deal a severe blow to the whole world movement to improve Human Rights."[161] He concluded,

The blame for this sorry story, if blame there be, must lie with those who, many years ago, decided that in emergency conditions in Colonial-type situations we should abandon our legal, well-tried and highly successful wartime interrogation methods and replace them by procedures which were secret, illegal, not morally justifiable and alien to the traditions of what I believe still to be the greatest democracy in the world.[162]

On the day the Parker Report was published, March 2, 1972, the government adopted the minority report recommendations. The prime minister announced, "[T]he Government, having reviewed the whole matter with great care and with reference to any future operations, have decided that the techniques . . . will not be used in future as an aid to interrogation." He added, "If a Government did decide . . . that additional techniques were required for interrogation, then I think that . . . they would probably have to come to the House and ask for the powers to do it."[163] The prime minister issued a directive prohibiting coercive interrogation and, particularly, the five techniques. The government also instituted mandatory medical examinations, comprehensive record keeping, and immediate reporting of complaints of ill treatment. Following the direct rule, the Attorney General of the United Kingdom issued a directive outlining the proper treatment of individuals taken into custody. The Director of Public Prosecutions would prosecute reports of ill treatment.[164]

There are many possible reasons for the government's decision. More, rather than less, violence had followed the use of the interrogation measures. A number of ministers apparently had not been aware of the exact techniques being used in the province. And outside the British state, international pressure was mounting: in 1971, the Republic of Ireland lodged a formal complaint against the United Kingdom at the European Commission of Human Rights. The Commission determined that the use of severe beatings and stress positions (such as forcing detainees to kneel on the floor with their foreheads on the ground and their hands clasped behind their backs) amounted to inhuman or degrading treatment, and unanimously agreed that the combination of the five deep interrogation techniques amounted to torture.[165] In 1976, the application evolved into formal proceedings before the European Court of Human Rights.

The Case of Ireland *v.* United Kingdom. The European Court subsequently found the United Kingdom in breach of Article 3 of the European Convention on Human Rights, which provides that "no one shall be subjected to torture or to inhuman or degrading treatment or punishment."[166] Although the European Court did not agree with the Commission that the severe beatings at Palace Barracks amounted to torture, it did find them to be inhuman treatment.[167] In a 16-1 vote, the European Court determined that the five deep interrogation techniques, "applied in combination, with premeditation and for hours at a stretch . . . caused, if not actual bodily injury, at least intense physical and mental

suffering to the persons subjected thereto and also led to acute psychiatric disturbances during interrogation."[168] The European Court added, "The techniques
were also degrading since they were such as to arouse in their victims feelings
of fear, anguish and inferiority capable of humiliating and debasing them and
possibly breaking their physical or moral resistance.[169] The court also found
that the extrajudicial use of detention and interrogation violated Article 5 of
the ECHR, which reads:

1. Everyone has the right to liberty and security of person. No one shall be deprived of
   his liberty save in the following cases and in accordance with a procedure prescribed
   by law:
   (a) the lawful detention of a person after conviction by a competent court;
   (b) the lawful arrest or detention of a person for non-compliance with the lawful
   order of a court or in order to secure the fulfillment of any obligation prescribed
   by law;
   (c) the lawful arrest or detention of a person effected for the purpose of bringing him
   before the competent legal authority on reasonable suspicion of having committed
   an offence or when it is reasonably considered necessary to prevent his committing
   an offence or fleeing after having done so . . .
2. Everyone who is arrested shall be informed promptly, in a language which he under-
   stands, of the reasons for his arrest and of any charge against him.
3. Everyone arrested or detained in accordance with the provisions of paragraph 1 (c)
   of this Article (art. 5–1-c) shall be brought promptly before a judge or other officer
   authorised by law to exercise judicial power and shall be entitled to trial within a
   reasonable time or to release pending trial. Release may be conditioned by guarantees
   to appear for trial.
4. Everyone who is deprived of his liberty by arrest or detention shall be entitled to take
   proceedings by which the lawfulness of his detention shall be decided speedily by a
   court and his release ordered if the detention is not lawful.

Neither the 1922–43 SPAs nor the later 1973 Northern Ireland (Emergency
Provisions) Act provided for anyone who was arrested to be promptly informed
of the reason for the arrest.[170] Under the 1972 DTO, and later the 1973 EPA, the
detainee could not initiate proceedings; nor could he contest the "lawfulness"
of the detention – either during the first 28 days or during the extension. Once
the detention order was issued, the detainee could take the matter to an appeal
tribunal, but the requirements of Article 5(4) – that a decision be speedily
delivered – was not met.[171] The narrowness of the Northern Ireland courts'
inquiry in the previous habeas corpus cases – particularly McElduff, Moore,
and Kelly – troubled the European Court. It concluded that "[t]he judicial
review of the lawfulness of the measures in issue was thus not sufficiently wide
in scope, taking into account the purpose and object of Article 5 para. 4 (art. 5-4)
of the Convention."[172]

Even as the European Court came to these conclusions, it also was of the
unanimous opinion that between August 1971 and March 1975 there was a
state of emergency in the United Kingdom within the meaning of Article 15 of
the ECHR – a provision that comes into play only "in time of war or other

public emergency threatening the life of the nation." The United Kingdom had entered formal derogations to this effect on August 20, 1971; January 23, 1973; and August 16, 1973, fulfilling the requirements of Article 15.[173] The European Court would not evaluate the effectiveness of the policies adopted by the British government at such a time,[174] and wrote, "It is certainly not the Court's function to substitute for the British Government's assessment any other assessment of what might be the most prudent or most expedient policy to combat terrorism. The Court must do no more than review the lawfulness, under the Convention, of the measures adopted by that Government from 9 August 1971 onwards."[175] Although the United Kingdom had derogated from Article 5 of the ECHR, the extrajudicial deprivation of liberty exercised from August 1971 to March 1975 did not – owing to the margin of appreciation left to states under Article 15 – amount to a breach of the ECHR.[176]

Aftermath. Although the five deep interrogation techniques were formally defunct, claims of mistreatment during lengthy, unsupervised periods of detention continued.* From August 1971 to November 1974, 2,615 complaints against the police were made, 1,105 of which alleged ill treatment or assault.[177] Between March 1972 and November 1974, 1,268 complaints against the army were made; of these just over one thousand were forwarded to the Director of Public Prosecutions (DPP). In total, between April 1972 and the end of January 1977, the DPP prosecuted 218 security force members for assault; 155 were convicted.

Even after this period, however, reports of physical abuse continued.[178] Through the late 1990s, the Committee for the Administration of Justice received evidence reporting on psychological and occasional physical abuse. In 1994, for instance, the police chased a republican suspect, David Adams, who hid under a van. He was pulled out by the legs, made to kneel, handcuffed, and hooded. When he gave a false name, the police grabbed his head and pounded it on the ground, telling him that the only good Fenian is a dead one. He was beaten about the head and torso, and his lung was punctured by one of the ribs thus broken. When he arrived at the interrogation center at Castlereagh, he was bleeding profusely. A number of officers took turns running and jumping on his left leg until it broke. The case went to court, where the High Court awarded Adams £30,000. In March 1996, James McDonnell, a prisoner in Maghaberry prison, died. An autopsy found 11 broken ribs and damage to McDonnell's voice box – sustained in the course of an altercation with prison officials after being informed of his father's death. Neither the Adams case nor the McDonnell

---

* For example, Noel Bell, of the "Armagh Four" (four members of the Ulster Defense Regiment convicted of murdering a Catholic), wrote of his interrogation, "I was slapped on the face, punched repeatedly on the chest and testicles until I fell to the floor. I was repeatedly told how I was supposed to have committed this murder on a guy I didn't even know. . . . I was physically and psychologically tortured, brainwashed and degraded until I put my name to a prepared statement in order to get peace." Kieran Cooke, *Echoes of Guildford for the Armagh Four*, Fin. Times (London), Nov. 16, 1989, at 10.

case resulted in any prosecution or discipline of the officers responsible. According to the Committee for the Administration of Justice, between March 1996 and September 1998, there were seven deaths in Maghaberry, some in suspicious circumstances.[179]

Certain institutional features may have played a role in perpetuating the problem. Even when challenged, the Diplock courts in Northern Ireland routinely accepted confessions obtained from interrogation sessions and, at the same time, increasingly relied solely on confessions made during interrogation for convictions.[180] (One study conducted in 1980 found that 86 percent of the evidence presented against suspects in the Diplock system consisted of statements made during interrogations – yet only 30 percent had supporting evidence.[181] Just over a decade later, another study found that most prosecutions relied upon a confession by the defendant. In 85 percent of the cases, the statements were uncorroborated – with a conviction rate of around 95 percent.[182])

Calls for the closing of interrogation centers, however, went unmet.[183] Most claims against the Royal Ulster Constabulary were settled out of court, with 86 percent of the complaints withdrawn – because, the independent commission for police complaints explained, raising objections was an insurgency tactic – not because detainees were further intimidated by the RUC.[184]

MEETING THE ISLAMIST THREAT IN THE UNITED KINGDOM

September 11 shook the United Kingdom, a country long familiar with a terrorist conflict in which – to paraphrase Brian Jenkins' now famous remark from the 1970s – paramilitaries wanted a lot of people watching, not a lot of people dead.[185] This new kind of terrorist wanted both. More Britons died in the World Trade Center attack than in any other terrorist incident in British history.[186] And although the 9/11 attack had been on foreign soil, al Qaeda quickly made it clear that the United Kingdom, too, was a prime target. The government began to focus on the possibility that there were already Islamist terrorist operatives within domestic bounds. September 11 had been carried out by foreign nationals. It was to this community the government looked to ascertain the possible threat.

The state here faced a dilemma: where it did not have a strong enough case to charge a suspect with a crime, or where the intelligence services needed to protect their sources or information-gathering methods, or where suspicion rested on intercept evidence that was not admissible in court, there were significant barriers to initiating a criminal prosecution. Furthermore, any attempt by the government to deport non-British subjects back to their home country, where they might face torture or even death, would be blocked by the nation's international obligations.[187] To address this problem, two months after 9/11 the state reintroduced indefinite detention – a move to which the Law Lords strongly objected. In 2004 and 2005, they ruled against the government in two important cases: the first dealing with the use of indefinite detention; the second with whether the government could detain individuals on the grounds of information obtained by torture.

Indefinite Detention Revived

The 2001 Anti-Terrorism, Crime, and Security Act (ATCSA) gave the British Secretary of State the authority to specially designate ("certify") foreign individuals reasonably suspected of being a terrorist,[188] and defined "terrorist" broadly, to include anyone with links to international terrorist organizations.[189] Where either a point of law or practical considerations prevented deportation, the legislation provided for indefinite detention.[190] As a safeguard, the statute allowed an appeal to the Special Immigration Appeals Commission (SIAC).[191] The powers were to be in place for 15 months. To ensure that the state was in good standing with its international obligations, the United Kingdom formally derogated from Article 5(1) of the ECHR.[192] It was the only European state to do so (Spain, despite the March 11, 2004, Madrid bombings that left 191 dead and 1824 injured, did not derogate; neither did Germany, even after it became clear that active al Qaeda cells had been operating within the state).

Although by most calculations, the United Kingdom did not make extensive use of these powers (with 17 people later being subject to detention[193]), a broad range of opponents in the United Kingdom and overseas condemned them. Prominent Christian, Jewish, and Muslim leaders, as well as human rights activists, called for their repeal.[194] In Parliament, the Joint Committee on Human Rights repeatedly berated the government for retaining the provisions.[195] The Committee of Ministers of the Council of Europe criticized the ATCSA, as did the European Commission Against Racism and Intolerance and the UN Committee Against Torture.[196] In a thinly veiled slight, the Parliamentary Assembly of the Council of Europe resolved, "In their fight against terrorism, Council of Europe members should not provide for any derogations to the European Convention on Human Rights."[197]

Britain's Privy Counsellor Review Committee considered the provisions unsustainable over the long term as a way to deal with terrorist suspects.[198] The committee argued from two central principles: "that the individual has a right to liberty and to privacy; and that the authorities have a duty to take the steps necessary to protect society from terrorism."[199] As much as possible, ordinary criminal justice ought to suffice. Where special needs existed, extraordinary authority could be used as long as counterterrorist law was kept distinct from ordinary criminal law, limited to terrorism, accompanied by specially designed safeguards, and coordinated with the international community.[200] Civil liberties would suffer less harm if the state were to impose restrictions on a suspect's freedom of movement (e.g., curfews, tagging, daily reporting to police station) and ability to use financial services, communicate, or associate freely (e.g., requiring them to use only certain specified phones or bank or internet accounts, which might be monitored) – all such freedom subject to the provision that if someone broke the order, he or she would be subject to detention.[201] The committee expressed concern that, some two years into the operation of detention, the state was not engaged in a good-faith effort to negotiate with foreign governments for the eventual deportation of suspects.[202] Nor was there "a sufficiently proactive, focused, case management approach to determining whether any particular suspected international terrorist should continue to be detained." The government, moreover, had apparently ceased to consider alternatives.[203]

Yet alternatives did exist. In 2004, the Northern Ireland Human Rights Commission issued a report, *Countering Terrorism and Protecting Human Rights*, in which it proposed a number of solutions to the dilemma: the state could use intercept evidence in court, and legislation could be introduced to protect witnesses, informers, and undercover agents and to allow cases based on intelligence sources to progress through the judicial system. The commission suggested that a special mechanism for review of contingency plans be instituted in the event of an attack, and that anti-jury-tampering measures be applied. For individuals detained and suspected of terrorist involvement, the commission recommended, among other things, that only evidence not obtained under torture be allowed – and that 14-day detention exist only as long as an emergency was in place.

The press release detailing these recommendations coincided with the Law Lords' consideration of the detention of foreign terrorist suspects.[204] In December 2004, the Law Lords held that the powers of detention were incompatible with Articles 5 and 14 of the ECHR.[205] The former deals with the right to security and liberty of person (see page 59), whereas the latter states, "The enjoyment of the rights and freedoms set forth in this Convention shall be secured without discrimination on any ground such as sex, race, color, language, religion, political or other opinion, national or social origin, association with a national minority, property, birth or other status."[206]

Because of the constitutional importance of the case, an extraordinary nine Law Lords sat – eight of whom found the provisions both disproportionate and discriminatory.[207] Even while ruling against the state, however, the judiciary demarcated political questions as falling within the government's domain. In other words, the decision whether a state of an emergency existed fell outside judicial competence, but liberty rights fell squarely within it.

European jurisprudence set the framework. The Lords looked to the meaning of public emergency in *Lawless* v. *Ireland* – a case relating to the internment of a suspected member of the Irish Republican Army between 1954 and 1957.[208] There, a public emergency amounted "to an exceptional situation of crisis or emergency which affects the whole population and constitutes a threat to the organized life of the community of which the State is composed."[209] More than a decade later, the European court had set the upper limit, specifically in the *Greek Case*: "[T]he emergency must be actual or imminent, its effects must involve the whole nation, the continuance of the organized life of the community must be threatened, [and] the crisis or danger must be exceptional, in that the normal measures or restrictions, permitted by the Convention for the maintenance of public safety, health and order, are plainly inadequate."[210]

In casting his opinion, Lord Bingham recognized that the decision whether a state of emergency existed fell outside judicial competence.[211] Instead, the question to be addressed by the court was the extent to which the measures adopted were *strictly required by the exigencies of the situation*. According to Bingham, the threat "did not derive solely from foreign nationals or from foreign nationals whom it was unlawful to deport."[212] Nor was there evidence that, even if fewer British nationals posed a threat, the magnitude or nature of the threat from them differed considerably from that presented by noncitizens.[213] The fact that these individuals would otherwise be released, free to pursue their "criminal designs" elsewhere, proved "hard to reconcile with a belief" that they had the "capacity to inflict serious injury to the people and interests of this country."[214] The actual text of the statute, moreover, did not limit the certification process to al Qaeda[215] (violent animal rights activists, for instance, could be similarly certified and detained). Lord Bingham recognized that the government had guaranteed that the measures would not be used for non-al Qaeda-related detentions. But he found it unacceptable "that interpretation and application of a statutory provision bearing on the liberty of the subject should be governed by implication, concession and undertaking."[216]

The case proved a battleground for institutional political legitimacy. Lord Bingham flatly rejected the Attorney General's attempt to distinguish between democratic institutions and the courts. Although judges were neither elected nor answerable to Parliament, and although they dwelt in different domains, "the function of independent judges charged to interpret and apply the law is universally recognized as a cardinal feature of the modern democratic state, a cornerstone of the rule of law itself."[217] Bingham continued, "The Attorney General is fully entitled to insist on the proper limits of judicial authority, but he is wrong to stigmatize judicial decision-making as in some way undemocratic."[218] He found the Attorney General's suggestion "particularly inappropriate," when Parliament gave the courts the authority – indeed the responsibility – of determining the extent to which domestic law infringed the ECHR. In other words, it fell to the judiciary to demarcate the bounds of a rights-based state.[219]

The Law Lords found that the measures were not just disproportionate, but unfairly discriminated against noncitizens. Article 14 of the ECHR affirmed the principles of equality and nondiscrimination.[220] Seven Law Lords followed suit: Lord Nicholls of Birkenhead wrote, "Indefinite imprisonment without charge or trial is anathema in any country which observes the rule of law. It deprives the detained person of the protection a criminal trial is intended to afford"; as a result, "[w]holly exceptional circumstances must exist before this extreme step can be justified."[221] But years had elapsed since 9/11. Citizens – namely, British Islamists – were not subject to the extraordinary powers. Nicholls wrote, "The government has vouchsafed no persuasive explanation of why national security calls for a power of indefinite detention in one case but not the other."[222] Where, as here, insufficient weight had been accorded to human rights, the court's duty was to intervene.[223]

Lord Hoffman also underscored the importance of this "ancient liberty ... freedom from arbitrary arrest and detention."[224] Quite ignoring the Irish experience, Hoffman announced that indefinite executive detention flew in the face of history ("Nothing could be more antithetical to the instincts and traditions of the people of the United Kingdom"[225]) and went one step further: "The real threat to the life of the nation, in the sense of a people living in accordance with its traditional laws and political values, comes not from terrorism but from laws such as these. That is the true measure of what terrorism may achieve. It is for Parliament to decide whether to give the terrorists such a victory."[226]

For Lord Rodger of Earlsferry, the magnitude of 9/11 mattered.[227] The courts lacked the government's access to intelligence reports and "expertise."[228] And where national security decisions came before them, the judiciary "must accord an appropriate degree of deference to the measures adopted by the government and by Parliament."[229] But even under limited judicial scrutiny, the conditions of the ECHR had not been met.

The Lords' decision, handed down on Charles Clarke's first day as Home Secretary,[230] quashed the derogation order and resulted in a declaration of incompatibility with the European Convention on Human Rights.[231] The government accused the judiciary of not understanding national security.[232] In defiance, the state continued to hold the detainees, prompting the resignation of Ian MacDonald and Rick Scannell – special advocates who had been given security clearances to represent the detainees before the Special Immigration Appeals Commission.[233] Then in January 2005, Clarke proposed universal control orders to replace the detention of foreigners – a measure that, though met with controversy, succeeded in becoming law (see page 67).

Torture Revisited

As the same time as they were pondering the issue of detention, the Law Lords were also scrutinizing the Special Immigration Appeals Commission to decide whether evidence procured by torture, without the complicity of British authorities, could be used as a basis for detention. The use of torture in the United Kingdom was already illegal under both domestic and international law.[234] Where British officials were not, however, actually engaging in such acts, and information was obtained by the use of torture, or inhuman and degrading treatment, in other states, the law was not as clear. It fell to the judicial House of Lords to determine whether Britain could take into account information thus obtained. In December 2005, Britain's highest court overturned the lower courts' findings and stated that information obtained by torture could not be taken into account in determining whether to detain foreign terrorist suspects.[235] Again, an extraordinary number of Lords – seven – heard the case.

In their decision, the Law Lords looked to the common law, the European Convention on Human Rights, and principles of international law. Lord Bingham noted that, since 1640, no lawfully sanctioned torture had existed in England, "and the rule that unsworn statements made out of court are inadmissible in court was well-established by latest the beginning of the 19th century."[236] English criminal law excluded confessions when challenged – unless the prosecution could prove, beyond reasonable doubt, that the confession had not been obtained by coercion or any method likely to render it unreliable.[237] Although confessions differed from general evidence, Lord Bingham found it significant that the common law treated oppression as going to the question of whether such information was even admissible – not to the amount of weight to be accorded a confession. The exclusionary rule – that such information would have to be excluded from the trial altogether – could be transferred, and practical reasons for doing so existed. Notoriously unreliable, such statements violated important judicial principles and cultural norms: exemption from self-incrimination and the protection of individuals while in police custody.[238] The endorsement of such behavior raised moral concerns: Bingham cited US Supreme Court Justice Felix Frankfurter's opinion in *Rochin v. California* (1952), which referred to "conduct that shocks the conscience." Frankfurter had underscored the importance of the "general principle" that "States in their prosecutions respect certain decencies of civilized conduct."[239] One could argue that "civilized" meant "British." And it was at the heart of British culture to embrace certain norms. For Frankfurter, due process rested on whether actions had offended "those canons of decency and fairness which express the notions of justice of English-speaking peoples even toward those charged with the most heinous offenses."[240]

Such canons of decency could be said to spring from the English tradition of honor. Lord Hoffman explained, "The use of torture is dishonourable. It corrupts and degrades the state which uses it and the legal system which accepts it." The United States' recent use of coercive interrogation, and the practice of rendering people to third countries, had brought, he said, "dishonour" on America.[241]

The corrosive effect of the use of torture was a serious problem in counterterrorism. Lord Hope of Craighead declared, "Once torture has become acclimatised in a legal system it spreads like an infectious disease, hardening and brutalising those who have become accustomed to its use."[242] If such conduct were to gain judicial approval, it would lie about "like a loaded weapon ready for the hand of any authority that can bring forward a plausible claim of an urgent need."[243]

As a matter of other international law, the ECHR was not alone in condemning torture. The 1945 United Nations Charter underscored the importance of individual dignity and worth. It was succeeded by the 1948 Universal Declaration of Human Rights and the 1966 International Covenant on Civil and Political Rights, each of which affirmed that no person should be subjected to inhuman or degrading treatment – or torture.[244] Lord Bingham concluded, "There can be few issues on which legal opinion is more clear than on the condemnation of torture."[245] Even complicity stood beyond the pale: "the *jus cogens erga omnes* [international law demanding compliance from all states] nature of the prohibition of torture requires member states to do more than eschew the practice of torture."[246] The United Kingdom had a duty "to reject the fruits of torture inflicted in breach of international law"[247] – a duty the threat of terrorism did not override.[248] Lord Bingham noted that the English abhorrence of torture "is now shared by over 140 countries which have acceded to the Torture convention."[249] The issue was not about evidence, he stated, but one of constitutional principle.[250]

While agreeing on the decision not to admit such tainted evidence, the Law Lords disagreed about the most appropriate test for determining how to identify it. For Lord Bingham and some others, the burden of proof lay on the accused, or his special advocate, to demonstrate that information central to his detention might have been obtained under torture – for instance, by showing that the information plausibly came from a country known for engaging in the practice. But a plurality – Lord Carswell, Lord Brown of Eaton-under-Heywood, and Lord Rodger of Earlsferry – cast their votes with Lord Hope.[251] SIAC should ask whether it is "established, by means of such diligent inquiries into the sources that it is practicable to carry out and on a balance of probabilities, that the information relied on by the Secretary of State was obtained under torture"; and if it was, the information could not be admitted as evidence.[252]

Control Orders

Addressing the Law Lords' concern about discrimination, the control orders that Home Secretary Charles Clarke proposed in January 2005 could be applied either to British subjects or to foreigners. These orders would, like the American preemption doctrine, "be preventative, designed to disrupt those seeking to carry out attacks, whether here or elsewhere, or who are planning or otherwise supporting such activities."[253] A clamor of protest arose immediately.[254]

Lawyers, Members of Parliament, civil liberties groups, and the press protested what was deemed "house arrest." The Law Society, which represented approximately 90,000 solicitors in England and Wales, condemned it as an "abuse of power."[255] Politicians such as David Blunkett (a former Home Secretary), John Denham (chair of the Home Affairs Select Committee), Robert Marshall-Andrews (a Labour MP for Medway), and Diane Abbott (a Labour MP for Hackney North and Stoke Newington) found the proposal objectionable.[256] David Davis, the shadow Home Secretary, argued, "Throughout our history, millions of British subjects have sacrificed their lives in defence of the nation's liberties and it would be a sad paradox if we were to sacrifice the nation's liberty in defence of our own lives today."[257] The decision to include British nationals was of particular concern.[258] Former members of SIAC and special advocates appointed under the ATCSA also demurred, as did the directors of Liberty, Amnesty International, and other organizations.[259]

There were strong arguments in the critics' favor. For one, control orders raised legal complications. Lord Lloyd explained that Britain would be violating Article 5 of the ECHR, requiring another derogation.[260] MPs expressed concern that Article 6 (right to fair trial), Article 8 (respect for private and family life), Article 10 (freedom of expression), and Article 11 (freedom of association) might similarly be implicated.[261] Even members of the prime minister's own party expressed concern that such orders would be open to legal challenge.[262] The parliamentary Joint Committee on Human Rights issued a report arguing that the new orders might breach European human rights law. Completely ignoring the Northern Ireland experience – where restriction orders were used with some regularity from 1922 forward – the report announced that Clarke's view was "eccentric" and would "subvert" the British constitution: "It is a long-established principle of the British constitution that, outside the field of immigration, the executive has no power to detain individuals without prior judicial authorisation or in circumstances where it is intended to bring the individual before a court."[263]

The practical effect of control orders also left something to be desired. Opponents pointed to the risk of alienating or radicalizing the Islamic minority, possibly further undermining security.[264] The Earl of Onslow drew a parallel to the Troubles, pointing out that internment had not just failed in Northern Ireland, but had been counterproductive. He added, "It was also against the law and against every single tradition with which we should be proud to associate ourselves."[265] Control orders could prove "a very effective recruiting sergeant" for terrorist organizations.[266] In a statement – utterly ironic considering that the Tory party had defended its use of internment and executive detention in Northern Ireland for decades – Michael Howard said that the Tories would reject the use of control orders issued by the Home Secretary because they would not allow liberty to be deprived "on the say-so of a politician."[267]

House arrest, without any opportunity to confront the accused or have guilt demonstrated in a court of law, was seen as unjust.[268] For the Opposition, it violated four central principles: the presumption of innocence, the right to know charges against oneself, the right to know and be allowed to challenge any evidence brought, and the criminal standard of proof (beyond reasonable doubt). Instead, a balance of probabilities would suffice to limit the inquiry to whether a suspect was more likely than not to have links to terrorist organizations – while essentially criminal penalties applied. Mere reasonable suspicion would be sufficient, limiting the possible scope of subsequent judicial review. These lowered standards underscored the risks of secret evidence – which had been publicly castigated by prominent attorneys who had served in the SIAC regime. Ian MacDonald explained to Members of Parliament that the system carried "an inherent risk that you end up with quote shoddy and misleading intelligence. There is no way you can ever be sure that that is accurate information on which you are acting."[269] David Davis noted that incarceration, like terrorism, could destroy lives.[270]

Newspapers the width and breadth of Great Britain denounced control orders.[271] In an editorial titled "An affront to justice – House arrest proposal smacks of political repression," Glasgow's *Herald* compared the measures to those used in the apartheid era, in Communist China, and in Myanmar.[272]

Others found parallels to Robert Mugabe in Zimbabwe, Vladimir Putin in Russia, Colonel Gaddafi in Libya, and General Musharraf in Pakistan.[273] The *Daily Post* in Liverpool suggested that "the so-called war on terror is hardly worth fighting if the freedoms and rights being threatened disappear as a result. The strategy of putting people behind bars without charge or trial on the basis of a political – as opposed to judicial – decision, is abhorrent regardless of the threat being posed to the nation. It is the very stuff of which dictatorships such as Saddam's were made."[274] The *Guardian* lamented, "Today MPs will be asked to abolish the presumption of innocence for British citizens."[275] Even the foreign press viewed the proposal as ill conceived.[276]

Initially, the government held its ground. Clarke invoked the traditional dichotomy: "I would urge you, when you consider this difficult question of the balance of liberty and security, even for UK subjects to recognize the obligations we all have to put security at the centre of our preoccupations."[277] Muslims had nothing to fear unless they were "explicitly involved in promoting terrorist activity."[278] The prime minister thought it better to err on the side of caution: "What we are desperate to do is to avoid a situation where, at a later point, people turn round and say: If you had only been as vigilant as you should have been, we could have averted a terrorist attack."[279]

But gradually, the government backpedaled. First, it dropped the concept of "house arrest," claiming never to have used the phrase.[280] Then, Blair agreed to meet with the Opposition.[281] It was the first meeting between Michael Howard and Tony Blair since the former had taken over Conservative leadership.[282] Charles Clarke similarly agreed to meet with David Davis, the Shadow Home Secretary.[283]

The Liberal Democrats also objected to the proposed control orders,[284] seeing them as involving too much executive power without sufficient judicial check.[285] Moreover, they wanted intercept evidence to be admissible in court and offered the judiciary as an alternative route to deal with national security terrorist threats.[286] Ireland and the United Kingdom were among the only "major western democracies" that refused to allow such evidence in court.[287] Senior police officers supported this effort.[288] Newspapers applauded the political resistance.[289]

The government, however – backed by its intelligence agencies, MI5, MI6, and Government Communications Headquarters (the central agency for signals intelligence) – refused to allow intercepts.[290] Clarke said it "would not assist in getting further prosecution."[291] (A government review found that allowing intercepts "would not have allowed any of the suspects held at Belmarsh to be tried in court."[292]) Human intelligence, according to Clarke, was more effective in the fight against terror.[293] Allowing such evidence might also hurt Britain's relationship with foreign intelligence bodies, upon which, quite apart from foreign relations generally, the United Kingdom depended for information. The Security Services expressed concern about how much of their time and resources would be diverted to preparing cases to take to court – when, instead, they could be hitting the pavement to get leads.[294] Gwyn Winfield, the publisher of the defense journal *Resilience*, added, "Telephone tapping is among the lowest forms of intelligence available."[295] It required human intelligence to give it meaning. But supplementing intercepts with intelligence in the course of judicial proceedings could put sources at risk – and reveal the methods used by the security services.

The Prevention of Terrorism Act

Despite strong opposition, the Government persisted. It resurrected the title of an old piece of counterterrorist legislation, the Prevention of Terrorism Act, and on February 21, 2005 announced that it would drive the measures through Parliament within a fortnight.[296] (With the existing detention orders on the remaining 10 foreign nationals due to expire on March 10, the state threatened that the suspects would walk without new legislation.[297]) Adding insult to injury, the Government allowed just two days for the discussion in the House of Commons.[298] Such "contempt for historic rights" raised hackles in the first chamber – as well as in the House of Lords, where the rapidly approaching end of the session meant that there would be little time to consider the bill.[299] The Opposition complained about such extraordinary powers being "rammed" through the political process.[300]

The Government went on the offensive: the day it published the bill, the Home Office issued briefing papers to Members of Parliament, detailing the "unprecedented and potent threat from international terrorism."[301] In Westminster, Charles Clarke warned that terrorists could strike during the general election campaign.[302] And in an effort to head off amendments, the government accused MPs of playing politics with national security.[303]

A massive public relations campaign paralleled the political maneuvering: Tony Blair went on Radio 4's *Woman's Hour*, stating that the threat was well in excess of intelligence officials' statements.[304] He pleaded that "you have got to give us power in between just surveying them and being sure enough to prosecute them beyond reasonable doubt. There are people out there who are determined to destroy our way of life and there is no point in us being naïve about it."[305] The government rolled out top cops to back its case: Sir John Stevens, former Chief of the Metropolitan Police, insisted that control orders were necessary to restrain some 200 trained operatives.[306] Sir Ian Blair, Stevens' successor, said greater vigilance was needed. "The main opposition to the bill," he wrote, "is from people who simply haven't understood the brutal reality of the world we live in and the true horror of the terrorism we face."[307] Release of the 10 suspects held at Belmarsh, without control orders, would be a "grave threat to national security."[308] Tony Blair told the press that it came down to leadership: "It is time to be strong."[309]

But the bill did not apply just to Islamist militants. When asked if the Home Secretary would use the orders against G8 protestors, who objected to policies set by the world's leading industrialized nations, the prime minister responded, "I couldn't rule it out."[310] So everyone's rights were at stake, and the opposition parties fought back. In a rare expression of solidarity, the Conservative Party and the Liberal Democrats tabled a joint amendment that criticized the bill as excessive, granting judicial rights to the executive, and infringing individual rights. The House of Commons defeated the amendment 316 to 216 – a majority of just 100. The Prevention of Terrorism Bill was then given its second reading, which passed more narrowly, by a majority of 76 (309 to 233). Notably, 32 Labour MPs voted against the Government.[311]

A popular revolt supported the political stonewalling. Lord Haskins (a Labour Party donor, and Blair's former advisor), three Bishops, the actress Honor Blackman (who played James Bond's girl Pussy Galore), Mike Leigh (the Oscar-nominated film director of *Vera Drake*), Sir Ian McKellen (actor), Peter Gabriel (musician), Frederick Forsyth (novelist), Sir David Hare (playwright), and Jazz-Funk DJ Mr. Scruff all took umbrage. Along with hundreds of lawyers, including such prominent ones as Mr. Guy Mansfield (chair of the Bar Council), Professor Ronald Dworkin, Professor Conor Gearty, and Lord Lester of Herne Hill, they signed a statement that described the proposed law as the "stuff of nightmares" and called for an "end to detention without trial, respect for precious British values of freedom, justice and the presumption of innocence, and the recognition that human rights must not and need not be sacrificed for effective security."[312] The document concluded, "Visible injustice debases our democracy and undermines our safety. Indefinite detention without trial is always wrong. We call on our politicians to think again."[313] Local papers began quoting the Magna Carta.[314]

Anger was directed at not just the inroads into liberty rights but also at the seeming contradiction: either the people were dangerous, and so ought not to be allowed to roam free; or they were not, and the control orders were abusive. The widest circulating tabloid, the *Sun* – a generally conservative paper to boot – demanded, "What the heck is going on?" The *Daily Mirror* argued that the bill put the "country at greater risk, not less." And the *Daily Mail*, generally right of center, opined, "What this sorry saga has revealed is a shaming litany of official arrogance, gross Government incompetence, outrageously bungled legislation and an almost contemptuous disregard for the legal safeguards that have been part of our constitutional fabric for centuries."[315]

One of the most contentious aspects of the proposed legislation stemmed from the role of the judiciary. Judges could review the decision, but would play no role in the initial act; and so as long as "reasonable grounds" existed for the order, it would stand.[316] A poll conducted by the *Daily Telegraph* found that three-quarters of the public felt that where suspected terrorists could not be brought to trial but intelligence indicated their involvement in terrorism, it may be necessary to restrict their movement. One-third of those polled considered the insertion of the judiciary preferable to unilateral executive action[317] – sentiments the MPs echoed. The shadow Attorney General, Dominic Grieve, for instance, noted that, while control orders may be "unpleasant, repellent and disgusting," if they must be instituted, it would be better to have a judge, not the Home Secretary, make the decision.[318]

Although to some extent the judiciary represented a safeguard on the possible abuse of executive power, the argument for involving the courts hinted at a deeper perception of the role of the judiciary in protecting liberty rights. Looked at in a slightly more cynical way, the judiciary offered legitimacy – and bringing judges into the process at the beginning could help avoid later rulings that might undermine government policy. The Liberal Democrats pointed out that "it will be far better for the upholding of the authority of government, of any party, for ministers to have their proposal endorsed by the judiciary, rather than what has happened to many Home Secretaries, which is to have their decision overturned by the courts."[319]

The government did not want the judiciary to be engaged in the process, but Clarke – under pressure and fearing a fight in the House of Lords – reluctantly proposed some judicial involvement at an earlier stage.[320] His effort to mollify his opponents failed spectacularly – if for no other reason than his arrogance and the manner in which he introduced the quasi-amendment – which would have to be carried through by the House of Lords (thus reducing the importance and impact of the Commons' debate[321]). During the Second Reading of the bill, Clarke, on his feet for 90 minutes, was "frequently interrupted in an increasingly tetchy House."[322] The concessions did not go far enough: only serious control orders would benefit from judicial involvement early in the process, and suspects still would not be told of the evidence against them.

Clarke essentially proposed in exchange for vows of future amendments that the House approve the Bill – an extraordinary request. Dominic Grieve complained, "We are being asked to pass this legislation, which is of huge constitutional and legal significance, and we are being asked to do it on the basis of promises which will be fulfilled elsewhere.[323] Kenneth Clarke, the former Tory Home Secretary, was outraged: "[I]t reduces our proceedings to a farce."[324] The Home Secretary became defensive – he was sick of barristers talking down to him. The shadow Attorney General pointed out that it was because Charles Clarke did not comprehend the principles at stake: namely, due process. Clarke whipped back, "I do understand what is at stake. I understand the issues very well."[325] Sixty Labour MPs, including four ex-cabinet ministers, rebelled, and Clarke watched his party's 161-person majority plummet to 14.[326] But Labour held on: with a vote of 267 to 253, the bill progressed to the second chamber.[327]*

Predictably, the House of Lords proved sensitive to questions regarding the role of the judiciary – but, unlike the Commons, they took umbrage with the manner of judicial involvement. Peers expressed concern that using the courts as a rubber stamp would erode their political legitimacy. The former Master of the Rolls, Lord Donaldson of Lymington, said it would be "totally unacceptable" for a judge to have to meet with Home Secretary and agree to a control order:

---

* Interestingly, more than 150 MPs did not vote, including 16 Liberal Democrats. The Conservative Party also did not have full attendance. *MPs Let Us Down: Why Should We Vote If They Don't?* THE OBSERVER, Mar. 6, 2005, p. 24.

"That is an affront to the fundamental position of judges, which is that they are umpires – they do not play."[328] For Lord Lloyd of Berwick, the insertion of judges would be "a charade" and "a sham," as they are not experts in risk assessment.[329] Lloyd continued, "[I]t is essentially a political decision, which would expose judges to a political backlash of just the kind from which it is our duty to protect them."[330]

The unrepresentative House of Lords was indeed "a strange place to be debating fundamental questions of liberty,"[331] but it was there, not in the Commons, that a rancorous discussion over the rights at stake broke out. The Tory spokesperson Baroness Anelay of St Johns explained, "[W]e believe that the Home Secretary has settled on the wrong answers, ones that may sacrifice essential and long standing principles of liberty and justice."[332] Baroness Kennedy of the Shaws, a Labour peer, recognized that terrorism presented a risk; but so did injustice, and the erosion of civil liberties was a cause for concern.[333] The Labour peer Baroness Mallalieu agreed, "It is wrong to take away or curtail anybody's freedom without due process of law. That's one of the basic principles of our constitution."[334] Remarkably, Baroness Margaret Thatcher, known for her hard line as prime minister against Northern Irish paramilitaries, argued *for* the rights of terrorist suspects.[335] Lord Thomas of Gresford, the Liberal Democrat spokesman in Lords, objected to placing the right to security above individual liberty: "[S]ecurity is no justification for the breach of fundamental principles which underpin our democratic system; no deprivation of liberty by Ministerial say so, no midnight, secret knock on the door, no gulags in Siberia or in Guantánamo."[336] A report from the House of Lords Constitution Committee recommended that because of the rights at stake, the powers granted should be temporary and renewed annually with a five-year maximum.[337] Control orders "should be regarded at best as an exceptional response to an emergency, not as a permanent feature of statute law, available for use by any government far in the future."[338]

The fact that the Lords, a generally uncontentious lot, proved more willing than the MPs to fight for basic liberties reflected the second chamber's growing willingness to confront the state where civil liberties were at stake.[339] To some extent, the trend related to the 1998 Human Rights Act, and the expanding role the Law Lords played in determining whether legislation was compatible with the ECHR. Recent reforms, though, also played a role: Labour removed most of the hereditary peerships. Down from 1,300 in 1999, by 2006 the number of peers had plummeted to 700.[340] Some commentators suggest that the remaining peers tended to attend regularly, and act with greater independence.[341] No party, moreover, controlled a majority: in the context of 206 Labour peers, 205 Conservative peers, and 191 cross-benchers, the Liberal Democrats, with 74, held the balance.[342] Simultaneously, counterterrorist measures were increasingly challenging civil liberties, bringing together Conservatives concerned about traditional freedoms, Liberal Democrats opposed to government policy, and cross-benchers drawn from the judicial system itself.[343]

Government ministers, however, remained largely impervious to the peers' demands. The *Independent* reported, "When they did respond, they made matters, if anything, worse."[344] The result was "politics at its fiercest and most raw." A "remarkably united Upper Chamber" was "pitted against a sharply divided Commons." The Conservatives, headed "by a former hard-line home secretary" was "defending civil liberties and leaving Labour to argue for the primacy of national security." In the meantime, the prime minister argued that freedom from terrorism was "the most important consideration" – outshining civil liberties concerns.[345]

By March 9, 2005, the Lords had inflicted five "humiliating" defeats on Labour – and their strength was growing.[346] The government refused to sunset the control orders, insisting that annual review would be sufficient to guard against abuse; it rebuffed efforts to require that, before assigning control orders, the Director of Public Prosecutions have no reasonable prospect of using criminal law to prosecute.[347] In response to the civil liberties objection, the prime minister hauled out the famous dichotomy: "I believe [the powers in the bill] are a proper balance between the civil liberties of the subject and the necessary national security of this country."[348] Labour then suspended the debates – though supposedly done to make adjustments to the text, this decision allowed the Lords even less time to consider the bill.[349]

The House of Lords voted 249 to 119 against the government for imposing control orders, a vote that led journalists to contemplate "the muddle, incompetence and myopia that have characterized the sloppy handling of this vital issue."[350] Voting against Blair were 24 peers from his own party; the defection of some of these peers – such as Lord Irvine, the former Lord Chancellor and the Prime Minister's former mentor– proved particularly embarrassing.[351] The tabloids for once applauded the House of Lords, saying that it "showed justified contempt for the idea that ministers should be able to place suspects under house arrest without going to court."[352] The *Evening Standard* proclaimed that "giving politicians the right to detain people on secret evidence from the security services goes against centuries-old principles of British justice"; to bring the point home, it adapted the National Lottery slogan: "It could be you."[353]

With the clock ticking, for more than 30 hours the bill flew back and forth between the two chambers, continuing the longest parliamentary "day" in 99 years. Arguments raged behind the speaker's chair.[354] Labour fought against increasing the standard of proof for lower level control orders, maintaining that "grounds for suspicion" would be sufficient. Davis retorted for the Tories, "Rejecting the balance of probabilities means that the government is willing to put a control order on someone who is probably not a terrorist. That is a formulation for many miscarriages of justice."[355] Lord Thomas, the Liberal Democratic spokesman, alleged that Labour was treating the British people like sheep.[356] As the debate became increasingly rancorous, defiant peers refused to concede: some set up camp beds in the library, and one lord had his heart pills biked in to London from his home in Essex.[357]

The government finally conceded that for the most serious control orders, known as "derogating" orders, judges would decide in the first instance whether control orders would be necessary. Where an emergency existed, a high court judge would confirm the decision within seven days. For nonderogating control orders, which would be issued by the Secretary of State, the onus lay on the target to appeal the decision.[358]

But the government flat-out refused to sunset the powers. The Home Secretary argued that there were already five or six review procedures in place: the legislation required the Home Secretary to report to Parliament every three months on the operation of control orders. An independent commissioner would be required to review the use of the powers every year. Derogating orders could only be put into place if the United Kingdom derogated – at which time Parliament would have to approve. The government vowed to revisit the subject at the next session. And the future general election would provide an additional, democratic check.[359]

Finally, the debate came to a close. Although the Lords had been successful on some points, a battle of attrition wore them down. Acutely aware of its lesser political status, the second chamber did not as a general matter block government legislation. Eighteen days after the introduction of the bill, it received Royal Assent.

In the end, the government broke its promise. It did not return to the Lords the following session to revisit the issue of control orders. Instead, it introduced a new bill into the House of Commons, extending the use of restriction provisions to individuals associated with, but not convicted of, involvement in drug running – a stark example of counterterrorist provisions seeping over into the criminal realm.

US DETENTION OF FOREIGN NATIONALS AT GUANTÁNAMO BAY

Three days after the hijacked planes flew into the World Trade Center and the Pentagon, US President George W. Bush declared a national state of emergency.[360] Congress authorized the president "to use all necessary and appropriate force against those nations, organizations, or persons he determines planned, authorized, committed, or aided the terrorist attacks . . . or harbored such organizations or persons, in order to prevent any future acts of international terrorism against the United States by such nations, organizations or persons."[361] The Joint Resolution helped lay the legal groundwork for the United States' subsequent war in Afghanistan. John Yoo, Deputy Assistant Attorney General, cited the document and the War Powers Resolution, as overt congressional acknowledgment of the president's "broad constitutional power" to preempt and retaliate against terrorists and those who harbor them.[362] On October 7, 2001, Bush announced that the US military had begun military strikes in Afghanistan.[363]

Six weeks later, on November 13, 2001, the President issued a Military Order stating that a "compelling government interest" required the indefinite detention of noncitizens.[364] These noncitizens included not only members of al-Qaeda but also anyone who "has engaged in, aided or abetted, or conspired to commit, acts of international terrorism, or acts in preparation therefore, that have caused, threaten to cause, or have as their aim to cause, injury to or adverse effects on the United States, its citizens, national security, foreign policy, or economy" and anyone who had knowingly harbored an international terrorist. Some detainees would be tried by military tribunals, presided over by three military officers. Their rights under the ordinary criminal system would not apply: "Given the danger to the safety of the United States and the nature of international terrorism," Bush said, "it is not practicable to apply in military commissions under this order the principles of law and the rules of evidence generally recognized in the trial of criminal cases in the United States district courts."[365]

As in the United Kingdom, these policies ignited a battle among the branches of government – a battle whose immediate focus was counterterrorism but that had implications well beyond the terrorist threat. At stake was the authority of the judiciary to protect individual rights in the face of an extreme assertion of executive power. And it was a complex set of rights involved: not just liberty rights were threatened but also free speech, freedom of association, and freedom of religion. In this struggle two of the branches shared a political party, making them less a check on each other and more cohorts in undermining the traditional balance of power that had been carefully crafted by the Framers. The repercussions of these policies were not only domestic but also international, radically diminishing the nation's stature in the world. In December 2001, Secretary of Defense Donald Rumsfeld announced that the detainees would be moved for interrogation to Guantánamo Bay[366]* – "the least worst place [according to him] we could have selected."[367]

As a purely practical matter, Guantánamo Bay had both drawbacks and advantages. For one, it shared a land mass with a hostile communist country.† For another, it lacked adequate facilities: from 1994 to 1996, the base held 50,000 Haitian and Cuban refugees.[368] Accommodations would have to be built for the influx of troops – and for a significant number of high-security

---

* Reports on the number of detainees held by the United States by the end of December 2001 vary widely. The *Austin American-Statesman* claimed that the United States held just 45 detainees – 8 on the USS *Peleliu* in the Arabian Sea, and 37 at a Marine camp near Kandahar. Bob Dart, "Afghan Prisoners Will Be Held at U.S. Base in Cuba," *Austin American-Statesman* (Texas), Dec. 28, 2001, at A9. The *Guardian* put the number closer to 7,000. *U.S. Questions 7,000 Taliban and al-Qaida Soldiers*, GUARDIAN (London), Dec. 21, 2001, at www.guardian.co.uk.

† In 1898, 600 Marines seized the island during the Spanish-American War. Five years later, President Theodore Roosevelt signed an agreement with Cuba that imposed a "lease" on part of the island – in return for 2,000 gold pieces per year. Renegotiated in 1934, the United States would only give back the land if both countries agreed. Treasury began sending checks for $4,085, which Fidel Castro annually tore up without cashing. *First 'Bad Guys' from al – Qaida Arrive in Cuba for Questioning*, COMMERCIAL APPEAL (Memphis, TN), Jan. 12, 2002, at A1. *See also* Larry Luxner, *Camp Delta at "Gitmo," Afghanistan Worlds Apart*, WASH. TIMES, Apr. 29, 2003, at A12.

prisoners.* The number of detainees in US custody was increasing by 20 to 25 people per day[369] and had, by mid-January, tipped 500.[370] The Pentagon estimated that facilities for up to 2,000 prisoners would have to be constructed.[371] When and if tribunals began, witnesses would have to be flown potentially thousands of miles, at significant expense, to testify.[372]

As for its advantages, Guantánamo Bay lay outside domestic borders – reducing potential threats to the American judiciary while circumventing potential legal challenge to the prisoners' continued detention. (The day after Rumsfeld's announcement, John Yoo and Deputy Assistant Attorney General Patrick F. Philbin wrote to William J. Haynes II, the Department of Defense's General Counsel, claiming that US federal courts lacked jurisdiction over any habeas petitions that may be made from the island. Although the authors hedged their language, this claim became central to the Bush administration's legal strategy.)[373] Guantánamo Bay was thousands of miles from the war zone and surrounded by open water, electric fences, and mine fields – diminishing the likelihood of prisoner escape or assault by the Taliban or al Qaeda.[374] As a security matter, the island base gave the United States more control than it had in Afghanistan, where in November 2001 hundreds of people, including a CIA agent, had died after a prisoner uprising at Mazar-e Sharif.[375] In December more than a dozen had lost their lives when al Qaeda captured weapons from Pakistani guards,[376] and even after the plane took off from Kandahar with the first transfer of detainees, rebels attacked the air strip.[377] Steve Lucas, speaking for US Southern Command in Miami, reflected, "For the movement of these kinds of prisoners, people who are murderously suicidal, I don't think there's precedent."[378]

In moving the detainees, the military adopted special security measures. The detainees' beards were shaved, and they were shackled, sedated, and hooded for the 24-hour flight.[379] After finding that some detainees had tuberculosis, the military placed surgical masks over detainees' mouths.[380] When they arrived on the island, the US military imprisoned them in six- by eight-foot wire cages,[381] "exposed to rain, wind, and Guantánamo's notoriously ravenous mosquitoes"[382] and provided only with sleeping mats and blankets.[383] "We've been told this is a tough group of people, and we're prepared to secure them here," said Navy Lieutenant Bill Salvin.[384] The *Boston Globe* reported, "They will be kept apart in the cage-like cells except for meals, showers, and brief exercise periods."[385] Roberto Nelson, a Navy spokesman, hailed them as "violent, desperate, and suicidal – 'the worst of the worst.'"[386] More than a year into the operation, Major General Geoffrey Miller, the Commander of the Joint Task Force at Guantánamo Bay, said, "Every detainee in this camp is a threat to the United States."[387]

---

* Camp X-ray, the initial temporary facility, was replaced by Camp Delta, a long-term detention site, for which Halliburton, Vice President Cheney's former company, provided most of the construction. Charlie Savage, *Guantánamo's 'Child Soldiers' in Limbo*, BOSTON GLOBE, Nov. 16, 2003, at A1.

This claim has, however, turned out to be as misleading as Britain's had been about its IRA prisoners (see page 41). Interrogation logs show that the military did transfer some valuable detainees: Mohamed al-Qahtani, believed to be a "20th hijacker"[388]*; Fazel Mazloom, the Taliban army's former chief of staff, was believed to have been involved in an al Qaeda attack on Ahmed Shah Massoud, a Northern Alliance leader, just before 9/11[389]; and Awal Gul, who helped bin Laden move from Sudan to Afghanistan in the 1990s.[390] The United States placed other Taliban officials, such as the former ambassador to Pakistan, on the island as well.[391]

But not everyone captured and transferred to Guantánamo Bay was a "seasoned thug," "who drilled intensively at Osama bin Laden's camps in the sinister arts of murder with bare hands and construction of hairbrush bombs."[392] By March 2002, the *Washington Post* reported, "Some appear to be naïve teenagers whipped into religious frenzy and dispatched to holy war by wily elders."[393] Major General Michael Dunlavey, who oversaw interrogations at Camp X-ray in Guantánamo Bay, acknowledged in March 2002, "We do have a small percentage who are people who got caught up in the excitement of the moment."[394] (It later emerged that in the spring of 2002 Dunlavey went to Afghanistan to protest the transfer of "Mickey Mouse" [absurdly low-level] detainees to an already overcrowded facility.[395]) By December, at least 59 detainees (nearly 10%) were regarded as having no meaningful connection to al Qaeda or the Taliban.[396] *All* of them had been recommended for repatriation *prior* to their transfer to Guantánamo,[397] and classified reports described them as farmers, cobblers, taxi drivers, and laborers.[398]

US intelligence officers in Afghanistan "became increasingly dismayed" at the type of prisoner being sent to Guantánamo Bay. One said, "We saw it as having huge potential for eroding public trust" – devastating efforts to win hearts and minds.[399] A list of people whom military officials thought should be excluded from transfer began to circulate; it included the suspects' occupations, where they were captured, their alibis, and a summary of their initial interrogation. Military officials began to withhold detainees' names "from prison rosters until they could be evaluated. That way, they didn't officially exist and, if deemed harmless, could be released before their names got caught up in the system."[400]

The detainees ranged in age from 13 to somewhere in the seventies.[401] Later the children were separated from the other prisoners and placed in "Iguana House."[402] Although Rumsfeld eventually acknowledged that they were not all hard-core terrorists, he still held to the line that the first transfers were.[403] But this assertion, too, fell short of the truth: the first prisoner to be released, for example, in April 2002, was insane. He ate his own feces and urinated in his canteen – and then drank it.[404] A Pakistani intelligence report later claimed

---

* The existence of a "20th hijacker" stems from a theory that one of the planes destroyed on 9/11, United Airlines Flight 93, was missing a person. Qahtani is not the only person to be considered as the "missing" member. Zaccarias Moussaoui, Ramzi Binalsibh, Saeed al-Ghamdi, Mushabib al-Hamlan, and others have been considered in this category.

that privately, "The U.S. authorities have agreed that most of the Pakistanis are innocent and they were at the wrong place at the wrong time."[405] Many of them had been security guards, cooks, or drivers for the Taliban and were captured when General Rashid Dostum's Northern Alliance forces took over the city of Kunduz in October 2001. Reward money also appears to have determined who was handed over to the United States. The Pakistani report says, "Dostum's troops buried hundreds of wounded Pakistanis alive and locked thousands in containers without air inlets resulting in deaths of hundreds due to suffocation. Those who remained alive were sold to the U.S. for $20,000 to $30,000 per head."[406] By the summer of 2002, Pakistan was negotiating the release of 54 of 61 Pakistanis held at Guantánamo Bay.[407] By February 2006, by the Pentagon's own figures, only 8% of the individuals held at the base were classified as al Qaeda suspects.[408]

Not only were many of those held low-level operatives or innocent, but the US government sent the true "worst of the worst" elsewhere. In December 2002, the *Washington Post* reported that the United States was running secret detention centers overseas and quoted Rumsfeld: senior al Qaeda members were "treated in a totally different way, in a very careful way."[409] Some suspects and facilities were under CIA, not Pentagon, control,[410] leading some counterterrorism experts to suggest that Guantánamo's inmates were "among the least significant of the detainees captured since the Sept. 11 attacks."[411] At these secret sites, the CIA isolated and disoriented prisoners, convincing them that they were in the control of other regimes.[412] Among these detainees were Abu Zubaydah, believed to have taken over al Qaeda operations after Mohammed Atef was killed in an air strike; Suleiman Abdalla; and Ramzi bin al-Shibh.[413]

Part of the reason people not central to al Qaeda ended up at Guantánamo Bay was structural: the criteria for transfer there left little opportunity for cases to be considered individually. Then, upon arrival, the prisoners were not given the opportunity to contest their detention; nor did a review body examine each case. Like the intelligence available on Northern Irish paramilitarism in the early 1970s, little was known early on about al Qaeda or the region – and any information might be valuable. In addition, no one wanted to be responsible for the next attack.[414]

What was to happen afterward to the detainees remained a matter of speculation. Rumsfeld laid out the options: they might be tried by military tribunal or civil court, or transferred to other countries for prosecution, or simply be held indefinitely.[415] Until this decision was made, the prisoners would be treated in a manner "reasonably consistent with the Geneva Conventions."[416]

Suspending the Geneva Conventions

As Donald Rumsfeld's remarks hinted, behind the scenes in Washington, a fierce debate was raging. Unbeknownst to the public, two days before the first detainees arrived, a series of legal memoranda began shuttling among the White House and the Departments of Defense, Justice, and State, addressing whether the Geneva Conventions ought to be applied to individuals detained as part of the global war on terror. This discussion unwittingly echoed the debate that had begun in the United Kingdom three decades earlier, but been set to one side. The United States, however, waded further into its depths. The four Geneva Conventions of 1949 address the treatment of noncombatants: wounded soldiers on the battlefield, wounded or shipwrecked soldiers at sea, prisoners of war, and civilians under enemy control. Two common articles appear in all four conventions:

Art. 2: In addition to the provisions which shall be implemented in peace time, *the present Convention shall apply to all cases of declared war or of any other armed conflict which may arise between two or more of the High Contracting Parties, even if the state of war is not recognized by one of them.* The Convention shall also apply to all cases of partial or total occupation of the territory of a High Contracting Party, even if the said occupation meets with no armed resistance.

Art. 3: *In the case of armed conflict not of an international character occurring in the territory of one of the High Contracting Parties*, each Party to the conflict shall be bound to apply, as a minimum, the following provisions: (1) Persons taking no active part in the hostilities, including members of armed forces who have laid down their arms and those placed 'hors de combat' by sickness, wounds, detention, or any other cause, shall in all circumstances be treated humanely, without any adverse distinction founded on race, color, religion or faith, sex, birth or wealth, or any other similar criteria. To this end, the following acts are and shall remain prohibited at any time and in any place whatsoever with respect to the above-mentioned persons: (a) violence to life and person, in particular murder of all kinds, mutilation, cruel treatment and torture; (b) taking of hostages; (c) outrages upon personal dignity, in particular humiliating and degrading treatment; (d) the passing of sentences and the carrying out of executions without previous judgment pronounced by a regularly constituted court, affording all the judicial guarantees which are recognized as indispensable by civilized peoples.[417]

The Bush administration eventually determined that, as a matter of policy, the Geneva Conventions did apply to the wars in Afghanistan and Iraq. At the same time, the president asserted his broad authority to suspend the treaty, declaring that it did *not* apply to "enemy combatants" detained by US forces.

The discussion leading to this conclusion raised important legal and political arguments that I explore later. The key point is this: as a policy matter, the decisions both to withhold the Conventions and to increase pressure on military interrogators to obtain information led to a series of abuses for which the United States has paid – and is paying – a high price.

The Legal Arguments. In early January 2002, in the first internal memo, John Yoo, Deputy Assistant Attorney General, and Robert J. Delahunty, Special Counsel at the Office of Legal Counsel, wrote to the General Counsel at the Department of Defense. Yoo and Delahunty started with the US War Crimes statute that, consistent with Geneva Convention requirements, criminalizes "grave breaches" of all four Conventions by any US national or member of the Armed Forces.[418*]

Yoo and Delahunty next asserted that neither Common Article 2 nor Common Article 3 applies to the global war on terror: although Common Article 3 binds the United States as a High Contracting Party "even if other parties to the conflict are not parties to the convention," it requires only that certain minimum standards be met in the case of civil war. When juxtaposed to the language of Common Article 2 ("between two or more of the High Contracting Parties"), the language of Article 3 ("not of an international character") could be taken to mean within the borders of one state.[419] Yoo and Delahunty suggested that the drafters of the Geneva Conventions had in mind just two forms of armed conflict: between Nation States (and thus regulated by Article 2) and "large-scale civil war within a Nation State (subject to Article 3)."[420] Situations like the global war on terror "would have been simply unforeseen and, therefore, not provided for."[421] Al Qaeda was not a state and thus could not claim protection under Common Article 2. Even if al Qaeda were to claim to be an irregular force, the network did not meet the requisite criteria. Geneva Convention III defines lawful combatants as follows:

(1) Members of the armed forces of a Party to the conflict as well as members of militias or volunteer corps forming part of such armed forces.
(2) Members of other militias and members of other volunteer corps, including those of organized resistance movements, belonging to a Party to the conflict and operating in or outside their own territory, even if this territory is occupied, provided that such militias or volunteer corps, including such organized resistance movements, fulfill the following conditions: (a) that of being commanded by a person responsible for his subordinates; (b) that of having a fixed distinctive sign recognizable at a distance; (c) that of carrying arms openly; (d) that of conducting their operations in accordance with the laws and customs of war. (3) Members of regular armed forces who profess allegiance to a government or an authority not recognized by the Detaining Power.... (6) Inhabitants of a non-occupied territory, who on the approach of the enemy spontaneously take up arms to resist the invading forces, without having had time to form themselves into regular armed units, provided they carry arms openly and respect the laws and customs of war.[422]

Yoo and Delahunty said that al Qaeda did not meet these criteria; further, under the 1907 Hague Convention, the "laws, rights, and duties of war" apply only to regular or irregular militias when they meet four conditions: "command by responsible individuals, wearing insignia, carrying arms openly, and obeying

---

* The Geneva Conventions offer slightly different definitions of "grave breach." A grave breach under the third Convention is "willful killing, torture or inhuman treatment, including biological experiments, willfully causing great suffering or serious injury to body or health, compelling a prisoner of war to serve in the forces of the hostile Power, or willfully depriving a prisoner of war of the rights of fair and regular trial prescribed in" the treaty. Geneva Convention III, art. 130. *See* hwww.icrc.org/Web.

the laws of war."[423]* Al Qaeda members, in contrast, did not follow the laws of war.

Underlying this memo was the idea that the Geneva Conventions were in essence a contract. Where the language does not explicitly address international terrorism, the terms ought not, with time, be read expansively. This approach was at odds with that taken by various bodies in regard to human rights – whose protection during wartime was the purpose of the common articles.[424] The application of Common Article 3 to civil war involves substantial interference in state sovereignty: that is, even where a conflict is purely internal, the High Contracting Parties must submit to international standards. To expect the Conventions to not apply then to noninternal conflicts, on the basis of rejecting an expansive reading, runs somewhat counter to logic.[425]

Yoo and Delahunty, though, took a positivist position. As a policy matter, significant disadvantages would accompany acquiescence to a treaty whose legal implications remained cloaked from view. The Geneva Conventions, moreover, do contain a mechanism for amendment: in the event that a country wants the provisions to be applied to different forms of international conflict, then steps can be taken to gain the agreement of states party to the provisions.

Where Yoo and Delahunty were on weakest ground was in relation to the Taliban. They claimed that, since, like al Qaeda, the Taliban did not meet any of the requirements of a regularly constituted militia – as laid out in Geneva Convention III and the Hague Convention – they were unlawful combatants.[†] The problem with Yoo and Delahunty's assertion was that the Taliban did act primarily as a military organization: its members openly carried arms and could be identified by black headdresses; they followed a chain of command (the United States claimed to have the army's former chief of staff at Guantánamo Bay);[426] and professed allegiance to a government or authority not recognized by the United States – and thus belonged squarely under Article 4(A)(3) of Geneva Convention III. As a movement resisting the American occupation of Afghanistan, they also fell within Article 4(A)(2), which similarly applied to that nation's Karzai government – which in turn evoked Common Article 3 (applying to insurgents within domestic bounds.)

The Office of Legal Counsel argued, though, that not only did the Geneva Conventions not apply, but that, even if they did, the president had the authority to suspend the treaty.[427] Where Afghanistan either could not fulfill its obligations or was in material breach of the treaty, the president could declare it null and void. As a domestic matter, his power to do so stemmed from Article II of

---

* Yoo/Delahunty further asserted that, by not falling within the meaning of Common Articles 2 or 3, Article 4 ceased to apply. However, even if Article 4 were read to be jurisdictional as well as substantive, they did not meet the conditions created by the 1907 Hague Convention.

† In *United States v. Lindh*, the U.S. District Court for the Eastern District of Virginia came to a similar conclusion. *United States* v. *Lindh*, 1:02-cr-00037-ALL (January 15, 2002), documents cited at www.notablecases.vaed.uscourts.gov/.

the Constitution. As a matter of international law, the United States could not denounce the Conventions (a process explicitly prescribed). But, in accordance with the Vienna Convention on the Law of Treaties, which in 1969 codified customary international law, the United States could simply suspend the treaty's application.[428]

The problem with this argument was that whereas the Vienna Convention explicitly prohibits the suspension of humanitarian treaties,[429] Common Articles 2 and 3 of the Geneva Conventions focus exclusively on humanitarian concerns. It could be argued, in response, that the Geneva Conventions are not part of the human rights regime; that, instead, they form the core of the laws of war – an alternative regime that operates at a time of conflict. But if the international legal system is binary – that is, it operates under either the laws of war or the laws of peace – then, under the former, the conflict is covered by the Geneva Conventions, a position at odds with Yoo and Delahunty's broader claim. If the latter, then the humanitarian regime stands, dictating how the United States is to treat individuals associated with al Qaeda and the Taliban.

The Geneva Conventions, moreover, require that the High Contracting Parties respect the provisions "in all circumstances."[430] The treaty does provide a process for the states party to it to withdraw their assent; thus, *expressio unius est exclusio alterius* [the expression of one thing being the exclusion of the other], the inclusion of a particular mechanism to withdraw altogether from the treaty implies the exclusion of informal suspension. This lack of suspension as a remedy for a state, moreover, does not mean that no remedy exists when a signatory to the treaty is in material breach: a state can withdraw from the treaty through the formal mechanisms provided therein, or try to pursue matters through an international tribunal, or can exercise economic and diplomatic pressure.

Yoo and Delahunty concluded their memo with a discussion of customary international laws of war. If the Geneva Conventions do not apply, and the US War Crimes Act thus lacks import, the question remained whether, under domestic law, customary international law binds the executive. The authors argued that international law does not rise to the level of a federal statute. What they did not consider is whether – where Congress has not spoken to reinforce customary international law – its violation by the United States brings the country into breach of international law. Where customary international law overlapped with *jus cogens* [the body of international norms from which derogation is not permitted], universal jurisdiction could be established, making it possible for legal action to be brought in any country that was protesting the American violation of the laws of war.

In summary, although valid legal arguments undergirded the contractual reading of the Geneva Conventions and their application to al Qaeda, much weaker claims supported the administration's decision to withhold the treaty's protections from the Taliban. As a policy matter, the reinterpretation was to prove devastating.

Dissent Overruled. Nine days after Yoo and Delahunty sent their memo, President Bush formally determined that the Geneva Conventions applied neither to al Qaeda nor to the Taliban.[431] Donald Rumsfeld wrote to Richard Myers, chairman of the Joint Chiefs, directing that members of neither entity be granted prisoner of war status. Detainees, nevertheless, were to be treated "humanely and, *to the extent appropriate and consistent with military necessity*, in a manner consistent with the principles of the Geneva Conventions."[432] Not only did this language leave a gaping hole in how prisoners ought to be treated but it also made a number of people within the executive branch uneasy – of whom the most influential was the Secretary of State.

General Colin Powell was thoroughly familiar with the conduct of war: for 35 years he served in the Army, spending time in Korea and undertaking five tours in Vietnam. He was awarded a Bronze Star with a "valor" designation, issued for acts of bravery and heroism in the course of combat. And he understood the policy world as well. In 1989, he became the youngest officer in US history to be chairman of the Joint Chiefs of Staff. Throughout his tenure, he advocated containment and diplomacy over violence.[433] In January 2002, he became an important dissenting voice within the administration.

Powell entreated the president to reconsider the decision not to apply the Geneva Conventions.[434] Sensitive to the importance of the instrument – particularly in the midst of hostilities – he requested that the United States treat both al Qaeda and the Taliban as prisoners of war. He argued that all enemies captured were entitled to individual hearings before a military board – although he conceded that, after such a hearing, individuals could be removed from that category.[435] The presumption lay in the direction of international law.

In contrast, however, many in the administration – including the Office of Legal Council, the Secretary of Defense, and members of the Department of Justice – saw the battle against al Qaeda outside the contours of international law.[436] Alberto Gonzales, White House Counsel and a man known for his loyalty to the president, pointed out the advantages of the president's determination not to apply the Conventions – foremost among which was that it preserved his flexibility. The country found itself in "a new kind of war," in which a premium was placed on "the ability to quickly obtain information from captured terrorists and their sponsors in order to avoid further atrocities against American civilians." This type of combat rendered the Geneva Conventions "quaint."[437]

Gonzales drew the president's attention to certain legal advantages: not applying the treaty diminished the threat of criminal prosecution under domestic law – particularly, the War Crimes Act – owing to the vagueness of many of the terms, such as "outrages upon personal dignity" and "inhuman treatment."[438] The executive might want to push the boundaries: "[I]t is difficult to predict the needs and circumstances that could arise in the course of the war on terrorism."[439]

Gonzales recognized some drawbacks as well: this would be the first time that the United States had denied the applicability of the treaty, and doing so would preclude the United States from claiming its protections or using the War Crimes Act against enemy forces within domestic bounds. The political fallout might be considerable.[440] Other countries might follow suit, looking "for technical 'loopholes' in future conflicts to conclude" that they were not bound by the Conventions – and it might prevent even allies from turning over terrorist suspects. The determination "could undermine U.S. military culture which emphasizes maintaining the highest standards of conduct in combat, and could introduce an element of uncertainty in the status of adversaries."[441]

For Gonzales, though, these arguments were unpersuasive. This "new type of warfare," which was not even contemplated in 1949, required a new approach.[442] By maintaining a policy of treating detainees humanely, the United States could claim the same for its soldiers – and, in any event, could bring war crimes charges against anyone mistreating American troops.[443]

What Gonzales did not acknowledge, and what Powell was more attuned to, was the strength of the Geneva regime. The treaty, at the core of the international laws of war, served as an authority on which the United States could draw and demand compliance. Gonzales also discounted how other states would respond, and assumed that simple reassurances would be sufficient to convince them that America continued to respect the Geneva Conventions and other "recognized standards."[444] Such a pick-and-choose approach to international law, however, was not likely to be regarded with great respect. Nor was the United States' insistence on abdicating responsibility in one area likely to strengthen its claims to be upholding it in another. Gonzales, who, unlike Powell, had never served in the armed services, also discounted the possible affect on military disci-pline. For Gonzales, the more nebulous "commitment to treat the detainees humanely and, to the extent appropriate and consistent with military neces-sity, in a manner consistent with the principles of" the Geneva Conventions would be sufficient.[445] But who would determine "the extent appropriate and consistent with military necessity"?

Gonzales claimed that the military would remain bound to apply the prin-ciples of the Geneva Conventions because the president had directed them to do so – yet failed to acknowledge that the president himself had sanctioned a way to avoid such principles. It is this license that created the permissive environment in which subsequent abuses occurred.

After reading a draft of Gonzales's memo, Powell asked him to reconsider his position.[446] Powell was concerned that Gonzales had neither presented the full range of options available to the president nor identified the significant advan-tages and disadvantages of each option. Instead, Gonzales's memo focused on the first option – saying that the Geneva Conventions did not apply to the conflict, but that, nevertheless, all detainees would be treated consistent with their principles. A second option would have been to say that the treaty did "apply to the conflict in Afghanistan, but that members of al Qaeda as a group and the Taliban individually or as a group" did not deserve prisoner of war status.[447] For Powell, the second option also preserved flexibility and did not raise any significant risk of the domestic prosecution of officials. The first carried a higher price: it would reverse more than a century of US policy. It would have immediate and negative consequences on US foreign policy. It would make military cooperation with allied countries harder to sustain. And it would hurt extradition. It could, moreover, open US troops to prosecution and make the executive more vulnerable to domestic and international legal challenge. The second option would give the United States more credibility and moral authority, putting the country in a better position to request and obtain international support. It would be the strongest legal foundation on which to move forward.[448]

Though not entirely alone in his concerns or in suggesting that the Geneva Conventions as traditionally applied might be sufficient,[449] Colin Powell found himself in the minority. The day after Powell wrote to Gonzales, Donald Rumsfeld announced from Guantánamo Bay that the prisoners "will not be determined to be POWs."[450] President Bush met with the National Security Council to consider the detainees' "unlawful combatant" status. But he held to the previous course: "We are not going to call them prisoners of war," the president said. "And the reason why is, Al Qaeda is not a known military. These are killers, these are terrorists, they know no countries. The only thing they know about a country is when they find a country that's been weakened and they want to occupy it like a parasite."[451] Bush glossed over Powell's dissent: "A couple of things we agree on. One, they will not be treated as prisoners of war; they're illegal combatants. Secondly, they will be treated humanely. And then I'll figure out – I'll listen to all the legalisms and announce my decision when I make it."[452]

As the winds blew against the treaty, Attorney General John Ashcroft weighed in on the side of damage control. In his view, a presidential determination that Afghanistan was a failed state would minimize legal exposure to "liability, litigation, and criminal prosecution."[453] Acting under the Attorney General's advice, on February 7, 2002, President Bush made a formal determination: "I accept the legal conclusion of the Attorney General and the Department of Justice that I have the authority under the Constitution to suspend Geneva (Conventions) as between the United States and Afghanistan, but I decline to exercise that authority at this time."[454] He reserved the right to do so "in this or future conflicts."[455] He walked a fine line between the Department of State, the Office of Legal Counsel, and the White House: although the Geneva Conventions applied as a general matter to the war in Afghanistan, they would not be applied to al Qaeda, by virtue of the group's not being a High Contracting Party.[456] Nor would the Taliban fall under their protections "because, among other reasons, the relevant conflicts are international in scope and common Article 3 applies only to 'armed conflict not of an international character.'"[457] Taliban detainees would be treated as "enemy combatants" and be exempt from prisoner of war status under Article 4.[458] Nevertheless, the United States supported Geneva and its principles. *The armed forces* would "continue to treat detainees humanely and, *to the extent appropriate and consistent with military necessity*, in a manner consistent with the principles of Geneva."[459]

This language validated Rumsfeld's classified order of January 19, 2002. It left open what behavior might be appropriate, as well as what circumstances would meet the standard of necessity. It stopped short of addressing nonmilitary actors, such as the Central Intelligence Agency. And it left some observers lamenting, "The Guantánamo Bay issue is one of the worst cases of 'do as I say, not as I do' recorded by the U.S. in recent times."[460]

Habeas Corpus and Judicial Review

Although it was the Bush administration's line that the trade-off between national security and the rights of the detainees demanded that the former be given priority, that dichotomy pales beside the actual dynamics in play at the time. At stake was the distribution of federal power: the administration claimed unilateral authority to hold detainees indefinitely; and neither congressional statute nor judicial oversight, it asserted, could restrict the executive from acting under its wartime authority. The House of Representatives and the Senate, controlled by the same party that sat in the White House, did little to contest the administration's claims. The White House further pointed to the Authorization for Use of Military Force to say that Congress expressly granted the executive the power to detain combatants. Although, as in the United Kingdom, the courts were willing to push back on the executive, a brief examination of important decisions and their aftermath shows how limited the courts' role really is.

The Cases of Rasul *and* Hamdi. The first two cases to come before the Supreme Court were handed down June 28, 2004: *Rasul* v. *Bush*, brought by Australian and Kuwaiti citizens detained in Guantánamo Bay,[461] and *Hamdi* v. *Rumsfeld*, involving a US citizen, captured in Afghanistan in November 2001 and transferred to Guantánamo Bay.[462] (The military later moved Yaser Hamdi to the United States, where the government detained him for nearly three years as an unlawful enemy combatant, without ever formally bringing charges.) In both cases, a 6-3 majority said that the executive branch had exceeded its authority by seeking unilateral powers of detention and interrogation. It lay within the Court's domain to establish the boundaries among the three branches and to consider challenges to the legality of the detentions.

Justice John Paul Stevens, writing for the majority in *Rasul*, considered the government's objection: that in an earlier case, *Johnson* v. *Eisentrager* (1950), the Supreme Court had denied its own jurisdiction.[463] Stevens characterized *Eisentrager* as a statutory holding whose predicate no longer obtained: according to the Court, *Eisentrager* was based upon the idea – since overruled – that a federal court's statutory jurisdiction extended only as far as its territory. The Court's subsequent precedents construed habeas as conferring jurisdiction even outside domestic bounds.[464]

Stevens also distinguished *Eisentrager* from the contemporary situation: the earlier case involved German citizens, captured by US forces in China, tried and convicted of war crimes by an American military commission headquartered in Nanking, and incarcerated in occupied Germany.[465] In contrast, in *Rasul*, the petitioners were not nationals of countries at war with the United States. They denied that they were involved in any acts of aggression against America. They had not been afforded access to any tribunal – much less charged with or convicted of wrongdoing. For more than two years, moreover, they had been imprisoned in territory over which the United States exercised exclusive jurisdiction and control. (The US agreement with Cuba expressly grants the United States complete jurisdiction and control over the island base. It can claim this indefinitely, if it so chooses).[466] Justice Stevens – joined by Justices Sandra Day O'Connor, David Souter, Ruth Bader Ginsburg, and Stephen Breyer – found no impediment to detainees using the federal habeas statute to obtain relief.*

In the second case, the court considered a habeas petition from an American citizen being held as an enemy combatant. Justice O'Connor, writing for the majority, held that due process requires that citizens be given a meaningful opportunity to contest the factual basis for their detention,[467] but that Hamdi had not been given the opportunity to go before a review board to contest his detention. O'Connor wrote, "An interrogation by one's captor, however effective an intelligence-gathering tool, hardly constitutes a constitutionally adequate fact-finding before a neutral decision-maker."[468] In other words, the Constitution guarantees an independent review by neutral adjudicators – a requirement not canceled by a high level of threat. For O'Connor it was precisely during times of emergency that the "nation's commitment to due process" must be upheld.[469] "[A] state of war," she wrote, "is not a blank check when it comes to the rights of the nation's citizens."[470]

Rasul and *Hamdi* were hailed by legal commentators as an "historic pair of decisions affirming due process rights even in a time of war."[471] Tony Mauro, a Supreme Court analyst, reported that the decision "repudiated the Bush administration's view that enemy combatants and detainees can be held indefinitely without access to federal court habeas corpus review."[472] By March 2006, more than 200 prisoners in Guantánamo Bay had filed habeas proceedings in Washington, D.C.[473]

The Executive's Response. In May 2004, anticipating the Court's decision, Deputy Secretary of Defense Paul Wolfowitz created an administrative review board (ARB). The ARB would annually conduct a fact-based, nonadversarial review of each detainee's case, a review in which he would be allowed to

---

* Justice Kennedy filed a concurring opinion, saying that he would follow *Eisentrager* as the governing framework. Courts should be reluctant to go into this realm; however, in this case extraordinary circumstances held: the petitioners had not even been given an opportunity to challenge their detentions through any judicial process; and, as Stevens recognized, they were being held in territory over which the United States had jurisdiction. 542 U.S. 466, at 485–88. Justice Scalia filed a dissenting opinion, in which Justices Rehnquist and Thomas joined. 542 U.S. 466, at 488–506.

participate, and at whose conclusion he would be released, transferred, or further detained. The aim would be to determine to what extent prisoners posed a threat to the United States, and whether some other reason existed to continue to hold them.[474]

Not only did the Court's ruling draw attention to such due process concerns as notice and the opportunity to be heard, but more specifically, O'Connor's plurality opinion in *Hamdi* suggested that Army regulation 190–8 might be a potential basis for these to be observed. Accordingly, on July 7, 2004, the military created a second administrative body – a Combatant Status Review Tribunal – to give a detainee the opportunity to contest his status as an enemy combatant. Detainees would be informed of their right to do so and to seek a writ of habeas corpus in US courts. The order called for three officers, none of whom had daily involvement with the detainee, to staff the tribunal. One would be a judge advocate, with the senior ranking officer serving as the president. A military officer would be assigned to each detainee to prepare for hearings before the tribunal. Detainees would also be given the right to testify, call witnesses, and introduce evidence. The tribunal would deliberate in secret and then issue its decision. Only those detainees who met the criteria for enemy combatant – understood as "an individual who was part of or supporting Taliban or al Qaeda forces, or associated forces that are engaged in hostilities against the U.S. or its coalition partners"[475] – were granted a subsequent review.

Over the first six months, the Combatant Status Review Tribunal held approximately 558 hearings; of these, 520 detainees continued to meet the criteria for enemy combatant status. The 38 who were no longer deemed enemy combatants were forwarded to the State Department, putting it in a quandary similar to the United Kingdom's (see page 62): because the United States was signatory to the Convention Against Torture, the State Department would not send the individuals back to countries where they were more likely than not to be tortured. By March 2006, the State Department had received assurances that 29 of those considered innocent of terrorist activity would not be mistreated. (Unlike the United Kingdom, no formal memoranda of understanding were signed – nor were the agreements greeted with the same public outcry that accompanied Britain's efforts to return individuals to countries known for torture). However, nine individuals remained in US custody for want of such assurances.[476]

Congress and the 2005 Detainee Treatment Act. Even as the military adjusted to meet the requirements of the judicial ruling, the administration tried to narrow the scope of judicial review. A Republican-controlled Congress wrote into the 2006 Defense Appropriations Act a new Detainee Treatment Act to address a broad range of subjects related to the treatment of detainees. This legislation both placed restrictions on the treatment and interrogation of individuals in US custody (see page 95) and sought to regulate judicial review. To this purpose, the legislation specified the following:

Except as provided in section 1005 of the Detainee Treatment Act of 2005, no court, justice, or judge shall have jurisdiction to hear or consider – (1) an application for a writ of habeas corpus filed by or on behalf of an alien detained by the Department of Defense at Guantánamo Bay, Cuba; or (2) any other action against the United States or its agents relating to any aspect of the detention by the Department of Defense of an alien at Guantánamo Bay, Cuba, who – (A) is currently in military custody; or (B) has been determined by the United States Court of Appeals for the District of Columbia Circuit in accordance with the procedures set forth in section 1005(e) of the Detainee Treatment Act of 2005 to have been properly detained as an enemy combatant.[477]

The Detainee Treatment Act gave the Court of Appeals for the District of Columbia Circuit the "exclusive jurisdiction to determine the validity of any final decision of a [Combatant Status Review Tribunal] that an alien is properly designated as an enemy combatant."[478] This court, too, was given exclusive jurisdiction to determine the validity of any final decision of a military commission. The scope of review was limited to only

(i) whether the final decision [of the military commission] was consistent with the standards and procedures specified in the military order referred to in subparagraph (A); and (ii) to the extent the Constitution and laws of the United States are applicable, whether the use of such standards and procedures to reach the final decision is consistent with the Constitution and laws of the United States.[479]

In other words, only habeas cases could come before the D.C. Circuit appellate court – and the scope of the review would be limited. Even as the president signed the new law, a case to test the administration's move was pending before the courts.

The Case of Hamdan *v.* Rumsfeld. In November 2001, Salim Ahmed Hamdan, Osama bin Laden's former bodyguard and driver, was captured in Afghanistan; just over six months later, he transferred to Guantánamo Bay. In 2003, the president declared him eligible for trial by military commission. It was a full year before Hamdan was charged with a crime: one count of conspiracy "to commit . . . offenses triable by military commission."[480] Like Rasul and Hamdi, Hamdan filed a petition for writ of habeas corpus. He claimed that neither a congressional act nor the common law allowed for the state to try him for conspiracy – an offense not considered a violation of the law of war. He also contended that the procedures used for military tribunals violated basic principles of military and international law: the right to see and hear the evidence against oneself. The administration argued in response that the Detainee Treatment Act meant that the courts could not review Hamdan's claims. The judiciary, moreover, lacked the authority to second-guess the president, as commander-in-chief, during times of war.

On June 29, 2006, the Supreme Court handed down its decision. The Detainee Treatment Act (DTA) did not deprive the Supreme Court of jurisdiction: Hamdan's case was already in motion when the DTA went into effect. Military commissions, moreover, had not been expressly authorized by

Congress. Separation of powers had been built into the Constitution specifically to prevent the executive from overreaching. Justice Stevens wrote that while the Constitution makes the president the "Commander in Chief" of the Armed Forces, it reserves to Congress a range of powers related to war – such as the power to "declare War . . . and make Rules concerning Captures on Land and Water," to "raise and support Armies," to "define and punish . . . Offences against the Law of Nations," and "To make Rules for the Government and Regulation of the land and naval Forces."[481] Stevens quoted Chief Justice Salmon P. Chase in *Ex parte Milligan* (1866) as follows:

> The power to make the necessary laws is in Congress; the power to execute in the President. Both powers imply many subordinate and auxiliary powers. Each includes all authorities essential to its due exercise. But neither can the President, in war more than in peace, intrude upon the proper authority of Congress, nor Congress upon the proper authority of the President.[482]

It was not for Congress to direct military campaigns; nor for the president, without congressional approval and outside of compelling necessity, to construct tribunals.[483] The president's Military Order of November 13, 2001, did not issue under federal law – nor was it required by military necessity. The executive would have to try the prisoners under regularly constituted courts-martial, or obtain permission from the legislature to proceed with an alternative structure. The military commissions' procedures, moreover, violated the Uniform Code of Military Justice. And they failed to satisfy the Geneva Conventions.

Here, the Court disagreed with the Office of Legal Counsel by ruling that Common Article 3 does apply to al Qaeda suspects detained in Guantánamo Bay. Justice Stevens wrote, "The term 'conflict not of an international character' is used here in contradistinction to a conflict between nations."[484] He explained,

> Common Article 2 provides that "the present Convention shall apply to all cases of declared war or of any other armed conflict which may arise between two or more of the High Contracting Parties." 6 U.S.T., at 3318 (Art. 2, ¶ 1). High Contracting Parties (signatories) also must abide by all terms of the Conventions vis-à-vis one another even if one party to the conflict is a nonsignatory "Power," and must so abide vis-à-vis the nonsignatory if "the latter accepts and applies" those terms. *Ibid.* (Art. 2, ¶ 3). Common Article 3, by contrast, affords some minimal protection, falling short of full protection under the Conventions, to individuals associated with neither a signatory nor even a nonsignatory "Power" who are involved in a conflict "in the territory of" a signatory. The latter kind of conflict is distinguishable from the conflict described in Common Article 2 chiefly because it does not involve a clash between nations (whether signatories or not). In context, then, the phrase "not of an international character" bears its literal meaning.[485]

The official commentaries provided with Common Article 3 did indicate that its central purpose is to protect rebels involved in one type of "conflict not of an international character" – that is, a civil war. But the commentaries also clearly stated "that the scope of the Article must be as wide as possible."[486] Furthermore, language that would have limited the scope of the provision was dropped from the final text. The Court noted the apparent absence of any need to depart from regularly constituted rules and procedures for courts-martial, and explained, "Common Article 3 obviously tolerates a great degree of flexibility in trying individuals captured during armed conflict; its requirements are general ones, crafted to accommodate a wide variety of legal systems. But *requirements* they are nonetheless. The commission that the President has convened to try Hamdan does not meet those requirements."[487] Stevens concluded, "[I]n undertaking to try Hamdan and subject him to criminal punishment, the Executive is bound to comply with the Rule of Law that prevails in this jurisdiction."[488]

Congress and the 2006 Military Commissions Act. The Bush administration did not take kindly to the Court's ruling, and Congress – controlled by the same party that sat in the White House, with its members facing reelection – proved a willing and able partner. The subsequent 2006 Military Commissions Act (MCA) went beyond the Detainee Treatment Act and tried to strip the courts of *any* authority over detainees held in Guantánamo Bay outside the contours of the earlier legislation. The MCA read as follows:

No court, justice, or judge shall have jurisdiction to hear or consider an application for a writ of habeas corpus filed by or on behalf of an alien detained by the United States who has been determined by the United States to have been properly detained as an enemy combatant or is awaiting such determination.[489]

The legislation stripped US courts of jurisdiction not only over habeas claims but also over any action "against the United States or its agents relating to any aspect of the detention, transfer, treatment, trial, or conditions of confinement of an alien who is or was detained by the United States and has been determined by the United States to have been properly detained as an enemy combatant or is awaiting such determination."[490] To avoid the loophole exploited in *Hamdan* v. *Rumsfeld* – that the case was pending at the time of the statute's enactment – the new legislation applied "to all cases, without exception, pending on or after the date of the enactment of this Act which relate to any aspect of the detention, transfer, treatment, trial, or conditions of detention of an alien detained by the United States since Sept. 11, 2001."[491]

Following the Supreme Court's remand in *Hamdan* v. *Rumsfeld* – and the Military Commissions Act – Judge James Robertson of the D.C. District Court, who had held *for* Hamdan in the first case, found that he lacked jurisdiction to consider Hamdan's further habeas claim because Congress, through the MCA, had clearly deprived federal courts of jurisdiction. Robertson analyzed the MCA's plain language and declared it "so clear that it could sustain only one interpretation": that the courts' jurisdiction over pending habeas petitions from "enemy combatants" had been retroactively withdrawn.[492] Although that interpretation did not fully suspend the writ consistent with the Suspension Clause of Article I of the Constitution, Hamdan, as an alien involuntarily detained in Guantánamo Bay, lacked any *constitutional* entitlement to habeas that would survive Congress's statutory withholding of the right. Unlike the other four times in which Congress had authorized a suspension, "neither rebellion nor invasion was occurring at the time the MCA was enacted."[493] Congress, moreover, had not made any findings of the predicate conditions. The situation was analogous to the enemy combatants in *Johnson* v. *Eisentrager*: Hamdan's "connection lack[ed] the geographical and volitional predicates necessary to claim a constitutional entitlement to habeas corpus."[494] Hamdan appealed.

International Fallout and Its Effect on US Policy. The decision to detain terrorist suspects for an indefinite time alienated allied and nonallied countries that the United States needed in its war against the global threat. The government initially refused to release detainees' names or nationalities, but early rumors suggested that 25 countries' nationals were located in Guantánamo Bay.[495] Gradually, such countries as Australia, France, Britain, Saudi Arabia, Sweden, and Yemen came forward to confirm that their nationals were being held.[496] Many gained access to them.

Among the first to arrive was the United Kingdom.[497] Although cautious formal support followed, as Geoff Hoon, the United Kingdom's Defence Secretary, issued a statement backing the detention of enemy combatants,[498] this support was far from unconditional. Foreign Secretary Jack Straw announced that, if the United States wanted to maintain "moral ascendancy," it would have to treat the detainees humanely.[499] The conservative *Washington Times* translated Straw's language as "firing a warning over the Atlantic."[500]

Outside of official government circles, the British response proved substantially less amenable to the US position. The Labour back-bencher Jeremy Corbyn denounced the transfers as "illegal."[501] The families of some of the Britons detained accused Prime Minister Blair of "aiding and abetting" the United States in its unlawful detentions.[502] Lord Steyn, one of Britain's most senior Law Lords, considered the detentions "a monstrous failure of justice" and the proposed tribunals "kangaroo courts"[503] – "a pre-ordained arbitrary rush to judgment by an irregular tribunal which makes a mockery of justice." These were strong words from someone intimate with the careful language of the law.[504] The *Sunday Mirror*, a tabloid press, put the point more strongly: "These prisoners are trapped in open cages manacled hand and foot, brutalized, tortured and humiliated."[505]

Pressure built on the Labour government – particularly as news emerged that two of the six initial detainees who would undergo military tribunals were British.[506] (Moazzam Begg and Feroz Abbasi were believed to have pled guilty after lengthy interrogation and segregation;[507] the latter, at age 23, was reported to have attempted suicide and had a nervous breakdown while in US custody.[508]) The *Guardian* reported that "outrage over Guantánamo Bay" had become "an embarrassing political problem for Tony Blair, with MPs from all parties condemning the U.S. for a regime that broke international laws"[509]; and that it was "damaging America's standing abroad."[510] Lord Peter Goldsmith, Britain's Attorney General, made several trips across the Atlantic to try to negotiate the release of the men.[511] Straw met with Secretary of State Powell to demand that either the United States establish fair trials consistent with international standards or that the country return British nationals to the United Kingdom.[512] Rumsfeld retorted that the United States would return the detainees on the condition that the British government would prevent them from walking free.[513] But British officials could not guarantee that all the detainees would face trial: they did not know whether US evidence could be used in British courts, as torture and inhuman and degrading treatment violated the European Convention of Human Rights.[514]

The White House eventually caved in and directed Rumsfeld not to prosecute Begg and Abbasi – and to begin negotiations with Lord Goldsmith.[515] After an 18-month stalemate, the Pentagon conceded, granting Begg and Abbasi their own lawyers.[516] In March 2004, the United States released a number of the Britons without charge.[517]

As the detainees returned home, they painted vivid pictures of their detention: Tarek Dergoul, age 26, claimed to have been interrogated at gunpoint, beaten, and subjected to inhumane conditions.[518] Jamal Udeen, returned the same day, told the *Mirror* that his interrogators tried to get him to sign a confession, but he refused. He alleged that he was then beaten and isolated for a month for refusing an injection, and that he was interviewed around 40 times by US agents, up to 12 hours at each stint – and 9 times by MI5 and British consular officials.[519] Two of the "Tipton Three" – Shafiq Rasul, age 26, and Asif Iqbal, age 22 – sent a letter to President Bush and the US Senate Armed Services Committee, saying that during their interrogations they had been chained to the floor so long that at times they had urinated on themselves.[520] (At Guantánamo Bay, Major General Geoffrey Miller had initiated the practice of short-shackling, whereby a detainee was forced to squat without a chair, hands chained between his legs to the floor; if the prisoner fell, the chains would cut into his hands.)[521] Rasul and Iqbal claimed to have been tricked into false confessions.[522] Along with the third man from the Midlands town of Tipton, Rhuhel Ahmed, they asserted that they were repeatedly beaten and deprived of sleep, photographed naked, and subjected to unnecessary anal searches.[523] Although American interrogators had showed them an al Qaeda training video from 2000 and claimed they were in the film, one of the men had been working at an electrical goods store in the United Kingdom when the movie was made, whereas the other two had been in trouble with the police.[524] Yet after three months in isolation, Rasul admitted to being in the video.[525] He also alleged that a fellow inmate was beaten until the other prisoners thought he had died; for days he was left in the same clothes, covered in blood.[526]

In addition to the United Kingdom, Saudi Arabia demanded the return of its nationals – by January 2002, 100 of 158 prisoners.[527] Yemen, Morocco, Spain, Sweden, and Pakistan sent officials to interview their citizens.[528] The *Scotsman* reported, "When the first pictures were beamed around the world from the camp of the masked boilersuited detainees, their hearing muffled and shackled at their hands and feet, there was uproar. . . . As time passed, repeated allegations of torture further tarnished the already criticized regime at Guantánamo Bay."[529] Bill Butler, the Chair Emeritus of the International Commission of

Jurists, condemned the United States, which had "devised a criminal juris-diction whereby we can lease property anywhere in the world and create a Devil's Island where individuals have no access to the U.S. court system."[530] World leaders urged the United States to treat the detainees as prisoners of war.[531] The Parliamentary Assembly of the Council of Europe – a body rep-resenting many of America's closest allies – passed a resolution declaring that "the combat against terrorism must be carried out in compliance with national and international law and respecting human rights."[532] The *San Francisco Chronicle* noted the "growing international clamor" that was "calling into question the treatment of prisoners held at the makeshift jail at Guantánamo Bay."[533]

International concern heightened when it was revealed, in answer to an off-hand question from a foreign journalist, that there were children at the base: three detainees under the age of 16, and between two and five teenagers aged 16 to 18 lived at the facility.[534] James Ross, legal adviser for Human Rights Watch in New York, said, "The U.S. military is exacerbating an already con-tentious situation. The detention of youths reflects our own broader concerns that the U.S. never properly determined the legal status of those held in the Afghanistan conflict."[535] What made the presence of minors particularly note-worthy was that the United States had recently ratified the optional protocol to the Convention on the Rights of the Child, which protected children in the midst of armed conflicts.[536] Concern for these minors deepened as reports of abuses began to circulate.[537]

International dissent was not unanticipated. And it mirrored distress within the United States itself: officials at the highest levels of government disagreed about whether to apply the Conventions. While the Attorney General, the Assis-tant Attorney General at the Office of Legal Counsel, and the White House Counsel claimed a new kind of war – one where the old rules did not apply – the Secretary of State, the Legal Advisor to the Chair of the Joint Chiefs of Staff, and a number of military attorneys disagreed. The presidential determination only added to the complexity by – in what appeared to be a quasi-compromise – blurring the conditions and limits not only of detention and but of interrogation as well.

COERCIVE INTERROGATION AND TORTURE IN THE GLOBAL WAR ON TERROR

The issue of interrogation and the use of torture in connection with it stirred up even more dissent at home and abroad. As the first detainees reached Guantánamo Bay, US Brigadier General Mike Lehnert declared, "The ques-tioning that goes on is within the bounds of normal legal procedures that are in effect within the United States." There would be "no torture, whips . . . no bright lights, drugging." Lehnert proudly stated, "We are a nation of laws."[538] Two elderly men released early on reported that they had not been treated poorly. One, Faiz Mohammed, explained, "They treated us well. We had enough food. We could pray and wash five times a day. We had the Qu'ran and read it all the time." And the other, Mohammed Sediq, acknowledged that the guards treated Islam with respect.[539]

There may be several reasons for this initial conservatism. It may have stemmed, in part, from a certain stasis and the legacy of the Geneva Conventions: for more than a half-century, military personnel had been trained in the treaty requirements. The US Army's own manual banned "[t]he use of force, mental torture, threats, insults, or exposure to unpleasant and inhumane treatment of any kind,"[540] and declared such treatment illegal and "neither authorized nor condoned by the U.S. Government."[541] The manual considered coercive techniques ineffective.[542] It summarized, "[F]rom both legal and moral viewpoints, the restrictions established by international law, agreements, and customs render threats of force, violence, and deprivation useless as interrogation techniques."[543]

The initial conservatism may also have been tied to a broader culture: the United States had signed the Convention Against Torture. The federal government routinely denounced other nations for their use of inhuman and degrading treatment, and torture; and in October 1999, the State Department declared, "No official of the government, federal, state or local, civilian or military, is authorized to commit or to instruct anyone else to commit torture. Nor may any official condone or tolerate torture in any form."[544] There were no exceptions. Furthermore, "United States law contains no provision permitting otherwise prohibited acts of torture or other cruel, inhuman or degrading treatment or punishment to be employed on grounds of exigent circumstances (for example, during a 'state of public emergency') or on orders from a superior officer or public authority, and the protective mechanisms of an independent judiciary are not subject to suspension."[545] The State Department noted the strong and clear protection against torture afforded by the Eighth Amendment, prohibiting cruel and unusual punishments,* which include conditions of confinement – such as deprivation of food, warmth, and exercise, as well as excessive force by prison officials, inadequate training of guards, and inadequate medical care.[546]†

---

* This includes inhuman punishments, those that "fail to comport with human dignity, and punishments which include undue physical suffering. It covers punishments which, although not physically 'barbarous,' involve the unnecessary and wanton infliction of pain, or are 'grossly disproportionate' to the severity of the crime." Moreover, "[T]he Eighth Amendment forbids public officials from deliberately inflicting pain on prisoners in an unnecessary and wanton manner, such as through beatings." U.S. Department of State, Initial Report to the UN Committee Against Torture (Oct. 15, 1999), citing *Hudson* v. *McMillian*, 403 U.S. 1 (1992).

† Although the Eighth Amendment applies only to the punishment of those in US custody, "[t]he due process clauses of the Fifth and Fourteenth Amendments may reach actions that are technically outside Eight Amendment purview, such as excessive use of force by law enforcement personnel during the investigative or pretrial states." Pretrial detainees – that is, individuals lawfully arrested but not yet tried – enjoyed equivalent protections. Id., citing *Hamm* v. *DeKalb County*, 774 F.2d 1567, 1573–74 (11th Cir. 1985) ("[S]tates may not impose on pretrial detainees conditions that would violate a convicted person's Eighth Amendment rights.") Owing in part, perhaps, to the absence of a Supreme Court decision directly on this point, the law is slightly more complex: *Rochin* v. *California* forbids conduct that "shocks the conscience." *Rochin* v. *California*, 342

This conservatism may also have been related to the necessity to ensure that information gleaned from interrogations would be obtained legally to be admissible in court. One of the options for the detainees, it will be recalled, was, eventually, to have them stand trial. (In February 2002, the general counsel at the Department of Defense asked the Office of Legal Counsel whether the self-incrimination clause of the Fifth Amendment would reach interrogations conducted at Guantánamo Bay.[547*])

But in the months that followed the presidential determination denying the applicability of the Geneva Conventions, there was a steady erosion of detention and interrogation standards. It began by the president's counsel asking the Office of Legal Counsel to issue an opinion on the appropriate standards for interrogation and to consider their relationship to US obligations under the Convention Against Torture.[548] The subsequent legal redefinition proved instrumental in shifting interrogation standards and also evoked a much deeper and older constitutional argument about separation of powers. Even as the rules changed and acrimonious exchanges shot back and forth among the branches, the sudden influx of detainees overloaded newly created structures. Interrogation techniques developed in relation to Afghanistan migrated to Iraq, where, under minimal supervision, even harsher interrogation methods emerged. "Black" sites, run by the CIA outside of military control (see page 107) created further opportunities for abuse. All this led to an international backlash that undermined US foreign policy and hurt its ability to respond to the terrorist threat.

The Convention Against Torture (CAT)

One hundred and forty-one states worldwide are party to the Convention Against Torture and Other Cruel, Inhuman or Degrading Treatment or Punishment, which defines torture as the following:

[A]ny act by which severe pain or suffering, whether physical or mental, is intentionally inflicted on a person for such purposes as obtaining from him or a third person information or a confession, punishing him for an act he or a third person has committed or is suspected of having committed, or intimidating or coercing him or a third person, or for any reason based on discrimination of any kind, when such pain or suffering is inflicted

---

U.S. 165 (Jan. 2, 1952). However, the case law suggests that even dreadful acts, if done for legitimate governmental purposes, may be exempt from this category. *See, e.g., Chavez v. Martinez,* 538 U.S. 760 (2003) (addressing coercive interrogation in the course of medical treatment for potentially fatal injuries); and *Sacramento v. Lewis,* 532 U.S. 833 (May 26, 1998) (finding in relation to a high-speed chase that only direct efforts to cause harm that are not related to the legitimate object of the arrest meet the shocks the conscience test).

* Jay Bybee responded that where interrogation served the purpose of obtaining information, the constitutional rule of conduct established in *Miranda v. Arizona* did not apply. If prosecution were to follow, within domestic bounds, failure to "mirandize" suspects would result in the exclusion of coerced confessions; but the final forum for prosecution had not been decided. *United States v. Bin Laden,* S.D.N.Y., No S(7) 98 Cr. 1023 (2/13/01).

by or at the instigation of or with the consent or acquiescence of a public official or other person acting in an official capacity.[549]

CAT requires the states party to it to take preventive measures to ensure that torture does not occur in any territory under their jurisdiction.[550] It adds, "*No exceptional circumstances whatsoever, whether a state of war or a threat of war, internal political instability or any other public emergency, may be invoked as a justification of torture.*"[551] CAT requires states to train their civil, military, medical personnel, public officials, and others involved in the custody, interrogation, or treatment of detainees to ensure that they do not violate the Convention.[552]

Not only does the instrument ban torture, but it requires the states party to it to "undertake to prevent in any territory under its jurisdiction other acts of cruel, inhuman or degrading treatment or punishment which do not amount to torture as defined in Article I, when such acts are committed by or at the instigation of or with the consent or acquiescence of a public official or other person acting in an official capacity."[553] Where reasonable grounds exist that torture or cruel, inhuman, or degrading treatment has occurred, "Each State Party shall ensure that its competent authorities proceed to a prompt and impartial investigation."[554] All acts of torture or complicity in torture, moreover, are to be a violation of domestic criminal law.[555]

In 1994, the United States ratified CAT and entered a handful of reservations. The ban on cruel, inhuman, or degrading (CID) treatment would be considered consistent with Fifth, Eighth, and/or Fourteenth Amendment jurisprudence.[556] The purpose of this reservation was, according to Abraham Sofaer, the State Department's legal advisor when the United States signed CAT, "to ensure that the same standards for CID would apply outside the United States as apply inside."[557] To constitute torture, "[A]n act must be specifically intended to inflict severe physical or mental pain or suffering."[558] This definition includes prolonged harm caused by the *threat* of severe physical pain or imminent death, or the threat that *others* would suffer from the same. Torture applies "only to acts directed against persons in the offender's custody or physical control."[559] For an official to be complicit, he must, prior to the act, be aware of it "and thereafter breach his legal responsibility to intervene to prevent such activity."[560] The United States also entered a reservation declaring Articles 1–16 of the treaty to be nonself-executing – they would have to be implemented by domestic law to be binding.

The statute implementing CAT goes further in some areas than the Convention itself: it omits any reference to information gathering in its definition of torture. Instead, the intentional infliction of *any* "severe physical or mental pain or suffering (other than pain or suffering incidental to lawful sanctions) upon another person" in the state's custody or control amounts to torture.[561] The legislation defined "severe mental pain" consistent with the reservation. It became an offense to commit or attempt to commit torture even outside US jurisdiction. Violation carried a fine and/or imprisonment of up to 20 years.[562] If a tortured individual died, the state could seek life imprisonment or the death penalty for whomever was responsible for the torture. (Conspirators would be subject to the same penalties).[563] The United States claimed jurisdiction where the accused was a national of the United States.[564]

Applying the New Standards

Following the presidential determination that withheld the Geneva Conventions from detainees, the Counsel to the President asked the Office of Legal Counsel to clarify the standards for interrogation and to compare these with the US obligations under CAT. Subsequent memos crucially broadened the acceptable limits on questioning.

Jay Bybee, the Assistant Attorney General for the Office of Legal Counsel, answered the initial request by stating that the Convention text "prohibits only the most extreme acts by reserving criminal penalties solely for torture and declining to require such penalties for 'cruel, inhuman, or degrading treatment or punishment.'"[565] This wording required that domestic law only outlaw torture – not cruel, inhuman, or degrading treatment. For Bybee, for an act to be considered torture, a person accused of inflicting it must act "with the specific intent to inflict severe pain, the infliction of such pain must be the defendant's precise objective."[566] Mere knowledge that such pain would result would be insufficient.[567] The hurt must be "difficult to endure" and "equivalent in intensity to the pain accompanying serious physical injury, such as organ failure, impairment of bodily function, or even death."[568] Mental pain or suffering, in turn, "must result in significant psychological harm of significant duration, e.g., lasting for months or even years"[569] – and must come from one of the predicate acts listed in domestic law: threat of imminent death, threat of torture, psychological torture, the use of drugs or other procedures to thoroughly disrupt the senses or alter an individual's personality, or threatening to do any of these to a third party.[570]

Following the Bybee memo, a series of communications focused on what techniques would be allowed in the "new" environment. Lieutenant Colonel Diana E. Beaver, legal counsel at Guantánamo Bay, explained that as a result of the 2002 presidential determination, there was "no established clear policy for interrogation limits and operations."[571] The Secretary of Defense had yet to issue guidelines for acceptable techniques.[572] Beaver considered a range of approaches, such as waterboarding (a technique that is used to simulate drowning and sometimes causes death), 20-hour interrogation, stress positions, exposure to cold weather and water, light and sound assaults, and scenarios designed to convince detainees that they, or their family members, are in imminent threat of death or severe pain.[573] She concluded that, where conducted with proper oversight and as part of "an important governmental objective" (not solely to cause suffering), these techniques were legal. The commander of Guantánamo Bay, Major General Michael Dunlavey, agreed with Beaver's assessment and sent her memo to General James T. Hill, the commander of Southern Command, for approval. Hill was not convinced and asked the chairman of the Joint Chiefs of Staff for guidance in identifying lawful counter-resistance techniques.[574] In December 2002, Rumsfeld, acting on the advice of his General Counsel, William Haynes, approved Category I and some Category II and III measures, such as the use of dogs and removal of prisoners' clothing.[575]

News of the techniques being used in Guantánamo Bay slowly leaked to the public, generating increased concern about US actions.[576] In December 2002, the news that military coroners had determined that the death of two Afghans held by the United States at Bagram air base had been homicides[577] provoked further questions about the treatment of prisoners. At that time, the United States held about 650 detainees.[578] Interviews conducted by Human Rights Watch and a reporter from the BBC recounted prisoners' experiences: Alif Khan, an Afghan businessman arrested when a taxi in which he was a passenger was stopped by local forces, explained how he had been transferred to the Americans, hooded, repeatedly interrogated, and forced to kneel with his hands above his head until he became unconscious. He was injected and then transferred to Guantánamo where prisoners were held in cages.[579] He said, "Two men in cells next to me went crazy. They tried to kill themselves."[580] Another detainee talked about being loaded into a container, in which dozens of people died. He reported, "They gave us pills that made us feel numb or made us drunk. I saw one person try to commit suicide by drinking shampoo. A Pakistani wrapped his bed sheets around his neck, but he was rescued by the guards."[581] Another reported that, under repeated interrogations, "I started hearing noises and seeing ghosts."[582] He, too, spoke of injections and pills:

After I received an injection, my eyes would remain fixed upward, and my muscles would get stiff. I would stay like that for a day and sometimes longer, until I was given another injection, which would relax me, and then I could move my eyes and muscles again. Sometimes they would give me pills after the first injection. I saw other prisoners receive injections as well.[583]

He tried three times to commit suicide. Yet another prisoner spoke about being gassed – and injected: "Guards would enter the cell with sticks and masks, and two or three of them would hold a prisoner while one of them injected him in any part of his body. Immediately after the injection, the person would faint. Then he was put into isolation. Twice they injected me and took me to the isolation room, a dark room with cold air blowing. I saw other prisoners who were beaten until blood was running from their heads. . . . The questions were the same."[584]

One of the most notorious prisoners, Mohamed al-Qahtani, tried to enter the United States just weeks before 9/11 – while Mohammad Atta waited for him outside an airport. Although al-Qahtani was turned away, he was later seized fleeing Tora Bora (a chain of caves in the White Mountains of Afghanistan to where al Qaeda members fled after the US invasion) and, in February 2002, was transferred to Guantánamo Bay. In June 2005, his interrogation logs became public.[585] A military inquiry found that in November 2002 interrogators had created a special plan for al-Qahtani[586]: according to the Schmidt Report, al-Qahtani's "ability to resist months of standard interrogation in the summer of 2002 was the genesis for the request to have authority to employ additional counter resistance interrogation techniques."[587] He was questioned 18–20 hours daily for 48 of the 54 days between November 23, 2002, and January 16, 2003,[588] and was held in isolation from August 8, 2002, until January 15, 2003.[589]

This report documented the techniques used on al-Qahtani: interrogators threatened him with military working dogs,[590] he was straddled by a female interrogator,[591] and he was subjected to extreme temperatures (apparently resulting on different occasions in a drop in body temperature to 95 to 97 degrees and hospitalization due to episodes of bradycardia – a condition where the heart beats unusually slowly, at less than 50 to 60 beats per minute).[592] He was "forced to wear a woman's bra and had a thong placed on his head during the course of the interrogation...was told that his mother and sister were whores...[and] was told that he was a homosexual, had homosexual tendencies, and that other detainees had found out about these tendencies."[593] Finally, al-Qahtani was tied to a leash and forced "to perform a series of dog tricks,"[594] compelled to dance with a male interrogator, repeatedly subjected to strip searches, required to stand naked in front of women,[595] and, on 17 occasions, had water poured over his head.[596]

Although the techniques used against al-Qahtani met the requirements laid down by Secretary Rumsfeld, the combination of techniques and the duration of their use – as with the deep interrogation techniques used in Northern Ireland in the early 1970s – fundamentally changed the nature of the interrogation. The Schmidt Report concluded that "the creative, aggressive, and persistent interrogation of the subject...resulted in the cumulative effect being degrading and abusive treatment." Of particular concern was "the combined impact of the 160 days of segregation from other detainees" and the persistent interrogation – 48 of 54 consecutive days.[597]

The military at no time claimed that al-Qahtani's interrogation prevented future attacks or yielded particularly important information about al Qaeda's funding. Nor, even in its official statement defending the techniques, did the Department of Defense.[598] Al-Qahtani later repudiated his statements, which had identified some 30 fellow prisoners as Osama bin Laden's bodyguards[599] (claims the Pentagon had seized on to justify the continued detention of the other men). The nature and method of al-Qahtani's interrogation now make it unlikely that the state will be able to bring him to trial.

Soon, many of the techniques used on al-Qahtani and other prisoners at Guantánamo Bay – including the same five deep interrogation techniques used in Northern Ireland in the early 1970s and found to be inhuman and degrading treatment – were transferred to Abu Ghraib.

Iraq and the Revision of Interrogation Standards. On January 15, 2003, Rumsfeld rescinded his permission to use the previously approved Category II and III techniques. In the future, these were to be used only on a case-by-case basis, after direct approval from the Secretary of Defense.[600] Requests were to be accompanied by "a thorough justification for the employment of those techniques and a detailed plan" for their use.[601] In the interim, Rumsfeld created a working group of military lawyers to examine "the legal, political, and operational issues relating to the interrogations of detainees held by the U.S. Armed Forces in the war on terrorism."[602]

Six weeks later, toward the end of February, the working group, chaired by Mary L. Walker, General Counsel for the Air Force, issued the first of two reports, this one on the legal arguments put forward by the White House. This document focused on the necessity defense – one squarely based on the security or freedom dichotomy. Should security needs dictate, a broader array of interrogation techniques would be admitted. The report identified two factors crucial to determining military necessity: whether officials felt *certain* that particular individuals had the information necessary to prevent an attack and *the likelihood of the attack's occurring and the potential scale of devastation*.[603] The report noted that military courts tended to resist the necessity defense. Judicial concern centered on the extent to which the rule of law would be replaced by private moral codes. The report warned about the possible "adverse effects" coercive interrogation could have on the "culture and self-image" of the armed forces, which had in the past, where the laws of war had been violated, been damaged. Should such techniques be brought to light, they would undermine not only the confidence of those responsible for the interrogation but also the public's confidence in the war on terrorism – and the military's role in it.[604]

The working group found, as a legal matter, that the CAT bound the United States to the extent that interrogation techniques were in accord with the Fifth, Eighth, and Fourteenth amendments. (This demand applied only to cruel, inhuman, and degrading treatment – not to torture). The report noted that physical brutality and psychologically coercive interrogation techniques may meet the "shock the conscience standard" established in domestic law, thus violating substantive due process.[605] The working group raised, for the first time, the Uniform Code of Military Justice, which applies to all active duty US forces,[606] and considered the Army Field Manual as well.

Less than two weeks after the report was issued, the United States attacked Iraq.[607] On April 4, 2003, the working group issued a second report, further relaxing the interrogation standards in light of increased security concerns. The introduction declared, "This assessment comes in the context of a major threat to the security of the United States by terrorist forces who have demonstrated a ruthless disregard for even minimal standards of civilized behavior, with a *focused intent to inflict maximum casualties* on the United States and its people, including its civilian population." It added, "In this context, intelligence regarding their capabilities and intentions is of vital interest to the United States and its friends and allies."[608]

Thus, the invasion of Iraq – even with the extremely tenuous link to weapons of mass destruction, which turned out not to exist at all – caused a recalculation in the security/freedom equation that allowed for ever more permissive interrogation standards. With the Geneva Conventions set to one side, *even though the United States was engaged in a formal war*, new rules, made up on the fly, would apply.

The new report suggested that interrogations might be required "beyond that which may be applied to a prisoner of war who is subject to the protections of the Geneva Conventions,"[609] and it evaluated "useful techniques" of interrogation, based on a list of 35 different types.* The lawfulness and effectiveness of any one of these techniques depended on the specific context in which they were used and on procedural protections – which would demonstrate whether the interrogator had any intention to inflict significant mental or physical pain.[610] The report acknowledged that using the techniques in combination changed their quality. And it contemplated the "ticking bomb" scenario: "Interrogation of an individual known to have facts essential to prevent an immediate threat of catastrophic harm to large populations may support use of 'exceptional' techniques, particularly when milder techniques have been unavailing."[611]

A detailed chart noted that some of the techniques examined, such as removing clothing or increasing anxiety by using aversions (such as setting aggressive, snarling guard dogs opposite prisoners deathly afraid of dogs) might violate both the CAT and domestic law. As a policy matter, these and other techniques departed from those acceptable to major partner states. The new report noted that coercive interrogation might affect the government's ability to prosecute detainees,[612] and it both included a more detailed treatment of the possible affirmative defenses that could be offered for the use of torture and analyzed different legal technicalities that could be used to create a "good faith defense against prosecution." In addition, this report recommended that the more exceptional techniques be limited in use and only applied outside US geographic bounds.

Rumsfeld responded to the report by issuing a new list of approved interrogation techniques.[613] He echoed President Bush's February 7, 2002, order, urging that the military "continue to treat detainees humanely and, to the extent appropriate and consistent with military necessity, in a manner consistent with the principles of the Geneva Conventions." Where military necessity required,

---

* These included Direct (questioning), Incentive/Removal of Incentive, Emotional Love (playing on a detainee's love for a group/individual), Emotional Hate (playing on detainee's hate for a group/individual), Fear Up Harsh, Fear Up Mild, Reduced Fear, Pride and Ego Up, Pride and Ego Down, Futility, We Know All, Establish Your Identity (convince detainee that interrogator has mistaken detainee for someone else); Repetition Approach, Rile and Dossier (convince detainee interrogator has damning/inaccurate file that has to be fixed), Mutt and Jeff, Rapid Fire, Silence, Change of Scenery Up, Change of Scenery Down, Hooding, Mild Physical Contact, Dietary Manipulation, Environmental Manipulation, Sleep Adjustment, False Flag (convince detainee that individuals from another country are interrogating him), Threat of Transfer, Isolation, Use of Prolonged Interrogations, Forced Grooming, Prolonged Standing, Sleep Deprivation (not to exceed four days), Physical Training, Face slap/Stomach slap, Removal of Clothing, Increasing Anxiety by Use of Aversions. "Working Group Report on Detainee Interrogations in the Global War on Terrorism: Assessment of Legal, Historical, Policy, and Operational Considerations, Apr. 4, 2002," reprinted in *The Torture Papers: The Road to Abu Ghraib*, 341–43 (Karen J. Greenberg & Joshua L. Dratel, eds., 2005).

interrogators could remove comfort items; isolate a prisoner; and use incentives, rewards, and different scenarios, such as pride and ego down – a humiliation technique in which the interrogator attacks the prisoner's self-worth to encourage him to vindicate himself and thus reveal important information. Additional techniques required a written request to the chairman of the Joint Chiefs of Staff, which would be forwarded to the Secretary of Defense. He concluded, "Nothing in this memorandum in any way restricts your existing authority to maintain good order and discipline among detainees."[614]

Rumsfeld's memo, translated to the field, sowed confusion about what would, and would not, be allowed. On September 10, September 14, October 12, and October 16, interrogation policy in Iraq changed, as different techniques were added. The memo's language proved contradictory.[615] A later military review reported, "Anecdotal evidence suggests that personnel were confused about the approved policy from as early as 14 September 2003."

Abu Ghraib. Until the spring and summer of 2004, detailed information about how detainees inside Iraq were being treated was not readily available.[616] The memos I have cited remained secret. Members of the media and outsiders were allowed into Guantánamo Bay only in tightly controlled conditions. As tens of thousands of people began to pass through American hands, though, more stories began to circulate about prisoners' experiences.

The administration initially denied any mistreatment. President Bush announced in June 2003 that the United States would not violate the Convention Against Torture.[617] In December of that year, the Pentagon and the CIA claimed that they did not use torture against detainees.[618] Colin Powell later told ITV1's *Tonight with Trevor McDonald*, "Because we are Americans, we don't abuse people in our care."[619]

Then in April 2004 pictures of the abuses in Abu Ghraib burst upon the public. The Pentagon's immediate defense of its practices (e.g., hooding, sleep and dietary deprivation, stress positions, isolation for more than 30 days, and intimidation using dogs), as being consistent with international law[620] was met with skepticism, anger, and outright condemnation. The *Washington Post* lambasted the government and, asserting that the techniques had migrated from Guantánamo Bay to Iraq, noted, "Once a government opens the door to abusive treatment of prisoners, it creates a climate in which those abuses are likely to be practiced far more widely and with less exactitude than it intends."[621]

When the Pentagon caved in and announced it would abandon the techniques, it only fed – rather than assuaged – public anger.[622] How far had the government gone in sanctioning and using cruel and inhuman treatment – or torture? The public demanded information. The administration balked. Attorney General Ashcroft protested that such data was privileged.[623] Nevertheless, during the first two weeks of June 2004, executive documents leaked into the public domain.[624] Polls showed "increased national unease with the Bush administration's stand on the war in Iraq and the war on terror."[625] The White

House partially conceded, releasing hundreds of pages of documents aimed to show that, although the United States had used aggressive tactics, it had not condoned torture.[626] The incomplete information left Democrats unpersuaded. Senator Patrick Leahy (D.-VT) scoffed, "The stonewalling in the prison abuse scandal has been building to a crisis point. Now, responding to public pressure, the White House has released a small subset of the documents that offers glimpses into the genesis of this scandal. All should have been provided earlier to Congress, and much more remains held back and hidden away from public view."[627] Finally, the executive relented and initiated a series of inquiries to look into the abuses.[628] The picture that emerges from these reports is that techniques the military initially used in Guantánamo Bay were carried to Iraq, where an emphasis on interrogation, confusion about who was in charge, minimal discipline and oversight, and overextended resources resulted in serious abuse.

In autumn 2002, Major General Geoffrey Miller took over the Guantánamo Bay operation – just prior to the Secretary of Defense's authorization of Category I and II and some Category III techniques – with the mandate to gather as much intelligence from the detainees as possible. After twelve months at Guantánamo, Miller and approximately two dozen staff members went to Iraq, where the military had been unable to generate sufficient intelligence to counter growing resistance.[629] Miller found chaos: virtually no oversight of the prisons, overcrowded facilities, exhausted personnel, 120 degree temperatures, and no guidelines for interrogating low-level operatives.[630] He reported back to Lieutenant General Ricardo Sanchez that the conditions were not conducive to obtaining information.[631] Although a significant number of Iraqi detainees had no connection to al Qaeda, Anser Al Islam, or other terrorist organizations, Miller recommended using police guards to interrogate the internees.[632]

In October 2003, Sanchez responded to Miller's report by issuing guidelines for interrogation that included stress positions for up to 45 minutes and threatening with guard dogs. The following month, Sanchez issued an order for military intelligence to take over operational control of Abu Ghraib, with the military police in support – in essence transposing their roles. There followed a series of gross abuses.

To look into these abuses, the military commissioned a handful of inquiries, prominent among which was one conducted by Major General Antonio Taguba, who wrote a scathing, 53-page report on the treatment of prisoners at Abu Ghraib. He found that, between October and December 2003, "numerous incidents of sadistic, blatant, and wanton criminal abuses were inflicted on several detainees."[633] Detailed witness statements, graphic photographs, and written confessions substantiated the claims, which included punching, slapping, and kicking detainees; stomping on their feet; and videotaping and photographing naked prisoners.[634] Military police arranged detainees in sexual poses and photographed them, forced male detainees to wear women's underwear and to masturbate, and placed naked male detainees in a pile and jumped on them.[635] The guards positioned one detainee naked on a box with a sandbag on his head and attached wires to his fingers, toes, and penis as though he were being electrocuted.[636] Taguba reported sex between a male military police officer and a female detainee and the use of military working dogs without muzzles to intimidate and frighten detainees – in at least one case biting and seriously injuring the detainee – and that a dog chain had been placed around a detainee's neck, with a female officer holding it while posing for a picture; there were also photographs of dead Iraqi detainees.[637]

In addition to the substantiated abuses, he also found credible several more allegations, which included the sodomizing of a detainee with a chemical light and perhaps a broomstick, and the breaking and pouring of the contents of chemical lights on prisoners.[638] Detainees had been threatened with a charged 9-millimeter pistol; others had been beaten with a broom handle and a chair.[639] Some had had cold water poured on them while naked.[640] Males had been threatened with rape, and a military policeman had been allowed to stitch up a detainee whose skin had split when he was thrown against the cell wall.[641]

These abuses were all tied to the military police. Sanchez separately ordered Lieutenant General Anthony Jones and Major General George Fay to examine the role of military intelligence. The men noted that at the formal end of the Iraqi war (as declared by President Bush on May 1, 2003, aboard the *USS Abraham Lincoln*), the United States held only 600 enemy prisoners of war and criminals; in contrast, during the US occupation of Iraq in the fall of 2003, there was an exponential increase in the number of detainees.[642] The abuses took place in an environment that was undermanned and had an increasing number of missions; nevertheless, "[t]he primary causes are misconduct (ranging from inhumane to sadistic) by a small group of morally corrupt soldiers and civilians, a lack of discipline on the part of the leaders and Soldiers of the 205th MI BDE [Military Intelligence Brigade] and a failure or lack of leadership."[643] Issues related to command and control, doctrine, training, and soldiers' inexperience contributed to the abuse.[644]

This "small group" included at least 27 military intelligence personnel who "allegedly requested, encouraged, condoned or solicited military police personnel to abuse detainees and/or participated in detainee abuse and/or violated established interrogation procedures and applicable laws and regulations during interrogation operations at Abu Ghraib."[645] Most of the violent sexual violations occurred outside the established, scheduled interrogations "*and did not focus on persons held for intelligence purposes.*"[646]

The key to this abuse of prisoners lay both in the ambiguity resulting from the lifting of the Geneva Conventions and in the transfer of nontraditional and more extreme techniques from Afghanistan and Guantánamo Bay.

Jones and Fay divided the abuses into two categories: "intentional violent or sexual abuses" and "incidents that resulted from misinterpretations of law or policy or resulted from confusion about what interrogation techniques were permitted by law or local SOPs."[647] Although some of the practices in the second category violated international law, they were believed at the time to be condoned by the US military.

In addition to the Taguba Report and the Jones/Fay document, which provide two official government analyses of what occurred in Iraq, human rights bodies and nongovernmental organizations also conducted fact-finding missions. The International Committee of the Red Cross, for instance, documented beatings, threats, humiliation, sleep deprivation, burns, and stress positions inflicted on detainees.[648] The organization highlighted this treatment's psychological effects, finding that prisoners exhibited "signs of concentration difficulties, memory problems, verbal expression difficulties, incoherent speech, acute anxiety reactions, abnormal behaviour and suicidal tendencies,"[649] and concluded, "These symptoms appeared to have been caused by the methods and duration of interrogation."[650]

Ghost Detainees, Black Sites, and Extraordinary Rendition.

By November 2005, the United States had detained approximately 70,000 people worldwide, of whom some 10,000 were still in US custody.[651] But these figures do not tell the whole story. In the first place, they do not include all of the prisoners held. To give interrogators more flexibility, some detainees were never recorded. Others were held at undisclosed sites run by the Central Intelligence Agency around the world. In a process called "extraordinary rendition," hundreds more were transferred to countries that were known not to hesitate at inflicting torture.

In respect to the first point, the Taguba Report noted that "ghost detainees" – prisoners in CIA custody, whose presence was secret, whose names were never entered into official records,[652] and who were hidden from the International Committee of the Red Cross – were held in Iraq. General Paul Kern, who oversaw one military investigation into US interrogation policies, found "perhaps up to 100" ghost detainees in Iraq.[653]

The CIA was, of course, operating outside the minimal guidelines established to replace the Geneva Conventions. The presidential determination, which had specified that *the armed forces* would "continue to treat detainees humanely and, to the extent appropriate and consistent with military necessity, in a manner consistent with the principles of Geneva," said nothing about the CIA and the role it would play in obtaining information from detainees. Cofer Black, who served as the director of the CIA's Counterterrorism Center from 1999–2002, testified to Congress, "[T]here was a 'before' 9/11 and 'after' 9/11. After 9/11 the gloves come off."[654] According to *ABC News*, the rules for the CIA differed from those binding the military. By mid-March 2002, the CIA had been authorized to grab and shake prisoners, slap them on the belly in a manner that caused pain and triggered fear but that avoided internal injury, force them to stand for more than 40 hours at a time, subject them to 50 degree climates while dousing them with cold water, and use waterboarding.[655]

In addition to Abu Ghraib, the military and the CIA ran an international network of detention facilities in Afghanistan, Iraq, Jordan, Romania, Poland, Thailand, Qatar, and elsewhere.[656] There were, for instance, at least 17 detention facilities in Iraq and another 25 in Afghanistan.[657] Some of the other sites were known; but many were not.[658] These ranged from operations "as small as shipping containers" to large complexes.[659] The *New York Times* wrote that the location of some of these sites was so secret that "one official said he had been told that Mr. Bush had informed the CIA that he did not want to know where they were."[660] The *Washington Post* explained that the purpose of these facilities was "to hold suspected terrorists or insurgents for interrogation and safekeeping while avoiding U.S. or international court systems."[661]

As for those detainees subject to extraordinary rendition to other countries, the United States had significantly increased their number. Regular rendition – that is, transfer of an individual outside of extradition, removal, or exclusion proceedings – was first authorized by President Reagan in 1986 to apprehend and bring to justice individuals suspected of complicity in the 1983 Marine barracks bombing in Lebanon.[662] In the early 1990s, renditions were similarly conducted under a law enforcement rubric, with the aim of bringing suspects to the United States or elsewhere for trial or questioning.[663] Presidential Decision Directive 39, signed by President Bill Clinton in 1995, set the policy: "When terrorists wanted for violation of U.S. law are at large overseas, their return for prosecution should be a matter of the highest priority and shall be a continuing central issue in bilateral relations with any state that harbors or assists them."[664] Michael Hurley, a staff member of the 9/11 Commission, explained, "If extradition procedures were unavailable or put aside, the United States could seek the local country's assistance in a rendition, secretly putting the fugitive in a plane back to America or some third country for trial."[665] According to George Tenet, the former director of Central Intelligence, the CIA took part in approximately 80 renditions before 9/11.[666]

Not all of these renditions appear to have been conducted with an eye toward trial. Michael Scheuer, a former CIA agent who helped create the rendition program, said that at times the CIA was reluctant to bring cases to court: too much information about intelligence gathering would be revealed, and standard criminal procedure would be too restrictive. Instead of rendering suspects to the United States, the CIA decided to transfer them to Egypt – a strategic ally that had less compunction about using coercive interrogation and a mutual interest in stopping the activities of Islamist groups. Jane Mayer of the *New Yorker* reported that "[a] series of spectacular covert operations followed." In the summer of 1998, for instance, the CIA worked with Albanian intelligence to intercept communications between Dr. Ayman Muhammad Zawahiri, a central member of al Qaeda, and Islamist militants. The United States convinced Egypt to help with the interrogation of the militants – who were flown to Egypt, tortured, and some killed. Mayer writes,

On August 5, 1998, an Arab-language newspaper in London published a letter from the International Islamic Front for Jihad, in which it threatened retaliation against the U.S. for the Albanian operation – in a "language they will understand." Two days later, the U.S. Embassies in Kenya and Tanzania were blown up, killing two hundred and twenty-four people.

After 9/11, the scope and frequency of so-called extraordinary rendition (that is, the transfer of individuals not to stand criminal trial, but to be interrogated by other states "in circumstances that make it more likely than not that the individual will be subjected to torture or cruel, inhuman, or degrading treatment"[667]), expanded. Just after the attacks, President Bush reportedly signed a new, still-classified directive that exempted the CIA from needing to obtain case-by-case approval from the White House.[668]

On the record, government officials still acknowledge only regular rendition.[669] But off the record is a different story. In an interview with the *Washington Post*, one diplomat noted that such renditions became common after 9/11: they "allow us to get information from terrorists in a way we can't do on U.S. soil."[670] Another official explained, "We don't kick the [expletive] out of them. We send them to other countries so they can kick the [expletive] out of them."[671] According to *Newsweek*, when the CIA Director George Tenet was asked whether the United States intended to try to remove prisoners from regimes where they were likely to face torture, he replied that there were times when more aggressive interrogation might be desirable.[672] Although the CIA refuses to say how many people have been rendered since 9/11, Scott Horton, who helped prepare a study done by New York University Law School and the New York City Bar Association, put the total at approximately 150.[673] (These numbers, however, may be conservative: in February 2007 the European Union endorsed a report that put the number of CIA flights within the 14 member states that had allowed rendition to occur within their territories at 1,245.[674])

As a legal matter, the NYU study argues that extraordinary rendition violates domestic and international law.[675] In 1998, Congress passed the Foreign Affairs Reform and Restructuring Act, which brought the United States into compliance with the CAT.[676] Regulations under this statute prohibit the removal or extradition of an individual to a country where he is more likely than not to be subjected to torture. The most common states to which suspects are sent are Egypt, Morocco, Syria, and Jordan – all countries repeatedly accused by the US State Department of using torture during interrogation.[677] Indeed, many of those detainees rendered and subsequently released reported being tortured. (Mamdouh Habib, for instance, detained in Afghanistan in late 2001, was sent to Egypt, where he was strapped to the ceiling and given an electrified barrel to stand on – giving him the option either to hang painfully or be electrocuted. He was also blindfolded, locked in rooms flooded with water, and guarded by German shepherds that, he was informed, had been trained to sexually assault people.[678] After 40 months' imprisonment, he was released without charge.[679] Khaled al-Masri, a Lebanese-born German, was pulled off a bus on the Serbia-Macedonia border in December 2003 and sent to Afghanistan, where he was beaten and drugged. After five months of interrogation, he was released without charge.[680]) The NYU report found that the practice also violated the UN Convention Against Torture and Other Cruel, Inhuman or Degrading Treatment or Punishment, the International Covenant on Civil and Political Rights, the Geneva Conventions of 1949, and the Refugee Convention of 1951.[681]

Responsibility for these policies lay in the highest levels of the US government. Military and CIA lawyers developed the programs and the rules of detention and interrogation; the Department of Justice's Office of Legal Counsel acquiesced. In some cases the White House General Counsel or the president himself reportedly authorized the operations.[682]

The World Balks

The interrogation procedures adopted by the United States had adverse political, diplomatic, and legal consequences. In July 2004, the International Committee of the Red Cross found the techniques to be cruel, inhuman, and degrading treatment – and the involvement of psychiatrists in the interrogations to be "a flagrant violation of medical ethics." Four months later, the *New York Times* leaked the report.[683] The news was picked up around the world.[684] The United Nations also issued a document charging that the interrogation practices in Guantánamo Bay amounted to torture, and called for those who had ordered and condoned such practices to be brought to justice "up to the highest level of military and political command." Drawing on interviews with former detainees, the 54-page report called for the facility to be closed "without further delay" – and for US personnel to be trained in the acceptable and unacceptable limits of interrogation in international law. The White House immediately dismissed the UN's findings, saying that they were based on false information from suspected terrorists. Scott McClellan, the White House spokesman, added, "We know that Al Qaeda detainees are trained in trying to disseminate false allegations," and explained, "These are dangerous terrorists that we are talking about.... Nothing has changed in terms of our views."[685]

Concern extended beyond international organizations and into the state system – bringing with it legal and political costs. In May 2005, for example, a Swedish parliamentary investigator concluded a 10-month examination of the CIA transfer, through its territory to Egypt, of Ahmed Agiza and Muhammad Zery, who had lived in Sweden for extended periods and had sought political asylum there. These men were tortured in Egypt and later released with no charge. The Swedish Parliament also held hearings on the state's acquiescence in the operation.[686] In July 2005, the attorney general of Bobigny, France, initiated an investigation into CIA flights through LeBourget Airport. Four months later, a Spanish attorney opened investigations into CIA flights through the Canary Islands. And in November 2005, the European Union Justice Commissioner, Franco Frattini, announced that any EU country complicit in running black prisons within domestic bounds would be suspended from voting on EU matters.[687]

Condoleeza Rice, who had replaced Colin Powell as Secretary of State, initiated a trip through Europe to try to soothe America's allies. This, she said, is a "war of ideas": "The U.S., and those countries that share the commitment to defend their citizens will use every lawful weapon to defeat these terrorists. Protecting citizens is the first and oldest duty of any government. Sometimes these efforts are misunderstood."[688] Rice spoke of "the hard choices involved," and threatened,

Some governments choose to cooperate with the U.S. in intelligence, law enforcement, or military matters. *That cooperation is a two-way street. We share intelligence that has helped protect European countries from attack, helping save European lives. It is up to those governments and their citizens to decide if they wish to work with us to prevent terrorist attacks against their own country or other countries, and decide how much sensitive information they can make public.*"[689]

Apparently, if European countries wanted help from the United States, they should drop the matter.

Europe, however, did not drop the matter. Instead, it took increasingly prominent legal and political actions at both a state level and in collective European bodies – resulting in precisely the scenario Gonzales ignored in his memo, which dismissed the importance of international law (see page 84). In November 2006, for instance, a criminal complaint, requesting that the German Federal Prosecutor open an investigation, was filed in Berlin on behalf of 12 Iraqi citizens. The suit called for the criminal prosecution of high-ranking US officials for authorizing war crimes. (The complaint was filed under Germany's Code of Crimes Against International Law, which extends universal jurisdiction for war crimes, crimes of genocide, and crimes against humanity.[690]) Germany issued arrest warrants for 13 US citizens wanted in connection with an alleged CIA abduction of a German citizen as well. In February 2007, Italy indicted 31 people in a CIA rendition case – including 26 Americans, all but one of whom were CIA agents.[691] The Swiss government in turn authorized its prosecutors to investigate a US flight that went through Swiss airspace during a detainee transfer from Italy to Germany. The Portuguese general prosecutor opened an investigation into CIA flights suspected of rendering detainees, leaving open the possibility that criminal charges would be brought.[692]

Even America's closest ally in Europe caved to public pressure. The United Kingdom established a parliamentary group to look into CIA use of British airspace. Led by a Conservative, Andrew Tyrie, the group was strongly critical of the United States. A broad array of British political leaders expressed open disdain for US methods. The Attorney General, Lord Peter Goldsmith, repeatedly criticized US policies.[693] Harriett Harman, Britain's Constitutional Affairs Minister and a close political ally of the prime minister, considered Guantánamo Bay "a legal no man's land. Either it should be moved to America and then they can hold these people under the American justice system or it should be closed."[694] Sir David Omand, the former director of Government Communications Headquarters, who now teaches at King's College, London, concluded that the United States was making the same mistakes that the United Kingdom had made in the 1970s. (Omand worked in Northern Ireland at the Ministry of Defence when the coercive interrogation techniques were introduced – and was responsible for defending them to the European Court of Human Rights).[695] Coming to the same conclusion was Lord Lloyd of Berwick, a Lord of Appeal in Ordinary who conducted the United Kingdom's comprehensive *Inquiry into Legislation Against Terrorism*.[696]

It was not just individual countries that took a stand: in June 2006, the Council of Europe issued a broad report, condemning European involvement in rendition. This was swiftly followed by a Council of Europe Resolution by the Parliamentary Assembly of the Council of Europe, demanding that treaties concerning American military bases in Europe be amended to include human rights clauses – and that all bilateral agreements between the United States and European countries regarding the stationing of US forces in Europe and the use of military and other infrastructures be reevaluated.[697] Then in February 2007, the European Parliament adopted by a significant majority a scathing report, condemning both US rendition and acquiescence by European states.[698]

Such inquiries and legal actions were not limited to America's European allies. In February 2004, for example, the Canadian government, under immense public pressure, initiated a formal inquiry into the American rendition of Maher Arar, a 34-year-old Canadian of Syrian birth.[699] (Arar was detained in September 2002 at John F. Kennedy airport while on a connecting flight home.[700] He was interrogated for 13 days and then put on a plane that flew to Washington, D.C., and then to Jordan. Arar overheard the pilots identify themselves as "the Special Removal Unit."[701] He ended up in Syria, where, for the next 10 months, he was tortured.[702] In October 2003, he was released without charge.[703]) The Canadian Commissioner reported on September 18, 2006, "I am able to say categorically that there is no evidence to indicate that Mr. Arar has committed any offence or that his activities constitute a threat to the security of Canada."[704] Although no Canadian officials had actively participated or acquiesced in the rendition, "[i]t is very likely that ... the US authorities relied on information about Mr. Arar provided by the [Royal Canadian Mounted Police.]" That information turned out to be misleading: it portrayed Arar "in an unfair fashion and overstated his importance to the investigation. Some of this inaccurate information had the potential to create serious consequences for Mr. Arar in light of American attitudes and practices at the time."[705]

Charges of American duplicity followed closely on the legal and political actions taken abroad. The US State Department had, over the years, taken a leading role in condemning the cruel, inhuman, or degrading treatment and torture practiced by other nations. Its annual human rights reports called attention to their use of sleep deprivation, confinement in contorted positions, stripping, blindfolding, and threatening with dogs – all methods *approved* by the US Secretary of Defense in December 2002.[706] Similarly, even as senior administration officials claimed to respect the rule of law (thus, Condoleeza Rice at the start of her European tour said, "We believe in the rule of law"),[707] the administration's simultaneous decision *not* to follow that law deeply hurt the country's international standing. Paul Hunt, the United Nation's special *rapporteur* on the right to health, explained, "The rule of law cannot be applied selectively. A state cannot apply the rule of law in one place, but not to another, to one group of people but not another. The rule of law is not to be turned on and off like a tap."[708] The Council of Europe – representing many of the US's closest allies – passed a resolution condemning the US decision not to follow international law.[709] Human rights bodies around the world decried American actions – Kenneth Roth of Human Rights Watch, for instance, called them "shameful."[710] European Judge Michel Picard, president of the Human Rights Chamber in Bosnia-Herzegovina, said, "It's clear that the world is not safe anymore because of the behaviour of the United States. When the United States feel that they do not have to comply with laws in any country of the world, because of the fight against terrorism, it shows that everything can happen everywhere."[711]

The *Independent* in London concluded that Guantánamo Bay had "gravely diminished the moral authority of the US around the world."[712] In Australia, the *Canberra Times* opined, "The illegality of the American conduct taints its moral and practical capacity to try (and, if appropriate, punish) these prisoners. It also raises fundamental questions about the purity of the Western cause, and the capacity of those who support that cause, to posit Western conduct against the barbarism of its enemies."[713]

The American press proved sensitive to the international charges. The *Washington Post* wrote,

> It may or may not be true that such techniques, when practiced under close supervision by highly trained interrogators, are effective. The administration has offered no evidence that they are, and many outside experts believe otherwise. But the administration hasn't limited its system to Guantánamo Bay or to senior al Qaeda detainees.... The result has been outrages that have done far more damage to the United States than any intelligence collection could justify.[714]

The system "brought international opprobrium on the United States. It generated domestic skepticism of its commitment to the rule of law in fighting terrorism."[715] The *Columbus Dispatch* noted, "The Bush administration has made a hash of the public-relations war, and that is hurting the war against terrorism. The refusal to provide any meaningful information about the Guantánamo prisoners reinforces suspicions of Americans and the world that while the United States preaches democracy and the rule of law on one hand, it practices something different on the other."[716]

Indeed, the country's efforts to extradite terrorist suspects from other countries suffered: European countries were barred by the European Convention on Human Rights from transferring individuals where there was the likelihood that they would be subjected to cruel, inhuman, or degrading treatment or to torture. It was for precisely this reason that, in 2003, Germany delayed extradition of two al Qaeda suspects, Sheik Muhammad Ali Hassan al-Mouyad and Muhammad Moshen Yahya Zayed,[717] and required assurance from the United States that the two would not be tried by a military tribunal.[718] Senior military commanders in Iraq acknowledged that the abuses had damaged their reputations all over the world.[719]

Congress Speaks: The 2005 Detainee Treatment Act Revisited

The international and domestic outrage at the revelation of these interrogation practices turned largely on international obligations – both under the Geneva Conventions and the Convention Against Torture. In regard to the former, a tenuous link, at best, had been drawn by the US administration between Iraq and the war on terror – making it unclear why the United States did not apply the Conventions to those detained in Iraq. In regard to the latter, the administration had claimed that in the war on terror, CAT could not diminish the president's authority as commander-in-chief.

When it ratified CAT, the United States had entered a reservation specifying that the Convention would be read as far as it was compatible with the Fifth, Eighth, and Fourteenth Amendments (see page 96). At his confirmation hearings for Attorney General, Alberto Gonzales offered a surprising and novel interpretation of this reservation, insisting that it meant that CAT *would be applied only within domestic bounds*, as the Fifth and Eighth Amendments do not attach outside US territory.[720] According to a clarification subsequently provided by the Department of Justice, "[T]he Senate intended that Article 16 [of CAT] not impose any new obligations on the United States beyond what was already required by the Constitution"; thus, "Article 16 would not apply outside 'territory under [U.S.] jurisdiction.'"[721] In other words, the administration claimed that the reservation meant that the geographic reach, not the substance, of the Fifth, Eighth, and Fourteenth Amendments would apply. Abraham Sofaer, who had been General Counsel at the State Department when the United States signed the Convention, wrote to Senator Patrick Leahy, explaining that the reservation *had* meant that *substantively*, not geographically, the Convention would accord with US law.

Calls for new legislation to prevent the use of torture erupted.[722] Senator John McCain (R.-AZ), himself a prisoner of war during the Vietnam War and subjected to torture, successfully amended the fiscal year 2005 Defense Appropriations Bill to prohibit "cruel, inhuman, or degrading treatment or punishment of persons under custody or control of the United States government." Section (b) read, "Nothing in this section shall be construed to impose any geographical limitation on the applicability of the prohibition against cruel, inhuman, or degrading treatment or punishment under this section." Nor would the law be superseded by subsequent statutes, unless they directly repealed the section. The legislation specifically defined cruel, inhuman, and degrading treatment as treatment prohibited by the Fifth, Eighth, and Fourteenth Amendments, "as defined in the United States Reservations, Declarations, and Understandings to the United Nations Convention Against Torture and Other Forms of Cruel, Inhuman or Degrading Treatment or Punishment."

Vice President Dick Cheney lobbied hard against the new law, saying that, although the United States did not torture people, it needed broad flexibility. When the amendment passed, President Bush – although he signed the bill – attached a statement reiterating the previous, internal memos:

The executive branch shall construe Title X in Division A of the Act, relating to detainees, *in a manner consistent with the constitutional authority of the President to supervise the unitary executive branch and as Commander in Chief and consistent with the constitutional limitations on the judicial power*, which will assist in achieving the shared objective of the Congress and the President, evidenced in Title X of protecting the American people from further terrorist attack.[723]

The executive refused to concede.

The judiciary, for its part, has yet to address, specifically, coercive interrogation. Although in *Hamdan* v. *Rumsfeld*, the Supreme Court stated that the Geneva Conventions applied to prisoners held in Guantánamo Bay, two cases – those of Maher Arar and of Khalel El-Masri – specifically on rendition were dismissed by the courts under the state secrets privilege. In the first case, Maher Arar, the Canadian who had been rendered to Syria, brought suit in the Eastern District of New York, pursuant to the 1992 Torture Victims Protection Act (which, ironically, former US President George Bush, Sr., had introduced to help victims of torture seek redress in US courts).[724] The government moved to dismiss Arar's lawsuit on the grounds that it would jeopardize national security.[725] District Court Judge David Trager agreed, and noted, "One need not have much imagination to contemplate the negative effect on our relations with Canada if discovery were to proceed in this case and were it to turn out that certain high Canadian officials had, despite public denials, acquiesced in Arar's removal to Syria."[726] Another lawsuit was brought on behalf of Khaled El-Masri, a 42-year-old German citizen who, while on vacation in Macedonia, was abducted, drugged, and transported to a secret CIA prison in Afghanistan. Several months later, he was taken to Albania and released, with no crime charged. The district court dismissed the case on the grounds of national security: "[T]he substance of El-Masri's publicly available complaint alleges a clandestine intelligence program, and . . . any admission or denial of these allegations by defendants in this case would reveal the means and methods employed pursuant to this clandestine program and such a revelation would present a grave risk of injury to national security."[727]

PARALLEL COSTS

The parallels between the United Kingdom and the United States are, indeed, startling, as both countries paid a heavy price, both at home and abroad, for using indefinite detention and coercive interrogation.

Domestic Political Power

In the first place, the reductive "security or freedom" framework frequently called upon to justify extreme provisions does not take into account the distribution of power among the branches of government.

Following the September 11 attacks, the Bush administration claimed expansive authority under Article II of the Constitution – to the exclusion of the other two branches. The legislature, for the most part, was complicit: it did not pass a single law between 2001 and 2005 that limited or even regulated the executive branch in the exercise of the detention and interrogation program. In 2005, the Military Commissions Act actually *strengthened* the administration's hand against the judiciary – perhaps to be expected since the same party controlled the legislature as lived in the White House. The statute retroactively legalized the administration's actions. Congress did eventually make efforts to control the manner of interrogations. However, the 2005 Detainee Treatment Act came late in the game and was vigorously fought by the administration, subsequently watered down, and accompanied by a signing statement to protect executive autonomy. (The exact status of these signing statements is a matter of controversy.) In September 2007, efforts in the Senate to repeal the MCA provisions blocking habeas corpus petitions from Guantánamo Bay detainees failed.[728]

The judiciary, for its part, largely limited its involvement to habeas petitions from Guantánamo Bay – a base that houses only 500 of more than 10,000 people detained worldwide. Even here, the courts' role gradually narrowed; for, like the British Government in 1972, the White House responded to the habeas cases by issuing new orders and by forcing new statutes through the legislature, underscoring the executive's intent to circumvent the courts in the future. In April 2007, the Supreme Court denied certiori in the cases of *Boumediene v. Bush* and *Al Ohah v. United States* on the grounds that under the MCA, other remedies were available.[729]* Beyond habeas claims, the judiciary did not address a considerable range of issues that accompanied the executive branch's decision to create a new, worldwide detention, interrogation, and judicial system. The two cases on rendition that did come before the courts were dismissed on grounds of state secrets. El-Masri appealed, but in October 2007 the Supreme Court denied his petition for a writ of certiorari.[730]†

In the early 1970s, the United Kingdom's legislature also proved complicit in continuing detention policies. As in the United States, habeas proceedings in England quickly stalled over jurisdictional questions. In Northern Ireland, the courts were limited to inquiring whether the 1922–43 Special Powers Act regulations were *ultra vires*. This was a narrow inquiry, as later noted by the

---

* This does not mean that the courts had no role to play – indeed, at the end of June 2007, the Court reversed its earlier denial. It consolidated the cases, and granted each applicant one hour's oral argument, which the Supreme Court heard in December 2007. Boumediene v Bush, 127 S.Ct. 3078 (Mem), 75 USLW 3705, 75 USLW 3707, U.S., June 29, 2007 (NO. 06-1195). Transcript of argument available at http://www.supremecourtus.gov/oral_arguments/argument_transcripts/06-1195.pdf.

† In November 2007 Arar's attorneys appeared before a panel of three judges in the Second Circuit to try to re-open his suit against senior US officials. As of the time of writing, their opinion has not been issued. (Mike Rosen-Molina, Arar Lawyers urge Federal Appeals Court to Reinstate Extraordinary Rendition Lawsuit, Nov. 9, 2007, available at http://jurist.law.pitt.edu/paperchase/2007/11/arar-lawyers-urge-federal-appeals-court.php).

European courts; although not altogether ineffective, neither was it particularly forceful. The state, moreover, essentially overrode judicial considerations by forcing subsequent legislation through Westminster that retroactively legalized army actions in Northern Ireland. It was the European Court of Human Rights, not Parliament, that pushed back on the use of deep interrogation.

After the incorporation of the 1998 Human Rights Act, the role assumed by the Law Lords changed. What is now playing out, in part because of the government's counterterrorist agenda, is a massive battle over the distribution of power among the Law Lords, the House of Lords, and the government. At issue as well is the legitimacy of each branch; the House of Lords, for instance, proved particularly reluctant to involve the judiciary in the issuance of control orders, preferring that political questions be kept within the executive. The implications of the constitutional questions that now hang in the balance go well beyond counterterrorist concerns.

What is important here is not just the judiciary acting as constituted courts, but the judges' actions in an advisory capacity. For, unlike the United States, the United Kingdom government has routinely made use of independent inquiries to examine the impact of past policies and to articulate future options. The Compton Committee confirmed the interrogation techniques that were being used; the Parker Committee issued both a majority and a minority report addressing the Geneva Conventions and whether the five techniques should be abandoned; the Diplock Committee considered judicial alteration to facilitate the move away from internment; the Gardiner Committee looked at how to balance civil liberties and human rights against ongoing security concerns; and in 1996 Lord Lloyd led an inquiry into permanent counterterrorist law. The commissions were all staffed by senior and respected members of the judiciary, chosen not for political affiliation but for prominence. And their recommendations were routinely accepted by both Labour and Conservative governments.

For the United Kingdom as well as the United States, the very use of coercive interrogation discounted the future influence of the judiciary. Such devices make it difficult to bring terrorist suspects to trial.[731] To some extent, the disjuncture reflects the difference between approaches: intelligence gathering focuses on heading off threats – not on prosecuting suspects.[732] In both states, domestic law outlaws the fruits of coercive questioning. As an international matter, the Convention Against Torture demands, "Each State Party shall ensure that any statement which is established to have been made as a result of torture shall not be invoked as evidence in any proceedings, except against a person accused of torture as evidence that the statement was made."[733] The European Convention on Human Rights similarly condemns the use of such information. This issue was the one at the heart of the negotiations between Rumsfeld and Goldsmith, who could not guarantee that Britons returned to the United Kingdom from Guantánamo Bay would be able to stand trial (see page 93).[734] The use of coercive questioning also harmed the ability of both countries to extradite suspects from even allied states. Although such barriers can be surmounted – for instance, by a formal agreement that suspects will not be subjected to inhuman and degrading treatment – their presence discourages the use of judicial mechanisms and undermines the strength of the judiciary.

Innocent Victims

Beyond the power struggles within the state itself, these policies harmed many innocent people who were caught up in their net. In the late 1960s and early 1970s, the United Kingdom interned thousands of people with no involvement in republican activity. More than three decades later, the United States similarly detained thousands of people innocent of any involvement in terrorism.* In both contexts, when this information became public, it exacerbated domestic and international concern.

To some extent, detention of the wrong people may – when the executive is essentially given a blank check – be inevitable. Terrorism is, by its nature, clandestine. States rarely have the information they need to apprehend those responsible – especially in close-knit communities, which are notoriously difficult to penetrate to gain human intelligence. Protections otherwise afforded the innocent are not present. Terrorist organizations, moreover, tend to go to ground just before an attack, making it particularly difficult, in the immediate aftermath, to apprehend those responsible for it.[†]

Furthermore, the promise of reward money corrupts the process, particularly where a state lacks the necessary intelligence capability and where people are poor and tempted to sell someone to the state for economic gain. After 9/11, for instance, the United States dropped pamphlets in Afghanistan and Pakistan, offering money for al Qaeda or Taliban operatives.[735] One detainee, an Afghan shopkeeper, said he was falsely identified, and passed a polygraph confirming his story.[736] Another prisoner in Guantánamo Bay claimed that his ex-wife sold

---

* Documents show that taxi drivers, goat herders, bakers – people at the wrong place at the wrong time, and low-level Taliban fighters – ended up in indefinite detention in Guantánamo Bay. Alif Mohammed, for example, accused of having a satellite phone to orchestrate ambushes, claimed to be a tinsmith; Taj Mohammed, a goat herder, was accused of being linked to al Qaeda through Lashkar-e-Tayyiba; Mohammed Nasim of Warzai claimed to be a poor farmer; and Allah Nasir claimed to be a shopkeeper. Partial list of detainees at Gitmo, compiled from transcripts released to AP under court order by DoD, approx. 5,000 pages. The *National Journal* reviewed the legal records of 132 men being held on the island and found more than half of them were not accused of fighting against the United States. Many had been picked up in Pakistan – and the only evidence against them had been obtained from fellow inmates, subjected to hundreds of hours of harsh questioning. Denis Staunton, *Amnesty Report Calls for Closure of Guantnamo*, IRISH TIMES, Feb. 6, 2006, at 10.

† Al Qaeda, for instance, has in the past used a special communication mode called alarm communication, for "when the opposing security apparatus discovers an undercover activity or some undercover members. Based on this communication, the activity is stopped for a while, all matters related to the activity are abandoned, and the Organization's members are hidden from the security personnel." AL QAEDA MANUAL, located by Manchester (England) Metropolitan Police during search of a member's home. Computer file described as "the military series" related to the "Declaration of Jihad." UK/BM-29–30, Translation into English, available at www.usdoj.gov.

information to US soldiers.[737] Yet another, Shah Zada, who was arrested in January 2003 with three other men, claimed that the Afghans sold him to the United States for $15,000.[738] Abdul Matin, a science teacher, said that when he refused to give Afghan authorities a bribe of $30,000, he was handed over to the US military.[739] The likelihood that innocent people may be swept up in the counterterrorist net enhances the necessity of properly protecting terrorist suspects.

The Psychological Effects of Indefinite Detention

Beyond the anxiety about physical safety, indefinite detention's long-term psychological effect on suspects can – even without coercive interrogation – be devastating. The European Court of Human Rights brought these effects to public notice in *Ireland* v. *United Kingdom*. But the problem was not limited to the treatment of Northern Irish detainees. Many people subject to detention and then control orders in the United Kingdom after September 11 became severely mentally disturbed.[740] Mahmoud Abu Rideh, for instance, one of the first post-9/11 detainees, was transferred to Broadmoor psychiatric hospital.[741] When released on bail, subject to a set of strict conditions, he overdosed on pills and had to be rehospitalized.[742] Another man collapsed and had to be taken to the hospital for treatment for psychiatric difficulties,[743] and a third was deemed severely disturbed because of the experience.[744] By March 2005, 4 of the 10 placed under control orders were suffering from acute psychiatric or other medical problems.[745] In February 2006, Lord Carlile of Berriew expressed concern about the "potential psychological effects" of restriction.[746]

Neither have those at Guantánamo Bay been exempt from this danger. On July 2, 2002, there occurred the first in a series of suicide attempts.[747] Over the next few months, guards prevented loss of life or serious medical consequences – until the 11th attempt on January 16, 2003, when a man in his twenties tried to hang himself;[748] after two and a half months, he came out of a coma with brain damage.[749] A sudden surge in attempted suicides followed.[750] In response, the Pentagon announced that it would build a new mental ward, with approximately 35 cells and staffed by psychiatrists, psychologists, and nurses.[751] Suicide attempts continued through the summer of 2003,[752] culminating in August 2003 when 23 detainees tried to kill themselves over an eight-day period.[753] By November 2003, psychologists had 110 people on a watch list, around 25 percent of whom were prescribed psychotropic medication.[754] Military police said that the efforts by detainees to take their own lives were "emblematic of the stressful conditions" at Guantánamo Bay.[755] Correctional psychology experts suggested that the risk of suicide increases in individuals experiencing the hopelessness and stress of indefinite detention and being separated from contact with the outside world.[756] Earlier, in October 2003, the International Committee of the Red Cross broke its traditional code of silence to express concern about Guantánamo Bay prisoners' mental health, attributing it to uncertainty about their fate.[757]

Minority Concerns

These techniques and measures have been applied – by both the United Kingdom and the United States – almost exclusively against one community. Although it can be argued in excuse that the terrorists came from these communities, the fact that in each case a minority group is being targeted somewhat undercuts the security or freedom assumption: that is, every citizen or resident is not being asked to sacrifice his or her freedom; only certain individuals are. Moreover, not one kind of freedom is being constricted, but several are, owing to the interwoven nature of rights. Added to this are concerns related to social cohesion, along with the danger to security posed by further radicalizing the population.

In the late 1960s and early 1970s, the United Kingdom's measures in Northern Ireland further alienated Catholics from the state and breathed new life into the republican movement. After 9/11, the state again applied extended detention to individuals drawn from a minority – this time, the Muslim, Arab community in Great Britain. As the bombings of July 7, 2005, demonstrated, there was a threat from Islamists – and not just from noncitizens, but from Islamist British subjects as well. The government had to walk a fine line between neutralizing the threat and alienating Islamic moderates. A poll published in the United Kingdom in 2006 found that around 7 percent of Britain's 1.6 million Muslims (approximately 100,000 people) considered suicide bombings justified in certain circumstances.[758] In 2005, a YouGov poll found that 24 percent of British Muslims were sympathetic to the motives of the July 7 bombers, and 32 percent agreed with this statement: "Western society is decadent and immoral and Muslims should seek to bring it to an end."[759] Perhaps because of concerns about radicalization, of the one hundred or more radical Islamists on the government's list, fewer than two dozen found themselves subject to control orders.[760] The carefulness of this approach was extremely important. At stake was the position of the minority community within the social fabric of the state – and a wide range of rights were implicated. Secret evidence and lowered standards of proof affected due process.

As a broader matter, in respect to liberty rights, it was very difficult for targets to exculpate themselves – when they had no idea what the evidence was against them. Neither could the appointed advocate tip the state's hand and request alibis or information that would negate the state's claim. Even if such data became secretly available, the sudden release of a detainee had a political cost and thus created an institutional incentive against lifting the orders – heightened by the traditional tendency of the executive to err on the side of caution when a terrorist attack seemed likely. Although detention might end with prosecution, it was the police, not the Director of Public Prosecutions, who were required to evaluate whether prosecution was a plausible alternative to control orders; yet the necessary intelligence might not have been in law enforcement's domain. An end to the fight against terror might also lead to the lifting of the orders, but in the face of ongoing threats, this was a politically untenable position. Deportation might be another option – but would apply only to non-British subjects (at a time when the number of British citizens subject to control orders was increasing)[761] – and required that a watertight memorandum of understanding be signed with a country that routinely practiced torture. For one commentator, this situation left but two options: death or "descent into madness."[762]

Physical freedom, though, was not the only right on the line. Individuals subject to control orders had to endure the stigma subsequently attached to their names.[763] Even nonderogating control orders placed under partial surveillance anyone with whom a detainee associated, creating social pressure on individuals to avoid contact with that person. The case of the alleged plot to blow up Manchester United football ground provides a good example. This plan apparently never existed. But as the Centre for Policy Studies explained, "The reporting of this incident was inflammatory and misleading. It caused needless alarm among millions of TV viewers and newspaper readers. It stirred up anti-Islamic prejudice. It ruined the lives of several of the suspects. They lost their homes, their jobs and their friends as a result. They have never received a personal apology, either from the police or from the press."[764]

The police themselves have expressed concern about the impact of post-9/11 measures on the minority community. Lord Condon, commissioner of the Metropolitan Police from 1993–2000, raised concern that although short-term extended detention may give the state an advantage, over the long term it would be a strategic disaster: "Even though in one, two or three individual cases an extension to 90 days may help, my fear is what that might generate in terms of helping in the propaganda of terrorism."[765] It may "encourage ... martyrdom rather than prevent ... it."[766] George Churchill-Coleman, the former head of Scotland Yard's antiterror squad, suggested that the new measures were impractical, unethical, and likely to marginalize Britain's Muslims even more: "I have a horrible feeling that we are sinking into a police state."[767] Irene Kahn, from Amnesty International, expressed concern that ethnic minorities were being alienated.[768] Tarique Ghaffur, Britain's most senior Asian Muslim police officer, condemned the disproportionate use of stop and search powers.[769] Although the government set up a series of working groups to look into the impact of these provisions on the Muslim community, the Labour government hardly seemed serious about addressing this issue: the seven task forces were given just three meetings and six weeks to deliver their conclusions.[770] Two weeks into their discussions, Blair unveiled a 12-point counterterrorist plan – without canvassing the task forces for their views on the substantive changes proposed.[771]

Like Britain, the United States also has focused its detention powers on individuals drawn from the Muslim community. Although I have thus far focused on operations outside domestic bounds, within American borders the government followed September 11 by also detaining more than 1,200 noncitizens indefinitely. The Department of Justice refused to release the names or locations of those held for questioning. Some individuals were kept in detention up to three years. The state also made a list of all males, aged 18–35, who entered the United States on certain dates – and undertook to interview every person on the list. And it began an extensive registration program for foreign visitors.

A special project on the impact of post-9/11 measures on this community directed by the US Social Science Research Council found that the Muslim and Arab communities' capacity to discuss religious and political issues had been severely restricted. The Casey Foundation surveyed more than two dozen mosques and found that every one of them had lost contributions. Muslim newspapers saw the sudden withdrawal of advertisers, who did not want to risk being accused of association with suspected terrorists – a charge hard to refute, but one with unfortunate consequences.[772] Louise Cainkar, a prominent scholar on the Arab American community, reported from interviews with Islamic religious leaders that there were "widespread community fears of the federal government...feelings of being watched and followed, [and] reductions in charitable giving."[773] In other words, a wide range of concerns – free speech, freedom of association, freedom of religion, and the right to privacy – were implicated in part because of the detention provisions adopted. There is a security issue here as well: the United States needed this community to help determine the best response to the al Qaeda threat, to glean information, and to gain the advantage of language and other knowledge held by the minority group. Alienating Arabic and Muslim people was thus extremely costly.

These actions were all taken within America's borders. Other steps, taken abroad, reinforced the impression that the United States was waging a war on Islam – further alienating important communities. Methods of interrogation that involved female interrogators touching men sexually, wearing miniskirts, and smearing fake menstrual blood on detainees did little to counter the charge.[774]

A typical incident centered on allegations that guards at Guantánamo Bay had desecrated the Qur'an: in Islam, the text, believed to have been given to the Prophet by the Archangel Gabriel, is considered sacred – literally, the word of God. Believers are careful about how they handle the book; nonbelievers are not supposed to touch it. A *Newsweek* story in spring 2005 reported that guards had stepped on the Qur'an, urinated on it, and flushed it down a toilet. The Pakistan Embassy in Washington, D.C., called for an inquiry and sought assurances that "perpetrators of the sacrilegious act" be "dealt with firmly."[775] The administration hastened to reassure Pakistan that any soldiers responsible for such actions would be held accountable, and that it valued Pakistan's assistance in the war on terror[776] – words that proved woefully inadequate.

At a press conference on May 6, 2005, Imran Khan, a prominent Pakistani cricket star-turned-politician, held up a copy of *Newsweek* and declared, "Islam is under attack in the name of the war on terror."[777] Riots erupted in many Islamic countries.[778] In Afghanistan, 17 people died.[779] For days, English and Urdu papers in Pakistan focused on the issue, which captured the attention of the Pakistani Parliament.[780] Islamists charged President Pervez Musharraf with colluding with the United States against Islam – and thus drove the legislature into passing a unanimous resolution condemning the actions of guards at Guantánamo Bay.[781] Musharraf and his prime minister, Shaukat Aziz, subsequently expressed "profound shock and dismay" at the reports,[782] declaring that "the entire Muslim ummah [worldwide community of believers], including the Pakistanis" was "deeply hurt by reports of the alleged incident"[783] and that people of faith must be given due respect.[784]

Although US officials tried to blame *Newsweek*, saying that the magazine had sullied America's reputation abroad,[785] reports of desecration of the Qur'an by guards at Guantánamo Bay had been circulating for years. (Asif Iqbal, one of the Britons who had been released, gave a deposition, upon his return to the United Kingdom, saying that guards kicked the book and threw it in a toilet.[786] Nasser Nijer Naser al-Mutairi, a Kuwaiti, said that mistreatment of the text had led to a hunger strike at the prison, that had ended only after a formal apology – a story confirmed by a former interrogator.[787] Other prisoners made similar allegations.[788]) Indeed, the US government's own documents recorded such instances: FBI reports showed one incident in which guards "flushed a Koran in the toilet."[789] Another noted guards desecrating the text.[790] Furthermore, before publishing the article, *Newsweek* had provided an exact copy of it to the Pentagon, which had not objected to the text.[791]

The incident became a lightning rod for discontent over US detention and interrogation policies and links between the United States and Islamic states. At that point, more than 40 people had died in US detention facilities.[792] The *International Herald Tribune* suggested, "The real source of outrage is the United States' failure to properly investigate, much less address, such claims after years of consistent reports."[793] It concluded, "One of the dangerous results of the now tarnished image of the United States is that it plays into the hands of politicians who stoke religious anger in the Muslim world."[794] The *Gulf News* explained that, more than three and a half years after September 11, "there are many more Muslims today who are skeptical of the United States than ever before. Many Americans who re-elected US President George W. Bush for a second term probably failed to recognize the harm that has been inflicted upon their country's relations with the outside world in conducting the so-called war on terror."[795]

The Bush administration went on the offensive. Secretary of State Condoleeza Rice announced, "The United States of America is one of the strongest defenders of human rights around the world. We've fought hard and worked hard even in the circumstances of a new kind of war (on terrorism) to treat people humanely."[796] She added, "[S]ometimes bad things happen." [797] In an interview with *Larry King Live*, Vice President Dick Cheney went further, declaring the reports of the Qur'an being mishandled and detainees beaten as "peddling lies."[798] A Pentagon spokesman, Bryan Whitman, denounced the *Newsweek* article as "irresponsible" and "demonstrably false."[799] The White House pressured *Newsweek* for the anonymous source on which Michael Isikoff, the author of the piece, had based his account – and the source backed down. *Newsweek* retracted a portion of the article and apologized.[800] Scott McClellan, White House spokesman, blamed the magazine for America's tarnished reputation and the deaths resulting from the riots.[801] Rice stated, "[I]t's appalling that this story got out there," and hoped that "everybody will step back and take a look at how they handled this – everybody."[802] Rumsfeld warned, "People need to be very careful about what they say, just as they need to be careful about what they do."[803]

But some of the allegations were substantiated in a three-week formal inquiry conducted by Brigadier General Jay W. Hood, commander of the Joint Task Force, Guantánamo Brigade. Guards had, indeed, kicked, stepped, and urinated on copies of the Qur'an[804] – incidents, though, that Hood dismissed as "rare, isolated and largely inadvertent." He claimed that, to the contrary "respect for detainee religious beliefs [has been] embedded in the [Guantánamo Bay] culture from the start."[805]

Whether there were one, two, ten, or a hundred such incidents, the cumulative effect of the treatment given those in detention polarized world opinion and hurt the ability of the United States to fight terrorism. *New York Times* columnist Bob Herbert wrote, "[T]he image of the United States has deteriorated around the world. The U.S. is now widely viewed as a brutal, bullying nation that countenances torture and operates hideous prison camps at Guantánamo Bay, Cuba, and in other parts of the world – camps where inmates have been horribly abused, gruesomely humiliated and even killed."[806] The "huge and bitter protests" that met the allegations of mistreatment of the Qur'an reflected growing rage at "the atrocious treatment of detainees, terror suspects, wounded prisoners and completely innocent civilians in America's so-called war against terror."[807] The *Washington Post* asserted, "The hundreds of suspected enemy combatants who have been held incommunicado or subjected to abuse and torture, and the scores who may have been unlawfully killed, represent the single greatest failing of the United States in the war on terrorism."[808] The *Columbus Dispatch* recognized that "reports of abuses at Guantánamo, Afghanistan and Iraq have poisoned the Muslim world with a virulent form of anti-Americanism."[809]

Rumsfeld admitted that Abu Ghraib had been "unhelpful" to US efforts in Iraq, and Pentagon officials insisted that, although members of Congress could view photos from the prison, they ought not to describe them in detail, so as to prevent further repercussions against US persons abroad.[810] Moazzam Begg, a Briton released from Guantánamo Bay, said he saw things "that you would believe were out of a Nazi manual, or a Stalinist detention camp. Is this going to proliferate terrorism, and hate and ignorance? Yes."[811] Tarek Dergoul, a British citizen held for nearly two years in Guantánamo Bay before being released without charge, became during that time "a devout and intensely political Muslim."[812] "I now look on America," he said, "as a terrorist state because that's what they have done – terrorised us."[813]

International Repercussions and Foreign Policy Considerations

In addition to the social and political repercussions of both countries' use of extended detention and coercive interrogation, legal implications demand scrutiny. A number of lawsuits against the United States are currently pending even in its closest allies.

And US foreign policy goals have been undermined in a range of ways. For one example, the use of cruel and inhuman interrogation and the rendering of suspects to third countries for torture made liberal democracy less attractive – at a time when, for political and economic reasons, the United States was trying to encourage other countries to adopt such a regime. The use of these practices prevented the United States from being able to take a leading role in convincing other countries – such as Cuba, Russia, Malaysia, and China – to improve their human rights records. Egypt began justifying its use of torture. Malaysia pointed to Guantánamo Bay and said that indefinite detention was fine. Russia defended its treatment of Chechnya. And the Cuban dictator Fidel Castro announced that President Bush had "no moral authority to accuse" Cuba of human rights violations.

Indefinite detention and coercive interrogation are frequently justified as necessary wartime measures to combat the danger of terrorism. These techniques, which are some of the most extreme state responses to terrorist threat, have often put the military in the frontlines with, at times, disastrous results. Not that the military should not play a key role in responding to terrorism, but everyone involved needs to have clear rules and be fully aware of the significant risks in order to mitigate them before they undermine the state.

3

Financial Counterterrorism

"[A] foreign entity without property or presence in this country has no constitutional rights, under the due process clause or otherwise."
People's Mojahedin Organization of Iran v. U.S. Department of State, 1999

"It is during our most challenging and uncertain moments that our nation's commitment to due process is most severely tested; and it is in those times that we must preserve our commitment at home to the principles for which we fight abroad."
Justice Sandra Day O'Connor, *Hamdi v. Rumsfeld*, 2004

"President George W. Bush's order freezing terrorist assets is directed as much against international banks and governments as Osama bin Laden's network."
Richard Wolffe, FINANCIAL TIMES (London), 2001

The United Kingdom and the United States have at least four goals in going after terrorist finance: to deprive terrorists of resources, to track operatives, to chart relationships, and to deter individuals from supporting terrorist organizations. Although these aims are critical to the success of a state's counterterrorist strategy, both countries have tried to fulfill them – as they have other counterterrorist objectives – in ways that not only erode the civil rights of their citizens, weakening the standards meant to protect them, but involve significant political, international, and humanitarian costs as well.

In the United Kingdom, the powers to interrupt the flow of funds to paramilitary organizations held by the Northern Ireland executive, and later by the British government, had for decades gone largely unused. In the mid-1980s, the anti-drug campaign led the state to increase its power to interrupt drug finances and to rethink its approach to dealing with terrorist finances. Regulatory authority, forfeiture provisions, and investigatory powers transferred from the anti-drug realm to counterterrorism, where they intensified before crossing back into drug trafficking statutes. The Police Service Northern Ireland made greater use of the powers available, but it still did not put its full weight behind the antiterrorist finance law. The September 11 attacks accelerated the trend toward greater state authority and pushed counterterrorist initiatives further into nondrug and nonterrorist-related offenses. The law moved from criminal law to civil law as a way to address criminal finance, weakening the burden of proof, the presumption of innocence, evidentiary rules, and the standards for determining the criminal origin of property.

The United States turned more recently than the United Kingdom to countering terrorist finance. As an administrative matter, before September 11, federal agencies paid minimal attention to this field. As a legal matter, it was only in 1995 that the executive branch began maintaining a Specially Designated Terrorist List – on which Osama bin Laden did not appear until 1998. The mid-1990s also saw the introduction of the Antiterrorism and Effective Death Penalty Act. As in the United Kingdom, these counterterrorist provisions drew inspiration from anti-drug statutes. After September 11, the state aggressively redirected its administrative, legal, and, to some extent, political agenda toward stemming terrorist finance. Title III of the 2001 USA PATRIOT Act, and the issuance of Executive Order 13,224, under the International Emergency Economic Powers Act, subsequently weakened individual rights. It became easier for the executive branch to avoid not just criminal law but the judicial system altogether in its efforts to prevent the flow of funds. In the process, the state replaced a criminal law standard with an intelligence one: mere *links* to known terrorists became sufficient to "prove" financial support, and administrative procedures replaced judicial processes. Having passed the initial legislation giving the executive these powers, Congress played almost no oversight role in their implementation.

PARAMILITARY FUNDING IN NORTHERN IRELAND

Britain's antiterrorist finance regime has exhibited an almost symbiotic relationship between anti-drug and antiterrorist finance measures since the mid-1980s, leading to a steady expansion in the number and range of related offenses, investigatory authorities, regulatory provisions, and powers of forfeiture. September 11 caused no seismic shift, as it did in the United States; it merely accelerated an existing trend. With the obscuring of the line between terrorism and ordinary criminal activity, many of the more extreme provisions transferred into broader efforts to prevent crime.

This evolution had important consequences in the British legal and administrative realm. The United Kingdom shifted its emphasis from criminal to civil standards, divorcing financial forfeiture provisions from conviction of any underlying offense. Simultaneously, the burden of proof, presumption of innocence, evidentiary rules, and the standards employed to determine the criminal origin of property weakened. Perhaps of greatest concern is the recent relaxation of client-attorney privilege attached to state investigatory powers in Northern Ireland. Although the statutory instrument currently applies only to the province, the history of British antiterrorist finance measures suggests that such powers may one day extend throughout the United Kingdom.

Northern Ireland paramilitary organizations get most of their money from domestic operations, such as bank robberies, tax fraud, and black taxis. Only a small amount comes from overseas. Although traditionally these groups have not needed a lot of money to mount operations, their shift in the late twentieth century to political activity increased their need for resources. Terrorist organizations on both sides of the religious divide increasingly turned to organized crime to fund their ventures, creating a murky overlap between ordinary criminal activity and terrorist intent.

One of the most extraordinary cases began on the evening of December 19, 2004, when Belfast temperatures hit an icy zero degrees Celsius. Armed men, posing as police officers, knocked at the home of Chris Ward, a 23-year-old Northern Bank official. The intruders took him to his supervisor's home while Ward's family stayed behind at gunpoint. The men arrived with Ward at Kevin McMullan's home in Loughinisland, County Down, where they took McMullan's wife away to a secret location as a hostage. On Monday morning, acting on the kidnappers' instructions, Ward and McMullan arrived at work as usual. Toward closing time, after sending a messenger and three employees home, Ward and McMullan entered the vaults that serviced the bank's 95 branches across Northern Ireland. They stacked 24 boxes of money onto trolleys and wheeled them to a loading bay. Men in a white Ford Transit van with false registration plates met them and drove away with £26.5 million pounds sterling and more than £1 million in euros and US dollars.[1]

Nearly 50 police officers began working around the clock to find the culprits. In just over a fortnight, the police service amassed 560 exhibits and carried out 100 interviews. On January 7, 2005, the Chief Constable issued his interim report: Provisional Irish Republican Army (PIRA) was responsible, and would they please give the money back?[2]

Surprisingly, PIRA did. Not all of it, but a month later a "police officer" telephoned and directed the ombudsperson to five shrink-wrapped £10,000 bundles stuck in toilets at the Newforge Country Club – a law enforcement sports association in south Belfast. Hugh Orde, the Chief Constable, reflected, "I'm not particularly impressed... but I did ask them to give the money back."[3]

As the security services redoubled their efforts, republican panic set in. Down in County Cork, a burned bank note drifted over a garden wall, and the suspicious neighbor alerted the Garda Síochána. Officers arrived to find someone shoving Northern Bank notes into a bonfire.[4] Across the Channel, reports began to circulate about efforts to buy English houses with Northern Irish currency.[5] And in March 2005, "a disproportionate amount of Northern Ireland sterling changed hands" during the four-day Cheltenham horse race festival.[6] In the meantime, more than 100 Gardaí took part in Cork and Dublin raids, uncovering £2.3 million linked to a PIRA money-laundering ring. Unfortunately, it appeared to be the wrong one.* As of the spring of 2007, investigators have established no formal link between this money and the robbery.

PIRA made a half-hearted attempt to distance itself from the incident, and issued the lengthy statement, "We were not involved," signed by P. O'Neill, the IRA's historical *nom de plume*. Ian Paisley, Jr., scoffed, "P. O'Neill obviously stands for Pinocchio O'Neill."[7] The Irish Taoiseach (Prime Minister), the Secretary of State for Northern Ireland, the United Kingdom Independent Monitoring Commission, the Irish Garda Síochána, the Northern Ireland Police Service, and, indeed, most members of Dáil Éireann and Westminster seemed to agree.[8]

The amount of money in the vault took everyone – including, apparently, PIRA – by surprise.[9] The terrorists had a real problem: the entire annual operating budget of the organization throughout the 1980s and 1990s routinely came in under £5 million.[10] Even multiple robberies each year (including three in Belfast earlier in 2004) comprised only a small portion of the total. Two immediate complications ensued: what to do with the unanticipated money and how to withstand the assault from the security establishment on both sides of the border, awakened by the sheer volume involved. Of the £26.5 million, some £16.5 million were new notes, making them difficult to move without being identified.[†] As for the remaining £10 million, Northern Irish promissory notes proved more or less useless outside the province: most commercial and retail establishments, even in Great Britain, refuse to accept them, forcing individuals to exchange them for legal tender at banks. And Northern Bank upped the ante: three weeks after the robbery, it announced the recall and replacement of £300 million in bank notes with currency bearing a new logo, new colors, and different prefixes on the serial numbers.[11] Britain and Ireland initiated one of the largest investigations in either state's history. The Police Service Northern Ireland recovered the kidnappers' feces from McMullan's sewage system for DNA analysis and began poring over hundreds of hours of closed-circuit television footage.[12] It decided not to retire more than 800 reservists as previously planned – ensuring continued scrutiny of the Provisional IRA.

Despite these drawbacks, however, in many ways the heist brilliantly played to PIRA's advantage. For one, its sheer audacity and apparent success – without

---

* Although the Republic of Ireland announced that the money "absolutely" came from the heist, only £60,000 worth of the bank notes even bore the bank's insignia. *See* Angelique Chrisafis, *Raids May Yield IRA Link to Robbery*, GUARDIAN (London), Feb. 18, 2005, at 2; Martin Hodgson, *The Editor: What They Said About . . . IRA Finances*, GUARDIAN (London), Feb. 21, 2005, at 18; Gemma Murray, *Notes "Absolutely" Linked to Bank Raid*, BELFAST NEWS LETTER, Mar. 3, 2005, at 4. *But see Minister Names MPs as Members of IRA Ruling Army Council*, BELFAST NEWS LETTER, Feb. 21, 2005, at 8; *Police Quiz Seven Over "IRA Cash,"* BBC News, Feb. 18, 2005, available at www/newsvote.bbc.co.uk.

† Within three days of the raid, police released the serial numbers on the £16.5 million. *See* Jonathan McCambridge & Maureen Colemann, *Bank Heist Swoop; Police Raid Home of Leading Republican*, BELFAST TELEGRAPH, Dec. 24, 2004; Jonathan McCambridge, *Stolen Note Alert*, BELFAST TELEGRAPH, Dec. 24, 2004.

loss of life – earned the grudging respect of both security forces and the mainstream media.[13]* "Gerry, Gerry give us a loan" turned up scrawled on walls in the North, referring to Gerry Adams, the president of the Provisional IRA's political arm.[14] Republicans, feeling the weight of pressure for decommissioning, considered it a slap in the face of the British government.[15] Indeed, it had an immediate and profound impact on the peace process.[16] While it could be argued that the heist undermined the republicans' position by portraying them as common criminals,[17] the sophistication of the raid and the resources it produced elevated them to a force to be taken seriously. The British government decided to interpret the raid as a sign of PIRA's capability, not of its intention.[18]

To some extent, 10 Downing Street did not have a choice: it needed republicans at the negotiating table. Sinn Féin swept the April 2005 Northern elections, pushing aside the nationalist Social Democratic Labour Party's efforts to capitalize on the robbery.[19] In a crucial by-election south of the border, Sinn Féin *gained* 13 percent of the first-preference votes.[20] Simultaneously, for the first time since the drawing of the border in 1922, the Northern Ireland police and the Garda Síochána signed an agreement to exchange personnel, furthering PIRA's goal of an integrated Ireland.[21] Nor did the raid appear to dent Sinn Féin's fundraising ability abroad.[22] Although Washington banned Gerry Adams from fundraising during his traditional March tour of the United States (and disinvited him to the White House St. Patrick's Day party), this appears to have been just a temporary slap on the wrist.[23] And, as of the spring of 2007, the only money that has resurfaced is the £50,000 deliberately placed in the toilets of the police officers' club.

The Northern Bank robbery and the subsequent unfolding of events illustrate the difficulties of preventing terrorist groups from obtaining and transferring funds. There are many soft targets. In a nationalist conflict fought over state legitimacy, the political costs of robbing the state or multinational corporations may be low. Sympathizers may see such operations as victimless. Weaknesses in the private sector's record keeping may make it difficult to recover assets. And the movement of funds across international borders – as in respect to the United States and the al Qaeda network – may create jurisdictional and administrative difficulties, exacerbated by inconsistent domestic legal structures. Northern Irish terrorist groups, which have always taken advantage of the international border with the Republic, also are beginning to operate on a more global scale.

But raids like the one on the Northern Bank, although a traditional form of paramilitary funding, are far from the only option. In the early twentieth century, the Irish Republican Army also robbed in-transit services, bookmakers,

---

* Within a week of the incident, Cliff Goodwin (an English author) and Justin Stanley (an American producer) had signed agreements to turn it into a book, SPECTACULAR, and then a film. Goodwin announced, "As a writer, this is a tremendous story. I appreciate there are victims involved but I will make my book as accurate and interesting as possible." *Bank Raid Story to Hit Big Screen*, BELFAST NEWS LETTER, Feb. 1, 2005, at 4.

retail establishments, and post offices.[24] It exacted fines from the local population and solicited "voluntary" donations.[25]* Branches of IRA groups in Great Britain funneled money back to the island,[26] and prominent republicans traveled to the United States to raise money.[27]†

The terrorist demand for financial resources – at least in the early to mid-twentieth century – was not a constant; on the contrary, following the Civil War in the South, only three republican campaigns emerged. This changed, however, with the dawning of the Troubles in the late 1960s and the assumption of direct British rule. For the next three decades, violence raged. With the growth of paramilitary organizations came the diversification of funding streams. The number of armed robberies and the percentage they contributed annually to paramilitary coffers declined: extensive sentences specifically for terrorist-related robberies and modern forensic techniques (which made it easier for the police to identify the culprits) increased the risk to those engaged in such operations. Simultaneously, protection rackets made paramilitary robberies on their own turf somewhat of a moot point, and led to more sophisticated forms of organized crime.[28] Already in control of local communities, terrorists used that power to make more money, which reinforced their social and economic dominance – while undermining their claims to be engaged in political, not criminal, pursuits.[29]

On the domestic front, tax fraud, extortion, drinking clubs, taxi companies, smuggling operations, drug trafficking, and kidnapping opened new revenue streams.[30] "Voluntary" contributions supplemented these sources, as did contract bombing – where individuals paid for paramilitaries to destroy their businesses and then claimed insurance or compensation.[31] Intellectual property theft also provided a source of funds, as did forgery.[32] Most recently, law enforcement has witnessed a movement by paramilitaries into high technology. As of 2003, approximately 25 percent of the cases undertaken by the Police Service Northern Ireland Computer Crime Unit related to terrorism.[33]

Although most paramilitary money derives from domestic operations, neither republicans nor loyalists limit their fundraising efforts to them. The IRA, for instance, initially drew money from the Irish government – with or without sanction.[34] In the early 1970s, on the grounds that Libya would fight

---

* In 1934, for instance, the organization attempted to run the "Cambridge Sweep" to raise proceeds for the paramilitary movement. The tickets featured a picture of a soldier in a green IRA uniform trampling on the Union Jack, with the General Post Office in Dublin, the site of the 1916 Easter Rising, burning in the background. *Sweepstake Tickets Seized: Irish Republican Army Scheme*, THE TIMES (London), Aug. 24, 1934, at 14.

† Between 1820 and 1920, approximately five million Irish left the "Emerald Isle" for Boston, Providence, New York, Philadelphia, and elsewhere. This community proved to be a rich source of funds for the fledgling republican movement. *Irish Look Back from America*, THE TIMES (London), Mar. 18, 1959, at 11. Even as late as 1940, the Irish government was "certain that large sums of money in dollars were coming in from America" to regenerate republican coffers. *Public Safety in Eire: Emergency Powers Demanded*, THE TIMES (London), Jan. 4, 1940, at 8. *See also Irishman with an Iron Cross: Alleged Funds for the I.R.A.*, THE TIMES (London), June 22, 1940, at 3.

the United Kingdom everywhere, Moammar Gaddafi began sending money, arms, and equipment to the PIRA.[35] Republican arms also arrived from the Czech Republic.[36] Loyalist paramilitaries raised money in Canada and obtained weapons from South Africa.[37]

By far the most publicized and well-known source of funding, though, resides in the United States. The Irish Northern Aid Committee (Noraid), founded in 1969 by Irish civil war veterans, has at times provided important ideological and financial support to the PIRA.[38] With one or two exceptions, the United States initially turned a blind eye to Noraid – which claimed that all donations went to humanitarian aid for people in Northern Ireland.[39] Gradually, however, it became clear that Noraid's claims fell somewhat short of the truth: by the early 1970s, Noraid was supplying more than 50 percent of the resources required for the PIRA's armed campaign.[40]

Diplomatic pressure from Britain paid off. Spurred, too, by the growing disillusionment of the Irish American community with PIRA's tactics, the United States began to take a more active role in stemming the flow of money. In 1983, the Reagan administration closed six years of negotiations with an extradition agreement.[41] The FBI became more focused on Noraid's role in arms smuggling, and in 1982, the judiciary ruled that Noraid would have to comply with the 1938 Foreign Agents Registration Act and register as PIRA's agent.[42] By the mid-1980s, less than £135,000 of PIRA's annual budget came from the United States.[43] In 1994, Gerry Adams launched a new fundraising organization to replace Noraid: Cairde Sinn Féin now funnels money to the republican political arm.[44] The American government later blocked all assets held by the Real IRA, the Continuity IRA, the Loyalist Volunteer Force, the Orange Volunteers, the Red Hand Defenders, and the Ulster Defence Association/Ulster Freedom Fighters.*

Terrorist campaigns do not require extensive funding. The annual estimated costs of PIRA run at only £1.5 million. The Ulster Volunteer Force, a loyalist paramilitary, requires between £1 and £2 million. Even the Ulster Defense Association, the largest loyalist group, requires only £500,000 per annum. These represent the largest and most complex terrorist operations – some, such as the Continuity IRA, run on a budget of £30,000 or less.[45]

Although terrorism itself does not require exorbitant amounts of money, politics does – as became clear as paramilitaries moved into the political realm. In the 1980s, Gerry Adams noted that £2 million in operating funds would prove woefully inadequate to run a £5–10 million political machine. His personal attention to this issue resulted in the "slow but steady and noticeable 'professionalization' of the IRA's handling of its finances."[46] To meet increased demand, paramilitaries began to diversify their funding schemes, learning, in a Darwinian sense, from their own – and other groups' – successes and failures.

---

* Although Noraid gained notoriety for its assistance to republicans, loyalist paramilitaries also obtained arms and funding from the United States. Friends of Northern Ireland, for instance, located in the vicinity of Chicago, had as its aim the provision of a gun to every Protestant household in Northern Ireland. Robert Fisk, *Mr. Whitelaw Expected to Relax the Ban on Parades in Ulster*, THE TIMES (London), Apr. 5, 1973, at 1.

THE STATE'S RESPONSE

It is difficult to unravel the United Kingdom's efforts to interrupt terrorist finance in the first three-quarters of the twentieth century. From 1922 to 1972, the Northern Ireland Executive maintained extensive authority to seize private assets, but very little information appears in the public record offices in Belfast or London that details the manner in or extent to which such powers issued. In part this may be because the 1922–43 Special Powers Acts and Regulations did not require the Civil Authority to lay property seizure or arrest orders before Stormont, the Northern Ireland Parliament; nor did they demand their promulgation in the *Belfast Gazette* or local newspapers. Journalists, in turn, made only random and limited references to state actions in this area.[47] From the mid-1960s forward, the lack of information may have been due to the persistent omission of monetary property rights in civil liberties concerns: neither the Northern Ireland Civil Rights Association nor the Standing Advisory Commission on Human Rights addressed the issue. In its well-known semi-monthly accounting of events related to the Troubles, *Fortnight* makes not one reference in relation to the seizing of assets from 1970 through 1974. Instead, property rights only appear relative to security force destruction of personal property in the course of search operations.[48]

Another, and perhaps more convincing, reason for the lack of information on these powers may be that the British state, although it had the authority to take possession of resources supporting the commission of violence, simply did not use this authority. Faced by the need to disperse riots, find gelignite, and defuse bombs, the state may have assigned a low priority to examining revenue streams.

This explanation does not elucidate the apparent lack of use of these powers during the substantial periods of relative calm in Northern Ireland. For this reason, I suggest – although I am happy to entertain contrary theses – that the lack of emphasis on and use of such powers merely reflected a cultural norm. That is to say, under Stormont, certain ways of dealing with the threat from republicanism became standard. Officials may have seen emphasizing the financial underpinnings of the movement as pointless: terrorist operations did not require tremendous amounts of money, and it would have been difficult to trace such funds prior to the growth of the modern banking and credit industries. The government also may have deemed this approach an inefficient way to prevent attacks – particularly when the Executive could simply imprison suspects and hold them indefinitely without judicial interference.

From the mid-1980s forward, however, the emphasis shifted. A steady ratcheting of state authority occurred within counterterrorist legislation and between counterterrorist law and drug trafficking statutes. Particularly in relation to drug trafficking, the cultural norms changed, making it possible to monitor financial institutions more closely. On its face, this shift influenced, and then was influenced by, antiterrorist finance provisions. Contemporary events assisted in this evolution: the peace process, discussed in Chapter 1, brought with it an increased demand for money to fund political activities – as well as the need to satisfy claims to legitimacy in order to participate in the negotiations. These changes forced paramilitaries between a rock and a hard place: deviations from the law became important propaganda tools by which the state could undermine groups' participation in the dialogue.

Statutory Measures Before September 11

Two seminal pieces of legislation comprise Westminster's counterterrorist efforts before the introduction of the Terrorism Act 2000: the 1973 Northern Ireland (Emergency Provisions) Act (1973 EPA) and the 1974 Prevention of Terrorism (Temporary Provisions) Act (1974 PTA). The former applied to Northern Ireland; the latter primarily to Great Britain, with some overlap to Northern Ireland. Although technically both statutes operated under sunset provisions, they never lapsed. On the contrary, successive Secretaries of State called for the extension of the powers, in a dialogue punctuated by Parliament reissuing the statutes with amendments.

Two points are of note. First, the EPA's powers went well beyond those incorporated into the PTA. This was a conscious decision made by the British government to limit inroads into property rights in Great Britain. The state accepted that this meant it would not be able to cut off terrorist funding entirely. Reginald Maudling, appointed Home Secretary in 1970, gave voice to the concern that both efficacy and individual rights would be sacrificed should the state seriously attempt to stop all resources flowing to republicans:

It is admittedly offensive that the IRA factions . . . should flaunt themselves over here and openly collect money for their subversive purposes. But there has to be a stronger reason to take extraordinary powers than the removal of such flaunting and collecting, especially since the powers would not by their mere assumption remove the activities, but would have to be exercised with a thoroughness that would quickly give rise to objections of a different kind.[49]

There seems to have been fairly widespread public agreement with this approach. Even the *Times* of London, not known for being a hotbed of radicalism, suggested that as long as the IRA was not trying to exploit legal loopholes regarding proscription, ordinary powers were sufficient to prevent paramilitaries from obtaining resources in Great Britain. The *Times* also raised concerns regarding individual rights:

[I]n conditions of free political debate and in the absence of an overwhelming public conviction concerning the objectives of policy, recourse to unaccustomed powers of coercion, the suspension of normal rights and safeguards, may confuse and embitter opinion in a way that actually works to the advantage of those against whom the special measures are directed.[50]

For most of the Troubles, then, the EPA contained the more extreme powers related to antiterrorist finance.* Nevertheless, they were exercised only rarely.

Second, despite reductions in violence related to Northern Ireland, the powers included in both statutes steadily expanded. An inverse relationship between the level of violence and the state focus on terrorist funding followed. This effect is likely due to the influence of drug trafficking and money laundering provisions in the final decades of the twentieth century (see page 135). It may also reflect the state's decision to counter rising levels of violence not with financial provisions but, first and foremost, with measures implicating life and liberty.

Property Rights and Asset Forfeiture: Laying the Groundwork. The 1973 EPA provided the British government substantially broader powers to interfere with property in Northern Ireland than it could exercise in the rest of the United Kingdom. Drawing heavily from the 1922–43 Special Powers Acts, the 1973 EPA provided that "[a] constable may seize anything which he suspects is being, has been or is intended to be used in the commission of a scheduled offence."[51] The legislation authorized any member of Her Majesty's forces to enter any premises to detain, destroy, or move any property, or to "do any other act interfering with any public right or with any private rights of property."[52] Although the statute also required that the state pay compensation for real or personal property taken, occupied, destroyed, or damaged, this provision did *not* apply when it was a question of maintaining public order or preventing terrorist violence.[53] These powers remained untouched into the twenty-first century.[†] The Prevention of Terrorism Act, in contrast, did not include an equivalent right to state interference with property, nor did subsequent iterations of the statute build one into the law.

The 1973 EPA also had special financial provisions related to proscribed organizations. The legislation allowed the court to demand the forfeiture of assets where an individual, convicted of membership in an illegal organization, controlled money or property that benefited the list of banned entities: Sinn Féin, the IRA, Cumann na mBan, Fianna na hÉireann, Saor Éire, and the UVF.

---

* The only real exception to this came in 1989, when the PTA introduced the offense of financing terrorism and associated forfeiture provisions. Within two years, however, the EPA not only adopted these powers, but, as this chapter discusses, it expanded them in important ways.

† The only amendment came in 1987, when Parliament set a time limit for filing for compensation where no offense against the legislation might be involved. *See* Northern Ireland (Emergency Provisions) Act (Amendment), 1975, ch. 62; Northern Ireland (Emergency Provisions) Act, 1978, ch. 5. It is possible to trace the sections through the different Acts. E.g., § 11(3) became § 13(3); § 17 became § 19(1); and § 25 became § 28. Northern Ireland (Emergency Provisions) Act 1987, ch. 30; Northern Ireland (Emergency Provisions) Act, 1991, ch. 24. § 19(1) became § 24(1); in addition, the right to compensation previously in § 28 is enumerated in § 63(1). Northern Ireland (Emergency Provisions) Act, 1996, ch. 22; Northern Ireland (Emergency Provisions) Act, 1998, ch. 9.

The legislation made it an offense to solicit or invite financial or other support for a proscribed organization, or knowingly to make or receive any contribution to the resources of the same. Criminal penalties applied.*

An important point here is that, under the 1973 EPA, charges of contributing to a proscribed organization amounted to a scheduled offense: those accused of this crime automatically entered the Diplock court system, losing their right to trial by jury. Other important legal restrictions applied, such as limits on bail and the use of *in camera* and *ex parte* proceedings.[54]

Unlike the 1973 EPA, the 1974 PTA did not initially allow the court to order the forfeiture of proscribed organizations' assets. And, although it also made it an offense to raised funds for, or contribute to, a proscribed organization, only one group graced the list: the IRA.[55] In 1976, however, the new PTA added a forfeiture provision that allowed the state to seize any money or other property controlled by an individual convicted of membership, where such resources were intended for use in Northern Ireland terrorism.[56] Similarly, the statute made it an offense to solicit contributions for a proscribed organization if the solicitor intended, knew, or suspected that the resources would be funneled to terrorist ends.[57] Although the 1976 statute limited this provision to solicitation within the United Kingdom, Westminster dropped this requirement in 1984 – while still restricting its application to proscribed organizations.[58] Five years later, however, the state's powers were significantly broadened.

Anti-Drug Trafficking and Counterterrorism: 1985–91. New standards for inroads into individual property rights, set by the British effort to stem growing drug abuse, quickly seeped over into efforts to interrupt the flow of funds to terrorist organizations. These initiatives began in May 1985, when the House of Commons Home Affairs Committee warned that unless the United Kingdom took immediate, preventive measures, within five years the country would face a drug crisis on par with that in the United States.[59]

Within weeks, Leon Brittan, Home Secretary, unveiled extraordinary powers to stem the flow of illicit substances. Commentators immediately labeled the new measures draconian. They had a point: the legislation authorized courts to seize assets, required a reform of banking law to allow the state to undertake a closer examination of financial records, reversed the burden of proof (requiring drug barons to prove, after conviction, that any of their assets *not* subject to forfeiture were obtained in a manner unrelated to trafficking), and created a new offense of handling assets made from trading in hard drugs.[60] By autumn a new bill sat before Parliament.[61]

Perhaps the most controversial aspect of what became the Drug Trafficking Offenses Act centered on the freezing and seizure of assets. The legislation

---

* Summary conviction yielded six months' imprisonment and a £400 fine. Indictment resulted in up to five years' imprisonment plus fine. *See* 1973 EPA *supra* note 51, § 19(1). In 1978, Westminster increased imprisonment on indictment to 10 years; but these powers otherwise remained largely constant through the twenty-first century.

empowered the court to impose a confiscatory fine equal to the proceeds of trafficking and then hold the debt against all the accused's property, unless that person could prove that the items had *not* come into his or her possession through drug money. The legislation granted law enforcement and customs the authority to gather new information, and gave the state the ability to freeze assets, even *prior* to arrest, for anyone "reasonably suspected of involvement in drug trafficking or money 'laundering.'" The action was ancillary to criminal proceedings. Should the criminal proceedings collapse or end in an acquittal, then the Restraint Order must immediately be discharged. Sentence enhancements of up to 10 years' imprisonment applied.

The 1989 PTA drew inspiration from these anti-drug laws. It severed the dependence of the financial provisions on a list of proscribed organizations and created a new offense of financial contributions to acts of terrorism. This included Northern Ireland-related violence as well as international terrorism, where such acts constituted triable offenses within the United Kingdom. (The legislation, however, specifically exempted other acts of terrorism related to British domestic matters.)[62] Simultaneously, the statute expanded judicial forfeiture powers.

The 1989 PTA divided financial assistance to terrorism into four offenses: the first, as discussed, focused on contributions toward acts of terrorism. The second broadened the previous offense of contributing resources to a proscribed organization to include entering into an arrangement making money or property available to an illegal group.[63] The third offense targeted the mass of accountants, fund managers, and other professionals employed by terrorist organizations, and placed beyond the pale anyone who assisted in any way with the management of terrorist funds.[64] The statute significantly increased the penalties associated with the first three offenses.* As to the fourth offense, where previously the PTA required disclosure of information related to *acts* of terrorism, the 1989 PTA expanded this requirement to criminalize failure to disclose information about terrorist *funds*.[65] Shortly thereafter, the British government extended this requirement to include the mere *suspicion of financial assistance* for terrorism.[66] This section essentially removed any contractual obligations that might otherwise apply to parties engaged in interactions with terrorist entities.

Conviction for any of these offenses made possible the court-ordered forfeiture of one's assets. As with the drug laws, there was an important shift in the burden of proof: where before the state would have to prove the defendant *intended* the resources under his or her control to benefit a proscribed organization, from 1989 the court became entitled, as under the 1986 Drug Trafficking Offenses Act, to assume "in the absence of evidence to the contrary... that any money or property" in the defendant's control could be used for terrorist

---

* From five years' imprisonment and a fine on indictment (the penalty previously applied, for example, to the second offense), the penalty increased to 14 years' imprisonment plus fine. Prevention of Terrorism (Temporary Provisions) Act, 1989, § 11.

ends. The statute only required the court to give the owner of the property "an opportunity to be heard."[67]

In 1991, the EPA followed suit – and went one step further. A new section retained the provisions related to proscription, but added a new set of powers and offenses dealing with terrorism. Thus, incorporating the four offenses of the 1989 PTA, the statute added two more: the first made it illegal to help anyone retain the proceeds of terrorist-related activities;[68] the second outlawed concealing or transferring the proceeds of terrorist-related activities.[69] Each new offense became scheduled, moving related cases into the Diplock realm.

Where the forfeiture provisions of the PTA *allowed* the court to demand assets, new confiscation powers in the EPA *required* the court to make confiscation orders. Instead of narrowly tying its provisions to resources actually linked to acts of terrorism, the EPA allowed the court to *assume* that whatever resources had arrived into a defendant's possession in the six years prior to conviction, or in any time that had elapsed since conviction (above a £20,000 minimum), could be seized. Realizable property included *any* property held by the defendant, plus any property held by someone else to whom the defendant had directly or indirectly made a gift. The statute placed the burden on the defendant both to refute the prosecution's claims regarding which assets applied and to demonstrate that such an order would be unfair or oppressive.[70] Schedule 4 of the act further provided for the court to issue a restraint order, prior to conviction, on any specified realizable property. Courts could conduct these procedures *ex parte*. Violation could result, on indictment, in up to 14 years' imprisonment plus fine.[71]

An interesting question here is why weren't the powers subsequently used? There were cases of individuals who allowed their homes to be used in the commission of terrorist acts; but as true finance offenses, they were not prosecuted until the early twenty-first century. Interviews with individuals deeply involved with the process suggest that the police service used general investigators. To prosecute purely financial offenses, the state needed financial investigators – and a strategy that placed priority on confronting terrorism using these tools. The legislation did go some way toward meeting this issue: it expanded the state's investigatory powers, allowing the Secretary of State to appoint an individual to report on terrorist financing. The act required suspects, when requested, to produce information to investigators, except where legal privilege or banking obligations of confidence applied.[72] In 1996, investigators became authorized to remove any requested documents, unless reasonable cause existed that such information might be subject to legal privilege.[73]

Racketeering in Northern Ireland. Coinciding with the influence of drug provisions on the broader counterterrorist considerations was a shift in the state's approach to terrorism. Up to this time, despite the presence of legislative authorities granted to prosecutors and the court, the Northern Ireland bureaucracy did not treat stemming the flow of funds as a matter central to state security. On the contrary, in 1977 a Housing Executive memorandum showed that, far from cracking down on paramilitary funding, during the 1975 ceasefire, government ministers actually ordered the protection of PIRA members' jobs – regardless of claims of fraud.[74]

In the late 1970s and early 1980s, the state took some steps to counter specific schemes: for instance, the Northern Ireland Housing Executive, particularly vulnerable to tax exemption certificate fraud, began to require that sublet work be approved by a supervising officer and that subcontractors register with the Executive. The introduction of licenses for drinking clubs and slot machines similarly attempted to interrupt these sources of income.[75] Yet not all of these measures were properly enforced.

In 1983, the provincial focus began to shift. In February of that year, an important Northern Ireland Office study drew attention to paramilitary financial flows. The report noted that PIRA's resources derived from bank robberies on both sides of the border, extortion rackets, tax exemption frauds, and gaming machines. Overt streams of cash arrived from clubs, social functions, shops, direct collections, subscriptions, and overseas sympathetic contributions. The Royal Ulster Constabulary (RUC) responded by creating a general racketeering squad, labeled "C19" and known locally as the "Al Capone squad." But this unit, responsible for all racketeering, had only 15 officers and 2 supervisors.[76] And most of the officers assigned to the units were mainstream detectives – not financial investigators. In 1988, the RUC further reformed its bureaucratic structure, forming a specialist unit to tackle terrorist financing.[77]

Reflecting these changes, in 1987 Westminster introduced provisions specifically targeted at preventing paramilitaries from running protection rackets. The EPA prohibited security services from operating without first obtaining a certificate from the Secretary of State. It required companies to supply the government with the identities of their employees, partners, and officers. Businesses had to report any new hires, officers, or partners. The Secretary of State retained the authority to withdraw the certificate, which was renewed annually, at any time. The 1987 EPA made it illegal to promote or employ any security firm that did not have a special certificate. Criminal penalties on summary conviction of six months plus fine applied.[78] The state continued its effort to target this type of fundraising by strengthening its protections for victims to encourage them to come forward with more information.[79]

Counterterrorism and Anti-Drug Trafficking: 1993–2000. In 1993, Westminster revisited the issue of drug trafficking and passed measures that further limited property rights. The Criminal Justice Act provided for prosecutors to apply for a confiscation order to a court – which can then grant the order where satisfied on the basis of the evidence that the confiscation order meets the statutory provisions.[80] It also allowed the court to postpone determinations for up to six months from the date of the conviction.[81] Although legislation in respect of ordinary crime and terrorism was dealt with in two separate parts of the Home Office, the provisions that appeared in counterterrorism statutes then appeared in drug law. Echoing the 1991 EPA, the Criminal Justice Act strengthened assumptions about the proceeds of drug trafficking: instead of providing that the court *may* assume that property derives from trafficking, it *required* the judiciary to assume that all property flowed from illicit proceeds, unless the defendant could prove otherwise or injustice would result.[82] The statute expanded the number of people who could have their assets frozen or confiscated to anyone who knowingly acquired or used property related to drug proceeds.[83] Like the 1989 Prevention of Terrorism Act, the legislation created an offense in connection with money laundering, making it illegal for *anyone* to fail to disclose knowledge or suspicion of money laundering – or to notify suspects that they are under investigation.[84] The legislation gave the Commissioners of Customs and Excise the power to initiate prosecution for drug offenses.[85]

Critically, the legislation amended the 1988 Criminal Justice Act to create a new and weaker standard of proof. Although some practitioners would argue that the legislation merely did what the government thought it had earlier achieved but the courts had said it had not – because it was not explicit on the face of the earlier legislation – the inclusion of the new standard in the measure itself did weaken the earlier standard. The state formally adopted a civil, not criminal, standard to determine whether a person benefited from drug proceeds and thus forfeited his or her possessions.[86]

Part IV of the legislation addressed, specifically, the financing of terrorism and further signaled a merger between counterterrorist law and drug trafficking law. It amended the 1991 EPA to give courts more flexibility to confiscate whatever amount they might consider appropriate. Bringing counterterrorist law into line with drug trafficking law, the legislation changed the standard of proof to the "balance of probabilities" for determining the following: whether a person benefited from terrorist-related activities, the value of the proceeds of those activities, and the amount of the required payment under a confiscation order.[87] Instead of the six months' postponement allowed for ordinary crime, the legislation allowed the court to postpone any final decision on assets already confiscated for "such period as it may specify."[88] The legislation lifted any barrier to self-incrimination, requiring the defendant to provide the court with any information it requested.[89] And it created a duty of disclosure, requiring certain professionals to inform a constable when they know or suspect an individual is acting in a proscribed manner.[90]

Within a year, yet another important statute entered the books. The 1994 Drug Trafficking Act consolidated the 1986 Drug Trafficking Offenses Act and provisions in the 1990 Criminal Justice (International Cooperation) Act dealing with illicit trafficking. Part I again addressed confiscation orders, expanding court authority to confiscate without any application from a prosecutor. The idea was to avoid having the court hamstrung by the fact that a prosecutor had not taken the appropriate steps. The statute required the court to determine whether the defendant benefited from drug trafficking (defined broadly as receiving any payment or other reward at any time in connection with drug trafficking). If the defendant had, the court could then order him or her to pay the requested amount. The standard of proof for determining both whether the individual benefited and the amount to be recovered again lay in the civil realm: the balance of probabilities.[91] The statute required the court to assume that any property received six years prior to the date of conviction came free of other interests in it, and that all expenditures during that time derived from drug proceeds.[92] These provisions essentially expanded the drug trafficking powers to equal those that the Proceeds of Crime Act had introduced for terrorist offenses. Notably, changes in the confiscation legislation were strongly influenced by international events such as the Vienna Convention and, later, the activity of the Financial Action Task Force – actions themselves heavily influenced by the United States.

The Drug Trafficking Act also went further: like the 1991 EPA, it included tainted gifts as seizable items.[93] And, again drawing from the 1991 EPA, a prosecutor's statement asserting that the defendant benefited from drug trafficking and estimating the value of the proceeds became sufficient to reverse the burden of proof, forcing the defendant to answer the charges and indicate evidence on which he or she would rely to refute them. (A "prosecutor's statement" is the term given to the results of a financial investigator's evidence. It spells out exactly what bank account and property dealings evidence has been obtained by Production Orders – that is, subpoenas – and is then offered to the court by the prosecutor). In keeping with counterterrorist law, where mere reasonable cause sufficed to establish that a defendant had benefited from drug trafficking, the statute authorized the High Court to issue a restraining order to prohibit any person from dealing with any realizable property held by a specified person either before or after the date of the order.*

In addition to these changes, the 1994 Drug Trafficking Act gave HM Customs and Excise officers the authority to seize cash if any reasonable grounds existed for suspecting that the money directly or indirectly represented drug proceeds. In the event of such a seizure, the magistrates' court would make a forfeiture order, which the affected individual had to appeal within 30 days.[94] Interestingly, this provision stemmed from a recommendation made by US Customs to a British Parliamentary Select Committee, indicating that the United Kingdom had a gap in its anti-drug law.[95]

The final section of the statute laid out a series of offenses connected to the proceeds of drug trafficking: it criminalized concealing or disguising any property, or converting or removing property from British jurisdiction, to avoid prosecution or the enforcement of a confiscation order. If a third party knew, or had reasonable grounds to suspect, that certain property related to drug proceeds, he became barred from acquiring, using, or taking possession of it. Criminal penalties applied to these offenses, as well as to the failure of any professional to report incidents of actual or suspected drug money laundering.[96]

---

* The restraint order, which could only be made on application by a prosecutor, could be presented *ex parte* to a judge *in camera*, but it still had to provide notice to all persons affected by the order. Drug Trafficking Act, 1994, ch. 37, §§ 25–26.

In the mid-1990s, as political violence seemed to be coming to an end, the British government began contemplating the introduction of permanent counterterrorist law. Lord Lloyd's report, issued in 1996, became a basis for the subsequent 2000 Terrorism Act. In 1998, before the government could introduce the legislation, however, the Real IRA killed 28 people in Omagh. In Parliament, Prime Minister Tony Blair angrily announced that "we must take exceptional measures to mop up the last recalcitrant and renegade terrorist groups that are prepared to threaten the future of Northern Ireland."[97]

The subsequent 1998 Criminal Justice (Terrorism and Conspiracy) Act gave the court the power to order the forfeiture of *any* property used in connection with the activities of the Real IRA or other similar groups – a power that included both deliberate and unwitting aid. In other words, if the Real IRA were to bury a steel drum containing weapons in a ditch on the edge of a farm, the farmer could technically lose the land. Moreover, the statute increased already severe penalties to emphasize the "gravity of the offense."[98] It left the forfeiture decision entirely to the discretion of the courts. Introducing these provisions, Jack Straw suggested that, because they retained judicial discretion, they were not that extreme compared to those simultaneously under consideration in Ireland.[99] The act applied throughout the United Kingdom, with its provisions subject to annual renewal.

Members of Parliament expressed concern at the time that the measure's interference with property might run afoul of the ECHR. Simply allowing someone to appear before a judge does not ensure a balanced trial. Moreover, "[w]here people have different interests in a piece of property – land, a house or a car – one cannot just seize it under the European convention if that will punish another person."[100] Nevertheless, the legislation flew through Parliament under extraordinary procedures, attracting the most attention not for its financial provisions but for its extraterritorial authority and the relaxed rules of evidence it adopted for convicting defendants of terrorist offenses.

Finally, in the year 2000, the Terrorism Act became the first permanent counterterrorist law in the United Kingdom. The financial clauses maintained the importance of intent in determining whether an offense warranted forfeiture.[101] These measures also included judicial checks and balances on the determination to seize assets.[102] Although the legislation broadened the number of people authorized to confiscate cash at the borders, it required HM Customs and Excise to apply to a magistrate's court immediately for an order to detain the money for up to three months, after which officials would either return or permanently seize the assets. The court could grant the request only if reasonable grounds existed to suspect that the cash related to terrorism, and if continued retention was necessary pending further investigation. The legislation required the court to serve notice on anyone affected by the subsequent order, and granted an opportunity for appeal within 30 days.[103] The statute also attached interest requirements to offset the disadvantage created by the temporary suspension of property rights. The statute created a duty of disclosure, but it made a professional exemption for legal advisors who obtained relevant information in privileged circumstances. And although law enforcement agencies could approach financial institutions for customer information, the legislation inserted a warrant process and limited the type of information they could obtain.[104]

Notably, the statute avoided some of the most extreme measures previously in place, dropping the EPA's broad powers regarding the suspension of property rights and eliminating the 1998 Criminal Justice (Terrorism and Conspiracy) Act provisions allowing the state to seize property unwittingly related to terrorist crime. In part these changes may have been a result of the lengthy and public consultation process that preceded the statute's introduction. They may also have reflected the perception that, with the peace process well underway, the threat from terrorism had decreased. This is not to say that the measures were optimal, but that the effort to balance state power with judicial protections reflected the importance of due process considerations.

The Organized Crime Umbrella. While permanent counterterrorist law allowed the state to respond to international terrorism and recalcitrant splinter organizations, the United Kingdom still faced the problem of paramilitary participation in ordinary criminal enterprises. The professionalism and strength of these organizations presented a particular challenge, for which ordinary criminal law appeared insufficient. The numbers here are significant: approximately 230 organized criminal gangs operate in Northern Ireland, two-thirds of whom have ties to republican or loyalist paramilitaries.[105] Some 97 percent of the population considers organized crime a severe threat.[106] Indeed, approximately 85 of the identified gangs conduct what intelligence refers to as top-level activities.[107]

In September 2000, Adam Ingram, the Minister of State for the Northern Ireland Office, said that the government had to look beyond terrorism to organized crime more generally, and announced a new bureaucratic entity, the Organized Crime Task Force (OCTF) to address the legacy of the Troubles. The OCTF would include government, law enforcement, and various other agencies working to drain criminals' financial resources.[108] In May 2004, the group identified its top priorities as reducing extortion, intimidation, and blackmail; disrupting the supply of illegal drugs; reducing the loss to the Exchequer from fuel smuggling and dilution; and interrupting alcohol and tobacco smuggling. The task force also targeted money laundering and the forfeiture of criminal assets and singled out for special attention intellectual property crime and in-transit robberies for special attention.

To provide the statutory authority, in March 2001 the Home Secretary announced a new instrument specific to Northern Ireland: the Financial Investigations (Northern Ireland) Order. The draft Proceeds of Crime Order would apply to the United Kingdom more broadly.[109] These legal instruments transferred powers previously reserved for counterterrorist law and drug forfeiture provisions to the broader criminal realm.

Prior to this time, the main Northern Ireland legislation addressing criminal – as opposed to terrorist – finance was the 1996 Proceeds of Crime (Northern

Ireland) Order. Article 49 allowed the state to appoint a financial investigator
to assist the police in determining the proceeds related to criminal activities.
The financial investigation powers, set out in schedule 2, included the ability
to issue a general bank circular to identify accounts held by named individuals.
Such authority could be exercised only following a county court judge's ruling
that the appointment of a financial investigator would substantially enhance
the investigation. Between August 1996 and December 2000, judges used this
power modestly, appointing financial investigators in only 28 cases. These investigators issued 23 general bank circulars that, in turn, identified more than 1,200
previously unknown accounts linked to people under investigation.

In 2001, the Financial Investigations (Northern Ireland) Order further
expanded these powers. The new order granted HM Customs and Excise the
ability, previously reserved for the police, to apply for the appointment of
a financial investigator to assist with investigations into proceeds of crime.
Investigators received the same access to material under production orders as
was previously available only to law enforcement.[110] The statutory instrument
widened the range of financial institutions to which investigators could issue
a general bank circular, and thus made it possible for the state to demand
information from anyone possibly engaged in business with the accused.[111]*
Customs officers could now issue general circulars to financial institutions and
solicitors, demanding information.[112]

Most controversially, one portion of the order granted the state the power to
issue a general solicitors' circular, directly affecting client-attorney privilege.[113]
Solicitors became required to report the names of their clients. Ingram suggested
that this measure addressed quirks unique to Northern Ireland, where there are
two systems for registering land. Registration of title is not compulsory, and
any inquiry regarding land ownership can be made only in reference to the
property itself – not to the owner. When the Law Society of Northern Ireland
and the Human Rights Commission took a different view of the weakening of
client-attorney privilege, Ingram responded angrily and asserted that no client-
attorney privilege exists where an issue relates to furthering criminal intent. He
cited drug trafficking statutes as precedent for the move:

> The obligation on solicitors to report to the police or NCIS any suspicious transactions
> as defined by our current money laundering offenses has effectively weakened the duty
> of confidentiality that solicitors owe to their clients. Therefore, there has already been
> an acceptance in law of the need to tackle organized crime.[114]

Even if the law did recognize a need to address organized crime, however,
Ingram's answer avoided the key issue: the new powers narrowed client-
attorney privilege prior to any judicial finding of wrongdoing.

The proposed powers generated heated debate. Although Ingram acknowledged the individual rights concerns, he suggested that they were overridden by

---

* Prior to the order, the scope was restricted to banks and building societies. The state wanted to
  extend it to securities, futures, options, and insurance markets, so as to include investment firms,
  insurance companies, and others in the regulated financial sector.

the right of British subjects not to suffer from organized crime.[115] He cited the fact that a county court judge had been inserted into the process for appointing a financial investigator as a safeguard, as well as the requirement that, before issuing a circular, investigators have reasonable grounds to believe a person has benefited from serious crime. And he noted that the power to issue a solicitors' circular would be unique to Northern Ireland – and thus unwittingly emphasized the two-tiered system of justice within the United Kingdom.

The issue of rights figured significantly in the Parliamentary Northern Ireland Grand Committee, which considered the measures. Although the Ulster Democratic Unionist Party, Sinn Féin, and the Social Democratic Labour Party did not show up for the hearing, William Ross of the Ulster Unionist Party welcomed the order: "The Minister was right to declare that there is always a conflict between the protection of individual rights and what is good for the community." Although this was *not* what the minister had said, Ross went on to suggest that "even the European convention on human rights recognizes that the prevention of crime is sufficient reason for interfering with the right of criminals to a private life." Ross saw the issue as a conflict of entitlements: "[T]he right of society to fight crime successfully is pitted against an individual's right to privacy in his legal affairs." He ended his address with this sentence: "I appreciate that the Government wants to tread cautiously because of the conflict – it is at the heart of the matter – between freedom, the necessity of privacy, and the need to investigate crime and prosecute those who are engaged in it in a proper manner that will give confidence to people."[116]

The existence of the solicitors' circular underscores the growing pressure on the legal profession. What began as an indemnity under counterterrorist law for a solicitor to come forward morphed into a duty to disclose information not obtained under legal privilege. In 2001, state authority expanded further to allow the government to request specific information from a solicitor.[117] Two years later, the Home Secretary issued yet another White Paper, this time entitled "One Step Ahead: a 21st Century Strategy to Defeat Organized Criminals." In this document, the state explained that because defendants could exploit legal safeguards, the government wanted to turn the tide. In practice this meant that the state saw financial institutions and lawyers, both considered the "regulated" financial sector, as an extension of its intelligence-gathering arm. If they refused to participate, they would be found guilty of an offense. This approach makes it difficult for an attorney to advise a client under state scrutiny without "prejudicing an investigation." In 2005, the government's Criminal Justice Order extended the solicitors' circular concept to the Assets Recovery Agency in civil recovery investigations. As of winter 2006, however, a solicitors' circular order had yet to be obtained.

Expansion of Counterterrorist Finance Law After September 11, 2001

Despite the careful consideration legislators gave to counterterrorist finance in preparation for the 2000 Terrorism Act, counterterrorist law was further expanded after the attacks in the United States. Perhaps most importantly, the

2001 Anti-Terrorism, Crime and Security Act (ATCSA) enabled the UK government to confiscate any money it believed to be related to terrorist operations, *whether or not a court had brought proceedings in regard to an offense connected with the cash*.[118] The statute completely blocked the judiciary from playing a role in the freezing of assets of non-UK entities: where the Treasury reasonably believed a non-UK person posed a threat to the British economy, British nationals, or United Kingdom residents, the Secretary of the Treasury could issue a statutory instrument seizing that individual's assets. At the end of 28 days, each House of Parliament had to pass a resolution for the order to continue.[119]

The legislation also expanded the function of freezing orders: not only did their issuance result in a suspension of access to funds but they could also require persons to disclose information. There were criminal penalties of up to two years' imprisonment for failing to abide by the order – or provide the requested data.[120]

The legislation went further, however, and expanded the number of people who could seize cash beyond HM Customs & Excise and related functions to any authorized officer.[121]* The statute also amended the 2000 Terrorism Act by allowing law enforcement agencies to apply for an open warrant, essentially giving the state the ability to conduct ongoing account monitoring, rather than requiring the appropriate officer to seek judicial approval each time he or she sought information related to a terrorist investigation. The order can be in place for only 90 days, although renewal is possible.

The ATCSA further amended the Terrorism Act by making it an offense for any person in the "regulated sector" to fail to inform law enforcement promptly where reasonable grounds exist for suspecting that another person has committed an offense relating to terrorism or laundering terrorist funds. Although the duty of disclosure overrides statutory or professional limits,[122] failure to disclose is excusable where the person "is a professional legal adviser and the information or other matter came to him in privileged circumstances."[123]

While the powers expanded, though, some individuals intimately involved in their exercise suggest that their actual impact has been minimal. Of greater importance, it is suggested, was the opening of the information gateway between the tax authorities and the police, which previously the government had been unable to accomplish.[124]

In respect to the monitoring and interception of criminal finance, 9/11 did not so much lead to new measures as accelerate a process already in motion. In June 2000, a government report argued that the state had hitherto dramatically underutilized its potential to recover criminal assets.[125] Soon thereafter, as I have said, Ingram announced legislation to address this problem. The resulting 2002 Proceeds of Crime Act (POCA) essentially applied extraordinary state powers, previously limited to terrorist and drug activity, to mainstream criminal

---

* Detention of the money beyond the initial 48 hours, however, would still require the approval of a magistrate's court.

behavior.* Simultaneously, it rejected pursuing criminal finance through the criminal law system, opting instead for the civil domain and its softer protections of individual rights.[126]

The legislation granted the executive broad powers and limited judicial intervention. Where the courts did become involved, Parts 2, 3, and 4 of the act turned them into a "one-stop shop," allowing the prosecution to "'purchase' pre-trial restraint of assets, criminal conviction, sentence, and, ultimately, confiscation of the restrained assets."[127] Proceedings would no longer be split between the High Court (for the freezing and receivership elements) and the Crown Court (for the actual confiscation hearing). Instead, all proceedings would take place in the Crown Court. Under Part 5 of the legislation, the civil recovery scheme would remain in the High Court, to which other serious civil cases are assigned. This portion of the act severed assets recovery from any sort of criminal conviction[128] and adopted the more lenient civil standard of proof – a "balance of probabilities" – instead of "beyond reasonable doubt." By consciously sidestepping criminal law, the state did *not* have to presume the innocence of the accused. The House of Lords, the Privy Council, and the European Court of Human Rights had all previously held similar confiscation provisions outside the scope of criminal law (where criminal confiscation proceedings had been held under a civil standard of proof because they were post-conviction) – and thus not subject to the presumption of innocence as embodied in Article 6(2) of the ECHR.[129]

Previously the 1996 Drug Trafficking Act had *required* the court to consider that any property received in the six years prior to a case was derived from crime. In contrast, the 1988 Criminal Justice Act had *allowed* for judicial discretion in that determination. POCA combined and extended these regimes: where the court is satisfied that the criminal lifestyle provisions apply due to the type or number or value of offenses of which the defendant is convicted, the assumption is that the defendant has benefited from crime. The statute reversed the burden of proof, creating the "criminal lifestyle" standard and requiring self-incrimination under production and disclosure orders.[130] The statute *obliged the court to assume that all expenditures in the six years prior to the case came from property obtained through criminal conduct.*[131] On appeal, the court could confirm, quash, or vary a confiscation order.[132] Jane Kennedy, the Minister of State for the Northern Ireland office, hailed the legislation as "a formidable addition to our arsenal."[133]

To administer this new regime, the statute created the Assets Recovery Agency (ARA), a nonministerial department that reports to the Home Secretary, although it maintains operational independence. The ARA operates throughout

---

* For example, the statute defines money laundering offenses strictly in relation to the crime: "A person commits an offense if he (a) conceals criminal property; (b) disguises criminal property; (c) converts criminal property; (d) transfers criminal property; (e) removes criminal property from England and Wales or from Scotland or from Northern Ireland." Proceeds of Crime Act, 2002, Part VII, § 327.

the United Kingdom, with its main branch located in Great Britain and a sub-sidiary office in Northern Ireland.[134] Its strategic aim is to interrupt criminal activity by recovering criminal assets and to promote financial investigations as a key element of criminal cases. The agency takes on cases referred by the police, HM Customs and Excise, the prosecution authority, and other law enforcement. The system creates an alternative to criminal law: the state must have attempted and failed to prosecute through the criminal system, or else prosecution must not be feasible. The minimum amount of recoverable property is set at £10,000, and must include items other than cash or negotiable instruments (although these could be included if other property also is at issue). The organization is staffed by lawyers, accountants, ex-police investigators, forensic accoun-tants, and Customs and Excise and Inland Revenue personnel. External advisors drawn from the private sector and the Treasury Solicitor's Office also assist.

The agency opened for business on January 13, 2003. Between February of that year and the following May, it received 142 referrals from other agencies. But when asked in March 2005 which assets of PIRA, Real IRA, Continuity IRA, Official IRA, Irish National Liberation Army, Ulster Defense Association (UDA), and Ulster Volunteer Force had been seized or frozen by the Assets Recovery Agency, Ian Pearson, the Parliamentary Under-Secretary of State for Northern Ireland, provided less than impressive figures: he put loyalist assets under interim receiving orders at £350,000, with another £1.25 million agreed for recovery; Republican cases, in turn, had netted only £173,332 in frozen funds and £225,000 agreed for recovery.[135] David Burnside, from South Antrim, pointed out in response, "If ever there were a description of the tip of an iceberg, that is it." One Slab Murphy (rumored to be so called because of his habit of dropping cement blocks on his enemies' legs) runs a smuggling operation along the border with the Republic of Ireland that nets around £40 million – making almost meaningless the paltry £225,000 recovered from Republicans.[136]

Pearson replied to the criticism that it was, as yet, early in the program. He had a point: the organization was still in its infancy, and initially only 10 people worked there (as opposed to more than 50 in its southern counterpart).[137] The ARA, moreover, was not the lead agency for terrorist assets: this role was held by the Police Service Northern Ireland. Pearson was optimistic about the future – and he had reason to be: considerable incentives exist for the agency to pursue more, rather than fewer, funds. The statute made the ARA self-financing, thereby creating an incentive for aggressiveness in the organization. To some degree, this seems to have worked: by March 31, 2004, although its business plan only targeted £10 million in frozen assets, the ARA had frozen £14.8 million.

Nevertheless, its overall "success" in the paramilitary realm leaves some-thing to be desired. Going by the ARA's public press releases, only two cases, both loyalist, appear thus far to relate directly to paramilitaries: in the first, a UDA case in South-East Antrim, the agency obtained assets held by David and Pauline Hill in the United Kingdom and United States. In March 2005, the agency wrestled about £4.8 million in assets from Colin Armstrong and

Geraldine Mallon, both of whom had links to the Ulster Volunteer Force and later the Loyalist Volunteer Force, when the organization split.[138] The reason for the sparseness of cases is complex. It may directly relate to the Police Service Northern Ireland's continued lack of real attention to this issue, as the ARA's ability to act is limited to some extent by the financial information submitted.

The Effects of Expanding Laws

In many ways, antiterrorist finance represents one of the most benign options available to the state in its response to terrorist threat: these initiatives are largely seen through the prism of terrorism-as-crime, not as war. But although their aim is relatively uncontroversial, the adverse consequences of the actual steps taken have been considerable. As the antiterrorist finance regime in the United Kingdom has moved from criminal law to civil law standards, the forfeiture of one's property ultimately has become divorced from one's conviction for any underlying criminal offense. With the presumption of innocence no longer applying, the burden has shifted to those seeking to *prevent* the state from claiming their assets to prove that such property does not relate to criminal activity. Simultaneously, the standard for determining the criminal origin of property has weakened: now a balance of probabilities applies, instead of beyond reasonable doubt.[139] The number and range of offenses related to the financing of criminal activity have rapidly expanded as well.

Not only has the United Kingdom eroded these entitlements and, consequently, property rights, but the state has also created institutions with a vested interest in aggressively wielding investigatory powers and pursuing forfeiture proceedings. Although, in one sense, these initiatives are meant to strengthen the state's ability to respond to a very real threat, their transfer to the ordinary criminal system means their repercussions spread beyond it. Yet little attention has been paid to the broader impact of these authorities. Perhaps of greatest concern has been the weakening, in Northern Ireland, of client-attorney privilege as part of the state's investigatory powers – a development that, to judge by the history of antiterrorist finance legislation – may eventually extend throughout the United Kingdom.

Instead of stopping to question the significant expansion in state powers, British efforts to address the flow of criminal funds continue apace. On April 1, 2003, new Money Laundering Regulations entered into force.* These regulations require that anyone in the course of relevant business comply with identification procedures, record-keeping procedures, internal reporting procedures, and training.[140] All money service operators and high-value dealers must register with HM Customs and Excise, which can impose civil fines and penalties

---

* These regulations replaced the Money Laundering Regulations 1993 and 2001. The idea was to bring them into line with Directive 2001/97/EC of the European Parliament and of the Council, amending Council Directive 91/308/EEC on the prevention of the use of the financial system for money laundering.

for noncompliance.[141]* In the legislative realm, a consultation paper issued in March 2004 floated new proposals looking at standards for compelling witnesses, admitting evidence, increasing sentencing, and restricting licenses. Conspiracy law and proposals for a National Witness Protection Program also graced the text. And the administrative structure continues to evolve: in February 2004, the government announced the formation of the Serious Organised Crime Agency, which draws from responsibilities divided among the National Crime Squad, the National Criminal Intelligence Service, HM Customs and Excise, and the Immigration Service. Chaired by the Home Secretary, the Serious Organised Crime Agency focuses on developing national strategies and encouraging communication across bureaucratic barriers. Aspects of this regime have proven unhelpful and even counterproductive in the effort to prevent terrorist organizations from raising money and transferring funds, as I discuss further in the American context.

ANTITERRORIST FINANCE IN THE UNITED STATES

In the United States – unlike the United Kingdom, where September 11 accelerated a trend already under way – there was an abrupt change of course in respect to countering terrorist finance. Prior to the attacks, the administrative structure all but ignored the subject: the Department of Justice tended not to bring criminal charges for contributions to terrorist organizations.[†] Since terrorism did not require much money, it was the popular belief that there were more efficient ways of preventing attacks. Not a single unit at FBI headquarters focused on the financing of terrorist organizations; nor did the Criminal Division of the Department of Justice have a national terrorist financing program.[142] Consequently, the FBI lacked the detailed intelligence necessary to conduct a successful anti-finance campaign. Turf battles, the scourge of the bureaucratic state, compounded the issue.

The CIA, for its part, had little insight into the financial underpinnings of groups associated with al Qaeda. Like the FBI, the CIA did not consider interrupting the flow of money a high priority – but for different reasons. The

---

* A money service operator is anyone who accepts deposits, carries out long-term insurance contracts, deals in investments as principal or agent, arranges deals in investments (manages them, safeguards, or administers them), establishes collective investment schemes, advises on investments, or issues electronic money. A "high value dealer" is anyone dealing in goods by way of business when the transaction involves more than £15,000.

† Successful prosecution required the state to trace donor funds to particular terrorist attacks. The Department of Justice found it easier to use minor charges to disrupt operations. On the more serious cases, the FBI was concerned that if it opened a criminal investigation, it would not be able to use broader powers under the Foreign Intelligence Surveillance Act to place suspects under surveillance. The FBI also claimed (after the fact) that the political climate would not have allowed them to go after religious charities. John Roth, Douglas Greenburg & Serena Wille, *National Commission on Terrorist Attacks Against the United States, Monograph on Terrorist Financing: Staff Report to the commission*, Aug. 21, 2004, at 32, available at http://www.9–11commission.gov.

general – and, it turned out, erroneous – belief was that, at least in regard to al Qaeda, money came directly from bin Laden.[143] Also, the complicated manner in which terrorists obtained and transferred funds made efforts to follow the money less effective than other approaches to addressing the threat. The CIA did have a virtual station (ALEC station), initially named the Counter Terrorism Center (CTC) – Terrorist Financial Links, but it dealt only with financial matters connected to other agency efforts. The ALEC station director, moreover, strongly believed that money did not reveal much about an organization's plans. The Office of Transnational Issues, within the Directorate of Intelligence, ran an Illicit Transaction Group that addressed terrorist finance – but it was not considered part of the CTC.[144]

The story was similar for other bureaucratic entities with a vested interest in the matter. Although the National Security Agency did have a handful of people addressing terrorist finance, its foreign language capabilities were not particularly strong. The Treasury Department's Office of Foreign Assets Control (OFAC) ran the Foreign Terrorist Asset Tracking Center, but herculean battles following the 2000 Bremer Commission report limited OFAC's operations – which, in any event, were confined to US borders. FinCEN, the Treasury's Financial Crimes Enforcement Network, born in 1990, tended to focus on Russian money launderers and other high-profile crimes. The only federal organization seriously addressing the issue was the National Security Council (NSC): after the 1998 East Africa bombing, Richard Clarke started an NSC-led interagency group on terrorist financing, which also included the Treasury, the CIA, the FBI, and the State Department. The task force initially focused on determining bin Laden's assets. (It was this group that later discredited the CIA's assumption regarding al Qaeda funding.)

A legal framework addressing terrorist finance also was developed rather late in the day. In the mid-1990s, the first efforts to address nonstate actors' funding emerged, and focused narrowly on specific actors. The financial regulatory regime, for its part, existed quite separately and almost wholly in the realm of drug trafficking and money laundering.

After September 11, however – with Title III of the USA PATRIOT Act and Executive Order 13,224 leading the charge – the administrative structure suddenly and dramatically began to focus on the issue, placing increased pressure on allied and nonallied states to introduce new structures to stem the flow of funds to international terrorist organizations.

Measures Before September 11

Three legislative streams constituted the general framework for US regulatory and investigative powers in respect to terrorist finance before the attacks of September 11, 2001. The first originated with the 1917 Trading with the Enemy Act (TWEA), which gave the president the ability to "investigate, regulate...prevent or prohibit...transactions" during war or national emergencies.[145] Congress wanted to prevent individuals located within the

United States from conducting transactions with declared enemies. Initially viewed as an instrument of war, in 1933 the legislature amended the statute to apply during any national emergency. Abuses during the Nixon era led to its revocation and replacement with the 1977 International Emergency Economic Powers Act.[146] In the final decade of the twentieth century, the executive issued an order under this statute that created a list of Prohibited Persons and Specially Designated Terrorists whose financial transactions could be banned. The second legislative stream, the 1996 Antiterrorism and Effective Death Penalty Act (AEDPA), created two lists of entities against which financial strictures applied: state sponsors of terrorism and designated foreign terrorist organizations. Statutes related to drug trafficking and anti-money laundering are the third tributary leading to post-9/11 antiterrorist finance efforts.

Lists Under the International Emergency Economic Powers Act (IEEPA). The 1977 IEEPA required that any economic regulation introduced by the president arise from extraordinary threats located wholly, or mostly, outside the United States. Once the president declares a national emergency in regard to the specific threat, a broad range of powers goes into effect: the president can designate individuals or entities he or she considers a national security threat, freeze their assets, and block transactions between them and every US person by making it illegal to make or receive any contribution of funds, goods, or services to or from those included on the list.[147] The president must report the order within 10 days to the Treasury's Office of Foreign Assets Control. This agency then informs banks, whose refusal to comply may result in criminal or civil penalties. Early uses of the IEEPA applied to Libya and Cuba; in the 1990s, however, the executive began to go after nonstate actors: first, Palestinian organizations, and, later, drug traffickers like the Cali cartel in Colombia.

In January 1995, President Clinton issued Executive Order 12,947 under the IEEPA. This instrument blocked all US assets of specified terrorists or groups threatening to use force to disrupt the Middle East peace process,[148] and prohibited all US persons from engaging in transactions with entities included on the Specially Designated Terrorist List. The justification for the Executive Order was the centrality of peace in the Middle East to US national security. Although the Clinton administration did not originally include Osama bin Laden on this list, Executive Order 13,099 added him and a number of his key aides after the 1998 East Africa bombings.[149] Then in 1999 the executive authorized OFAC to block financial transactions with the Taliban in retribution for their protection of bin Laden.[150]

Two cases in the 1980s tested executive authority to act under both the Trading with the Enemy Act (TWEA) and the IEEPA. In the first, the Supreme Court upheld executive authority to freeze assets to create a bargaining chip for foreign relations.[151] From this case it became clear that although Congress intended the IEEPA to limit the president's power during peacetime, the statute did not reduce overall executive power to control foreign assets. In the second, the Court held that the sanctions regime against Cuba had properly moved from the Trading with the Enemy Act to the IEEPA.[152] These two decisions, in addition to the removal of the legislative veto in *INS* v. *Chadha* (1983),[153] afforded the executive significant discretionary power. As long as the president declares a national emergency, he or she has the power to place sanctions on recalcitrant actors and to request that OFAC issue regulations. Only rarely have the courts scrutinized these decisions.[154]

Designated Foreign Terrorist Organizations. The second stream of authorities stems from the 1995 Oklahoma City bombing. Although US nationals planned and carried out the attack, many of the provisions that Congress subsequently incorporated into the 1996 Antiterrorism and Effective Death Penalty Act (AEDPA) dealt with foreign threats. Two sections – 312 and 302(a) – related to antiterrorist finance.

The first section made it a criminal offense – with criminal penalties – for US persons (except as approved by Treasury in consultation with the State Department) to engage in financial transactions with the governments of states designated under the 1979 Export Administration Act as international state sponsors of terrorism. Cuba, Iran, Iraq, Libya, North Korea, Sudan, and Syria almost immediately found themselves on the list. (Afghanistan was on a special "not cooperating fully" list.)

Section 302(a), which provided a legislative supplement to Executive Order 12,947, created another set of powers particularly relevant to counterterrorism.[155] This measure made it a crime to provide "material support or resources to a foreign terrorist organization." US law defined "material support" broadly to include currency or financial securities, financial services, lodging, training, expert advice or assistance, safe houses, false documentation or identification, communications equipment, facilities, weapons, lethal substances, explosives, personnel, transportation, or any other physical assets, except medicine or religious materials.[156]* A federal court later determined that material support also included food and shelter.[157] For a group to qualify, it must be foreign, engage in terrorism or terrorist activity, and threaten national security or the safety of US nationals.[158]† Criminal penalties apply. In October 1997, Secretary of State Madeline Albright issued a list of 30 entities. Two years later, the State Department reissued the list, reducing it to 27. Not until late October 1999 did al Qaeda join the other designated groups.

By May 2000, it was clear that, according to the courts, these extraordinary powers lay firmly within the executive domain. For non-US persons, the

---

* The court later held that the terms "personnel" and "training" in the definition of material support were impermissibly overbroad and thus void for vagueness under the First and Fifth Amendments; but these could be severed from the statute. *Humanitarian Law Project* v. *Reno*, 9 F. Supp. 2d 1176, 1205 (C.D. Cal. 1998). *See also Humanitarian Law Project* v. *Reno*, 205 F.3d 1130 (9th Cir. 2000), *cert. denied*, 532 U.S. 904 (2001); *Humanitarian Law Project* v. *U.S. Dep't of Justice*, 352 F.3d 382 (9th Cir. 2003) (again affirming the lower court's ruling on this point).

† For discussion of the procedure followed, see State Department Office of Counterterrorism, *Fact Sheet on Foreign Terrorist Organizations*, Aug. 9, 2002, available at www.state.gov.

judiciary could speak only to an extremely narrow set of issues: whether the entities listed were "foreign" and "engaged in terrorist activities." The US Court of Appeals for the Fourth Circuit explained, "[A] foreign entity without property or presence in this country has no constitutional rights, under the due process clause or otherwise."[159] As long as it *appeared* that the Secretary of State came to her conclusions based on some sort of information, the court had no power to review the actual decision.

The Fourth Circuit seemed concerned that its decision not be taken as an endorsement of the executive's findings: "In so deciding we are not . . . allowing the reputation of the Judicial Branch to be 'borrowed by the political Branches to cloak their work in the neutral colors of judicial action.' *We reach no judgment whatsoever regarding whether the material before the Secretary is or is not true.*"[160] The court appeared uncomfortable with AEDPA's procedures and the executive's manner of implementing them: "As we wrote earlier, the record consists entirely of hearsay, none of it was ever subjected to adversary testing, and there was no opportunity for counter-evidence by the organizations affected."[161] Nevertheless, "As we see it, *our only function is to decide if the Secretary, on the face of things, had enough information before her to come to the conclusion that the organizations were foreign and engaged in terrorism.*"[162] Thus, although the Secretary of State might be wrong, it did not lie within the court's purview to exonerate foreign organizations. The question whether US persons could fall within the statute's remit, for the moment, remained open. But not for long.

In a rare exception to judicial deference on these matters, in June 2001 the Court's decision in *National Council of Resistance* v. *State* suggested that the truncated procedures adopted in AEDPA did deny US persons due process.[163] Under the existing procedures, organizations could be designated on the basis of classified information immune to challenge, with an extremely limited scope of subsequent judicial review.[164] The Supreme Court, however, again left open a significant question: What procedures, at what point, *would* satisfy due process? Only broad guidelines, involving notice and an opportunity for meaningful review, followed. The Court hedged even these guidelines, though, with language recognizing "the privilege and prerogative of the executive" and the desire of the court "not . . . to compel a breach in the security which that branch is charged to protect." This case came down three months before September 11. The Supreme Court has yet to determine exactly which procedural devices the executive must grant to designated groups or individuals to protect their interests and at what point such devices must be given.[165]

Courts have repeatedly, however, upheld the narrow interpretation of the judicial role.[166] The courts also view political advocacy for foreign regimes as outside the remit of the First Amendment.[167] Similarly, it is not up to the judiciary to consider whether the humanitarian efforts of designated organizations stand separate from their violent activities.[168] Nevertheless, for "material support or resources" to designated foreign entities to be a crime, the executive must supply proof that individuals charged with violating AEDPA know about either the organization's designation or the unlawful activities that led to its inclusion on the list[169]:

[G]uilt is personal, and when the imposition of punishment on a status or on conduct can only be justified by reference to the relationship of that status or conduct to other concededly criminal activity ... that relationship must be sufficiently substantial to satisfy the concept of personal guilt in order to withstand attack under the Due Process Clause.[170]

Because Congress included the word "knowingly" in the statute, the court read the law to include a *mens rea* requirement – literally, a "guilty mind." The individual had to intend the action to be in furtherance of the group's illegal activity. Conduct regulated by statute did not fall into the "public welfare" category of conduct excepted from the knowledge requirement:

Thus, to sustain a conviction ... the government must prove beyond a reasonable doubt that the donor had knowledge that the organization was designated by the Secretary as a foreign terrorist organization or that the donor had knowledge of the organization's unlawful activities that caused it to be so designated.[171]

Money Laundering. The third stream of legislative authority stemmed from efforts to prevent money laundering, particularly as it related to drugs. These provisions tended to focus on creating a paper trail to help the state detect and investigate violations of the tax and criminal law. Together with the 1998 Money Laundering and Financial Crimes Strategy Act, which required Treasury to work with state and local officials to write a national money laundering strategy, three pieces of legislation – the Bank Secrecy Act, the Anti-Drug Abuse Act, and the Housing and Community Development Act – created the due diligence standard to which banks were held before September 11.[172]

The first of these measures, the 1970 Bank Secrecy Act and Regulations, emphasized money laundering and the use of secret foreign accounts.[173] The legislation required financial institutions (defined by Treasury) to file Suspicious Activity Reports (SARs) for questionable transactions. The rationale ran thus: private industry stands in a better position than the state to detect illicit movement of money, and having a nongovernment entity file the reports protects customer privacy. The statute required that the financial entity "know" its customers; that is, the beneficial owner of the account, the source of the funds, and whether the transaction reflected the customer profile. The bank, in turn, could more effectively limit its exposure to risk. Criminal penalties, civil fines, and administrative sanctions could accompany the failure to file SARs within 30 days or to have an appropriate system in place. The SAR scheme made it more difficult for money launderers, drug dealers, and fraudsters to use the US banking system.[174]

Constitutional challenges to the statute on grounds of privacy and a Fourth Amendment property interest in bank records failed.[175] Legislators responded with the 1978 Right to Financial Privacy Act, which limited the state's ability to request and obtain financial records.[176] It required investigators, for the most part, to make requests in writing and compelled banks to provide notice to customers when the state requested their records. The regulatory scheme in the Bank Secrecy Act can nevertheless be viewed as a way around these procedures or, for that matter, grand jury subpoena.

In 1986, the second important piece of legislation, the Anti-Drug Abuse Act, included a set of provisions aimed at further emasculating money laundering schemes.[177] Three new criminal offenses made it illegal knowingly to assist in laundering, to handle transactions of more than $10,000 derived from criminal proceeds, or to structure transactions to dodge statutory reporting requirements. The statute upped the ante on the criminal and civil penalties, including the forfeiture of "any property, real or personal, involved in a transaction or attempted transaction" that violated the reporting rules.[178] The legislation also gave Treasury the authority to require financial organizations to file geographically focused reports on suspect regions.

In the third significant measure in 1992, Title XV of the Housing and Community Development Act gave regulators the ability to close accounts and seize the assets of financial institutions that violated money laundering statutes.[179] This legislation essentially expanded the application of SARs to an even broader range of financial institutions.[180] Outside of general guidelines, though, the legislation left it to the banks to determine what amounted to suspicious activity.

The financial industry vigorously opposed the bill that preceded this law. But Congress was looking for a tighter relationship between the state and private industry. As a result, the final statute required institutions to maintain records of wire transfers so that the state could produce such information later as evidence in court. Congress compromised by making vague rules on the format and content of such records, leaving their exact structure up to the individual institutions. Subsequent regulations from Treasury and the Federal Reserve proved equally broad. Nevertheless, the statute introduced an interesting administrative penalty, forbidding anyone convicted of money laundering from engaging in business with a federally insured entity without explicit authorization from the state.[181] And it required a joint advisory board to oversee the Bank Secrecy Act, drawing its members from Treasury, Justice, the Office of National Drug Control Policy, and financial institutions.

These shifts proved to be an iron fist in a velvet glove: the statute gave Treasury the ability to interfere in the running of financial institutions, requiring them to institute anti-money laundering programs, designate compliance officers, train employees on a regular basis, and assent to an independent audit. The legislation created an indemnity from any civil suits, thus meeting a long-standing concern of the American Bankers Association, which was uncomfortable about the legal implications of such inroads into personal privacy. The legislation also made it illegal for employees to discuss with customers any grand jury subpoenas – any violation again involving criminal penalties, civil fines, and administrative penalties.

Prior to September 11, the general trend was toward giving prosecutors more discretion in using these powers. Courts, in turn, tended increasingly to decide ambiguities in favor of prosecutors.[182] Unlike the pre-September 11 terrorist measures, money laundering statutes required only that the money be traceable to a specified unlawful activity – not that the defendant be tied to the commission of the act.

Even though these measures had teeth and were steadily becoming sharper, they appear almost mild in light of the dramatic changes after the attacks. The financial industry had managed to fend off stronger attempts by the state to involve itself in the financial world. In 1994, for instance, Congress directed Treasury to begin regulating "money services businesses" (e.g., check cashers, wire money transfers, money orders, and traveler's checks). Three years later, Treasury drafted regulations, but the rules were not issued until 1999, with implementation set for December 31, 2001. The Bush administration planned to follow in the Clinton administration's footsteps, delaying implementation once more until late 2002 to give the government the opportunity to "educate" these businesses about their obligations.[183] Where Treasury attempted to embed itself further into the already regulated financial industry, it came up short: in 1998, Treasury proposed stronger "know your customer" requirements, which would have required banks to obtain extensive private information, such as where money came from and to whom it was going. More than 200,000 negative responses – stretching from left to right on the political spectrum – bombarded the department.[184] As Congress began openly contemplating rolling back the current controls, Treasury abandoned ship.[185] Efforts to get the Money Laundering Control Bill of 2000 through Congress also failed; this statute would have given the Treasury Department control of foreign banks with accounts in the United States. Before moving to the regulatory and investigative measures the United States introduced in response to the September 11 attacks, though, we need to take a brief look at al Qaeda's funding to understand the impact of subsequent provisions.

Al Qaeda Funding

Like the Provisional IRA and other paramilitary organizations in Northern Ireland, al Qaeda does not require an inordinate amount of money to carry out its attacks. The September 11 Commission estimated that the 1998 East African embassy attacks required just $10,000. The 2002 Bali bombings cost al Qaeda only $20,000. Despite the devastation caused in 2001 to the World Trade Center and the Pentagon, the total amount spent on the actual operation ran between $400,000 and $500,000.[186*] This does not mean that money is

---

* This number excludes overhead costs, such as recruitment and training. For detailed discussion of the value of money to terrorists, *see* Rex A. Hudson, The Sociology and Psychology of Terrorism: Who Becomes a Terrorist and Why 14–19 (1999); and Raphael Perl, *Terrorism, the Future, and US Foreign Policy*, Issue Brief for Congress IB95112, at 4 (Apr. 11, 2003).

unimportant to al Qaeda – indeed, internal memos suggest otherwise.[187] But when small amounts of money are transferred, it makes it difficult for states to intercept the funds.

The structure of the network further compounds such efforts. Al Qaeda comprises loosely affiliated groups that more closely resemble a movement than an organized entity. Most of its operations are self-financed: the group carrying out the attack raises its own funds through a variety of legal and illegal sources. This distinguishes al Qaeda from many of the Northern Ireland groups, which tend to obtain funds from a central organization. Although a financial committee reported to Osama bin Laden before September 11, even then central financing was limited, and groups on the periphery developed their own revenue streams.[188] Since the attacks, al Qaeda has become even more diverse and less tied to a central structure. As William Wechsler, director of the task force examining bin Laden's finances, explained, the network has become "a constant fundraising machine."[189]

US awareness of this machine, as I previously noted, came rather late in the game: it was not until 1998, following the East Africa bombings and the listing of al Qaeda as a terrorist organization, that the White House asked the National Security Council (NSC) and the CIA's Illicit Transactions Group to find out how the network operated.[190] Until then, the CIA and others mistakenly assumed that most of the money came from bin Laden's pocket.[191] Although the Africa bombing trials in early 2001 generated more information,[192] not until September 11 did the Bush administration become resolute about finding the money. Yet, even months later, Kenneth Dam, Deputy Secretary of the Treasury, admitted that the United States lacked a complete picture.[193]

Government expenditures and independent donations from Saudi Arabia appear to be critical in al Qaeda's funding and development. The Staff Report to the September 11 Commission claimed, "Over the past 25 years, the desert kingdom has been the greatest force in spreading Islamic fundamentalism, while its huge, unregulated charities funneled hundreds of millions of dollars to jihad groups and al Qaeda cells around the world."[194]* After five months of analyzing documents and interviewing government officials, U.S. NEWS AND WORLD REPORT came to a similar conclusion. The news magazine found that Saudi money flowed to 20 different states, which had training camps and where weapons purchases and recruiting activities occurred.[195] In 2002, the United Nations Security Council reported that jihadists had secured $300–$500 million over the previous decade, the bulk derived from Saudi donors and charities.[196] Saudi money has not just gone to militants. Between 1975 and 2002, Saudi

---

* The Staff Report to the September 11 Commission found that no foreign government directly funded al Qaeda, but it went into detail on many of the Saudi links highlighted earlier and classified the sections of the final report that deal directly with Saudi Arabia. John Roth, Douglas Greenburg & Serena Wille, *National Commission on Terrorist Attacks Against the United States, Monograph on Terrorist Financing: Staff Report to the commission*, Aug. 21, 2004, at 4, 22–24, available at www.9–11commission.gov.

Arabia spent more than $70 billion on foreign aid – more than two-thirds of which went to spreading the (fundamentalist) Wahhabi sect worldwide.[197] Alex Alexiev, a former CIA consultant on religious conflict, referred to the program as "the largest worldwide propaganda campaign ever mounted."[198] In 2002, AIN AL-YAGEEN, a weekly Saudi paper, claimed that the money helped to build approximately 1,500 mosques, 210 Islamic centers, 202 colleges, and 2,000 schools – all outside of Islamic states.[199]

In respect to these efforts and to the many charitable organizations run and funded by Saudis, there are two particularly important points. First, although many of the summaries tend to place all Saudi sources into one box, there are considerable differences among the members of the Saudi royal family, between the state and private donors, and among different initiatives. Second, many of the charitable and religious donations provide critical humanitarian services to hospitals, orphanages, and disadvantaged communities. This nuance is an important part of responding to terrorist finance. Failure to be aware of it may mean that funding that ought to be encouraged dries up, or that devastating political, economic, or humanitarian consequences may follow.

But what complicates the picture is that a significant number of the charitable organizations funded by Saudi resources also funnel money to violent struggles. A 1996 CIA report found that, of the 50 Islamic charities engaged in global assistance, approximately one-third had links to terrorist organizations. The grand mufti of Saudi Arabia has overseen some of the largest Islamic charities, such as the Muslim World League (with 30 branches worldwide) and the International Islamic Relief Organization (with offices in more than 90 different states).[200] *U.S. News and World Report* tied these organizations directly to terrorist movements.[201] The New York Council on Foreign Relations put the point strongly: "[I]t is worth stating clearly and unambiguously what official US government spokespersons have not: For years, individuals and charities based in Saudi Arabia have been the most important source of funds for al Qaeda; and for years, Saudi officials have turned a blind eye to this problem."[202]

With some $600 billion in Saudi money in US banks and the stock market, successive administrations have avoided looking too closely into the Saudi role.[203] The Carlyle Group, for instance – advised by former President George H.W. Bush, former Secretary of State James Baker, and former Secretary of Defense Frank Carlucci – made millions from its Saudi links.[204] The CIA instructed its station chief in Riyadh not to focus on Islamic extremists – even after East Africa – because of political sensitivities.[205] The 1998 NSC report provided a breakthrough of sorts – but the Clinton administration made only meager attempts to follow the money. Vice President Al Gore met with Saudi Crown Prince Abdullah in Washington, D.C., and set up a visit for US counterterrorist specialists to meet with Saudi officials in Riyadh.[206] The NSC's William Wechsler and Treasury's Richard Newcomb subsequently traveled to Saudi Arabia and met with top security and banking officials.[207] But Saudi Arabia has sharp divisions between law enforcement and the banking industry and minimal regulation of its financial sector. On the US side, the State Department, concerned about the impact of ending the organizations' legitimate charitable efforts, argued against freezing their assets.[208]

Saudi Arabia is not by any means the only source of funding that strengthened what became al Qaeda.[209] Money flowed from the Persian Gulf, Egypt, South Asia, Africa – and the United States. During the Cold War, for instance, the United States and Saudi Arabia put a $3.5 billion package together to back the mujahideen in Afghanistan – a group to which Osama bin Laden belonged. When the Soviets left Afghanistan in 1992, he traveled to Sudan, where he established a corporate shell, Wadi al-Aqiq, parent to a number of subsidiary firms.* Jamal Ahmed al-Fadle, the Chief Financial Officer of Wadi al-Aqiq, reports that the parent company's bank accounts stretched from Sudan to Hong Kong and Malaysia, with several accounts in London at Barclays Bank.[210]

Bin Laden's personal business, however, proved to be far less important in funding al Qaeda than were charitable organizations located in Saudi Arabia and elsewhere. In drawing from these sources, al Qaeda benefited from one of the five pillars of Islam: *zakat,* or charitable giving, which requires that adherents give at least 2.5 percent of their income to charity and humanitarian causes.[211]† As a legal matter, the net effect of this system – where the donors to charities were indeed focused on humanitarian assistance, but their money was skimmed at the end of the cycle – was that those donors, lacking the intent to support violent causes, were not necessarily culpable.[212]

As money from legitimate business mingled with illegitimate funds, al Qaeda moved resources through both regulated and unregulated systems.‡ It appears likely, for instance, that al Qaeda has benefited from the trade in drugs, diamonds, and other commodities. Although the September 11 Commission found "no persuasive evidence" that the drug trade provided an important source of revenue for al Qaeda, nor that the network was substantially involved with "conflict diamonds," these conclusions do not match those of a wide range of reports in the press and, in any event, are not necessarily true of the

---

* Taba Investment, a currency trading firm, was located in Kenya, where the company dealt in gems. Ladin International Co. focused on import-export business. Al-Hijra Construction built bridges and roads. Other businesses traded in commodities like palm oil and sugar. Robert Clow, Andrew Edgecliffe-Johnson, Adrian Michaels & Richard Wolffe, *Team Set Up to Block Terrorist Funds*, FIN. TIMES (London), Sept. 17, 2001, at 6.

† Although I recognize that the 9/11 Commission is not an authoritative source on Islamic jurisprudence, and that its analysis may in some respects be misleading, I reference the document here as it calls attention to religious considerations and their relationship to antiterrorist finance concerns.

‡ To fund September 11, for instance, the organization used approximately a dozen hawaladars, as well as wire transfers, physical deposits of traveler's checks, physical movement of cash, and access to foreign funds via debit and credit cards. None of the individual transactions exhibited particularly unusual traits. John Roth, Douglas Greenburg & Serena Wille, *National Commission on Terrorist Attacks Against the United States, Monograph on Terrorist Financing: Staff Report to the commission*, Aug. 21, 2004, at 13, available at www.9-11commission.gov.

post-September 11 environment.* Indeed, Islamist groups appear to be increasingly interested in this realm.[213]

Increased reporting requirements for the regulated sector followed the attacks (see page 160), pushing Islamists toward the unregulated sector. Alternative remittance systems deserve brief attention here. Although no broad agreement exists on a definition, common elements mark them. Most developed along ethnic lines well before the West adopted a formal banking structure. Their defining feature is the ability to move value without moving currency, primarily through netting or book transfers.[214] They often rely upon personal connections.[215] They tend to work like this: an immigrant living in, for instance, the United States, can go to a trusted dealer and give the individual $250 to send back to the immigrant's mother living in, say, India. The dealer then contacts a dealer in India, who physically hands $250 to the immigrant's mother. The transaction between the two dealers amounts to ledger entries. Occasionally the two dealers may transfer money between them to even outstanding balances. But no actual transfer of money takes place at the time of each individual remittance.

These systems are fairly widespread: the International Monetary Fund and the World Bank estimate that the total amount of money flowing through them numbers in the tens of billions of dollars.[216] India alone estimates that up to half of its economy (roughly equivalent to the entire Canadian economy) goes through this type of system. Pakistan puts its national total at around $7 billion.[217] Although the extent of the alternative remittance system in the United States is unknown, in 2004 the Inter-American Development Bank put the total remittances just from Latin American immigrants at approximately $30 billion.

Alternative remittance systems are attractive: they are reliable and efficient and available 24 hours a day, seven days a week. With minimal paperwork, they offer anonymity and cost less than formal banking. In the United Kingdom, for instance, where Western Union would charge £10 to send just £50 to

---

* Various treatments of the subject point to the end of the Cold War (and the drying up of funds to insurgent groups) as the impetus for increasing links to the drug industry. *See, e.g.,* Rex A. Hudson, *A Global Overview of Narcotics-Funded Terrorist and Other Extremist Groups* (Library of Congress Report, May 2002), available at www.loc.gov/rr; *see also Moving Target*, ECONOMIST (U.S. Edition), Sept. 14, 2002 (discussing al Qaeda's use of drug trafficking); Terrence Henry, *Al Qaeda's Resurgence: The Ever Resilient Terrorist Group Continues to Adapt – and Is Rapidly Breeding a Full-Fledged Movement*, ATLANTIC MONTHLY, June 1, 2004, at 54 (reporting al Qaeda's drug activities in Kandahar, Afghanistan as yielding some $24 million per year). *See also* Thomas Catan & Michael Peel, *U.S. Suspects al-Qaeda African Diamond Link*, FIN. TIMES (London), June 30, 2004, at 11. Frank Wolf, the chair of the House Commerce-Justice-State and Judiciary Appropriations Committee, expressed surprise that the September 11 Commission would be skeptical of such a link, and said that he had seen "pretty definite" evidence that it exists. *Id.* As a result, to head off increasing public criticism that the diamond trade provided a rich source of income to terrorist organizations, the World Diamond Council adopted a system of warranties. Mark Huband, *"Conflict" Diamonds Spur Code of Practice*, FIN. TIMES (London), Oct. 30, 2002, at 13.

Bangladesh, hawaladars charge only £0.50.[218] They also offer a way for customers to circumvent limits in currency exchange regulations.[219] And remittances are becoming an increasingly important source of money for poorer regions, where formal banking systems have yet to be established. Wealthy countries are estimated to send $1\frac{1}{2}$ times the total in formal government foreign aid through individuals' remittances.[220]

Significant variation exists among individual dealers. In some cases, they keep better records than commercial banks, share them more readily, and carefully screen customers. In others, the dealers' record keeping, amenability to government oversight, and due diligence fall somewhat short of the formal banking standard. One important consideration in the following discussion on counterterrorist financial legislation is whether it has been counterproductive. The presence of incentives to further cloak operations and keep minimal records only reduces the state's ability to trace money through the system – an objective becoming increasingly important as alternative remittance systems become the preferred mode of transferring terrorist funds.

Measures After September 11

In the abrupt recasting of the US antiterrorist framework in the fall of 2001, concern about the funding of terrorist operations swept through the federal government. Three of the five subsequent National Security Strategy documents addressed the issue.[221] And although the National Money Laundering Strategies had previously omitted discussion of terrorist finance, from 2002 on it became a central focus of the report.[222]

Gone was the lethargy that previously marked the administrative realm. The Department of Justice immediately created what became the Terrorist Financing Unit to coordinate a "national effort to prosecute terrorist financing." The FBI established a Financial Review Group to centralize the investigation into the money funding the September 11 attacks. Renamed the Terrorist Financing Operations Section (TFOS) and housed in the FBI's counterterrorist division, the unit included staff from Customs, the IRS, banking regulators, FinCEN, and the Office of Foreign Assets Control. TFOS was the first single-office coordinating effort to deal with terrorist finance.[223] In addition to it, the FBI ramped up its joint terrorism task forces (JTTFs), first created in 1980, by doubling their number after September 11 and establishing a national JTTF in Washington, D.C. The Departments of Homeland Security, Immigration and Customs Enforcement, and the IRS Criminal Investigative Division subsequently took part in JTTF meetings, which increasingly focused on terrorist finance.

Other organizations followed suit. The CIA formed a new section focused on terrorist financing. The FBI, the National Security Agency, the Department of Defense, and the CIA all participated, with the aim of collecting intelligence, understanding financial networks, finding terrorist money, and disrupting operations. Immediately following September 11, the Financial Crimes Enforcement Network set up a Financial Institutions Hotline (1-866-556-3974), so that the banking sector could report to law enforcement any suspicious transactions in which terrorist activity might be involved.[224] Treasury formed the Financial Action Task Force to identify and prioritize which groups should fall subject to blocking orders. In March 2003, Treasury created a new Executive Office for Terrorist Financing and Financial Crimes,[225] which works with other agencies at Treasury and other executive branch agencies, as well as with the private sector and foreign governments, to prevent terrorists from taking advantage of the international financial system.

Despite the incessant "Kumbayaa" refrain emanating from federal corridors, however, in many instances cooperation proved short-lived. Perhaps the best example of this situation is Operation Green Quest. US Customs created the program to identify patterns in counterfeiting, credit card fraud, drug trafficking, cash smuggling, illicit charities, and formal and alternative financial institutions.[226] The bureaucratic barriers – at least for the moment – appeared to come down, as prosecutors from Justice and investigators from IRS, Customs, the FBI, and other agencies came together in common cause.[227] But the cowboy-like approach of the new entity, underscored by a series of raids in March 2002, quickly alienated federal agencies, civil rights organizations, and the US Muslim community. Green Quest's expansionist tendencies raised hackles: in January 2003, the program doubled in size, utilizing some 300 agents and analysts nationwide. Three months later, it followed Customs into the Department of Homeland Security (DHS) fold. The Department of Justice (DoJ), keen to rein in the maverick organization, objected. Michael Chertoff, chief of the Criminal Division (and, as fate would have it, future Secretary of the Department of Homeland Security), and Deputy Attorney General Larry Thompson pushed the White House to relocate Green Quest at the DoJ. The DHS, however, angrily pushed back and alleged that the FBI was trying to sabotage investigations by refusing to turn over information.[228]

Bickering between the two agencies ultimately led, in May 2003, to the signing of a formal memorandum of agreement between the Attorney General and the Secretary of the DHS. In a nutshell, the DoJ won, becoming the lead federal law enforcement agency in the national effort to interrupt terrorist finance[229] – and leaving the DHS to play ball according to the rules set by the FBI.[230]

The DHS, however, did not take defeat lying down. Although the Memorandum of Understanding required that Operation Green Quest cease as of June 30, 2003, and that the DHS investigate only matters related to terrorist finance with the consent of the FBI, by July 2003 Immigration and Customs Enforcement had launched its own initiative: Operation Cornerstone.[231] Its basic premise was to find and eliminate financial system vulnerabilities that either attract criminals or provide a target for terrorists. The DHS called it "a new financial crimes investigative initiative," whose aim was to "[i]dentify vulnerabilities in financial systems through which criminals launder their illicit proceeds, bring the criminals to justice and work to eliminate the vulnerabilities." The DHS also announced a new initiative meant to build bridges with private industry: SHARE (Systematic Homeland Approach to Reducing Exploitation).[232] In addition to these initiatives, DHS complained to Congress that the memorandum hurt its ability to conduct investigations into financial crime.

The Senate responded by directing the Government Accountability Office (GAO) to evaluate the impact of the memorandum on the Secret Service. Dodging the administrative bullet, the GAO responded that since the agreement related only to the FBI and Immigration and Customs Enforcement (ICE), questions involving the Secret Service were irrelevant. As for the other claims, the GAO could not determine that ICE's mission or role in investigating nonterrorism-related crimes had been harmed.[233] The GAO also noted, albeit with politically guarded administrative language, that the Memorandum of Understanding had served to make things worse.[234] The report warned, "Our interviews with FBI and ICE officials...indicated that long-standing jurisdictional and operational disputes regarding terrorist financing investigations may have strained interagency relationships to some degree and could pose an obstacle in fully integrating investigative efforts."[235]

Administrative infighting aside, the fact that federal agencies cared enough to fight over these new initiatives illustrates the focus placed on interrupting financial flows. The executive, however, was not alone in its response. The USA PATRIOT Act and the wide-ranging powers contained therein, on the one hand, allowed the federal government access to private financial information and, on the other, gave it the ability to suspend property rights without reference to the judiciary. Both the regulatory elements of the statute and the provisions giving the state broader surveillance authorities were of consequence. Post-9/11 changes to the IEEPA also bear discussion.

The USA PATRIOT Act: Financial Provisions. Just two months before the passage of the USA PATRIOT Act, Treasury Secretary Paul O'Neill had announced that he would ease the US regulatory regime and depend upon international cooperation, rather than threats of sanctions, to combat illicit money flows.[236] He had also tried to stop the National Security Council's proposed terrorist asset tracking center.[237] The USA PATRIOT Act turned the administration's policy 180 degrees. The sheer breadth of the measures taken – and, indeed, the fact that an entire section was focused on antiterrorist finance – emphasized its centrality to the state's counterterrorist strategy.[238] Simultaneously, the statute collapsed the anti-money laundering and counterterrorist financial enforcement regimes, crashing together the three streams that had previously flowed into antiterrorist operations.[239] The length of the statute and the rate at which it rushed through Congress meant that, even years later, the private sector was still struggling to come to grips with its implications.[240]

The USA PATRIOT Act made changes in four key financial areas: it broadened executive powers under the International Emergency Economic Powers Act, it significantly expanded the state's regulatory regime, it strengthened forfeiture powers and shifted the burden of proof, and it introduced broad extraterritorial authority. The legislation also required Treasury to submit a series of reports, most of which contemplated the introduction of further measures.[241]

In the first area, the USA PATRIOT Act made three important changes to the IEEPA.[242] It amended the previous statute to allow the executive branch to submit classified evidence *in camera* and *ex parte*. It allowed the state to block assets during the course of an investigation – which in practical terms meant indefinitely and thus gave the government an important bargaining tool to use against an accused during an investigation. The statute included neither humanitarian exceptions nor provision to set funds aside for legal defense. And it authorized the president, "when the United States is engaged in armed hostilities or has been attacked by a foreign country or foreign nationals," to "confiscate any property, subject to the jurisdiction of the United States, of any foreign person, foreign organization, or foreign country that he determines has planned, authorized, aided, or engaged in such hostilities or attacks against the United States."[243] The statute thus required neither any link between the assets and any particular act of violence nor any proportionality between the amount of property seized and the crime. The language also had the significant effect of removing the judiciary from the proceedings altogether, concentrating power in the executive.

Perhaps the most important – and certainly the most extensive – shift came in the second area: increased regulatory powers. The USA PATRIOT Act required banks, savings associations, credit unions, securities broker-dealers, mutual funds, futures commission merchants, and introducing brokers to enhance their customer identification measures.[244] They had to use the full and accurate name of each customer and to record their date of birth and Social Security and passport numbers.[245] Such lists, which had to be maintained for five years, made it easier to link up different accounts and transactions at different entities.

These requirements fell just short of the "know your customer" proposal defeated two and a half years before. *All* financial institutions in the United States (the above, plus casinos, money services businesses, mutual funds, and operators of credit card systems), as well as numerous businesses (insurance companies; unregistered investment companies; investment advisors; commodity trading advisors; dealers in precious metals, stones, or jewels; travel agents; vehicle sellers; and all those involved in real estate closings and settlements) became required to institute anti-money laundering programs.[246]

The statute also expanded the number of entities required to file Suspicious Activity Reports.[247] Where the Bank Secrecy Act of 1970 had required banks and credit unions to report $10,000 or more in cash transfers, now "any person who is engaged in a trade or business" that has received more than $10,000 in cash must file a SAR. Given that $10,000 in the 1970s is the equivalent of $2,625 today, this means that, together with the documentation that accompanies credit card purchases, the government can now trace a significant portion of consumers' buying habits and purchases.[248]

The statute both required nonfinancial trades or businesses to file currency transaction reports with FinCEN[249] and brought all unlicensed money-transmitting businesses into the regulatory tent.[250] The legislation further demanded that all financial institutions behave with due diligence in completing transactions that bear a resemblance to money laundering schemes.[251] Entities with correspondent accounts also have to apply due diligence procedures to detect and report money laundering activity.[252]

Concerned that offshore banking, subject to minimal supervision, provided terrorists and criminals with too much anonymity (making it difficult to trace the proceeds of crime), Congress amended the Bank Secrecy Act and gave the Secretary of the Treasury discretionary authority to place restrictions on foreign jurisdictions, institutions, or types of account if they pose a "primary money laundering concern" to the United States.[253] (No terrorist link need be found.) Treasury could require financial institutions to maintain additional records for certain transactions, to identify foreign beneficial owners of accounts located at US financial institutions, and to identify customers using foreign accounts at banks within the United States. (Treasury has used these powers only twice since September 11, neither of which related directly to terrorism.[254]) The statute essentially forbids correspondent accounts – defined broadly to include most relationships that a US financial entity can have with a foreign financial institution – with shell banks (unregulated entities with no physical presence in any jurisdiction), where such banks are not recognized or regulated by depository institutions.[255]

Such rules serve a dual purpose: they alert Treasury to possible criminal activity and provide law enforcement with a paper trail for use in investigations. To assist in the latter aim, Title III further allows Treasury to specify any region, entity, person, or account; financial institutions can then be required to search their records to determine whether they contained any information relevant to a suspect.[256] The legislation demands that entities report any positive matches within two weeks or, in an emergency, within two days. Law enforcement can then file a subpoena to obtain the data. Failure to disclose information opens individuals to criminal and civil penalties.

This power, used extensively after passage of the statute, quickly became known in some circles as a "Google search."[257]* The statute sets no bounds on who can make such requests, allowing everyone from law enforcement to the Postal Service to file to obtain information about any offense related to money laundering – a category that includes some 200 different crimes. This power immediately created a problem for banks, which were inundated with requests – often several each day, addressed to the wrong people, and vaguely worded. The American Bankers Association complained and said that Treasury should narrow the scope of the requests, create standardized forms, and specify the time period within which it needs the information to distinguish between urgent and nonurgent requests.

On November 19, 2002, only 15 days into the operation of this power, FinCEN announced a moratorium on requests made directly to financial institutions,[258] and inserted itself into the process, requiring a form from law

---

* Treasury issued regulations under this section on September 26, 2002, encouraging public/private cooperation and permitting the sharing of information between government agencies. 31 C.F.R. §§ 103.100, 103.110 (2002).

enforcement requesting customer account information and asserting that it relates to money laundering or terrorist investigations. FinCEN then would go to banks to obtain the information (making FinCEN, in effect, an information broker[259]). By 2003, FinCEN had supported more than 2,600 terrorism investigations and received more than 2,600 SARs on possible terrorist financing.[260] In that year, it forwarded such searches on 962 suspects, two-thirds of whom appeared to have no relation to terrorism.[261]

The third significant alteration introduced by the USA PATRIOT Act centered on expanding the list of predicate offenses for the freezing and forfeiture of property. New "specified unlawful activities" for criminal money laundering provisions include foreign criminal offenses, foreign public corruption, extraditable offenses, some export control offenses, computer offenses, customs and firearm offenses, and felony violations of the Foreign Agents Registration Act of 1938.[262] Foreign predicate offenses occurring inside the United States fall under the new rubric.[263] The aim of adding these offenses was to prevent corrupt foreign officials from taking advantage of the US banking system.[264] The statute also includes illegal money remission business[265] and bulk cash smuggling of greater than $10,000 across domestic borders.[266] Penalties include forfeiture of the amount smuggled plus up to five years' imprisonment. Where the money may not be available, the state can essentially bill the individual for the total – this is known as "value" forfeiture. There are also civil forfeiture penalties.

Although the statute does provide an opportunity for individuals to contest the forfeiture of assets, it shifts the burden of proof. A target can file a claim under the Federal Rules of Civil Procedure and assert an affirmative defense – either that the property is not subject to confiscation or that the owner is innocent. But the statute simultaneously allows the court to consider evidence otherwise inadmissible under the Federal Rules of Evidence, where the judiciary considers it reliable and compliance with the Federal Rules would jeopardize US national security. This provision places the onus on individuals whose assets have been confiscated to demonstrate that the state should not have seized their property or that they are innocent owners – while simultaneously allowing evidence to be used against them that normally would be impermissible in a court of law.

The fourth way in which the USA PATRIOT Act shifted the law centers on extraterritorial jurisdiction. The legislation brings within reach of the judiciary foreign persons laundering money in the United States, foreign banks, and other entities.[267] The statute empowers the courts to seize assets pending trial for use in any final judgment. It also amends the existing forfeiture law to give the government control over assets deposited overseas.[268] The mechanism allows the state, where a foreign bank has a correspondent account in the United States, to seize that account, requiring the bank to debit the terrorist account located overseas. Critically, the state could block such assets during an investigation. Although meant to address an emergency, the state could exercise the procedures indefinitely – a possibility that quickly became a source of much concern. In cases of a potential conflict of laws between foreign jurisdictions and the United States, the statute grants the Attorney General, as opposed to the court, discretion to determine the most appropriate course of action. The same section requires US and foreign banks to maintain and make certain records available to the courts, with severe penalties for failure to comply.

USA PATRIOT Act: Surveillance Provisions. Although part of the USA PATRIOT Act specifically grants the federal government the authority to go after the financial underpinnings of terrorist organizations, other sections of the legislation give the government broad surveillance authorities. These are relevant here because, as recognized by senior civil servants in the United Kingdom,

Financial investigations are information-intensive. They involve both public and private sector material, for example taxation records and bank account information, which demonstrate money movements, together with any relevant information as to lifestyle.... The investigator seeks to discover where money came from, who obtained it, when it was received and where it was stored, deposited, or transformed into other forms of property.[269]

Although in Chapter 4 I go into more detail on these provisions, one instrument figures largely in the effort to track terrorist finance as well. National Security Letters (NSLs), a form of administrative subpoena and one for which no warrant is required, allow the executive branch to serve certain institutions with, literally, a letter, demanding certain records. Under the USA PATRIOT Act and subsequent legislation, the specific individual served with such a subpoena is barred – at the risk of criminal penalties – from discussing it with anyone. By 2006, the executive branch was issuing approximately tens of thousands of such letters – each of which could obtain millions of records – per year to a wide range of institutions, banking and otherwise. By this time the program was arousing considerable controversy.

The impact of NSLs on the financial industry is not insubstantial: In June 2006, the *New York Times* reported that just after September 11 the Bush administration had served an NSL on a Belgian banking cooperative called Swift that routes approximately $6 trillion per day between thousands of financial institutions worldwide.[270] The surveillance program collected information on international transactions, including those entering and leaving the United States. The Central Intelligence Agency, under Treasury's guidance, ran the program. At the outset, lawyers at the Department of Justice and Treasury debated whether the operation had to comply with the laws restricting government access to private financial records. In the end, they decided that it did not: Swift was defined not as a bank or financial institution, but because it routed transactions, as a messaging service.[271]

The Swift banking incident highlights an important legislative weakness: absent any statutory reporting requirement, the executive branch simply did not inform Congress about the existence of the program. Senator Arlen Specter, the Republican chairman of the Senate Judiciary Committee, later objected that the administration began telling members of Congress only after the

New York Times began making inquiries.[272] Representative Sue Kelly, the Republican chairwoman of the House Financial Services oversight panel, confirmed that the administration had failed to brief the appropriate committees.[273] The Democratic Representative Barney Frank, who said that the administration had offered to brief him only after the *New York Times* inquiry, declined the invitation because the administration had also said that Frank would not, following the briefing, be allowed to discuss the matter.[274] So the legislature, which was not even told about the secret program (despite laws to the contrary), was barred from publicly doing anything about it even when its members were finally informed.

The Swift banking operation was not the only financial surveillance program in place. The US government, for instance, reached agreements with companies to provide the state with access to ATM transactions, credit card records, and Western Union wire payments.[275] But it was by far the largest effort underway. Two years into its operation, Swift officials, concerned that they were breaking the law, tried to end the program. The US executive intervened, and the program continued with some new controls, including an auditing firm to verify that the searches conducted were based on intelligence leads about terrorist suspects.[276] According to Swift, the range of information made available to the United States narrowed.

When the story broke in the *New York Times*, the White House went on the offensive, immediately accusing the newspaper of hurting the United States – and helping terrorists. President Bush stated, "We are at war with a bunch of people who want to hurt the United States of America. And for people to leak that program and for a newspaper to publish it does great harm to the United States.... [T]he fact that a newspaper disclosed [that we are trying to follow the money] it makes it harder to win this war on terror."[277] Vice President Dick Cheney took a similar line: "What I find most disturbing is the fact that some of the news media take it upon themselves to disclose vital national security programs, thereby making it more difficult for us to prevent future attacks against the American people."[278] Dana Perino, the deputy White House press secretary said, "We know the terrorists pay attention to our strategy to fight them, and now have another piece of the puzzle of how we are fighting them."[279] John Snow, Secretary of the Treasury, wrote, "The decision by the *New York Times* to disclose the Terrorist Finance Tracking Program ... was irresponsible and harmful to the security of Americans and freedom-loving people worldwide."[280] Representative Michael Oxley of Ohio, Republican chairman of the House Financial Services Committee, accused the newspaper of "treason."[281] Officials defended the program, saying that it provided "a unique and powerful window into the operations of terrorist networks."[282] It led to the capture of Riduan Isamuddin, also known as Hambali, who was believed to have coordinated the 2002 Bali bombing; as well as of Uzair Paracha, who, prosecutors say, agreed to launder $200,000 for an al Qaeda operative in Pakistan.[283] But many officials also expressed unease and strong concern about the program's power to invade people's privacy.[284]

The International Emergency Economic Powers Act. Less than two weeks after the attacks, under the authority of the IEEPA, President Bush issued Executive Order 13,224 – an initiative he proudly referred to as "draconian."[285] It essentially replaced a criminal law standard with an intelligence norm. It also made it illegal for anyone to attempt to alleviate any humanitarian suffering resulting from the seizure of assets.[286]

The instrument begins innocuously enough: it declares a national emergency and creates a Specially Designated Global Terrorist list, blocking "all property and interests in property" of designated terrorists and individuals contributing material support to terrorism.* This list includes al Qaeda and its associated groups, Osama bin Laden, and his supporters. The order provides a list of specified foreign persons whom the Secretary of State has determined pose a risk to national security, foreign policy, the economy, or US citizens.

From there, however, the order becomes considerably more extreme: it incorporates a list of persons the Secretary of the Treasury has determined to be acting for or on behalf of the persons listed under the order (or subject to it) or assisting in, sponsoring, or providing financial, material, or technological support for those listed – and *any persons Treasury determines to be otherwise associated with those listed.* Thus, any business that has not ceased to interact with the listed entities can itself be listed and have its assets frozen. Also, mere association – and not demonstrated material support – can be sufficient for the state to confiscate all property. Moreover, once property is blocked, the Executive Order makes it illegal for anyone to deal in the blocked assets or for any US entity to try to avoid or conspire to avoid the prohibitions – *or to make donations to relieve human suffering to persons listed under the order or determined to be subject to it.* Any foreign banks that refuse to provide information to the US government risk the freezing of their assets and transactions within the United States.

Executive Order 13,224 centers on two goals: stopping the money flow to al Qaeda and convincing the public that something is being done.[287] In regard to

---

* Thereafter, the White House continued the emergency on an annual basis. The first extension was issued September 18, 2003. Notice of Sept. 18, 2003, Continuation of the National Emergency with Respect to Persons Who Commit, Threaten to Commit, or Support Terrorism, 68 Fed. Reg. 55,189 (Sept. 22, 2003). The second was issued September 24, 2004. Message from the President of the United Sates transmitting Notification that the National Emergency Declared with Respect to Persons who commit, threaten to commit, or support terrorism is to continue in effect beyond Sept. 23, 2004, pursuant to 50 U.S.C. 1622(d), H.R. Doc. No. 108–217, at 3 (2004); Continuation of the National Emergency with Respect to Persons who Commit, Threaten to Commit, or Support Terrorism, H.R. Doc. No. 108–217, at 1. Additionally, on January 23, 1995, in Executive Order 12,947, President Clinton declared a national emergency under the IEEPA for a threat to the Middle East; this was modified August 20, 1998, by Executive Order 13,099 (which added four people, including bin Laden). Exec. Order No. 12,947, 60 Fed. Reg. 5079 (Jan. 23, 1995); Exec. Order No. 13,099, 63 Fed. Reg. 45,167 (Aug. 25, 1998). President Bush continued this emergency on January 16, 2004, for another year. Notice of Jan. 16, 2004, Continuation of the National Emergency With Respect to Terrorists who Threaten to Disrupt the Middle East Peace Process, 69 Fed. Reg. 2,991 (Jan. 21, 2004), available at www.whitehouse.gov.

the former, the Treasury's Office of Foreign Assets Control could already target Osama bin Laden and al Qaeda under Executive Order 12,947.[288] Executive Order 13,224, however, both divorces the terrorist list from the Middle East peace process and also makes it illegal for *all* US actors, and not just financial institutions, to engage in business with the listed entities.

In regard to the second goal, the signing of this document turned into a public relations exercise *extraordinaire*. On September 24, 2001, President Bush announced, "At 12:01 a.m. this morning a major thrust of our war on terrorism began with the stroke of a pen. Today, we have launched a strike on the financial foundation of the global terror network."[289] He went on to say, "Just to show you how insidious these terrorists are, they oftentimes use nice-sounding, nongovernmental organizations as fronts for their activities. We have targeted three such NGOs."[290] Bush threw the gauntlet: "If you do business with terrorists, if you support or sponsor them, you will not do business with the United States of America."[291] Paul O'Neill echoed this sentiment:

> If you have any involvement in the financing of the al Qaida organization, you have two choices: cooperate in this fight, or we will freeze your U.S. assets; we will punish you for providing the resources that make these evil acts possible. We will succeed in starving the terrorists of funding and shutting down the institutions that support or facilitate terrorism.[292]

Despite these bellicose remarks, the administrative structure designed to implement the measures fell short. An Office of Foreign Assets Control (OFAC) report in April 2004 showed only 4 staff members dedicated to terrorist finance – as opposed to 12 people enforcing trade embargos on Cuba.* Although there was a sudden surge of names on the list, the average number added monthly quickly dwindled.[†] By May 2002, the Department of Treasury had blocked the assets of 210 groups and people, freezing $34 million. Allied countries blocked another $82 million.[293] On average, the executive added 6 people a month thereafter, bringing the total to 397 by January 2005.[294]

---

* Between 1990 and 2003, only 93 terrorism-related investigations took place at OFAC, as opposed to some 10,683 Cuba-related investigations during the same time period, and fines for Cuba-related offenses amounted to $8 million dollars, whereas those charged with terrorism paid only $9,425. Mark Frank & Richard Lapper, *U.S. Squeeze Angers Cubans: Bush Clampdown is Seen as Blow to Family Ties*, Fin. Times (London), May 10, 2004, at 4.

† The initial register froze the assets of 27 people and groups suspected of terrorist finance. Exec. Order No. 13,224, 66 Fed. Reg. 49,079 (Sept. 25, 2001), available at www.treas.gov/offices/. *See also* Mike Allen & Steven Mufson, *U.S. Seizes Assets of Three Islamic Groups*, Wash. Post, Dec. 5, 2001, at A1. Of these, 12 were individuals and 15 were organizations. Less than a month later the administration added another 39 names to the list. U.S. Dep't of the Treas., Office of Foreign Assets Control, *Terrorism: What You Need to Know About U.S. Sanctions* (2005), available at www.treas.gov/offices. *See also* Joseph Kahn & Judith Miller, *U.S. Freezes More Accounts: Saudi and Pakistani Assets Cited for Ties to Bin Laden*, N.Y. Times, Oct. 13, 2001, at A1; Richard Wolffe, *U.S. Freezes Assets Linked to Terror Network*, Fin. Times (London), Oct. 13, 2001, at 1. Roughly a fortnight later another 22 names issued, and within five days 62 more individuals and entities found their assets blocked. The pace continued, but the number of entities added each time diminished. By May 2002, 210 names and groups found themselves on the list.

Not all of those on the list relate to September 11: included on it, for instance, are the Continuity IRA, the Loyalist Volunteer Force, GRAPO (the First of October Anti-Fascist Resistance Group), the Communist Party of the Philippines, and the Communist Party of Nepal. The bulk, however, bear some link to Arab states or the Islamic faith. According to the *Washington Post*, by September 2002 the government was monitoring more than 500 hundred Arab and Muslim businesses in the United States.[295] It was this scrutiny, and the federal government's loose standards, that led to a drop in contributions to Islamic charities.[296] Treasury issued "voluntary best practices guidelines" containing a thinly veiled threat: they called for "rigorous, self-imposed financial oversight; high levels of disclosure and transparency; and immediate severing of all ties to any foreign recipient associated with a terrorist organization." The document continued, "Although wholly voluntary, if implemented with sufficient resources and diligently adhered to in practice, the guidelines offer a means by which charities can protect themselves against terrorist abuse, enhance donor confidence, and significantly reduce the risk of a blocking order."[297] The standards the government used, and the basis on which it made its decisions, fall short of the democratic norms it otherwise endorses.

THE EROSION OF COMPLEX RIGHTS

Although financial counterterrorist laws may be causing an incremental erosion of areas already subject to substantial government control or regulation, they have infringed on a broad range of rights – free speech, religion, privacy, and property – all important to the overall health of a democracy. They have caused other political and humanitarian damage as well.

Consider the United States. In the First Amendment to the Constitution, free speech includes the solicitation of funds, long considered a necessary constituent for the effective flow of information and the ability of citizens to advocate different positions.[298] But what about contributing funds to groups with an expressive component? None of the central First Amendment cases address contributions to groups *outside* the United States that have a mix of legitimate and illegitimate functions. As a statutory matter, as I have noted, the judiciary has shown great deference to the executive in this area. Yet the measures have had a practical and detrimental effect. Contributions to religious and charitable Islamic organizations, and interactions with Islamic businesses, have slowed. Islamic publications have seen the sudden withdrawal of advertisers.[299] The findings from the Casey Foundation survey in respect to mosques' loss of funds, and Louise Cainkar's report about the Islamic community's "fears of the federal government"[300] are borne out by statistics: the Treasury Department, through April 2005, lists 743 people and 947 organizations with frozen assets. Of these, 98 percent (725) of the people and 96 percent (907) of the organizations appear to be Muslim or Arab.[301] Because of the reduced standard of proof required to freeze assets – namely, mere association – a number of prominent banks have adopted internal policies that require employees to refuse interaction with Islamic and Arab enterprises.[302]

As for freedom of religion, many Muslims have found it more difficult to fulfill their religious duty to support Islamic charity work.[303] Although this may not be a constitutional issue, it does bring the state into conflict with well-established religious beliefs.

Privacy also, long read into the penumbra of the rights afforded by the Constitution, has been affected by these provisions. Under Title III of the USA PATRIOT Act, any federal agency can now obtain sensitive and private data without any subpoena or judicial intervention, as long as it is investigating one of some 200 possible offenses. Admittedly, subpoenas themselves do not provide a particularly meaningful protection for privacy: they require only that the information be relevant to the investigation. (In the next chapter, I look in more detail at, particularly, administrative subpoenas, which issue in a range of areas outside the National Security Letters I have discussed.) Nevertheless, the antiterrorist finance provisions have had at least an incremental impact on individual privacy rights.

Ironically, it was precisely because of privacy concerns that many of the provisions adopted *after* September 11 – and marketed as central to the administration's counterterrorist effort – had previously been rejected as part of the anti-money laundering scheme. David Aufhauser, General Counsel at Treasury, for instance, announced that with 24-hour surveillance the state could "home in on and bomb terrorists on the basis of a clue as tiny as a tyre-track in a desert." He told an audience of international bankers "that they should use the same sort of technology on their customers."[304] In January 2002, Assistant Attorney General Michael Chertoff notified the Senate Banking Committee that, in relation to the USA PATRIOT Act's new information-gathering powers, "[t]he principal provisions of the Right to Financial Privacy Act no longer apply to letter requests by a government authority authorized to conduct investigations or intelligence analysis for purposes related to international terrorism."[305]

These provisions put banks in a difficult position: customers, in the absence of a subpoena, might mount a legal challenge to the bank's decision to hand information to the government. How could the institutions ensure the security of customers' financial data?[306] On the other hand, there were strict penalties for the failure to turn information over when requested. And it was bad for business to be associated with terrorist groups.

Many of the new powers, moreover, had to be tailored to specific sectors, creating a dense and complex web of federal powers. Treasury released hundreds of pages of regulations. To assist in complying with the statute, a cottage industry sprang up that further burdened the right to privacy. For example, Bridger Tracker Online 5.5 software takes the identification requirements in §326 of the USA PATRIOT Act and allows banks to compare their lists and account or transaction information against more than 20 different federal watch lists. By January 2005, more than 80 percent of US banks used the program. The company boasts that the software helps institutions better "know your customers."[307] Nevertheless, its accuracy could be presented only in relative terms: "With its sophisticated and proprietary fuzzy logic, Bridger Insight yields false positive rates three times lower than competitive products."[308] The upshot of these changes was that, as privacy rights narrowed, Treasury became privy to everyday financial transactions, and private companies became an extension of the state's counterterrorism efforts.[309]

These developments are at odds with the importance of privacy not just to the liberal, democratic state but also to international banking and finance.[310] In the past, the idea of third-party records as being voluntary applied because individuals willingly relinquished them. But now, the reporting requirements for financial institutions curtail the judicial assumption of voluntariness.[311]*

Property may be the most significant right affected by antiterrorist finance measures, though it is often left off the litany of rights frequently associated with counterterrorist concerns. As with the other rights involved, I am not here making a constitutional claim, and I recognize that the inroads into property rights in this area may be incremental. The regulatory state is, after all, in part characterized by its regulation of the economic sector, a task that affects a range of financial transactions. In respect to the regulation of property, the government has the authority to block assets during the pendency of an investigation. Where probable cause exists, the government can seize substantial portions of a suspect's property. (In such a case, controversy frequently centers on different rights: thus, rules allowing the state to seize guns may be discussed under the right to bear arms – not as an aspect of property rights.)

Nevertheless, and although title may not be lost under Executive Order 13,224, the government *can* impose indefinite forfeiture. Under the USA PATRIOT Act, the state can block assets "during the pendency of an investigation," on whose length no limits are set. The courts have held that indefinite forfeiture does not constitute a taking, as it does not permanently vest property in the United States.[312]

Although I have used an American model to make the point, in the United Kingdom, too, standards have been lowered. The Terrorism Act of 2000, for instance, employs a civil law standard that deviates from the criminal law requirement. The state can divest individuals suspected, but not convicted, of terrorist activity of their property.

Underlying my argument is concern that if antiterrorist finance is designed to promote democratic values, attention must be drawn to where these values

---

* In 1976, *U.S. v. Miller* [425 U.S. 435 (1976)] reaffirmed that customer bank account records are *not* the private papers of the customer. An individual has neither ownership nor possession of such records, reasoned the Court; therefore, the records are simply the "business records of the bank." This line of argument and the precedents that have developed it extend back through the eighteenth century. The crucial element in this traditional view is that the individual, lacking a "proprietary" interest in a bank's records of his or her account, has no legal right to challenge access to those records by government or anyone else. The Privacy Protection Study Comm'n, Personal Privacy in an Information Society: The Report of the Privacy Protection Study Comm'n ch. 9, at 4 (1977), available at www.epic.org; *see* WILLIAM BLACKSTONE, 3 COMMENTARIES ON THE LAWS OF ENGLAND 382 (1854); S.F.C. MILSOM, HISTORICAL FOUNDATIONS OF THE COMMON LAW 372 (1969).

are not served. Well-established doctrines of the legitimate right of government to restrict free speech, narrow privacy rights, or deprive individuals of their property are not inconsistent with this approach.

In addition to the rights affected by antiterrorist finance measures, three other developments that have accompanied antiterrorist initiatives undermine a democracy's health: the elimination of intent, the use of secret evidence, and the stigma associated with designation. None of these developments occurs as a result of routine regulatory or administrative procedures.

The Elimination of Intent

Even as antiterrorist finance provisions affect property rights, intent has all but dropped from the equation. Executive Order 13,224, for instance, does not include any requirement that the individual involved *knowingly* assist terrorist activity. But how can the state infer intent from mere associational links? Unlike drug laws, where possession may be the trigger for asset forfeiture, more nebulous accusations appear sufficient for the executive to deny individuals access to their assets.

In the case of the Benevolence International Foundation, for instance, the FBI claimed that its founder, Enaam Arnaout, had links to bin Laden in the 1980s. Considering the $3.5 billion US aid package for mujahideen in Afghanistan at the same time, these links hardly appear to be adequate justification for the expropriation of all of Arnaout's resources. Indeed, the state never was able to bring criminal charges on these grounds; instead, it simply suspended his access to his property until it could bring suit on different charges.

The standard is low. Although people may be involved in raising money for Islamic causes, and may share a common religion, and may even disagree with US foreign policy, they are not necessarily terrorists. Banks, moreover, carry out business with numerous customers, whose behavior they cannot hope to regulate outside their direct relationship. There is the example of Al Taqwa, a financial network based in Switzerland and the Bahamas, that the Bush administration alleged had ties to terrorism. The administration claimed that Hamas maintained accounts there, that in October 2000 Al Taqwa extended a clandestine line of credit to "a close associate" of Osama bin Laden, and that the chairman of the bank provided financial assistance to bin Laden and al Qaeda in late September 2001.[313] On November 7, 2001, Treasury froze the assets of organizations and individuals associated with Al Taqwa.[314] When the Swiss Banking Commission audited the firm of Youssef Nada, who owned al Taqwa, however, it found no evidence of money laundering or of other organizations using the bank as a front company.[315]

Efforts to target such businesses inflict real economic costs: Arab Bank, the third largest Arab lender, first established a New York office in 1982; but, in February 2005, the bank cited the "litigation environment in the US" as the reason why it would begin shutting down its US operations. The bank claims that it was unaware that payments from a Saudi charity in the West Bank and

Gaza Strip were going to the families of suicide bombers. Shukry Bishra, the chief banking officer, stated, "We have zero role in determining who receives the payments and why that beneficiary received the payments." He suggested that the US government used the courts "to target Arab individuals, banks, and governments."[316]

This argument does not, however, carry weight in the prevailing political attitude in Washington. President Bush stated in November 2001, "We fight the terrorists and we fight all of those who give them aid. America has a message for the nations of the world: . . . If you feed a terrorist or fund a terrorist, you're a terrorist, and you will be held accountable by the United States and our friends."[317] Nearly two years later he reiterated,

I want you to know, the doctrine that says, "Either you're with us, or you're with the terrorists," it still stands, and we enforce it every single day. If you harbor a terrorist, if you feed a terrorist, if you finance a terrorist, you're just as guilty as the killers who struck America on September the 11th, and we'll hold you accountable as well.[318]

Although this language may be effective political rhetoric, as legal doctrine it leaves something to be desired. There is an enormous difference between making contributions that eventually flow to terrorist activity and actually, intentionally, funding such activity. By the Bush administration's own admission, the shift to eliminating intent gives the state unprecedented power to go after private assets.[319] The courts, moreover, have been loath to interfere in this realm, seeing it as firmly the executive's.

It is important at this point to distinguish between punishing individuals aiding designated state sponsors of terrorism (or giving direct aid to individuals engaged in terrorism) and the forfeiture or blocking of assets of an individual merely associated with someone suspected of terrorism. In the former instance, an individual does not need to share a *mens rea* – that is, the guilty state of mind – to be found in violation of the law. The transfer of assets to the named state or individual constitutes a crime. In the latter instance, however, one does not need to have actually helped further terrorist offenses, but can lose access to one's assets merely through association. This provision is equivalent to saying that, once a terrorist state has been so designated, if one knows anyone of that nationality one could lose one's home – and is as preposterous. If the actual funding of terrorists or terrorist organizations is not to be a necessary condition to freeze an individual's assets, mere association, without intent, seems a weak basis on which to seize or freeze them.

Secret Evidence and Due Process Concerns

The USA PATRIOT Act §106 explicitly amended the IEEPA to allow the executive to submit classified evidence *in camera* and *ex parte*.[320] The movement to the civil realm is important here: the courts have held that because terrorist financial freezing does not fall under criminal law, the defendant's claim to a Sixth Amendment right to confront his or her accusers does not apply.[321]

As a constitutional matter, strong arguments can be raised on both sides of the divide: on the one hand, it is well established that temporary and permanent aliens have a Fifth Amendment right to due process.[322] The Supreme Court has routinely held that the ability to confront witnesses and answer evidence is central to due process.[323] But a constitutional argument can be made to the contrary that, according to the Foreign Intelligence and Surveillance Act and IEEPA-related cases, the discretionary use of secret evidence is permitted: where the latter allows for it, the former demands it. Indeed, in the national security realm, the courts historically have been reluctant to interfere in such due process claims. The case of *Benevolence International Foundation, Inc. v. John Ashcroft* (2002), although decided on different grounds, cited precedent for allowing secret evidence.[324] In *Global Relief Foundation, Inc. v. Paul O'Neill* (2002), the court denied the plaintiff's motion not to allow *in camera* and *ex parte* proceedings, and suggested that just because the judiciary considers secret evidence does not mean that it relies exclusively on it.[325] The use of such information may be necessary where "acute national security concerns" are at issue. Many contend that terrorism is different from ordinary crime and requires some sort of mechanism whereby law enforcement can work with intelligence information.

The general rule appears to be that a court cannot dispose of the merits of a case on the basis of secret evidence.[326] Yet this principle is under attack. In antiterrorist finance cases it has brought since September 11, the government has not only asserted the right to secret evidence but also claims that it is entitled, on the strength of such evidence, to obtain summary judgment.[327] This concern about secret evidence is not peculiar, of course, to financial antiterrorist measures; it is a recurring theme in the counterterrorist initiatives taken, since September 11, by both the United States and the United Kingdom.

Aside from the purely legal question of whether secret evidence and *ex parte* proceedings can be used in antiterrorist finance efforts, the fact they are used suggests that it might be wise to maintain a higher standard than that employed in regulatory or administrative procedures. The risks of not doing so are significant – as the United Kingdom learned in the so-called Supergrasstrials in Northern Ireland. In the early 1980s, Britain attempted to crack down on terrorist suspects by allowing individuals to turn witness for the state: much of their secret evidence, which was used to convict scores of individuals, turned out, however, to arise from personal vindictiveness. Likewise, in the United States: the government detained Hany Kiareldeen, a Palestinian living in New Jersey, after an informant accused him of meeting with one of the individuals convicted in the 1993 World Trade Center bombings. When Kiareldeen realized that the main source of the information was his wife, with whom he was locked in a bitter child custody battle, he informed the judge, who began to question the evidence in more depth. The state released Kiareldeen.[328]

The problem of vindictiveness is not insurmountable: one possible solution, put forward in the Benevolence International Foundation memo, might be for the prosecution to issue a statement of undisputed facts, which can then be used to build the case and would give the defense the opportunity to counter the charges.[329] Nevertheless, the law as currently written incorporates no such protection.

Other concerns underscore the importance of maintaining a stronger due process standard. For example, the encroachment on property rights goes well beyond ordinary regulatory regimes, even as courts deny protections ordinarily connected with such invasive mechanisms in criminal law. Deferring to OFAC regulations, the judiciary has interpreted interest in property in its broadest sense: "an interest of any nature whatsoever, direct or indirect," which could include "any other property, real, personal, or mixed, tangible or intangible, or interest or interests therein, present, future, or contingent."[330] The only check on this system is that a mid-level government official makes the decision, and an informal audit revealed that officials omitted even this minimal administrative record on at least three occasions.*

Searches conducted in the course of antiterrorist finance efforts may be extensive, and the impact of freezing assets substantial. In December 2001, Larry Thompson, the Deputy Attorney General, authorized a Foreign Intelligence Surveillance Act search of the offices of the Global Relief Foundation (GRF) and its director's home.[331]† From the former, the FBI collected records, video equipment, financial literature, promotional books, tapes, email, and computers, as well as servers, modems, a cell phone, hand-held radios, a credit card imprinter, and diskettes; and from the director's home, it took computers, diskettes, video photographs, documents, records, audio tapes, cassette tapes, date books, a cell phone, a camera, a Palm Pilot, credit cards, foreign currency, and $13,030. The federal government simultaneously froze all GRF assets, forcing the organization to close, and Immigration and Naturalization Services deported a key GRF fundraiser. In January 2002, GRF sued the state and requested a return of the materials seized, but the suit failed.[332] The court held that a federal agency's interpretation of its own regulations must be given controlling weight when challenged unless it was plainly erroneous or inconsistent with the regulation, especially in matters involving foreign policy and national security.[333]

The Staff Report for the September 11 Commission highlighted "the highly deferential standard of review afforded to the President in the exercise of his

---

* In the case of the Illinois charities, the suspension of assets lasted 10 or 11 months – hardly the pressing emergency to which the measure was meant to apply. John Roth, Douglas Greenburg & Serena Wille, *National Commission on Terrorist Attacks Against the United States, Monograph on Terrorist Financing: Staff Report to the commission*, Aug. 21, 2004, at 51, available at www. 9-11commission.gov.

† GRF, which began operating in 1992 as a domestic, nonprofit enterprise headquartered in Illinois, funneled millions of dollars to alleviate human suffering in 25 states. In 1995, it funded programs in Chechnya, Bosnia, Pakistan, Kashmir, and Lebanon. In 1996, it expanded to Afghanistan and Azerbaijan; in 1997, to Bangladesh; in 1998, to Iraq and Somalia; in 1999, to Albania, Belgium, China, Eritrea, Kosovo, and Turkey; and in 2000, to Ethiopia, Jordan, and Sierra Leone. It also funded programs in Gaza and the West Bank. *Global Relief Found., Inc.* v. *O'Neill*, 207 F. Supp. 2d 779, 785 (N.D. Ill. 2002).

Commander in Chief powers under IEEPA."[334] The writers reflected, "Although effective in shutting down its targets, this aggressive approach raises potential civil liberties concerns, as the charities' supporters insist that they were unfairly targeted, denied due process, and closed without any evidence they actually funded al Qaeda or any terrorist groups."[335] Thus, this deference allows the state to waive the notice requirements otherwise inherent in due process.[336]

The current system is operating with a certain conflict of interest, which further distinguishes antiterrorist finance from other administrative and regulatory measures. Defendants who have had their assets frozen must apply to OFAC for a license to release funds. The license dictates who can represent the defendants, how much money the defendants can spend, and which issues they can raise – thus basically putting executive branch officials in control of who can sue them, the terms upon which they are sued, and how vigorously the lawsuit is pursued.[337] And no one can step up to pay for legal fees: the Executive Order makes any such support illegal, a prohibition raising issues related to the rule of law. The courts have yet to rule on the merits of the claim that this requirement violates a Fifth Amendment right to due process and a First Amendment right to sue for redress. (The one case to address this issue, *Benevolence International Foundation*, ended up with a plea bargain.[338])

Stigma

Even if no criminal charges follow, the stigma of investigation, particularly in relation to terrorism, is hard for an individual or a business to counter. For example, Bob Simon, from CBS's *60 Minutes*, claimed during one show that several Muslim groups in Herndon, Virginia, had terrorist ties. Reported on the basis of an anonymous source (who turned out to be Rita Katz, a private analyst who monitors chat rooms and sends translated documents to government agencies[339]), the story suggested that the groups invested in Mar-Jac Poultry, a chicken-plucking farm in Gainesville, Georgia, where possibly millions of chickens had gone "missing." Customs agents raided the farm but found nothing. Mar-Jac filed suit against the network and the city of Atlanta. Because of the investigation, the poultry farm is facing bankruptcy, and banks, "wary of being accused of financing terrorism, may cut its credit lines."[340] In the case of Global Relief Foundation, although the state never brought criminal charges, the stigma attached to the GRF undermined its operations. But the courts have ruled that the mere statement that such groups are under investigation, without more defamatory statements, is insufficient to counter legal claims.[341]

THE POLITICAL AND HUMANITARIAN COSTS

The political and humanitarian costs of the British and American antiterrorist finance provisions go well beyond the security or freedom rubric. Exercise of the powers – particularly in the absence of direct evidence of a person or business's participation in terrorist activity – may alienate international partners.

And domestic and international populations that the states need to help respond to terrorist claims may find ethnic targeting and the states' refusal to respond to humanitarian issues unacceptable. Such behavior underscores terrorist assertions that, since September 11, have painted Western states as going after individuals – and states – on the basis of race and religion.

More than 80 percent of the money the United States blocked after September 11 came under government control within the first three months.[342] The state's immediate and sudden creation of lists of individuals and entities for the purposes of asset blocking, however, appeared to be done on the basis of insufficient evidence. Early cases quickly demonstrated the weakness of the US charges against those the state accused of complicity in terrorist aims. And lower standards of proof did nothing to increase international confidence in US standards of justice. As I have noted, the initiatives essentially replaced a criminal law standard with an intelligence one, making mere links to terrorists or terrorist organizations a sufficient basic for the seizure of assets. Together with the targeting of a specific ethnic and religious community – which would cause considerable domestic unrest in states with a larger proportion of their population drawn from the Arab, Muslim community – the lack of due process is disturbing. Simultaneously, the Bush administration refused to provide additional information on which the claims had been made. The Staff Report for the September 11 Commission found the following:

These early missteps have made other countries unwilling to freeze assets or otherwise act merely on the basis of a U.S. action. Multilateral freezing mechanisms now require waiting periods before money can be frozen, a change that has eliminated the element of surprise and virtually ensured that little money is actually frozen.[343]

A United Nations monitoring panel established in January 2004 to determine whether and to what extent financial measures had been effective against al Qaeda concluded that the network had successfully evaded sanctions, while the financial sanctions regime itself had lost credibility.[344]

In respect to apparent errors on the part of the United States, the case of the London-based Palestinian Relief and Development Fund known as Interpal underscores important differences between the United Kingdom and the United States. First registered in the United Kingdom in August 1994, Interpal "provides aid to, assists, guides and comforts poor and needy Palestinians in the West Bank and Gaza strip, Jordan and Lebanon. It aims to relieve the hardship and suffering of these distressed persons by co-operating or working with other charitable organizations in the region." Its income between January 2000 and December 31, 2001, was more than £4 million. On August 21, 2003, President Bush accused the group of sending funds to Hamas. The Charity Commission for England and Wales, which registers charities, responded within three days by temporarily freezing Interpal's bank accounts. Its subsequent investigation, however, failed to find any evidence to back this claim. In September 2003, the United Kingdom released the organization's assets and closed its inquiry, announcing, "The US authorities were unable to provide evidence to support allegations made against Interpal within the agreed time scale."³⁴⁵ The Commission stated that it was "alert to the possibilities of charities being used to further or support terrorist activities"; that it was willing to look at the US allegations and work with law enforcement for investigation; but that "[t]he Commission's own work reveals that connections or links between registered charities in England and Wales and terrorist organizations are very rare."³⁴⁶

The Netherlands is another allied state to depart from the American approach. When Aqeel al-Aqeel, the former director of al-Haramain, filed a lawsuit against four US officials for including him in the Specially Designated Global Terrorist list, and the United States refused to release any evidence implicating him, the Dutch government unfroze his assets.³⁴⁷

Perhaps the best example of apparent errors in judgment is US action taken against al-Barakaat. Its name meaning "the blessing" in Arabic, al-Barakaat served as the principal banking system in Somalia. Founded by Ahmed Nur Ali Jumale in 1985, by September 11 it had more than 180 offices in 40 different states, with its headquarters in the United Arab Emirates. The US government alleged that from 1992 Osama bin Laden served as both a customer and a silent partner of the organization, which supposedly had close links to al-Itihaad al-Islamiya, a group of Islamists whom the Defense Intelligence Agency considered a major threat in Somalia. In July 1999, the FBI in Minneapolis opened a full field investigation and found other al-Barakaat branches in San Diego, Washington, D.C., Charlotte, Cincinnati, New York, and Seattle. The following year, it opened a criminal investigation.

Following September 11, al-Barakaat became one of the first organizations to have its assets frozen. On November 7, 2001, federal agents broke into eight al-Barakaat offices around the United States and seized their records. President Bush held a press event, alleging that Jumale was a friend and supporter of bin Laden and estimating that some $25 million went through his organization to terrorist operations. Jumale, and others the state associated with the network and placed on the list, could not so much as buy a stick of gum in the following months without violating Executive Order 13,224. After five months of trying to get its assets unfrozen (and OFAC not returning its calls), the organization brought suit.

In the interim, the FBI began to realize the contradictoriness of the information it had collected from the United Arab Emirates (UAE) and various intelligence bodies. Out of tens of thousands of al-Barakaat documents, nothing appeared out of order. It turned out that bin Laden had not been in Afghanistan with Jumale. The UAE fully cooperated with the investigation. Despite scores of interviews with individuals involved in the case (including Jumale) and unfettered access to the organization's records, the "FBI could not substantiate any links between al-Barakaat and terrorism."³⁴⁸

The United States did not just go after the US assets of those associated with al-Barakaat. It placed three Swedish citizens and one Canadian on a UN list of designated terrorists. In January 2002, the Swedes petitioned OFAC and the UN to remove their names. Canada also moved to take its citizen off the list. Sweden unsuccessfully tried to persuade the Security Council to use criminal evidentiary standards for constructing the list. The United States vigorously opposed this effort, on the grounds that most of the names would be removed. The Swedish effort spurred France to try to persuade the Security Council to establish even basic rules, such as criteria for sanctions and a procedure for review. Eventually the United States removed five people from the list and said it would consider other appeals.[349] The UN, in turn, created an evidentiary requirement for the list as well as an appeals procedure. The Swedes brought suit in the European Court of Justice, claiming a violation of due process.[350] The case became a lightning rod for human rights and due process violations associated with US actions taken since September 11. Well-known Swedes collected money for the men's defense, and a prominent attorney took the case. One of the men, Abdirisak Aden, had run for office in the 2000 Swedish elections; none of them had criminal records.

Ultimately, this designation, and many of those made immediately after September 11, undermined US efforts to stem the flow of funds to terrorist organizations. The Staff Report of the September 11 Commission later described the atmosphere as chaotic and emphasized the use of the antiterrorist finance efforts as a public relations exercise: "The goal set at the policy levels of the White House and Treasury was to conduct a public and aggressive series of designations to show the world community and our allies that the United States was serious about pursuing the financial targets. It entailed a major designation every four weeks, accompanied by derivative designations throughout the month." The result, even by Treasury's standards, was the inclusion of weak cases. The National Security Council had been behind the push to designate as many entities as possible: "Some believed that the government's haste in this area, and *its preference for IEEPA sanctions, might result in a high level of false designations* that would ultimately jeopardize the United States's ability to persuade other countries to designate groups as terrorist organizations." The report concluded, "Ultimately ... this proved to be the case with the al-Barakaat designations.[351]

Here the executive's bypassing of judicial mechanisms, in relying on less robust standards, made more likely a wrongful designation – with detrimental consequences for the United States. By 2004, the United Nations recognized that its list, largely constructed by the United States, had "begun to lose credibility and operational value" and needed updating.* By 2004, not a single person on the list had been stopped by the travel ban.[352] In March 2006, a UN Security Council report expressed concern about the program's effectiveness.[353] The Council of Europe issued a report that said the UN list violated the European Convention on Human Rights: it provided neither any protection against

---

* Only 21 states submitted names for the list – most of which originated from the United States – including approximately 174 people and 111 groups associated to al Qaeda. Stephen Fidler & Haig Simonian, *IMF Chief Urges United Response to Slowdown*, Fin. Times (London), Oct. 6, 2001, at 1.

arbitrary decisions, nor did it include mechanisms to ensure that the allegations made by governments were accurate.[354] The individuals targeted, moreover, had no recourse against national governments.

The credibility gap meant not only that states tended to be uncooperative but also that those people and organizations responsible for intentionally funding terrorist operations continued to act with impunity: more than two years after the attacks, for example, Youssef Nada and Ahmed Idris Nasrddin, both of whom were central to al Qaeda's international financing, remained in business in several European states.[355] Al Taqwa, supposedly shut down, continued to operate.[356] And a number of individuals placed on the lists began to bring suit.[357]

The alienation of allied (and nonallied) states is particularly important. On the one hand, the lack of evidence provided means that, in complying with US requests, an Islamic state looks as though it is simply "caving in to Western demands at the expense of Muslim tradition," risking "a backlash against the governments."[358] Indeed, Islamic banks are beginning to go on the offensive.[359] As governments prove reluctant to trust the United States, the US government is forced to adopt more coercive methods to achieve its objectives – methods that involve expansion of extraterritorial powers, as in the antiterrorist finance provisions in the USA PATRIOT Act. Such coercion, however, consumes political advantage that might be better applied to more effective ways to interrupt terrorist operations. And it creates a gulf between countries. A *Financial Times* article of September 25, 2001, suggested that the network was directed not just toward al Qaeda, but against international banks and governments.[360] This is a dangerous perception to cultivate when one needs international allies to counter a global terrorist threat – or to pursue other, equally or even more important foreign policy objectives.

But this is a perception steadily gaining ground. The Swift bank data operation (see page 164) generated further unease among the US's European partners. The European Parliament demanded that the European Commission, the European Central Bank, and each of the European Union's 25 member states disclose the extent to which they were aware of the "secret agreement" between Swift and the United States.[361] Although the resolution was not binding, according to the European Union's Justice and Security Commissioner's spokesman, it has "political teeth."[362] Jean-Marie Cavada, a French lawmaker, said, "Now we discover that our powerful friend and ally is rifling through our private bank accounts."[363] Giusto Catania, a prominent member of the European Parliament, said that it was the flip side of rendition – both operations trying to "extort information."[364] "The "secret, routine, and massive access" by US agencies to Swift banking codes – needed to transfer in and out of European financial institutions – is "unacceptable," stated Peter Hustinx, the Brussels official responsible for EU data oversight."[365] Criminal complaints against Swift were subsequently filed in every member state of the European Union.[366] A European Union panel that prepared a formal report on the operation expressed "serious doubts" about the legality of the program under European law.[367]

Not only do such measures alienate important allies in the battle against terrorism but the manner of their implementation also bolsters some of Osama bin Laden's claims. Specifically, the campaign against Muslim charities does little to counteract the assertion that the United States is targeting Muslims. As the Staff Report to the September 11 Commission notes, "[T]he campaign has aroused controversy on various political, religious and humanitarian grounds and is viewed in some quarters as broadly anti-Islamic."[368] For example, the Al Sanabil Association for Relief and Development, established in 1993 in response to the UN Relief and Works Agency's (UNRWA) budget cuts, sponsored 1,200 Palestinian families, spending approximately $800,000 in 2003 on orphans and $55,000 on needy patients. The organization also distributed food and home appliances to displaced persons. Treasury froze the group's assets in August 2003, claiming that its funds went through Hamas. As a result, UNRWA could not provide even basic needs for the more than 1.3 million Palestinian refugees in Lebanon, Syria, Jordan, West Bank, and the Gaza Strip whom it had previously helped. Considerable publicity in the region drew attention to US actions – and to the lack of evidence to support its allegations.[369]

Also, the Benevolence International Foundation (BIF), a nonprofit charitable organization founded in 1992 and run by US citizens, raised millions for humanitarian aid in 11 locations: Pakistan, Bosnia, Azerbaijan, Tajikistan, Yemen, Bangladesh, Turkey, Dagestan, Georgia, China, and Ingushetia.[370] When OFAC froze the organization's assets in 2001, the BIF offered to have the FBI itself take the money overseas to a Charity Women's Hospital in Daghestan and a children's tuberculosis hospital in Tajikistan, both of which would otherwise be forced to close. OFAC refused the request. Most employees had to be let go, and the charity was unable to raise new funds to support its humanitarian relief. With all the frozen funds having to be spent on BIF's legal fees, US action proved devastating for the regions BIF had previously served. Such actions, like the clause in the Executive Order explicitly banning assistance for humanitarian need, are counterproductive.

US policy since September 11 also brings the United States into conflict with Islamic states that depend upon the flow of alternative remittances for the health and welfare of their populations. In addition to foreign policy considerations, the United States has an interest in ensuring that many of these regions remain economically viable and tied to US influence as a way to obviate a vacuum into which extremist movements can move.

For example, aid agencies in Somalia became concerned that shutting down al-Barakaat, the largest remittance company in the country, would push the state into the hands of extremists. Approximately $500 million per year – far in excess of the foreign aid given to the region – flowed through al-Barakaat, which ran highly efficient transfers and was used by the United Nations itself. The humanitarian costs of shutting it down would be considerable: with an economy already driven into the ground from war, weather, and border closures, at least 50 percent of the Somali population, according to Save the Children, depended upon funds from abroad for their basic existence. Blocking these funds does not marginalize fundamentalists; it makes them more powerful. The United States ignored these claims, however, taking the absurd position that since Western Union operated along the borders, and Moneygram had one office in Mogadishu, money would continue to flow to the region.[371] These more expensive and limited alternatives, however, proved inadequate to address the significant need within Somalia.

It is not just Islamic states with the potential to host fundamentalist movements that suffer from the US stringent financial measures. For example, they affect Latin America as well. In 2000, the Bureau for International Narcotics and Law Enforcement Affairs spent roughly $11 million to counter drugs, terrorism, and money laundering in the Bahamas, Central America, and South America.[372] The United States used its post-September 11 authority to target financial institutions in the region.

Bush downplayed the region's concerns,[373] but the powers are available; and to ensure compliance with the new regulatory regime, remittance businesses will incur new expenses. The effect is felt well beyond the counterterrorist realm. Latin American immigrants in the United States, for instance, send an average of $250 each to their home states 8–10 times each year, but transfer fees raise the costs to up to 20 percent of the value they send. Increased regulatory requirements make remittances – which exceed US foreign aid to the region – even more expensive.[374] Latin American institutions may reject legitimate business they would have accepted in the past. States may opt to introduce even stricter rules than those in the United States to retain other economic benefits of association with Washington – with potential economic consequences. Just as Mexico is recovering from the 1994 peso crisis, these policies may trigger an economic downward spiral, destabilizing the Mexican economy.[375] Concerns abound elsewhere: in 2003, the Cuban expatriate community in the United States sent some $1 billion to Cuba. In May 2004, the administration announced new limits on this transfer: remittances were capped at $1,200 per year, and an expatriate was allowed only one visit to Cuba every three years, instead of annually, as previously. Cubans in the United States reacted strongly to what they soon saw as a humanitarian crisis.[376]

Financial assets are essential for terrorist groups: they cannot operate without money, even though the amount necessary may be small. If terrorist organizations do decide to take up weapons of mass destruction, particularly those using fissile material, the importance of money may well increase. For now, the real problem is that financial counterterrorism has significantly expanded executive power in the United Kingdom and the United States, with little resistance from either the legislature or the judiciary – and with adverse effects on a range of rights and with severe political and humanitarian consequences.

4

Privacy and Surveillance

"To refer to the more or less indiscriminate storing of information relating to the private lives of individuals in terms of pursuing a legitimate national security concern is . . . problematic."

Judge Luzius Wildhaber, *Rotaru* v. *Romania*, 2000

"We must build a 'system of systems' that can provide the right information to the right people at all times. Information will be shared 'horizontally' across each level of government and 'vertically' among federal, state and local governments, private industry, and citizens. . . . We will leverage America's leading-edge information technology to develop an information architecture that will effectively secure the homeland."

US National Strategy for Homeland Security, 2002

"The act of turning the military loose on civilians even if sanctioned by an Act of Congress, which it has not been, would raise serious and profound constitutional questions. Standing as it does only on brute power and Pentagon policy, it must be repudiated as a usurpation dangerous to the civil liberties on which free men are dependent.

Justice William O. Douglas, *Laird* v. *Tatum*, 1972

"[The enemy moves in] a shadowy underworld operating globally with supporters and allies in many countries. Including, unfortunately our own. . . . Contrary to popular belief, there is no absolute ban on [military] intelligence components collecting US person information."

Robert Noonan, Deputy Chief of Staff for Intelligence, Department of the Army, 2001

"You have zero privacy anyway. Get over it."

Scott McNealey, CEO Sun Microsystems, 1999

Published in 1949 at the dawn of the Cold War, George Orwell's *1984* forewarned against the corrosive impact of broad state surveillance.[1] The novel's main character, Winston Smith, a citizen of Oceania (a fictional representation of the United States and United Kingdom), lived under the all-seeing eye of Big Brother. Nearly two decades after Orwell wrote *1984*, Vance Packard warned in *The Naked Society* about the growing danger of electronic devices.[2] Alan Westin's *Privacy and Freedom* subsequently admonished that failure to pay attention to increasing inroads into privacy could have far-reaching implications.[3] In 1984, Congress, finally alarmed by the growth of technology, held hearings on the subject. In opening the proceedings, Representative Glenn English, a Democrat from Oklahoma and former staff sergeant in the US Army Reserves, suggested that, although Orwell's "totalitarian world of constant fear, repression, and surveillance" did not yet exist, the technology that would enable such a world did: "The issue that we must face is how to control the technology before it controls us."[4]

At the time of the congressional hearings, only 45 percent of the public knew how to use a computer, but 69 percent felt that an Orwellian society was at hand.[5] Since then, national security claims, counterterrorist law, and advancing technology have pushed the United Kingdom – and particularly the United States – much further down the Orwellian path.

Consider first the United Kingdom. Unlike the United States, Britain does not have a long history of clashes among the executive, legislative, and judicial branches of government over the collection of information. Indeed, until relatively recently it had *no* law governing the gathering of information on the public by the police and intelligence services. Except for extraordinary stop and search powers for terrorist-related offenses and warrants for police interference with property, surveillance techniques used by the state (physical searches of property, the interception of communications, the use of electronic bugs, and the running of covert human intelligence sources) – indeed, the very existence of the intelligence services – were not recognized by statute.

This lack of recognition certainly did not mean that no surveillance occurred. To the contrary, surveillance took place within the ring of secrecy. Shaped by the country's experiences in World War II and the Troubles in Northern Ireland, surveillance was broadly accepted as the executive's responsibility.[6] It was not routinely challenged in court nor rigorously examined by Parliament: not a single select committee even oversaw such authorities. Information about these programs, in light of strong official secrets legislation (discussed in detail in the next chapter), was on a need-to-know basis.

Then in the 1980s, changes to the constitutional structure of the United Kingdom shifted the legal landscape. Britain's increasing ties to the European Commission and European Court of Human Rights, and the latter's stronger protections for privacy pushed the state in a new direction. The European Court objected to the absence of any statutory framework and the lack of legal safeguards. The state subtly resisted: on the surface, it met successive demands by the European Court – while simultaneously expanding its executive surveillance authorities. Yet pressure from Europe did lead to a series of domestic statutes that put the intelligence services on a legal footing and created oversight mechanisms – mechanisms that are lacking in the American context. The Continent also nudged the United Kingdom toward stronger data protection than is the case across the Atlantic.

Although British law thus does provide some protection against executive abuse of surveillance authorities, and is in some ways more robust than the law in the United States, surveillance continues to be conducted in a closed culture: it is devilishly difficult to get information about actual operations underway. Parliament continues to exercise minimal public scrutiny of the executive. Only snippets of information emerge. Yet changes to the law even prior to 9/11 suggest strong interest in data-mining activities. And the most recent Interception of Communications Commissioner's report indicated that nearly a half-million requests for communications information had been lodged by the government in 2005 and the first few months of 2006.[7] The United Kingdom, moreover, by no means eschews the broad use of surveillance to monitor individuals as they move through public space. Here, port and border controls and closed-circuit television figure largely.

In contrast to the United Kingdom, the United States has a long public history of aggressive surveillance, public debate on the matter, and the institution of laws to restrict efforts by the executive to obtain information. But following September 11, Congress rolled back previous checks on the executive, gave it substantially more surveillance authority, and then – as I discuss in this chapter – failed to oversee these powers sufficiently.

Often missed in discussions about the USA PATRIOT Act, though, is the fact that its surveillance provisions are in many ways just the tip of the iceberg. The behemoth Department of Defense (DoD) has now shifted its attention to the homeland. After 9/11, the newly formed Northern Command established two intelligence-gathering centers within domestic bounds, and the Pentagon authorized the creation of Counterintelligence Field Activity to collect and analyze information from law enforcement, the military, and intelligence agencies. Other DoD entities followed suit: the National Security Agency began monitoring telephone traffic; the Defense Intelligence Agency scanned Internet activity to identify Americans linked to international terrorism; and the National Geospatial-Intelligence Agency began collecting information on 133 US cities, thus acquiring the capability to identify the occupants of each house, their nationality, and their political affiliation. Outside of the DoD, the Departments of Justice, Homeland Security, Treasury, and Transportation, among others, have created similar programs.

In addition to actual surveillance operations, there are underway in the United States dozens of known federal data-mining operations, analyzing information to discern social network patterns and to try to anticipate and avert threats. The granddaddy of these operations is John Poindexter's Total Information Awareness (TIA) – launched in 2002 and designed to link *all* government and commercial databases available worldwide.[8] The Information Awareness Office, which oversaw TIA, used an official logo that neatly captured this vision: at the top of the Illuminati pyramid an eye spread its gaze over the world, while at the bottom the Latin phrase *Scientia est Potentia* proclaimed "Knowledge is Power."

The Information Awareness Office was right: knowledge is power. And using information to find out what terrorist organizations are planning is, in many ways, at the heart of the counterterrorist battle. But the ability to fight terrorism is not the only kind of power generated by information. And the data now available – for whatever purpose – eclipse what previously could have even been obtained.

What matters is not just that more people know how to use computers than they did in 1984, but how those computers are being used.* The type of material available has changed: nearly 82 million Americans go online for spiritual or religious purposes.[9] Some 44 percent of American Internet users contribute their thoughts to the online world.[10] The most popular uses of the Internet center on the most personal of matters, such as financial records, access to medical information, letters to friends and family, and gift purchases.[11] Not only does Internet use leave a trail but digitization also allows medical, educational, financial, and other records to be recorded, analyzed, and shared.

The evolution in telephony means that not just voice but also data and images can be transferred at the speed of light: just one of Cisco Systems's CRS-1 routers can move the *entire* Library of Congress in 4.6 seconds.[12] From circuit-switched networks, technology has morphed to allow for packet-switched designs, making the movement of data even more efficient.[13] Satellites break physical constraints. These and other technologies have dramatically increased the number of people using electronic communications. In 2007, for instance, the number of people using just mobile phones – not computers or land lines – is expected to hit 2 billion.[14]

The trails left by all these activities can be picked up and followed by private industry and the government. Here, the United States, in particular, lacks the privacy protections afforded to European consumers. Acxiom, Choicepoint, Lexis-Nexis, and other US firms now comprise a multi-billion dollar information industry. Infobase, just one of Acxiom.com's products, provides "[o]ver 50 demographic variables . . . including age, income, real property data, children's data and others."[15] It contains information on education levels, occupation, height, weight, political affiliation, ethnicity, race, hobbies, and net worth."[16] For a fee, Docussearch.com will provide any customer with the target's Social Security number, previous addresses, date of birth, names of neighbors, driver records, current address and phone number, current employer, driver's license number, license plates/vehicle VINs, unlisted numbers, beepers, cell phone numbers, fax numbers, bankruptcy and debtor filings, employment records, bank

---

* In 1981, only 300 computers linked to the Internet; by 1993, approximately one million computers had joined it. As of January 2000, some 72.4 million were connected. Randall L. Sarosdy, *The Internet Revolution Continues: Responding to the Chaos*, Metropolitan Corp. Couns., Sept. 2000, at 15.

account balances and activity, stock purchases, corporate bank accounts, and credit card activity.[17]

The US federal government buys access to this digital market. Choicepoint, one of the industry's leaders, claims that it contracts with at least 35 federal agencies. These include a number of organizations that deal in counterterrorism, such as the Department of Justice, the FBI, the Drug Enforcement Agency, the US Marshals, the IRS, the Bureau of Citizenship and Immigration Services, and Alcohol, Tobacco, and Firearms.[18]

These and other technologies mean that in some computer file there is a digital copy of what each of us does. Combined with other files holding similar information, a copy of one's life – oneself – can be constructed. None of the ordinary activities that any one of us engages in – going to school, seeking medical care, buying food, reading, or writing letters – is new. But the recording of this information, its integration, and its swift recall – by private or public entities – are unprecedented. Access to such data gives others insight into who you are, who you have been, and who you are becoming. It allows people to get inside your mind and to learn about how you react, what your emotional states are, what issues you care about, and what drives you. A critical point here is that *the information is individualized*. It relates specifically to you, and can be recalled specifically in relation to yourself.

The combination of national security, counterterrorist law, and technology has brought both countries to a point where psychological – not just physical – surveillance is possible. When the stated aim of a government is to get inside citizens' heads – and to figure out from an individual's emotional, social, intellectual, and physical history what one is going to do before one does it – we have left the old world behind. This capability represents something different in kind, not degree, from the past. And its potential costs go well beyond those captured in the security or freedom dichotomy.

In respect to the issue of costs, it is worth remembering that benefits – particularly with surveillance – tend to be hidden from view, whereas potential harms are more visible. In other words, surveillance is part of a secret world that occasionally becomes public, but that, in the main, operates under the radar. Citizens will never know about many terrorist operations that covert intelligence helped foil. On the other hand, the act of looking for terrorists – the proverbial needle in the haystack – may well involve obtaining information about a large number of people.

But this parallel consideration does not negate the fact that such programs reach deep into the social and political fabric of the state. What is the state's aim in gathering data? How is the information being used? How long is it retained? Who sees it? These questions, particularly in the American context, have not been squarely addressed; nor has either state confronted the potentially profound social and political effects of such provisions. To the extent, moreover, that the public discourse focuses on one particular information-gathering operation, the broader picture – and the cumulative effects of surveillance operations – goes unaddressed.

BRITISH STATUTORY AUTHORITY FOR INTELLIGENCE GATHERING

British law provides separately for the interception of communications, property interference, and covert surveillance. Successive cases at the European Court of Human Rights put pressure on the state to place the intelligence services on a statutory footing and to begin legislating for the use of information-gathering authority. *Malone*, *Hewitt and Harman*, *Halford* and *Khan* proved instrumental in this regard and led to the 1985 Interception of Communications Act; the 1989 and 1996 Security Service Acts; the 1994 Intelligence Services Act; and the 2000 Regulation of Investigatory Powers Act.

The Interception of Communications

British legal scholars are sharply divided over the origin of executive authority to intercept communications and continue to speculate about whether the power finds its locus in royal prerogative, in statutes governing preservation of the state and public order, in common law, or in custom – a natural evolution from the state's monopoly on the postal system.[19] Indeed, two secret committees (one each in the House of Lords and the House of Commons), which in 1844 were given the task of determining the law with respect to opening letters, dodged the question of the origins of the power by simply recognizing its existence.[*]

As a purely substantive matter, written documents and letters were the first kinds of communication to be intercepted. The state's authority to do so was virtually uncontested. The ordinance establishing the first Post Office referred to it as "the best Means to discover and prevent any dangerous and wicked Designs against the Commonwealth."[20] Subsequent legislation reaffirmed this power: an Act of Parliament in 1660 agreed *mutatis mutandis* with the content of the ordinance.[21] Three years later, the Crown issued a Royal Proclamation announcing that only the Principal Secretary of State could open packages and letters.[22] Similar language marked the 1710 statute "for establishing a General Post Office for all Her Majesty's Dominions," 1837 Post Office (Offences) Act, 1908 Post Office Act, and, more recently the 1953 Post Office Act. Under this statute, only an express warrant issued by a Secretary of State could authorize the interception and opening of any letter, postcard, newspaper, parcel, or telegram.[23] Four years later, the Birkett Committee concluded that for centuries the state had frequently used the power to intercept letters and packages, that the authority was well known to the public, and that "[a]t no time had it been suggested with any authority that the exercise of the power was unlawful."[24] The interception of telephone communications has a similar history.

---

[*] The House of Lords commented, "[T]he Power appears ... to have been exercised from the earliest Period, and to have been recognized by several Acts of Parliament. This appears to the committee to be the State of the Law in respect to the detaining and opening of Letters at the Post Office and they do not find any other Authority for such detaining or opening." BIRKETT REPORT, ¶ 15 (cited in note 19).

From the start of telephone service in the early twentieth century until 1937, the state, the Post Office, and the general public simply assumed that any entity operating the telecommunication network had the authority to intercept messages.[25] Such surveillance did not, therefore, require any warrants from the Secretary of State; rather, the intelligence services and law enforcement simply contacted the Director-General of the Post Office if they needed any information.[26] In 1937, the policy changed to reflect the Home Secretary's view that the powers granted to the Secretary of State in regard to the post and, later, to telegrams logically extended to telecommunications.[27] For nearly 50 years, however, no explicit, statutory authority could be found for the interception of wire communications. Instead, British administrative procedures guided state agencies.

Administrative Practice Before 1985. Under the administrative procedures, any agency that wanted to intercept communications had to provide to the Secretary of State the name, address, and telephone number of the target to be intercepted. Occasionally, one warrant would include several people.[28] The standard practice was for the Secretary to ascertain whether such intercepts would be necessary for either the prevention or the detection of serious crime or to protect national security.[29] What constituted a serious crime reflected changing political and cultural norms: during World War II, for instance, efforts to get around rationing constituted a serious offense. Participation in lotteries, a severe crime in 1909, had by 1953 become a way to pass the time. And the standards for obscenity gradually relaxed.[30]

From 1937 to 1957, the Metropolitan Police and HM Customs and Excise submitted the majority of the warrant requests.[31] From time to time, the Home Office admonished these and other agencies for making too many requests: in September 1951, for example, the Home Office issued letters saying that interception was an "inherently objectionable" practice, and suggested that "the power to stop letters and intercept telephone calls must be used with great caution."[32] The Secretary laid down three conditions for law enforcement to meet. First, the offense had to be really serious: that is, an individual with no previous record could reasonably expect at least three years' sentence, or the offense, of lesser gravity, involved a significant number of people. Second, for Customs and Excise, the Secretary of State narrowed "serious crime" to cases involving "a substantial and continuing fraud which would seriously damage the revenue or the economy of the country if it went unchecked." Third, the requesting agency had to have tried normal methods of investigation and failed, or alternatively, other methods had to be unlikely to succeed. The Home Office also declared that good reason must exist to believe that interception would result in conviction.[33]

Separate arrangements governed warrants sought by MI5, an organization that traced its history back to the creation in 1909 of the Secret Service Bureau. By 1914, the Bureau had evolved into the Directorate of Military Intelligence

Section 5 (MI5), which dealt with domestic counterespionage, and the Directorate of Military Intelligence Section 6 (MI6), which addressed external operations. In 1952, Sir David Maxwell Fife, the Home Secretary, issued a directive to the Director-General of MI5, indicating that the organization would report directly to him – although MI5 continued to be considered as part of the United Kingdom's Defence Forces. According to the 1952 directive, the mission of the Security Service was to defend the realm "from external and internal dangers arising from attempts at espionage and sabotage or from actions of persons and organizations whether directed from within or without the country which may be judged to be subversive of the state."[34] To grant a warrant, the Secretary of State required that applications relate to an investigation into major subversive or espionage activity likely to hurt national security, and that the material thus yielded would be of use to MI5 in carrying out its duties. Whereas the Secretary of State preferred that more conservative means of gathering the information be first attempted, or be unlikely to succeed, the Home Office gave greater weight to the collection of information than to the need to secure convictions.[35] All warrants issued by the Secretary of State authorized interception for an indefinite period.

For the Metropolitan Police, HM Customs and Excise, or MI5 to obtain a warrant, each organization had to cross a series of bureaucratic hurdles. All three agencies had internal vetting structures.[36] The first two organizations then forwarded the successful bids for a warrant to the Home Office Criminal Department for approval, after which an application went to the Permanent Under-Secretary of State. (MI5 forwarded the application directly to the Permanent Under-Secretary of State.) If satisfied that the requirements had been met, the Under-Secretary then forwarded the request to the Secretary of State for final approval.

The net result of this carefully constructed process was that the Secretary of State ended up rejecting few applications[37] – a claim echoed in the US Department of Justice's later defense of the almost nonexistent refusal by the FISA courts to grant a warrant (see page 232). Additional procedures within the agencies and the Home Office kept the matter under advisement: from 1956 forward, the Metropolitan Police undertook a weekly review of outstanding warrants; Customs and Excise considered theirs quarterly; MI5 reviewed them on a biannual basis; and the Permanent Under-Secretary conducted a quarterly examination.[38] Home Office policy required that, except in extraordinary circumstances, any information gleaned from interception be excluded from judicial proceedings or as evidence in any other formal inquiry.[39]

Across the agencies, as telecommunications grew in social importance, action in the administrative warrant realm moved away from postal intercepts and toward telephone conversations. In 1937, the total number of warrants for mail openings issued by the Home Secretary in England and Wales eclipsed the number issued for telephone wiretaps: 556 warrants were approved for postal intercepts, whereas a mere 17 applied to telephones. Within less than two decades, the numbers had reversed, with wiretaps exceeding mail openings. The number of taps steadily expanded from 299 in 1965 to 468 by 1975. In 1995, the Home Secretary authorized 910 taps; by 2000, this number had increased to 1,559.*

Throughout this period, with no law sanctioning the intercept regime or providing a remedy for violations, it technically remained legal to place phone taps even in the absence of an authorizing warrant. This gap caused the Birkett Committee to suggest in 1957 that Parliament "consider whether legislation should be passed to render the unauthori[z]ed tapping of a telephone line an offence."[40] But it was not until the United Kingdom fell afoul of European law, nearly three decades later, that Westminster began to take up the issue.

The Interception of Communications Act (1985). The first important case to make it to the European courts stemmed from efforts by the London Metropolitan Police to ascertain whether an antiques dealer, suspected of handling stolen property, was, in fact, doing so. In 1978 the target of the surveillance, James Malone, took the police to court, alleging that the state had violated his rights.[41] Malone claimed relief under both English law and the European Convention on Human Rights.

Under the former, Malone argued that it was unlawful for anyone, including the state, to intercept communications without the consent of those involved – a claim that arose from the rights of property, privacy, and of confidentiality. The police disagreed: no statute made government wiretapping illegal. In fact, broad recognition in the administrative rules that such tapping occurred suggested that no immunity existed.

Malone argued also that the state's actions had violated Article 8 of the ECHR, which reads as follows:

1. Everyone has the right to respect for his private and family life, his home and his correspondence.
2. There shall be no interference by a public authority with the exercise of this right except such as is in accordance with the law and is necessary in a democratic society in the interests of national security, public safety or the economic well-being of the country, for the prevention of disorder or crime, for the protection of health or morals, or for the protection of the rights and freedoms of others.[42]

---

* These numbers do not reflect the total number of wiretaps issued in the United Kingdom: they omit warrants issued in Scotland, although a similar pattern existed there. *See* Regulation of Investigatory Powers Act, 2000, c. 23 (Eng.), available at www.opsi.gov.uk/acts; Interception of Communications Commissioner, Report, 2001, H.C. 1243, available at www.archive2.official-documents.co.uk. The numbers also neglect those issued by the Secretary of State for Northern Ireland, which have never been published, as well as by the Foreign Secretary, which have been withheld from public scrutiny since 1984. Equally absent is the number of wiretaps placed, but not specifically authorized or penalized, by domestic law. *See* Statewatch News Online, Telephone Tapping and Mail-opening Figures 1937–2000, www.statewatch.org (last visited Mar. 9, 2006).

Malone also asserted a violation of Article 13, which requires that the state provide a remedy:

Everyone whose rights and freedoms as set forth in this Convention are violated shall have an effective remedy before a national authority notwithstanding that the violation has been committed by persons acting in an official capacity.[43]

As a domestic matter, the English jurist, Sir Robert Megarry, heard the case. He responded to Malone's claims by announcing, first, that he was unconvinced that the electronic impulses transmitted over the wires constituted property. On the right to privacy, the oft-repeated recognition that no blanket right to privacy exists in English law – not least in the recently published HALSBURY'S LAWS OF ENGLAND – defeated any suggestion of an express right. The claim to an implicit right also failed. Like the American court in *Olmstead*, a 1928 case in which the court held that the wiretapping involved did not qualify as a search, Megarry asserted that interception outside the bounds of one's premises did not constitute trespass. Nor could the intercept be understood as eavesdropping: Described in 1809 by Blackstone as the act of listening under walls or windows or the eaves of a house and framing slanderous and mischievous tales, the offense had since been abolished by the 1967 Criminal Law Act.[44] The right of confidentiality, still in its infant stages, also did not apply, as – owing to extension lines, private switchboards, and crossed lines – no realistic person would expect not to be overheard when speaking on a telephone.

In regard to the second assertion, violation of the ECHR, the English court recognized a case directly on point. In 1979, the European Court had found in *Klass* v. *the Republic of Germany* that although Germany had not actually placed wiretaps on the five citizens claiming relief, the European court could still examine the legal structure of the surveillance system.[45] German law required the state to inform the citizens after the fact, where it would not jeopardize the purpose of the surveillance, that their communications had been intercepted. It also required, *inter alia*, that there be an imminent danger to state security, that other methods of obtaining the information be unavailable, and that the surveillance cease as soon as the requisite conditions cease. These safeguards meant that the statute, which fell afoul of Article 8(1), nevertheless met the criteria for necessity laid out in Article 8(2). The European court also required that there be an effective remedy before a national authority, bringing such measures into line with Article 13.

Megarry, comparing the German case to Malone's circumstances, recognized that British surveillance practice had no statutory basis – nor was there any legal remedy for perceived rights violations – suggesting that the use of intercepts fell afoul of the ECHR. The judge, however, bristled at the suggestion that European law carried any weight in the domestic realm. Megarry wrote, "Any regulation of so complex a matter as telephone tapping is essentially a matter for Parliament, not the courts; and neither the Convention nor the *Klass* case can, I think, play any proper part in deciding the issue before me."[46] Although, then, wiretapping may be "a subject which cries out for legislation," the court's hand's were tied. Malone appealed to the Continent.

In 1984, the European Court of Human Rights found for Malone.[47] The year in which the case reached the court's docket loomed large: Louis-Edmund Pettiti, a French judge on the court, wrote in his concurrence that "the mission of the Council of Europe and its organs is to prevent the establishment of systems and methods that would allow 'Big Brother' to become master of the citizen's private life."[48] He noted the continuing "temptation facing public authorities to 'see into' the life of the citizen."[49]

The UK government responded to the European Court's decision by introducing new law. The 1985 Interception of Communications Act made it a crime to obtain communications en route, other than as specified under statute.[50] To meet the requirements of Article 13 of the ECHR, the statute also established a complaints body. Any citizen, suspecting interception of his or her mail or telephone conversations, could file a complaint with a special tribunal, which was empowered to use judicial review mechanisms to ascertain whether the individual was, in fact, under surveillance and, if so, whether proper procedures had been followed. Where an individual was not under surveillance, the tribunal could only confirm to the applicant that no violations had occurred – not that they had not been the target of surveillance. In the event of surveillance and actual violations, the tribunal would inform the applicant and the prime minister, quash the warrant, destroy any information intercepted, and compensate the applicant. A senior member of the judiciary, serving as commissioner, would generate an annual report that, after the deletion of national security concerns, would be laid before Parliament. In the first six years of the statute's enactment, the tribunal uncovered a number of what it considered to be minor mistakes (such as the wrong phone tapped), but no blatant violations. In the interim, the number of warrants issued steadily increased.[51]

The Security Service Act (1989 and 1996) and the Intelligence Services Act (1994).

Soon after the adoption of the 1985 legislation, Westminster introduced measures to place the intelligence agencies on more secure legal footing. Once again, the European Court of Human Rights played a key role.

Harriet Harman, one of the Britons who brought suit, read Politics at the University of York.[52] From 1978 through 1982, she was a legal officer of the National Council for Civil Liberties (NCCL), an organization that, for 50 years, had been at the forefront of monitoring civil and political rights, lobbying, submitting evidence to formal inquiries, conducting research, holding conferences, issuing publications, and taking cases to court.[53] From 1983 through mid-1984, Harman served as General Secretary of the NCCL. Her time at the organization overlapped with that of Patricia Hewitt, who studied at Cambridge University and worked from 1978 to 1982 as a legal officer of the NCCL.

In the mid-1980s, the women brought suit against the government, claiming to have been placed under surveillance by MI5.[54] The applicants pointed to statements by Cathy Massiter, a former MI5 intelligence officer, who had mentioned in passing in March 1985 – and later swore in an affidavit – that the Security Service considered Harman and Hewitt to be "Communist sympathisers" owing to their participation in the NCCL. Although the women were not members of the Communist Party, the NCCL had been "assessed as a subversive organisation."[55] (Formally, the government, following a long-standing policy, neither confirmed nor denied that the applicants themselves were the subject of surveillance either while at the NCCL or after leaving the organization.)

MI5 still lacked, at the time, a statutory basis for the authority it exercised under the 1952 Fife Directive. Thus, as a legal matter, Security Service members had only the same search and arrest authorities extended to all British subjects[56] – a technicality that did not, however, appear to cause the Security Service much concern. (Just five years after the Fife Directive, a Privy Counsellor Committee had found that MI5 routinely intercepted communications.[57]) Hewitt and Harman appealed to the European Court of Human Rights, which found that the 1952 directive did not count as a legally enforceable rule.[58] It failed to give British subjects a sufficient idea of the powers of the state; nor was there an effective remedy under English law.[59]*

Even as *Hewitt and Harman v. United Kingdom* wound its way through the European courts, a domestic case involving an exposé written by a former intelligence agent raised government concern about the legal protections offered to the state. *Spycatcher* essentially drew attention to the flip side of the concern: the absence of legislative authority meant not just that Britons lacked protections, but that intelligence agencies also were limited in the legal devices available to protect them.[60]

Peter Wright, who had worked from 1955 to 1976 for MI5, decided upon his retirement to Tasmania that he would blow the whistle on the secret programs underway. After failed efforts to stimulate parliamentary inquiry into MI5's involvement in apparently dirty operations – such as an assassination attempt on the Egyptian president, efforts to remove Harold Wilson's government from power, and politically motivated burglaries of party headquarters and trade unions – Wright decided to publish a tell-all account.[61] Efforts by the government to obtain an injunction to prevent publication were met by unwieldy domestic and international legal barriers, so that the state was forced to rely on the Victorian law of breach of confidence and, later, contempt of court.[62]

---

* In a twist of fate, both Harman and Hewitt, previously suspected of subversive activity, went on to serve as Labour MPs. In 2001, Harman became Solicitor General and, in 2005, Minister of State in the Department of Constitutional Affairs – overseeing the criminal justice system. Two years later Harman became Deputy Leader of the Labour Party and Leader of the House of Commons. *See* www.harrietharman.org. In 2001, Hewitt was admitted to the Privy Counsel, the most trusted of British institutions. In 2005, she became Secretary of State for Health and – despite her own objection to being the object of state surveillance in the 1980s – has consistently supported the distribution of identity cards throughout the United Kingdom. *See* Patricia Hewitt, Secretary of State for Health, available at 10 Downing Street, www.pm.gov.uk; and The Public Whip: Policy report – 'Identity cards – Against introduction' compared to Patricia Hewitt MP, Leicester West, available at www.publicwhip.org.uk.

(See Chapter 5 for more detailed discussion of this case.) In the end, as a practical matter, state efforts to block publication were largely unsuccessful.

Accordingly, in 1989 the government took steps to place MI5 on a statutory basis. The Security Service Act, updated in 1996, reflected the organization's origins: it stated as MI5's object the protection of national security "against threats from espionage, terrorism and sabotage, from the activities of agents of foreign powers and from actions intended to overthrow or undermine parliamentary democracy by political, industrial or violent means."[63] Where an operation required agents physically to interfere with property, MI5 would have to obtain a warrant from the Secretary of State.[64] The statute required that the application made to the Secretary of State include a description of the case, the name of the person or organization targeted, the property involved, the operational plan, and a risk assessment. The Secretary of State must be satisfied that the search is necessary, "of substantial value" to MI5 in discharging its duties, and "cannot reasonably be obtained by other means."[65] The warrant is valid for a period of up to six months from issue, but can be renewed for another six-month period if considered necessary by the Secretary of State.[66]* To bring the powers into line with the European Convention, the new statute also provided for an Independent Commissioner to annually review the exercise of the powers, with a final report to be laid each year before the House of Lords and the House of Commons. The government met the dictates of the European Court by providing a tribunal for investigating complaints as well.

MI5, of course, is not the only organization that physically interferes with property in the conduct of domestic information gathering. Although the English constitution long ago addressed the conditions under which law enforcement – that is, the police – have to obtain a warrant, the 1984 Police and Criminal Evidence Act spelled out the basic rules.[67] The 1997 Police Act subsequently expanded the number of law enforcement bodies that could obtain permission to gain entry to include the police, the National Criminal Intelligence Service, the National Crime Squad, and HM Customs and Excise.[68] Formal implementation of these measures began in February 1999.[69]

To obtain a warrant, the officer must be satisfied that the action will be "of substantial value in the prevention or detection of serious crime, and that what the action seeks to achieve cannot reasonably be achieved by other means."[70] The legislation defines serious crime as violent acts, events that result in substantial financial gain, or conduct by a large number of people in pursuit of a common purpose. It also includes *any* offense for which a person above the age of 21 with no previous convictions would likely receive at least three years'

---

* The procedure on renewal is much the same as on initial application, except that the request states whether the operation has produced intelligence of value since its inception, and has to show that it remains necessary for the warrant to continue to have effect for the purpose for which it was issued.

imprisonment.[71] In the event that a dwelling, a hotel bedroom, or an office is to be inspected, or where confidential information is likely to be acquired, prior approval must be granted by a commissioner.* The statute empowers the commissioner to quash the warrant where reasonable grounds exist for believing the authority sought does not meet statutory requirements. In all cases, the officer authorizing the intrusion must notify a commissioner.

Although the protections relating to MI5 and law enforcement's exercise of power are not watertight (as I discuss later in this chapter), their presence and the fact that they were created in response to European pressure are important – as is the fact that the European Court of Human Rights continued to influence British surveillance law, even after the intelligence services were placed on a statutory basis.

The Regulation of Investigatory Powers Act (2000)

The 1989 and 1996 Security Service Acts and the 1994 Intelligence Services Act empowered first MI5, and later MI6 and Government Communications Headquarters, to apply through the Secretary of State for telegraphic intercepts. By the mid-1990s, however, with momentum gaining ground for the incorporation of the European Convention of Human Rights into domestic law, gaps in British law remained. A landmark case reached the European Court directly on point, highlighting what still needed to be done in domestic law to bring it into line with the Convention.

Alison Halford, a graduate of Notre Dame Convent Grammar School and former member of the Women's Royal Air Force, had in 1962 joined the police force. For the next three decades, she dedicated her career to the police service, rising to the rank of Assistant Chief Constable for Merseyside.[72] The most senior female police officer in the United Kingdom – and the first woman in British history to reach her rank – Halford failed eight times in seven years to obtain a promotion to Deputy Chief Constable either in Merseyside or elsewhere.[73] In 1990, she initiated proceedings in the Industrial Tribunal, claiming gender discrimination and, two years later, finally obtained a hearing. To prepare for the case, the Chief of Police for Merseyside took the liberty of placing secret wiretaps on Halford's home and work telephones.[74]

Halford sought relief in the European Court, which held that the interception of communications over private telecommunications systems fell outside the scope of the 1985 Interception of Communications Act.[75] But since no remedy at either common law or within domestic statutory law existed, the European Court found a violation of Article 8(1), saying that phone calls made from work or home could be considered "private life" and "correspondence."[76] As it was

---

* If, however, it is not reasonably practicable for a commissioner to grant prior approval, an urgent, 72-hour approval can be authorized by designated officers within the law enforcement bodies, for later approval by a commissioner. Police Act 1997, c. 50, §§ 94–95.

a public authority interfering with private life and correspondence, such actions had to be taken in accordance with the law – and the domestic statutes did not provide adequate protection.[77] The case drew attention to two problems: the codes of practice under which the police operated, and the remedy afforded by the law. With the 1998 Human Rights Act – and the incorporation of the European Convention into domestic law – looming large, the case forced the Labour government to bring forward new legislation.

The 2000 Regulation of Investigatory Powers Act (RIPA) subsequently became the primary legislation for surveillance and the interception of communications.[78] The formal drafting process began in June 1999 when the Home Office issued a consultation paper on the interception of communications. Although RIPA's aim, purportedly, was to establish the safeguards required by the Convention, the state used the occasion as an opportunity to update its ability to respond to (and take advantage of) new technologies. The government drew attention to the increase in the number of companies offering fixed line services, the mass distribution of mobile phones, the evolution of satellite technology, the growth of Internet communications, and the diversification of the postal network to include nonstate-run companies.[79] Six changes that significantly expanded state power followed.

First, the state proposed to expand the interception of communications sent via post or public telecommunication systems to *all* communications by telecom operators or mail delivery systems. Second, the state sought to relax warrant applications, tying them not to addresses, but to individuals, with a list of addresses and numbers attached and easily amendable by lower level officials.[80] (The USA PATRIOT Act similarly introduced the so-called roving wiretaps into domestic law [see page 235].) Third, to give the state flexibility to respond to emergencies, the authority to request wiretaps would be extended from the Senior Civil Service to the head of the agency involved. Fourth, the Labour government wanted to expand the length of time for which a warrant operated: under the previous statutes taps stayed in place only for a two-month period, with monthly renewals in cases of serious crime, and on a six-month basis for matters of national security or economic well-being. The state proposed to change the length of time, for serious crime, to three months, to be renewed every three months, and, for matters of national security and economic well-being, to six months, to be renewed every six months.* Fifth, the government also proposed to expand its intercept authority to include private networks, with the aim of making it legal for businesses to record communications to create a paper trail of commercial transactions and business communications in both public and private sectors. Sixth, where previously communications data could be turned over voluntarily, the state wanted to compel targets to do so. The new legislation ultimately forced Internet Service Providers (ISPs) to attach devices to their systems to enable communications to be intercepted

---

* This brought the interception of communications into the same time frame as intrusive surveillance device provisions, discussed in the subsequent text.

en route.[81] ISPs began automatically rerouting all Internet traffic – from email to click streams – to the Government Technical Assistance Center at MI5's London headquarters,[82] and no effort was made to insert any form of prior judicial sanction into the process.

It is notable that *none of these alterations addressed concerns raised by the European Court*, but, rather, expanded existing powers – even though their original impetus was actually to introduce safeguards on privacy to bring British law into line with the Convention.

In line with the latter's requirements, the legislation did create judicial and administrative oversight functions. The new Interception of Communications Commissioner (ICC), who replaced the IOCA Commissioner, was required to review the Secretary of State's decisions in regard to communications intercepts. Twice a year, the ICC began visiting the Security Service, Secret Intelligence Service, Government Communications Headquarters, NCIS, Special Branch of the Metropolitan Police, Strathclyde Police, Police Service for Northern Ireland, HM Customs and Excise, Foreign and Commonwealth Office, Home Office, Scottish Executive, and Ministry of Defence. These organizations forward a complete list of warrants issued since the last visit; the commissioner then selects which cases he would like to inspect – sometimes at random, sometimes for specific reasons. The ICC reviews the files, supporting documents, and the product of the interception to ensure that the procedure complies with RIPA. He also speaks to the Home Secretary, Secretary of State for Northern Ireland, Secretary of State for Defence, and First Minister for Scotland. In 2003, the commissioner also visited communications service providers (such as the Post Office and major telephone companies), which are the entities responsible for executing the warrants.

A new Intelligence Services Commissioner, in turn, replaced the two commissioners previously established by the 1989 Security Service Act and the 1994 Intelligence Services Act, combining in one person responsibility for intrusive surveillance and interference with property.[83]

The legislation also established a universal complaints tribunal to protect both public and private information. This Investigatory Powers Tribunal replaced the Interception of Communications, the Security Service, and the Intelligence Services tribunals, as well as the complaints function under the 1997 Police Act and complaints lodged under the 1998 Human Rights Act.*

Like the earlier provisions, these safeguards had weaknesses. First, consider the commissioners' annual reports. Like those generated under the 1985 Interception of Communications Act, the ICC's reports, which focus on the use of surveillance authority by law enforcement organizations, frequently refer to a "significant number of errors" in the operation of the intercepts – errors either human or technical that resulted in the destruction of the information

---

* This body has not found any violations of RIPA or the 1998 HRA. *See, e.g.,* INTERCEPTION OF COMMUNICATIONS COMMISSIONER, REPORT, 2003, H.C. 883, at 6–7, available at www.archive2.official-documents.co.uk.

intercepted.[84]* But these reports do not address substantive violations, and the portions that might have sensitive information remain classified.

The annual reports generated by the Intelligence Services Commissioner, in turn, which focus on intrusive surveillance and interference with property, stand out in their use of the cut-and-paste function, simply repeating from year to year the legal authorities under which the intelligence services conduct surveillance. The reports consistently omit even the broadest information: in the first ever report on MI5's actions, as required by the previous act, the Right Honorable Lord Justice Stuart Smith considered it "not in the public interest" to provide even the total number of warrants issued, as there were only a "comparatively small number of warrants issued under the 1989" legislation. Subsequent reviews, even after RIPA, similarly resisted providing such information, concerned that doing so would "assist the operation of those hostile to the state."[85] The handful of paragraphs addressing errors made by the intelligence services (which, each year, can be counted on one hand) carry similar language to this effect: "As it is not possible for me to explain any details of these breaches without revealing information of a sensitive nature, I have referred to them in more detail in the confidential annex."[86] The reviewers simply assure the public that any errors are solely due to administrative hiccups and that the powers themselves have been exercised in good faith.

Those conducting the reviews, although senior members of the judiciary, are not experts in surveillance technology. Nor are they given sufficiently large staffs, with specialists in cryptography, computer science, or other relevant disciplines – despite the complexity of the technologies involved.

Although the law requires the Investigatory Powers Commissioner for Northern Ireland, who focuses on the operation of the security services in the province, to lay annual reviews of surveillance powers exercised in Northern Ireland before the Northern Ireland assembly, RIPA allows the commissioner to exclude any information that may be prejudicial to the prevention or detection of serious crime or the continued discharge of the functions of any public authority[87] – apparently a large amount of material, as little information is made public. Annexes to the Chief Surveillance Commissioner's annual review, the Interception of Communications Commissioner's annual review, and the Parliamentary Intelligence and Security Committee, which performs oversight of MI5, MI6, and GCHQ, are confidential.

Second, the broader information made public tells us little about the powers specifically related to terrorism and national security – an exception permitted by Article 8(2) of the ECHR. The ICC, for instance, does not disclose the

---

* As of the present time, under RIPA 2000, there are four commissioners: the Interception Commissioner (replacing the Commissioner under IOCA 1985; previously High Court judge; Lord Lloyd 1986–91; Lord Bingham 1992–93, Lord Nolan 1994–2000, and Lord Justice Swinton-Thomas, 2001–06), the Intelligence Services Commissioner (replacing two different commissioners under the Security Service Act 1989 and ISA 1994), the Investigatory Powers Commissioner for Northern Ireland, and a Chief Surveillance Commissioner (has functions under the Police Act 1997, now Parts II and III of RIPA).

number of warrants issued by either the Foreign Secretary or the Secretary of State for Northern Ireland – the two secretaries most likely to be dealing with terrorism. The rationale is that "[i]t would greatly aid the operation of agencies hostile to the state if they were able to estimate even approximately the extent of the interceptions of communications for security purposes."[88] The government does not consider a similar risk, however, to accompany the release of information related to warrants issued by the Home Secretary or the First Minister for Scotland; nor does it consider the release of information related to property warrants – and broken down into offenses that include drug crimes, terrorism, and the like – to compromise the state.

Third, although the ICC and the Intelligence Services Commissioner inspect the agencies engaged in the interception of communications, the results of their inspections remain secret.

Fourth, the effectiveness of the Investigatory Powers Tribunal that RIPA provided, to inquire into and oversee remedies for violation of the statute, is open to question. Like the bland nature of the annual reports, this is not a new weakness: the complaints tribunal established under the 1989 Security Service Act, for instance, considered some 338 complaints between 1989 and 1999, with 3 left outstanding.[89] In none of these cases did the tribunal find in favor of a complainant.[90] In similar fashion, until the 2005–06 report, on no occasion did the Investigatory Powers Tribunal direct a finding in favor of an applicant.[91] (Finally, in February 2007, the tribunal reported a finding in favor of two complainants who filed a joint application.)[92] If anything, RIPA made it harder to ascertain the effectiveness of the oversight authorities: Where information was previously broken down by the agency exercising the powers – as the reporting requirements for each tribunal took place under different statutes – the information is now combined, with only the total number of complaints made available.[93]

Despite these concerns, some aspects of the legislation did carry benefits. The statutes formalized what before had been general guidelines adopted, exercised, and modified by the Secretary of State and thus, to this extent, did increase procedural protections. Part I of RIPA reiterated from the 1985 legislation, for instance, that it is a criminal offense for any person, without lawful authority, to intercept any communication sent via public post or telecommunication in the course of their transmission.[94] To be lawful, interception must be undertaken in accordance with a warrant issued by the Secretary of State. The grounds for granting the warrant collapsed into one category national security, the prevention or detection of serious crime, safeguarding the economic well-being of the United Kingdom (in relation to persons outside the British Islands), or giving effect to any international mutual assistance agreement in relation to serious crime.

RIPA requires the Secretary of State to be satisfied that no other reasonable means exists for obtaining the same information. The conduct authorized must be proportionate to the aim of the investigation. The warrant must specify the conduct that will be undertaken, how related communications data will be obtained, and the individuals who must assist in giving effect to the warrant. Although roving wiretaps can be sought, as a matter of practice the application is not open-ended: the agency requesting the wiretap must state that the target will be using, for instance, the following numbers or staying at the following addresses.[95]

The informal procedures continue to require a range of officials to sign off on the operations. Those authorized to request interception warrants include the Director-General of MI5, the Chief of MI6, the Director of GCHQ, the Director-General of the National Criminal Intelligence Service, the Commissioner of the Police of the Metropolis, the Chief Constables of the Northern Ireland and Scottish police forces, the Commissioners of Customs and Excise, the Chief of Defence Intelligence, and, for cases involving mutual assistance, any competent authority of countries outside the United Kingdom.[96] It is up to the Secretary of State to examine and approve the number of persons to whom the material is made available and the extent to which the information is released or copied, as well as the number of copies made.[97]

The new legislation required that the agencies conducting intercept activities conform to, and ensure that their practices were in accord with, the legal authorities. It also limited the operation of the warrants: where before codification warrants were granted indefinitely, first the 1985 legislation and later RIPA specified the acceptable periods before the warrant would have to be reviewed.

Although the codification in law of the previous Home Office measures does not, as a substantive matter, offer more rigorous standards of protection to the targets of surveillance than existed prior to the European Court's findings, the use of primary legislation means that the procedures for granting warrants are publicly available and must pass parliamentary approval to be altered. The oversight bodies, moreover, although reporting to the government, provide protections that otherwise did not exist – and that continue not to exist on the other side of the Atlantic. The deterrent value here of the commissioners' visits is of note – they create a fair amount of anxiety within the target agency to ensure that they "pass" the external audit. As the auditor is drawn from a different institutional background, the review also functions to allow individuals outside the target institution's culture to evaluate the use of the powers. The reviews also create the opportunity for the government to receive independent advice that may allow it to alter course.

Finally, RIPA specifically excludes any information gathered from the interception of communication – or the fact that it has been gathered – from being used as evidence in court.[98]* Anyone revealing it becomes subject to criminal penalties.[99] Arguments can be made both ways as to whether the exclusion of intercepts benefits or hurts targets of surveillance. On the one hand, the state can use the information to find a place and time for obtaining further information;

---

* The legislation exempted proceedings before the Tribunal, the Special Immigration Appeals Commission, or the Proscribed Organisations Appeal Commission.

and the fruits of such surveillance remain admissible. On the other hand, private aspects of an individual's life, even those not at all related to the crime suspected, may enter the surveillance record. This provision thus prevents such information from surfacing directly in a court of law. But keeping the surveillance out of court means that the manner by which information is gathered remains cloaked – which is, of course, the primary argument put forward for preventing it from entering official records.[100] Although the inclusion of this limitation has proven to be highly controversial, and multiple reviews have argued for its repeal, the state has held its course.[101]

Electronic Bugs and Encrypted Data

Throughout most of the twentieth century, Home Office guidelines, not statutes, governed law enforcement's use of electronic surveillance. Part III of the 1997 Police Act introduced the first statutory controls, including a Code of Practice on Intrusive Surveillance, which entered into force in February 1999.[102]* Similarly, until 1994, no law regulated MI5's use of covert surveillance. That year the Intelligence Services Act required authorization by the Secretary of State.[103] RIPA amended and expanded these statutes. Before delving into the details of the current authorities, however, I look first at a case considered by the European Court of Human Rights, which demonstrates where the authorities introduced between 1989 and 1997 fell short of Convention demands.

On March 14, 1994, an English court sentenced Sultan Khan, a British national, to three years in prison for dealing drugs in a case that relied heavily on information obtained from an electronic bug that the police placed in his home.[104] The Appeal Courts dismissed Kahn's appeal but raised the issue, as a point of law, whether the product of covert surveillance could be introduced as evidence in a criminal trial. Although the House of Lords again dismissed the appeal, it addressed the question at hand. The Lords asserted that English law admits of no general right to privacy – and that, even if such a right does exist, common law requires that improperly obtained evidence be admitted at trial, according to judicial discretion. Lord Nolan, writing for the majority, added, "The sole cause of this case coming to the House of Lords is the lack of a statutory system regulating the use of surveillance devices by the police." He noted that "[t]he absence of such a system seems astonishing, the more so in view of the statutory framework which has governed the use of such devices by the Security Service since 1989, and the interception of communications by the police as well as by other agencies since 1985."[105] In January 1997, Kahn lodged a complaint

---

* Various nonstatutory codes of practice also were developed at this time by the Association of Chief Police Officers in England and Wales, the Association of Chief Police Officers in Scotland, and HM Customs and Excise. The Code has been replaced by the Covert Surveillance Code of Practice (Surveillance Code) issued under the Regulation of Investigatory Powers Act. 2000, c. 23, § 71(5) (Eng.), available at www.opsi.gov.uk.

with the European Commission of Human Rights, claiming, *inter alia*, a violation of Article 8, focusing on the right to respect for private life, and of Article 13, requiring an effective domestic remedy.

In April 1999, the European Court held that the surveillance in question
clearly violated Article 8(1).[106] The question was whether it fell sufficiently
within Article 8(2) – namely, whether it was "in accordance with the law" and
"necessary in a democratic society" for one of the purposes specified in that
section. Drawing on *Halford*, the Court noted that "in accordance with the
law" requires both compliance and attention to whether it reflects the rule of
law: that is, that the law has to be sufficiently clear as to inform the public of
the authorities claimed by the state. But, like the previous state of affairs in
relation to the interception of communications, no statutory scheme for electronic bugging existed. Neither did the Home Office guidelines governing covert
surveillance carry the force of law – nor did the public know what the guidelines were. The Court unanimously ruled that the practice violated Article 8.
The Court also found in the applicant's favor with respect to the claim
under Article 13: while the English judiciary could have excluded the evidence
under the Police and Criminal Evidence Act, the only redress to violations of
that statute was to file a complaint with the Police Complaints Authority –
hardly an impartial body.[107] On May 12, 2000, the Court awarded Khan
£311,500.

The *Khan* case, reflecting the state of law prior to the RIPA, revealed the stark
difference between British practice and European standards. RIPA addressed
this disparity by creating a new regime to address electronic bugging. As with the
interception of communications, however, the government did not just address
the issues raised by the European Court; instead, it used the occasion as an
opportunity to expand on the existing guidelines to allow for broader surveillance authority.

Part II of RIPA focused on the three types of covert surveillance: intrusive,
directed, and covert human intelligence surveillance. The level of authorization
that must be obtained and the circumstances under which public authorities can
authorize information gathering vary depending on the type of surveillance and
on the entity undertaking it. The legislation covers operations undertaken by
MI5, MI6, and Government Communications Headquarters, as well as "public
authorities" – all in all, more than 950 entities, ranging from local authorities
and health trusts to the National Crime Squad and the Metropolitan Police.
In 2004, the government further expanded the public authorities to which the
legislation applied, bringing under its remit such varied bodies as the Postal
Services Commission and Office of Fair Trading.[108]

The first area, intrusive surveillance, covers any covert search conducted on
residential property or in private vehicles, in which either an individual or a
device collects the information. A gadget not physically located on the property
or in the car, which delivers the same quality of information as though it were
physically present, counts as intrusive. The authorizing officer must be assured
that the surveillance is necessary on the grounds of national security or to

prevent or detect serious crime. The statute also requires that the officer be satisfied that the operation is proportionate to its aim. Outside of emergency situations, the approval of a commissioner is required prior to implementation.*

Although the legislation established commissioners to oversee the process, it is not clear how much of an impact they have. In the first year of the statute's operation, for instance, the commissioners refused prior approval only in one case (out of 371 authorizations for property interference and 258 authorizations of intrusive surveillance) and did not overturn any of the 46 emergency authorizations.† Outside of prior approval, the commissioners also have the ability to terminate an authorization or renewal either where no reasonable grounds exist for believing that the authorization meets the required criteria or where an emergency authorization is found to be wanting. In the first year of the statute's operation, the Commission refrained from overturning any intrusive surveillance warrants. In his annual review of these powers, the chief commissioner, Andrew Leggatt, interpreted these numbers as indicating "that applications continue to be properly considered by the agencies before they are authorised."[109] This trend continues.[110]‡

The second category, directed surveillance, focuses on information sought in the course of an investigation or operation where private data are likely to be gathered. Electronic bugs placed in work areas or nonprivate vehicles fall into this category. The process for obtaining warrants duplicates intrusive surveillance requirements with two critical differences in the criteria. First, unlike intrusive surveillance, the senior authorizing officer or (for the intelligence services) the Secretary of State does not need to take into account whether the information could reasonably be obtained by other means. Second, many more entities can request a directed warrant than can request an intrusive one – a circumstance in line with the broader number of aims such warrants can seek. Whereas intrusive warrants are limited to issues of serious crime, national security, and the economic well-being of the United Kingdom, directed warrants may, in addition, be directed toward public safety, the protection of public health, the assessment or collection of taxes or duties, and any other purpose

---

* Subsequent guidelines constructed by the commissioners' office state that it is not necessary to obtain authorization through the Secretary of State when hostages are involved; the suspects in such circumstances are considered to be engaged in crime, and are thus stripped of any claim to privacy. The victims, in turn, would be unlikely to object to any invasion of their privacy if it meant being freed from captivity. CHIEF SURVEILLANCE COMMISSIONER, REPORT TO THE PRIME MINISTER AND TO SCOTTISH MINISTERS, 2002–2003, H.C. 1062, at 4, available at www.archive2.official-documents.co.uk.

† The reason for refusal centered on timing: the public authority initiated the surveillance *prior* to obtaining commission approval, as required by law.

‡ These numbers do not include renewals, which, at least in regard to the Police Act, are increasing: 437 in 2001–02, 543 in 2002–03. *Id.* at 3. The total renewals are decreasing, however, in intrusive surveillance: from 102 in 2001–02, the total dropped to 80 in 2002–03. *Id.* at 4. In his annual review of these powers, the Chief Commissioner, Andrew Leggatt, attributes this decline and the drop in urgent requests to "improved knowledge and efficiency as well as to an increasing familiarity with the requirements of authorization." *Id.* at 3.

specified under order by the Secretary of State. Accordingly, many more authorizations are made for directed than for intrusive surveillance. (In 2001, for instance, public authorities and intelligence agencies obtained some 28,000 directed authorizations, as opposed to 493 intrusive ones.)*

The third category, covert human intelligence sources (CHISs), addresses the process via which public authorities develop relationships with individuals to facilitate the secret transfer of information. As with intrusive surveillance, proportionality is required. The statute requires that the public authority establish a manager for day-to-day contact with the CHIS, a handler for general oversight, and a registrar to maintain records on the source; and that access to the records be limited to a need-to-know basis. CHIS authorizations include the broader aims of directed surveillance, extending such information-gathering powers to public safety, public health, the collection of taxes, and other purposes as may be issued under order by the Secretary of State. On average, public authorities and the intelligence services recruit between 5,000 and 6,000 new sources annually. For each of the three categories, authorization lasts for three months, with three-month renewals possible. In an emergency, authorization can be granted for a 72-hour period.

The role of the commissioners here again is at least questionable. It could be argued that the oversight conducted by the office is significant: records of all surveillance must be kept by the public authority for review by the commissioners. But, in the rare instance that the Commission does quash an authorization (only a handful of instances in the five years that have elapsed since RIPA), law enforcement and public authorities can appeal to the Chief Surveillance Commissioner. And the standard of review is remarkably weak: where the Chief Surveillance Commissioner is satisfied that reasonable grounds exist for believing that the requirements have been satisfied, he can modify the commissioner's decision. There is, though, some oversight of this process in that the Chief Surveillance Commissioner then reports his findings directly to the prime minister.[111]

In addition to reporting statistics and reviewing applications for authorization, the commissioners also conduct general inspections of law enforcement agencies and public authorities making use of the surveillance powers. Again, an argument could be made that this is an effective oversight mechanism: the Surveillance Commissioners annually inspect approximately 60 law enforcement entities and 270 public authorities. With this rigorous schedule, as of the spring of 2007, all 442 local authorities in Great Britain have undergone at least one inspection. However, it takes years to inspect all the agencies, and the results of these inspections are not made public. Rather, the Commission forwards a report to the Chief Officer and, where necessary, requests that the

---

* In 2004, the state narrowed this requirement for local authorities to allow them to conduct direct surveillance or use covert human intelligence sources only for preventing crime or disorder. Regulation of Investigatory Powers (Directed Surveillance and Covert Human Intelligence Sources) Order 2003, available at www.opsi.gov.uk.

entity develop an action plan to address any issues raised. Some flavor of these reviews comes through in the commissioner's annual report, where he or she has highlighted a number of bad practices, such as "insufficiently specific applications and authorisations, exceeding the terms of the authorisation, delegation of reviews by authorising officers, codes of practice not readily available to practitioners and inadequate RIPA training and education."[112] The inspections also revealed a significant number of basic errors, such as the entry of wrong addresses, mistakes in the vehicle identification numbers specified in the authorization, and the use of the procedures for intrusive surveillance when the situation warranted only directed surveillance authority.

The importance of these reviews should not be underestimated; it is likely that the presence of external inspectors creates a certain apprehension in the target agencies prior to inspection and creates a relationship that encourages entities to redress errors. But the insistence that reports on these agencies be made available only to the entity being inspected somewhat detracts from the public's ability to judge a report's effectiveness.

The final area to examine in this context is encrypted data. Section III of the Regulation of Investigatory Powers Act created a duty of disclosure: those possessing encryption keys became required to hand them over to the state where it was necessary for national security, where it would help to prevent or detect crime, or where it would be in the interests of the economic well-being of the United Kingdom. One may also be required to do so where the information sought is central to the exercise of public authority, statutory power, or statutory duty. The duty of disclosure must be both proportionate to what its imposition seeks to achieve and the only reasonable way in which the information can be obtained.[113] Criminal penalties of up to two years' imprisonment and a fine follow violation of the statute. The legislation also makes it illegal to tip anyone off to the fact that the state is seeking the information – an offense that is treated as even more serious than not providing the keys and can be punished by up to five years' imprisonment and a fine.[114] RIPA places a duty on law enforcement and public authorities to use the keys only for the purpose for which they are sought, as well as to store them in a secure manner. The records of a key must be destroyed as soon as it is no longer needed to decrypt the information.[115]

Although the powers were supposed to begin in 2004, the Home Office deferred implementation of Part III. Chief Surveillance Commissioner Leggatt explained that terrorists and criminals had not, as predicted, yet moved fully into the encryption realm. In the meantime, the National Technical Assistance Center, a Home Office facility that handles complex data processing, "is enabling law enforcement agencies to understand protected electronic data, so far as necessary." Leggatt added, "I am assured that the need to implement Part III of RIPA is being kept under review."[116] In the spring of 2007, the Home Office announced its intention to bring Part III of RIPA into force, toward which end it has issued a draft code of practice. However, as a technical matter, it has remained in abeyance.

The upshot of RIPA is that, although MI5 still needs a warrant to read the content of the information obtained from ISPs, such authorization is *not* necessary for the agency to monitor patterns, such as Web sites visited, to and from whom email is sent, which pages are downloaded, of which discussion groups a user is a member, and which chat rooms an individual visits. It is too early to gauge how these powers will measure up against the ECHR. Nor is it clear how the European Court will respond to the gag orders included in the legislation.

Both business and civil liberties groups object to the legislation, which the government presented with little public discussion and no evidence about the level of threat posed over the Internet by terrorists, pedophiles, and other criminals. Nor did the government present evidence that would suggest that the need for these measures outweighs their impact on privacy.

DATA PROTECTION

As with intercepts and electronic bugs, European jurisprudence has influenced the United Kingdom's treatment of third-party information: the extent to which such data are protected and how long they are kept. Here British standards are significantly more protective of individual privacy than those in the United States. In the United Kingdom, the focus is not on mining massive amounts of information already available, but instead on what information must be made available when requested through controlled intelligence-gathering authorities.

European Union Norms and Rules

Many scholars have written persuasively and at length about the different approaches to privacy, and the different legal regimes that spring from them, taken by the European Union and the United States.[117] It is not that one has failed and one has succeeded. "That," observed one scholar, "is hogwash. What we must acknowledge, instead, is that there are, on the two sides of the Atlantic, two different cultures of privacy, which are home to different intuitive sensibilities, and which have produced two significantly different laws of privacy."[118] The European culture of privacy can be seen as protecting human dignity – not as protecting individuals against state interference[119] – thus making entirely acceptable a high level of government involvement in protecting consumers' privacy.[120]

This contrast is perhaps seen most clearly in the realm of third-party data protection. What some call a "command and control model with precise rules governing the handling of personal information"[121] stems from the history of the European Union. The 1957 Rome Treaty incorporated unifying principles:

The Community shall have as its task, by establishing a common market and an economic and monetary union and by implementing the common policies or activities ... to promote throughout the Community a harmonious and balanced development of economic activities, sustainable and non inflationary growth respecting the environment, a high degree of convergence of economic performance, a high level of employment and of social protection, the raising of the standard of living and quality of life, and economic and social cohesion and solidarity among Member States.[122]

The legal institutions subsequently developed were designed to cross national borders and led one academic to conclude, "This unified approach has allowed Europe to take the lead in formulating a harmonized legal regime for the information age."[123] Since the turn of this century, the European Commission, tasked with creating free competition, has approved a range of high-technology measures – for example, the E-Commerce Directive, E-Signatures Directive, Distance Selling Directive, Data Protection Directive, Database Protection Directive, and the Copyright Directive.[124]

As early as the 1970s, specifically in the realm of data protection, member states began developing national measures to regulate the collection, use, and storage of information.[125] Although these measures did not initially provide a uniform level of protection, efforts to harmonize the national laws led to the introduction in 1995 of the European Union Data Protection Directive.[126]

This instrument achieved its purpose of protecting individual privacy against industry by addressing both the processing of personal data ("any information relating to an identified or identifiable natural person") and the movement of such information.[127] The directive defines "processing" broadly to mean "any operation or set of operations which is performed upon personal data, whether or not by automatic means, such as collection, recording, organization, storage, adaptation or alteration, retrieval, consultation, use, disclosure by transmission, dissemination or otherwise making available, alignment or combination, blocking, erasure or destruction."[128] It required that each member state adopt a national law consistent with the agreement by October 1998. It laid out a set of principles with which such laws must conform: "Personal data must be processed fairly and in a manner consistent with specified, explicit and legitimate purposes, maintained accurately, updated periodically, erased or rectified in a timely manner, and kept anonymously when identification of data subjects is no longer necessary." Processing may take place only when the following conditions are met:

(a) the data subject has unambiguously given his consent; or (b) processing is necessary for the performance of a contract to which the data subject is party or in order to take steps at the request of the data subject prior to entering into a contract; or (c) processing is necessary for compliance with a legal obligation to which the controller is subject; or (d) processing is necessary in order to protect the vital interests of the data subject; or (e) processing is necessary for the performance of a task carried out in the public interest or in the exercise of official authority vested in the controller or in a third party to whom the data are disclosed; or (f) processing is necessary for the purposes of the legitimate interests pursued by the controller or by the third party or parties to whom the data are disclosed, except where such interests are overridden by the interests or fundamental rights and freedoms of the data subject which require protection under Article 1(1).

The consent clause essentially means that the EU has adopted an "opt-in" standard, which requires a subject to express consent and makes data processing dependent on the will of the individual involved.[129]

The directive further requires that certain types of information be given even more protection. Race, ethnicity, political or religious affiliation, health, and membership of unions cannot be processed without explicit consent or in a handful of special cases. Data controllers must provide certain information to the target – such as the reason for the processing, who will see the information, and what rights the subject has. In the event that the processor does not comply with the law, the data may be erased.[130] The directive also requires that controllers take appropriate data security measures.[131]

In the United States, in contrast, notions of privacy are grounded more in liberty than in dignity.[132] As a result, "[p]reserving both individual autonomy and commercial flexibility has traditionally been paramount, and industry has historically been trusted to police itself, particularly where such self-policing would support continued growth and development of the Internet."[133] US industry has thus embraced the twin principles of self-regulation and government restraint in dealing with information held by third parties[134] – an approach that has made for fragmented federal law, where a wide range of statutes cover discrete corners of privacy concerns.[135] Although Congress has made some movement toward a more unified approach, no statute as yet provides a comprehensive federal framework for the collection and use of personal information.[136] Most applicable law stems from the states[137] – further complicating the American approach, which tends to give subjects the opportunity not to "opt in" to data processing, but instead emphasizes an "opt-out" standard.[138] As one scholar explains, "Under the 'opt-out' approach, an individual has the right to demand that the collection and/or the commercial use of personal information about him be stopped or curtailed."[139]

The difference between the European Union and the United States matters in that the European directive requires that member states ensure that any personal information transferred to a third country be subjected to a similar level of protection. Article 25 requires that member states allow transfers of personal data to countries outside of the European Union "only if . . . the third country in question ensures an adequate level of protection."[140] Adequacy depends upon a range of factors, such as the nature of the information, the rules of law in force in the country receiving the data, and the security measures in place.

The low level of protection for private information in the United States means that European entities may be barred by law from passing on information to US actors. The European Union's standards could severely hamper the ability of the United States to do business in Europe. One scholar concludes, "This could create major problems. A large international bank with customers in the EU and processing centers in the United States could not transmit information concerning those customers across the Atlantic. A credit reporting company could not report personal credit information gathered in Europe to the United States."[141]

In other words, the more that American counterterrorist law lowers protections on personal information, the greater the risk of potentially harmful economic effects – yet nowhere is this risk considered in the security or freedom rubric often used as a shorthand to evaluate whether further incursions into privacy ought to be allowed. And the potential consequences are substantial: in 2003, the value of US trade with the 15 member nations of the European Union was more than $400 billion.[142] One estimate put the total value of all transactions between these countries and the United States at $1.7 trillion[143] – a value that is expected to increase. A high percentage of the commercial traffic depends upon the transfer of data.[144]

Faced with the possibility that American companies would be blocked from transferring critical information out of Europe, the US Commerce Department negotiated Safe Harbor, an agreement in which US companies would take reasonable steps to ensure data integrity.[145] Information coming from the European Union to Safe Harbor companies can continue without special approval. These Safe Harbor companies annually certify to the Department of Commerce that they are in compliance with the principles laid out in the agreement.[146] So far, this agreement has held. But the legal issues that would accompany any challenge to it are extremely complex and have yet to be worked out. It is not clear which jurisdiction would win in a battle over data protection.[147] And reviews of Safe Harbor are mixed: some see it as a good compromise; others consider it satisfying to none of the parties involved. Friction continues, for instance, over the Safe Harbor companies' failure to incorporate the data protection principles into their written privacy policies.[148]* Nevertheless, as one commentator noted, "A surprising absence of interference by European authorities with information flowing from the EU to the United States has occurred."[149] One explanation may be that currently it is simply not in the EU's business interests to do so and that, for the time being, discrepancies between the American and the European regimes can be overlooked. Nevertheless, the potential cessation of data flow, as a legal matter, is still on the table.[150]

British Data Retention Law

The Regulation of Investigatory Powers Act of 2000 provides, as I have discussed, for the government to obtain communications data – including the

---

* Those tensions have only grown in the aftermath of September 11. James Q. Whitman, *The Two Western Cultures of Privacy: Dignity Versus Liberty*, 113 YALE L. J. 1151, 1157 (2004) (citing, e.g., Peter Gola & Christoph Klug, Die Entwicklung des Datenschutzrechts in den Jahren 2001/2002, 55 Neue Juristische Wochenschrift [N.J.W.] 2431, 2431–32 (2002); and Adam Clymer, *Privacy Concerns: Canadian and Dutch Officials Warn of Security's Side Effects*, N.Y. TIMES, Feb. 28, 2003, at A14).

type of equipment used and the location of the user, information about telephone subscribers, itemized telephone bill logs, email headers, Internet protocol addresses, and postal envelope information. The statute defines the conditions under which such data can be obtained:

(a) in the interests of national security
(b) for the purpose of preventing or detecting crime or of preventing disorder
(c) in the interests of the economic well-being of the United Kingdom
(d) in the interests of public safety
(e) for the purpose of protecting public health[151]

The difficulty that quickly became apparent after RIPA's passage was whether private companies would be able to meet the demands for information if and when they were made by the state. The industry trend at the time, toward reducing the amount of data required for billing purposes, was – together with pressure from the privacy lobby – leaning on companies to retain less customer information.[152]

In addressing this concern, the 2001 Anti-Terrorism Crime and Security Act required that communication service providers retain data for a specified period to ensure the fulfillment of requests made under 2000 RIPA. Some scholars attribute the inclusion of this passage to lobbying done by the National Criminal Intelligence Service on behalf of the police, Customs and Excise, the Security Service, the Secret Intelligence Service, and Government Communications Headquarters, which called for a minimum 12-month retention by the communication service provider, followed by six-year storage, either in-house or by a trusted third party.[153] What is fascinating about the expansion is the rationale offered by the NCIS:

Communications data is crucial to the business of the Agencies. It is pivotal to reactive investigations into serious crime and the development of proactive intelligence on matters effecting not only organized criminal activity but also national security. At the lower level, it provides considerable benefit to the detection of volume crime.... Short term retention and the deletion of data will have a disastrous impact on the Agencies' intelligence and evidence gathering capabilities.[154]

This language hints at a general data-mining approach to the detection of crime – one similar to that of its US counterpart.[155]

To carry out the retention provisions, the ATSCA empowered the Secretary of State to issue a voluntary code of practice, a draft of which the Home Office published in March 2003, to be followed by implementation via statutory instrument. In the event that the code proves inadequate to force communication service providers to turn over information, the legislation empowers the Secretary of State to issue compulsory directions.[156] In the case of a recalcitrant service provider, civil proceedings for an injunction or other relief may be initiated by the Secretary of State.[157]

Like many information-gathering authorities in the USA PATRIOT Act, the ATCSA does not retain only terrorism data. A late amendment requires that the information "may relate directly or indirectly to national security" for prosecution – however, "may" also suggests "may not."[158] The government strenuously opposed even the limited amendment – much less efforts to restrict data retention solely to counterterrorist concerns.[159] Counsels' advice to the Information Commissioner on the data retention provisions in the ATCSA noted that it is "an inevitable consequence of the scheme envisaged by ATCSA that communications data" retained for an extended period will be "available for production in accordance with a notice issued under section 22 RIPA for a purpose with no connection whatever to terrorism or national security."[160]

The requirement that data be retained received a boost the following year when the European Union issued a directive regarding the processing of personal data and the protection of privacy in the electronic communications sector. Echoing Article 8 of the ECHR, Article 15(1) of the directive allows for information to be archived in the interests of national security, defense, or public security or for the prevention or detection of criminal offenses.[161]

The ATCSA retains more information than is necessary – while it remains relatively easy for anyone desiring anonymity on the Internet to dodge state grasp. Traditional email systems include the name of the sender and the receiver and require individualized login and password information – but it is entirely possible for other people to access these accounts. Email systems – such as Earthlink, Hotmail, and Yahoo! – allow individuals to obtain accounts under an alias. A user can access these accounts via a public terminal and thus remain anonymous. Individuals surfing the Web can use sophisticated browsers that cover their trail. Guardster.com "offers free anonymous Internet Web surfing to everyone."[162] Other sites, such as Anonnymizer.com, the-cloak.com, and anonymous.com, offer similar services. Special programs, such as Anonymity 4 Proxy, allow a user to scan servers and confirm their anonymity.[163] Users can obtain fake IP addresses, block cookies, and change their browsers to mask personal information. Although such legislation as the ATCSA may catch some terrorists, anyone engaged in terrorism is likely to use these relatively accessible tools to ensure the privacy of their planning.

This likelihood raises the issue whether the measures are proportionate – especially in light of the state's ability to introduce statutory instruments under RIPA to expand the number of entities that can demand that the stored communications include public authorities that are not related to national security. The Leading and Junior Counsel from Matrix Chambers, a prominent practice at Gray's Inn (one of the four Inns of Court to which barristers are called), advised the Information Commissioner, upon being approached for analysis, of the following:

There is, in Counsel's view, no doubt that both the retention of communications data on behalf of a public authority, and the disclosure of such data to a public authority constitute an interference with the right to respect for private life and correspondence enshrined in Article 8(1) of the European Convention of Human Rights.[164]

Indeed, the European Court has found that "states do not enjoy unlimited discretion to subject individuals to secret surveillance or a system of secret files. The interest of a State in protecting its national security must be balanced against the seriousness of the interference with an applicant's right to respect for his or her private life." The president of the European Court of Human Rights, Judge Luzius Wildhaber, continued,

[T]here has to be at least a reasonable and genuine link between the aim invoked and the measures interfering with private life for the aim to be regarded as legitimate. To refer to the more or less indiscriminate storing of information relating to the private lives of individuals in terms of pursuing a legitimate national security concern is . . . evidently problematic."[165]

The European Court also reads the Convention as requiring that the new measures be necessary; however, the 2001 ATCSA, introduced nine months after the 2000 Terrorism Act came into effect, hardly addressed a serious gap in the law. There was not enough time to establish this failure – and certainly no evidence of it has been made public since.*

Another aspect of proportionality concerns whether the potential impact of the provisions on the privacy of individuals could prove incompatible with the European Convention of Human Rights[166] – an issue raised in November 2001 by the UK Information Commissioner. This issue echoes the 1998 Data Protection Principles, raising the question about whether Britain's measures are at odds with the EU directive of 1995. In particular, the latter's first principle requires a legitimate basis for processing; the third ensures that the information collected be relevant and not excessive in relation to the purpose, and the fifth demands that personal information not be held any longer than is necessary for processing. Professor Clive Walker suggests that these provisions "would almost certainly forbid the blanket storage of logs recording such details as web-sites browsed or email addresses."[167]

SURVEILLANCE IN PUBLIC SPACE

Although surveillance oversight mechanisms and data protection laws appear more robust in the United Kingdom than in the United States, and information on the number and range of programs in place in the former is muted, Britain nonetheless conducts broad surveillance. Indeed, the state collects significant amounts of data – and maintains the ability to track individuals as they move through public space, through extraordinary port and border controls, as well as through the use of closed-circuit television.

---

* The only cases made available, in an attempt to convince Internet companies to retain records, cited instances in which records more than 15 months old were sought in non-national security-related investigations. *See* Stuart Miller, *Internet Providers Say No to Blunkett*, GUARDIAN (UK), Oct. 22, 2002, at 9.

Port and Border Controls

In 1974, the United Kingdom supplemented its general immigration law with special port and border controls that allow it to collect low-level intelligence[168]: that is, information on a broad number of people that, isolated, may appear innocuous, but that can be used to piece together patterns, gain insight into relationships, and hence to understand basic social interactions. The tools used to accomplish this information gathering involve both "carding" – a process whereby travelers fill out information on a card and return it to the examining officer – and allowing officers to detain and question travelers. The information thus obtained can then be compiled with other information to fill out a picture.

The heavy use of these powers on the Irish community led in the 1980s and 1990s to protest and controversy. In his exhaustive review of counterterrorist powers in 1996, Lord Lloyd of Berwick addressed this concern and recommended that the state scale back the powers, introduce a code of restraint to counter the stereotyping, and reduce the amount of time travelers could be detained from 24 hours to 6.[169]

The subsequent Terrorism Act of 2000 did reform port controls. It reduced detention to nine hours and provided for the Secretary of State to order the repeal of the carding procedure.[170] It required that the use of carding be effected via affirmative parliamentary procedures to underscore that they would be used only when security demanded it. Lord Bassam of Brighton, a Labour Whip, explained, "Objections have included that its use can delay journeys on occasions and that it can appear to be used disproportionately against Irish people." He continued, "Even when a carding order is in force, that is not to suggest that blanket carding of all flights and sailing will take place simply as a matter of course."[171]

Despite these reassurances, as Professor Clive Walker observes, "the promise of restraint was not met."[172] The subsequent secondary instrument continued the powers in much the same fashion as before. The process allows the examining officer (constable, immigration officer, or a designated officer from HM Customs and Excise) to question passengers, regardless of whether there are any grounds for suspicion.[173] The power can be used within a mile of the border between Northern Ireland and the Republic of Ireland, as well as at all sea and air ports within the United Kingdom – for both domestic and international travel.[174] Anyone stopped for questioning is required to do the following:

(a) give the examining officer any information in his or her possession that the officer requests
(b) give the examining officer on request either a valid passport that includes a photograph or another document establishing his or her identity
(c) declare whether he or she has with him or her documents of a kind specified by the examining officer
(d) give the examining officer on request any document that he or she has with him or her and is of a kind specified by the officer[175]

Failure to cooperate would, presumably, be sufficient grounds to execute an arrest.[176] To determine whether additional questioning is necessary, the legislation also provides for the examining officer to search the passengers, the vessel, and any cargo.[177] Property can be seized for up to seven days.[178]

In 2001, the Anti-Terrorism Crime and Security Act made further changes to the law, giving officers the ability to exercise port controls not just for those entering the United Kingdom or traveling between Northern Ireland, Great Britain, and the British islands, but also for flights within Great Britain or Northern Ireland, as well as any movement of ships or boats within the country.[179] The carriers are responsible for providing passenger information when requested in writing by an examining officer.[180] All information can be shared with the Secretary of State, HM Customs and Excise, constables, the director of the National Criminal Intelligence Service or the National Crime Squad, or individuals designated by the Secretary of State.[181]

As recommended by Lord Lloyd, the government did develop a code of practice for the exercise of these powers, which states the following:

Examining officers should . . . make every reasonable effort to exercise the power in such a way as to minimize causing embarrassment or offence to a person who has no terrorist connections. The powers to stop and question a person should not be exercised in a way which unfairly discriminates against a person on the grounds of race, color, religion, creed, gender or sexual orientation. When deciding whether to question a person the examining officer should bear in mind that the primary reason for doing so is to maximize disruption of terrorist movements into and out of the United Kingdom.[182]

The Code provides further guidance:

The selection of people stopped and examined under the port and border area powers should, as far as is practicable given the circumstances at the port or in the area, reflect an objective assessment of the threat posed by various terrorist groups active in and outside the United Kingdom. Examining officers should take particular care not to discriminate unfairly against minority ethnic groups in the exercise of these powers. When exercising the powers examining officers should consider such factors as:

- known and suspected sources of terrorism
- any information on the origins and/or possible location of terrorist groups
- the possible nature of any current or future terrorist activity
- the means of travel (and documentation) that a group of individuals could use
- local circumstances, such as movements, trends at individual ports or parts of the border area.[183]

Closed-Circuit Television

Surveillance cameras were first introduced into the United Kingdom in 1956, and the country now leads the world in the per capita concentration of public surveillance devices.[184] In 1999, the British government appropriated £153 million to develop a closed-circuit television (CCTV) network.[185] By 2003, two and a half million, or roughly 10 percent of the globe's total number of CCTVs operated on British soil.[186] In 2003, according to the *National Geographic*, this number topped four million.[187] The net effect is substantial: each person traveling through London is caught on film approximately 300 times per day.[188] These devices do not just watch and record; some use facial recognition technology to scan the public against a database of persons sought by the state.* In East London alone, approximately 300 cameras incorporate this technology.

Although the systems aim to deter and detect ordinary crime – and thereby increase residents' sense of security – no statistics are available on the cameras' effectiveness. However, CCTV has played a role in counterterrorism: in Northern Ireland, for instance, the Casement Park trials (in which the state prosecuted individuals for complicity in the 1988 Provisional Irish Republican Army murder of two soldiers in civilian dress, who drove their car into the middle of a funeral procession) centered primarily on footage obtained from CCTV; and in Britain, Jan Taylor and Patrick Hayes were convicted for the 1993 Harrod's bombing in part because of evidence procured from surveillance cameras.[189] After the King's Cross bombing in July 2005, police review of CCTV tapes played a significant role in piecing together the events leading up to the attack and helped to identify a suspected handler.

London is not alone in its surveillance efforts. Scotland maintains approximately 10,000 cameras to monitor traffic speed and parking structures.[190] Some 75 cities in total in the United Kingdom have public CCTV systems, with a number of private actors following suit. And the cameras have overwhelming support: approximately 95 percent of all local governments regard them as a viable means to enforce the law.[191] In Newham, for instance, where $30 million went into installing the devices, police claimed an 11 percent drop in assaults, a 49 percent drop in burglaries, and a 44 percent drop in criminal damage through the end of 1994.[192] These statistics, however, are not hard and fast; and at this point, there is not enough information to isolate CCTV as causing the drop in crime in these cities. Some observers suggest that the drop in crime could be due to a number of initiatives undertaken at the same time – or part of general trends that can be seen even in areas where cameras are lacking.

The primary legislation governing CCTV is the 1998 Data Protection Act (DPA), which mirrors the European directive. The DPA incorporates rights of access to information and regulates data controller behavior. It also provides for special exceptions – amongst which is national security.[193] Data controllers – in this case, those overseeing CCTV – must act in accordance with specified principles, including fair and lawful processing, the acquisition of information only for specific and lawful purposes, and the processing of information only

---

* Facial recognition technology is a form of biometric identification. Algorithms map relationships between facial features, can identify from live video or still images, up to a 35-degree angle, and compensate for light conditions, glasses, facial expressions, facial hair, skin color, and aging. *Find Criminals, Missing Children, Even Terrorists in a Crowd Using Face Recognition Software Linked to a Database*, PRNewswire, Nov. 16, 1998.

in a manner compatible with that purpose. The information gathered must be proportionate to the purpose for which it is processed, and those obtaining the data may not hold them any longer than necessary for the stated purpose. The legislation grants targets of surveillance particular entitlements – such as the right to know when a controller is processing their personal data, and the ability to prevent the information from being used for direct marketing. The statute requires that no significant decision involving the information be made solely via automation. The target has the right to require the destruction of inaccurate information. And the legislation allows subjects to go to court to remedy a breach of it.

In keeping with RIPA 2000, the Chief Commissioner recommends that where CCTV is to be used at a crime hotspot, and if it is likely that private information will be gathered, the police ought to apply for directed surveillance. The Chief Commissioner's assumption is that a judge will go easier on public authorities who have sought a warrant.[194]

Although the European Court has not adjudicated on the general presence of the cameras, it has ruled against Britain's use of specific footage. In *Peck* v. *United Kingdom* (2003), the facts of which occurred prior to the 1998 Human Rights Act, CCTV caught the applicant wielding a knife in preparation for suicide. The police immediately went to the scene and prevented Peck from hurting himself. Although the police did not charge him with a criminal offense, the local council later released the tape to the media, which aired footage of Peck with the knife (but not the actual suicide attempt) on national television. The government also used a photograph of the applicant as part of a public relations exercise to demonstrate the effectiveness of the cameras. The state did not mask this man's identity when it released the information to the public.

When the applicant's efforts to seek relief through the domestic judicial system failed, he appealed to the European Court. The British government asserted that because the event occurred in public, the state's action had not compromised the applicant's Article 8 right to a private life. The Court noted that Peck was not a public figure and not attending a public event, but was, rather, walking late at night in a state of considerable distress. Although disclosure had a basis in law, was foreseeable, and sought to uphold public safety and the prevention of crime, it failed on the grounds of proportionality.* The local council could have tried to mask the applicant's identity or sought his consent. Advertising the effectiveness of the system did not present a compelling enough reason to violate Peck's rights under Article 8. The European Court also determined the lack of domestic remedy to be a violation of Article 13, and in 2003, it awarded Peck €11,800 for nonpecuniary damages and €18,705 for expenses.[195]

---

* The High Court had held that under the Criminal Justice and Public Order Act 1994, x. 163, the local council could use CCTV to prevent crime; and through the Local Government Act 1972, s. 111, could distribute the footage. *See* Michael Cousens, Surveillance Law (2004), at 56.

In handing down its decision, the European Court emphasized the importance of recording the information: had the cameras simply been observation devices, the monitoring of public space would not give rise to privacy concerns. The recording of the information, however, even though it was in a public arena, mattered, and its dissemination meant that Peck's action had a much broader audience than would otherwise have been the case.

Similar CCTV systems that are beginning to spring up in the United States are not protected by any legislation even approximating the United Kingdom's Data Protection Act. The city of Washington, D.C., for instance, plans to take advantage of more than 1,000 video cameras, "all linked to central command station accessible to not only the District police but the FBI, the Capitol Police, the Secret Service, and other law enforcement agencies."[196] The public learned about the placement of these devices, and plans for expanding the system only after the initial group had been put into place. What began as 13 cameras owned by the Metropolitan Police Department became linked to several hundred cameras in schools and public transportation.[197] The National Park Service, in turn, spent some two to three million dollars to install cameras at major memorial sites on the Washington Mall.

In 2002, at the first congressional hearings to be held on the matter, Chief of Police Charles Ramsey said that the department made use of the cameras 24/7 only during heightened alert or large-scale events.[198] The National Park Service, as of the time of the hearings, had yet to decide how long to keep the recordings. The associate regional director of the National Capital Region, National Service, John Parsons, tied the existence of these cameras to the terrorist threat: "We are convinced by studies and consultants that these icons of democracy are high targets for terrorist activities. And that is the sole reason that we have made the decision to go forward with planning for these cameras."[199]

Chicago presents a more extreme case. As of December 2005, the police had the ability to monitor some two thousand cameras.[200] By 2006, the city had added another 250.[201] What makes these numbers even more significant than those for Washington, D.C., is the technology attached: software programs cue the cameras, which are trained on sites considered terrorist targets, to alert the police automatically when anyone wanders in circles, lingers outside, pulls a car over onto a highway shoulder, or leaves a package and walks away.[202] The city consciously modeled this plan after London's, as well as after systems in place in Las Vegas and currently being used by Army combat teams.[203] When fully implemented, the Chicago system will be one of the most sophisticated in the world, particularly with respect to its ability to monitor the thousands of cameras in motion – subjecting citizens to almost constant surveillance in public space. Dispatchers who receive an image will have the ability to magnify it up to 400 times. And the total cost to the city? $5.1 million for the cameras; another $3.5 million for the computer network.[204] Discussing plans to expand the project and place cameras on public vehicles, such as street sweepers, Mayor Richard M. Daley defended the eye of the state: "We're not inside your home or your business. The city owns the sidewalks. We own the streets and we own the alleys."[205]

Washington and Chicago are not alone: more than 60 urban centers in the United States use CCTV for law enforcement purposes.[206] Baltimore, Maryland, has perhaps the next most extensive system.[207] But it is not just large cities that have jumped on the CCTV train. Yosemite airport, for instance, combines CCTV with facial recognition technology to scan for terrorists.[208] These systems make it increasingly difficult for individuals to retain their anonymity as they move through public space. There are legitimate law enforcement interests in this surveillance – such as to prevent and detect crime, reduce citizens' fears, and aid in criminal investigations. Yet even electronic surveillance companies admit that "[o]verall, it is fair to say that no jurisdiction is currently keeping the kind of statistical data that can be analyzed in such a way to demonstrate the effect of CCTV."[209]

THE AMERICAN SURVEILLANCE CULTURE

During most of the twentieth century, the surveillance culture in the United States was considerably more public than in the United Kingdom, and the manner in which the executive exercised surveillance authorities more contested. From the beginning of the Red Scare early in the century, periodic efforts by Congress and the judiciary to exercise control over the executive through statutory law and common law were met by the executive branch's determined efforts to continue on its path. Thus, in May 1908, Congress barred the Department of Justice from employing the Secret Service in an intelligence-gathering function. The Attorney General responded by going around the ban and creating new positions – special agents – to conduct investigations; within a year, these became concentrated in the newly formed Bureau of Investigation.[210]

Over the next decade, extensive acts of violence – some engineered by anarchists, others by ordinary criminals – increased.* In response, Attorney General A. Mitchell Palmer – assisted by young J. Edgar Hoover – amassed information on citizens and initiated a series of purges, arresting and deporting thousands of "undesirable aliens." In one day alone, federal agents rounded up some 4,000 people in 33 cities.[211] This period set a precedent for the extraordinary use of executive power during peacetime to counter a threat to national security. It also resulted in a public backlash against the overzealous Palmer.

In 1924, a new attorney general, Harlan Fiske Stone, came to office determined to clamp down on domestic intelligence gathering. He demanded that the Bureau of Investigation's director resign, initiated an immediate review of all people working at the agency, and insisted that only "men of known good

---

* On May Day 1919, for instance, 36 bombs entered the postal system, addressed to prominent Americans. A month later, one found its way to Palmer's home. In 1920, a wagon bomb exploded in lower Manhattan, killing more than 30 people and injuring hundreds more. The attack caused some two million dollars in damage. *House of Morgan Bombed*, www.pbs.org/wnet (last visited Mar. 3, 2006).

character and ability" – and preferably legal training – be given positions.[212] J. Edgar Hoover became the new director of the bureau, which retained the extensive dossiers it had built up between 1916 and 1924. But when the Treasury Department's Bureau of Prohibition merged with the Bureau of Investigation (BI) into a new Division of Investigation, in June 1933, it brought with it policies that allowed for routine interception of electronic communications. Rather than changing the Bureau of Prohibition's policies, the BI – renamed in 1935 the Federal Bureau of Investigation – adapted to bring its practices into line, returning to the previous practice.[213]

This policy shift was soon endorsed at the highest levels of government. In 1936, President Roosevelt met with Hoover to discuss "the question of the subversive activities in the United States, particularly fascism and communism."[214] He wanted Hoover's organization to provide him with detailed information on the threat – "a broad picture of the general movement and its activities as may affect the economic and political life of the country as a whole."[215] Hoover obliged by sending to all field offices a letter that ordered them "to obtain from all possible sources information concerning subversive activities being conducted in the United States by Communists, Fascists, representatives or advocates of other organizations or groups advocating the overthrow or replacement of the Government of the United States by illegal methods."[216] He established a procedure that provided for the systematic collection and reporting of data. And he emphasized the importance of secrecy, "in order to avoid criticism or objections which might be raised to such an expansion by either ill-informed persons or individuals having some ulterior motive." Wary of the legislative branch, Hoover continued, "Consequently, it would seem undesirable to seek any special legislation which would draw attention to the fact that it was proposed to develop a special counter-espionage drive of any great magnitude."[217]

The field offices complied. They carefully shielded the Bureau's surveillance program from public scrutiny, as they obtained data from "public and private records, confidential sources of information, newspaper morgues, public libraries, employment records, school records, et cetera."[218] Some information related to entirely lawful (and constitutionally protected) activities. Child care centers, political reelection campaigns, Christian organizations, and the NAACP, for instance, all merited attention.[219]

After World War II, Congress renewed its debate on the use of wiretaps. But, as the Iron Curtain descended, anti-communist fever swept the United States. The House of Representatives' Dies Committee, formed in 1937 to look into subversive elements, turned in 1946 into the permanent House Committee on Un-American Activities. When the Judith Coplon espionage case burst onto the national scene, Hoover's tactics appeared warranted.

On the one hand, the case proved the presence of subversives – Judith Coplon having, through her job at the Justice Department, funneled FBI reports to the Soviet Union's KGB. On the other hand, it exposed Hoover's surveillance to the eye of the courts. The appeal court determined that the wiretap evidence against Coplon could not be admitted – and that her arrest without a warrant violated federal law. Yet the judiciary's ability to rein in the executive was limited: although the court dismissed all charges, the Bureau, undeterred, continued to wiretap.[220]

In the early 1950s, the conflict between personal privacy and the Red threat came to a head. Efforts by the highest court in the land to stem intrusions into citizens' private lives, though, fell on deaf ears. The issue was larger than just counterespionage or counterterrorism. The issue centered on privacy rights. Justice Robert H. Jackson wrote,

Science has perfected amplifying and recording devices to become frightening instruments of surveillance and invasion of privacy, whether by the policeman, the blackmailer, or the busybody. That officers of the law would break and enter a home, secrete such a device, even in a bedroom, and listen to the conversation of the occupants for over a month would be almost incredible if it were not admitted.[221]

Herbert Brownell, who had become Attorney General in 1953, took the offensive. He responded to Jackson's remarks with a memorandum to the Director of the FBI demonstrating contempt for the judiciary – and clearly setting national security apart from ordinary criminal investigation: "[F]or the FBI to fulfill its important intelligence function, considerations of internal security and the national safety are paramount and, therefore, may compel the unrestricted use of this technique in the national interest."[222] New "emergency anti-Communist" legislation would legalize electronic surveillance.[223] The Republican leader of the House, Charles Halleck, threw down the gauntlet: all "loyal" citizens would see the administration's proposal as an "anti-traitor bill."[224]

Despite executive efforts to steamroll Congress, public concern about the executive branch surveillance of law-abiding citizens (read legislators) spurred a series of hearings. These surprised the country with the extent of the surveillance programs underway and (although the private sale of surveillance devices soared) made for a consensus, from radical left to hard right, that they should be somehow controlled.[225] In June 1965, President Johnson issued an unpublished memorandum banning wiretapping. Yet, once again, he carved out an exception for national security.[226]

Although surveillance was exercised in respect to national security, it also reached well beyond that realm into the ordinary criminal one and, thus, was a much bigger issue. In addition, concern about surveillance and its inroads into privacy increased in concert with the development and spread of the technologies that were making eavesdropping and wire intercepts possible. Furthermore, the executive consistently claimed that its authority to protect the nation was not limited by either the legislature or the judiciary. It was thus not the Fourth Amendment that mattered, but, rather, the president's Article II authorities. Indeed, court opinions appeared to recognize repeatedly an exception where surveillance was conducted under the auspices of national security. Two columns on the legal ledger emerged.

In 1967, in *Katz* v. *United States*, the Supreme Court wrestled with developing technology and recrafted the contours of the Fourth Amendment.[227] As the Court replaced the previous "trespass doctrine" with one based on a "reasonable expectation of privacy," the Fourth Amendment came to protect "people, not places."[228] Justice Potter Stewart, writing for the Court's majority, explained, "What a person knowingly exposes to the public, even in his own home or office, is not a subject of Fourth Amendment protection. But what he seeks to preserve as private, even in an area accessible to the public, may be constitutionally protected."[229] The "presence or absence of a *physical* intrusion" mattered naught in consideration of the Fourth Amendment.[230]

As important as the case was to ordinary criminal law, though, it raised the question whether national security concerns fell within its remit. Justice Byron White in his concurrence emphasized that the presumption against warrantless searches *could* be overcome by pressing need, and continued, "We should not require the warrant procedure and the magistrate's judgment if the President of the United States or his chief legal officer, the Attorney General, has considered the requirements of national security and authorized electronic surveillance as reasonable."[231]

Justice William O. Douglas, joined by Justice William J. Brennan, objected to White's assertion and pointed out a certain conflict of interest: "Neither the President nor the Attorney General is a magistrate. In matters where they believe national security may be involved they are not detached, disinterested, and neutral as a court or magistrate must be."[232] The constitutional responsibility of the executive is to "vigorously investigate and prevent breaches of national security and prosecute those who violate the pertinent federal laws."[233] Douglas concluded,

Since spies and saboteurs are as entitled to the protection of the Fourth Amendment as suspected gamblers like petitioner, I cannot agree that where spies and saboteurs are involved adequate protection of Fourth Amendment rights is assured when the President and Attorney General assume both the position of adversary-and-prosecutor and disinterested, neutral magistrate.[234]

The national security issue proved contentious, and a sort of de facto double standard evolved. According to the Court, physical surveillance and electronic bugging became subject to a "reasonable expectation of privacy" test. But wiretapping and surveillance where national security might be involved were on a different side of the legal ledger – a side where much looser considerations would satisfy the demands of Article II.

Although after *Katz*, the executive jumped on the bandwagon and gave lip service to the Court's concern, once again it retained for itself the very exception that had led to such widespread use of wiretaps: national security. President Lyndon Johnson announced the following in his 1967 State of the Union address:

We should protect what Justice Brandeis called the "right most valued by civilized men" – the right of privacy. We should outlaw all wiretapping – public and private – wherever and whenever it occurs, *except when the security of the nation is at stake* – and only then with the strictest governmental safeguards. We should exercise the full reach of our Constitutional powers to outlaw electronic "bugging" and "snooping."[235]

The following year Congress introduced the Omnibus Crime Control and Safe Streets Act.[236] Title III of this statute, which went beyond the Supreme Court's decision, continues to govern the use of wiretaps for ordinary criminal law investigations. It created prior judicial authorization and established the circumstances under which an intercept order could be issued. The legislation requires probable cause that a crime has been or is about to be committed. The communications to be intercepted have to be relevant to the particular offense. The officer applying for the warrant has to specify the person, location, description of communications, the name of person requesting the warrant, and the length of time it is to last, with a 30-day limit. Any extensions are subject to earlier restrictions.[237] Title III limits wiretaps to 26 specified crimes, including murder, kidnapping, extortion, gambling, counterfeiting, and drugs – all, coincidentally, activities associated with terrorist organizations. Moreover, Title III makes a wiretap even harder to obtain than an ordinary search warrant, which has to indicate that normal investigative procedures will not suffice. Nevertheless, Congress *specifically excepted national security*, leaving such investigations firmly in the executive domain.[238]

In a landmark decision handed down in 1972 – and in another attempt by the judiciary to rein in the executive branch – the Supreme Court held that Title III *does not* authorize the executive to engage in electronic surveillance for national security purposes; rather, it simply reflects congressional neutrality.[239] This decision left the Court open to consider whether warrantless domestic wiretapping for national security falls exclusively within the constitutional remit of the executive. The Court determined that it does not. Although the duty of the state to protect itself has to be weighed against "the potential danger posed by unreasonable surveillance to individual privacy and free expression,"[240] such "Fourth Amendment freedoms cannot properly be guaranteed if domestic security surveillances may be conducted solely within the discretion of the Executive Branch."[241]

Justice Jackson, again writing for the Court, recognized that executive officers could hardly be regarded as neutral and disinterested: "Their duty and responsibility are to enforce the laws, to investigate, and to prosecute. . . . [T]hose charged with this . . . duty should not be the sole judges of when to utilize constitutionally sensitive means in pursuing their tasks."[242] He highlighted the dangers: "[U]nreviewed executive discretion may yield too readily to pressures to obtain incriminating evidence and overlook potential invasions of privacy and protected speech."[243] Domestic security surveillance thus did not fall under one of the exceptions to the warrant requirement under the Fourth Amendment.[244] Jackson rejected the government's suggestion that national security matters are "too subtle and complex for judicial evaluation."[245] Nor did he accept that "prior judicial approval will fracture the secrecy essential to official intelligence gathering."[246]

Once again, the executive branch largely ignored this decision. Wiretapping of domestic individuals and organizations, under the guise of national security, continued. The Federal Bureau of Investigation, the National Security

Agency, the Central Intelligence Agency, and the Department of Defense all held their course. Although much has been written about the executive excesses that occurred during this time, a handful can illuminate the breadth and depth of the abuses that occurred under the executive's Article II claims.

Executive Excesses (1945–75)

In the excesses occurring between 1945 and 1975, where surveillance, conducted under the auspices of national security, became an instrument of political power, these stand out: the NSA's Operation SHAMROCK and Project MINARET; the FBI's COINTELPRO, with its focus on left-leaning organizations and individuals; the CIA's Operation CHAOS; and the US Army's Operation CONUS. Each operation began as a limited inquiry and gradually extended to capture more information from a broader range of individuals and organizations. Each targeted American citizens. And each remained insulated, until Senator Frank Church's hearings in 1975, from legislative or judicial oversight.

Operation SHAMROCK began in World War II, when the military placed censors at RCA Global, ITT World Communications, and Western Union International. Keen to maintain the flow of intelligence at the close of the war, the Department of Defense told the companies to continue forwarding intercepts; from 1949 until 1975, the project continued (from 1952 under the control of the National Security Agency) without the knowledge of subsequent presidents. To keep the project under the radar, the NSA deliberately refrained from formalizing the relationship in any (traceable) document.[247] By the 1970s, from the magnetic tapes that recorded all telegraph traffic, the NSA was selecting approximately 150,000 messages per month for its analysts to read and circulate.

SHAMROCK put the government in the position of asking private industry to break the law – not execute it. The United States Code prohibited the interception or decryption of diplomatic codes or messages[248] and also outlawed the transfer of information "concerning the communication of intelligence activities of the United States or any foreign government" to unauthorized persons.[249] Although the law required the president to designate individuals engaged in communications intelligence activities, from 1949 forward no president was even aware that the companies and their executives surveilled all telegraphs entering, leaving, or circulated within the United States. The project is also notable in that it gave the companies a political interest in guaranteeing that certain administrations would remain in office – thus ensuring that that they, the companies, would not be subject to criminal prosecution.

Whereas SHAMROCK was a broad information-gathering effort, the NSA also undertook Project MINARET, which placed under surveillance "individuals or organizations involved in civil disturbances, anti-war movements, [or] demonstrations."[250] Project MINARET maintained a Top Secret classification. Its charter specified that although the NSA had instigated the project, it would not be identified with it.[251] The NSA initially focused on American citizens traveling to and from Cuba, but it then expanded the target list to individuals believed to threaten the president. The FBI added domestic and foreign entities, saying that they were "extremist persons and groups, individuals and groups active in civil disturbances, and terrorists."[252] The Bureau of Narcotics and Dangerous Drugs extended the remit to include "the abuse of narcotics and dangerous drugs."[253] In 1971, the executive branch specifically requested that the NSA monitor international terrorism.[254] And by 1971, the program extended to *all* criminal activity, as well as to foreign support for, or basing of, subversive activity.[255] In October 1973, the NSA terminated the program, having placed under surveillance hundreds of thousands of Americans engaged in constitutionally protected political protest.[256]

Vast and expensive as this machinery was, it appears to have been relatively ineffective. When pressed repeatedly whether acts of terror in fact had been prevented, General Lew Allen, the first director of the National Security Agency ever to testify to Congress, told Representatives that only *one* event had been so disrupted.[257] Moreover, rather than information coming bottom-up (from the surveillance being conducted to concluding what threats faced the state), considerable pressure ran top-down to find something linking foreign organizations to civil disturbances.[258] While at some level this approach makes sense – indeed, management of the intelligence community requires strategic guidance on where resources ought to be placed – at the other extreme, ideology becomes a driving force and makes for skewed intelligence, with little basis in substantive threats.[259] Indeed, strong political pressure from the top has played out through many major intelligence-gathering operations.

In addition to the NSA's surveillance operations, Hoover's Federal Bureau of Investigation ran – without either the president or the Attorney General knowing about it – an operation code-named COINTELPRO.[260] Court records show that from 1936 through 1976, the FBI disrupted domestic organizations.[261] These programs involved a wide range of activities aimed at left-leaning organizations and the antiwar movement: the FBI provided their leaders' past criminal records and "derogatory material regarding . . . marital status" to the media; it sent anonymous letters to exacerbate racial tensions and made false claims about members of these organizations[262]; and it distributed fake newspapers on campuses and contacted the Better Business Bureau in New York City with untrue allegations to interrupt organizations' fundraising efforts.[263] According to Professor Geoffrey Stone, a prominent legal scholar, the FBI "caused antiwar activists to be evicted from their homes; disabled their cars; intercepted their mail; wiretapped and bugged their conversations . . . prevented them from renting facilities for meetings; incited police to harass them for minor offenses; sabotaged and disrupted peaceful demonstrations; and instigated physical assaults against them."[264] The judiciary that explained the agency conducted interrogations to "enhance the paranoia in [Leftist] circles and . . . to get the point across there is an FBI agent behind every mailbox."[265] The organization extended its interviews to the workplace, where it questioned supervisors, as well as religious organizations and neighborhoods.

These disruptive actions complemented the general surveillance of groups considered a threat to the state. As with Operation SHAMROCK and Project MINARET, the number of people targeted gradually expanded. Initially, the FBI focused on just the Communist Party of America, but soon included the Socialist Workers Party and, in 1964, the Ku Klux Klan and other Aryan organizations.

While these groups may be exactly the types of organization we might want the government to be monitoring, the salient point about these surveillance programs is that – whatever their initial motivation and target – they almost inevitably tend to expand. By 1965, the civil rights movement had become a focus, with leaders such as Martin Luther King, Jr., and organizations such as the NAACP coming within the Bureau's remit. In the late 1960s, the FBI further extended its list to include "Black Nationalist" groups, such as the Southern Christian Leadership Council, the Student Nonviolent Coordinating Committee (SNCC), and the Nation of Islam.* Prominent leaders – H. Rap Brown (SNCC and later a member of the Black Panthers), Elijah Muhammad (Nation of Islam), and Malcolm X (Nation of Islam until his 1964 founding of the Organization of Afro-American Unity) – were all observed around the clock. The FBI also became suspicious of all "dissident" parties within the Democratic bloc, such as Students for a Democratic Society.† Although, after an extensive investigation, the FBI concluded that the Communist Party was *not* behind the antiwar movement, it continued to attend and record teach-ins and antiwar rallies.[266]

Successive presidential directives provided general authority for the FBI to conduct investigations into espionage and sabotage; however, the manner in which it carried out such investigations involved outright violations of American law. A notable example of such violation involved the Socialist Workers' Party (SWP), which first came under Hoover's eye in 1940.

Article II of the SWP's constitution called for "the abolition of capitalism through the establishment of a Workers and Farmers Republic."[267] The organization sought what it considered a democratically elected government: a series of elected local councils would then elect the central government. It supported the freedom to form political parties and also advocated "basic individual rights and freedoms such as freedom of speech and religion and due process of law."[268]

---

* The Southern Christian Leadership Council was founded in 1957 and led by Martin Luther King, Jr. In 1960, the Student Nonviolent Coordinating Committee formed and began focusing on nonviolent actions, particularly in the South, to protest white domination. Clayborne Carson, *Civil Rights Movement*, www.liberationcommunity.stanford.edu. (last visited Mar. 3, 2006). Clayborne Carson, *Civil Rights Movement, in* ENCYCLOPEDIA OF THE AMERICAN CONSTITUTION 411–12 (Leonard W. Levy et al. eds., 2000). Nation of Islam was a black religious organization, founded in 1930 and led by Elijah Muhammad. Claude A. Clegg, *Message from the Wilderness of North America: Elijah Muhammad and the Nation of Islam, c. 1960*, 1 J. MULTIMEDIA HIST. 1 (1988), available at www.albany.edu/jmmh.

† Tom Hayden founded the SDS in 1959. A Kent State protest led by the SDS gave rise to a violent National Guard reaction that further divided the country. After a number of splinter groups broke off from the organization, and a power struggle for control emerged, by 1972 the organization ceased to operate. *Old American Red Groups*, www.reds.linefeed.org (last visited Mar. 3, 2006).

Despite its overarching goal, however, the organization was not engaged in violence. SWP leaders stated under oath that terrorism contradicted their central philosophy,[269] and outside of court they repeatedly criticized terrorist attacks, such as the 1972 Black September attack on Israeli Olympians and the assassination of the Spanish prime minister two years later. Members spent most of their time debating Marxist theory, the war in Vietnam, the plight of agricultural workers in California, and the civil rights movement – all "unquestionably lawful political activities," the District Court wrote, "which a group such as the SWP has a clear constitutional right to carry out."[270]

Nevertheless, for 36 years, the FBI kept the SWP under strict surveillance and, in the process, committed more than 204 burglaries. Agents broke into SWP and Young Socialist Alliance offices in New York, Newark, Chicago, Detroit, Boston, and Milwaukee, as well as members' homes in Detroit, Newark, Hamden (Connecticut), and Los Angeles.[271] "Black bag" jobs – the Bureau's shorthand for break-ins in which they stole or photocopied papers – yielded 9,864 documents, which contained information on topics that ranged from the group's activities, finances, and legal matters to members' personal lives.[272] These break-ins also allowed the FBI to hide surveillance devices. Between 1943 and 1963, agents conducted approximately 20,000 wiretap days and 12,000 electronic bug days on the SWP alone.[273] The FBI clearly knew that the break-ins violated the law – as an internal memorandum dated July 19, 1966, noted:

We do not obtain authorization for "black bag" jobs from outside the Bureau. Such a technique involves trespass and is clearly illegal; therefore, it would be impossible to obtain any legal sanction for it. Despite this, "black bag" jobs have been used because they represent an invaluable technique in combating subversive activities of a clandestine nature aimed directly at undermining and destroying our nation.[274]

To get past the legal issues, the FBI followed what it called a "Do Not File" procedure: the Special Agent in Charge prepared an informal record of all "black bag" operations, which he placed in his personal safe. Bureau Inspectors would then read the memorandum and destroy it.[275]

In addition to direct surveillance, the FBI ran approximately 1,300 informants – most of whom were paid – to gather additional information and, through them, obtained some 12,600 additional documents.[276] Informants further provided the Bureau with records on what occurred at the SWP's meetings, and intimate information on its members and their families, such as "marital or cohabitational status, marital strife, health, travel plans, and personal habits."[277] The FBI also paid SWP members to disrupt SWP operations by discouraging recruitment, lowering dues, and diminishing how much people contributed.[278]

The result: in more than 30 years – out of 1,300 sources and thousands of reports and documents – not a single informant reported any instance of "planned or actual espionage, violence, terrorism, or efforts to subvert the governmental structure of the United States."[279] Nor did the Bureau bring a single prosecution against any member of the SWP.

In 1973, the SWP filed suit against the Attorney General. Complicated by the Department of Justice's efforts to maintain strict secrecy under the claim of national security, the case took 13 years to reach the Supreme Court. Much of the information about these surveillance efforts has emerged in the years since. At the time they were being conducted, the public had no idea of their extent, until the Citizens' Commission to Investigate the FBI (an antiwar group) broke into an FBI office and stole roughly one thousand pages of confidential information.[280] In April 1971, Hoover announced the cessation of COINTEL-PRO. Despite this announcement, and the FBI's claim that it had terminated "domestic security" break-ins, such actions – and various other surveillance programs – continued.[281]

Like the NSA and the FBI, the CIA also ran many domestic counterintelligence projects, among which was one code-named Operation CHAOS.[282] This project owed its existence to pressure from the Johnson and Nixon administrations to find a link between the antiwar movement and overseas actors.[283] In the process of gathering data, the CIA placed under surveillance more than 300,000 American citizens, with an average of one thousand individual reports per month flowing from it to the FBI.[284] The CIA also shared specific information with the White House. Like the FBI with respect to "black bag" jobs, the agency was entirely aware that its actions pushed legal bounds.[285] Nevertheless, the Attorney General consistently claimed that, under his Article II authority, the president has the power to authorize electronic surveillance of US citizens without court order.[286] Efforts to challenge Operation CHAOS in court hit a brick wall: because the information had been classified at the highest level, claimants could not gain access to it to demonstrate that particular individuals had been targeted.[287]

The military also conducted surveillance. Operation CONUS maintained files on more than 100,000 political activists and orchestrated data exchange between some 350 military posts. The list of targets included senators (Adlai Stevenson III, J. William Fulbright, and Eugene McCarthy), the Congressman Abner Mikva, the singer Joan Baez, and the civil rights leader Martin Luther King, Jr., as well as civil liberties organizations, such as the American Civil Liberties Union, Americans for Democratic Action, the NAACP, the American Friends Service Committee, and the Southern Christian Leadership Conference.[288] Army Intelligence agents attended meetings and submitted reports to headquarters, describing the name of the organization, the date of the gathering, the speakers, the attendees, and any disorder. The Army drew from open sources and law enforcement databases. The substance of the reports ranged from targets' political views to their sex lives and financial status.[289]

In 1972, the Supreme Court addressed the constitutionality of this program.[290] Chief Justice Warren E. Burger, writing for the Court, indicated that *surveillance alone*, particularly when drawn from open source material, did not prove a chilling effect on First Amendment activities. The claimants had not demonstrated any illegal wiretap or electronic bugging, breaking and entering, or concrete damage.[291] Justice William O. Douglas, in a vigorous dissent, wrote the following:

> The act of turning the military loose on civilians even if sanctioned by an Act of Congress, which it has not been, would raise serious and profound constitutional questions. Standing as it does only on brute power and Pentagon policy, it must be repudiated as a usurpation dangerous to the civil liberties on which free men are dependent.[292]

CONUS used undercover agents to infiltrate civilian groups and open confidential files. Stealth and secrecy, coupled with cameras and electronic ears, allowed the Army to gather information, which it then distributed back to civilian law enforcement agencies. Douglas thundered, "This case involves a cancer in our body politic. It is a measure of the disease which afflicts us."[293] He protested, "The Constitution was designed to keep government off the backs of the people. The Bill of Rights was added to keep the precincts of belief and expression, of the press, of political and social activities free from surveillance. The Bill of Rights was designed to keep agents of government and official eavesdroppers away from assemblies of people."[294] The purpose of such provisions "was to allow men to be free and independent and to assert their rights against government. There can be no influence more paralyzing of that objective than Army surveillance."[295]

The foregoing programs were far from the only surveillance operations underway.[296] President Nixon, for instance, used the Internal Revenue Service (IRS) to collect information on and audit people placed on watch lists.[297] And in 1970, the Department of the Treasury and the FBI initiated programs to try to obtain citizens' library records.[298] But as rumors about the extent of the projects underway began to circulate, Congress entered the ring. Between 1965 and 1974, the legislature held 47 hearings and issued reports on privacy-related issues[299] among which Idaho's Senator Frank Church's hearings between 1973 and 1976 stood out, becoming symbols of an era of government abuse of power. From assassination to covert operations, the proceedings shed light on the darkest corners of the executive branch.

Not everyone felt such inquiry appropriate. In words echoed by today's counterterrorist debates, Senator John Tower, a Republican from Texas, drew attention to the "very powerful adversary" the United States faced, and suggested that this enemy "would not hesitate to resort to military means to achieve its political objectives." The communist threat jeopardized "the peace and security of everybody," making it impossible to distinguish between war and peace.[300] Indeed, the tone of the hearings was, at times, almost apologetic for daring to ask questions. Concern centered on attempting to "balance the right to privacy against the need for national security."[301]

Although cognizant of these reservations, the Church Committee persevered. It found that the executive had undertaken covert surveillance of citizens purely on the basis of political beliefs, even when such ideas posed no threat of violence or illegal actions.[302]

The executive responded to the public outcry that followed the Church Committee's findings with a series of actions to curb surveillance. In 1976, President

Ford banned the NSA from intercepting telegraphs and also forbade the CIA from conducting electronic or physical surveillance of American citizens. Clarence Kelly, whom President Richard Nixon had nominated to take over the FBI after Hoover's death in 1972, publicly apologized for the Hoover era.[303] Attorney General Edward Levi, like Harlan Fiske Stone after the Red Scare in 1920, introduced guidelines that required the FBI to have "specific and articulable facts" indicating criminal activity before opening an investigation. Although they lacked legal force, the guidelines could serve in a judicial setting as a way to calibrate the organization's actions.[304] Since 9/11, every one of these protections has been eliminated, as I discuss later in this chapter.

Although the executive also said that it wanted to protect privacy more generally, subsequent legislation introduced by the Nixon administration – to put it mildly – lacked teeth.[305] The Privacy Act ostensibly regulated the collection, maintenance, use, and dissemination of citizens' personal data.[306] But it allowed the CIA to exempt its files from any legal requirement to provide citizens access to them.[307] Any agency with law enforcement, prosecution, or probation activities could withhold identification information, criminal investigative materials, and reports assembled between arrest and release.[308] Moreover, *any national security information* held by any agency could be exempted, as well as any Secret Service files or law enforcement material.[309] The statute allowed data to be shared within and between government agencies.[310] Although the kind of information that could be obtained had to be gathered for a lawful purpose, what constituted a "lawful purpose" was left up to the agency. Citizens could request information about files on themselves, but the legislation failed to include any timeframe for a response. Finally, Congress left implementation to an understaffed, underfunded Office of Management and Budget.[311]

With these gaping holes, it is not surprising that a commission appointed in 1977 by President Jimmy Carter found that the difficulty with the Privacy Act was "that agencies have taken advantage of its flexibility to contravene its spirit."[312] The review added, "The Act ignores or only marginally addresses some personal-data record-keeping issues of major importance now and for the future."[313] Consequently, the legislation "has not resulted in the general benefits to the public that either its legislative history or the prevailing opinion as to its accomplishments would lead one to expect."[314] In 1986, the US General Accounting Office similarly reported on the poor implementation of the Privacy Act.[315] The Department of Justice noted in 2004 that "[t]he Act's imprecise language, limited legislative history, and somewhat outdated regulatory guidelines have rendered it a difficult statute to decipher and apply. Moreover, even after more than twenty-five years of administrative and judicial analysis, numerous Privacy Act issues remain unresolved or unexplored."[316]

Congress Responds: The 1978 Foreign Intelligence Surveillance Act (FISA)

As the extent of the domestic surveillance operations emerged, Congress attempted to scale back the executive's power while allowing for flexibility to address national security threats.[317] The legislature focused on the targets of surveillance, limiting the new law, the Foreign Intelligence Surveillance Act of 1978, to foreign powers and to agents of foreign powers, which included groups "engaged in international terrorism or activities in preparation therefor."[318] Congress distinguished between US and non- US persons, creating tougher standards for the former.[319] FISA considered as falling under the new restrictions any "acquisition by an electronic, mechanical, or other surveillance device of the contents of any wire or radio communication," as well as other means of surveillance, such as video.[320] Central to the statute's understanding of surveillance was that, by definition, consent had not been given by the target. Otherwise, the individual would have a reasonable expectation of privacy, and under ordinary circumstances, the Fourth Amendment would require a warrant.[321]

FISA provided three ways to initiate surveillance: Attorney General certification, application to the Foreign Intelligence Surveillance Court (FISC), and emergency powers. Of these, FISC serves as the principal means by which surveillance is conducted.* To open surveillance on a suspect, the executive branch applies to the court, a judicial body that operates in complete secrecy, for approval.† The application must provide the name of the federal officer requesting surveillance and the identity of the target (if known), or a description of the target.[322] It must include a statement of facts supporting the claim that the target is a foreign power (or an agent thereof), and that the facilities to be monitored are currently, or expected to be, used by a foreign power or

---

* Under the first, the president, through the Attorney General, has the authority to collect information related to foreign intelligence – *without judicial approval* – for up to one year. The Attorney General must attest in writing, and under oath, that the electronic surveillance will be directed at communications between foreign powers or from property under their control; that "no substantial likelihood" exists that a US person will be party to the communications; and that every effort will be made to minimize the acquisition, retention, and dissemination of information relating to US persons. *Id.* § 1802(a)(1), (h)(1), (a)(2). Under the third approach, emergency powers, in which the Attorney General reasonably determines that "an emergency situation exists with respect to the employment of electronic surveillance to obtain foreign intelligence information," he or she must inform a judge that the decision has been made to engage in the activity. The Attorney General has 24 hours from the initiation of authorization to submit a full application. In the event that the application is ultimately denied, an exclusionary rule applies to any information gathered in the interim. Although the law requires that, in the event that the application is denied, notice be given to the target of emergency surveillance, such notice may be suspended for 90 days and, thereafter, indefinitely, subject to an *ex parte* showing of good cause. 50 U.S.C. §§ 1805(f), (j); 1811.

† After 9/11, Congress expanded FISC, which initially consisted of 7 United States district judges from different circuits, to 11 judges, 3 of whom have to reside in the vicinity of Washington, D.C. *Id.* § 1803(a). The judges serve a maximum of seven years. *Id.* § 1803(d). Consistent with the original statute, three additional judges, all chosen by the Chief Justice, constitute a special review panel. *Id.* § 1803(b). Writs of certiorari can be submitted from this court to the Supreme Court. Although initially only the president or Attorney General filed applications, in 1979 President Jimmy Carter issued an Executive Order extending the number of officials authorized to certify the application to the court to include the secretaries of State and of Defense, the directors of the CIA and the FBI, the deputy secretaries of State and of Defense, and the deputy director of the CIA. Exec. Order No. 12,139, 44 Fed. Reg. 30,311 (1979).

its agent.[323] Probable cause must be presented – not that the individual has committed or is about to commit a crime (the standard for Title III warrants) – but that the individual qualifies as a foreign power and will be using the facilities surveilled.[324] The application must describe the "nature of the information sought and the type of communications or activities to be subjected to the surveillance." Importantly, the court is *not* required to determine whether any foreign intelligence information is likely to be uncovered.[325] The application requires a designated national security or defense officer to certify that the information is related to foreign intelligence, and that "such information cannot reasonably be obtained by normal investigative techniques."[326] It must specify how the surveillance is to be effected (including whether physical entry is required),[327] and all previous applications involving the "persons, facilities, or places specified in the application," as well as actions taken by the court on these cases, must accompany the application.[328] The form includes an estimate of the time required for surveillance and requires an explanation why authority should not terminate at the end of the requested period.[329] Finally, if more than one surveillance device is to be used, the applicant must address the minimization procedures – that is, what steps will be taken to minimize the intrusiveness of the surveillance – and describe the range of devices to be employed.[330] Finally, the judge may request additional data.[331]

In 1994, Congress amended the statute to allow for warrantless, covert physical searches (not just electronic communication intercepts) when targeting "premises, information, material, or property used exclusively by, or under the open and exclusive control of, a foreign power or powers."[332] The statute requires that there be no substantial likelihood that the facilities targeted are the property of a US person.[333] Applications must include the same information as for electronic surveillance.[334] Twice a year the Attorney General informs Congress of the number of applications for physical search orders; the number granted, modified, or denied; and the number of physical searches that ensued.[335]

In addition to the above powers, FISA provided the authority for the installation and use of pen register and trap and trace devices for international terrorism investigations.[336] (Pen registers obtain the number dialed from a particular phone; trap and trace devices act as a caller ID record.) The Attorney General, or a designated attorney, must submit an application in writing and under oath either to the FISA court or to a magistrate specifically appointed by the Chief Justice to hear pen register or trap and trace applications on behalf of the FISA court.[337] The application must include information to show that the device has been, or will in the future be, used by someone who is engaging or has engaged in international terrorism or is a foreign power or agent thereof.[338] Thus, a US citizen, thought to be engaged in international terrorism, may be the target of the pen register or trap and trace device. The government is not required to ever inform individuals targeted under this power that they have been placed under surveillance. The order can be granted for up to 90 days, with an additional 90-day extension.[339] As with electronic surveillance, in the event of an emergency the Attorney General can authorize the installation and use of a pen register or trap and trace device without judicial approval.[340] A proper application must be made to the appropriate authority within 48 hours.[341] Information thus obtained *can* be used in court proceedings, although reasonable effort must be made to inform the target that the government "intends to so disclose or so use such information."[342]*

More than two decades before 9/11, then, Congress created a tool for the executive to obtain information to prevent acts of international terrorism. The system, like Britain's, was not without its drawbacks. For one, the court often seemed to serve the executive branch as a rubber stamp: between 1979 and 2003, FISC denied only 3 of 16,450 applications the executive branch submitted.[343] Like British intelligence officials, US officials claimed that this record simply reflected the professionalism of the executive branch: an application that would not pass muster would simply be stopped before reaching the court.[344] Although this ratio did not significantly differ from that for ordinary wiretap applications, in light both of the lower standards of proof required and of the increasing tendency to use FISA for US persons and criminal investigations, it can be considered problematic.

Here is another drawback: the fact that the executive relied increasingly on these powers suggests, at the outside, that it was taking an end run around ordinary Title III searches. Between 1978 and 1995, the executive made just over five hundred new applications per year. Since 1995, however, the numbers have steadily grown, with a sudden burst since 9/11: in 2002, the number leaped to 1,228; and in 2003, to 1,727 applications. For the first time in history, in 2002 and 2003, the Department of Justice requested more wiretaps under FISA than under ordinary wiretap statutes – a circumstance suggesting a significant shift in the government's strategy for gathering information. Under FISA, law enforcement must cross a much lower threshold and is not subject to the same Fourth Amendment restrictions as in the ordinary criminal code (a subject to which I return, on page 234, in considering the impact of the USA PATRIOT Act and the Department of Justice's use of FISA as a tool in ordinary criminal prosecution).

In sum, while FISA pushed back on the worst excesses of the McCarthy era, efforts by the executive to obtain personal information continued.[345] And then came the attacks of September 11, 2001.

---

* Following the 9/11 attacks, Congress relaxed the requirement for factual proof: the applicant no longer must demonstrate why he or she believes that a telephone line will be used by an individual engaged in international terrorism. Instead, the applicant must demonstrate only that the information likely to be gained does not directly concern a US person and will be relevant to protect against international terrorism. This provision, hotly contested by civil libertarians, was scheduled to sunset on December 31, 2005; but See Uniting and Strengthening America by Proving Appropriate Tools Required to Intercept and Obstruct Terrorism Act of 2001 (USA PATRIOT Act), Pub. L. No. 107–56, § 215, 115 Stat. 272 (2001) (codified as amended at 50 U.S.C. §1861 (2000 & Supp. 2001)); 18 U. S. C. § 214 (2000). Congress made it permanent. USA PATRIOT Improvement and Reauthorization Act of 2005, P.L. 109–177, § 102, 120 Stat. 192 (2006).

THE USA PATRIOT ACT AND ITS SURVEILLANCE PROVISIONS

The three most important surveillance provisions in the USA PATRIOT Act – passed soon after 9/11 – and the 2006 USA PATRIOT Improvement Act are alterations to FISA, the introduction of delayed-notice search warrants, and the extended use of National Security Letters. The 2006 act did provide, as its title suggests, some improvement for individual rights – while simultaneously making almost all of the temporary powers permanent.[346]

Alterations to the Foreign Intelligence Surveillance Act

The 2001 USA PATRIOT Act made two important changes to FISA: it allowed applications where foreign intelligence constituted only "a significant purpose" for an investigation, and it authorized the state to obtain tangible objects, such as computer disks and drives. Where previously FISA applications required that the gathering of foreign intelligence be "the" sole reason for search or surveillance, the new legislation allowed for applications when foreign intelligence provided merely a significant reason.[347] The Attorney General quickly seized on this power and issued guidelines that said such authorization could be sought even if the primary ends of the surveillance related to ordinary crime.[348] These guidelines effectively collapsed the wall between the FBI's prosecution and intelligence functions.

Although FISC had functioned secretly for nearly three decades, in May 2002 it published an opinion for the first time to protest Attorney General Ashcroft's guidelines.[349] The court required that the state rebuild the wall between the Bureau's prosecution and intelligence functions. FISC centered its directive on the statutory minimization requirement and raised concerns about abuse: it noted, for instance, that in September 2000, the government had admitted that it had made "misstatements and omissions of material facts" in 75 of its counterterrorism applications.[350] The court recognized the reasons a wall had been placed between intelligence gathering and criminal investigations, and suggested that "the 2002 procedures appear to be designed to . . . substitute FISA for Title III electronic surveillances and Rule 41 searches."[351] By removing the wall, "criminal prosecutors will tell the FBI when to use FISA (perhaps when they lack probable cause for a Title III electronic surveillance), what techniques to use, what information to look for, what information to keep as evidence and when use of FISA can cease because there is enough evidence to arrest and prosecute."[352] Such measures did not appear to be reasonably designed "to obtain, produce, or disseminate foreign intelligence information."[353] And so, the court imposed conditions.

For the first time in the history of FISC, the government appealed. The executive argued that Congress's intent in changing the wording from "the" to "a significant" reason was, *precisely*, to eliminate the wall between intelligence and law enforcement agencies.[354] The executive branch claimed, moreover, that attempts to impose minimization were so intrusive as to "exceed the constitutional authority of Article III judges."[355]

Six months later, the three-judge appellate court appointed by Chief Justice William Rehnquist issued its first opinion – one that reversed the lower court's ruling.[356] The appellate court suggested that FISA was never meant to apply only to foreign intelligence information relative to national security, and that it could also be used for *ordinary criminal cases*.[357] The court went even further: it interpreted the USA PATRIOT Act to mean that the *primary* purpose of the investigation could, indeed, be criminal investigations – "[s]o long as the government entertains a realistic option of dealing with the agent other than through criminal prosecution."[358] Stopping a conspiracy, for instance, would suffice.[359] To reach this conclusion, the appellate court rejected the Fourth Circuit Court's finding in *United States* v. *Troung* (1980), which rejected warrantless search and surveillance once a case crossed into a criminal investigation.[360] The appeals court suggested that the *Troung* ruling may even have been at fault for contributing "to the FBI missing opportunities to anticipate the September 11, 2001 attacks,"[361] and added that "special needs" may provide further justification for departing from constitutional limits.[362] John Ashcroft hailed the decision, which reversed two decades of court policy, as "a giant step forward."[363]

This reversal raises deeply troubling constitutional issues.[364] The Fourth Amendment jurisprudence requiring that a warrant be issued by a neutral and detached magistrate means that the individual who will execute the warrant meet the standard of probable cause, and that the applicant designate the places to be searched and the items to be seized.[365] FISA had previously withstood constitutional challenge precisely because of its very purpose of sustaining national security, which allowed it to fall outside the ordinary criminal law warrant requirements.[366] By allowing FISA to be used for ordinary criminal investigations, though, the appeals court eliminated a key characteristic differentiating the ordinary criminal standard from FISA's looser requirements.

The second significant change to FISA rested on the type of information that the executive could obtain. Although FISA granted broad access to electronic surveillance, it did not specifically empower the state to obtain business records. After the 1995 Oklahoma City bombing, Congress expanded FISA orders to include travel records.[367] The USA PATRIOT Act provided further access to *any* business or personal records[368] and also changed the standard under which FISC would be *required* to grant the order. Where previously specific and articulable facts had to demonstrate that the target represented a foreign power (or an agent thereof), the new legislation eliminated the need for a particularized showing.[369] Thus, under the PATRIOT Act, the person seeking the records only has to say that the "records concerned are sought for an authorized investigation . . . to protect against international terrorism or clandestine intelligence activities." What constitutes an investigation is wholly within the domain of the executive branch – a definition that Attorney General John Ashcroft relaxed following the passage of the USA PATRIOT Act (a preliminary investigation is now sufficient.) This means that FISA can be used to gather records of individuals who are not themselves the target of any investigation or an agent of a foreign power. In fact, entire databases could be obtained in this manner, as long as "an authorized investigation" exists.[370]

Not only did the USA PATRIOT Act make these changes to FISA but the manner in which the executive obtained authorization for surveillance also shifted after 9/11. As I have discussed, surveillance of non-US persons can be initiated both by an application to the FISA court or, in an emergency, by the Attorney General. In the statute's first 23 years, Attorneys General sporadically made use of the emergency category and, in total, issued approximately 55 such orders. In the 18 months following 9/11, however, this number dramatically increased: in 2002 alone, Ashcroft signed more than 170 emergency foreign intelligence warrants.[371] This important alteration has largely escaped public notice.

Delayed-Notice Search Warrants

A second innovation in the USA PATRIOT Act affected the notice requirement for physical searches. Section 213, which applies to all federal criminal investigations – not just those conducted for counterterrorism – eliminates the "knock and announce" requirement long considered integral to determining whether a search warrant is deemed reasonable. In delayed-notice, or "sneak and peek" search warrants, to prevent individuals from learning that the state has appropriated their property or placed them under surveillance, the government must only demonstrate reasonable cause to believe that notice may cause an adverse result. Although delayed notice was already provided by the 1986 Electronic Communications Privacy Act and endorsed by the Second and Ninth Circuit Courts of Appeal, the USA PATRIOT Act allowed notice to be suspended indefinitely. This provision was not subject to a sunset clause.

The delayed-notice search warrants are notable in that, as with roving wiretaps, the USA PATRIOT Act was not their first appearance on the legislative stage.[372] The FBI had previously proposed them in anti-drug bills and then attached them to a Bankruptcy Bill – all efforts at legalization that Congress had previously rejected. After 9/11, however, not only did the legislature acquiesce but it also failed to limit the new powers to terrorism. Section 213 can be used by law enforcement for any crime on the books. Since the statute's passage, the state has used it to break into a judge's chambers, to look into health care fraud, and to investigate check swindling.[373] In July 2005, the Justice Department told the House Judiciary Committee that only 12 percent of the 153 delayed-notice search warrants it received were related to terrorism investigations.[374] What was illegal in the break-ins conducted under COINTELPRO has now become legal.

In its 2006 renewal of the USA PATRIOT Act, Congress added "enhanced oversight" of these powers. The legislation requires the judiciary to report the following information to the Administrative Office of the courts, within 30 days of issuing a delayed-notice search warrant: the fact of the warrant application; whether it was granted as applied, or was modified or denied; the length of the delay in notifying the subject of the search; the number and duration of any extensions; and the offense specified in the warrant or application.[375] Beginning in September 2007, this information is being provided to Congress as well.[376]

National Security Letters

The third, and most significant, surveillance provision in the USA PATRIOT Act augmented the FBI's ability to bypass warrant requirements – under both Title III and FISA. Section 505, innocuously entitled "Miscellaneous National Security Authorities," enhanced the amount and type of information that could be obtained via National Security Letters (NSLs), bringing Internet Service Providers within its remit and expanding the information that could be obtained to include credit card records, bank account numbers, and data pertaining to Internet use (such as protocol addresses and session times).[377] Critically, the statute placed an indefinite gag order on anyone served with such administrative subpoenas.* It also broadened the range of officials who could request the information: where previously requests had to provide specific and articulable facts that established the target as a foreign power (or agent thereof), the new NSL powers merely have to be *relevant* to any "authorized investigation to protect against international terrorism or clandestine intelligence activities."[378]† The Bush administration quickly attempted to make NSLs

* National Security Letters draw their authority from one of four sources. The 1947 National Security Act authorizes investigative agencies to request financial records and information, consumer reports, and travel records for individuals with access to classified information, where such individuals are under investigation for sharing the information with foreign powers. National Security Act of 1947, 50 U.S.C. § 402 (2000). The Fair Credit Reporting Act provides for the FBI and certain government agencies to obtain consumer information in the course of investigations into international terrorism. Fair Credit Reporting Act of 1970, 15 U.S.C. § 1681 (2000). The 1978 Right to Financial Privacy Act allows for the FBI to obtain financial records as part of their investigation into international terrorism and espionage. Right to Financial Privacy Act of 1978, 12 U.S.C. § 3401–22 (2000). And, prior to 9/11, the Electronic Communications Privacy Act empowered the FBI, in the course of investigations into international terrorism or espionage, to request electronic communication related to agents of a foreign power from banks, credit agencies, and Internet Service Providers. *See* Electronic Communications Privacy Act of 1986, 18 U.S.C. § 2709 (2000). Although the Fourth Amendment applies to administrative subpoenas, because they are constructive searches, courts have *not* in the past required either a warrant or probable cause for them to be issued. Instead, the subpoena must only be "reasonable": that is, it falls within the agency's remit, the request is finite, and information is relevant to an appropriate inquiry. What makes such subpoenas constitutional, however, is that the party subpoenaed must have the opportunity to "obtain judicial review of the reasonableness of the demand prior to suffering penalties for refusing to comply." *Doe*, 334 F. Supp. 2d at 495 (2004) (quoting See v. City of Seattle, 387 U.S. 541, 544–45 (1967)). Even if review is granted *after* a subpoena is issued, a neutral tribunal can determine whether its issuance is compatible with the Fourth Amendment. Unlike NSLs, most administrative subpoenas either do not require secrecy or they limit it to particular circumstances. *Id.* at 485.
† Section 505 expanded *who* could request the information from requiring that the request be made by an FBI official at the level of Deputy Assistant Director or above, to allowing *any* FBI Special Agent in charge of a field office to issue NSLs to obtain consumer reports, financial

available to the CIA and the Pentagon, without intervention from the Department of Justice.[379]

The application of NSLs to Internet Service Providers immediately implicated a broad range of institutions. The legal definition means that traditional ISPs – such as America Online, Juno, and UUNET – as well as companies whose cables and phone lines carry the traffic, would qualify.[380] It also incorporates companies that provide email but are not ISPs, like Microsoft and Netscape, and captures both any service that creates mailing lists, such as the Yahoo! Groups service, and *any library, school, or company* that provides physical access to the Internet.[381] Indeed, there is evidence that some portion of the hundreds of NSLs served immediately after 9/11 related to libraries.* A study conducted by the University of Illinois found that in the first 12 months, federal agents made at least 545 visits to libraries to obtain information about patrons, affecting just over 10 percent of the libraries polled.[382]† Libraries, however, did not have the sole honor of receiving NSLs. In December 2003, the FBI sent letters to hotels in Las Vegas, requiring them to turn over all customer records between December 22, 2003, and January 1, 2004.[383] In similar fashion, the FBI obtained data from airlines and hotels in the vicinity.[384] Even these few letters implicated an estimated 270,000 people – with no individualized suspicion to back them.[385] Internet Service Providers, too, have been inundated with requests. Mr. Al Gidari, a Seattle privacy lawyer who represents America Online, AT&T Wireless, and Cingular, reported that "[d]emands for information have soared as much as five times over pre-September 11 levels."[386] The

---

records, or electronic communications. Memorandum from Gen. Counsel, Nat'l Security Law Unit, Fed. Bureau of Investigation, to All Field Offices National Security Letter Matters, Ref: 66F-HQ-A1255972 Serial 15 (Nov. 28, 2001), available at www.sccounty01.co.santa-cruz.ca.us. The practical effect of this, in the words of the Department of Justice, means that the FBI could issue an NSL stating, e.g., "[a] full international terrorism investigation of subject, a U.S. person, was authorized . . . because he may be engaged in international terrorism activities by raising funds for HAMAS." *Id.*

* A joint Freedom of Information Act request filed by the ACLU, the Electronic Privacy Information Center, the American Booksellers for Free Expression, and the Freedom to Read Foundation yielded five pages (entirely redacted) of institutions on which NSLs had been served between October 2001 and January 2003. These pages are available at www.aclu.org/patriot_foia/. The lower court interpreted the missing names as numbering in the "hundreds." *Doe*, 334 F. Supp. 2d at 502.

† Although the § 215 changes to FISA would also have allowed the FBI to obtain library records, it appears that the FBI made use of NSLs instead. In response to an inquiry from James Sensenbrenner, chair of the House of Representatives Judiciary Committee, Daniel J. Bryant, the Assistant Attorney General, suggested that "the more appropriate tool [than § 215] for requesting electronic communication transactional records would be a National Security Letter (NSL)." Letter from Daniel J. Bryant, Assistant Attorney Gen., to F. James Sensenbrenner, Jr., Chairman, Comm. on the Judiciary, U.S. House of Representatives (July 26, 2002), available at www.lifeandliberty.gov. A memorandum from Attorney General John Ashcroft to the Director of the Federal Bureau of Investigation, Robert Mueller, supports this reading; it confirmed that, as of 2003, § 215 had yet to be used. Memorandum from John Ashcroft, Attorney Gen., to Robert Mueller, Dir. of the Fed. Bureau of Investigation (Sept. 18, 2003) available at www.cdt.org/security/.

Associated Press noted, "At one major Internet backbone provider, requests for information 'have gone through the roof.'"[387]

By 2004, the FBI was issuing tens of thousands of National Security Letters each year – 56,000 in 2004 alone, a number that eclipsed the 8,500 issued in 2000, prior to 9/11.[388][*][†] The issuance of NSLs had become routine procedure for ordinary criminal activity – during both preliminary investigations and the "threat assessment" stage – far before a formal criminal investigation commenced. Over five dozen FBI supervisors had obtained the authority to issue NSLs. There is no statutory limit on how much information can be gathered or how many people can be targeted by each one of these letters.

Perhaps of most concern in respect to individual rights is the lack of control over who has access to the information, how long it is kept, and the manner in which it is used. In 2003, Attorney General John Ashcroft withdrew a 1995 guideline that required the FBI to destroy NSL information on American citizens or residents if such data proved "not relevant to the purposes for which it was collected."[389] In its place, Aschroft *required* the FBI to keep all records collected, and authorized it to disseminate such information to any federal agency. The same order stipulated that the Bureau use "data-mining" technology to trawl through its rapidly expanding files to try to find links between people. In January 2004, the FBI created the Investigative Data Warehouse, which uses the same technology that the CIA depends upon – and is barred from using in similar fashion on American citizens.[390] The Attorney General also changed the guidelines to allow the FBI to incorporate commercially available databases, such as ChoicePoint and Lexis Nexis. (See page 257 for more on data mining.)

An important aspect of the collection of this information is that it is subject neither to prior judicial review nor to detailed congressional oversight. In four years, the FBI has provided Congress with only classified statistics on the total number of NSLs issued, the type of information obtained (financial, credit, or

---

[*] In 2007 the Inspector General of the FBI reported that after the USA PATRIOT Act, the number issued steadily increased to 39,000 in 2003, and 56,000 in 2004. In 2005, the number dropped to 47,000 – still considerably above the 2000 level. *FBI Abused PATRIOT Act Powers, Audit Finds*, GUARDIAN, Mar. 9, 2007, available at www.guardian.co.uk. These numbers are larger than, although they do not contradict, the number first published by Barton Gellman, a reporter for the *Washington Post*, who said that more than 30,000 NSLs were being issued per year. *The FBI's Secret Scrutiny: In Hunt for Terrorists, Bureau Examines Records of Ordinary Americans*, WASH. POST, Nov. 6, 2005, at A1. Gellman's story played a key role in drawing attention to the issue and generating a chain of events that culminated in Congress demanding that the Inspector General prepare a report on the use of NSLs.

[†] The FBI numbers reflect only the Bureau's use of the power; they do not include efforts by the Department of Homeland Security, which presumably also has authority under the USA PATRIOT Act, to issue NSLs. Nor do those numbers include letters issued by the Department of Defense or the Central Intelligence Agencies – organizations that, the *New York Times* reported in January 2007, have been issuing noncompulsory NSLs to obtain citizens' banking and credit records. Military intelligence officials estimate that the letters were used in approximately 500 investigations between 2002 and 2007, putting the likely number of NSLs issued by the Pentagon in the thousands, as multiple letters are sent for each investigation. Eric Lichtblau & Mark Mazzetti, *Military Expands Intelligence Role in U.S.*, N.Y. TIMES, Jan. 14, 2007.

communication), and the number of US persons targeted – reports that omit an entire category of NSLs, as well as other federal agencies' use of the same. Although in 2004 Congress requested the Attorney General to describe the scope of NSLs and provide the "process and standards for approving" them, more than 18 months passed without a reply. As for the NSLs' effectiveness in counterterrorism, the Bush administration has not publicly offered a single example of the use of one having interrupted a terrorist attack.[391]

Despite the gag order, to date two cases have made it to the courts. The first, *Doe v. Ashcroft* (2004), involved an Internet Service Provider. From the beginning, the plaintiff was in a precarious position: according to the original USA PATRIOT Act, an individual served with an NSL could not disclose to *anyone* that the FBI had requested this information[392] – a stipulation that ostensibly included an attorney or, even, a court of law. (The renewal statute now allows individuals served with an order to discuss the matter with an attorney and anyone necessary to obtaining the information requested.[393])

In this case, the FBI telephoned Doe and told him that he would be served with an NSL.[394] The document, printed on FBI letterhead, directed him to provide certain information and informed him that the NSL provisions in the USA PATRIOT Act prohibited Doe or his employees "from disclosing to *any person* that the FBI has sought or obtained access to information or records."[395] The FBI instructed him to deliver the records in person, not to use the postal system, and not to mention the NSL in any telephone conversation.[396] Doe spoke with attorneys at the ACLU, refused to provide the information requested, and instead brought suit.[397]

The District Court held that the provision that barred recipients from disclosing receipt of an NSL, as applied, violated the Fourth Amendment: it did not allow for any judicial process.[398] Judge Victor Marrero, who wrote the opinion, noted that in nearly 20 years, not a single judicial challenge had been brought to the issuance of an NSL.[399] He suggested that "it would be . . . naïve to conclude that §2709 NSLs [the specific administrative subpoena amended by the USA PATRIOT Act], given their commandeering warrant, do anything short of coercing all but the most fearless NSL recipient into immediate compliance and secrecy."[400] The court subjected the gag order, which counted as both a prior restraint and a content-based restriction, to strict scrutiny.[401] It found that the indefinite ban on disclosure was *not* narrowly tailored to further the government's interest in pursuing its counterterrorist strategy.[402] Even where secrecy was no longer justifiable, the gag order would stand.[403] Marrero objected:

[A]n unlimited government warrant to conceal, effectively a form of secrecy per se, has no place in our open society. . . . When withholding information from disclosure is no longer justified, when it ceases to foster the proper aims that initially may have supported confidentiality, a categorical and uncritical extension of non-disclosure may become the cover for spurious ends that government may then deem too inconvenient, inexpedient, merely embarrassing, or even illicit to ever expose to the light of day.[404]

"At that point," the court concluded, "secrecy's protective shield may serve not as much to secure a safe country as simply to save face.[405]

In the second case, *Doe v. Gonzales* (2005), FBI agents served George Christian, who managed 36 Connecticut libraries' digital records, with an NSL, which demanded "all subscriber information, billing information and access logs of any person" using a particular computer at one of the branches.[406] Like the plaintiff in the earlier lawsuit, Christian refused to provide the FBI with the records. Instead, his employer, Library Connection Inc., brought suit.[407]

Once again, the case turned on the gag order. Christian claimed that it amounted to a prior restraint, which caused irreparable harm: it made it impossible for him to participate in the public debate surrounding the introduction of no less than eight bills before Congress that were aimed at further tailoring NSL powers.[408]

The district court granted the preliminary injunction against the government to prevent the gag order from going into effect.[409] The court reasoned that it looked as if Doe were likely to succeed on the merits, and that irreparable harm would result if he were not able to participate in the dialogue.[410] As a content-based prior restraint, the order had to pass strict scrutiny; but although the state had a general interest in national security, no specific harm would be caused by revealing Doe's identity.[411] The district court concluded, "Especially in a situation like the instant one, where the statute provides no judicial review of the NSL or the need for its non-disclosure provision . . . the permanent gag provision . . . is not narrowly drawn to serve the government's broadly claimed compelling interest of keeping investigations secret."[412] The court considered the measure "overbroad as applied with regard to the types of information that it encompasses."[413]*

A panel of the Second Circuit reversed the district court's decision and granted the motion to stay the injunction, pending an emergency appeal.[414] Justice Ruth Bader Ginsburg, who sat as Circuit Judge for the appeal, refused to hold that vacatur of stay was warranted.[415] She noted the speed with which the case was going through the Court of Appeals and recognized that the American Library Association, of which the entity in question was a member, was free to note in its lobbying efforts that one of its member had been served with an NSL.[416]

As perhaps suggested by the number of NSL-related bills circulating in 2005, the effort to expand National Security Letter authority did not stop with the

---

* The court found the ban "particularly noteworthy" in light of the fact that proponents of the Patriot Act have "consistently relied on the public's faith [that the Government will] apply the statute narrowly." *Id.* (quoting Emergency, at 26 (quoting Attorney General John Ashcroft, Remarks at Memphis, Tennessee: Protecting Life and Liberty (Sept. 18, 2003)), available at www.usdoj.gov (last visited Oct. 7, 2005) (characterizing as "hysteria" fears of the executive's abuse of the increased access to library records under the Patriot Act and stating that "the Department of Justice has neither the staffing, the time[,] nor the inclination to monitor the reading habits of Americans. No offense to the American Library Association, but we just don't care.")

USA PATRIOT Act. Neither that statute nor the 1986 Electronic Communications Privacy Act imposed penalties for refusal to cooperate. In 2003, the Department of Justice prepared to close this loophole. Section 129 of the leaked draft "Enhancing Domestic Security Act" – colloquially known as USA PATRIOT II – provided for criminal penalties.[417] Although leading Republicans and Democrats in Congress immediately condemned PATRIOT II, in September 2004 Representative James Sensenbrenner introduced the "Anti-Terrorism Intelligence Tools Improvement Act of 2003," which provided for up to five years in prison for a violation of the gag orders.[418] The session closed before the bill passed, but in March 2006 the administration managed to incorporate a penalty of up to five years' imprisonment and/or a fine, into the USA PATRIOT Act renewal statute.[419]

In November 2001, one month after President Bush had signed the USA PATRIOT Act, the Department of Justice constructed a new interpretation of the United States Code: where before NSLs could be used only in a formal investigation, they now could be used in any preliminary inquiry.[420] The "certification" process, meant to provide a check on the use of these powers, became a rubber stamp: the Department of Justice provided all field offices with a boilerplate paragraph to be inserted into all NSLs at paragraph two.[421] The language of this paragraph, drafted in Washington, D.C., helped to ensure that the proper requirements for certification would be met – regardless of the actual state of the inquiry or investigation being conducted by the field office.[422] The Department of Justice also instructed the field offices not to include a date range for credit record requests, "because these requests seek all records where the consumer maintains or has maintained an account."[423] The Attorney General granted more than five dozen supervisors the authority to issue NSLs.

The most notable expansion of executive power occurred in December 2003 when the Bush administration quietly signed into law the Intelligence Authorization Act for Fiscal Year 2004.[424] The legislation included one sentence that modified a section of the 1978 Right to Financial Privacy Act. The net effect of the almost inscrutable language of this law was to allow the FBI to issue NSLs in a domain where previously only Treasury and Intelligence agents could go.[425] Although one could argue that there is nothing wrong with this – why shouldn't the FBI be able to act like the other two agencies? – the central point remains that this law further expanded executive authority.

Along these lines, the Intelligence Authorization Act also empowered all of these agencies to issue NSLs to a broader range of institutions. The obscure cross-reference in the text to "section 5312 of title 31" means that NSLs can now be issued to banks, credit unions, thrift stores, brokers in securities or commodities, currency exchanges, insurance companies, credit card companies, dealers in precious metals, stones, or jewels, pawnbrokers, loan or finance companies, travel agencies, any business that transfers funds, telegraph companies, car, airplane, and boat sellers, real estate agents, the US Postal Service, state and local government entities involved in the preceding, and casinos.[426] Like the NSLs to electronic communications service providers, a gag order prevents these entities from revealing that they have received a demand for information.

When the House of Representatives passed the first version of its renewal bill, Sensenbrenner argued for the permanent entrenchment of the extraordinary search authorities, claiming that there was no evidence that the powers had been abused, and asserting that they had been subjected to "vigorous oversight."[427] This claim ran somewhat counter to reality: efforts by minority members of the Senate Intelligence Committee even to obtain hearings on the use of surveillance authorities – including the NSLs – had met with little success.[428] Aside from the difficulty intrinsic in the fact that one party controlled both the executive and the legislature, the USA PATRIOT Act contained minimal requirements for congressional oversight.

The 2006 renewal statute partially addressed this deficiency. For NSLs, it required the Attorney General to submit an aggregate report to Congress each April, laying out the total number of NSLs made by the Department of Justice.[429] It also required the Inspector General of the Department of Justice to audit "the effectiveness and use, including any improper or illegal use" of NSLs it issued.[430] This task included reviewing the NSLs issued from 2003 to 2006; describing any "noteworthy facts or circumstances" (such as the illegal use of the power); evaluating how useful NSLs are as an investigative tool; examining how the information is collected, retained, and analyzed – by DoJ and others; and examining how such information is used.[431] The report, which was to be unclassified but could contain a classified annex, was to be submitted within a year to the Judiciary Committees and Select Committees on Intelligence in House and Senate.[432] The statute also required the Attorney General and Director of National Intelligence to submit a joint report on the feasibility of applying minimization procedures to protect the constitutional rights of US persons.[433]

The required Inspector General's report proved to be more effective than years of (almost no) congressional oversight. The audit found 22 possible violations of internal regulations in a sample of 293 NSLs[434] – a drop in the bucket of the more than 30,000 issued annually. FBI Inspector General Glenn Fine found previously unreported potential violations in approximately one-quarter of the 77 cases he reviewed.[435] According to the WASHINGTON POST, this audit revealed that "FBI agents used national security letters without citing an authorized investigation, claimed 'exigent' circumstances that did not exist in demanding information and did not have adequate documentation to justify the issuance of letters."[436] In a number of instances, the Bureau used "exigent letters" to get information in a hurry, promising the recipients that grand jury subpoenas or National Security Letters would soon be sent – but neither ever materialized. Fine found that the FBI offices maintaining the case files did not maintain accurate records of even the number of NSLs issued – omitting about 20 percent of the total number in their reports to FBI Headquarters.[437]

The FBI responded to the Inspector General's report by promising to do better. According to a press release issued the same day that the news was released, FBI Director Robert Mueller was implementing steps to strengthen internal controls, changing policies and procedures to improve oversight of the NSL approval process, barring some practices, and ordering an immediate review.[438] On March 20 and 21, 2007, the House and Senate Judiciary Committees held hearings in which Fine and the FBI's General Counsel testified.[439]

Outside of requiring the Inspector General to report, the renewal act provided a limited number of other protections, such as exempting libraries that function as traditional book lenders and offer Internet access from being served with NSLs, allowing the appeal of gag orders, and not requiring that the recipient of the NSL provide the FBI with the name of any attorney consulted about the search.[440]

Despite these welcome provisions, the broader power to collect massive amounts of information on citizens remains. Minimal restrictions are placed on who sees the information, how long it is kept, and the purposes to which it is directed. And a classified annex means that substantial amounts of information may still be kept secret from public scrutiny. The renewal act, moreover, provides for a one-year delay before a gag order can be appealed.[441] Notably, although enacted in response to 9/11, the USA PATRIOT Act powers are not limited to terrorism. According to the Department of Justice, Section 210 of the legislation, for instance, which gives investigators access to Internet subscriber information, was used to convict the father of a 13-year-old girl in Indiana, who had produced child porn and posted it on the Internet.[442] Similarly, a West Virginia man who abducted and sexually assaulted his estranged wife was captured as a result of information obtained under section 220 of the USA PATRIOT Act.[443]

These important statutory changes, and their use beyond the terrorism realm, represent just the tip of the iceberg. For beneath the USA PATRIOT Act, surveillance programs are being exercised deep within the executive branch.

SURVEILLANCE OPERATIONS UNDER OTHER AUSPICES

Although the USA PATRIOT Act has become the poster child for federal surveillance, it is not the only source of that surveillance; nor is it in many ways the most important one. Many people do not realize that many of the entities that make up the US intelligence community are actually located within the Department of Defense; after 9/11, these organizations turned their gaze on the domestic realm. In addition, the Departments of Justice, Homeland Security, Transportation, and the Treasury, as well as other entities, have expanded their domestic surveillance, using authorities that fall outside of the USA PATRIOT Act, to pursue their agendas. In this section, I discuss programs initiated by the Department of Defense, the attorney general's guidelines and programs initiated by the FBI, the Department of Justice's citizen reporting programs, various watch lists, and a few ongoing surveillance programs. Though these programs represent only a handful of the activity in this area, they demonstrate the remarkable depth and breadth of the programs that have been launched at the federal level and that directly affect individuals within the state.

The Department of Defense

The National Security Agency, the National Reconnaissance Office, the National-Geospatial Intelligence Agency, the Defense Intelligence Agency, and the Northern Command Intelligence Units are all part of the US intelligence community and are all also located within the Department of Defense.[444] Each of these organizations has, since 9/11, expanded its domestic role.

Perhaps the most well known initiative is the National Security Agency's Domestic Surveillance Program – which, under a 2002 presidential order, began monitoring the international telephone calls and email of thousands of individuals within the United States – bypassing the FISA courts altogether.[445] The Bush administration defended NSA's program, saying that the Authorization for the Use of Military Force, issued by Congress, provided adequate authority for it. Although constitutional concerns might arise in the state's exercise of broad surveillance, the administration was not overly concerned. John Yoo, the Justice Department lawyer who, as discussed in Chapter 2, had co-written the memo arguing that the Geneva Conventions did not apply to al Qaeda and the Taliban, explained in 2002 that, owing to the danger of potentially catastrophic attacks, "the government may be justified in taking measures which in less troubled conditions could be seen as infringements of individual liberties."[446] The following year in an unrelated court case, the Justice Department submitted a brief asserting that "the Constitution vests in the President inherent authority to conduct warrantless intelligence surveillance (electronic or otherwise) of foreign powers or their agents, and Congress cannot by statute extinguish that constitutional authority."[447]

Although Yoo's position reflected that of the administration, some senior officials privately expressed concern that the program was not legal. And history repeated itself. The NSA went to some lengths to mask the existence of the program – even from the eyes of the FISA court. As in the McCarthy era in the 1950s, the possibility that a change in political leadership could entail criminal prosecution of individuals involved in the surveillance effort gave intelligence agents a vested interest in keeping the Democratic party out of the White House. Officials admitted that federal officials feared that if Senator John Kerry were to win the 2004 presidential election, the NSA would be subjected to public scrutiny.[448]

Also as in the McCarthy era programs, the NSA operation put private industry in the potential position of breaking the law: in August 2006, Detroit District Court Judge Anna Diggs Taylor ruled in a related case that the program violated the First and Fourth Amendments of the Constitution, as well as FISA.[449] In January 2006, the Electronic Frontier Foundation lodged a class action lawsuit against AT&T for collaborating with the NSA wiretapping and data-mining program. AT&T moved to dismiss the case on grounds that it had simply done what the state told it to do; the government argued, in addition, that allowing the trial to go forward would reveal "state secrets" and harm national security.

US District Judge Vaughn Walker issued a decision in July 2006 denying these motions.

Other Department of Defense programs that went outside the law in their efforts at domestic surveillance, and news of whose operations has leaked into the public domain, are TALON and CIFA. The former had been authorized in the spring of 2003 by the Deputy Secretary of Defense, Paul Wolfowitz, as the Threat and Local Observation Notice (TALON) program – "to capture non-validated domestic threat information, flow that information to analysts, and incorporate it into the DoD terrorism threat warning process."[450] A little more than a year later, in June 2004, 10 activists went to Halliburton to protest the firm's "war profiteering": that is, it was charging too much for food distributed to US troops in Iraq.[451] The protesters wore papier-mache masks and handed out peanut butter and jelly sandwiches to employees[452] – an incident that made its way into a TALON report. And like all TALON reports, the information was forwarded to Counterintelligence Field Activity (CIFA) – a post-9/11 Pentagon creation charged with putting such data in a central database and sharing it with the Defense Intelligence Agency, the Joint Intelligence Task Force Combating Terrorism, and other organizations.[453]

TALON, which grew out of Operation Eagle Eyes (a sort of military neighborhood watch program, which I discuss on page 253), gathers information from "concerned citizens and military members regarding suspicious incidents."[454] The reports are not validated and "may or may not be related to an actual threat."[455] They focus on nonspecific threats to the DoD's interests: suspected surveillance of DoD facilities and personnel, tests of security, unusual repetitive activity, bomb threats, or any other suspicious activity or incident "reasonably believed to be related to terrorist activity directed against DoD personnel, property, and activities within the United States."[456] In his May 2003 memo establishing the program, Wolfowitz made it clear that rapid reporting mattered more than careful detail. He supplied a list of the types of information to be included – among other items, the date, location, criteria for inclusion, classification level, source and assessment of credibility, and details of the act in question – essentially, the who, what, when, where, why, and how of potential threats to the United States.[457]

Although overinclusiveness may be considered inevitable in the collection of counterterrorist information, the degree to which surveillance overreaches its target does depend to some extent on the framework established. TALON, like many other surveillance programs underway, had little to limit its reach. In late 2005 and early 2006, a few hints emerged to show how broadly military personnel interpreted suspicious activity – activity, that is, that could "reasonably" be believed to be related to terrorist activity. In Florida, a TALON report was filed when fewer than two dozen people protested outside a military recruiting office at the local mall.[458] The librarian who had organized the event seemed surprised that the gathering, at which a "Bush Lied" sign was displayed, presented a national security threat.[459]

In April 2006, a Freedom of Information Act request submitted by the Legal Defense Network yielded documents showing TALON reports filed on lesbian, gay, bisexual, and transvestite student groups opposed to the military's "Don't Ask, Don't Tell" policy.[460] One group, New York University's Outlaw – a decades-old student organization found at law schools throughout the United States – attracted attention in part because of its name.[461] The agent filing the TALON report, unaware that the name referred to the intersection between coming out and legal issues, wrote, "The term 'outlaw' is not defined in the posting . . . the term 'outlaw' is a backhanded way of saying it's all right to commit possible violence and serve as vigilantes during the symposium. Therefore, it is possible that physical harm or vandalism could occur at this event."[462] A later update to the file noted that the term might "refer to members of the gay community that are now 'out' in the open that are studying at law schools." It continued, "However, per the original source there is almost nothing about the term 'outlaws' available with conventional Internet search engines . . . the source believes there is still a potential for confrontation at NYU."[463] (This is an extraordinary claim: a June 2006 Google search for "outlaw law schools" yielded more than 1.5 million hits in 0.53 seconds. Admittedly, 14 months had elapsed since the original TALON report, and some portion of the hits are not directly on point for Outlaw groups at law schools. But it seems at least unlikely that at the time there were not enough references on the Internet to allow an intelligence officer to ascertain the nature of the NYU student group's activities.)

These incidents were simple matters of overreaching. They were not isolated, but were tied to the overly broad nature of the programs, to the emphasis on speed at the expense of accuracy, and to lack of effective oversight. They also reflect a clear pattern: the tendency of surveillance programs to expand along political lines. NBC reported on December 13, 2005, that of some fifteen hundred "suspicious incidents" included in a sample of TALON database entries from July 2004 to May 2005, some four dozen focused on antiwar meetings and protests and on opposition to military recruiting.[464]

TALON and CIFA also are among other initiatives that stem from a broader, more far-reaching reorientation of the military to domestic affairs. After 9/11, the Bush administration pronounced the continental United States a military theater, and the Pentagon created Northern Command (Northcom).[465] Based in Colorado Springs, Northcom maintains intelligence centers in Colorado and Texas, where the military analyzes data from CIFA, the FBI, and other domestic agencies.[466] The 290 intelligence agents who staff these centers outnumber both the people at the State Department's Bureau of Intelligence and Research and the intelligence agents at the Department of Homeland Security.[467]

According to the Department of the Army's Deputy Chief of Staff for Intelligence, Robert W. Noonan, military intelligence agents not only are allowed to collect information about US persons, but can "receive" any information "from anyone, anytime." In his November 2001 memo, Noonan wrote that the enemy moves in "a shadowy underworld operating globally with supporters and allies in many countries. Including, unfortunately our own."[468] Military intelligence would, he said, "play a pivotal role in helping to defeat" the terrorist threat; he continued, "Contrary to popular belief, there is no absolute ban on intelligence components collecting US person information."[469] Noting that his staff had received reports indicating that military intelligence (MI) personnel had declined "to receive reports from local law enforcement authorities, solely because" they contained personal information, Noonan hastened to reassure the agents: he said that not only could they receive the data ("Remember, merely receiving information does not constitute 'collection' . . . collection entails receiving 'for use'") and retain it where it related to foreign intelligence and counterintelligence, but MI could transmit or deliver the information to others.[470] In January 2002, an official from the Army Inspector General's office, Michael Varhola, again raised the issue in a circular. He complained that "unfortunately some individuals find it easier or safer to avoid the issue altogether by simply not collecting the data on citizens they may need to do their complete jobs."[471] By February 2002, Wolfowitz had created CIFA to coordinate military intelligence.[472]

Military domestic surveillance initiatives did not stop there.* And CIFA, intended as a clearinghouse for information from other organizations,[473] took on a broader role. By August 2006, the organization had grown to incorporate nine directorates. Although its budget remains classified, congressional sources suggest that CIFA spent more than $1 billion over its first four years.[474] One counterintelligence official reported that there were 400 full-time employees and between 800 and 900 contractors working at the site.[475] CIFA's mission is to "transform" counterintelligence by "fully utilizing 21st century tools and resources."[476] The Pentagon boasts that it uses "leading edge information technologies and data harvesting," and exploits "commercial data," whereby it contracts with White Oak Technologies, MZM, and other companies to collect information. CIFA considers counterintelligence to include not just data collection but also activities that "protect DoD and the nation against espionage, other intelligence activities, sabotage, assassinations, and terrorist activities."[477] Their motto is reported to be "Counterintelligence 'to the Edge.'"[478]

In January 2006, Paul Wolfowitz acknowledged in a memo that the DoD may have obtained and retained information on US citizens that it ought not to have.[479] Stephen A. Cambone, the Undersecretary of Defense, ordered a formal review,[480] which determined that CIFA did indeed have data that violated regulations – specifically, a ban on retaining information on US citizens more

---

* In 2004, for instance, the Marine Corps expanded its domestic intelligence gathering; it now oversees the "collection, retention and dissemination of information concerning U. S. persons" (as stated in the April 2004 order approving the program). Walter Pincus, Pentagon Will Review Database on U.S. Citizens; Protests Among Acts Labeled 'Suspicious.' WASH. POST, Dec. 15, 2005, at A1. The order suggests that Marine Intelligence will be "'increasingly required to perform domestic missions' . . . 'as a result, there will be increased instances whereby Marine intelligence activities may come across information regarding U. S. persons.'" *Id.* (quoting April 2004 order).

than 90 days, unless it was "reasonably believed" to be linked to terrorism, criminal wrongdoing, or foreign intelligence.[481] In January 2006, Deputy Defense Secretary Gordon England issued a memo ordering that CIFA "purge such information from its files," and recommending refresher training courses on the regulations.[482]

Despite these clear instances of overreaching, efforts to expand CIFA's purview continue. CIFA has allegedly contracted with Computer Sciences Corporation to buy "identity masking" software, enabling it to create false Web sites.[483] Toward the end of 2005, a presidential commission on intelligence suggested that CIFA be empowered to conduct domestic criminal investigations as well as clandestine operations.[484] Its law enforcement authorities would extend to crimes such as treason, espionage, and terrorism.[485] The commission found that such an expansion would not require any congressional approval; rather, a presidential order and a Pentagon directive would be sufficient to provide the requisite authority.[486] The 2006 Intelligence Authorization Bill included a provision that would allow the FBI, with the approval of the Director of National Intelligence, to share information with the Pentagon and the CIA.[487] (The Pentagon must, for now, report such information exchanges to Congress.[488]) In spring 2006 rumors began circulating about the possible merger of CIFA and the Defense Security Service, an entity that holds the data generated by background checks on defense contractors and their employees.[489] And in January 2007, when the *New York Times* reported that the Pentagon had issued potentially thousands of National Security Letters, military officials revealed that over the following year the information would be fed into CIFA's database – even where the information had demonstrated suspects' innocence.[490]

In addition to the NSA and the Pentagon, even the DoD's National Geospatial-Intelligence Agency has taken an active role in domestic surveillance. It is now gathering information on 133 cities in the United States *with the aim of being able to re-create a map of each region, down to the identity of each person in every home, as well as their national background and political affiliation*.[491] In February 2007, the Defense Intelligence Agency, in turn, announced its intent to hire some 1,000 new analysts, engineers, acquisition specialists, and other professionals. Most of the positions are in the Washington, D.C., area.[492]

Many of these programs – and the larger matter of the military's movement into this realm – have gone relatively unnoticed by the Senate or the House. Neither chamber has conducted an inquiry into DoD's changing domestic surveillance role.[493] The full extent of the programs underway has yet to be made public: in addition to the content of the reports, even the *number* of annual TALON reports is classified.[494] Yet the intrusion on individual privacy may be significant: according to the Inspector General's newsletter, for instance, just one military service taking part in this program – the Air Force – generated 1,200 reports during the 14 months that ended September 2003.[495]

Attorney General Guidelines and FBI Surveillance

Not only does the FBI enjoy broad authority now to initiate investigations but it also has various tools on which it can draw to do so: for example, the Carnivore/DCS1000, keystroke programs, and such instruments as the Terrorism Information and Prevention System (TIPS) and federal watch lists. Through the use of these tools, enhanced by the weakening of the Attorney General's guidelines, the executive continues to increase its power under the claim of counterterrorism – with scant oversight from either Congress or the courts.[496]

After the Church hearings in the middle 1970s, the Attorney General strengthened the guidelines that governed FBI investigations. Of the weakening of those guidelines that thereafter occurred, by far the most significant took place after 9/11. Of the two documents Ashcroft issued, the first (see page 233) eliminated the wall between prosecution and intelligence investigations, leaving either side able to initiate, operate, continue, or expand FISA searches or surveillance. The second document gave the FBI the authority to enter anywhere open to the public (which includes surfing the Internet, attending religious gatherings, and taking notes at political meetings) to obtain data that *may* be relevant to criminal activity.[497] Since such entrance *did not require suspicion of actual criminal or terrorist activity*,[498] it allowed for what one commentator referred to as the "routine mining of commercial databases for personal information," without any limits on with whom or to what extent this information could be shared.[499]

Ashcroft's memo essentially collapsed the different stages of an investigation. Before June 2002, agents would have to check leads, then conduct a preliminary investigation, and, if enough evidence emerged, then move to open a full investigation. Now, from that date on, agents could rapidly move to the third stage.[500] The guidelines gave the Special Agent in Charge the authority to initiate and renew an investigation, so long as notification was sent to headquarters.[501] Perhaps the most startling aspect of the new guidelines is that they *require* the FBI to maintain a database of all investigations.[502] This information can be shared with the Department of Justice, other federal agencies, and state or local criminal justice agencies. The data collection powers are particularly strong where terrorism is concerned.[503]

As in the Vietnam era, the FBI appears to be using these powers to place antiwar demonstrators under surveillance. According to the *New York Times*, the Bureau is amassing "extensive information on the tactics, training and organization of antiwar demonstrators." The FBI defends its position, claiming it is simply trying to identify "anarchists and 'extremist elements'" – not monitor "the political speech of law-abiding protesters."[504] Yet during antiwar protests in New York City, questionnaires used by the police included queries on political party affiliation, voting record, and views of the president. In 2005, a Freedom of Information Act suit filed by the American Civil Liberties Union (ACLU) revealed that the FBI has expanded its surveillance to environmental and political organizations. The ACLU, Greenpeace, and other civil groups have been the target of Bureau surveillance.[505]

Among the tools the FBI has at its disposal for gathering data are Carnivore and Magic Lantern. The former's existence was revealed in July 2000 by Neil King of the *Wall Street Journal*.[506] Carnivore, introduced in 1999 by the FBI without Justice Department approval (or knowledge), monitors Internet Service Providers to intercept digital information. The Bureau activates the system "when other implementations (e.g., having an ISP provide the requested data) do not meet the needs of the investigators or the restrictions placed by the court."[507] Carnivore uses hardware, known as a "black box," and software, attached to an ISP's system, to collect email, instant messaging, chat room discussions, financial transactions, and Web sites visited.[508] Carnivore "chews all the data on the network" – while ostensibly eating only the particular information indicated in a court order.[509] Law enforcement can program it to collect all information to and from specified receivers and senders.

As news of Carnivore because public and generated concern, the FBI gave the system the relatively innocuous new name of "DCS 1000."[510] The House and the Senate held hearings to look into the matter, at which the FBI revealed that by September 2000 it had used the system 25 to 35 times.[511] Twenty-eight members of Congress wrote letters to Attorney General Janet Reno demanding that the program be terminated.[512] Instead, the Department of Justice suspended it, pending an independent, technical review[513] and, when the report concluded that the system was sound, reengaged Carnivore.[514] While the review noted that the information being gathered might exceed FBI authority, it notably failed to address the constitutional issues implicit in the operation of the program.

The agency's refusal to disclose more information led to Section 305 of the 21st Century Department of Justice Appropriation Authorization Act, which required a report at the end of fiscal years 2002 and 2003 on the operation of the program. Although in these reports the FBI announced that it had used DCS 1000 zero times in fiscal years 2002 and 2003, it had actually used commercially available software to undertake surveillance 13 times during that period.[515] This number does not include the number of times Internet Service Providers used their own software to intercept communications – such as those requested under NSLs.[516] It is understood that Carnivore's usefulness diminished greatly as the FBI began going directly to the ISPs for information.[517]

An Electronic Privacy Information Center Freedom of Information Act request in October 2000 yielded 729 pages of information on the system – of which 200 pages were blank, and another 400 were partially redacted.[518] The FBI, which justifies the system on the claim of national security, asserted that it could be programmed only to get specific information. However, as noted by Senator Patrick Leahy (D.-VT) and the formal review report, the system lacks procedural safeguards. The FBI determines which emails to obtain, according to classified FBI procedures.

As for Magic Lantern, it is an FBI keystroke logging program that does *not* require physical access to conduct surveillance of an individual's computer use.[519] The software targets a user's system through an email message, with the sender posing as a friend or family member. It is unclear whether the recipient needs to open the attachment or not.[520] The FBI also has the option of hacking a user's computer and placing the program directly on the hard drive. Magic Lantern captures keystrokes and, when the computer hooks up to the Internet, automatically sends the information back to the FBI. Although Magic Lantern might be caught by virus scans, the FBI approached companies that program against viruses, and requested them not to target the surveillance device; some agreed.[521] This program allows the FBI to break encryption by identifying pass phrases used to access information; it also can recreate emails and Word documents never printed or sent, as well as other information that was never meant to move beyond the immediate computer.

The courts addressed the constitutionality of keystroke programs in 2001 and determined that a key-logging device, *with a search warrant*, is not a violation of the Fourth Amendment.[522] The district court wrote that "we must be ever vigilant against the evisceration of Constitutional rights at the hands of modern technology. Yet, at the same time, it is likewise true that modern-day criminals have also embraced technological advances and used them to further their felonious purposes."[523] The government argued in the *United States* v. *Scarfo* that the key logger system (KLS) used in that case met Title III requirements: it did not record the user's entry while any modem on his or her computer was in operation. Similarly, the program did not actively seek out data already held on the computer. The court denied defense counsel access to the manner in which KLS operated as well as the nature and extent of the information obtained.

Citizen Reporting Programs

Complementing the FBI's efforts, the Department of Justice also runs its own surveillance operations. In January 2002, the department announced plans for the Terrorism Information and Prevention System (TIPS). "A national system for concerned workers to report suspicious activity,"[524] TIPS's aim was to recruit "millions of American truckers, letter carriers, train conductors, ship captains, utility employees and others" as informers.* The pilot program would have engaged 1 in every 24 Americans living in the largest 10 cities to report anything perceived as "unusual or suspicious." For seven months after the announcement, little happened. Then, just weeks before the DoJ launched TIPS, Ritt Goldstein wrote an article in an Australian newspaper, the

* Operation TIPS Web pages have since been removed from the Internet, although the original pages from July 16 and August 8, 2002, are available at www.thememoryhole.org/policestate/tips-changes.htm.

Sydney Morning Herald, that implementation would mean that "the US will have a higher percentage of citizen informants than the former East Germany through the infamous Stasi secret police"[525]: some 4 percent of Americans would report "suspicious activity."[526] After the Associated Press picked up the story, there was an immediate backlash.

A *Boston Globe* editorial led off: "OPERATION TIPS . . . is a scheme that Joseph Stalin would have appreciated."[527] Opposition spanned the ideological divide: in the House of Representatives, Republican majority leader Dick Armey and Representative Bob Barr condemned the program; their resistance was matched in the Senate by Democratic Senators Patrick J. Leahy, Edward M. Kennedy, and Charles E. Schumer.[528] The deliberate inclusion of professions with access to private homes, and the apparent intention to use TIPS to build a central database, caused particular affront. On July 25, Attorney General Ashcroft told the Senate Judiciary Committee that, although the FBI and its agencies would retain the information, he was not aware of any plans to build a central database.[529] Congress, unconvinced, shut down the program: "Any and all activities of the Federal Government to implement the proposed component program of the Citizen Corps known as Operation TIPS (Terrorism Information and Prevention System) are hereby prohibited."[530]

Congress's ban on TIPS turned out to be wishful thinking: although the Web site disappeared from cyberspace, a plethora of watch programs followed. Marine Watch sprang up in Maine, Ohio, and Michigan.[531] President Bush declared "Coastal Beacon," which coordinated reports of suspicious activity along the shores of Maine, to be "[o]ne of the most innovative TIP [*sic*] programs in the country."[532] The Department of Homeland Security, which funded Highway Watch, embraced the more than three million truck drivers integrated into the program as "a potential army of eyes and ears to monitor for security threats," and claimed that they are "naturally very aware of suspicious activity and behavior." The department added, "[T]ruck drivers are everywhere – ports, airports, malls, bridges, tunnels – thus giving greater range to homeland security observation efforts."[533] On March 15, 2004, the Transportation Security Administration (TSA) announced that another $19.3 million would assist the TSA and the American Trucking Associations to expand the operations. The press release stated, "This innovative program combines the training of highway professionals in safety and security awareness with information sharing and analysis networks, to assist in national security and road safety."[534] The expansion – indeed, the very existence – of the Highway Watch system is surprising in that the "Operation TIPS Fact Sheet" initially listed it as a TIPS system, making its continuation a violation of Congress's express prohibition.[535]

Proponents of these programs argue that, since the state has limited resources, enlisting the help of law-abiding citizens – many of whom are eager to help in some way – would dramatically increase law enforcement's ability to interdict crime. And past successes readily present themselves as justification for this claim: for instance, the "Neighborhood Watch" concept has proven effective in stemming ordinary crime.[536] Terrorism, in particular, depends upon surreptitious operations – such planning as may easily slip beneath the radar of law enforcement, which must focus on a range of different threats. The watch program approach counters the impersonalization created by social mobility and urbanization, returning society to an environment more like the small communities that characterize rural areas. If terrorists are prevented from blending into their surroundings, they lose the anonymity critical to their ability to mount attacks; and the potential devastation of an attack, owing to advances in weapons technology, makes it all the more urgent to try to prevent one. There are, moreover, many programs that encourage – or even demand – that individuals turn in information on fellow citizens: educators and teachers in California, for instance, are required by law to report child abuse.

Despite these arguments, however, the requirement that "suspicious activity" be reported can lead to considerable prejudice and abuse, both personal and political. According, for instance, to Operation Eagle Eyes ("an anti-terrorism initiative that enlists the eyes and ears of Air Force members and citizens in the war on terror")[537] potential terrorists include "[p]eople who don't seem to belong in the workplace, neighborhood, business establishment or anywhere else . . . people know what looks right and what doesn't look right in their neighborhoods, office spaces, commutes, etc., and if a person just doesn't seem like he or she belongs, there's probably a reason for that."[538] As the counterterrorist *Pentiti* trials in Italy or the Supergrass system (see Chapter 2) in Northern Ireland attest, such programs become a way for people to settle old scores – which bear no relation to terrorism.[539] This general risk, of course, is not limited to terrorism. Suspected child abuse may be reported out of spite – or an ex-spouse may turn his or her previous partner in to the Internal Revenue Service. But both of these systems are tied to concrete actions, and the law establishes opportunities to confront one's accusers and to defend oneself. Counterterrorism, in contrast, has fewer limits. The type of information necessary to identify a terrorist is not readily available to the public. In other words, most citizens are not intelligence officers and thus must rely on vague concepts, which may quickly degenerate into prejudice. Furthermore, there is little control over what happens to the information – how it is stored, whether and to what extent it is verified, who sees it, how long it is kept, and to what ends it is directed.

Even once ordered destroyed, such information may nevertheless haunt those to whom it relates. In the mid-1970s, the Church Committee hearings led to the order to destroy thousands of files held by the Los Angeles Police Department (LAPD).[540] In 1983, however, it emerged that an LAPD detective had stolen the files, kept them in his garage, and made the information available to the Western Goals Foundation.[541] This anti-communist, Cold War organization circulated the data to local police departments, the Secret Service, the FBI, the State Department, and the CIA.[542] Such systems may quickly take on racial overtones. Moreover, they increase fear and mistrust in society and may undermine social interactions. Ultimately, free speech suffers from all this – with people becoming reluctant to discuss issues either publicly or privately – as does, as a result, the democratic process.

TIPS is only one part of the Citizen Corps program handed down by Executive Order in the aftermath of 9/11. The Corps' stated goal is "to harness the power of every individual through education, training, and volunteer service to make communities safer, stronger, and better prepared for terrorism."[543] The Citizens' Preparedness Guide, issued by the USA Freedom Corps (with a foreword by John Ashcroft noting the need to change social behavior in the aftermath of 9/11), urges citizens to "[c]onsider incorporating your place of worship into your Neighborhood Watch programs."[544] Citizens are directed to contact law enforcement whenever they see "someone unfamiliar ... loitering in a parking lot."[545] The guide both recommends that Americans keep their yards clean and "[p]rune shrubbery,"[546] and urges that "[w]hen traveling" Americans should "dress conservatively."[547] While at one extreme, some of these recommendations help spread suspicion throughout the fabric of social life, at the other, many of them appear to have little real impact on terrorism.

Watch Lists

In the mid-twentieth century, as I have noted, the CIA, the FBI, the IRS, and the NSA all had "watch lists" that targeted American citizens.[548] It was not clear exactly how names got onto any of these lists, and the directors of the organizations did not review each name personally. The director of the National Security Agency from 1969–72, Vice Admiral Noel Gaylor, did not even know about the *existence* of the tabulations until a year after taking office. Instead, the lists were administered at a lower level, and agencies circulated among one another those names, which the NSA and others simply accepted on the assurance that their inclusion was somehow appropriate.[549]

Now, once again, the executive branch has begun to construct lists with minimal procedural safeguards. At least 12 exist at the federal level.[550] In 2003, the White House spearheaded an effort to compile a master list of terrorist suspects. Although the total number of individuals on the list is classified, it is believed to be in the hundreds of thousands.[551] Here I discuss one of the original lists, which colloquially came to be known as the "No Fly List."

As of September 11, 2001, the federal government had the names of 16 people on a secret "No Transport List"; this number – even if the names correlated – was not high enough to have prevented all 19 hijackers from boarding the planes on 9/11. By December 2001, this list had evolved into two sets of records: the "No Fly List" and the "Selectee List." Individuals on the first list were completely barred from flying; those on the second were merely subjected to further security measures. By the following year, these two lists combined contained more than one thousand names and, by April 2005, some 70,000 names.[552] For the program's first two-and-a-half years, however, the FBI and the Transportation Security Administration denied its existence.[553]

The transportation lists only began to attract broad public attention when prominent antiwar activists, such as Jan Adams and Rebecca Gordon, and political opponents of the Bush administration, such as Senator Edward Kennedy and the civil rights attorney David Cole, found themselves included.[554]

Distinguished Muslim Americans, such as the singer Cat Stevens and an Army chaplain, James Yee, were similarly singled out – as were two dozen students, chaperoned by a priest and a nun, on their way to a peace teach-in.[555] Documents obtained through an ACLU Freedom of Information Act request in 2004 demonstrated that even those people who were entering names and administering the list had no idea how every name had been added.[556] One particularly telling email suggested that its author would not risk flying on a commercial plane because of the haphazard manner in which the list had been assembled and the lack of procedural safeguards or mechanisms to facilitate getting off it.

Beyond the 70,000 people actually on the lists, there is substantial anecdotal evidence that individuals who share exact or similar names to those on the list also have become caught in the system. In Portland, Oregon, two comedians wrote a song about the plight of anyone named David Nelson:

> They call me David Nelson and my name has been besmirched
> When I fly across my country, I will always be strip-searched
> Somewhere a David Nelson is allegedly quite mean
> And the TSA ain't able to declare my person clean...
> I missed my flight from Texas and I missed my flight to Spain
> You'd think my second cousin was a Tikrit named Hussein
> I'm scrutinized and sanitized by security and then
> The next time that I fly, they have to do it all again.[557]

In response to a class action lawsuit filed by people caught in the name game, the TSA created an ombudsperson process, whereby individuals now can download and print out a Passenger Identity Verification Form and mail it, along with certain notarized documents, to the TSA. The organization then decides whether to undertake procedures to expedite your travel, but it is not required to do anything – nor is any criterion available as to how a decision is made. The process does not remove your name; rather, it differentiates you from others who may be on the list and saves your personal information, which is then forwarded to the airlines, in another, specially cleared list.

The No Fly List overlaps with the Computer Assisted Passenger Screening (CAPS) program, which draws information from a database to determine which individuals ought to be placed under further scrutiny.* The idea behind CAPS was to create a "vast air security screening system designed to instantly pull together every passenger's travel history and living arrangements, plus a wealth of other personal and demographic information" to "profile passenger activity and intuit obscure clues about potential threats."[558] Airlines would collect and provide the full name, address, phone number, and date of birth of people flying. The broader system would then use "data-mining and predictive software" to determine the degree of risk posed by an individual.[559]

The companies initially signed up to develop prototypes collected the information themselves, which ranged from land records and car ownership to

---

* The Federal Aviation Reauthorization Act of 1996 required the Federal Aviation Administration to help airlines develop CAPS as part of its overall security effort. Pub. L. No. 104–264, § 307, 110 Stat. 3213, 3253 (1996).

projected income, magazine subscriptions, and telephone numbers.[560] When interviewed about the system, the former acting administrator of the Federal Aviation Administration (FAA; and security consultant for the CAPS project) said, "This is not fantasy stuff.... This technology, based on transaction analysis, behavior analysis, *gives us a pretty good idea of what's going on in a person's mind.*"[561] In July 2004, Homeland Security Secretary Tom Ridge announced that CAPS II would be terminated, but other DHS officials said that only the name had been retired.[562] Indeed, Secure Flight, the FAA's latest project, bears a striking similarity to the previous project.[563]

The problems with the No Fly List generally, and Secure Flight in particular, loom large. It is not at all clear who runs the lists, how the information gets entered, who verifies it, what the criteria are for inclusion, and how the information is used subsequently. Passengers are not given the opportunity to challenge the relevant data or to confront those accusing them of being associated with terrorist activity. In July 2005, government auditors alleged that – in violation of existing privacy laws – Secure Flight held information on 43,000 people who were not suspected of terrorism.[564] Because the TSA refuses to comment on the criteria used, it also cannot reveal whether First Amendment activities are being used as a basis for inclusion. The existence of the lists shifts the burden of proof onto anyone wishing to travel: a traveler first has to prove that he or she is not the individual sought. Although at times it does make sense to place this burden on suspects, to do so broadly and on the basis of secret evidence is troublesome. It also is not clear where the information goes. Some of the watch lists run by the Departments of Defense, State, Justice, Transport, and Treasury include biometric and other personal data. Furthermore, much of the information is currently in the hands of private industry.

These widespread informer systems, along with such surveillance operations as TALON, Carnivore, and Magic Lantern, are all efforts to watch and record citizens' and noncitizens' actions, conversations, reading habits, spending habits, money flows, and the like. They are not the only programs underway; indeed, they are, in many ways, just the beginning. The federal government continues to announce – and to refrain from announcing – new initiatives. In May 2007, for instance, it emerged that the Department of Homeland Security had created a new unit designed to watch "homegrown terrorists."[565] According to *USA Today*, the new unit will focus on *all* forms of extremist activity.[566]

Outside of these and other developments lies another – and, in many ways, more important – phenomenon that has largely escaped public attention: the federal data-mining operations that have proliferated since 9/11. Remarkably, many of these programs have, as their *stated* aim, getting inside peoples' heads – to find out what individuals are thinking. They move surveillance from the physical to the psychological realm.

US DATA-MINING OPERATIONS

In 2004, the General Accounting Office (GAO) conducted a survey of 128 departments and agencies to determine the extent of federal data mining: the analysis of large amounts of information to generate new knowledge, to find previously unknown patterns, and to identify relationships.[567] The GAO uncovered 199 operations, 14 of which related to counterterrorism.[568] The CIA, for instance, runs Octopus and Quantum Leap.[569] The Defense Intelligence Agency (DIA) operates Insight Smart Discovery and Pathfinder. The Department of Education maintains Project Strikeback, which compares FBI and Department of Education files to find anomalies that signify possible terrorist activity. The Department of Homeland Security's Notebook I2 links people and events to specific data points. The Department of Justice has a Secure Collaborative Operational Prototype Environment to enable investigators to analyze multiple digital sources to find hidden patterns and relationships. Some rely in considerable measure on personal information. For example, the DIA's Verity K2 Enterprise trawls the intelligence community and the Internet to identify foreign terrorists or Americans connected to foreign terrorism. Eight of the 14 draw on privately held information to profile potential operatives.[570] And 12 get information from other agencies.[571]* In this section, I discuss a few of these – in particular, Total Information Awareness (TIA) and its offshoots – to illustrate the extent to which the state is actively seeking to develop psychological profiles, and to highlight the impact of these operations on individual privacy.

In 2002, as I noted earlier, John Poindexter initiated Total Information Awareness – a leviathan whose aim was to link every government and commercial database available worldwide.[572] Thus, trawling through multiple petabytes of data, TIA would uncover hidden patterns and give advance warning of a terrorist attack.[573]† The public balked at the TIA's flagrant disregard for privacy. On the Internet, Web sites immediately appeared dedicated to

---

* Nonterrorist government databases also can be used to mine data. The Department of the Treasury collects financial information from banks and financial institutions. The FBI maintains a criminal database with records, fingerprints, and DNA material. Health and Human Services has a "new hires" database that includes the name, address, Social Security number, and quarterly wages of every working person in the United States. The Department of Education maintains primary school through higher education records (which, since 9/11, the FBI can search without probable cause). And the Departments of Motor Vehicles have photographs of virtually every American over the age of 16. JAY STANLEY & BARRY STEINHARDT, AM. CIVIL LIBERTIES UNION, BIGGER MONSTER, WEAKER CHAINS: THE GROWTH OF AN AMERICAN SURVEILLANCE SOCIETY, 8 (2003), available at www.aclu.org.

† One petabyte would fill the Library of Congress' space for 18 million books more than 50 times. Some intelligence data sources "'grow at the rate of four petabytes per month.' Experts said those are probably files with satellite surveillance images and electronic eavesdropping results." Sniffen, *supra* note 569 (quoting the Office of Advanced Research and Development Activity). Deviance from social norms was to serve as an early indicator of terrorism. From human activity models, the ARM Program will develop scenario-specific models that will enable operatives to differentiate among normal activities in a given area or situation and activities that should be considered suspicious. The program aims to develop technologies to analyze, model, and understand human movements, individual behavior in a scene, and crowd behavior. The approach will be multisensor and include video, agile sensors, low power radar, infrared, and radio frequency tags. Information Awareness Office, Defense Advanced Research Project Agency, Report to Congress Regarding the Terrorism Information Awareness Program: Detailed Information 1 (2003) at 11.

collecting information on Poindexter: his telephone number, where he lived, where he shopped, what he bought, what his family did, and where he had last been spotted.[574] Poindexter changed his telephone number. And in May 2003, he renamed the program "Terrorism Information Awareness."*

On September 30, 2003, as it became clear that the new TIA shared much in common with the old TIA, Congress cut off its funding.[575] Nonetheless, many of its projects were simply transferred to other intelligence agencies.[576] Two of the most important moved to the Advanced Research and Development Activity (ARDA) division,† located at NSA headquarters.[577]

In 2002, the Defense Department awarded a $19 million contract to Hicks & Associates to build an Information Awareness Prototype System – the architecture underlying TIA.[578] An email to subcontractors from Brian Sharkey, an executive at the firm, said that the 2003 congressional decision to cut off TIA's funding "caused a significant amount of uncertainty for all of us about the future of our work." "Fortunately," he added, "a new sponsor has come forward that will enable us to continue much of our previous work."[579] According to the *National Journal*, the new source was ARDA.[580] Sharkey wrote that the new effort would be referred to as "Basketball" – a program described by the Defense Department, after Congress shut down TIA – in the same language used for the TIA Information Awareness Prototype System first awarded to Hicks & Associates.[581]

Another central TIA project, Genoa II, sought to develop the technology to help anticipate and preempt terrorism.[582] Intelligence sources confirmed to the *National Journal* that this project had been renamed "Topsail" and moved to ARDA.[583] In October 2005, a government press release announced that it had granted Science Applications International Corporation (a $7.8 billion company that works extensively with the Department of Defense and the US intelligence community) a $3.7 million contract under Topsail – with language describing the project virtually the same as previous descriptions of Genoa II.[584] When Democratic Senator Ron Wyden of Oregon in February 2006 asked the Director of National Intelligence, John Negroponte, whether it was "correct that when [TIA] was closed, that several . . . projects were moved to various intelligence agencies,"[585] Negroponte's deputy, General Michael V. Hayden, the former director of the National Security Administration, responded, "I'd like to answer in closed session."[586]‡

---

* A report submitted to Congress on the operation of the program bragged that TIA had already been used to analyze data obtained from detainees in Afghanistan and to assess "weapons of mass destruction in the Iraqi situation." *Id.* at 16.

† In 2005, ARDA, created in 1998 as a funding agency for the intelligence community, was renamed the Disruptive Technology Office (DTO). In December 2007, ARDA/DTO became part of the Intelligence Advanced Research Projects Activity, reporting to the Director of National Intelligence.

‡ In a classified annex to its legislation halting funding to the TIA, Congress created an exception, allowing funds to be used for "[p]rocessing, analysis, and collaboration tools for counterterrorism foreign intelligence." Department of Defense Appropriations Act, Pub. L. No. 108–87, § 8131,

The Technology and Privacy Advisory Committee (TAPAC), appointed by Secretary of Defense Donald Rumsfeld to analyze the use of "advanced information technologies to identify terrorists before they act,"[587] admitted in March 2004 that TIA-like activities "may be continuing."[588] TAPAC added that TIA is "not unique in its potential for data mining. TAPAC is aware of many other programs in use or under development both within DoD and elsewhere in the government that make similar uses of personal information concerning US persons to detect and deter terrorist activities."[589]

Indeed, the Homeland Security Act *requires* the Department of Homeland Security's Directorate for Information Analysis and Infrastructure Protection to do the following:

To access, receive, and analyze law enforcement information, intelligence information, and other information from agencies of the Federal Government, State and local government agencies (including law enforcement agencies), and private sector entities, and to integrate such information in order to – (A) identify and assess the nature and scope of terrorist threats to the homeland; (B) detect and identify threats of terrorism against the United States; and (C) understand such threats in light of actual and potential vulnerabilities of the homeland.[590]

Congress authorized $500 million for the Homeland Security Advanced Research Projects Agency to develop "data mining and other advanced analytical tools."[591]

Although many of the systems being developed remain screened from the public eye, hints of the scope of some of them occasionally surface. One little-known DHS project, for instance, is Analysis, Dissemination, Visualization, Insight and Semantic Enhancement (ADVISE).[592] According to the National Laboratories, ADVISE "is a thrust area that has been developed to support the full range of information fusion needs of the DHS." The past tense here matters: it is under "spiral development" – meaning that DHS implements it as the system evolves.[593]

ADVISE collects a broad range of information, such as financial records, blog postings, and news stories.[594] But it does not stop there. The model, as discussed by the National Laboratories, also includes multimedia, inferences, metadata, and history as types of information to be integrated into the system.[595] ADVISE then cross-references this data against intelligence and law enforcement records.[596] The system stores each cross-reference as an "entity." A report summarizing a 2004 DHS conference in Virginia said that the system would be able to retain information on approximately one quadrillion entities.[597] According to Joseph Kielman, who manages the DHS's Threat and Vulnerability, Testing and Assessment portfolio (which oversees ADVISE), the

---

117 Stat. 1054 (2004). The condition attached was that such tools could only be used where connected to "lawful military operations of the United States conducted outside the United States" or "lawful foreign intelligence activities conducted wholly overseas, or wholly against non-United States citizens." *Id.* § 8131 (b)(1)–(2).

aim is not just to identify terrorists, but to find new patterns that reveal their intentions and generate new knowledge.[598]

TIA, ADVISE, and the other data-mining efforts demonstrate that the government has an interest in, and is attempting to develop, a centralized clearinghouse for information. In July 2002, the National Strategy for Homeland Security recognized that, instead of residing in a central computer network, information exists in a variety of federal, state, and local databases. The strategy stated, "It is crucial to link the vast amounts of knowledge resident within each agency at all levels of government."[599] The document declared its intent:

We will build a national environment that enables the sharing of essential homeland security information. We must build a "system of systems" that can provide the right information to the right people at all times. Information will be shared "horizontally" across each level of government and "vertically" among federal, state and local governments, private industry, and citizens.... We will leverage America's leading-edge information technology to develop an information architecture that will effectively secure the homeland.[600]

Such a comprehensive architecture has serious implications for privacy and the role it plays in a democratic state – implications that include but stretch far beyond enabling a state to thwart terrorist threats.

Even seemingly limited programs are intrusive. After 9/11, for instance, the NSA assembled a massive database, into which it fed caller information allegedly obtained from Verizon, AT&T, and BellSouth.[601] Despite the administration's insistence that innocent Americans were not being monitored, it turned out that, indeed, millions of individuals and businesses had had their caller information recorded, retained, and mined.[602] Such information is far from innocuous. By plotting out call patterns, one can identify the key players in a social network – and which people are peripheral. The strength of the links between individuals (their connectedness), the placement of relations within the network, and how close each individual is to others in the network can be analyzed by means of complex mathematical equations.[603] Thus, if the state is looking to figure out which individuals are indispensable to an organization, even ordinary caller identification information can help it quickly determine where to focus its resources: remove the node, and you sharply curtail communication among individuals. Similarly, for dispersed networks that depend upon key people being connected, taking out the middle connections can break up an organization. And for those individuals who have the closest connections to others in a network, eavesdropping on their conversations would provide the greatest return for resources in terms of information gleaned.

Such social network analysis can be extremely helpful in determining, for instance, al Qaeda communication patterns. Certainly central members of the administration referred to al Qaeda in these terms: "Al Qaeda," John Yoo wrote, is "a network." He continued, "[T]he US should destroy the hubs of the network. Only a coordinated, simultaneous attack on several major hubs will leave a network in isolated and relatively harmless pieces." But network analysis could equally be used to analyze connections among domestic organizations – including political opponents. The collection of such information could quickly and effectively help, for instance, a political party maintain power – a goal that has nothing to do with terrorism. When, as I have written before, a political party wants to remain in power to prevent such programs from becoming publicly known, and when there is minimal oversight of such data collection and analysis, the risk is all the greater that it will use these tools for purposes other than to combat terrorism.

BRITISH AND AMERICAN OVERSIGHT COMPARED

The American surveillance oversight structure leaves much to be desired. Consider first the legislature: 17 congressional committees have the responsibility of overseeing at least one intelligence agency.[604] Any one program may fall within the purview of several bodies: the NSA's wiretap program, for instance, could be considered to come within the domain of the House or the Senate's Armed Services, Intelligence, or Judiciary committees.[605]

On the one hand, many of these committees have substantial powers: they can hold hearings, place witnesses under oath, and subpoena those reluctant to appear. Anyone who refuses to attend can be held in contempt of Congress and penalized (albeit subject to a separation of powers challenge). The legislature holds the purse strings and can shut off money to the executive branch as well.

On the other hand, the committee oversight structure has in many ways failed since 9/11. Between 1998 and 2001, Congress held 51 hearings on the right to privacy. But from 2002 through 2004 – even as the powers of the executive branch to conduct surveillance were increasing dramatically – there were only 16 hearings on this matter.[606] Congress simultaneously diminished its interest in the oversight of military intelligence: on this topic, there were, between 1998 and 2001, 33 hearings; from 2002 to 2004, only 13.[607] In contrast, its concern about terrorism, and the risk posed by terrorist threats, skyrocketed: between 1998 and 2000, 25 hearings were held, as opposed to 134 between 2001 and 2004.[608] Congress's emphasis was clearly on the threat terrorists posed – and not on the dangers of rapidly expanding executive strength.

There are a number of possible reasons for legislators' reluctance to examine surveillance. Politics, in counterterrorism, often carries more weight than the letter of the law. After 9/11, the Senate and the House of Representatives were controlled by the Republican Party, which also held the White House, and that party was little inclined to work against the president on surveillance matters.* Not that the Republicans in Congress did not oppose the president on every issue – even on national security: the line-item veto and the structure of the Department of Homeland Security, for instance, proved particularly divisive

---

* From September 2001 to October 2006, Republicans controlled the House of Representatives; from November 2002 to October 2006, they held a majority in the Senate.

even within the Republican Party. But in the realm of information gathering, the Republicans' oversight was limited.

Their reluctance may have stemmed from a shared belief that, as a constitutional matter, Article II gives the president the exclusive authority to conduct national security surveillance.[609] Or it may have been tied to the aggressive policy adopted by the White House, that anyone opposing its policies was sympathetic to terrorists. Or the explanation may be more direct: in at least one case, Senator Arlen Specter, the Republican Chair of the Judiciary Committee, was prevented by Vice President Dick Cheney from subpoenaing telecommunications executives to testify about the NSA program.[610] Reluctance may also relate to the deeper concern that any legislators who weaken intelligence-gathering measures would have to bear the responsibility for the next attack – making for a chancy record for future campaigns.*

Whatever the reason behind that lack of political will – and rules that allowed that deficit to dominate – committees tasked with overseeing intelligence agencies did not perform their duties. At the start of the 108th Congress, House rules did not require the chairs of the committees to consult the opposition to determine what hearings would be held and what witnesses would appear.[611] In spring 2006, Senator Ron Wyden, a Democrat on the Senate Select Committee on Intelligence, commented that it was impossible to get the majority party to agree to hearings on National Security Letters.[612] (The party change in Congress in 2007 was not accompanied by a shift in the rules. On the contrary, Representative Henry A. Waxman, a California Democrat who became chair of the Committee on Oversight and Government Reform, expressed his delight that it was now the Democrats' turn to block efforts by Republicans to hold hearings.[613]) Neither did the General Accounting Office, Congress's tool for holding executive agencies accountable, perform detailed audits of how the rapidly expanding surveillance powers were being used. Although the GAO has broad authority to evaluate, for example, CIA programs, as a practical matter it has not audited the agency since the early 1960s.[614] When the agency does ask even for more limited information, it has no control over whether the CIA provides the data, partially provides it, or declines to provide it altogether.

Efforts to strengthen Congress's role in the intelligence realm have, for the most part, revolved around making the transfer of intelligence more efficient – not on strengthening the balance of power between the branches. Both the 9/11 and the WMD Commissions, for instance, called for the reform of congressional oversight.[615] But the 2004 Intelligence Reform and Terrorism Prevention Act reorganized the structure of the intelligence community and created the National Counterterrorism Center, directing it "[t]o conduct strategic operational planning for counterterrorism activities, integrating all instruments of

---

* These characteristics may also go some way toward explaining why, more than a year after the NSA revelations became public, the Democratic Party, which had by then obtained a majority in Congress, had done little to change the actual programs in place. Eric Lichtblau, *Despite a Year of Ire and Angst, Little Has Changed on Wiretaps*, N.Y. TIMES, Nov. 25, 2006, A1.

national power, including diplomatic, financial, military, intelligence, homeland security, and law enforcement activities within and among agencies"[616] –
words hardly suggesting strengthened oversight of the exercise of such national
power. Efficiency, too, characterized the creation, in the same legislation, of a
Director of National Intelligence. The aim was to encourage the sharing and
coordination of information – not to provide a check on the manner in which
surveillance was conducted.

As far as purse strings go, a considerable amount of money has been shifted
below the line – beneath congressional scrutiny. And multiple committees
meant, for many years, multiple sources of funding. In January 2007, the House
finally formed the Appropriations Select Intelligence Oversight Panel – a sort of
hybrid created to satisfy turf battles between the Committee on Appropriations
and the House Permanent Select Committee on Intelligence.[617] On this panel
sit 10 members of the Appropriations Committee, 10 members of the Defense
Appropriations Subcommittee, and 3 from the Permanent Select Committee on
Intelligence. But like the other committee assignments, the Speaker of the House
makes appointments to this panel and selects its chair and ranking members.
And although the panel can hold hearings and receive testimony, it cannot
issue subpoenas or require the attendance or testimony of witnesses. Its primary purpose is simply to review budget requests and to make the appropriate
recommendations.[618]

In the United Kingdom, where the government holds plenary power in Parliament – and where there is a strong culture of allowing the executive to control
surveillance – legislative oversight also is not strong. Until recently, although
various committees occasionally considered specific aspects of intelligence gathering, no parliamentary committee conducted broad oversight. The Intelligence
and Security Committee (ISC) that now oversees MI5, MI6, and Government
Communications Headquarters (GCHQ) was created just over a decade ago
by the Intelligence Services Act and is not a typical select committee of Parliament. Select committees, creatures of the legislature, typically make their
own rules, employ their own staffs, and operate as they deem fit. The ISC, in
contrast, is composed of members appointed by the government. The prime
minister requests reports and decides which parts, if any, will be made public.
The committee meets in the cabinet office, not in Parliament – and although the
committee can initiate its own reports, it operates within the ring of secrecy, a
classified realm. Although recently there have been calls to have this committee
led by a member of HM Opposition, the past two chairs have been drawn from
the prime minister's own Labour Party.

The Public Accounts Committee, the most senior committee in Parliament,
does regularly review the intelligence agencies' budgets. The chair of this committee, by a tradition that reaches back to the Victorian era, is held by a senior
member of the Opposition; and the deputy, or vice-chair, is always drawn from
the government. These two officers are given access to an external audit of the
agencies prepared by the National Audit Office (NAO), whose Comptroller
and Auditor General are appointed by the Public Accounts Committee. These

appointments tend to be apolitical and very influential – the current individual who holds this office has been in it for 15 years. Unlike the American congressional budgetary committees, the senior staff members of NAO have access to the intelligence agencies' expenditures that occur below the line. Theoretically, the team of auditors who specialize in intelligence could go to an MI6 station overseas and ask where the money went. (Notably, though, they do not routinely see how all the money is spent – and the services would be particularly careful, if such a request were made, to maintain security.) The NAO reports are then forwarded to the Public Accounts Committee, which, unlike the US Congress, does not have the power to authorize spending. Instead, the government presents the budget, which the committee scrutinizes after the fact.

What about the judiciary? The history of surveillance provisions in the United States illustrates the weak role played by US courts. Hampered by executive stonewalling, as well as by an institutional concern that the judiciary is not particularly well placed to second-guess national security policy, the federal courts do not play a central role. Instead, primary responsibility lies with the Foreign Intelligence Surveillance Court, whose terms of reference are narrow and that has allowed all but three warrant applications to move forward. The appellate Foreign Intelligence Surveillance Court, moreover, ruled that even applications where the primary purpose is not related to terrorism or the acquisition of foreign intelligence would be allowed to proceed.

In the United Kingdom, it was the European Court of Human Rights, not the domestic courts, that drove the state to adopt statutory safeguards. Here the most important function of the judiciary has fallen outside its traditional role: the two intelligence commissioners – one overseeing the interception of communication, the other electronic bugs and other surveillance – are statutorily required to be former senior members of the judiciary.[619] They are selected because of their stature – not because of political affiliation or ideological stance. The structure matters: upon appointment, judges cease to align themselves with a particular party. Then, in determining who will serve as a commissioner, it is the Lord Chief Justice, not the prime minister, who draws up a list of candidates. Unless there is good reason for the government or Lord Chancellor to object, individuals on the list are then appointed to each post. By law, the intelligence services must open their records to the commissioners, who annually inquire into whether the information provided to the Home Office was accurate, whether the operations were conducted properly, and whether the records of the agencies are in order.[620] They recommend how to avoid mistakes in the future. A commissioner's arrival at an agency is seen as a major event – any mistakes found would be considered a scandal, and, if they were reported, even privately, the government would have to act. Although the public reports sometimes withhold information, the sense within the security services is that if the government does not act, the judges could go public. They are seen as highly independent. As one former director of the Government Communications Headquarters put it, "It is inconceivable that you would find the UK agencies going outside RIPA and running black operations that they were not prepared to tell the commissioner about. It would be more than their jobs were worth."[621] Since the commissioners inspect *all* agencies engaged in surveillance, everyone – from MI6 to the local egg inspector – gets audited.

Separate annual reports on counterterrorist legislation more broadly provide an additional check on the system. These reviews are conducted, again, by senior members of the judiciary, who look at the operation of powers in counterterrorist law. For much of the Troubles, this meant that both the 1973 Northern Ireland (Emergency Provisions) Act et seq. were reviewed by one individual, and the 1974 Prevention of Terrorism (Temporary Provisions) Act et seq. by another. In 2000, these acts became combined in the 2000 Terrorism Act. Reviews of this legislation, and of the subsequent 2001 ATCSA, followed. These reviews supplement the commissioners' reports; and although they do not speak specifically to the intelligence operations covered by RIPA, they do address related areas, such as the use of extended detention as a form of surveillance.

The United States, hampered by separation of powers concerns, has no equivalent, external judicial audit function. Instead, audits are conducted *within the intelligence agencies themselves*. Although this check is not to be discounted – it was the Department of Justice's Inspector General who, under statutory requirement, revealed information to Congress about the FBI's misuse of National Security Letters (see page 236), neither should too much reliance be placed on it. The DoJ is not the only entity with an Inspector General (IG): the CIA has one, who is appointed by the president and confirmed by the Senate. But the breadth of powers afforded to the IGs is limited: the Defense Intelligence Agency, the National Reconnaissance Office, the National Security Agency, the National Geospatial-Intelligence Agency, and the Director of National Intelligence have administrative IGs who are appointed by the head of each agency and have even less autonomy than the CIA's Inspector General.[622]

Outside of the Inspectors General, the President's Foreign Intelligence Advisory Board (PFIAB) analyzes the "quality, quantity and adequacy of intelligence collection, of analysis and estimates, of counterintelligence, and of other intelligence activities."[623] Its 16 members serve at the pleasure of the president.[624] It is an optional advisory board: President Jimmy Carter, for instance, elected not to have a PFIAB. Carter did, however, continue the Intelligence Oversight Board (IOB) – a standing committee within the PFIAB that advises the president on the legality of certain foreign intelligence activities and occasionally conducts inquiries into covert operations.[625] According to the Executive Order establishing the IOB, its responsibilities include preparing reports for the president on any activities believed to be unlawful or contrary to Presidential Directive, reviewing the intelligence community's internal guidelines, and reviewing the practices and procedures of the Inspectors General and the General Counsel.[626] These reports, however, are specifically for the president and not for outside consumption.

Finally, in respect to the United Kingdom's executive structures, its administrative warrant system remains within the executive branch – unlike FISA, which exercises a semi-judicial check on the US executive. Unlike FISA warrants, however, British surveillance warrants last for a limited time, and applications for them have to be signed off by a range of Home Office officials. Although most warrants ultimately go to the Home Secretary, any Secretary of State – such as the Secretary of State for Foreign Affairs or for Northern Ireland – can approve one. Each one of these officials is answerable to Parliament.* For the Secretary of State to approve the application, the statute requires that he or she consider the surveillance necessary to help the intelligence agency in carrying out its functions, and that the objective cannot reasonably be achieved by other means.[627] Further, it is the practice that, informally, for the most sensitive areas (namely, counterterrorism), senior officials from the security services routinely meet with those approving the warrants. They talk through whether the warrants were successful and what events followed. This practice ensures that the senior officials who are scrutinizing the applications understand both the background to the cases and why the authorities are being sought.

Although this entire process takes place within the executive branch, officials from a different agency exercise judgment on whether the intelligence gathering is being done in a manner consistent with necessity and the law. And since civil servants in the Home Office who are involved in this process tend to hold their positions for several years, there is quite a bit of continuity in the process, which may ensure that, by the time an application gets to the Secretary of State, it is fairly clear why it should be approved – although sometimes one is turned down. Granted, a number of investigations do not come under RIPA – for instance, if the police need details of a target's bank account, they can separately obtain the authority to request those details if there is reasonable cause to believe that the individual is engaged in illegal activity. But the specific techniques covered by the surveillance statutes were thought to be the ones that required political authorization. The reason is fairly straightforward: the Secretary of State, who is answerable to Parliament, can be caught out publicly for any mistakes made in the operation of this system. This accountability, again, although its strictness ought not to be overemphasized, is a strength.

THE POLITICAL, SOCIAL, LEGAL, AND ECONOMIC CONSEQUENCES

Rights, as I discussed in Chapter 1, do not exist in isolation. And these surveillance measures have a significant impact on a host of interrelated entitlements and state mechanisms. Failure to address this issue has had far-reaching effects on the political, legal, social, and economic fabric of the state.

One danger lies in the possibility that inaccurate information may become part of an individual's permanent digital record. Mistakes happen, of course, in all systems – tax, regular policing, eyewitness testimonies, and the like – but

---

* There is additional emergency provision for such warrants to be signed outside of regular working hours, and RIPA 2000, sec. 5 (1)–(2). The legislation provides for emergencies when the Secretary of State is not available. RIPA 2000, § 6.

counterterrorism has certain characteristics that not only make such errors more likely but also mean that they will not be fixed. Owing to counterterrorism's lack of openness, absence of public access, and denial of due process, individuals on whom information is gathered have little opportunity to confront their digital accusers.

Counterterrorist data-mining operations in particular, which use many sources of information, raise issues related to people's having similar records– as, notably, in the operation of the "No Fly List" since 9/11. Substantive difficulties also arise in respect to third-party collection points. A system is only as good as the entity gathering the information. Yet a host of possibilities – from the deliberate entry of false information and the acquisition of data under circumstances of duress (such as torture) to simple mistakes – could corrupt the data, making their use in further analysis somewhat of a moot point. Many of the current systems neither ensure accuracy in third-party collection nor identify the collection point to allow later users of the data to go back to verify them – much less to ensure that the same error is not repeated as data transfer through the system. Since a target rarely knows that the data have been gathered, he or she is unlikely to challenge them. This danger becomes even more pronounced in light of the possibility that hackers may deliberately penetrate data systems to alter or retrieve information.

There is some question whether inaccurate information can be used to convict individuals of criminal offences. The US Supreme Court found in 1995, for instance, that the exclusionary rule does not apply to errors made by court employees.[628] In his dissent to this opinion, Justice John Paul Stevens admonished that the Court's position "overlooks the reality that computer technology has changed the nature of threats to citizens' privacy over the past half century."[629] Justice Ginsburg, also dissenting, referred to the "potential for Orwellian mischief" represented by increasing reliance on technology.[630]

We know that mistakes are made. Twenty years ago, the FBI conducted a study that revealed that approximately 12,000 invalid or inaccurate reports on individuals wanted for arrest were being circulated to law enforcement agencies daily.[631] Databanks have since only increased in size.

There is an additional danger in relation to a contextual data merger. Taking information gathered for one purpose and applying it to another risks changing its meaning. Say a student takes Islamic history courses and obtains high marks. Curious, then, about areas she has studied, she applies for a grant to travel to Egypt, where she hopes to see the pyramids. When she gets there, she happens to meet someone in a café, who is on the US list of terrorist suspects. Individually, each point of information may have an entirely different meaning: top grades in history may suggest that she is simply a good student. A plane ticket for a week in Egypt may simply look like a holiday. And a cup of coffee in a café may be just that. But each piece of data taken together, in the context of a terrorist threat, could put her in a difficult position, with her rights very much at risk. As I discussed in chapter 3, for instance, under Executive Order 13,224, her assets could be frozen indefinitely.

Not only is there a problem with the transfer of the wrong information but the shadow of too much information also looms large. Thus, one Privy Counsellor Review committee commented, "The East German Government may have had files on a quarter of their population, but it failed to predict or prevent its own demise. If there is too much information, it can be difficult to analyze effectively and so can generate more leads than can be followed up or trigger too many false alarms."[632] The United States has gone much further down the path of massive information gathering; however, the nature of debates in Parliament – and recent revelations from the British commissioner indicating that massive numbers of communication records had been sought by the state – suggest that the United Kingdom may be just as susceptible to this concern.

In addition to these individual issues, the concentration of information-gathering authorities in the executive weights the balance in power in its favor in respect to the other two branches of government.[633] In the United States in the past, such accumulations of power have been used for political reasons, with private information – from Hoover to Nixon and beyond – becoming an instrument of control. The veil drawn over access to this information may harden to an impenetrable wall, with the judiciary – or the legislature – loath to second-guess those responsible for ensuring national security. Executive privilege and access to confidential information may prove sufficient to convince the other branches (and, indeed, the public at large) of the truth of national security claims. Assertions, by both the United States and the United Kingdom, regarding the presence of weapons of mass destruction in Iraq are only the latest example in a long series of such claims. In *Korematsu v. United States* (1944), the judiciary deferred to executive claims regarding secret privileged information to allow the widespread detention of Americans of Japanese descent during World War II.[634] The secret materials turned out not to exist.

Furthermore, particularly in the United States, these powers have been widely used not just to counter national security threats but also to prevent dissent. The effort to root out Communists during the Cold War resulted in actions against civil rights leaders, the women's movement, and various political parties that disagreed with the administrations' policies. Although the United States did not cease to be a democracy in those years, nor was dissent entirely suppressed, such efforts did dampen the willingness of many people to engage in public discussion. Protecting our freedom to deliberate openly helps ensure that government policies are examined more fully, and that citizens have more information on which to base their decisions.

One of the technologies developed under the Total Information Awareness program (see page 257) enables the state to scan a crowd for deviant behavior – as an early indicator of terrorism. As a general principle, there are various situations in which we might want law enforcement to undertake precisely such efforts: when, for example, my brother, an undercover police officer, is stationed at a rock concert, his safety and that of the people around him depend on his being able to quickly identify potentially violent individuals. Similarly, we want systems to identify actions that indicate terrorist behavior – such as an unattended package at a politically important site. Deviant behavior is, however, a broad category: in some places, it could mean cross-dressing or passionately kissing a member of the same sex. Establishing programs that search for individuals departing from supposedly accepted social norms may increase the pressure on individuals to conform. We may already have such pressure – but one of the animating concepts of a liberal state is tolerance for diversity and the celebration of individual expression. Much as surveillance programs may encroach on such freedoms, the latter do not figure largely in the overall consideration of counterterrorist intelligence gathering and analysis.

A further difficulty is the possibility that information gathered for one purpose will be used for others. In late 1995 in Redwood City, California, for example, the police began installing listening devices to detect gunfire – devices that, the police later admitted, enabled them to listen in to conversations in private dwellings.[635] Such misuse is difficult to uncover when surveillance information is masked from public scrutiny. More specifically, *counterterrorist* provisions that allow the gathering of such data rarely include strictures on the *purpose* for which those data can be used.

The widespread collection of information also carries legal implications. No longer must the state demonstrate individualized suspicion to target individuals and invade their privacy. Instead, everyone in society becomes suspect; each person is forced to defend himself or herself when the state reaches its (potentially entirely mistaken) conclusions.

There are broader legal issues in the constitutional realm. Statutory provisions for surveillance, for instance, provide a way for the state to go around the Fourth Amendment, which offers individuals protection against unwarranted state interference. The executive acts instead under Article II, claiming considerable leeway in its decision to do so.

Perhaps the loss of anonymity and movement into psychological surveillance press most heavily on the social sphere. The widespread collection of information makes people suspicious both of the state's intentions and of law enforcement. Of course, suspicion of the state is not a new phenomenon.* The difficulty now is that surveillance powers reside in the hands of state officials who exercise them in secret; the extent of their impact is unknown; and one has no reasonable opportunity to object. This situation leaves much to speculation, such as how far private rights are invaded, and whether they need to be at all.

In fact, the significant expansion in technology and the broader state access to private information after 9/11 have raised public concern. Resolutions against the USA PATRIOT Act, including five state-wide declarations, have been passed

---

* In 1844, a secret Committee of the House of Commons noted "the strong moral feeling which exists against the practice of opening letters, with its accompaniments of mystery and concealment." Report of the Committee of Privy Counsellors Appointed to Inquire into the Interception of Communications (1957), ¶ 133. The committee added, "There is no doubt that the interception of communications . . . is regarded with general disfavour. . . . Whether practised by unauthorized individuals or by officials purporting to act under authority, the feeling still persists that such interceptions offend against the usual and proper standards of behaviour as being an invasion of privacy and an interference with the liberty of the individual in his right to be 'let alone when lawfully engaged upon his own affairs.'" *Id.*

in 401 cities and counties in 43 states.[636] Cities that have condemned the broader surveillance measures include New York City and Washington, D.C. – the targets of the 9/11 attacks. By the end of 2003, the federal legislature, picking up on this sentiment, had introduced nearly a dozen amendments to mitigate some of the act's more egregious provisions. From left to right, privacy advocates voiced their concern: in October 2002, House Majority Leader Dick Armey referred to the Justice Department as "the biggest threat to personal liberty in the country." The chairman of the House Judiciary Committee, Representative James Sensenbrenner, threatened to subpoena the Attorney General to get answers to questions about the department's use of the powers. Conservative commentators, such as William Safire, found themselves in the same camp as liberal icons, such as Senator Ted Kennedy of Massachusetts. And strange bedfellows began emerging: Conservative leader Bob Barr, for instance, became a formal advisor to the ACLU – which invited the head of the National Rifle Association to address its annual membership conference. These developments forced the Attorney General to go on the offensive. He initiated a speaking tour in 2003 to defend the USA PATRIOT Act,[637] and the DoJ launched a Web site, called "Preserving life and liberty," to defend the government's use of the legislation.[638]

As for law enforcement, the adversarial relationship created by the state's surveillance policies may seriously inhibit its ability to provide basic services. A startlingly good example here comes from the TIPS program, which initially planned to train first responders and firefighters to report on "suspicious" behavior (see page 251). Pressure also mounted on the police to begin collecting and reporting information relating to immigrant communities. These professions have access to private residences and so are in a better position to gather information otherwise masked from state view. The problem, of course, is that if people think that firefighters – or the police, for that matter – are coming to spy on them and possibly to turn them in to the authorities, people in need will not call them. The resulting adversarial relationship will only make it more difficult to provide basic services – which have nothing to do with terrorism and perhaps everything to do with, among other things, health, fire, and domestic abuse.

Then there is the issue of psychological surveillance, which the United States undertook in the twentieth century to try to get inside people's heads and find ways to control them. In Project CHATTER, run from 1947–53, the Navy administered "truth drugs" (Anabasis aphylla, scopolamine, and mescaline) to people in the United States and overseas. Project BLUEBIRD/ARTICHOKE, run by the CIA from 1950 to 1956, investigated "the possibility of control of an individual by application of special interrogation techniques," in which hypnosis and sodium pentothal were the chosen means. MKULTRA, overseen by the CIA from 1950 to the late 1960s, attempted to manipulate human behavior through chemical and biological weapons, as well as "additional avenues to the control of human behavior ... [such as] radiation, electroshock, psychology, psychiatry, sociology, and anthropology, graphology, harassment substances, and paramilitary devices and materials."[639] Although these projects began as efforts to defend the United States, that purpose was soon subordinated to perfecting techniques "for the abstraction of information from individuals whether willing or not."[640] Despite, or perhaps because of, the outright violations of individual rights that occurred during these earlier efforts, intelligence agencies made deliberate efforts to prevent citizens from even knowing about these programs. The CIA Inspector General wrote the following in 1957:

Precautions must be taken not only to protect operations from exposure to enemy forces but also to conceal these activities from the American public in general. The knowledge that the Agency is engaging in unethical and illicit activities would have serious repercussions in political and diplomatic circles and would be detrimental to the accomplishment of its mission.[641]

It would be naïve to assume that efforts to get inside terrorists' heads so as to anticipate their plans (a self-stated aim of the TIA as well as of the 2002 National Security Strategy) could avoid similar issues related to social control and secrecy. To the contrary, the use of such massive amounts of information, replete with social network analysis, could give certain individuals the ability to manipulate the social structure of the state.

Surveillance programs also undermine the equality of privacy. Not *all* citizens will be subject to psychological profiling; but once certain traits are identified (likely linked to age, religion, country of origin, nationality, or ethnicity), only certain portions of the population will lose the degree of privacy otherwise afforded the majority. Feelings of inequality and perceptions of injustice may make these groups less willing to participate in civic structures and less able to take advantage of state services when needed.

Among other social concerns, perhaps one of the most serious is the fact that one's past transgressions may become a scarlet letter, emblazoned on a citizen's chest, "visible to all and used by the ... powerful ... to increase their leverage over average people."[642] This circumstance would make somewhat obsolete the concept of paying one's dues – and then moving forward with a fresh start. As Alan Westin notes, "Part of the value of privacy in the past was that it limited the circulation of recorded judgments about individuals, leaving them free to seek self-realization in an open environment."[643] Thus, the relentless collection, storage, and recall of such information may make it difficult for people to overcome the past and to see themselves in a new, more positive light.

On the economic front, extensive surveillance may discourage innovation or harm commercial activity.* Encryption, for example, is an essential part of

---

* Not that there may not be good reasons for a state to want to have access to encrypted data: in the late twentieth century Aum Shin ri Kyo, for instance, used encryption to mask computer files that contained plans to carry out a biological attack on the United States. Dorothy E. Denning & William E. Baugh, Jr., *Encryption in Crime and Terrorism, in* CYBERWAR 2.0: MYTHS, MYSTERIES AND REALITY 167 (Alan D. Campen & Douglas H. Dearth eds., 1998). Ramzi Yousef, a member of al Qaeda partially responsible for the 1993 attack on the World Trade Center, encrypted files that detailed plans to bomb 11 planes over the Pacific Ocean. *Hearings on Encryption Before the H. Comm. on International Relations*, 105th Cong. (1997) (testimony of FBI Director Louis J. Freeh).

commercial security, allowing companies to develop strategies, make bids, and price parts and services without their competitors' knowledge.[644] The interception of this information – particularly in finance, where money ends up simply a matter of "bits and bytes" – may be devastating.[645] It may also raise difficult diplomatic issues: European alarm at Echelon, a massive international data-collection effort spearheaded by Britain and the United States, rests in part on concern about economic espionage.[646] And, as I discuss in the next chapter, reduced data protection in the United States may harm the country's ability to do business with its European partners.

Limits on the development of encryption may hurt domestic security firms' ability to compete in the international market. In congressional hearings, Sam Gejdenson, the ranking member of the House Subcommittee on International Economic Policy and Trade, suggested that the current situation mirrors Dick Cheney's efforts, when Secretary of Defense, to prevent the Secretary of Commerce from lifting controls on Intel 286 16-bit microprocessor computers – at a time when any civilian could buy an Intel 386 32-bit microprocessor device at Radio Shack in Beijing.[647] Gejdenson cited "a recent NEW YORK TIMES story of a German company basically sending its appreciation to the American government and the restrictions we placed on encryption because we are about to make them really rich."[648]

Powers of surveillance in the United Kingdom and the United States have played out in different ways. Yet both states now find themselves courting the shadow of Big Brother. The ease with which the two countries can obtain information rests in large part on the counterterrorist discourse. At stake are the balance among the branches and the social, legal, and economic fabric of the state. Equally important are the rights on the line. For privacy is an important aspect of the liberal, democratic state – yet it is the entitlement perhaps hardest hit in the counterterrorist dialogue. Encroachments on it, moreover, affect such vital other entitlements as freedom of speech, of association, and of religion. Surveillance is not alone in this effect. As I suggest in the next chapter, efforts to stifle speech carry equally far-reaching costs.

5

Terrorist Speech and Free Expression

"Congress shall make no law ... abridging the freedom of speech, or of the press."

US CONSTITUTION, First Amendment

"Islamic governments ... are established as they [always] have been by pen and gun[,] by word and bullet[,] by tongue and teeth."

AL QAEDA MANUAL

"Everyone has the right to freedom of expression. This right shall include freedom to hold opinions and to receive and impart information and ideas without interference by public authority. ... The exercise of these freedoms, since it carries with it duties and responsibilities, may be subject to such formalities, conditions, restrictions or penalties as are prescribed by law and are necessary in a democratic society, in the interests of national security, territorial integrity or public safety, for the prevention of disorder or crime ... "

European Convention on Human Rights, Article 10

"When you had a bomb outrage, and there are pictures of bodies [shown] to distressed and weeping relatives, and the next thing that happens on the screen, in people's living rooms, is somebody saying, 'I support the armed struggle' or 'They deserved it' – that I think is not only offensive, but it's wrong and it's perfectly reasonable to remove that."

Douglas Hurd, UK Home Secretary, 1988

"A person is guilty of an offence if he (a) uses threatening, abusive or insulting words or behaviour, or disorderly behaviour, or (b) displays any writing, sign or other visible representation which is threatening, abusive or insulting, within the hearing or sight of a person likely to be caused harassment, alarm or distress thereby."

UK Public Order Act, 1986

On June 16, 2002, Dennis Pluchinsky, a senior diplomatic security analyst at the US Department of State, wrote an article in the *Washington Post* calling for censorship. The text began, "I accuse the media in the United States of treason." Pluchinsky, who had worked on counterterrorism for 25 years, pointed to post-9/11 articles that revealed American vulnerabilities: "Our news media, and certain think tankers and academicians, have done and continue to do the target vulnerability research for them."[1]

Pluchinsky had a point. Terrorist organizations can and do use the media – and the protections afforded speech – to obtain and disseminate information, to organize and persuade others to join them, and to try to influence a state and its people.

In respect to the first purpose, Al Qaeda's training manual, recovered from a flat in Manchester, details how to make bombs, assassinate people, conduct espionage, and take hostages. It instructs how to avoid detection and withstand interrogation. And it offers advice on how to obtain operational data: "[N]ewspapers, magazines, books, periodicals, official publications, and enemy broadcasts," provide vital data. "[D]epending on the government's policy on freedom of the press and publication," the manual says, "at least 80% of information about the enemy" can be obtained – "without resorting to illegal means."[2] Operatives can get photographs of government and law enforcement personnel, data on state capabilities, information related to economic vulnerabilities, and announcements of events where the public can gain access to secure buildings. "These," the manual suggests, "may be used in assassination, kidnapping, and overthrowing the government."[3] With the proliferation of biological and nuclear weapons, the range of information considered dangerous expands. Municipal data, such as the location of water sources or air intake vents, may be essential to a group's ability to launch an assault. Articles relating discoveries even in basic biology may provide information whose use could be devastating.

Terrorist organizations can use the media to organize and to anticipate state surveillance as well. They can use coverage of past incidents to observe response times, staging grounds, and prophylactic measures used by first responders. Public commentary allows them to analyze their errors and gauge the success of future operations.

As for gathering other people to their cause, the al Qaeda manual suggests that the establishment of Islamic government has always depended not just on firepower but also on the ability to communicate ideas.[4] Indeed, Osama bin Laden quickly followed 9/11 with a prerecorded statement to persuade the world of his cause. The Islamist network is not alone: terrorist organizations, after all, seek ultimately to convince. In Northern Ireland, the Progressive Unionist and the Ulster Democratic parties inject into the political debate the aims of the Ulster Volunteer Force and the Ulster Defense Association. The Provisional Irish Republican Army runs the Irish Republican Publicity Bureau. And in the 1970s, left-wing organizations in the United States and the United Kingdom issued lengthy, turgid prose attempts to explain *why* they were doing *what* they were doing – an approach mimicked in 1995 by the Unabomber in his manifesto, "Industrial Society and Its Future."[5] If successful, terrorism may persuade people that violence is a legitimate way of redressing grievances.

The media may be complicit in its role: efforts to report in a neutral manner provide terrorists with a platform and thus help establish and expand a base of support, generating assistance, money, and recruits from an uncommitted or sympathetic audience. Unrestricted speech, moreover, leaves terrorist organizations free to coerce the government and the population, resulting in enough public anxiety to influence elections. It can spur a state to react aggressively and thus play into the hands of those advocating violence. Fear can undermine the economy, discouraging tourism, travel, and investment. And it can emasculate citizens' belief in liberal, democratic values.

If, however, terrorist organizations need free use of the media, so, too, does a liberal, democratic state need free speech. Democracy depends upon the citizens' ability to explore and challenge ideas – to, as the US First Amendment goes on to say, exercise their right "peaceably to assemble and to petition the Government for a redress of grievances." Laws constraining this entitlement tend – even as they may promise to ensure security – to undermine the health of the state itself.

This tension – between both terrorists and the state needing free expression – has been resolved differently on each side of the Atlantic: the United States is more protective of political speech than its British counterpart. Aside from political expression, one of the most pressing issues right now in both countries relates to what I term "knowledge-based speech" – that is, scientific information that can be used either for good or for ill.* Here, neither the United States nor the United Kingdom offers much protection. In addition, the secondary effect of such measures as executive detention, control orders, and antiterrorist financial initiatives – although not in themselves placing outright restrictions on speech – may have a significant chilling effect on it anyway. It appears increasingly likely, moreover, that the United States in particular will use criminal charges, such as conspiracy, to go after those suspected of terrorism. Here, broader standards allow First Amendment-protected activity to be used as evidence of participation in criminal enterprises. Evidentiary standards are also of concern – such as the waiving of the right to silence in the United Kingdom for those accused of membership in a terrorist organization. Finally, there are the issues of controlling employees' speech and of classified information.

In each of these areas, more than free speech is on the line. To mitigate the security risk posed by free expression, executive authority in both countries has expanded. The ability of the other two branches to limit it is most restricted

---

* This category is similar to what Professor Eugene Volokh of UCLA Law School defines as crime-facilitating speech: "any communication that, intentionally or not, conveys information that makes it easier or safer for some listeners or readers (a) to commit crimes, torts, acts of war . . . or (b) to get away with committing such acts." His term, however, suggests that the information itself plays a role in the commission of the crime, and thus risks biasing the discussion against allowing this language. The concept of knowledge-based speech avoids this bias, by focusing on the nature of the speech, which is rooted in data that can be used to assist, prevent, or accomplish goals that may or may not be related to criminal activity. *See* Eugene Volokh, *Crime-Facilitating Speech*, 57 STAN. L. REV. 1095, 1103 (2005).

where the state acts in a privileged position as either employer or information-holder. The record demonstrates extreme American and judicial deference in this area, resulting in a shift in the balance of power among the three branches – another result often lost sight of in the security or freedom rubric.

POLITICAL SPEECH

One of the chief harms of terrorist-related speech is the possibility that individuals dedicated to violence will be able to convince others of the justness of their cause – and thus gain either acquiescence or explicit support. In the United States, however, core political speech is now largely protected. It was not always this way. The country has a history of limiting political expression. But the judicial test used since 1969 to determine whether the state has infringed on political speech and the cultural norms resisting state encroachment have proven fairly robust at guaranteeing free expression.[6]

The United Kingdom has a longer history of restricting political expression. Initiatives equivalent to American sedition provisions can be found across the Atlantic in laws relating to treason, unlawful assembly, sedition, and prohibitions on music, monuments, and flags. As with the United States, a short discussion of its history helps provide a context for the United Kingdom's recent efforts to curb political speech: in the mid-1980s, a broadcast ban against terrorist organizations, and in 2006, prohibitions on the glorification of terrorism.

Sedition Versus Free Speech in the United States

From the earliest days of the American republic, questions arose about how much leeway to give dissenting voices. In 1798, the Federalists faced imminent war with France. Exasperated by Republican criticism of their policies, the Federalists introduced the Alien and Sedition Acts. This legislation made "any false, scandalous and malicious writing" against the government, either house of Congress, or the President, "with intent to defame . . . or to bring them . . . into contempt or disrepute; or to excite against them . . . hatred of the good people of the United States, or to stir up sedition" a high misdemeanor, with penalties ranging from fine to imprisonment.[7] The vice president, a Republican, was not granted the same protections. To further ensure that the Republicans would not have access to the same powers, the Federalists set the statute to expire on President John Adams' last day in office.[8]

This legislation ultimately backfired.[9] Public outrage carried Thomas Jefferson to the White House, and the new president pardoned those convicted under the statute, which to him represented a "nullity as absolute and as palpable as if Congress had ordered us to fall down and worship a golden image."[10] Congress repaid all fines – with interest.[11]

But for more than a half-century afterward, the shadow of government excess loomed large. During the Civil War, the Lincoln administration avoided the outright prohibition of political speech by suspending the writ of habeas corpus.[12]* When it is "politically inexpedient to legislate against disloyal utterances in general," other measures may prove more effective.[13] Indeed, the executive detained thousands of citizens – estimates run as high as 38,000 – many on the basis of speech.[14]† This figure eclipses the number of people prosecuted under the Alien and Sedition Acts or, later, the Espionage Act of 1917. But the suspension of the great writ demonstrated that "there is more than one way to skin a cat – or, in the more dignified language of political science, a powerful government in war time can find other means of dealing with disloyalty than through the courts."[15]

The May 1915 bombing of the *Lusitania* catapulted the United States into World War I and reinvigorated state efforts to restrict political speech. With the 1905–07 Russian Revolution just past and the October 1917 Revolution close at hand, Woodrow Wilson announced, "[I]f there should be disloyalty, it will be dealt with a firm hand of stern repression." Those daring to agitate "had sacrificed their right to civil liberties."[16]

The Assistant Attorney General, Charles Warren, drafted the 1917 Espionage Act, which made it a crime to "make or convey false reports or false statements with intent to interfere with the operation or success of the military or naval forces of the United States or to promote the success of its enemies."[17] Any "attempt to cause insubordination, disloyalty, [or] mutiny," or to obstruct recruiting or enlistment, became illegal.[18] This disaffection provision turned out to be of paramount importance in not allowing truth as a defense – and thus marked a significant departure from even the 1798 Sedition Act, which had made true statements exculpatory.[19]‡

To control public opinion, the Wilson administration created the Committee on Public Information. The panel hammered home two themes: hate the enemy, and be faithful to the United States. The Attorney General directed all "loyal Americans" to report any suspicions directly to the Department of Justice. A plethora of volunteer groups with Batman-like names formed – Sedition Slammers, Terrible Threateners, Knights of Liberty, and Boy Spies of America – and wiretapped, broke and entered, bugged offices, and examined bank accounts and medical records.[20]

---

* This does not mean no effort was made to enact outright speech restrictions. The Virginia Emancipation Debates heralded the introduction of southern state measures to prevent abolitionist speech from gaining ground. However, the northern states did not follow suit. Efforts to get Congress to pass similar statutes also met with little success. *See* MICHAEL KENT CURTIS, FREE SPEECH, "THE PEOPLE'S DARLING PRIVILEGE": STRUGGLES FOR FREEDOM OF EXPRESSION IN AMERICAN HISTORY 125, 152, 184, 229 (2000).

† The War Department, which acknowledged that it had incomplete records, reported more than 13,000 people detained without charge. GEOFFREY STONE, PERILOUS TIMES (2005), at 113–15.

‡ The legislation also empowered the Postmaster General to prevent from traveling through the mail documents expressly advocating or urging unlawful actions. Such actions had to be directed toward causing "insubordination, disloyalty, mutiny, or refusal of duty." GEOFFREY STONE, PERILOUS TIMES (2005), at 150. (quoting Gilbert Roe, an attorney representing the Free Speech League, testifying before the House Judiciary Committee).

The courts provided little respite from either statutory restrictions or overenthusiastic patriots. Although a few judges did take a clear stand for free speech, most did not. Instead, lower federal courts applied a "bad tendency" rationale: in other words, judges considered whether the "natural and probable tendency and effect of the words" were "calculated to produce the result condemned by the statute."[21] Anyone questioning the legal or moral aspects of the war threatened public order.[22] Juries narrowly determined as a question of fact whether the law had been violated, and a high conviction rate followed.

One of the first significant challenges to this statute – and to the bad tendency test – arose within a month of its passage. The New York postmaster decided that *The Masses*, a monthly revolutionary publication featuring antiwar poems, cartoons, and articles, fell afoul of the law. In granting the paper an injunction against the postmaster, Judge Learned Hand rejected the bad tendency test.[23] He pointed to the vague standards and broad discretion granted under the statute, and noted that it would be nearly impossible to refute charges. Only such speech "thought directly to counsel or advise insubordination," or that directly advocated "resistance to the recruitment and enlistment service," ought to fall under the legislation.[24] The circuit court stayed the injunction and overruled Hand's interpretation of the statute. But, in later years, his effort to distinguish between advocacy and discussion resurfaced.

In 1918, the executive strengthened its hand further. The Sedition Act became one of the most draconian pieces of legislation in American history. Members of Congress who attempted to oppose any portion of it immediately became seen as enemies of the state.[25] The new statute expressly prohibited *all* "unpatriotic or disloyal" language, regardless of whether immediate harm might follow.[26] Within a year, three important cases upheld the Espionage and Sedition acts and, under the bad tendency doctrine, found guilty those charged with their violation.

The first, *Schenck* v. *United States* (1919), involved distribution of a Socialist Party leaflet arguing that the Espionage Act ought to be repealed, and that the draft amounted to involuntary servitude – a violation of the Thirteenth Amendment. Although the pamphlet did *not* advocate breaking the law, Justice Oliver Wendell Holmes said that the pamphlet would not "have been sent unless it had been intended to have some effect" – to discourage people from complying with the draft.[27] In a passage recognizing that the leaflet would have been lawful had a war not been going on, Holmes famously remarked that "the character of every act depends upon the circumstances in which it is done." For Holmes, "The question in every case is whether the words used are used in such circumstances and are of such a nature as to create a clear and present danger that they will bring about the substantive evils that Congress has a right to prevent." It was "a question of proximity and degree."[28] Although the United States had already signed the armistice, the exigencies of the situation met the test.

One week later, the Supreme Court handed down a second ruling against a German-language newspaper that had prepared, but not published, a series of articles arguing that Wall Street had forced the United States into war. In

Frohwerk v. *United States*,[29] the Court convicted the author of conspiracy to violate the Espionage Act. Again writing for the majority, Justice Holmes acknowledged that no evidence had been provided that the article in any way *actually* affected the war; nevertheless, because it *might* have an impact, the government had the authority to ban it.[30]

That same week, the Supreme Court considered a third, high-profile case, this one against Eugene Debs, a Socialist Party official who had received one million votes in the 1912 presidential election. In a public address, Debs exhorted his audience, "[Y]ou need to know that you are fit for something better than slavery and cannon fodder."[31] Although Holmes acknowledged that this statement represented only a small portion of a much longer address, nevertheless the central issue was whether the purpose of Debs' speech was to oppose the war. *Schenck* provided the controlling opinion, and Debs received a 10-year sentence.

As the United States left World War I behind, the tide began to change. The shift first became evident in judicial dissents. The pivotal incident that made it to the courts involved Russian immigrants who had thrown English and Yiddish leaflets from a building, urging workers to stop making weapons that eventually would kill their fellows overseas.[32] Although the leaflets did not directly encourage draft dodging, the Court upheld their convictions under the Espionage Act. Somewhat surprisingly, though, Louis Brandeis, author of *Sugarman* v. *United States* (1919) (which had upheld the Espionage Act), and Holmes, author of *Schenck, Frohwerk*, and *Debs*, dissented.[33] Holmes wrote, "It is only the present danger of immediate evil or an intent to bring it about that warrants Congress in setting a limit to the expression of opinion."[34] Although either the intent of creating, or the actual creation of, a clear and present danger might prove sufficient, "nobody can suppose that the surreptitious publishing of a silly leaflet by an unknown man, without more, would present any immediate danger that its opinions would hinder the success of the government arms or have any appreciable tendency to do so."[35]*

The Red Scare, though, meant that not everyone shared Holmes's view that the "clear and present danger" had dissipated.[36] The growth of the Socialist Party, the formation of the Communist Labor Party, and the increasing number of labor strikes heightened concern.[37] Violence against prominent citizens resulted in widespread panic. Law enforcement intercepted more than 34 bombs addressed to Postmaster General Burleson, Justice Oliver Wendell Holmes, Senator Lee Overman, Attorney General A. Mitchell Palmer, John D. Rockefeller, and other prominent Americans.[38] As I noted in Chapter 4, Palmer responded by appointing John Edgar Hoover to head the General Intelligence Division in the Bureau of Investigation,[39] and the police simply picked up the clientele in "radical hangouts," such as pool halls, cafés, and bowling alleys.[40] In total, Palmer deported more than 3,000 aliens and charged more than

---

* Holmes's somewhat unexpected dissent signaled a split within the Court that continued in subsequent cases. *See, e.g., Schaefer* v. *United States,* 251 U.S. 466 (1920); *Pierce* v. *United States,* 252 U.S. 239 (1920); *Gilbert* v. *Minnesota,* 254 U.S. 325 (1920).

1,400 Americans with violations of the new criminal syndicalism statutes, which made it illegal to attempt to overthrow the government of the United States.[41]

In 1925, concern at the chilling effect of these statutes on free speech prompted the Supreme Court to consider whether the First Amendment applied to the states and not just to the federal government. In 1925 *Gitlow* v. *New York* held that Benjamin Gitlow's left-wing manifesto violated a New York criminal anarchy statute.[42] Although the prosecution failed to present evidence that the document had any appreciable effect, the Court upheld the statute saying that speech advocating the forceful overthrow of the government may be penalized regardless of success. Because the statute said that such actions were dangerous, they were to be considered presumptively valid. Punishment for such dangers before they actually occurred being reasonable, the Court lacked the authority to determine whether the outlawed actions would have had their intended effect.[43] Holmes again dissented, claiming that the case failed the clear and present danger test: the manifesto represented mere theory – not advocacy of a crime.[44]*

Although *Gitlow* (and later *Whitney* v. *California*[45]) essentially adopted Learned Hand's approach in the *Masses* case – that only express advocacy fell beyond the pale – this test proved not utterly useless: using this standard, in a series of cases, the court overturned three convictions.[46] Justices Holmes and Brandeis continued to attack the majority's position. By 1941, the Court acknowledged that "before utterances can be punished," the "substantive evil must be extremely serious and the degree of imminence extremely high."[47]

While the judiciary moved steadily, albeit slowly, in the direction of increasing protection for free speech, the political climate progressed down the opposite path. In 1940, Representative Howard W. Smith of Virginia took sedition by the horns. The Smith Act made it illegal for anyone knowingly or willfully to advocate, abet, advise, or teach the necessity or desirability of overthrowing the government through the use of force.[48] It also outlawed printing, publishing, editing, issuing, circulating, selling, distributing, or publicly displaying any written or printed matter endorsing the same.[49]

World War II drew to a close, but public fear of Communism lurked in the shadow of the Iron Curtain, and grew in strength. In 1950, Congress passed the Subversive Activities Control Act, which required the registration of all "Communists."[50] This statute created the Subversive Activities Control Board, which could declare any organization that refused to register voluntarily to be a communist organization. This designation barred any member of one from working in government or for private industry defense firms. The statute also authorized the executive detention of anyone believed to be likely to engage

---

* Two years later, Brandeis and Holmes's position in *Whitney* v. *California* again raised the issue of clear and present danger. 274 U.S. 357 (1927). Brandeis and Holmes refrained from dissenting, giving "great weight" to the fact that the state of California felt the need to introduce special legislation. However, they again put forward the clear and present danger test.

in espionage or sabotage, and omitted any form of judicial review or right to confront evidence. With the House of Representatives' Un-American Activities Committee leading the charge, all levels of government sought out disloyal citizens. These measures put a significant damper on free speech. By the time Congress considered the Communist Control Act of 1954,[51] not one Senator had the nerve to vote against it.[52]

In this atmosphere, the Supreme Court held that the First Amendment did *not* protect indoctrination in preparation for future, violent action.[53] Chief Justice Fred Vinson explained: "In each case [courts] must ask whether the gravity of the 'evil,' discounted by its improbability, justifies such invasion of free speech as is necessary to avoid the danger."[54] Justice Felix Frankfurter concurred: "The right of a government to maintain its existence – self-preservation – is the most pervasive aspect of sovereignty."[55]

At this time, the persuasive aspect of free speech appeared to threaten national security. By 1947, the Communist Party had swelled to some 60,000 members, reminding people all too clearly of Russia's overthrow in the early twentieth century. Czechoslovakia fell to the Communists in 1948; and in 1949, China – despite some three billion dollars in American aid – did as well, and the Soviet Union exploded its first nuclear bomb.[56] Korea represented a proxy battle, where the Soviet Union and the United States fought over opposing ideology. Justice Jackson described the enemy, "The Communists have no scruples against sabotage, terrorism, assassination, or mob disorder; but violence is not with them, as with the anarchists, an end in itself." He continued, "The authors of the clear and present danger test never applied it to a case like this, nor would I. . . . [I]t [would mean] . . . the Government can move only after imminent action is manifest, when it would, of course, be too late."[57]

In the short term, *Dennis* allowed the federal government broad leeway to go after communists. Indeed, arrests under the Smith Act accelerated. In the long term, however, this period came to be regarded as one of the most embarrassing in American history. It profoundly changed the relationship between the citizens and the state. Thousands of people employed in public and private industry lost their jobs and their reputations. Under the Truman administration, more than 4.7 million government employees came under scrutiny. The FBI conducted approximately 40,000 investigations, only 20 percent of which led to formal charges; 90 percent of these cases were cleared. Between 1947 and 1953, the federal government fired approximately 350 "disloyal" federal employees, whereas another 2,200 "voluntarily" resigned. Although the net result does not appear to be statistically significant, the social impact of the entire system was profound: a "sense of being 'watched'" permeated the United States, making it difficult for citizens to engage freely in even ordinary conversation. And the standard of what could be considered "disloyal" behavior steadily expanded: Truman broadened it in 1951, and then in 1953, Eisenhower issued Executive Order 10450, which defined it as "[a]ny behavior, activities or associations which *tend to show* that the individual is not reliable or trustworthy." He later amended the order to allow for automatic dismissal if anyone pled the Fifth Amendment. Under such loose standards, by 1956 the government had fired an additional 2,350 employees and accepted "voluntary" resignations from another 9,800. Despite these extreme measures, the state failed to uncover a single case of actual subversion or espionage.[58]

More than free speech suffered. Geoffrey Stone, a prominent First Amendment scholar who has written at length on this period of American history, concludes, "The loyalty program stifled meaningful debate, demanded conformity, and discouraged Americans from thinking, reading, talking, or acting in any way that was out of the 'mainstream' of contemporary political, cultural, or social thought. Perhaps most important, it reversed the essential relationship between the citizen and the state in a democratic society."[59]

The seminal First Amendment incitement case that continues to serve as the gold standard came in 1969. *Brandenburg* v. *Ohio* exonerated a Ku Klux Klan leader who had been convicted under an Ohio criminal syndicalism statute.[60] The Court held that advocacy of the use of force or unlawful activity was unprotected only where it is directed at inciting imminent, lawless action, and is likely to incite or produce such action.[61] This test means that the actor must *intend* the action to produce a certain effect – but does not require that the effect become manifest. In a subsequent case, the Court suggested that imminent lawless action amounts to a matter of hours – or at most, several days; it did not open the door to indefinite action.[62]

The *Brandenburg* decision has been hailed as a watershed in the development of First Amendment law. It tried to curb the executive's ability to restrain political opponents or people with unpopular ideas, while still leaving the door open to restricting the harmful speech that may emanate from groups that are, like terrorist organizations, bent on destroying the state.

Not that *Brandenburg* is cast in stone.* Although this case overturned *Whitney*, it stopped short of ruling on the fate of *Schenck, Dennis,* or *Yates.* To some extent, the decision not to repeal the earlier decisions stems from the definition of what constitutes a clear and present danger. As Justice Jackson was at pains to point out in *Dennis*, a very different situation prevailed in 1919 than in 1947. But by the mid-twentieth century, superpower rivalries had begun to

---

* In addition to my following arguments, it is possible that the contemporary environment makes it easier for speech to meet the *Brandenburg* criteria and thus lead to less protected speech. Modern means of communications, such as publication on the Internet – which, from the design of the site itself intent might be inferred – or participation in chat rooms dedicated to subversive ideas, make it easier to establish that a particular action has sought to incite unlawful behavior. While *Brandenburg* requires that the unlawful action sought be imminent, the nature of modern technology again changes the picture: If the Court interprets the initial posting as the relevant date, then the traditional standard would apply. However, with the almost constant transfer of information among Web sites, publication transcends a particular point in time. At the moment someone picks up the call to arms and acts on it, it may be easier to establish a point in proximity to that act. The likelihood of violence, in turn, rests in part on the precedent set by the last attack, combined with access to technical and operational information – data increasingly available in an age of expanded electronic communications. Finally, the Court has *not* distinguished among different kinds of advocacy (e.g., private nonideological versus public ideological) – an issue central to the threat posed by fundamentalist terrorism.

take form, communism was widespread, and the world stood on the edge of the nuclear age. We are now well into this nuclear age, attended by the growth of technologies that weaponize basic biological processes. Here let me note that the national security threat posed by terrorists wielding weapons of mass destruction, if credible, might be able to meet the clear and present danger test. As Stone has observed, as a pure historical matter, when fear has controlled the state, protections otherwise afforded recede.[63]

Yet, even so, strong judicial and cultural norms prevent the state from regulating core political speech. Unpatriotic, disrespectful, or patently offensive speech is constitutionally protected.[64] Abusive expressions or those contemptuous of public officials also fall under the courts' shield as long as they do not incite others to perform unlawful acts or to breach the peace. Perhaps the relaxation of these standards to address a unique national security threat ought to give us pause. We need to remember both how repressive of the free speech of political opponents – not just of those engaged in violence – these restrictions ended up being and the reluctance of the courts – as Frankfurter suggested in *Dennis* – to interfere in the executive determination of what constitutes a national security threat.

Offenses Against the State and Public Order in the United Kingdom

Although, like the United States, the United Kingdom also has mitigated its long tradition of suppressing political speech, it – unlike the United States – continues to prevent core political expression in respect to treason, unlawful assembly and public order, sedition, speech in the media, and any attempt to glorify terrorism. The European Convention of Human Rights, which otherwise protects free speech, provides an all-important exception where national security is on the line.

Treason. In English law, treason historically was the foremost offense against public order. Together with the law of prior restraint, it gave the state the ability to counter political challenge. Its essence lay in what the twelfth-century English jurist Ranulf de Glanville understood as *seditio exercitus vel regni* – or betrayal of the realm.[65] Peace was a privilege, granted by the king. War was a liability and a reversion to the state of nature, which lay outside the king's peace.[66] Any act threatening tranquility thus violated the allegiance owed to the king.[67]

Under common law, treason consisted, more specifically, of imagining the king's death, levying war, and giving aid to the king's enemy. Although the monarch initially left to judges' discretion to determine what qualified as a treasonous offense, confusion led to the enactment of the 1351 Treason Act, which limited treason to specific offenses.[68] This statute, shaped through subsequent judicial decisions, reinforced the relationship between the monarch and his or her subjects. The judiciary, however, considered it outside criminal law, as treason was an attack on the state itself – not on subjects within it.[69]

The sentence for treason was most severe. The motivating sentiment was that anyone convicted of the crime would find hell a relief.[70] (The punishment

involved drawing, hanging, disemboweling, burning of one's entrails [while still alive], beheading, and quartering – all at the same time.[71]) Successive monarchs expanded the list of treasonable offenses, which included acts startlingly similar to modern-day terrorism.[72] The Treason Act of 1795, for instance, made it illegal to depose or levy war against the king "in order, *by force or constraint, to change his measures or counsels,* or *in order to put any force or constraint upon, or to intimidate or overawe both houses or either house of parliament.*"[73]*
In 1848, fear heightened by the revolutions on the Continent again led to an expansion of treasonable offenses: conspiracy to commit treason became a felony, and included discussing the ideal form for English government.[74]

By the early twentieth century, treason was applied almost exclusively to Ireland – where it had a polarizing effect.[†] Although the 1848 statute was last used in Northern Ireland in the 1950s, it remained on the books until 1998 when it was amended, formally ending the use of the death penalty for treason in peacetime.[75]

In 2001, the *Guardian* newspaper tried to get the Attorney General to declare that the Treason Felony Act, and its prohibition on advocacy of different forms of government, violated the 1998 Human Rights Act. Alan Rusbridger, the editor of the *Guardian*, wrote to Lord Williams of Mostyn, "I write to give you notice that from December 6 . . . onwards the Guardian propose[s] to publish a number of articles which will invite and incite support for a republican government in the United Kingdom."[76] Rusbridger invited Mostyn to announce his intention not to apply the Treason Felony Act to prevent publications from advocating for an end to the monarchy.[77] Mostyn refused. So Rusbridger published the articles and sent them to the Attorney General, daring him to prosecute. The Attorney General replied, "Thank you for your letter of 6 December, enclosing a copy of the *Guardian.* I had in fact already read it. . . . It is not for any Attorney General to disapply an Act of Parliament: that is a matter for Parliament itself."[78]

The authors promptly took the Attorney General to court, requesting, *inter alia*, that the judiciary make a declaration of incompatibility with the Human Rights Act.[79] The Court of Appeals flippantly dismissed the case, underscoring the defunct nature of the crime:

There are powerful arguments against letting litigants occupy the time of the court with problems which do not affect them personally. There are people with pressing problems whose cases await solution. They are waiting longer because this case is being heard.

* Although more statutes followed the 1795 Act, treason remained frequently used and largely unchanged until the mid-nineteenth century. *See, e.g.*, Treason Act, 1817, 57 Geo. 3, c. 6 (Eng.)
† Of the 183 civilians tried by courts-martial following the Easter Rising, 90 received sentences of death. K. D. Ewing & C. A. Gearty, The Struggle for Civil Liberties, Political Freedom and the Rule of Law in Britain, 1914–45 (2000), p. 342. Alarmed by the public response to the first 15 executions, Prime Minister Herbert Asquith ordered a halt; but it was too late to stop the rising tide of public sentiment against the harsh penalties associated with treason. Conor Gearty, *The Casement Treason Trial in Its Legal Context*, Lecture Delivered at the Royal Irish Academy's Symposium on Roger Casement, Roger Casement in Irish and World History 9 & n.14 (May 6, 2000) (citing HC Debs, 11 May 1916, cols 935–70).

We do not understand the claimants to suggest that the uncertainty of our law as to treason has affected their decision to publish in the past or is likely to in the future. Their stance is that of the Duke of Wellington: publish and be damned. Nor is there any evidence to suggest that the existence of the 1848 Act causes them to sleep in their beds less soundly.[80]

The court continued, "Times have moved on. No one has been prosecuted under the 1848 Act for over 100 years."[81] As far as the Human Rights Act (HRA) went, "Parliament chose, for reasons which are readily understandable, not to amend all Acts which might require amendment in the light of our obligations under the Convention but instead to leave the Courts to do what they can with the help of section 3 of the HRA. This technique is valuable."[82] The act of using charges of treason to suppress political speech was dead. But treason is not the only crime designed to restrict free expression.

Unlawful Assembly and Public Order. English law differs from that in the United States, where unlawful assembly is not often invoked and disruption tends to be addressed under disorderly conduct statutes. In the United Kingdom, however, prior restraints were a powerful means of keeping people from gathering unlawfully. For, like other rights in the English constitution, historically the right to gather was a negative right.*

The question was whether an initial gathering could be considered unlawful in that its participants' conduct, or intent "to excite a breach of the peace on the part of opponents, fills peaceable citizens with reasonable fear that the peace will be broken."[83] Thus, for instance, if a lawful procession was planned, and an unlawful organization attempted to prevent it from occurring, the judiciary considered the original procession to be within its rights to proceed, despite a magistrate's order to the contrary.[84] The English constitution does not provide the state with the authority to convict a man "for doing a lawful act if he knows that his doing it may cause another to do an unlawful act."[85] As an Irish judge noted, the remedy for the protection of this right "is the presence of sufficient force to prevent [the unlawful] result, not the legal condemnation of those who exercise those rights."[86] However,

If there is anything unlawful in the conduct of the persons convening or addressing a meeting, and the illegality is of a kind which naturally provokes opponents to a breach of the peace, the speakers at and the members of the meeting may be held to cause the breach of the peace, and the meeting itself may thus become an unlawful meeting.[87]

Although, for the most part, the law requires that lawful assemblies be allowed, it provides a loophole for necessity: if dispersing a meeting provides the only way of preserving the peace, law enforcement may declare the gathering unlawful

---

* Professors Keith Ewing and Conor Gearty write, "The great British bluff on freedom is nowhere more clearly exposed than in relation to freedom of assembly. There is not and never has been a 'right' to demonstrate." K. D. EWING & C. A. GEARTY, FREEDOM UNDER THATCHER: CIVIL LIBERTIES IN MODERN BRITAIN(1990), p. 85.

and demand that it disperse.[88] The difficulty, of course, is determining what meets that necessity.

The most thorough use of the law of unlawful assembly to restrict terrorist-related speech occurred in Northern Ireland, where a second parliament, technically subservient to Westminster, operated between 1922 and 1972.* In Chapter 2, I discussed the 1922 Civil Authorities (Special Powers) Act, introduced by Stormont, which granted the executive extraordinary power to introduce whatever regulations it deemed necessary to preserve order and maintain peace.[89] In the more than 100 subsidiary measures that followed, not only did it become an offense to act against any regulation but it was also unlawful to incite or endeavor to persuade another person to commit an offense. The statute further provided, "If any person does any act of such a nature as to be calculated to be prejudicial to the preservation of the peace or maintenance of order in Northern Ireland and not specifically provided for in the regulations, he shall be deemed to be guilty of an offense against the regulations."[90]

Regulation 4 of the 1922–43 SPAs made it unlawful for three or more persons to gather to carry out any lawful or unlawful purpose in a way that endangered the public peace – or gave "firm and courageous persons" in the neighborhood grounds to apprehend a breach of peace.[91] Although the statutory instrument did not differ in any substantial way from the Northern Ireland government's common law powers to prevent unlawful assembly, the state regularly used it to prevent nationalists and republicans from gathering.

From 1922 to 1950, the Northern Ireland Ministry of Home Affairs prohibited more than 90 meetings, assemblies, and processions. There were bans on Easter commemorations (which hearkened back to the 1916 Easter Uprising in the South), unemployed workers' meetings, ceilidhs (Irish music and dancing), films, Gaelic Athletic Association events, anti-partition meetings, and St. Patrick's Day celebrations. In 1951, primary legislation replaced Regulation 4, making counterterrorist authorities permanent. Although a common law offense of unlawful assembly still existed, the Public Order Act became the primary vehicle for preventing marches and processions.[92] This statute allowed the state to regulate and prohibit not just gatherings, but any "provocative conduct."[93] Any Royal Ulster Constabulary officer or head constable could impose whatever conditions appeared appropriate, including banning a meeting. The legislation gave the Minister of Home Affairs the authority to suspend all processions in a certain area, or of a particular class, for up to three months. It outlawed threatening, abusive, or insulting words or behavior and prohibited

---

* Between December 1921 and May 1922, political violence killed 236 people and injured 346. Unionists, in control of the new provincial parliament, responded with the 1922 Civil Authorities (Special Powers) Act. Drawn largely from Britain's 1914–15 Defense of the Realm Acts and the 1920 Restoration of Order in Ireland Act, the statute included a one-year limit on its powers. Although violence ceased within six months, the Northern government renewed the statute annually from 1923 through 1927, extended it in 1928, and in 1933 made it permanent. *See* LAURA K. DONOHUE, COUNTER-TERRORIST LAW AND EMERGENCY POWERS IN THE UNITED KINGDOM 1922–2000 16–17 (2001).

individuals from allowing conduct leading to public disorder on any premises or land under their control.

As civil disorder grew, the unionist government gradually expanded its powers. In 1966, the Ministry of Home Affairs introduced Regulation 38, which gave law enforcement the authority to prevent three or more people from gathering where a breach of the peace might ensue.[94] In 1969, the ministry again extended its authority to restrict the public use of premises used for entertainment, exhibition, performance, or sports.[95] Then in 1970, the ministry gave the Civil Authority the explicit ability to prevent processions or meetings where such gatherings might give rise to public disorder *or* cause undue demands to be made on law enforcement.[96]

Almost all of the events outlawed under these regulations related to nationalist or republican aspirations, culture, or identity and, instead of threatening grave disorder, represented a political view that promoted disaffection with the government. Never did the Ministry of Home Affairs consciously ban a loyalist gathering, march, or procession, even when one might provoke the minority community. On the one occasion that a loyalist gathering inadvertently fell under an order issued to prevent nationalists and republicans from assembling, the Ministry of Home Affairs opted not to prosecute the hundreds of people who defied the ban; instead, it prepared an extensive apology to be given in the Northern Ireland House of Commons.[97]

The ministry received overwhelming support for these actions from the majority population: Orange Lodges routinely passed, and forwarded to the ministry, resolutions approving the bans. The Coleraine Drumming Club exhorted, "Long may you occupy the position to keep those Popish rebels in check. No Surrender. God Save the King."[98] The Falls Road Methodists felt "that if more of our leaders were as faithful and fearless in their duties, Ulster would truly be great."[99] Private letters were even more vitriolic: "I am proud to see that you . . . have got the guts to defy those who would desecrate the walls of the maiden city by their filthy flags and their disloyal music."[100]

In 1973, Westminster extended powers relating to unlawful assembly. Section 21 of the 1973 Northern Ireland (Emergency Powers) Act enabled the security forces to disperse any assemblies considered a threat to the peace.[101] The EPA increased the maximum penalty for riotous and disorderly behavior, from 6 to 18 months' imprisonment.[102] The statute also gave law enforcement the power to interfere with funerals to avoid potential serious public disorder or putting undue demands on HM forces or the police. The schedule left it to the discretion of the police to decide just what restrictions they would use.

Although the Northern Ireland Parliament made the most use of unlawful assembly provisions to prevent persuasive political speech, Great Britain made use of similar powers. These, too, began as emergency statutory instruments but transformed into primary legislation. And, as in the United States, World War I and growing fears about communist insurgency spurred their introduction.

In 1914, Regulation 9A of the Defence of the Realm Consolidation Act provided the British Home Secretary with the power to ban meetings and processions.[103] In 1921, Regulation 20 of the new Emergency Regulations extended this power.[104] It granted the authority to prevent public gatherings where the Home Secretary had reason to believe one would give rise to grave disorder, or that a procession would cause a breach of the peace. It entitled the police to take whatever steps deemed necessary to disperse the meeting. Although the state initially exercised the regulation's powers against their intended target, its use soon expanded beyond communists to include the 1926 Miners' General Strike, the National Unemployed Workers' Movement, and the British Union of Fascists.[105] This last gave rise to permanent public order legislation in the form of the 1936 Public Order Act, which quickly became the most important statute outside Northern Ireland for state control of public meetings.[106] It allowed any chief police officer, who reasonably apprehended that a procession "may occasion serious public disorder," to impose *whatever conditions* "appear[ed] to him necessary for the preservation of public order."[107] If insufficient, the officer could apply to the Home Secretary or local council for an order banning any meeting in the area for up to three months.*

The 1936 Act also created a statutory offense that the state came to use frequently.[108] Under the statute, it became illegal for anyone intentionally to provoke a breach of the peace or to break the peace through threatening, abusive, or insulting words or behavior or through any writing, sign, or other threatening, abusive, or insulting representations.[109] The key element here was the flexibility of the phrase "breach of the peace" – which came to include everything from nudity to meowing at a police dog.[†] For the Court of Appeal, a breach of the peace meant that "there has been an act done or threatened to be done which either actually harms a person, or in his presence his property, or is likely to cause such harm, or which puts someone in fear of such harm being done."[110] The requirement – that there be an *imminent* breach of the peace – was, however, rarely subject to judicial scrutiny; instead, the courts granted great deference to those entrusted with the law.[111]

In 1986, the British state revised the Public Order statute to consolidate previous measures, produce new authorities, and take account of competing rights within society. The balance tilted further in favor of the state: the statute replaced the common law offense of unlawful assembly with a "violent disorder" provision; introduced new offenses, such as unlawful assembly and riot; and required written notice to be submitted to the police at least six days prior to a planned procession.[112] And the statute expanded the powers to apply to

---

* Here, the statute differed substantially from its Northern Ireland counterpart: whereas in the Province, orders could be issued for specific meetings, in Great Britain, to prevent discrimination, *all* processions would have to be banned in specified areas. The first of these bans, in June 1937, brought the East End of London under a six-week ban. However, only sporadic use followed. Instead, custom dictated that the police simply increase their presence when disorder loomed.

† This phrase led Keith Ewing and Conor Gearty to suggest, "To the extent that freedom of expression figured at all, it was no more than as an implicit principle sitting silently in the gaps between the words. Not unnaturally, therefore, it was often squeezed." K.D. Ewing & C.A. Gearty, Freedom under Thatcher: Civil Liberties in Modern Britain (1990), at 88.

processions and meetings. No longer did law enforcement have to find a direct link to public disorder. Instead, it became sufficient for police to reasonably believe that there may be serious damage to property, serious disruption to the life of the community, or the intimidation of others "with a view to compelling them not to do an act they have a right to" – or not to – do.[113] Once satisfied, whatever conditions appear to the police "to be necessary to prevent such disorder, damage, disruption or intimidation, including conditions as to the route of the procession" may be imposed either in advance or at the time of the gathering.[114]

Perhaps the provision most threatening to freedom of speech and behavior is this one: "A person is guilty of an offence if he (a) uses threatening, abusive or insulting words or behaviour, or disorderly behaviour, or (b) displays any writing, sign or other visible representation which is threatening, abusive or insulting, within the hearing or sight of a person likely to be caused harassment, alarm or distress thereby."[115] Although in section 4 such insults must be connected with the threat of, or actual, violence, in section 5 all that is necessary is that they be *likely* to cause "harassment, alarm, or distress." Such likelihood included two men kissing in a park in the presence of two heterosexual males.[116] Perhaps more to the point of this book, a poster created by a republican organization in Northern Ireland – showing four boys throwing stones at a Saracen with these words printed underneath, "Ireland: 20 years of resistance" – fell afoul of section 5.[117] As actions leading to violence are already addressed under section 4, it is unclear exactly how far the police can go in ascertaining what constitutes "disorderly behaviour." No one, though, need actually be offended – it may just be a hypothetical person, who would likely be insulted by the behavior in question.[118]

The United Kingdom applies similar strictures to hate speech – another form of political expression and one treated by both Britain and the European Union as a crime – in sharp contrast to US law that, outside of direct fighting words, grants hate speech broad constitutional protection.[119] This distinction derives from a difference between First Amendment jurisprudence and the English constitution, which has a long tradition of preventing such utterances. Britain and Europe's attitude also must be understood in terms of their experience in World War II and the years before with the immediate threat posed by Adolf Hitler's rise to power. The 1965 Race Relations Act, for instance, outlawed any publication or pronouncement deemed "threatening, abusive or insulting" and intended to incite hatred on the basis of race, color or national origin.[120] The 1986 Public Order Act extended this stricture, making harassment illegal. Just over a decade later, this provision entered into its own with the Protection from Harassment Act.[121] The European Court found prohibitions on hate speech to be consistent with Article 10 of the European Convention for the Protection of Human Rights.

Similarly, although the 1998 Human Rights Act initially had some impact on Britain's public order law, questions remain regarding the extent to which the EU will limit broader strictures placed on political speech. Article 10 of the

ECHR states, "Everyone has the right to freedom of expression. This right shall include freedom to hold opinions and to receive and impart information and ideas without interference by public authority and regardless of frontiers."[122] Article 11 continues, "Everyone has the right to freedom of peaceful assembly and to freedom of association with others, including the right to form and to join trade unions for the protection of his interests." In 2001, the court applied Articles 10 and 11 to set aside a conviction for defacing an American flag, and suggested that the state's prosecution amounted to an undue interference with political speech.[123] A British subject with a long history of objecting to Britain's foreign policy toward Iraq also availed himself of Article 10 to overturn an injunction preventing him from protesting in Parliament Square.[124]

The ECHR, however, also allows for restrictions on this speech to be imposed in the interests of national security.[125] The state enjoys a certain "margin of appreciation" in determining the nature and breadth of a restriction on free expression; however, the European Court reserves a final say in whether the restrictions satisfy the two central requirements: that they meet a "pressing social need" and are proportionate to a legitimate aim.[126]

Sedition. Sedition is another way in which English law has restricted persuasive speech. The common law offense is defined as the "intention (i.) to bring into hatred or contempt, or to excite disaffection against, the King or the government and constitutions of the United Kingdom, or either House of Parliament, or the administration of justice."[127] Thus, not an actual incident of violence, but efforts to promote disaffection constitute the crime of sedition. The offense did not just protect the Crown or Parliament from unwanted criticism. It reinforced England's social and economic hierarchy: the charge included promoting "feelings of ill will and hostility between different classes of such subjects."[128] Although the judiciary exempted efforts to demonstrate that the monarch "has been *misled* or mistaken in his measures, or to point out errors and defects in the government or constitution *with a view to their reformation*,"[129] in practice, political considerations strongly influenced where the line was drawn.

For Blackstone, the law of sedition appeared consistent with liberty of the press: "Every freeman has an undoubted right to lay what sentiments he pleases before the public: to forbid this right is to destroy the freedom of the press: but if he publishes what is improper, mischievous, or illegal, he must take the consequence of his own temerity."[130] Prior restraint would make the licensor more powerful than the courts and the legislature in their power to restrict speech. Yet the good order of society required that some sort of restriction be available. Imposing restraints after the fact preserved liberty, making only the abuse "of that free will . . . the object of legal punishment. Neither is any restraint hereby laid upon freedom of thought or inquiry: liberty of private sentiment is still left; the disseminating, or making public, of bad sentiments, destructive of the ends of society, is the crime which society corrects."[131]

The issue, of course, was what counted as "improper, mischievous, or illegal." In 1792, for instance, Thomas Paine's *The Rights of Man* qualified. That same year, the English statesman Charles James Fox's Libel Act, which added the intent of the defendant to the elements of the crime, settled the controversy about whether to adopt a different definition of sedition.[132] And, like the 1798 Alien and Sedition Acts in the United States, this statute gave the jury, not the judge, the authority to determine whether a statement should be considered defamatory. This measure reduced judicial power and forced the law to conform to the general tenor of the times through the role of the jury. As it became more difficult to obtain a seditious libel conviction, prosecutions shifted to addressing issues of public order, such as unlawful assembly and seditious conspiracy.[133] By the late nineteenth century, these reforms had relegated purely political libel to the dustbin of history.

The law of seditious conspiracy centered on a similar principle: it made it illegal to conspire to effect a purpose "inconsistent with the peace and good government of the country." Such conspiracy had to be manifest by a person's making speeches, holding meetings, or taking other steps in concert with other people.[134] By the end of the nineteenth century, "the law as to seditious conspiracy [had become] of greater practical importance than the law of seditious libel."[135] It also bore an intimate connection to the law of unlawful assembly.[136] In the twentieth century, the state – relying on the elements of intent, the provocation of violence, and the use of force against the government – used seditious conspiracy against members of the Communist Party.[137]*

As with unlawful associations, the law of sedition took on a particular texture in Northern Ireland. Under the 1922–43 revisions of the Special Powers Act, Regulation 26 (and later Regulation 8) governed the restriction of printed matter. Like Regulation 4, which prevented meetings and assemblies, the unionist government used the publication restrictions almost exclusively against unpopular ideas. Regulation 26 allowed the Civil Authority to prohibit the *circulation* of newspapers and expanded in 1943 to prohibit the *publication* and circulation of any newspaper, periodical, book, circular, or other printed matter.[138]† In 1971, the unionists further amended the regulation to make it illegal to print, publish, circulate, distribute, sell, offer or expose for sale, or have in possession for purposes of publication, circulation, distribution, or sale, *any* document advocating the following: an alteration to the constitution or laws of Northern Ireland by some unlawful means, the raising or maintaining of a military force, the obstruction or interference with the administration of justice or the enforcement of the law, or support for any organization that participates in any of the above.[139] Additionally, any individual who the security forces reasonably believed had such a document in his or her possession, and refused to

---

* Although seditious libel traditionally related to attacks on state institutions, more attempts have been made to use it to address friction between groups within society. In 1989, for instance, a group of Muslims tried to prosecute the Indian novelist Salman Rushdie for seditious libel. *See, e.g., R. v. Chief Metropolitan Magistrate, Ex parte* Choudhury (1991) 1 QB 429.

† The unionist government revoked this measure in 1949 but reintroduced it five years later as Regulation 8. Revocation S.R.O. 147/1949, 20 August 1949; Reintroduced by S.R.O. 179/1954, 21 December 1954.

turn it over upon demand, would be found in violation of the offenses. The amendment exempted government ministers, the Northern Parliament, and the judiciary; it also lifted any requirement to issue subsidiary orders banning particular publications.[140]

Between the inception of the state and the expiration of the final order on December 31, 1971, the Northern Executive issued more than 50 orders banning in excess of 140 publications.[141] Most of these represented republican or nationalist views. A handful, such as *Workers' Life*, *The Irish World and American Industrial Laborer*, and *Irish Workers Weekly*, espoused socialist or communist ideals. Additional texts that fell subject to the censor included poetry, Gaelic Athletic Association scores, obituaries, quotations, coverage of recent government raids or actions, religious texts, calls to arms to fight the English, and the Irish Republican Army's position on social issues. Actual unrest had little to do with the decisions: the first publication ban came long after violence had come to a standstill.

Whereas Regulation 26 focused on printed materials, Regulation 26A, established in 1930, gave the executive the power to ban films and gramophone records.[142] Unlike Regulation 26, mere possession of a banned item constituted an offense. As the Ministry of Home Affairs understood it,

in the case of newspapers it was not desirable to make mere possession an offence, since individuals may be sent a single copy of a newspaper without any intention on their part of possessing or circulating it, but it is obvious that nobody becomes possessed of a cinematograph film or gramophone record unless by his own deliberate intention and with a previous knowledge of the subject.[143]

The primary purpose of Regulation 26A also differed: rather than focus on republicans or nationalists, it sought to halt any communist challenge to the state.[144] The Home Office in the United Kingdom had already banned a number of films under the Secretary of State's common law power, which, according to the authorities, formed part of the "inherent prerogative" of the Crown.[145] Unsure whether they could be applied to Northern Ireland, and concerned by the formation in 1929 of the Belfast Workers' Film Guild, the Northern Executive adopted similar powers. In the event, however, it was not a communist film banned under the regulation, but a republican one: on November 27, 1936, the Civil Authority banned *Ourselves Alone*, a work of fiction about Sinn Féin created by a British film company.[146]

Outside of Northern Ireland, the British state, in turn, had at its disposal the 1984 Prevention of Terrorism (Temporary Provisions) Act.[147] Section 11 of this statute required that anyone in possession of information that he or she knew to be, or had reason to believe might be, of material assistance in apprehending terrorists, or preventing an act of terrorism, contact officials immediately.[148] The government used this provision to intimidate the media into not allowing to appear on the air supporters of, or participants in, paramilitary movements.[149]* The prime minister saw the issue in black and white: "Either one is on the side of justice in these matters or one is on the side of terrorism."[150]

The Media Ban. Yet another tool the state has recently employed to prevent terrorist speech has to do with direct media restrictions. Although informal measures operated for some time, the media coverage following a Provisional Irish Republican Army attack in 1988 led to a six-year formal ban.[†] In October of that year, a PIRA Active Service Unit bombed the home of Sir Kenneth Bloomfield, head of the Northern Ireland Civil Service from 1984 to 1991; afterward, BBC Radio Ulster's *Talkback* featured Gerry Adams. On October 19, outraged at the publicity obtained by the organization, Home Secretary Douglas Hurd issued two notices – one each to the British Broadcasting Corporation and the Independent Broadcasting Authority – requiring them to refrain from broadcasting any statements made by a proscribed organization or by individuals supporting one. Hurd based his actions on a moral claim: it was not just offensive, but morally reprehensible, that individuals directly harmed in terrorist attacks would have to then be confronted with people celebrating the paramilitary victory.[151] The ban included proscribed organizations as well as Sinn Féin, Republican Sinn Féin, and the Ulster Defence Association – all of which claimed to be political arms of their paramilitary movements. Sinn Féin had, at the time, 60 councillors and one member of Parliament holding office.[152]

Three weeks after the government introduced the ban, and in the face of heavy criticism, it adopted new justifications – each based on the persuasive

---

* For instance, in 1979 a crew from the UK television show *Panorama* filmed an IRA roadblock in Carrickmore. The Attorney-General wrote to the BBC to underscore the effect of section 11. Again in 1988, the Royal Ulster Constabulary used it to obtain pictures from Independent Television News and the BBC that showed who killed two army corporals at a West Belfast funeral. K.D. EWING & C.A. GEARTY, FREEDOM UNDER THATCHER: CIVIL LIBERTIES IN MODERN BRITAIN(1990), at 241.

[†] In 1985, the Home Office pressured the BBC not to show *Real Lives: At the Edge of the Union*, which carried an interview with Martin McGuinness, a Sinn Féin leader and former member of the IRA Army Council. In the interview, McGuinness, an elected member of the Ulster Assembly, tried to justify IRA opposition to British rule in terms of the mistreatment of Catholics. Leon Brittan, the Home Secretary, announced that airing the program would be "wholly contrary to the public interest." The BBC delayed and then changed the segment. Joel Bellman, *BBC: Clearing the Air*, THE JOURNALIST, Jan. 1986, at 20. Similarly, in September 1988, at the urging of the British government, Channel 4 eliminated an *After Dark* program in which Gerry Adams was scheduled to appear. K.D. EWING & C.A. GEARTY, FREEDOM UNDER THATCHER: CIVIL LIBERTIES IN MODERN BRITAIN (1990), at 242–43. That same year, Sir Geoffrey Howe, Foreign Secretary, tried to prevent *Death on the Rock* (a program exploring the death of three PIRA operatives in Gibraltar) from being shown until after the inquest. *See* LORD WINDLESHAM AND RICHARD RAMPTON, THE WINDLESHAM/RAMPTON REPORT ON DEATH ON THE ROCK, ch. 11 (Faber & Faber, 1989). Although the chairman of the Independent Broadcasting Authority, Lord Thomson of Monifieth, refused to cancel the showing, the government then tried to discredit the program. DAVID FELDMAN, CIVIL LIBERTIES AND HUMAN RIGHTS IN ENGLAND AND WALES (2d ed. 2002), at 817.

aspect of speech. First, the government justified the restriction on the assumption that paramilitaries were using the airwaves to transmit threats and to create fear: thus, it was not that the individuals being interviewed were specifically threatening, but that they were contributing to a broad, generalized anxiety. Second, the state suggested that the "terrorists themselves draw support and sustenance from access to radio and television."[153]

Although the media strenuously objected to the restriction, they were careful not to run afoul of the law. The BBC and the IBA interpreted it as applying, for instance, to statements made in documentaries, "whether or not the speaker was dead, and even though he may have been dead for some time."[154] The BBC expressed concern about airing demonstrators singing Irish songs. In 1988, the IBA actually did ban the Irish rock band the Pogues' song *Streets of Sorrow* because it expressed sympathy for the Birmingham Six (who had been convicted of the 1974 Birmingham pub bombings in which 21 people died) and suggested that the Irish had not received equal justice.[155] (Ironically, three years later, British courts quashed these men's convictions, the traces of nitroglycerine found on them having come possibly from soap, and their "confessions" having been beaten out of them by the police.)[156] In November 1988, London's LBC independent radio station refused to allow the Dubliners' recording of the 1798 ballad *Kelly the Boy from Killane*.[157] Censorship did affect the publicity afforded the republican movement. Between October 1988 and March 1989, for instance, broadcast journalist inquiries to Sinn Féin (SF) dropped by 75 percent. At the February 1991 party conference, the political report urged, "The priorities for SF in the year ahead are to develop and strengthen our party organization, to improve our publicity output and to overcome the effects of censorship."[158]

But, though cautious, the media did not simply take the ban lying down; indeed, they took advantage of a loophole in the law. When it became clear that the order did not apply to the written media, broadcast authorities began subtitling interviews. They later used voice-overs to allow expression of the views of the parties prohibited from appearing on the programs.

The courts did little to push back on the executive: in 1991, the Law Lords upheld the Broadcasting Ban.[159] Three years later, the case reached Strasbourg, where the European Court decided that the restriction placed on Sinn Féin did not violate the European Convention for the Protection of Human Rights.[160]

The Glorification of Terrorism. Finally, there is the United Kingdom's recent decision to make it illegal to glorify terrorism. In the immediate aftermath of the July 7, 2005, bombings, the Labour Party worked to construct a cross-party counterterrorist initiative. But when ministers went on holiday, the media derided, "Let's Hope the Bombers are on Holiday Too." Trevor Kavanagh, the *Sun's* political editor, wrote an open letter beginning, "Dear MPs, Six Weeks Holiday is Enough for Anyone." The next day, as Blair flew to the West Indies with his family, a headline jeered, "Victory for Sun over New Terror Laws."[161]

Blair answered the media criticism by unilaterally laying out a 12-point plan to address terrorism. Among other provisions, the state would obtain new powers to deport foreigners for "fostering hatred."[162] And it would introduce the new offense of "glorifying terrorism." Home Secretary Charles Clarke explained, "People who glorify terrorism help to create a climate in which terrorism is regarded as in some way acceptable. They help to persuade impressionable members of their audiences that they have a moral duty to kill innocent people, in pursuit of whatever political or religious ideology they espouse."[163] These measures would be combined with others to give the United Kingdom the ability to counter al Qaeda.*

Blair's announcement helped considerably to stem the growing public frustration at seeing newcomers to the United Kingdom whip their followers into a vengeful fury. There were plenty of demagogues to choose from: in 2002 Hassan Butt, a Briton who went to Pakistan for militancy training when he was 20, called on three hundred people in Manchester to initiate terrorist attacks within Britain; he was "over the moon" about 9/11.[164] Abu Hamza urged adherents to attack "non-believers."[165] Abu Uzair called for jihad against the United Kingdom: "We don't live in peace with you any more," he said, "which means the covenant of security no longer exists.... Those four bombers that attacked London believed that there was no covenant of security. The banner has been risen for jihad inside the UK which means . . . it's allowed for them to attack."[166] Abu Abdullah, a Turkish Cypriot, wanted to transform Britain into an Islamic state.[167] Muhammed Al-Massari, a Saudi who had been given indefinite leave to remain in the United Kingdom, ran a Web site showing suicide bombings and beheadings – and the death of British soldiers in Iraq.[168] And Yasser al-Siri, an Egyptian who came to the United Kingdom for asylum, published a book in 2001 that called for the "killing of Jews and Americans wherever they are."[169]

Reflecting the growing public resentment, the *Daily Telegraph* voiced its approval that the government was beginning to demonstrate "a bit more steel in its dealings with Muslim extremists."[170] In particular, the way in which Labour dealt with the radical cleric Abu Qatada, taken into custody in August 2005 pending deportation, became a test of Blair's announcement that "the rules of the game have changed."[171] And the media wanted to do their part to help: when the Danish cartoon scandal broke in 2005 (the Danish daily *Jyllands-Posten's* publication of cartoons of Mohammed spurred riots worldwide that resulted in the death of more than 50 people in Asia, Africa, and the Middle

---

* Britain would automatically refuse asylum to anyone with terrorist links, consider stripping naturalized Britons of their citizenship as a penalty for terrorist involvement, and set a maximum time limit for deportation. Extended detention for terrorist suspects would be increased from 14 to 90 days. More control orders would be placed on British subjects, and greater use of the courts would be made for control orders. The government would proscribe Hizb-ut-Tahrir, the successor organization to Al Muhajiroun. Blair announced that the state also would establish a commission to ensure better integration of people of different faith – while pursuing the authority to shut down extremist mosques. And it would use biometric visas to strengthen border security. Paul Waugh, *100 More Hamzas Still in Britain*, EVENING STANDARD (London), Feb. 8, 2006, 1.

East),[172] Britain's *Sunday Times* monitored a public protest within the United Kingdom at which placards directed "slay those who insult Islam." The *Sunday Times* interviewed people there, and printed the names of those present – and then publicly offered its file to Scotland Yard.[173]

In February 2006, although the Conservative Party and the Liberal Democrats formally opposed the measures, and civil liberties groups mounted their opposition, Blair managed to get the glorification provisions through Parliament. The Terrorism Bill passed 315 to 277, providing Labour with a majority of 38. Only 17 back-benchers voted against the government.[174] The prime minister repeatedly emphasized the propaganda aspect of the legislation: it was part of being seen as tough on terror and would allow the government to go after those sympathetic to terrorists' aims.

In summary, by the mid-twentieth century, treason and sedition – two charges historically used to prevent persuasive political speech – had fallen by the wayside, whereas seditious conspiracy, unlawful assembly, and public order provisions remained central to the suppression of dissident political views. In Northern Ireland, the executive made further efforts to prevent the building of monuments and the flying of the Irish flag. After the implementation of direct rule, Westminster continued to use public order provisions to control political speech, and from 1988 to 1996, the British state instituted a media ban. The ECHR, although it guarantees freedom of expression, has thus far not put a strict limit on the exercise of these powers.

KNOWLEDGE-BASED SPEECH

In February 2001, the American Society of Microbiologist's *Journal of Virology* carried the five-page article, "Expression of a Mouse Interleukin-4 by a Recombinant Ectromelia Virus Suppresses Cytolytic Lymphocyte Responses and Overcomes Genetic Resistance to Mousepox."[175] The paper reported the results of Australian scientists' findings in 1999 that combining a gene from a rodent's immune system (interleukin-4) with the mousepox virus, and inserting the pathogen into mice, killed the mice. All of them – even the ones that were naturally immune or had been vaccinated against mousepox. Aside from a smattering of articles that focused mainly on the implications for recombinant DNA technology and the human smallpox virus, and related discussions on strengthening the Biological Weapons Convention, there was little public questioning in the United States or the United Kingdom whether the researchers should have published their findings in the first place.[176] Then came 9/11 and the subsequent spate of anthrax mailings in the United States that autumn of 2001. And everything changed.

In December 2001, rumors began to surface that the White House was pressuring American microbiology journals to restrict the publication of articles that might be helpful to terrorists.[177] Dr. Ronald Atlas, president of the American Society for Microbiology (ASM), contacted Dr. Samuel Kaplan, chair of the ASM Publishing Board, and reported that many people in the administration were upset with ASM for publishing the mousepox article.[178] Kaplan convened a meeting in December 2001 for the editors-in-chief of the ASM's nine primary and two review journals, cumulatively responsible for publishing some 70,000 pages of research each year. The Publishing Board reaffirmed its decision to print the piece, as it had contained important scientific information. Nevertheless, the group recognized that some information could be harmful in the hands of terrorists. Although the ASM code of ethics already stated that the organization was "dedicated to the utilization of microbiological sciences for the promotion of human welfare and the accumulation of knowledge," it changed its policy to require reviewers to consider the code in light of US national security.[179]*

Two aspects of the research gave the Australian article traction in the ensuing American political debate: fears about the implications for the possible reintroduction of smallpox and the low-cost, simple procedures used in the experiment. Many scientists regard smallpox as the most dangerous pathogen known to humans. In the twentieth century alone, approximately 500 million people died from the disease.[180] Almost three decades ago, in a political and medical triumph, scientists managed to eradicate it from the natural world. There are only two locations where, to public knowledge, the disease exists: a Russian laboratory in Siberia, and a Centers for Disease Control and Prevention facility in Atlanta, both of which are regulated by the World Health Organization. The United States administered its last vaccines, believed to be potent for three to five years, in 1972.[181] Even if freshly administered, these vaccines, discovered in 1796, would be unlikely to stop a modern, genetically engineered virus.[182] The experiment also underscored that even simple, standardized procedures, which could be replicated in a small space with limited (less than $1,000) funding, posed a significant threat to US national security.[183]

By March 2002, the argument over whether to introduce restrictions on microbiologists entered hyper-drive. The White House Chief of Staff told federal officials not to release any unclassified (but sensitive) information on biological weapons.[184] The newly formed Department of Homeland Security began developing an "information-security" policy that targeted foreign nationals. The 2001 USA PATRIOT Act tightened restrictions on foreign students and provided some $37 million for construction of the Student Exchange Visitor Information System to monitor university students. In May 2002, further measures required institutions of higher education to record information relating to international students – the subjects they studied, their workloads, and whether

---

* Between January 2002 and November 2004, this process isolated three articles dealing with anthrax, shigalatoxin, and botulinum toxin. In two cases, the editors contacted the authors to determine their intent. Although the journals did not require that the authors alter the text, the researchers changed the titles and headings prior to publication to bring the pieces into line with editorial policy. The author of the third paper, which focused on the aerosolization of botulinum toxin, included in the piece *additional* findings that demonstrated an *increase* in antigen properties, highlighting its nonviolent applications. The ASM published all three. Telephone Interview with Samuel Kaplan, Chair, Publishing Board, American Society of Microbiology, in Palo Alto, Cal. (Oct. 26, 2004).

they had changed their course of study.[185] In June, further legislation denied certain people (e.g., dishonorably discharged military personnel, drug users, terrorist suspects, and citizens from a list of "state sponsors of terrorism") access to particular substances. An onslaught of regulations followed.* The legislation further required that any genetic engineering experiments had to be cleared by the federal government.[186]

The drive to prevent microbiologists from publishing information reflects a long history of restrictions on knowledge-based speech on both sides of the Atlantic. In the United States, the Invention Secrecy Act, the Atomic Energy Act, and federal bomb-making provisions are precedents. The United Kingdom made use of various nonstatutory measures, such as the Voluntary Vetting Scheme and the D-Notice system and the Export Control Act to do the same. The *Brandenburg* case, focused on advocacy, has little to say about purely knowledge-based communication; on this issue, ECHR provisions that guard against inroads into political speech remain silent. Nevertheless, limitations in this area go to the heart of free speech and affect areas well beyond the security or freedom rubric.

Restrictions on Knowledge-Based Speech in the United States

That discoveries might be used either for good or ill is not a new idea. Concerned that "those inventions which are of most use to the Government during a time of war are also those which would, if known, convey useful information to the enemy," Congress introduced the 1917 Voluntary Tender Act, which gave the Commissioner of Patents the authority to withhold certification from inventions that might harm US national security, and to turn such inventions over to the US government for its own use.[187] The legislation required the government, if it made use of the discovery, to reimburse the inventor. If the invention fell into disuse, it was more or less a case of "too bad" for the inventor. The statute expired at the end of the war, and for more than two decades, there were no legislation or secrecy orders.

In 1940, prior to World War II, Congress reintroduced an amended version of the legislation,[188] which was to last only two years, with stronger sanctions (permanent denial of patent) for violation. The following year, Congress again strengthened the legislation with, *inter alia*, criminal penalties applied to violations.[189] A third set of revisions emerged the following year, extending the statute's life through the end of the war.[190] On November 30, 1945, the Commissioner of Patents rescinded 6,575 secrecy orders[191] – a move to which the

---

* For instance, in December 2002, 50 pages of the Federal Register directed that universities, private companies, and government laboratories with certain materials had to submit to unannounced inspections, register their supplies with the federal government, obtain federal security clearances and background checks for personnel, and secure certain substances. Daniel J. Kevles, *Biotech's Big Chill*, Tech. Rev. July-Aug., 2003, at 42.

Defense Department strenuously objected on grounds of national security.[192] As of December 31, 1945, some 799 secrecy orders remained.[193] Although the statute ceased to have force at the end of the war, the government claimed a continued national emergency, which remained in place until April 28, 1952.[194] During this time, the state issued more secrecy orders, with some 2,395 in place by 1951.[195] The following year the Invention Secrecy Act became the peacetime regulator of inventions that created threats – or opportunities – for US national security.

The 1951 Invention Secrecy Act established a prior restraint on government employees and – more pertinent to my subject – private inventors, to prevent them from publishing inventions deemed to be "detrimental to the national security."[196] When an inventor applied for a patent, the state had the opportunity to review the national security implications of the invention. If deemed a threat, the inventor could be forestalled from producing the device or sharing the information with anyone else. The statute provided for a right of appeal to the Secretary of Commerce under whatever rules he or she established. The orders lasted one year, but could be extended indefinitely once a determination was made that the release of the patent would threaten national security. The statute empowered the government to control efforts by the inventor to file for patents in foreign countries, with penalties ranging from fine and imprisonment to permanent loss of patent.[197] It also carried special emergency provisions to allow for secrecy orders during peacetime. In 1950, Truman declared a national emergency,[198] which lasted until 1979 and was the first time that the Invention Secrecy Act began operating as a peacetime measure.[199]

Congress's aim in enacting the measure was to help the United States develop new national security technology while denying other countries access to it.[200] And the state has not hesitated to use this measure. From 1959 until 1979, the annual number of secrecy orders for government employees *and* private inventors hovered between 4,100 and 5,000.[201] The ending of the emergency in 1979 marked the beginning of a federal reporting requirement.[202] However, statistics provided by the Patent and Trademark Office demonstrate not a *decrease* but an *increase* in the use of such orders.[203] Total secrecy orders nearly doubled in the span of just a decade: from 3,302 in 1981 to 6,193 in 1991.[204] An outcry erupted when the state provided this information to the Federation of American Scientists in response to a Freedom of Information request.[205]

Since the peak in the early 1990s, the annual number of secrecy orders has steadily decreased. A rather high average, though, persists: between 1991 and 2003, the state issued approximately 5,200 per annum. These aggregate numbers do *not* reveal the percentage of new orders that are placed on nongovernment-funded (private) research. From 1978 to 1979, approximately 15 percent of the new secrecy orders applied to these so-called John (or Jane) Doe orders. In 1982, this proportion hovered around 14 percent,[206] but by 1991, it had leaped to 75 percent (506 out of 774).[207] The Pentagon responded to the release of this information and the subsequent outcry by announcing that it would be limiting its use of secrecy orders.* But between 1997 and 2003, the number of John Doe orders reflected, in general, an upward trend, with an average of 46 new private patents denied per year for national security reasons.[208] Although the statute conferred a right of compensation, it is hard to claim for the Jane/John Doe inventions taken over by the state: the judiciary considers as equivalent to a state secret any information regarding the design, construction, and use of federal cryptographic encoding devices.†

The manner in which the state uses the secrecy orders effectively controls both ideas and technology. And history suggests that the government tends to err on the side of caution.‡ Certain areas of research, such as atomic energy and cryptography, consistently fall within their gamut. But the government has also placed secrecy orders on (the ill-fated) cold fusion, space technology, radar missile systems, and citizens' band radio voice scramblers.[209] Similar efforts to prevent the publication of optical engineering research and vacuum technology demonstrate the breadth of the national security net.[210]

In addition to formal strictures, the National Security Agency developed various informal techniques to prevent new discoveries with national security implications from reaching the public realm. The National Science Foundation submitted all applications for cryptographic research to the NSA for review. The agency also developed a more general volunteer vetting scheme, where scientists could submit articles prepublication to ensure that no information

---

* This may be related in some measure to efforts to modernize the military. Gary L. Hausken, *The Value of a Secret: Compensation for Imposition of Secrecy Orders Under the Invention Secrecy Act*, 119 MIL. L. REV. 201 (1988), at 202.

† In 1968, for example, Eugene Emerson Clift applied for a patent for a cryptographic device. The Commissioner issued a secrecy order, whereupon the inventor filed for reimbursement for losses incurred. The government withdrew the order and refused reimbursement. In the subsequent suit, the state denied having used the invention, but blocked efforts by the plaintiff to demonstrate state dependence on the cryptographic device. The court upheld executive privilege to maintain secrecy, saying that the state's need for secrecy outweighed the inventor's need for information. *Clift v. United States*, 808 F. Supp. 101, 103 (D. Conn. 1991).

‡ In 1978, for instance, Professor George I. Davida of the University of Wisconsin applied for a patent on a cipher device, an unclassified project on computer security that had been funded by the National Science Foundation. At the NSA's recommendation, the Commerce Department's Patent Office issued a secrecy order, prohibiting Davida from discussing his work. Wisconsin Chancellor Warner A. Baum, calling the order a threat to academic freedom, pressed the NSF to assist in protesting the order. The same year, the NSA issued a gag order against William Raike, Carl Nicolai, Carl Quale, and David Miller to stop them from marketing a "Phasorphone" – a device to protect private radio and telephone conversations. Gilbert, *supra* note 207, at 327–28 n.6; Judith Miller, N.Y. TIMES, May 31, 1978, at 1l Evans Witt, N.Y. TIMES, Sept. 26, 1978, at 57; Evans Witt, N.Y. TIMES, Oct. 11, 1978, at 84. The inventors charged that the secrecy order seemed to be "part of a general plan by the N.S.A. to limit the privacy of the American people. They've been bugging people's phones for years, and now someone comes along with a device that makes this a little harder to do, and they oppose this under the guise of national security." David Burnham, *The Silent Power of the NSA*, N.Y. TIMES, Mar. 27, 1983, at 6. The NSA reversed its decision, admitting that an inexpensive device meant to protect conversations against eavesdroppers failed to present a compelling national security threat. Evans Witt, N.Y. TIMES, Oct. 11, 1978, at 84.

damaging to national security would be released. In 1989, the NSA announced that this scheme had prevented approximately 7 percent of the papers submitted from moving forward.[211] The NSA also began to fund various unclassified research projects, "buying up" scientists who might otherwise develop technologies of concern – that is, putting them on government payroll for classified projects and, in the process, gagging them from speaking publicly on these issues.[212] The government also issued overt threats of more extensive, formal censorship. For example, in a speech to the American Association for the Advancement of Science, Vice Admiral Bobby R. Inman, former Director of the NSA and Deputy Director of the CIA, openly warned academics that failure to self-censor would lead to strict government controls: "Congress is ready to move to resolve the conflict between academic freedom and national security in favor of the latter." Failure to cooperate would mean that "far more serious threats to academic freedom would occur. . . . [T]he situation could well cause the government to overreact."[213] The breadth of innovations Inman included in this category was staggering: computer hardware and software, electronic gear and techniques, lasers, crop projections, and manufacturing procedures. The day of his speech, the American Association for the Advancement of Science passed this resolution: "Whereas freedom and national security are best preserved by adherence to the principles of openness that are a fundamental tenet of both American society and the scientific process, be it resolved that the A.A.A.S. opposes governmental restrictions on the dissemination, exchange or availability of unclassified knowledge."[214] This statement echoed other calls from prominent scientists, such as Edward Teller, warning against efforts to restrict scientific research.[215]

The 1954 Atomic Energy Act classified nuclear information from the moment of its birth: neither the state nor private actors could pass data to anyone lacking appropriate clearances.[216] Although as a prior restraint the legislation carried a "'heavy presumption' against its constitutional validity," the potential offensive use of a nuclear device against the United States and its citizens appears to satisfy this burden.[217] The legislation created a "Restricted Data" category that includes "all data concerning (1) design, manufacture, or utilization of atomic weapons; (2) the production of special nuclear material; or (3) the use of special nuclear material in the production of energy."[218] It grants the Atomic Energy Commission the authority to declassify information that it could demonstrate could be released "without undue risk to the common defense and security."[219] Scientists protested that secrecy would actually work against national security by retarding research efforts.[220] Private industry made almost no protest.[221]

In addition to the Restricted Data designation (preventing private research on atomic energy or weapons), at least twice, the US government has used informal pressure to censor publications on the subject. The first occurred in 1950 in connection with an article Dr. Hans Bethe wrote in *Scientific American*. The Atomic Energy Commission, which had obtained a prepublication copy of the article, requested that Bethe delete sensitive portions. It then demanded that the original article and printed plates be destroyed.

The second case arose in 1979, when the *Progressive* commissioned Howard Morland, a free-lance writer, to write a series on nuclear weapons.[222] The first piece presented no difficulties. The second, however, entitled "The H-Bomb Secret; How We Got It, Why We're Telling It," which included drawings of a nuclear weapon, worried the Department of Energy. When the Department offered to rewrite approximately 20 percent of the article, the *Progressive* refused. The state filed for, and obtained, an injunction.[223] The *Progressive* enjoyed a circulation of approximately 40,000 copies per month and had earned for itself some respect as a forum for the discussion of contemporary political affairs.[224] Nevertheless, the judge suggested that citizens could discuss proliferation and disarmament issues without intimate knowledge of how the H-bomb works (which was the subject of the article) or how to build one (which was not the subject of the piece, although it was frequently said to be).[225] The court explained, "What is involved here is information dealing with the most destructive weapon in the history of mankind, information of sufficient destructive potential to nullify the right to free speech and to endanger the right to life itself."[226] Although countries without the atomic weapon eventually might develop it, the court did not want to play a role in accelerating the process.

A third effort to restrict terrorist-relevant knowledge-based speech relates more generally to transmitting information about how to build conventional explosive devices and weapons of mass destruction. The relevant federal statute, passed in 1996, dates back to the April 1995 Oklahoma City bombing. Just under a month after the attack, Deputy Assistant Attorney General Robert Litt testified before the Senate Judiciary Committee's Subcommittee on Terrorism, Technology, and Government Information.[227] He raised the issue whether it was wise for bombmaking material to be available on the Internet. Three weeks later, Senator Diane Feinstein proposed an amendment to the bill that would become the 1996 Antiterrorism and Effective Death Penalty Act.[228] The amendment would have made it unlawful

for any person to teach or demonstrate the making of explosive materials, or to distribute by any means information pertaining to, in whole or in part, the manufacture of explosive materials, if the person intends or knows that such explosive materials or information will likely be used for, or in furtherance of, an activity that constitutes a Federal criminal offense or a criminal purpose affecting interstate commerce.[229]

Two days later, the Senate unanimously passed the bill; however, the conference committee subsequently replaced Feinstein's amendment with a new section that required the Department of Justice to conduct a study and report on the availability, and constitutionality, of restricting the dissemination of bomb-making instructional materials.[230] DoJ would provide information on all print, electronic, and film material; the extent to which domestic and international terrorist incidents used such data; the likelihood that such information might be used in the future; the relevant federal laws related to such material; the need and utility for additional laws to address this area, and an assessment of how far the First Amendment protects the holding and distribution of this information.[231]

On April 29, 1997, Attorney General Janet Reno submitted the report.[232] The DoJ noted the ease with which such information could be gleaned from "reference books, the so-called underground press, and the Internet."[233] It recognized that "[b]ombmaking information is literally at the fingertips of anyone with access to a home computer equipped with a modem."[234] One Web site alone yielded more than 110 different bombmaking texts (such as "Nifty Things that Go Boom"– believed to be a computer adaptation of *The Terrorist's Handbook*).[235]

Not surprisingly, circumstantial evidence suggested that a number of people found guilty of violent acts had access to similar material. The men indicted for the first bombing of the World Trade Center in New York in 1993, for instance, possessed information about explosive materials copied from American publications.[236] The arrest of Ray and Cecilia Lampley in 1995 interrupted their plan to use homemade C-4 (a plastic explosive used by the military) to attack either the Anti-Defamation League or the Southern Poverty Law Center. Agents found the *Anarchist's Cookbook*, along with Ragnar's *Big Book of Explosives* and *Homemade Weapons*, at their residence.[237] The Bureau of Alcohol, Tobacco, and Firearms found that 30 bomb investigations in 1985 and 1986 connected Internet bombmaking literature to the perpetrators.[238] The DoJ, however, could only find one case where chemical or biological weapons involved access to open source literature: the 1993 arrest of Thomas Lavy, who tried to cross the Canadian border with 130 grams of ricin, yielded *The Poisoner's Handbook*, *Silent Death*, and *Get Even: the Complete Book of Dirty Tricks*.[239] The report acknowledged that "no devices producing a nuclear yield have been constructed based on published bombmaking information."[240] Less convincingly, the report suggested that of the 117 nuclear terrorism threats since 1970, approximately half included reference to "fictional nuclear 'thrillers'" or contained "descriptive phrases gleaned from information in the public domain."[241] Law enforcement, the DoJ reported, expected this information to play a significant role in future acts of terrorism.

Federal law already prevented the use and dissemination of bombmaking information for criminal purposes. Conspiracy makes it illegal to plot to use explosives to commit "any felony which may be prosecuted in a court of the United States" – including offenses relating to the importation, manufacture, distribution, and storage of explosive materials.[242] In addition, "[a] person may not, as part of a conspiracy to commit an independently defined criminal offense, transmit information to a co-conspirator concerning how to make or use explosive devices."[243] The individual accused need not *actually* teach another how to commit the crime; rather, the disseminator must *know* what the other person intends to do with the information and *agree* with his or her co-conspirators that the offense will occur.[244] Solicitation measures also affect speech: federal law makes it unlawful to solicit, command, induce, or otherwise endeavor to persuade another individual to commit a felony involving physical force.[245] The DoJ recognized that many cases brought under this section could be restricted by *Brandenburg*, suggesting that persuasion would have to be accompanied by either threat or inducement.[246]

In addition to conspiracy and solicitation, two "aiding and abetting" statutes also prove relevant. One general federal prohibition states that "those who provide knowing aid to persons committing federal crimes, with the intent to facilitate the crime, are themselves committing the crime."[247] Although this includes speech, the DoJ suggested that it might not be effective as a way to prosecute the dissemination of explosive information: general publication or simply reckless behavior would be insufficient; an individual must intentionally or knowingly participate and share in the criminal intent, and the underlying offense must occur. In contrast, the 1996 Antiterrorism and Effective Death Penalty Act makes it unlawful to provide "material support or resources" to someone "knowing or intending that they are to be used in preparation for, or in carrying out," a specified list of terrorist offenses.[248] This provision exceeds the federal one in breadth: neither must the underlying offense occur, nor must specific intent to aid in the underlying offense be demonstrated.[249] The DoJ raised the questions, however, whether the courts would consider "training" to be distinct from "material support or resources," and whether a general manual on explosives would qualify as a "physical asset."[250]

Under *Brandenburg*, the Supreme Court would be unlikely to consider constitutional a prohibition on the general advocacy of illegal activity.[251] Similarly, the federal statutes I have addressed above stop short of preventing the general dissemination of information *per se*. And case law consistently protects such speech: In August 1981, for example, *Hustler Magazine* published "Orgasm of Death," which provided a detailed description of autoerotic asphyxia. The Fifth Circuit, indemnifying the magazine for liability from the subsequent death of a 14-year-old boy, stated, "The constitutional protection accorded to the freedom of speech and of the press is not based on the naive belief that speech can do no harm but on the confidence that the benefits society reaps from the free flow and exchange of ideas outweigh the costs society endures by receiving reprehensible or dangerous ideas."[252] Such "ideas" include instances of criminal violence, such as Michael Barrett's fatal stabbing in 1979 of 16-year old Martin Yakubowicz after seeing the film *The Warriors*, or James Perry's use of the information in the 1983 novel Hit Man to murder three people.[253]

Nevertheless, the Supreme Court has *never* held that lawfully obtained, truthful information is *always* constitutionally protected.[254] Such speech may be overcome by a "state interest of the highest order."[255] Justice Rehnquist, in a concurrence, commented that, "[w]hile we have shown a special solicitude for freedom of speech and of the press, we have eschewed absolutes in favor of a more delicate calculus that carefully weighs the conflicting interests to determine which demands the greater protection under the particular circumstances presented."[256] According to the DoJ, "keeping information on how to make explosives out of the hands of persons who want – or would be likely – to use that information in furtherance of violent crime" *does* constitute "a state interest of the highest order."[257] Thus, where one finds publication or expression "brigaded with action,"[258] the Constitution presents no impediment to its restriction. In *Brandenburg*, the Supreme Court *did* explicitly distinguish between "mere abstract teaching" and "preparing a group for violent action,"[259] and explained, "A statute which fails to draw this distinction impermissibly intrudes upon the freedoms guaranteed by the First and Fourteenth Amendments. It sweeps within its condemnation speech which our Constitution has immunized from governmental control."[260] Indeed, in *Dennis*, Justice Douglas specifically said that "the teaching of methods of terror and other seditious conduct should be beyond the pale."[261]

The DoJ cautiously endorsed new legislation prohibiting speech linked to unlawful activity.[262] "The more difficult question," the report suggested, "is whether criminal culpability can attach to general publication of explosives information, when the writer, publisher or seller of the information has the purpose of generally assisting unknown and unidentified readers in the commission of crimes."[263] This situation differs from one in which an individual prepares a *particular* group for violent action, but there is no "joint participation" in the crime.[264] Although the Court has not yet squarely addressed this issue, it has suggested that, in the context of a serious national security threat, motive matters: "[O]therwise privileged publication of information can lose its First Amendment protection when the publisher has an impermissible motive."[265] The DoJ then took the unusual step of suggesting that the District Court erred in *Rice v. Paladin Enterprises* (1996)[266] in ignoring the intent of the publisher: "At the very least, publication with such an improper intent should not be constitutionally protected where it is foreseeable that the publication will be used for criminal purposes; *and the Brandenburg requirement that the facilitated crime be 'imminent' should be of little, if any, relevance.*"[267] Thus, where the information lacks any other conceivable purpose, or where manuals actually assert as their purpose the facilitation of crime, the state ought to be able to use this "as probative evidence that the disseminator of accompanying information on the techniques of bombmaking intended by such dissemination to facilitate criminal conduct."[268] The "safest strategy," then – to avoid running afoul of constitutional requirements – would be to tie the prohibition of disseminating bombmaking information to knowledge of the person's intent to use the information illegally. Thus, a defendant would not have actually to know that some future event will occur, but would have to know only the other person's current intent. Therefore, the state would not have to demonstrate that the defendant was "practically certain" of the intent to engage in particular acts (the standard for future events), but only that there was a "high probability" that he or she currently intended to use the data for an illegal purpose.[269]

In 1999, Senator Feinstein attached her amendment to a (completely unrelated) private relief measure,[270] which focused on phosphate prospecting and compensation due to the Menominee Indian Tribe.[271] The Senate Judiciary Committee did not prepare any report on Feinstein's amendment; nor did it receive any attention in its presentation to either the Senate or the House. Instead, the Senate passed it by unanimous vote.

This measure makes it an offense "to teach or demonstrate the making or use of an explosive, a destructive device, or a weapon of mass destruction, or to distribute by any means information pertaining to, in whole or in part, the manufacture or use of an explosive, destructive device, or weapon of mass destruction" either knowing or intending "that the teaching, demonstration, or information be used for, or in furtherance of, an activity that constitutes a Federal crime of violence."[272]

The net effect of the statute has been to create a situation in which individuals of certain political persuasions are allowed to speak in a certain manner, whereas those of different political persuasions are not. For instance, on August 4, 2003, District Court sentenced Sherman Martin Austin, the 18-year-old owner of Raisethefist.com, for violation of this statute.[273] Austin's anarchist Web site had hosted and provided a link to *Break the Bank-DC S30 2001*,[274] which instructed activists on how to prepare for direct action against the World Bank and the International Monetary Fund in Washington, D.C. The manual instructed demonstrators to dress in black (the Black Bloc), to "unarrest" other protesters (by linking arms and pulling demonstrators away from the police), to change clothes when leaving the demonstration and how to shield against pepper spray, to build barriers against riot police phalanxes, and to build slingshots.[275] One chapter focused on homemade explosives, such as Molotov cocktails ("[t]he most popular choice in street fighting weaponry"[276]), smoke bombs (to shield against the media or police filming), and fuel-fertilizer explosives ("[t]hese will create an overwhelmingly large explosion and should be practiced in large faraway places like the desert before using"[277]). The instructions accompanying the different explosive devices lacked a certain sophistication. For instance, under Molotov cocktail, the author wrote the following:

The most high explosive and lethal mixture is ammonium-nitrate-based fertilizer mixed with gasoline. Just stuff the bottle with this mixture and light the fucker. This method should be made with a plastic bottle so that it will not break on impact. When you light it, the bottle will quickly explode so be quick. Using a fuse is a good idea.[278]

Such sites, however, appear amateur in comparison with the information on everything from pipe bombs and Molotov cocktails to high-end nuclear weapons currently available on mainstream Web sites such as CNN.com, Wikipedia.com, and HowStuffWorks.com.[279] Sites like Amazon.com readily sell books like *Silent Death* (reportedly used by Aum Shinrikyo in its 1995 sarin attacks on the Tokyo subway), *Home Workshop Explosives*, and the *Improvised Munitions Black Book*.[280] The real issue appears to be that Austin attached his manual to an acknowledged anarchist Web site. And so David S. Touretzky, a professor at Carnegie Mellon University who identifies himself as a Republican, freely posted the same material that led to Sherman's arrest – and to his serving time in jail.[281]

Restrictions on Knowledge-Based Speech in the United Kingdom

Like the United States, the United Kingdom also has restricted knowledge-based speech. One early initiative in this area came in 1912, when a series of informal meetings among press associations, the Secretary of the Admiralty, and the War Office led to the creation of Britain's "D-Notice system."[282]

This scheme initially focused on how to prevent the publication of state secrets by drawing on a D-Notice Committee to act as a filter prior to the release of government information. Concern quickly arose within military ranks, however, about data outside government control. The press balked at the idea of "consultation" in this area, saying it would be used to stifle criticism. World War I, though, soon overtook the discussions, resulting in formal, strict censorship of all media. After the war, Britain returned to using the D-Notice Committee. During World War II, the government again assumed control, only to return, after hostilities, to the voluntary "consultation" system.

The highly respected Chief Press Censor, Admiral George Thompson, ran the D-Notice program until the early 1960s. In 1962, the Radcliffe Committee on Security Procedures in the Public Service reviewed the scheme and issued a resounding endorsement, stating that it had "no hesitation in recommending the continuance of the system."[283] After Thompson's retirement, though, the program degenerated.* The state redrafted the guidelines and established 12 standing D-Notices. These suggested that publications related to defense plans; information about nuclear and conventional weapons systems; and radio and radar transmissions to civil defense, British intelligence services, and the (mysteriously named) "Whereabouts of Mr. and Mrs. Vladimir Petrov" first be submitted to the D-Notice Committee to ensure that they not breach national security.[284]

In 1993, the government renamed the system "DA-Notices." By May 2000, the standing notices had been consolidated to the present five: Military Operations, Plans, and Capabilities; Nuclear and Non-Nuclear Weapons and Equipment; Ciphers and Secure Communications; Sensitive Installations and Home Addresses; and United Kingdom Security and Intelligence Services and Special Forces.[285] With the exception of Ciphers and Secure Communications, the remaining notices specifically reference the threat posed by terrorism to the United Kingdom's national security.

---

* In 1967, an article in the DAILY EXPRESS alleged that the government opened cables and overseas telegrams. The state appointed a Committee of Privy Counsellors to determine whether Chapman Pincher, the journalist who wrote the piece, had violated the D-Notice system. Although the committee determined that he had not, the government countered with a White Paper saying that the article jeopardized national security. Cmnd 3309, 1967, Cmnd 3312. A subsequent inquiry led to the resignation of the D-Notice Committee Secretary, Colonel Lohan. Then, in 1971, a highly visible prosecution for a breach of section 2 of the 1911 Official Secrets Act again raised questions about the effectiveness of D-Notices. Technically, however, only information relating to British troops or strategic decisions counted – not (even privileged) information about the state of affairs in other nations.

The purpose of the system is "to provide to national and provincial newspaper editors, to periodicals editors, to radio and television organisations and to relevant book publishers, general guidance on those areas of national security which the Government considers it has a duty to protect."[286] It does not legally bind the participants. Neither does the system necessarily reflect the government's view whether certain information should be made publicly available; instead, it reflects the views of the advisory body. The D-Notice Committee labels the Notices issued to formal inquiries as "private and confidential," but their contents do *not* fall under the formal government security classification. Moreover, it is *not* an offense under the Official Secrets Act (OSA)[287] – nor is it considered a breach of the D-Notice system – to publish information found to breach one of the categories.

The government and the D-Notice Committee do not always agree – as occurred in two prominent cases. The first involved a BBC radio series, ironically named *My Country Right or Wrong*, which focused on issues raised by the infamous *Spycatcher* case (see page 322).[288] Although the series was cleared by the D-Notice Committee, the Attorney General forbade the BBC from showing it and announced in Parliament that the issue at stake was "the duty of the Government to protect the confidentiality that is owed to them by members and former members of MI5."[289] The state filed for an injunction based on the civil duty of breach of confidence.[290]

In the second case, *Lord Advocate v. Scotsman Publications Ltd. and Others*, Anthony Cavendish, a former MI6 official, sent 300 copies of his tell-all book to his closest friends and relatives for Christmas.[291] For some reason, though, the government did not respond to Cavendish; instead, it obtained injunctions against the *Observer* and the *Sunday Times* – and later the *Scotsman* – to prevent the information from being published again.[292] Although the Secretary of the D-Notice Committee had approved of the printed matter, the government claimed that it was not the content, but the disclosure itself that threatened national security.[293]

Even with these differences of opinion, one fascinating aspect of the system is that, for the better part of a century, it worked. Some commentators have suggested that this success owes much to the great regard shown past Secretaries, as well as to editors' wishes to do their part in protecting national security. The culture I referred to in the previous chapter here matters: the system developed in the face of the two world wars – both overwhelming national security concerns that threatened the life of the nation. To some degree, such compliance may also reflect editors' real fear of being prosecuted under the Official Secrets Act.[294] More recently, though, owing to its increasing efforts to pursue transgressions through civil penalties, the government has lost some of the trust the system previously enjoyed.[295] The net effect has been for publications to rely more heavily on legal advice than on the informal consultative committee.[296]

The D-Notice system is not the only control on knowledge-based speech. In 1994, the British government created the Voluntary Vetting Scheme to keep within the domestic sphere technologies related to weapons of mass destruction.[297] The scheme allows universities to "vet" potential students from overseas, by submitting their applications to the government for clearance. The government currently has 10 "countries of concern" and 21 "academic disciplines of concern."[298] Between April 1, 2002, and March 27, 2003, four universities in the United Kingdom referred more than 500 names to the state.[299] However, not all universities take part; in total, some 70 percent of all institutes of higher education participate in the program, which excludes the National Health Service and private commercial laboratories.[300] The Foreign Affairs Committee recently suggested that this program is ill suited to the terrorist threat, and recommended that additional steps be taken to increase government control over, particularly, biotechnology.[301]

The attacks of September 11, 2001, and the subsequent anthrax mailings in the United States, spurred further efforts to control knowledge-based information. In November 2002, in an unusual move, Lord May of Oxford, the president of the Royal Society, and Bruce Alberts, the president of the National Academy of Sciences, issued a joint editorial in *Science*. Timed to coincide with the Fifth Review Conference of the Biological and Toxin Weapons Convention, the editorial stated,

Every researcher, whether in academia, in government research facilities, or in industry, needs to be aware of the potential unintended consequences of their own and their colleagues' research.... [R]esearchers in the biological sciences...need to take responsibility for helping to prevent the potential misuses of their work, while being careful to preserve the vitality of their disciplines as required to contribute to human welfare.[302]

This statement reflected increasing focus on this issue within the Royal Society, with four times the number of reports on the topic in the four years following September 11, 2001, than in the previous five.[303]

In many ways, this joint statement can be seen as a call to head off formal state restrictions. On December 19, 2002, for instance, the House of Commons Science and Technology Committee announced the formation of an inquiry into Britain's scientific response to terrorism. The terms of reference included "what issues needed to be faced by the research community to ensure that their activities did not unwittingly assist terrorists' activities."[304] As in the United States, scientists emphasize responsibility but oppose formal restrictions. Scientific associations, as well as parliamentary committees, have endorsed the adoption of a code of ethics.

Britain's Society for General Microbiology (SGM), the American Society for Microbiology's counterpart, previously had no policy regarding the publication of sensitive biological research. A chance meeting in London between Dr. Ronald Fraser, SGM's Executive Secretary, and the editor of the *New Scientist*, however, led to an SGM Council discussion on February 21, 2003, regarding the development of such a policy and to its adoption on May 2, 2003.[305] This policy, strongly oriented toward the free publication of scientific research, notes that the "benefits [of scientific information] greatly outweigh the potential dangers."[306] It continues, "[The] SGM Council is against any blanket or external censorship of scientific publication in subject areas such as microbiology, as this would be a barrier to scientific progress. Furthermore, the potential benefits or dangers from a new discovery are not always possible to predict."[307] The SGM recognized that in "rare cases," "particular concerns" might arise; however, the decision should be left to "authors, editors, referees, and publishers," with the final decision on whether to publish left with the editor-in-chief of the journal in question.[308]

This policy, which applies through the SGM to the four main British academic microbiology journals and one quarterly magazine, attracted virtually no comment.[309] This lack of attention is not surprising, particularly in light of the extensive, new controls passed by Westminster. Parts VI and VII of the Anti-Terrorism, Crime and Security Act 2001 made it illegal to assist in the overseas development of chemical, nuclear, biological, or radiological weapons: "A person who aids, abets, counsels or procures, or incites, a person who is not a United Kingdom person to do a relevant act outside the United Kingdom is guilty of an offence."[310] The act also required any facility dealing with the pathogens listed in Schedule 5 to notify the government and to submit to random inspections. It required the directors of such premises to provide detailed information to the police about individuals working in the facilities, and empowered the Home Secretary to make a list of individuals who would not be allowed to work with certain substances.[311] Although early indications suggest that law enforcement is treading lightly, academics have articulated many concerns about the use of these powers.[312]

One significant formal stricture accompanies these informal limits on knowledge-based speech. A damning report on the sale of arms to Iraq issued in 1996 by Sir Richard Scott, a Lord Justice of Appeal, sparked concern over the export of British weaponry.[313] It took 9/11, though, to stimulate a formal government response. The resulting Export Control Act of 2002 carried with it considerable powers to prevent the transfer of scientific information.[314] The initial language in the bill – that the "Secretary of State may by order make provision for . . . the imposition of transfer controls in relation to technology of any description" – ignited concern about the implications for international collaboration and publication.[315] The final version created a check, providing that the Secretary of State

shall not make a control order which has the effect of prohibiting or regulating any of the following activities – the effect of interfering with – (a) the communication of information in the ordinary course of scientific research, (b) the making of information generally available to the public, or (c) the communication of information that is generally available to the public, unless the interference by the order in the freedom to carry on the activity is necessary (and no more than is necessary).[316]

The legislation came into force May 1, 2004. The Labour government noted that although, in *principle* the Secretary of State may not regulate basic scientific information, where such regulation is deemed necessary he or she has full authority to do so.[317] What makes this statute particularly threatening to

British scientists is that it regulates the transfer of both ideas and objects inside domestic bounds.[318] The jury is as yet out on its effect.

In summary, where the United States and particularly the United Kingdom retain, within broad limits, the ability to stifle persuasive speech, their authority to limit knowledge-based communications is less restricted – and may expand further under terrorist challenge, particularly in light of the proliferation of biological and nuclear weapons.

THE SECONDARY EFFECTS OF OTHER COUNTERTERRORISM MEASURES

There are a host of counterterrorism provisions that do not directly target speech, but that nonetheless significantly curb free expression within the state. The most significant may be those related to executive detention, proscription, and the rules of evidence – with initiatives affecting immigration, financial flows, surveillance, and the like exacerbating the impact of these.

The United States has thrice implemented widespread executive detention.* After 9/11, Attorney General John Ashcroft initiated the third and most recent

---

* First, during the Civil War, Lincoln oversaw more than 38,000 detentions, many carried out on the basis of otherwise protected First Amendment activities. GEOFFREY STONE, PERILOUS TIMES (2005), at 124. Second, in June 1940, the FBI initiated plans for the second major detention of American citizens. The Custodial Detention Program drew from a list of people arrested during the national emergency, and the executive branch detained 9,121 people. By presidential proclamation, all enemy aliens *not* interned – some 890,000 Italian, German, and Japanese nationals – suffered restrictions on their freedom of movement and could not own radios, cameras, or weapons. *Id.*, at 285–86. Following the attack on Pearl Harbor on December 7, 1941, Executive Order 9066 provided the military with the authority to "designate . . . military areas" from which "any or all persons may be excluded." Exec. Order No. 9,066, 3 CFR EO 9066 (1942). Over the next eight months, the army transferred more than 120,000 people of Japanese ancestry, two-thirds of whom were US citizens, to concentration camps. Although this action was initially upheld by the courts, the racism that motivated it – particularly in light of the lack of evidence of any threat posed by those interned – became a blight on American history. *See Hirabayashi v. United States*, 320 U.S. 81 (1943); *Korematsu v. United States*, 323 U.S. 214 (1944); *Ex parte Endo*, 323 US 283 (1944); *see also* GEOFFREY STONE, PERILOUS TIMES (2005), at 305–07. In 1976, President Ford issued Presidential Proclamation No. 4417, recognizing the error of EO. 9066. GEOFFREY STONE, PERILOUS TIMES (2005), at 305. In 1983, Congress's Commission on Wartime Relocation and Internment of Civilians concluded that "race prejudice, war hysteria and a failure of political leadership" drove the relocations. A joint Congressional Resolution recognized the "grave injustice . . . done" and apologized for exclusion, removal, and detention. *Id.* at 305–06. The judiciary took the unusual step of granting writs of error *coram nobis* – to set aside convictions for "manifest injustice" to Fred Korematsu and Kiyoshi Hirabayashi. The courts found that the government knowingly and intentionally failed to disclose vital information that would have exonerated the detainees. *Id.* at 307–07. In 1988, the Civil Liberties Act deemed the internment a "grave injustice . . . carried out without adequate security reasons," without any documented acts of "espionage or sabotage." Civil Liberties Act of 1988, Pub. L. No. 100–383, 102 Stat 903 (1988). A presidential apology and reparations for discrimination, loss of liberty, loss of property, and personal humiliation followed. GEOFFREY STONE, PERILOUS TIMES (2005), at 307.

program, which targeted – as I related in Chapter 2 – Arab males, aged 18 to 35, from 17 countries. In total, the Department of Justice detained approximately 1,200 non-US citizens – some for up to three years.[319] Subsequent antiterrorist immigration measures led to the detention of close to 4,000 more people.[320] The FBI began making regular visits to mosques, and the Department of Homeland Security obtained a breakdown of all Arab-Muslims in the United States by zip code.[321] Although not outright prohibitions on free speech, these measures inhibited the ability of individuals to express themselves without fear of state action. In this context, reliance on the *Brandenburg* decision seems somewhat misplaced.

The United Kingdom, too, has engaged in widespread detention, with internment occurring four times in Northern Ireland between 1922 and 1972 (see Chapter 2). On the last occurrence, Operation Demetrius led to the incarceration of hundreds of innocent people, and so enraged the communities in Northern Ireland that violence there spiraled out of control and forced Westminster to suspend the Northern Parliament. For the 50 years preceding this event, however, the state's power of detention, even if not exercised, served to dampen speech – as, indeed, have executive detention and control orders in the wake of 9/11. While detention itself does not target speech, it affects speech not protected by the free expression provisions of the European Convention of Human Rights.

The United States and the United Kingdom also have the authority to declare organizations unlawful. At first glance, this power may seem at odds with freedom of association – a right read into the First Amendment and embodied in the ECHR. The US Supreme Court has held, though, that the government *can* punish the member of a targeted group – even when that individual does not engage in illegal activities on its behalf – when he or she is active within it, knows its illegal aims, and intends to further them.[322]

Although there are constitutional limits on measures relating to domestic groups and organizations, the United States maintains a system of designated foreign terrorist organizations. In the 1970s, the state made its initial forays into this area with its proscription of the Palestinian Liberation Organization. After the Oklahoma City bombing, the 1996 Antiterrorism and Effective Death Penalty Act empowered the Secretary of State to "designate" foreign-based organizations engaged in terrorist activity, making it illegal for a person in the United States or one subject to American jurisdiction to provide funds or other material to anyone on the list.[323] Representatives and certain members of such an organization could be denied visas or excluded. American financial institutions became obliged to block foreign terrorist organization funds and to file a report with the Office of Foreign Assets Control in the Department of the Treasury. As of April 2005, some 40 organizations graced this list.[324] In *People's Mohjahedin Org. v. United States* (1999), the D.C. Circuit Court held that the judicial system could review the Secretary of State's determinations as far as the foreign nature of the organization and whether it engaged in terrorist activity, but not whether the organization proved a national security threat.[325]

The circuit courts are split, though, over how far to take this decision. The Ninth Circuit, for instance, held that "targeting individuals because of activities such as fundraising is impermissible unless the government can show that group members had the specific intent to pursue illegal group goals."[326]

English law had no such corresponding right of association until implementation of the Human Rights Act in October 2000. For centuries, the state maintained legislation proscribing membership even in domestic organizations. In 1799 and 1817, for instance, the United Kingdom suppressed secret societies; many in the British establishment believed that the republican movement in France and the Irish rebellion were linked.[327] A 1799 statute blacklisted the United Englishmen, United Scotsmen, United Britons, United Irishmen, and London Corresponding Society and noted that the members of these groups took unlawful oaths, used secret signs, and operated in stealth.[328] The legislation claimed that it was "expedient and necessary that...all societies of the like nature should be utterly suppressed and prohibited."[329] An 1817 statute similarly addressed political unrest.[330] These provisions remained in place until the late nineteenth century.

Prior to the formation of Northern Ireland, the British government also proscribed a number of organizations in Ireland. These bans, instituted under the Defence of the Realm Acts, remained in place through the adoption of Regulation 14 of the 1920 Restoration of Order in Ireland Act and then of Regulation 24 of the original schedule to the 1922 Special Powers Act.[331] Regulation 24 made it an offense for individuals sharing the objects of a listed organization to act to further them or to possess any document relating to the affairs of the organization. The burden of proof lay on the defendant, in whose quarters such documents might be found, to demonstrate that he or she was not associated with the group. Within days of the introduction of this regulation, the government expanded it, making it an offense to be a member of an unlawful association or to act to promote the aims either of an unlawful association or of a "seditious conspiracy."[332] As with the earlier regulation, under Regulation 24A possession of documents provided sufficient proof of membership. A third regulation, 24B, augmented proscription, making it illegal to refuse to recognize the court or to claim membership of an illegal organization during judicial proceedings.[333] Although the government withdrew Regulations 24 and 24B in 1949 and 1951, respectively, Regulation 24A remained on the books until the proroguement of Stormont.

Throughout this time, the Northern Executive periodically expanded the number of proscribed organizations to include both republican and left-wing organizations.* In 1966, the Northern Executive banned its first (and

---

* Such organizations include, for example, the Irish Republican Brotherhood, Irish Republican Army, Fianna na hÉireann, Cumann Poblachta na hÉireann, Saor Uladh, Sinn Féin, Fianna Uladh, Saor Éire, the National Guard Friends of Soviet Russia, the Irish Labour Defence League, the Workers' Defence Corps, the Women Prisoners' Defence League, the Workers' Revolutionary Party (Ireland), the Irish Tribute League, the Irish Working Farmers' Committee and the Workers'

penultimate) loyalist organization: the Ulster Volunteer Force. At the time of partition, II organizations remained on the list – 9 of which were republican in character.[334]* Owing to these measures, people were afraid to associate with particular groups – even for legitimate political or professional reasons: Sinn Féin recognized that "Section 31 is not only a bar or distorting factor on news reporting, it helps generate the atmosphere in which people are afraid to be seen as associated with Sinn Féin."[335]

Section 19 of the 1973 Emergency Powers Act, incorporating all of Regulation 24A's powers of proscription, added to them a measure that made it illegal for any person to solicit membership or funds for a proscribed organization. By making recruiting and fundraising an offense, instead of simply stifling any contrary speech as the unionist government had done, Westminster tried to separate paramilitary organizations from the communities whence they derived. Section 23A of the new legislation made it illegal for an individual to dress or behave in public "in such a way as to arouse reasonable apprehension that he is a member of a proscribed organization." The sectarian application of proscription aroused concern in reviews of emergency legislation.[336]† The government initiated 107 prosecutions in 1980, 71 in 1981, 137 in 1982, and 108 in 1983.[337] However, the provision acted as much as an effort to express outrage and moral disgust "at the barbarous acts of these organizations, and the revolting glee with which they claim responsibility for the organization, usually with personal anonymity, together with their public displays in particular areas,"[338] as it did as a means to prevent breaches of the peace.

The British government also made organizations in Great Britain illegal: like the EPA, the 1974 Prevention of Terrorism Act (PTA) provided for proscription. However, almost the sole purpose was to reflect the moral opprobrium of society. Roy Jenkins, Labour's Home Secretary from 1974 to 1976, sought to avoid seeing the "men of violence" gloat over the latest attack: "I have never

---

Research Bureau. LAURA K. DONOHUE, COUNTER-TERRORIST LAW AND EMERGENCY POWERS IN THE UNITED KINGDOM 1922–2000 (2000), at 100–03.

* In 1969, the application of these powers reached the highest court. The previous year, Michael Francis Forde, a Royal Ulster Constabulary district inspector, named John McEldowney as a member of the Slaughtneil Republican Club. Regulation 24A of the 1922–43 SPAs outlawed republican clubs. The state did not provide any evidence that the organization threatened peace, law, and order in the province. The police admitted that they were unaware of anything seditious in this particular club's pursuits. McEldowney claimed that under the SPAs, the criterion for banning an organization was *not* a general category (*i.e.*, "republican clubs") but rather its purpose and activities. The magistrate, agreeing with the defendant, dismissed the complaint. Forde appealed, and the case reached the House of Lords, where a majority found generic descriptions acceptable under the 1922–43 SPAs. *McEldowney v. Forde*, [1971] A.C. 632, at 645.

† The 1973 EPA outlawed Sinn Féin, the IRA, Cumann na mBan, Fianna na hÉireann, Saor Éire, and the Ulster Volunteer Force. By 1984, the British government had added the Red Hand Commandos, the Ulster Freedom Fighters, and the Irish National Liberation Army to the list. Northern Ireland (Emergency Provisions) Act, 1978 (Amendment) Order 1979 (S.KI. 1979, No. 746). For discussion of the orders proscribing the INLA, see 969 PARL. DEB., H.C. (5th ser.) (1979) 925–1070; 971 PARL. DEB., H.C. (5th ser.) (1979) 741–70.

claimed, and do not claim now, that proscription of the IRA will of itself reduce terrorist outrages. *But the public should no longer have to endure the affront of public demonstrations in support of that body.*"[339] Consequently, the British state outlawed only republican organizations. The 1974 PTA prohibited clothes that indicated membership in a proscribed organization. Possession of objects indicating membership shifted the onus to the defendant to prove that he or she was *not* a member of the group. As recognized in the House of Commons, "the open panoply of IRA activities was such an affront to our people that it had to be banned for that purpose."[340] Most recently, the 1998 Criminal Justice (Terrorism and Conspiracy) Act also allowed for proscription.[341]

Shifts in the rules of evidence also can contribute to the erosion of freedom of speech. Here, it is important to recognize that a different geopolitical situation holds today than it did in the early to mid-twentieth century – particularly in the United States. Like the communist threat, al Qaeda represents an international movement; however, the numbers have changed. This time, the great concern is not the massive recruitment of the domestic population, but the indoctrination of a small number of people from close-knit minority communities. In other words, an individual throwing pamphlets from the top of a tenement building is less likely now to seem threatening – as opposed to the person who quietly goes into a mosque and tries to recruit disaffected youth. Because of these changed circumstances, the government is more likely to use conspiracy provisions that address person-to-person persuasive speech than it is to focus on general advocacy efforts. Yet the relationship of *Brandenburg* to conspiracy law is not at all clear. For the most part, the free speech doctrine does not deal with solicitation of crime. As terrorist networks increasingly move away from large groups, the law likely to be applied to them moves away from *Brandenburg*.

Here, Congress has steadily weakened standards required by criminal law – especially in the relaxation of the bilateral requirement in conspiracy law, and the introduction and expanded use of the Racketeer Influenced and Corrupt Organizations (RICO) Act.[342] In relation to the first, although traditionally conspiracy required that two or more people agree for at least one conviction to follow, more recently a unilateral view of conspiracy has emerged: whether the other person had any intention of fulfilling that purpose proves irrelevant as long as the first person intends to fulfill it if possible.[343] (RICO is a statute Congress passed in 1970 that weakened federal conspiracy standards and was aimed at the Mafia world, though its use quickly went beyond that world.) RICO forbids the investment or "laundering" of racketeering profits in interstate commercial businesses, even where the business has a legitimate purpose wholly independent of racketeering activity.[344] It also bars the infiltration of legitimate enterprises by means of bribery, extortion, or other predicate acts or the corruption of a legitimate enterprise from within.[345] Congress wrote RICO to make personal involvement unnecessary. Law enforcement expanded on the concept of "enterprise" to include noncommercial enterprises. Agreeing with this interpretation, the courts have held that the enterprise need not have an economic motive. Although the statute requires two predicate acts, virtually simultaneous actions appear to suffice: in one Mafia hit case, for example, three assassinations performed at once established a pattern of behavior sufficient to satisfy RICO.[346] Once law enforcement makes the decision to pursue a case under the more expansive criminal law measures, the *Brandenburg* test can do little to guarantee the protections it claims.

General evidentiary rules also reverberate in free speech. Although the American judiciary, as a whole, prevents juries from imposing liability based on First Amendment activity, the state can introduce such activity as evidence of something else – for example, that a witness is lying, that a defendant has a bad character, or that co-conspirators have a previous association.[347] The First Amendment enters the scene only when speech tightly connects to what is being punished – not when used more generally as evidence of some mental state or past actions.[348] With regular rules of evidence "strongly weighted in favor of admission," defendants can thus *indirectly* be punished for First Amendment-protected activity.[349] This practice may chill some otherwise protected expression. It also may lead people to plea bargain or give up their right to a jury trial.[350]

Arguments in favor of the burden as currently written note that speech and expressive conduct help establish and ascertain motive and evidence of conduct. Individuals may be more likely to act on something they have said. Speech, moreover, demonstrates intent. Here, I return to the point where I left off in knowledge-based speech: that passing on to someone or an organization certain information with a specific political intent to destabilize the government is distinguished from passing on scientific information simply to share it. The issue of intent, in fact, comes up in lots of cases – from hate crimes to sex discrimination; and a long line of cases address the use of speech as evidence.[351]

But in the context of political crime, a political statement is not necessarily harmless – any more than is otherwise innocuous activity in the atmosphere of fear following acts of terror. Terrorism is a unique activity. The majoritarian bias traditionally attributed to juries works against the innocent and pressures people to cease and desist otherwise protected activities. It is for precisely this reason that the courts transferred to the state the burden of proof to demonstrate that a person is advocating overthrow of the government and to meet the standard of "clear and convincing" evidence.[352]

This situation is not without solutions. For instance, First Amendment activity can be distinguished from other forms of evidence and granted a stricter standard for admission.[353] By holding such activity presumptively prejudicial – unless its probative value significantly exceeds the prejudice so incurred – the courts would go some way toward alleviating this concern.[354] A less aggressive solution might be simply to exclude such evidence until the state demonstrates that it "substantially outweighs its prejudicial dangers."[355] Although outright prohibitions on speech might not be allowed, allowing evidence based on First Amendment activity in through the back door is risky.

Perhaps the most dramatic example of the state's lowering of evidentiary rules specifically to generate terrorist convictions occurred in the United

Kingdom. Following the 1998 Omagh bombing, the Terrorism and Conspiracy Act allowed a person's decision to remain silent in the face of questioning to be used as evidence of his or her guilt. This measure brought Britain into line with similar Irish legislation. Another provision in British counterterrorist law makes the accusation of a police officer evidence of one's membership in a terrorist organization.[356] The combined effect of these provisions is that if a police officer asks someone whether he or she is a terrorist, and that person remains silent – and the officer, in court, asserts that he or she is a terrorist – the court can consider the evidence sufficient proof that that person belongs to a terrorist organization. (As of spring 2007, the state had refrained from actually using this provision in the 1998 Act.)

Executive detention, proscription, and evidentiary rules only skim the surface of the counterterrorist measures that curtail free speech. The freezing of assets may make people afraid to contribute to charitable organizations. Restriction and exclusion orders may make individuals afraid to question state actions. Legislative inquiries into political beliefs or loyalty to the state, such as those in the United States at the height of the McCarthy era, may similarly stifle expression. Although arguments for and against these propositions are beyond the scope of this chapter, my point here is that appeal to cases like *Brandenburg* or the ECHR's commitment to free expression says little about counterterrorist provisions that, while not directly targeting this freedom, nonetheless dampen it. What is perhaps ironic is that some commentators, willing to give up other liberties directly entailed in counterterrorist measures, nevertheless draw the line at free speech. Yet once these other liberties begin to erode, similar erosion of free speech and expression becomes all but inevitable.

PRIVILEGED SPEECH

The measures discussed thus far relate to efforts by the United States and the United Kingdom to restrict speech in each state's exercise of its sovereign powers. Where these states act as employer, or as the holder of information, they have an even stronger power over their employees' speech and the release of information, which both states control through a nonstatutory classification system. Here, the courts are particularly deferential, and as with the other rights, state counterterrorist provisions affect others beyond the immediate one in question.

US Government Employment and Employees' Speech

The United States has at its disposal three ways to ensure that its employees toe the line with respect to terrorist-related speech. The first relates to the decision to hire (or fire) an employee based on expression outside the work environment. The government cannot deny employment to members of organizations such as the Communist Party, or to those who have refused to take an oath that they are *not* members of a "Communist front or subversive organization" simply on grounds of membership. The Supreme Court held such a stricture to be overbroad; however, if narrowed to "knowing" membership with a "specific intent to further unlawful aims," such speech would *not* be constitutionally protected and may lead to refusal to hire for – or dismissal from – government employment.[357] Although the Court distinguished between sensitive and nonsensitive positions in considering the constitutionality of retributive action based on group membership, it left the door open to a strong enough national security interest allowing the government to deny employment to a member with *no* specific intent, even though membership itself could not be *criminally* punished.[358]*

Another way the state may refuse employment centers not on group membership, but on an individual's refusal to answer certain questions. Here, again, the inquiry focuses on knowing membership.[359] The Court upheld the state's authority to inquire (and obtain an answer) about membership in specific organizations, the extent of an individual's knowledge of a group's aims, and that individual's intent to assist in carrying the goals to fruition. The net effect means that, although both knowledge *and* specific intent are necessary to deny employment, refusal to disclose these also may provide appropriate grounds for that denial.

The second way in which the state controls employees relates to sanctions placed on them for publicly speaking on certain matters while in the state's employ. Here, the state may *not* punish public employees' speech on matters of public concern, *unless the government demonstrates that some urgency or need outweighs the employee's First Amendment rights*[360]:

> [T]he State has interests as an employer in regulating the speech of its employees that differ significantly from those it possesses in connection with regulation of the speech of the citizenry in general. The problem in any case is to arrive at a balance between the interest of the employee, as a citizen, in commenting upon matters of public concern and the interest of the State, as an employer, in promoting the efficiency of the public services it performs through its employees.[361]

This standard applies equally to government contractors.[362] If the substance of the speech, however, does *not* address a matter of public concern, such speech remains unprotected.[363] Although a case could be made that matters related to terrorism generally are of public concern, arguments regarding the state interest in protecting itself would be more likely to win the day.

The third manner in which the state controls employees' speech, the nondisclosure agreement, prevents employees from revealing information *after* they leave government service. Early in the 1980s Congress resisted efforts to extend nondisclosure agreements to all executive branch employees, with the result that

---

* This does not mean that the doctrines of overbreadth and vagueness become meaningless; on the contrary, they apply whenever a First Amendment activity attends: "[T]he Constitution requires that the conflict between congressional power and individual rights be accommodated by legislation drawn more narrowly to avoid the conflict." *United States v. Robel*, 389 US 258 (1967), at 268 n.20.

now such contractual relationships depend upon the agency or department in question.* The Central Intelligence Agency provides a good example.

In the 1970s, the CIA began to require employees to sign a document saying that before publishing "any information or material relating to the Agency, its activities or intelligence activities generally," they would submit the document to the Publications Review Board. Material that had to be submitted included "all writings and scripts or outlines of oral presentations intended for non-official publication, including works of fiction," with publication understood as "communicating information to one or more persons."[364] Despite the fact that such guidelines would cover, as one civil libertarian put it, "even letters to your mother,"[365] the Fourth Circuit considered this agreement – at least, in relation to confidential documents that have not been released to the public – to be consistent with the First Amendment.[366] In 1976, to implement this policy, the CIA created the Publications Review Board, which – between 1977 and 1980 – found only 3 manuscripts unacceptable out of the more than 198 it reviewed. Authors withdrew an additional four manuscripts. Some portion of the controls instituted rested, not on national security concerns, but on public relations: on March 6, 1980, the CIA acknowledged to the House Intelligence Committee that it imposed stricter controls on its critics than on those who were part of the "old boy network."[367]

The Supreme Court considers the CIA's ability to create and enforce this program absolute and consistent with the Constitution. In 1975, for instance, Frank Snepp wrote the thriller *Decent Interval*, which the CIA claimed breached national security. The Court ruled that "even in the absence of an express agreement – the CIA could have acted to protect substantial government interests by imposing reasonable restrictions on employee activities that in other contexts might be protected by the First Amendment."[368] This ruling was extraordinary in that the Court made it without being presented with any evidence that the book had actually damaged national security.[369] Instead, the Court found, more broadly, that the CIA had a right to prevent publication. As Snepp had already published the manuscript, the Court ordered him to turn over to the government his earnings of $120,000 and to submit two manuscripts underway to the CIA.

This deference to the CIA extends – beyond pure publication and submission for review – to any requirements that it may place on authors. In the early 1970s, Victor Marchetti, an ex-CIA agent, submitted a co-written manuscript,

---

* The aborted effort, National Security Directive 84, *Safeguarding National Security Information*, available at www.fas.org, made employment where individuals had access to sensitive information conditional upon agreeing to lifetime prior review for any future publications. (The directive initially required that employees also submit to polygraphs as well, but under strong public pressure, the executive dropped this measure.) In 1981, Congress suspended the directive and held hearings on the subject. However, according to the General Accounting Office, at least 120,000 employees had already put their names on a lifetime censorship agreement – and to congressional horror, many had been asked to sign it *after* Congress had suspended the NSD. In February 1984, the executive withdrew the directive. As a result, instead of a blanket prohibition, individual agencies now require a nondisclosure agreement as a condition of employment.

The CIA and the Cult of Intelligence,[370] of which the reviewers directed him to remove approximately 15 percent to 20 percent.[371] Some of the required deletions – such as the sentence noting that Salvador Allende, a Marxist, was a central candidate in the Chilean election (prior to taking office) – simply related well-known public facts. After negotiations with Marchetti's attorney present, the CIA dropped 200 of the required deletions, leaving 168. The trial judge concluded that only 26 of these warranted censorship. The Fourth Circuit reversed, however, granting the CIA a "high presumption of regularity."[372]

Although the federal government has extensive authority to control employment in a manner that prevents speech supporting or possibly related to terrorist capabilities, it also has extensive power, outside of court documents, to control access to information already in its purview. The primary means through which it exercises this control is the classification scheme, which is based on the concept that secrecy breeds security. Classification is exercised by executive orders, a relatively recent phenomenon, not by congressional statutes.

Historically, classification lasted only one year unless the government made a further determination that declassification would threaten national security. Under President Jimmy Carter, classified information included data "owned by, produced for or by, or under the control of, the United States Government, and that has been determined pursuant to this Order or prior Orders to require protection against unauthorized disclosure."[373] Carter's order specifically excluded "basic scientific information not clearly related to the national security," as well as private research, conducted with open source material.[374] Where Nixon had allowed a 30-year automatic declassification, Carter created automatic declassification after 6 years, extendable up to 20 years. The order also emphasized the importance of balancing the public's right to know with identifiable damage that would be caused to national security.[375]

In 1982, President Ronald Reagan reversed the trend. Like Carter, Reagan endorsed three tiers: top secret, secret, and confidential; but in the third one, he eliminated the word "identifiable" from the harm reasonably expected to follow ("'Confidential' shall be applied to information, the unauthorized disclosure of which reasonably could be expected to cause damage to the national security").[376] The administration's chief concern was that it not have to identify a specific or precise damage that might follow from particular information being made public.[377] Thus, the default for "reasonable doubt" began to weigh in favor of secrecy – not of openness, as required under Carter. Reagan radically extended the period of classification from the six years established by Carter to indefinitely, subject to the discretion of national security officials.

After the attacks of 9/11, the US government immediately took steps to ensure that "sensitive but not classified" information under its control – even documents previously released into the public domain – be removed from public scrutiny. The State Department withdrew some 30 million pages of previously unclassified information and put the brakes on another 20 million pages already declassified and due to be released. The new review system created a five-year backlog.[378] The White House gave all federal offices until June 2002 to examine their Web sites for content that could be considered sensitive or pose a threat to public safety.[379] It required federal agencies to report their progress to the Office of Homeland Security. An avalanche of federal action swept from the Web documents relating to everything from environmental impact analyses to congressional reports.*

The percentage of government documents that are classified appears to be increasing annually, particularly in the past three years. The Information and Security Oversight Office reported that the government classified 11 million documents in 2002 and 14 million in 2003.[380] Although one might expect military operations to be accompanied by an increase in the information kept secret, some of the documents that are classified clearly violate the existing standards for what can and cannot be classified in times of war. For instance, section 1.7 of Executive Order 13292 requires that "[i]n no case shall information be classified in order to...conceal violations of law, inefficiency, or administrative error [or to] prevent embarrassment to a person, organization, or agency."[381] Yet the Taguba report on the torture of Iraqis (see Chapter 2), which found that "numerous incidents of sadistic, blatant, and wanton criminal abuses were inflicted on several detainees," was classified "secret."[382]

The most famous case dealing with classified documents suggests, though, that while the claim of national security may be necessary, it is not sufficient to prevent papers from entering the public domain. A high standard of proof must still be met to satisfy the burden of preventing publication.[383] In 1971, the *New York Times* and the *Washington Post* began to publish the Department of Defense's "History of U.S. Decision-Making Process on Viet Nam Policy,"[384] which provided penetrating insight into the war and made clear where the Nixon administration had lied to the American public about its operations overseas. The executive branch charged the newspapers with a violation of

---

* For example, the Agency for Toxic Substances and Disease Registry dropped a report critical of chemical plant security. Jay Lyman, *U.S. Pulls Information Off Web Since Attacks*, NEWSFACTOR NETWORK, October 4, 2001, available at www.newsfactor.com; *see also* Sabin Russel, *Watchdog Sites Shut Down in Interest of National Security*, NEWSFACTOR NETWORK, October 5, 2001. The Department of Energy, National Transportation of Radioactive Materials site replaced its text with the note: "This site temporarily unavailable, please contact Bobby Sanchez at 505 845 5541 if you have any questions." *See Chilling Effects of Anti-Terrorism: "National Security" Toll of Freedom of Expression*, ELECTRONIC FRONTIER FOUND, at www.eff.org (last visited July 17, 2005). The Bureau of Alcohol, Tobacco, Firearms, and Explosives withdrew pages and required that anyone seeking information send it a written request. *See ATF Online*, BUREAU OF ALCOHOL, TOBACCO, FIREARMS, AND EXPLOSIVES, at \ www.atf.treas.gov (last visited July 17, 2005). Citing increased security concerns, Congress suddenly classified three of the four Inspector General reports from the House of Representatives. *See Chilling Effects of Anti-Terrorism, supra.* The US Geological Survey required that more than 300 public and university libraries destroy material previously issued. *Federal Officials Order Libraries to Destroy CD-ROM with a Database on Public Water Supply*, STAR-TELEGRAM, Dec. 8, 2001. Steven Aftergood (who administers the Project on Government Secrecy for the Federation of American Scientists) pulled more than 200 pages off the Internet – such as floor plans of NSA and CIA facilities and images of foreign nuclear weapons plants. *See* David McGuire, *Anti-Secrecy Website Pulls Sensitive Information*, WASHINGTON POST.COM, Oct. 11, 2001.

the 1917 Espionage Act, which made it unlawful to publish, during war, any information the president declared was "of such character that it is or might be useful to the enemy," and filed for an injunction. Although the District Court refused to grant the request, the Second Circuit reversed that decision.

Within 18 days of the government filing, because of the unusual nature of the use of an injunction and the political importance of the documents, the Supreme Court held oral hearings and, 4 days later, handed down its decision. Six of the nine resulting opinions, and the *per curiam* (a decision issued on behalf of the Court and not attributable to any one justice), said the government had not met the "'heavy burden of showing justification'" for prior restraint on the press.[385] For the Court, the injunction amounted to a licensing scheme. The problem was that, regardless of whether it had been imposed unlawfully, its presence prevented the publisher from collateral attack – and thus created the odd situation that if the newspaper were to publish the account, and even if the government did not have the authority to prevent it from doing so, the publisher would still be held in violation of the law. While underscoring the strong presumption against prior restraints, however, the Court stopped short of creating a test tailored to the national security claim to justify such restrictions.[386] Over the objection of two justices (Justices Hugo Black and William O. Douglas) to *any* kind of prior restraint, the rest of the Court suggested that it might be justified if the state demonstrates with clear and convincing evidence that there would be an immediate and inescapable effect on national security.[387]

Although a sufficiently strong demonstration of harm to national security may satisfy the burden of proof for the imposition of prior restraint, a considerably lesser standard allows the state to prevent the disclosure of information relating to intelligence operations. Similarly, although the Espionage Act focused on the provision of information to foreign governments or saboteurs, information protected by security clearances falls under the statute – regardless of to whom it is given.[388] Thus, the United States charged Samuel Morison, an American intelligence agent who provided classified satellite photos to *Jane's Defense Weekly*, in London with theft of government property and espionage.[389] The state must demonstrate only that the information released is sufficiently "relating to the national defense."[390]*

The British Civil Service, *Spycatcher*, and the Official Secrets Act

Although, like the United States, the United Kingdom controls information within its purview through a nonstatutory classification system, it differs in the greater deference granted the British executive and the nature of the classification system itself. Underlying this distinction is a strong culture of secrecy,

---

* The government also has a broad capacity to restrict both public access to government property and press access to the military. *See* Barbara Cochran, *America's Free Press: Now More than Ever*, 4 THE CORNERSTONE PAPERS 1–2 (2002), available at www.mediainstitute.org.

discussed in the context of Chapter 4 as well, which manifests itself in various ways.[391]

Civil servants, for instance, act under strict limits – even in their personal capacity. Individuals in the "politically restricted" civil service category are not allowed to be parliamentary candidates, hold national office, or speak publicly on matters of national interest. Subject to the approval of the department, those who do *not*, as part of their work, speak on behalf of the government might be allowed to participate in local (but not national) politics. Upon receipt of permission to speak, civil servants must adopt only moderate positions. Limits on expression increase with rank.

In their professional capacity, civil servants fall under the Osmotherly Rules.[392] These bar officials from appearing before a select committee without ministerial approval, unless the committee issues a formal order. The official may not answer in his or her own right, but must respond in accord with how the minister directs.[393] The rules require that the official be helpful but refuse to answer where national security may be implicated. Thus, one cannot provide advice, address political controversies, reveal interdepartmental or interministerial communications, or discuss the level at which decisions have been made.

In addition to the Osmotherly Rules, upon entering, and once leaving, state employ, civil servants sign a nonlegal document that outlines conditions under which they might be subject to prosecution. Violations of this agreement result in breach of confidence and contempt of court proceedings – as demonstrated by the renowned *Spycatcher* case.[394] The courts, on this occasion, did not push back on the exercise of executive authority; to the contrary, the Law Lords accepted that an exceedingly general, long-term harm to the security services was sufficient to restrict former employees' speech – even when the information was already in the public domain.

The details of the case are relevant. From 1955 to 1976, Peter Wright worked for the British intelligence services.[395] When he joined and on his departure, he signed declarations that unless MI5 granted him explicit permission, or the information already existed in the public domain, he would not reveal information obtained during his employment.[396] Wright retired and moved to Tasmania, whence he sent a memo to the Chair of the Select Committee of the House of Commons requesting an inquiry into MI5.[397] He alleged the agency's involvement in an assassination attempt on the Egyptian president, in efforts to undermine Harold Wilson's government, and in burglaries of political party and trade union headquarters. Wright also reported that Sir Roger Hollis, the former head of MI5, was a double agent for the Soviet Union. Although this was not the first time such allegations had been made, Wright's position in the agency and the depth of details provided – as well as the timing – made the charges significant.[398] After Parliament made only cursory motions to address these issues, Wright decided to publish an exposé.[399]

In September 1985, the British government attempted to obtain an injunction. Wright agreed to wait to publish the account until the courts decided what to do.[400] In June 1986, the *Guardian* and the *Observer*, covering the legal proceedings, began to publicize Wright's allegations.[401] The Attorney General secured an injunction against the newspapers, which the Court of Appeal upheld. The court ordered that only information already in the public arena could be published. By March 1987, when it became clear that most of the data already were public, an Australian judge dismissed the injunction against Wright. The British government had *not* met the burden of demonstrating how the document would hurt national security.[402] In the interim, in April 1987, the *Melbourne Age*, the *Canberra Times*, the *Independent* (London), and two more British papers published synopses of the book – followed, in May 1987, by the *Washington Post*.[403] Claiming contempt of court, the British Attorney General immediately went after the British papers.[404] Soon afterward, Viking Penguin announced that the full account, *Spycatcher*, would be published in the United States.[405] Unable, because of the First Amendment, to go through American courts, Britain attempted to pressure the holding company that ran Viking not to publish the tract. The company refused to concede.

The editor of Britain's *Sunday Times* bought the rights to serialize the book and arranged for its publication in Britain. The first installment came out on the evening of July 12, 1987 – with a second publication the following morning – before the government could apply for an injunction. The next day, Viking published the entire work in the United States, where it became a best seller.[406] Although the Thatcher administration did not attempt to prevent import of the book, it continued to pursue contempt of court proceedings against the *Sunday Times*.[407] A series of appeals brought the case, at last, to the House of Lords, which not only upheld the decision to maintain an injunction but also insisted that even material publicly presented in the Australian courts could be enjoined.[408] As newspapers from Hong Kong to East Africa published excerpts, the Attorney General continued to pursue injunctions. These cases relied on the doctrine of breach of confidence and, relatedly, on contempt of court.[409]

The common law offense of breach of confidence, dating back to the Victorian period, focuses on publications of actual fact – not of opinion. The offense initially included matters relating to a broad range of communications, such as commerce, state information, and interfamilial conversations.[410] The modern formulation provides that "[i]f a defendant is proved to have used confidential information, directly or indirectly obtained from a plaintiff, without the consent, express or implied, of the plaintiff, he will be guilty of an infringement of the plaintiff's rights."[411] The elements include the confidentiality of the information, an obligation of confidence derived from circumstances in which the speech occurred, and breach of the obligation, without authorization, to the plaintiff's detriment.[412] Additionally, the information cannot already be public knowledge. Common law recognizes, however, that what might be public in some arena may nevertheless be confidential in another.[413] The court looks to the context to determine whether breach occurred.[414] Importantly, the charge does not require a formal contractual relationship.[415] To determine whether the offense has occurred, British courts balance the public interest in ensuring confidentiality with the public interest in having access to matters of public concern.[416]

Wright's duty centered on the facts that MI5 had employed him, and that national security interests required the state to prevent publications such as his from reaching the public domain.[417] The state claimed that the newspapers and publishers knew of this duty, and that they were required to meet it – making any breach a violation of their duty. Once the state enjoined the *Observer* and the *Guardian*, future efforts to publish would harm the substance of the suit, bringing such publications into contempt of court. The state's contention clearly did *not* turn on the secrecy of the information – 12 other books and 3 television programs had previously made the same allegations.[418] Instead, the national security interest at stake was to prevent others from publishing similar tell-all accounts, and thus revolved on the services' reputation and efficiency.

In sum, the Law Lords' finding suggests that a general, long-term prejudice to the reputation of the security services suffices to meet a national security claim. The case also demonstrates that contempt of court proceedings can be instituted with devastating effect.[419]*

The British state has no classification scheme equivalent to that of the United States; instead, it closes all government papers for 30 years. The Lord Chancellor may extend the period at the request or with the approval of the appropriate minister. Papers also may remain closed if a guarantee of confidence accompanied their receipt.[420] The basic mechanisms employed to protect closed papers are contempt of court proceedings (see page 323 et seq) and the Official Secrets Act (OSA). The latter, a criminal statute, dates back to 1889, when the

---

* A second, prominent case also demonstrates the extreme deference granted to the executive on issues of national security. In 1947, the British government founded an organization roughly similar to the US National Security Agency – the Government Communications Headquarters at Cheltenham – to conduct signals intelligence. By the late twentieth century, the GCHQ employed approximately 4,000 people, approximately 25 percent of whom conducted a one-day strike in 1981. See *Regina* v. *Secretary of State ex parte Council of Civil Service Unions*, [1984] I.R.L.R. 309 (Q.B. July 17, 1984), *rev'd*, [1984] T.L.R., No. 518 (C.A.), *aff'd* sub nom. *Council of Civil Serv. Unions v. Minister for the Civil Service*, [1985] A.C. 374 (1984). Although the British state did not want labor strikes to harm its intelligence functions, one small problem presented itself: the state had never admitted that the GCHQ conducted intelligence. In a 1983 paper, the government thus made passing reference to it – paving the way for the Minister for the Civil Service, in March 1984, to ban people working at the GCHQ from joining a union. The Council of Civil Service Unions, which represented six unions at the GCHQ, strenuously objected. Although the first court held that the government had to consult with the employees and their unions when rights were affected, the government won on appeal. The court's decision centered on a separation of powers claim: Lord Chief Justice Geoffrey Lane asserted that although other areas of Royal Prerogative might be fair game, the court could not inquire into "any action taken . . . which can truly be said to have been taken in the interests of national security." Charles D. Ablard, *Judicial Review of National Security Decisions: United States and United Kingdom*, 27 WM. & MARY L. REV. 753, 759 (1986) (citing [1984] T.L.R., No. 518 (C.A.)) The Law Lords upheld the decision of the lower court, saying that while normally the employees would have a legitimate expectation of consultation, under the excuse of national security the decision lay entirely in the realm of the executive.

legislation did not recognize "public good" as a defense. In 1911, on the brink of war, Westminster expanded the statute and rushed the bill through Parliament; subsequently, law enforcement applied OSA's powers to individuals who had nothing to do with the purpose for which the law was introduced. For instance, section 1 made it an offense for anyone "for any purpose prejudicial to the safety or interests of the state" to be in a military area or to obtain or communicate to anyone any information "which is calculated to be or might be or is intended to be directly or indirectly useful to an enemy."[421] Although Westminster intended this section to be used to prevent espionage, law enforcement later used it against the Campaign for Nuclear Disarmament, which gained access to intelligence and military facilities.[422]

Section 2 of the 1911 Act became notorious. Applying to *all* civil servants, it specified that any person *having information* in his or her possession by virtue of a contractual or employment relationship with the Crown could not communicate such information without authorization to anyone except for the person to whom state interests created a duty of disclosure. So, for instance, telling one's spouse the type of biscuits one ate at work qualified as an "official secret"; and both the employee *and* the spouse would be in violation of the statute.

Although this example may seem outrageous, the Law Reports show that national security does not have to be directly implicated for an individual to be found guilty.[423] From 1945 to 1971, the state used the OSA somewhat sparingly, with 23 prosecutions, 34 defendants, and 27 convictions;[424] and gradually, the charge fell into disrepute. However, in 1978, the state renewed its efforts, resulting in 29 prosecutions and 5 pending prosecutions over the next nine years.[425] The OSA proved to be both overinclusive and inefficient, as it blocked important information from reaching members of Parliament.

Three cases brought under the OSA demonstrate that the state frequently used its powers to save the government from embarrassment. For instance, in October 1983, Sarah Tisdall, a clerk at the Ministry of Defence, gave the *Guardian* a memo that reported the date on which American cruise missiles would reach the Royal Air Force Base at Greenham Common.[426] Although the court considered the *Guardian*'s defense – that the 1981 Contempt of Court Act laid out a "source protection law" that allowed the public release of information in the interests of national security – it ultimately rejected this claim on the grounds that someone had stolen the property to put it into the newspaper's hands.[427] The *Guardian* appealed. The House of Lords recognized that the actual memo was of little value and did not represent an attempt to undermine national security.[428] Nevertheless, three of the five Law Lords found that the evidence met the burden of necessity. Their decision drew heavily from the government's affidavit, which asserted, *inter alia*, that although *this* memo might not have represented a direct threat to national security, it would undermine allies' future confidence in the United Kingdom.[429] This claim, however, somewhat contradicted the substance of the memo, which was the blatant recognition of the political nature of the information and the recommendation that the date of arrival be kept secret – even from Parliament – until after the United States delivered the missiles.

A second case underscored the use of the OSA to hide state debacles and prevent members of Parliament from obtaining information. During the 1982 Falklands War, the British Navy sunk the *General Belgrano*, an Argentinian cruiser, killing 360 people.[430] An internal Ministry of Defence document showed that, contrary to the government's claim, the ship was *leaving* the exclusion zone when the Navy attacked. When, in May 1983, Tam Dalyell, a Labour MP, questioned Michael Heseltine, Secretary of State for Defence, about the incident, the latter refused to provide any information. Clive Ponting, who worked at the Ministry of Defence, gave the document to Dalyell. Ponting, who at the tender age of 38 had already been awarded an Order of the British Empire, said, "I did this because I believe that ministers within this department were not prepared to answer legitimate questions from a member of Parliament about a question of considerable public concern, simply in order to protect their own political position."[431]

The government initially prosecuted Ponting under the 1911 Official Secrets Act. But partway through the trial, after admitting that the document did not compromise national security, the state switched to the claim of breach of confidentiality. Heavy politics plagued the proceedings: for example, the Special Branch vetted more than 60 potential jurors – and, in the process, removed from service people whom noted scholars Keith Ewing and Conor Gearty accurately refer to as "dangerously independent minded persons."[432] During the trial, Merlyn Rees, former Secretary of State for Northern Ireland, supported Ponting, saying that civil servants' ultimate duty was to Parliament. The trial judge, Anthony McCowan, disagreeing, directed the jury that Ponting's duty was to the minister and did not extend to Parliament. The judge further suggested that whatever the government *claims* to be an issue of national security *makes* it national security.[433] Jurors, disgusted by the government's actions, acquitted.

The final case came to be known as the Zircon affair. In 1987, the BBC Documentary series *The Secret Society* revealed that the Ministry of Defence had neglected to mention to Parliament the introduction of a new £500 million electronic surveillance program.[434] The BBC, under government pressure, pulled the film. Although the filmmaker, Duncan Campbell, arranged for it to be shown in Parliament, at the last minute the government pressured the Speaker, who intervened to cancel the showing and referred the case to the Committee.

The Opposition was irate. Although Prime Minister Thatcher had obtained an injunction against Campbell, the filmmaker went on the run; and before he could be served, full details of the footage appeared in the *New Statesman*. Thatcher was scathing: "Unfortunately [] there seem to be people with more interest in trying to ferret out and reveal information of use to our enemies, rather than preserving the defence interest of this country, and thus the freedom which we all enjoy."[435] The Special Branch raided Campbell's home, the *New Statesman*'s offices, the home of a researcher working on the film, and the BBC – ostensibly for violation of the OSA. It also confiscated the remaining five films in the series, although the state did not allege that these other documentaries breached the OSA.

The state's response to these cases emphasized the notion that a civil servant's first responsibility is to the government in power, *not* to Parliament or to the public.

In 1985, Sir Robert Armstrong, the Cabinet Secretary, issued *The Duties and Responsibilities of Civil Servants in Relation to Ministers*.[436] Then, in 1989, the government wrote a new Official Secrets Act. Seen by one member of the House of Lords as owing rather "too much to obsessive resentment at the outcome of the *Spycatcher* and *Ponting* cases,"[437] the statute provided criminal sanctions for national security violations falling under any of the following classes of information: security and intelligence, defense, international relations, crime, or special investigation powers. It also outlawed any actual or potential harm to state interests – as determined by the government of the day. While mere receipt of information became insufficient to establish a violation of the law, further disclosure – either by an employee or by a member of the public – became illegal.[438] The state again used extraordinary procedures: after only two days in committee, the government guillotined this legislation.[439]

Professor David Feldman, a prominent British legal scholar, speculates in his exhaustive 2002 review of British civil liberties whether the new Official Secrets Act runs afoul of Article 10 of the ECHR, under which, for interference to be justified, the state must demonstrate the necessity of the measure in a democratic state. A two-pronged test applies: first, the response must be proportionate to a pressing social need to pursue a legitimate aim, and second, it must be compatible with liberal, democratic values.[440] Not only does the 1989 OSA not require that national security be damaged but it also prevents a defendant from demonstrating that his or her actions reflect a legitimate public interest. Feldman points to this last as evidence that the statute does *not* balance rights and interests in a matter compatible with the ECHR. The domestic statute captures anything in an individual's possession, regardless of whether it is still confidential. Feldman highlights the underlying concern that such legislation simply becomes a tool for state power: "successive governments have made selective use of secrecy obligations, authorizing disclosure, usually on a non-attributable basis, of information they wanted to be made public, and prosecuting when a disclosure disadvantaged them politically."[441]

The *Spycatcher* case did go to the European Court of Human Rights where a unanimous decision held against the United Kingdom. As Lord Lester of Herne related to the House of Commons, the European court ruled that the government's actions constituted a violation of Wright's right to free expression: the "restriction imposed by the British courts was not necessary in a democratic society, was disproportionate, was not reasonably proportionate to protect the legitimate aim of the state."[442]

The House of Lords recently considered another case that brought into sharp relief the relationship between the 1989 Official Secrets Act and the 1998 Human Rights Act. David Michael Shayler, a member of the Security Service from November 1991 to October 1996, signed an OSA declaration recognizing the sensitive nature of the information to which he was privy. Upon his departure from MI5, he signed a second OSA statement and swore that he had turned over all documents acquired during his service. Over the next year, however, Shayler made available to the *Mail on Sunday* documents that ranged from "classified" to "top secret." In August 1997, Shayler fled Britain for Paris; and soon thereafter, the paper published a series of articles by him and by journalists who had had the opportunity to read the sensitive documents. France refused extradition. Three years later, he returned to Britain to claim that his disclosures had been in the public and national interests: "I . . . rely on my right of freedom of expression as guaranteed by the common law, the Human Rights Act and Article 10 of the European Convention on Human Rights."[443]

The House of Lords, upholding the lower courts' decisions, announced that the defendant could *not* rely on the claim that disclosure served the national interest, and that sections 1(1) and 4 of the 1989 OSA did not permit this defense. Nor did this claim burden the prosecution to demonstrate that the release of the information *was* in the public interest. The 1989 OSA restrictions echoed the objectives of Article 10(2) of the ECHR: the limits were prescribed by law, directed to the protection of national security (a legitimate aim), and necessary for a democratic society to operate.* In determining the latter, in accordance with the European Court's decision in *Shayler*, the Lords looked to proportionality – whether "the interference complained of corresponded to a pressing social need, whether it was proportionate to the legitimate aim pursued and whether the reasons given by the national authority to justify it [were] relevant and sufficient under article 10(2)."[444] Lord Bingham wrote, "The acid test is whether, in all the circumstances, the interference with the individual's convention right prescribed by national law is greater than is required to meet the legitimate object which the state seeks to achieve."[445] Lord Hope of Craighead noted the special place of terrorism in the calculus of proportionality:

Long before the horrific events of 11 September 2001 in New York and Washington it was recognised by the European Court of Human Rights that democratic societies are threatened by highly sophisticated forms of espionage and by terrorism. The court held that they have to be able to take measures which will enable them to counter such

---

* The Lords cited the following European cases to support the claim to secrecy for efforts related to counterterrorism, criminal activity, hostile activity, and subversion: *Engel v. The Netherlands*, App. No. 5100/71, 1 Eur. H.R. Rep. 647, paras. 100–03 (1976); *Klass v. Federal Republic of Germany*, App. No. 5029/71, 2 Eur. H.R. Rep. 214, para. 48 (1978); *Leander v. Sweden*, App. No. 9248/81, 9 Eur. H.R. Rep. 433, para. 59 (1987); *Hadjianastassiou v. Greece*, App. No. 12945/87, 16 Eur. H.R. Rep. 219, paras. 45–47 (1992); *Esbester v. United Kingdom*, 18 Eur. H.R. Rep. CD 72, CD 74 (1994); *Brind v. United Kingdom*, 18 Eur. H.R. Rep. CD 76, CD 83–84 (1994); *Murray v. United Kingdom*, 19 Eur. H.R. Rep. 193, para. 58 (1994); *Vereniging Weekblad Bluf! v. The Netherlands*, App. No. 16616/90, 20 Eur. H.R. Rep. 189, paras. 35–40 (1995); *Shayler*, [2002] UKHL 11 at para. 26. According to the Lords, these decisions "insist on adequate safeguards to ensure that the restriction does not exceed what is necessary to achieve the end in question." *Shayler*, [2002] UKHL 11 at para. 26.

threats effectively. But it stressed in the same case that it must be satisfied that there exist adequate and effective guarantees that such measures will not be abused.[446]

The 1989 OSA did not completely restrict freedom of expression – rather, it only banned the release of the information in the absence of lawful authority to the contrary. Under the legislation, Shayler could have disclosed the information to a staff counselor, the Attorney General, the Director of Public Prosecutions, the commissioner of Metropolitan Police, the prime minister, or other ministers. If any one of these individuals had not taken effective steps to redress the grievance, Shayler could have sought official authorization to make the information available to a wider audience. If he had been refused without appropriate justification, he could have sought judicial review. The 1989 OSA had been designed to prevent unlawfulness or irregular behavior from going unreported. But employees had to go through these steps first – they could not immediately jump to public disclosure.

The extreme deference given to the executive in cases involving national security echoes a common refrain: "In the paradigm national security case, the outcome of a governmental application to restrain publication is likely to be a foregone conclusion in favour of the government."[447] As Lord Diplock commented, action required to ensure national security "is, par excellence, a non-justiciable question."[448] In other words, if the British government makes a content-based national security claim, the judicial track record suggests it will likely be successful.[449]

Calculating Costs

It is not just where the government already holds the information that deference to the executive branch, on both sides of the Atlantic, is shown. Yet bowing to the executive and allowing it to impose speech restrictions may carry enormous costs – well outside the traditional security or freedom framework.

Consider knowledge-based speech. The Invention Secrecy Act, the Atomic Energy Act, and the *Progressive* case came to define the American nuclear era. For fissile material, such protections may have made sense: speech restrictions introduced at the advent of the Cold War bought time to establish an international nonproliferation regime. The bomb had just been developed, and it was in the US national interest to prevent other actors from acquiring it. A short-term monopoly was possible. The invention's primary use was as a weapon. The science involved was complex, and its application limited. The stakes were high, and little would be gained by making the information widely available.*

---

* The atomic issue has not gone away. The British and American governments claim that al Qaeda is developing nuclear capabilities. In November 2001, US Special forces recovered documents from an al Qaeda house in Kabul that provided information on how to build nuclear weapons. A May 2003 unclassified report issued by the CIA Intelligence Directorate asserted that extremist organizations associated with al Qaeda "have a wide variety of potential agents and delivery means to choose from for chemical, biological and radiological or nuclear (CBRN) attacks."

Biological speech – and the issues surrounding it – presents an entirely different matter. It is not possible to establish a monopoly on biological research. Microbiology is ubiquitous, fundamental to the improvement of global public health, and central to the international development of industries such as pharmaceuticals and plastics. Whereas it is in the national interest to prevent terrorist organizations from obtaining biological weapons, it is not in the national interest to stunt research into (more likely) naturally occurring disease. The science involved, in contrast to the atomic project, is incremental – and each step has far-reaching implications. Dangerous as biological weapons may be, the dangers of restricting the information are equally great or greater. And unlike nuclear weapons, much may be *gained* by making biological data widely available.[450]

Naturally occurring diseases, for instance, wreak havoc on an extraordinary scale. In 1918, a natural outbreak of the flu infected one-fifth of the world's population and, within two years, killed more than 650,000 Americans. Twenty-five percent of the US population – some 20 million people – caught the virus, with a resultant 10-year drop in the average lifespan of an American citizen.[451] Nor is the threat posed by naturally occurring illnesses merely an artifact of history: every year, 5,000 people in the United States die from food-borne pathogens.[452] An extraordinarily large number of diseases exist, for which no treatment, much less a cure, has been found.[453]

Broad limits on research, or on publication of research, on the most deadly of these diseases might limit the information available to terrorist groups and organizations bent on destruction. But it may also prevent legitimate research into natural health threats. More than two decades ago, the American National Academy of Sciences recognized the unique, international character of biological research: informal global communication networks – such as circulation of material prior to publication, discussions at meetings, special seminars, and personal conversations – characterize the discipline.[454] Microbiology, perhaps more than any other scientific discipline, is both international *and* incremental: each advance depends upon the others' findings and access to their method of research.

Perhaps the best example centers on the mousepox case, already discussed. Because the research entered the public domain, and was not limited to just the Australian military and political realm (as it was initially), scientists around the world were able to begin working on the vulnerability. In November 2003, St. Louis University announced that it had uncovered an effective medical defense against a pathogen similar to, but more deadly than, that created in Australia. Funded by a grant from the American National Institute of Allergy and

Central Intelligence Agency, *Terrorist CBRN: Materials and Effects*, available at www.cia.gov (last visited Sept. 11, 2005); *see also* Bill Gertz, *CIA Says al Qaeda Ready to Use Nukes*, WASH. TIMES, June 3, 2003, available at www.washtimes.com. In January 2003, British officials showed members of the BBC material obtained from undercover agents in Afghanistan, who indicated that al Qaeda was obtaining radioactive isotopes from the Taliban to help construct a dirty bomb. Frank Gardner, *Al-Qaeda "Was Making Dirty Bomb,"* BBC NEWS WORLD EDITION, Jan. 31, 2003, available at www.news.bbc.co.uk.

Infectious Diseases, the project used mousepox and cowpox to determine what sort of genetic alteration to the human smallpox virus would make it more lethal to humans.[455] *New Scientist*, a British magazine, reported the new research.[456]

The idea that states are *more* likely to find solutions to vulnerability through free speech is not new. In the early 1980s, the joint Panel on Scientific Communication and National Security – created by the American National Academy of Sciences, the National Academy of Engineering, and the Institute of Medicine – addressed precisely this issue. After three classified briefings and numerous presentations from government and academia, the panel concluded that "security by secrecy" was untenable. Their report called instead for "security by accomplishment" – ensuring technological strength through advancing scientific research.[457]

It is time to think differently on both sides of the Atlantic about speech restrictions and to carefully consider the full costs of introducing them, with the intent of heading off a short-term terrorist threat – when what is at stake may be far more profound.

6

Auxiliary Precautions

"If men were angels, no government would be necessary. If angels were to govern men, neither external nor internal controls on government would be necessary. In framing a government which is to be administered by men over men, the great difficulty lies in this: you must first enable the government to control the governed; and in the next place oblige it to control itself."

James Madison, Federalist No. 51

The big question now is, What have we gained in terms of national security in return for the enormous price we have paid for counterterrorist law? There is no clear answer to this question.

It is possible that some of the provisions have been extremely helpful in curbing the threat. On June 15, 2004, MI5 placed under surveillance Dhiren Barot, also known as Abu Esa al Britani.[1] The Security Services subsequently lost track of him, but when a laptop captured in Pakistan revealed his involvement in a terrorist plot, authorities decided to capture him as soon as he resurfaced – as he did, in August.[2] A counterterrorist official later admitted, "It is no exaggeration to say that, at the time of the arrest, there was little or no admissible evidence against Barot."[3] But special powers of detention bought the state time to find enough material to bring charges; and over the next two years, careful examination of nearly 300 computers, 1,800 disks, CDs and hard drives, and other materials helped build a watertight case.[4] Barot, along with a number of co-conspirators, had been planning 11 simultaneous, coordinated attacks in Britain that ranged from packing limousines with gas cylinders and detonating a dirty bomb, to blowing up a device under the River Thames to flood the underground.[5] His primary aim was to "inflict mass damage and chaos" – on both the United Kingdom and the United States, where Barot had conducted reconnaissance and developed plans to bomb the International Monetary Fund and the World Bank in Washington, D.C., the Prudential building in New Jersey, and the New York Stock Exchange.[6] In November 2006, British courts sentenced Barot to life imprisonment.[7]

Barot's case became public, yet other benefits that follow from measures discussed in the preceding chapters may remain cloaked from view: the indefinite detention of noncitizens within the United States immediately after 9/11, or the control orders placed on prominent extremists in the United Kingdom in 2005, for instance, may have similarly interrupted terrorist cells before they could develop and execute plans to attack either country. Such outcomes may be known only to intelligence agencies and individuals with high-level clearances.

On the other hand, it may be hard to calculate gains with certainty. The tools used for analysis may be inadequate to the complexity of the task. Accounting measures in antiterrorist finance, for instance, rely on traditional money laundering metrics, which emphasize the total amount of money frozen and say little about whether the right people are being targeted or how important those who become caught in the system are to the flow of terrorist funds. Nor do they reveal the level of operations thereby aborted, if any are.

Of course, it also may be that we are gaining little or no benefit from some of the security measures I have discussed. The library provisions of the USA PATRIOT Act, for instance, have never been used by the state – nor have the property seizure laws introduced in the wake of the Omagh bombing in Northern Ireland. Yet both have become a permanent part of both countries' counterterrorist regimes. They may be acting as a deterrent – or they may not be. In other areas, such as coercive questioning, limited benefits may be substantially outweighed by the drawbacks.

It is not sufficient, however, to assume either that no counterterrorist laws work, or that they are all responsible for either the absence or the relatively isolated occurrence of attacks. Rather, calculating the benefits of the provisions – like calculating their costs – requires a nuanced approach.

What is clear is that, in both states, the executive has profited from counterterrorist law. Its strength relative to the other branches has grown, even as its absolute power in terms of what it can do with impunity to American citizens and British subjects has expanded. In the meantime, society has suffered: the measures have had harmful social, political, and economic effects. The provisions have narrowed not just one right, but a range of rights.

Concern about executive strength in the face of threats to national security is hardly new. James Madison revived the debate in Federalist No. 51, calling for the ratification of the US Constitution on the grounds that it was not enough simply to give the government the power to obtain order. It was also necessary to give it the ability to control itself. Although "[a] dependence on the people is, no doubt the primary control on the government," Madison warned, "experience has taught mankind the necessity of auxiliary precautions." What form ought such auxiliary precautions take to mitigate the risks, specifically, of counterterrorism?

It is important to try to create safeguards within the executive. The tradition in both countries, for instance, of protecting the independence of administrative agencies, may help offset political pressures to turn the bureaucracy to political advantage. Fortifying structural and cultural divisions between agencies may help check the exercise of power as well. It will be recalled that the United

Kingdom's administrative warrant system for surveillance, although not without its faults, requires that Home Office civil servants, who act independently of the intelligence services, laterally approve applications from MI5, MI6, and the Government Communications Headquarters. They also must make their case for approval vertically within their own organization. After the surveillance has occurred, intelligence agencies again debrief civil servants in other agencies to let them know whether it has yielded the expected results. In the United States, the Office of Management and Budget is in a position – owing to its recent effort to get intelligence agencies to use more complex performance standards (to determine the value of assets or targets, or to calibrate the information obtained relative to the counterterrorist aims of each organization)[8] – to potentially audit the exercise of surveillance.

These are just examples of checks that could be instituted within the executive – an immensely complex problem that deserves further scrutiny. Yet I am skeptical about the ability of the executive, as an organ, to limit its quest for more power. After all, because it falls directly to this branch to take responsibility for crime and threats to national security, it is to be expected that it would seek the broadest range of powers available.

The judiciary also has an important role to play in setting the limits of state authority. It was *Brandenburg* v. *Ohio* that established protections for political speech in the United States (see Chapter 5),[9] whereas *Hamdan* v. *Rumsfeld* restricted executive expansion in the context of habeas claims (see Chapter 2).[10] On the other side of the Atlantic, *A and others* v. *Secretary of State for the Home Department* led to the repeal of indefinite detention (see Chapter 2).[11] The courts' role, though, ought not to be overemphasized, as their ability to check the executive is, as I have shown, limited. And most of the remedies available to the courts are inadequate for stemming expansions in counterterrorist law. In other words, we should care about what the judiciary does and says, but not assume that it is the most important player, or even the final word, in respect to counterterrorism.

Instead, I see the legislature as the crucial player. This body acts as an enabler, providing the executive with legal legitimacy. It is the most representative of the people. It can lead and respond to them. And it has the authority to hold the government to account for the immediate and ongoing need for extraordinary provisions. The legislature can demand that the executive show that the powers are being used appropriately and demonstrate the efforts being made to mitigate the broader costs. Insisting that the government makes its case, releasing into the public domain whatever it can of relevant information, reverses the usual course of counterterrorism – where the executive is able to put through many of its demands immediately following a terrorist attack, leaving to those who find the provisions excessive and want to repeal them the impossible task of proving either that no violence will follow repeal or that some violence is acceptable. The legislature has the power to reverse the counterterrorist spiral.

I thus conclude this book by offering a series of recommendations that might help the legislative branch in each country address – within their respective constitutional constraints – the problems raised by counterterrorism measures and the expansion of executive power. I suggest that the legislatures should foster a culture of restraint; make sunset provisions a matter of last resort; reinforce transparency and accountability; draw a sharp line between criminal law, terrorism, and war; and discourage measures that further reduce the effectiveness or role of the courts. Although other options also flow from the history I have presented, these five are among the most pressing and offer, I believe, the strongest means of addressing these urgent problems.

My aim is to mitigate the costs of security measures without seriously reducing the government's ability to respond to real threats – ones that may be catastrophic. For what makes this issue critical at this moment is that, while both states have thus far responded to conventional terrorist threats, biological or nuclear weapons are hanging like a specter over the discussion. Five people died from anthrax attacks in 2001.[12] What would either the British or the American state look like if there were a biological attack and the number of deaths dramatically increased? In this chapter, I recommend several ways the legislative systems in both states can check the executive, mitigate the broader costs, and give each country the necessary flexibility to address terrorist threats.

RE-EMPOWERING THE LEGISLATURE

There is tension between the principles of democratic accountability and advocating that the legislature be less responsive to public demand. Yet, although we usually want our elected representatives to reflect public opinion, we do not necessarily want that following a terrorist attack. The aim of terrorism is to terrify people; and when people are afraid, they are likely to make hasty, short-sighted decisions. At such times, it is the legislature's task to weigh decisions carefully before cementing them into law.

With that task in mind, the legislature can mediate between representative democracy and the pressures of terrorism by emphasizing a culture of restraint that resists extraordinary procedures and encourages the immediate institution of an inquiry following a terrorist attack. It can reject sunset provisions and insist instead on obligatory reporting and stringent oversight. The legislature can reinforce transparency and accountability by strengthening the freedom of information regime in both states – and keeping the classification procedures firmly in sight. It can exercise vigilance in maintaining the lines between criminal law and counterterrorism, as well as within national security itself. And it can demonstrate a strong reluctance to alter judicial rules or to allow the executive to move into the judicial realm.

Fostering a Culture of Restraint

Perhaps the most important means of mitigating the adverse effects of counterterrorist provisions on either side of the Atlantic is to ensure that, before expanding the authorities available, each legislative body avoids extraordinary procedures and engages in thoughtful deliberation. Indeed, so quickly do legislatures – not just in America and Britain, but in other countries facing terrorism – tend to answer violence with provisions passed under extraordinary procedures, and so harmful are the subsequent effects of many of those provisions, that I feel that extraordinary procedures should be allowed only in the rarest of circumstances. And even then, the burden should be on the executive to demonstrate that *each* power it is requesting cannot be achieved by regular legislative action. Omnibus bills should not be rushed through, without due consideration for each of the many expansions in power being demanded; measures previously rejected precisely because of concerns about their impact on rights should be scrutinized even more closely. In brief, abbreviated procedures make for bad law. The more that legislators reject extraordinary procedures, they less likely are they to pass destructive laws.

This suggestion, I realize, goes against the tide: immediately after an attack, legislators are under enormous pressure not only to act, but, as I have said, to be seen to act, to respond. The immediate institution of an inquiry and the legislature's clear determination to hold hearings to gather information may help satisfy this public demand. Such an inquiry would have the benefit of independent evaluation and access to information at its most raw – treating the state's response to the terrorist (crime) as, in essence, an investigation. An inquiry may help prevent extraordinary powers from being rushed through without thoughtful consideration of their possible consequences and how they would be used for nonterrorist-related affairs. It may generate hard data for legislators, giving them a more concrete basis on which to determine the appropriate mechanisms needed for a long-term response to the threat. It may also require the government to demonstrate why certain provisions are necessary to respond to terrorism: that is, it may force the state to show that the costs are worth bearing, instead of immediately shifting to legislators the responsibility of demonstrating that the absence of the powers will not necessarily lead to more terrorism.

This proposal has precedent: within a week of the July 2005 London bombings, the United Kingdom's Intelligence and Security Committee wrote to the prime minister to inform him that it planned to conduct an inquiry.[13] The oversight body subsequently examined the government's counterterrorism strategy prior to July 7 and the nature and limitations of intelligence available at the time. It asked whether any intelligence was missed or overlooked and assessed the threat, the use of threat level designation systems, and how the state responded in the immediate aftermath of the attacks. Within 10 months of the attacks, the committee issued a public report. The sensitive nature of the ongoing criminal investigations did not create an insurmountable barrier: some of the information was held *sub judice* – under consideration by the court. Nor was the political nature of the issues to be tackled an obstacle. If anything, political sensitivities were higher than they might otherwise be, as the Labour government had *lowered* the threat level designation prior to the attacks. The inquiry addressed the concern that such an action might be seen as almost unpatriotic by highlighting that the fact of an investigation did "not overshadow the

essential and excellent work the Agencies have undertaken against the terrorist threat in the UK."[14] Theirs, moreover, was not the only such inquiry: in
September 2005, the London Assembly established a 7 July Review Committee
to focus on what lessons could be learned.[15] The Home Office also put together
an "Official Account" of the event.[16]

Not only is the institution of an inquiry tenable, but legislators can rise to the
occasion and refuse to pass measures without appropriate consideration. This
book opens with Representative James Sensenbrenner (R.-WI) drawing a red
line through the suspension of habeas corpus, as written into the first draft of the
USA PATRIOT Act. Sensenbrenner and Representative John Conyers (D.-MI)
subsequently went to great lengths, in the House Judiciary Committee, to craft
a law that introduced protections against abuse for every right subsequently
restricted. The executive branch, however, outmaneuvered Sensenbrenner and
Conyers and managed to introduce into the Senate a parallel bill that became
the nation's counterterrorist law. Unwilling to be seen as soft on terror, Congress
acquiesced.

Replacing Sunset Provisions with Obligatory Reporting Requirements

Although sunset provisions give the illusion of control, they actually reduce the
power of the legislature. The understanding is that, when the measures return,
the executive will have to make its case to retain the new authorities – which
the executive says are absolutely essential in the interim to fight off the short-
term threat. But the way it actually works is that, at the time of renewal, it is
extremely difficult for members of the legislature not to continue the temporary authorities. Not only did they previously vote *for* the measures – binding
them to their past decisions, but the burden shifts to those trying to oppose
the government to demonstrate that withdrawing the powers will not lead to
terrorism. Alternatively, they could argue that some level of terrorism is acceptable. But the former is impossible to prove and the latter politically untenable.
Either one supports the government seeking to extend the authorities that, the
public is assured, have been indispensable in the struggle against terrorism or
one is accused of helping the terrorists.

The language is infused with patriotism – and a moral quality. At the introduction of the 1974 Prevention of Terrorism Bill, Lord Hailsham, Lord Chancellor in Edward Heath's Conservative government, urged his fellow peers, "Apart
from [the Bill's] practical value . . . its moral impact is hardly less important and
would, I fear, be considerably blunted if we did not accede to the Government's
request to enable the Bill to receive the Royal Assent so as to place it on the
Statute Book tomorrow."[17] Withdrawing provisions therefore becomes seen as
retiring from the fight. Thus Lord Jellicoe later reported that proscription, one
of the measures in the 1974 statute, "enshrines in legislation public aversion to
organisations which use, and espouse, violence as a means to a political end."[18]
Sir George Baker similarly wrote in somewhat more colorful terms: "Proscription is an expression of the outrage of the ordinary citizen, who comprises the

overwhelming majority, at the barbarous acts of these organisations, and at the revolting glee with which they claim responsibility."[19] For, like British measures, those introduced in Northern Ireland also carried strong moral import. "I welcome the [Northern Ireland (Emergency Provisions) Act]," the Reverend Ian Paisley explained, "because it is a signal to the men of violence that the Government will not weaken in their fight."[20] Such statements continue to permeate the counterterrorist dialogue. The Labour Prime Minister Tony Blair, for instance, emphasized repeatedly in 2006 that the provisions banning the Glorification of Terrorism were important for the message they sent (see Chapter 5). And although the presentational aspect of counterterrorist law matters, the political stakes are high: thus, Nicholas Hawkins, who served in the Tory government in the Ministry of Defense, announced in Parliament, "Unless and until [Labour] support the Government on every piece of anti-terrorist legislation, the voters of Britain will never take seriously any of the weasel words of Labour Party's policy on crime. If the Opposition will not support us on measures against terrorism, they cannot be taken seriously."[21]

Because so much of the counterterrorist dialogue is cloaked in secrecy, the government rarely releases information showing just how helpful – or unhelpful – certain provisions are. Nor is there particularly strong pressure on the state to do so – especially when met by claims from the executive branch that even statistical reporting would undermine the state's counterterrorist efforts. Thus Britain refused to release the total number of wiretaps placed in Northern Ireland – and the Bush administration repeatedly ignored congressional efforts to find out even basic statistics on the exercise of delayed-notice search warrants. Even where measures have gone completely unused – such as indefinite detention in the United Kingdom in the 1980s, or the library provisions of the USA PATRIOT Act – and the legislators are so informed by the executive branch, such powers are *still* continued.

Not only are the measures not repealed, but the quality of the discussion substantially changes at the renewal debates. These debates tend to be ill attended and lack the energy that accompanies the initial introduction of a statute. What was extraordinary often becomes unexceptional.

In fact, by making powers temporary, the question changes: instead of asking what criminal law or national security provisions should be permanently entrenched – and, as a result, what safeguards must be included – legislators ask only what is necessary, in the short term, to address a specific threat. In other words, sunsetting takes the place of insisting on sufficient reporting requirements and oversight mechanisms.

This dynamic is so common as to lead me to conclude that under almost no circumstances ought sunsetting be allowed. I recognize that sometimes making powers temporary does help: it was because the USA PATRIOT Act provisions had to be renewed that Congress was able to revisit the use of National Security Letters and demand that the Inspector General issue a report on the matter. When that report was filed, it was revealed that the counterterrorist authority had become a routine tool for ordinary criminal investigations. This instance, and examples discussed in the previous chapters, suggest to me, though, that *it is the reporting requirement* that brings this information to light and then allows legislators to act. It also appears that, by integrating accountability into the law up front, the political implications of unified government, at least in the American context, may be somewhat mitigated. What keeps legislators from demanding regular reporting and clear lines of accountability is the assumption that sunset provisions will suffice to hold the executive accountable. But by enacting sunset clauses, legislators tie their own hands. The time period that lapses also matters: five years after the powers are introduced – or even two years, the typical period advocated for temporary powers – is late in the game to revisit how they are being used.

As for reporting requirements, what sorts of demands ought to be made on the executive branch? Legislators need to have information on how the powers are being used, whether and what level of terrorist operations are being interrupted, and to what extent the powers are bleeding over to other areas of the law. Mitigation steps also would prove helpful – that is, how the executive is taking steps to alleviate the adverse political, social, and economic effects of the provisions – as well as what less intrusive approaches have been tried or, if they have not, why they are not viable alternatives to more intrusive authorities.

To whom the reports are made, and whether they are public or not, also matters. Consider the US National Security Agency's warrantless surveillance of persons within the United States – the "Terrorist Surveillance Program" instituted by the president immediately after 9/11 (discussed in Chapter 4). The interception of telephone and other communications took place outside of the FISA court – indeed, the administration went to some lengths to mask the very existence of the program from the Foreign Intelligence Surveillance judges. The only oversight lay with Congress. Under the 1947 National Security Act, congressional intelligence committees must be "fully and currently" informed about intelligence gathering operations, "consistent with … protection from unauthorized disclosure of classified information relating to sensitive intelligence sources and methods or other exceptionally sensitive matters."[22] Reporting to Congress about covert operations, in contrast, can be limited by the president to the "Gang of Eight": the chairmen and ranking minority members of the congressional intelligence committees, the Speaker and minority leader of the House of Representatives, the majority and minority leaders of the Senate.[23]

In January 2006, the Congressional Research Service (CRS) released a report suggesting that the NSA surveillance program was intelligence gathering, not a covert operation. The administration, however, had not informed the congressional intelligence committees about the existence of the program. Instead, it had told 13 members of Congress, who had then been instructed not to divulge the existence of the program to anyone – including their fellow committee members. The CRS suggested, in the closing paragraph of its report, that limited disclosure may be allowed "in order to protect intelligence sources and methods" – but the law, on this point, was not clear; nor was it obvious whether a full program could meet this requirement, or whether the exception was limited only to particular aspects of the program itself. Clarification of these points would help ensure that the appropriate members of Congress are being informed.

Beyond this, the NSA example speaks to two very important points: first, reporting requirements must be deep enough to allow for scrutiny at an operational level. Like the Intelligence and, indeed, Appropriations Committees in Congress, the Office of Management and Budget was not even aware of the NSA wiretapping operation. The ability of the members of these committees to see acts carried out "below the line" is limited. The British system here, in some ways, is more robust: judicial reviewers do have the authority to inquire into specific operations – although the practical ability of reviewers to do this is limited by the resources available.

Second, at the other end of the spectrum, is the possibility that the cumulative nature of counterterrorist provisions is missed. Much of the debate in the United States over the NSA program – as framed by the White House – centered on whether US citizens should be allowed to communicate with members of al Qaeda with impunity. This discussion sidestepped the issue of allowing widespread wiretapping outside of any warrant requirement – much less the combination of such wiretapping with the plethora of intelligence-gathering operations and data-mining initiatives underway at the Department of Defense. These diversions and omissions suggest the importance of not just looking at the exercise of specific authorities, but of considering how reporting requirements fit with each other across different areas so that legislators can look at the broader picture to consider the cumulative effect of such measures.

Reinforcing Transparency and Accountability

Insisting upon deliberative processes and stringent reporting requirements is not sufficient to ensure that the executive branch is exercising its discretion in accordance with legislative intent. Also important is the degree to which the twin principles of transparency and accountability prevail. Their restriction severely reduces legislative power.

In regard to the former, the United Kingdom and the United States governments have a substantial amount of authority to prevent information in their possession from entering the public domain (see Chapter 5). But as executive power expands under the counterterrorist banner, it becomes particularly important for people to know the government is exercising its power – especially now that a number of executive bodies are actively trying to get inside people's heads, to know what they are going to do before they do it. Such psychological surveillance threatens a range of social and political interests – not least of which is legislative autonomy. Important in this connection are the Freedom of Information Act and classification procedures.

For even as executive power in the United States, in particular, is expanding, the ability of citizens to get information about how the government is using its power is contracting. The Freedom of Information Act, which dates back to

1966, gives individuals the right to obtain information from federal agencies.[24] After 9/11, changes to the administrative rules implementing the statute considerably weakened it.

Previously, Attorney General Janet Reno had created a "strong presumption of disclosure" and allowed for the discretionary release of information even in exempt areas to ensure the "maximum responsible disclosure."[25] But on October 12, 2001, Attorney General John Ashcroft issued a new memo that reversed this presumption.[26] He directed agencies to consider national security, effective law enforcement, and personal privacy. He also weakened the standard under which the Department of Justice would defend other agencies' decisions to withhold information. Where Reno required that, for an agency to be defended by the Justice Department in court, it must reasonably foresee that the disclosure would harm an interest protected by an exemption, Ashcroft indicated that Justice would defend it if any sound legal basis existed.[27]

A second memo in March 2002, from the Bush administration's Assistant to the President and Chief of Staff, to all heads of federal departments and agencies, further restricted the reach of the Freedom of Information Act (FOIA) and directed that the recipients safeguard all information relating to homeland security.[28] A joint memo, issued by the National Archives' Information Security Oversight Office and the Department of Justice's Office of Information and Privacy, accompanied the letter and provided additional guidance.[29] In 2003, a General Accounting Office Report found that approximately one-third of federal FOIA officers noticed a decrease in discretionary disclosures – a fact that most of the FOIA officers responding to the survey (75 percent) attributed to Ashcroft's policy.[30]

In November 2002, the new Homeland Security Act further dried up the information flow by including secrecy provisions to allow businesses to designate information supplied to the government as "critical infrastructure information" (CII).[31] The statute exempted private industry from all FOIA requests and private lawsuits and imposed criminal penalties for anyone revealing information designated CII.[32] The administration interpreted this latter provision in a later rule to mean that "any information voluntarily supplied to any government agency is protected . . . and therefore not subject to FOIA – if it is passed along to the Department of Homeland Security."[33] The argument that this information somehow protects the state from terrorism appears spurious: confidential trade information and sensitive data already enjoyed an exemption under FOIA. Both conservative and liberal commentators faulted this change – not least for making it difficult to protect nonnational-security-related environmental concerns.[34]

In the National Defense Authorization Act for Fiscal Year 2004, Congress made further provision to allow the National Security Agency automatically to refuse citizens' requests for information about how the agency works – its "operational files."[35] The Bush administration justified the measure in terms not of security, but of efficiency: "There's a better use of [the agency's] time and effort – the war on terrorism and so forth – than searching for records that are going to be denied anyway."[36] An impressive array of opponents lined up against the legislation: the Federation of American Scientists, the American Library Association, the American Society of Newspaper Editors, and the Electronic Privacy Information Center. While FOIA had provided a previous exemption to the CIA (in 1984), public hearings accompanied that decision. The National Imagery and Mapping Agency and the National Reconnaissance Office also had exceptions.[37] What concerned some observers about the NSA exception was that the organization already was notoriously difficult to penetrate.[38] And it had a long history of extraordinary abuse.[39]

The flip side of FOIA concerns, in the American context, is classification: the number of documents subject to it dramatically increased after 9/11. The government removed some 50 million pages of information, including congressional documents, environmental impact reports, and other data, from public view (see Chapter 5). Simultaneously, the state expanded its use of "For Official Use Only" – a rather murky designation that creates a strong reluctance to share information. The increasing secrecy surrounding executive branch activities insulates it not just from public inquiry, but from congressional inquiry – and, importantly, even if released to Congress, from legislators' ability to make the information public to bring public pressure to bear. Classification thus substantially reduces legislative power, for Members of Congress, answerable to their constituents, can be more sensitive to the inappropriate exercise of executive authority when such information is publicly known.

The United Kingdom also has some way to go in embracing a more transparent government. The country only recently joined the FOIA trend. For most of the state's history, the government simply released information when public access was considered appropriate.[40] As the campaign for freedom of information gained momentum in the 1990s, John Major's government came under increasing criticism for its secrecy. In 1994, he adopted the Code of Practice on Access to Government Information, which had no legal force and many loopholes.[41] Nevertheless, its flexible procedures did generate some revelations about government activity.* Three years later, the new Labour government published a white paper and vowed to put FOIA on a statutory footing.[42] The document recognized,

Unnecessary secrecy in government leads to arrogance in governance and defective decision-making. The perception of excessive secrecy has become a corrosive influence in the decline of public confidence in government. Moreover, the climate of public opinion has changed: people expect much greater openness and accountability from government than they used to.[43]

---

* According to the Parliamentary Ombudsman's Report (HC 91), in the first eight months of the code, some 2,600 requests under the code were made. Campaign for Freedom of Information, *The Campaign's views on the Operation of the Open Government Code of Practice, Evidence to the Select Committee on the Parliamentary Commissioner for Administration (the Ombudsman) on the Operation of the Code of Practice on Access to Government Information*, Mar. 16, 1995, available at www.cfoi.org.uk.

The government left implementation to Home Secretary Jack Straw, who, in November 1999, introduced a watered-down Freedom of Information Bill, which is constructive in that it establishes openness as the norm. Also, restrictions placed on the government fall under justiciable standards, with enforcement mechanisms to alleviate grievance. At a minimum, officials must respond in writing to all requests – with either an answer or an explanation why the information will not be provided – within 20 days of the original request.[44]

Although Westminster added some protections, the measure, like its American counterpart, has troublesome weaknesses in terms of exceptions.[45] The legislation specifically excludes any information supplied directly or indirectly by – or relating to – security, intelligence, criminal intelligence services and tribunals handling complaints about them, as well as any information a minister certifies requires exemption for reasons relating to national security.[46] It creates an exception for information related to defense.[47] Responding to the public scandals of previous decades, the legislation also excludes data provided in confidence.[48] The statute gives the Information Commissioner – also in charge of protecting data – the responsibility to encourage public authorities to act properly, to educate the public, and to arbitrate the authorities' claims to exemptions.[49] If, however, the commissioner directs an officer to comply with the act, the civil servant can avoid doing so by obtaining a national security certificate directly from the Secretary of State or one of his or her designated proxies.[50] Either party can appeal the Information Commissioner's decision to a tribunal established under the act.[51]

Where information cannot be released publicly, FOIA may be less relevant than clearances held by those conducting oversight. The Privy Counsel in the United Kingdom operates on the principle that certain public servants are trustworthy – literally, in the confidence of the Crown. What is remarkable about many of the devices developed within the United Kingdom is that political partisanship matters little.

Information about how the executive or government exercises its authority does, of course, go a long way toward holding those responsible accountable for the use of extraordinary authority. But the ability to call witnesses, and to identify a final individual who is publicly answerable for any misuse of authority, may be an even stronger protection. This consideration brings us to transparency's twin principle: accountability.

As I have said, here the United Kingdom's parliamentary system offers more protections than those in the United States. Ministers are directly accountable to Parliament for the exercise of counterterrorist provisions. In contrast, in the United States the fact that counterterrorist provisions tend not to name the office of those responsible for exercising specific powers, that calling executive branch officials to account is distributed broadly among different congressional committees, and that the House of Representatives' winner-takes-all system of rulemaking diminishes committee oversight during unified government make it difficult to assign blame or reward. Moreover, the public's ability to hold legislators to account for their failures to conduct effective oversight of the executive branch is limited. As some scholars have argued, "voters have no hope of apportioning responsibility for major national decisions among the hundreds of [Members of Congress], each of whom stands for reelection based largely on what she accomplished for her district and disclaims personal blame for broader government failures."[52] The legislature could address this situation by writing into the law clear lines of accountability in respect to the person or agency responsible for ensuring the appropriate use of new authorities – and then requiring that individual to answer to Congress, by law, regardless of which party controls the legislature.

Drawing Lines

In Northern Ireland, as a colloquial matter, a distinction can be drawn between terrorists and "ODCs" – ordinary, decent criminals. Although perhaps a facetious comparison, there are important differences between criminal enterprise and terrorism – just as there are differences between terrorism and all-out war. As a substantive matter, legislative reluctance to borrow measures from other areas and apply them to terrorism – and vice versa – may force a more careful examination of the consequences of new provisions and ultimately reduce the costs of counterterrorism. Here, antiterrorist finance provides a good example (see Chapter 3); but even within national security concerns, treating each type of terrorist threat as unique may help craft more effective responses without such widespread and adverse consequences.

Distinguishing Between Criminal Law and Counterterrorism: Financial Counterterrorism as an Example. Terrorism and money laundering are similar in that they use many of the same methods to hide and move money, depend on a lack of transparency and monitoring, and take advantage of the same systems – wire transfers, alternative remittance systems, bulk currency shipments, money transmitters, money changers, and commodity-based trade. Both may be political: money launderers may support candidates, use the media, and sponsor social projects in poor areas. Terrorist organizations obviously seek political ends, many engage in social support, and most have propaganda arms that deal with the media (see Chapter 5).

But money laundering and terrorism also have important structural differences in respect to the source and the volume of their money. Money laundering depends upon an underlying crime, whereas terrorist finance does not. Put somewhat crudely, the former takes dirty money and tries to make it clean, whereas the latter often takes clean money (e.g., a contribution to a charitable organization) and tries to make it dirty – that is, use it to fund violent attacks.[53] Victims, moreover, who otherwise might alert law enforcement to criminal activity are unlikely to speak up – they may not know where their money is going, or they may find out and be afraid to be considered complicit in the terrorist offense. Those involved in terrorist organizations are often less likely than those engaged in organized crime to have previous criminal convictions. And unlike money laundering, it is difficult, if not impossible, to discern patterns in financial transactions that would signify terrorist activity. New York Clearinghouse, an organization of the largest money-center banks, concluded, after a post-September 11 two-year study, that it simply cannot be done.[54] Despite repeated efforts to develop typologies appropriate to terrorist finance, the Financial Action Task Force Report reached a similar conclusion.[55] As a result, the profiles developed tend to rely on ethnicity and nationality, raising problems that range from inaccuracy and counterproductivity to the infringement of individual rights.[56] To monitor the possible use of legitimate funds for terrorist ends, therefore, the state must involve itself deeply in the private sector and examine an enormous amount of data in minute detail. The fact that approximately 12 million currency transaction reports are filed annually in the United States alone gives rise to privacy and bureaucratic efficiency problems that go well beyond those in the money laundering realm.[57]

As for the volume of money involved in each type of activity, the International Monetary Fund puts the total money laundered globally each year at around $600 billion; the amount of money flowing to terrorist organizations overall is unknown, although terrorists whose finances have been documented appear to require much less money than criminals do.[58]* PIRA operates on a budget of some £1.5 million, whereas the Real IRA and the Ulster Defense Association require only £500,000. To some extent this difference reflects the ends of the entities involved: profit primarily drives launderers, whereas terrorist organizations tend to be more interested in nonfinancial goals, such as obtaining political legitimacy or convincing a particular target population of their views. Unlike ordinary criminals, terrorists tend to avoid living conspicuous lifestyles that would alert authorities to the presence of extra income. Terrorist organizations tend to move money in smaller amounts and in ways that are harder to detect.

These structural differences between money laundering and terrorist finance play out in concrete ways. Whereas the purpose of money laundering investigations is to prosecute perpetrators and obtain funds, terrorist financing investigations also need to accomplish other important goals, such as interrupting the flow of money to a violent group or preventing a successful operation, whether or not they obtain a prosecution.[59] Stopping money from flowing through the regulated sector either by freezing it or by introducing sweeping regulations here undermines an important national security aim of the state: law enforcement does not just lose a conviction, but intelligence organizations may be unable to trace the funds to interrupt an operation or to find people linked to terrorist networks.† Indeed, because of the post-9/11 changes to the Western banking

---

* In 2003, financial firms in Europe and the United States spent more than $5 billion between them trying to prevent laundering activities. *Coming Clean; Money-Laundering*, ECONOMIST (U.S. Edition), Oct. 16, 2004.

† The benefits of retaining terrorist actors in the regulated sector are notable. For example, because they operated within the Western banking system, the September 11 hijackers Nawaf al Hazmi and Khalid al Mihdhar left a trail: they opened bank accounts in New Jersey and used debit cards to pay for their hotel room. Al Hazmi bought tickets on Flight 77 for himself and Salem al

system – instituted both by the United States and by the United Kingdom – groups linked to al Qaeda have changed their ways of raising money and transferring funds. Terrorist networks are turning to trusted hawaladars as well as to couriers.[60] To finance the Bali and Jakarta attacks, for instance, jihadists physically moved $100,000 and then $30,000 from the southern Philippines to Indonesia.[61] And terrorists transfer into gold increasing quantities of their funds.[62] Although these are more cumbersome ways of moving resources, these avenues also make it harder for the state to trace funds and find those responsible for terrorist violence.[63]*

Another way the structural differences play out can be seen in Suspicious Activity Reports (SARs), which can be extremely helpful for money laundering, but are ill suited to terrorism. Both countries have placed considerable emphasis on SARs. As far as the United States goes, however, SARs did not discover – nor should they have discovered, nor would they now discover – any of the financial activity in which the September 11 hijackers engaged.[†] Nevertheless, Title III of the USA PATRIOT Act expanded the number of organizations required to file SARs – a provision that dramatically increased the number of SARs filed from approximately 163,000 in 2000 to nearly 920,000 by 2005.[64] The *Economist* reported, "[B]anks in America and elsewhere are trying to cover themselves by filing ever more 'suspicious activity reports.' Regulators are swamped with information. Alas, most of it is useless."[65]

Hazmi, thus giving the authorities clues as to other perpetrators. Nawaf al Hazmi and another man who flew on Flight 77, Hani Hanjour, used the same address to open bank accounts at the same New Jersey bank. Another hijacker from that flight, Majed Moqed, used the same address to open an account at another New Jersey bank. This information, linking all five together, assisted federal law enforcement officers in quickly determining those who were responsible. National Commission on Terrorist Attacks Against the United States, Monograph on Terrorist Financing: Staff Report to the Commission, at 58–9, Aug. 21, 2004, available at www.9–11commission.gov.

* Simultaneously, al Qaeda has become more diffuse and harder to distinguish from the broader worldwide jihadist movement. An "array of loosely affiliated groups, each raising funds on its own initiative," has replaced the group's more centralized structure. National Commission on Terrorist Attacks Against the United States, *Monograph on Terrorist Financing: Staff Report to the commission*, at 29, Aug. 21, 2004, available at www.9–11commission.gov.

† Al Qaeda moved the money to fund September 11 in three ways: $130,000 was wired to hijackers in the United States from the United Arab Emirates and Germany; members physically carried cash/traveler's checks to the United States; and some established overseas accounts, which they drew on via ATM or credit cards in the United States. When they arrived in the United States, they opened bank accounts under their real names in both large national banks and smaller regional ones. While they lived in the United States, they made wire transfers of between $5,000 and $70,000, making the transactions virtually invisible in comparison to the billions of dollars moving daily through the international financial system. Their banking pattern – depositing a significant amount of money and then making smaller withdrawals – fit their student profiles. They did not use false Social Security numbers, and their grasp of the US banking system was not particularly sophisticated. National Commission on Terrorist Attacks Against the United States, Monograph on Terrorist Financing: Staff Report to the commission, at 53, Aug. 21, 2004, available at www.9–11commission.gov. *See also* Michael Peel & John Willman, *The Dirty Money That is Hardest to Clean Up: Financial Institutions are Keen to Eradicate Money-Laundering by Terrorists and to Freeze Assets*, Fin. Times (London), Nov. 20, 2001, at 16.

The United Kingdom also saw a sudden increase in reports of suspicious activity: In October 2001, the National Criminal Intelligence Service received 4,387 reports – more than four times the number filed in October 2000.[66] By June 2003, the NCIS was receiving around 7,000 SARs per month.[67] The cost of this expansion to both the United Kingdom and the United States (in terms of administrative overhead and diversion of resources) has yet to be determined. An independent audit by the Swiss Cooperative, KPMG International, however, raised concern about the low signal-to-noise ratio (number of true indicators of terrorist activity versus the number of reports filed) and the tendency of entities to over-report.[68] The quality of information contained in such reports on both sides of the Atlantic is, moreover, poor.[69]

Whether resources are better spent on SAR analysis or criminal investigation remains a matter of speculation. If SARs were unearthing terrorist activity, then analysis of them may be worth the expense. But financial institutions' tendencies to report appear in part to be tied to the political environment. In September 2001, for instance, only 27 SARs filed in the United States mentioned terrorism. The following month, 446 reports suddenly suggested connections between customers and violent organizations. While the numbers remained high for the next few months, they steadily declined and, by September 2002, were back down to 24.[70] The numbers remained low – until the advent of the war on Iraq and some well-publicized reports on state investigations into financial institutions with customers possibly linked to international terrorism.[71] At that point, the number of SARs citing possible terrorist links again skyrocketed.

Perhaps structure contributes to the apparent disconnect between financial institutions' ability to identify the flows of terrorist funds and the underlying terrorist threat. States, which are privy to classified intelligence material, are more likely than banks to know the identity of terrorist suspects. Without this information and lacking a reliable profile on which to base their decisions, financial institutions may thus revert to racial profiling.

Whether motivated by a desire to improve national security or by the fear of falling afoul of the measures adopted after September 11, financial institutions in the United States have been aggressive about filing SARs. By 2005, these institutions were submitting approximately 20 percent of their SARs in response to law enforcement inquiries and name matches with the Treasury Department's Office of Foreign Assets Control's specially designated terrorist list.[72] Eighty percent were voluntary. Depository institutions tended to focus on charitable organizations and Islamic foundations; on individuals presenting personal identification from Iraq, Afghanistan, and specific Middle Eastern states; and on wire activity to or from suspect states.[73] Casinos, in turn, focused on individuals connected with the Middle East – that is, those having Arab-sounding names or carrying passports from states considered suspicious.[74]

The filing of SARs based on these assumptions means that otherwise innocuous activity becomes suspicious merely through someone's ethnicity. And suspects' names quickly ascend the reporting chain. In the United States, the number of names forwarded to federal law enforcement for further action correspondingly increased with the number of SARs filed: from just 9,112 in all of 2000, the total increased to 13,649 in just the first 10 months of 2002.[75] Many of these reports concerned wire transfers to or from the Middle East. SARs, however, and documents that would disclose the existence of an SAR, are privileged from discovery in civil litigation – even if the discovery is necessary for an affirmative defense.[76] Moreover, from 2003, the United States began exchanging SARs with other states through the Financial Investigative Units. By operating under international treaties, such as the UN Convention on the Suppression of Financing of Terrorism, and under "soft law" (for instance, FATF's Forty Recommendations), the federal government can circumvent privacy laws that might otherwise block the transfer of financial data.[77]

The governments on both sides of the Atlantic are not unaware of the problem caused by the fourfold increase in SARs flooding the system. Britain's National Criminal Intelligence Service took the initiative to hold a series of seminars for private industry, specifying the conditions requiring a report to be filed. NCIS officials also began visiting institutions to encourage them to use common sense. By 2005, the US FinCEN had also taken concrete steps to reduce the sheer volume of filed information. In December 2004, to reduce duplicate reporting, FinCEN revised its guidelines to clarify that blocking reports filed with the OFAC satisfied the SAR reporting requirement.[78] In 2005, FinCEN lowered the information requirements of the SAR reporting forms by, *inter alia*, eliminating the "Continuation Sheet," which recorded traveler's checks, money orders, and wire transfer document numbers.[79]

Although these changes may help address some of the system's shortcomings, its general structural problem persists: SARs ineffectively address the ways in which terrorists, as opposed to money launderers, move money. And there is still no disincentive for financial institutions to file as many SARs as may possibly apply. They have nothing to lose by over-reporting, but incur considerable risk (that is, the freezing or forfeiture of their assets) if they neglect to report activity the state later deems suspicious. Indeed, the United States has indicated its willingness to go after such offenders: in 2002, Trustco Bank, N.A., in Glenville, New York, became the first institution cited for violating reporting requirements.[80*]

---

* A different approach for either state might be to increase the accountability of the filing banks: that is, over-reporting might incur some sort of penalty, or efficient reporting might be rewarded. But this policy would send a mixed message to financial institutions already thrust into the frontlines of intelligence gathering. Moreover, the large resources that such institutions would devote to compliance may adversely affect their ability to compete internationally. Such sanctions may also alienate private industry – at a time when the state needs its cooperation to head off real threats. Another strategy might be for intelligence or law enforcement organizations to share information and then target specific regions, banks, individuals, and charities – as is, for the most part, the current approach in the United States. But banks complain that intelligence services provide insufficient information. And there is evidence that this is the least effective of the current alternatives – that is, detection systems that "rely heavily on existing investigative methods," in contrast to reporting requirements, may be more effective than general reporting requirements in identifying people moving terrorist money and obtaining convictions. It is unclear whether this

This example, drawn from financial counterterrorism, is just one of many examples that could be used to highlight the basic problem: simply transferring to the counterterrorist realm tools that help the state respond to ordinary crime often carries substantial costs. Instead, legislators need to look at the provisions adopted and consider them, as much as possible, on their own merits, as crafted to meet the specific demands of the threat they are meant to counter.

Not only is it important to prevent the transfer of provisions from ordinary crime to terrorism but vigilance also should accompany the transfer of counterterrorist authorities to criminal law. In Chapter 1, I highlighted two reasons why counterterrorist provisions often move in this direction. The first is the tendency of provisions to become unexceptional, once they conceptually have been accepted within the terrorist realm. Thus, even if legislators include in counterterrorist law restrictions that prevent measures from being used for other purposes, ideas from counterterrorism subsequently creep into the code as legislators consider other laws. Why not apply provisions effective in the "war on terror" to the "war on drugs" – and from there to the "war on gangs" or the "war on crime"? Indeed, at a state level, we have statutes that refer to crimes such as "narco-terrorism" "environmental terrorism," and "school terrorism."[81] Even traditional criminal law offenses – such as kidnapping, stalking, sexual assault, and witness intimidation – in the late twentieth century became redefined as "terroristic offenses."[82]

The second way in which counterterrorist provisions creep into criminal law stems from legislators' decision not to limit the use of the provisions to counterterrorist efforts. As I have illustrated throughout the previous chapters, it is a mistake to rely on the administrative arm of government to voluntarily restrict the use of such provisions to terrorism – even where clear guidelines have been issued. The application of the provisions to ordinary crime takes away the very reason why extraordinary powers, using extraordinary procedures, have been approved. Once these powers enter the criminal law domain, it becomes exceedingly difficult for legislators to regain control of them.

The way for legislators to counter this circumstance is to build into statutes clear language limiting to terrorism the use of the powers. Vigilant oversight and skepticism about later efforts to transfer such authorities may also help counter the ratcheting effect.

Distinguishing Between National Security Threats: Knowledge-based Speech as an Example. Drawing a bright line between criminal law and terrorism, to the extent possible, is one way in which legislators can help mitigate the

is because of the ease of targeting individuals already suspected of criminal activity (Mariano-Florentino Cuéllar, *The Tenuous Relationship Between the Fight Against Money Laundering and the Disruption of Criminal Finance*, J. CRIM. L. & CRIMINOLOGY 311, 420–22 (2003)), or whether there is a more direct relationship between conducting investigations and then using finances to develop the case. Nevertheless, this approach may offer a more promising route to interrupting terrorist finance.

significant costs of counterterrorism. But even within national security considerations, one must carefully consider each measure and the particular terrorist
threat toward which it is directed. A good example here comes from knowledge-
based speech (see Chapter 5).

After the anthrax mailings in autumn 2001, it will be recalled, concern about
the ability of microbiologists to freely publish the results of their research centered in some part on the publication of the mousepox research, conducted
years earlier by Australian scientists. The argument for censorship of microbiologists grew straight from the approach adopted toward nuclear research
during the Cold War. Even individuals traditionally protective of free speech
suggested that some censorship should be imposed.

One approach was to argue for narrowly tailored restrictions that would
impose a small burden on legitimate research, but heavy burdens on would-be
terrorists. A "type of disease" framework, could be used: certain viruses might
be fair game, whereas information related to diseases selected by countries
as part of a weaponization program – such as smallpox – would be limited.
Restrictions might center on a "purpose of research" distinction: microbiologists seeking cures might be allowed to proceed, whereas those undertaking
research for offensive biological weapons would be restricted from publishing
(and perhaps from conducting) their research. Restrictions also could adopt a
"type of research" approach: genetic engineering, where the same could not be
found in nature, for instance, might be restricted.

Each of these approaches, though, assumes wrongly that microbiology can
be compartmentalized. One might learn extremely valuable information, for
instance, by studying particularly virulent diseases. Often states attempt to
devise ways of making weapons of existing devastating viruses; and with the
exception of smallpox, the continued presence of these diseases in nature means
that the threat from them may be greater than from a weaponized disease used
by a group intent on causing harm. Similarly, the attempt to isolate "purpose
of research" fails to reach the most basic of findings: how a disease works.
This information could be used to find a treatment – or cure – for a disease.
Perhaps the most promising test might be the "type of research" approach – but
here, too, it is short-sighted to assume that certain approaches to disease yield
only bad results. For instance, genetic manipulation may be unlikely to occur
naturally; however, stopping research in this area because of national security
considerations may prevent a state from being able to ensure the general health
of its population.

What is often forgotten in counterterrorism planning is that, although terrorism attracts a great deal of attention, its actual threat is limited. Relatively
few terrorist organizations have the intent, the knowledge, and the capability
to execute an attack using a weapon of mass destruction. Moreover, there are
limits on even these groups' ability to use such weapons. Terrorist groups have
constituents on whom they depend for their survival and to whom they must
constantly justify their use of violence. Immediately after 9/11, for instance,
Osama Bin Laden issued a video tape explaining al Qaeda's aims and grievances.

International agreements against the use of biological or nuclear weapons help place their use beyond the pale. It would take an extremely aggressive state action to spur the use of such instruments – because any group wielding them would have to justify its action to the community from which it seeks protection. While, then, terrorism using weapons of mass destruction remains a low probability/high consequence threat, any number of other threats – not least of which is a naturally occurring outbreak of disease – are high probability/high consequence ones. Thus, by cutting off research in microbiology, the state limits its ability to fend off more likely, and just as devastating, disease.

To judge by history, moreover, the people who are likely to be caught by restrictions on research are nonterrorist scientists – who have, indeed, been the only group to be legally hindered in their work by the strictures on handling controlled substances under the USA PATRIOT Act.[83] In contrast, terrorist organizations – some exceedingly well-funded ones – continue to conduct research and have access to information developed elsewhere. Even atomic information, tightly controlled in the United States, ended up being distributed.* And that was before the Internet. As Professor Mary Cheh, of George Washington University Law School writes,

> [S]ecrets often leak or, if they are important enough, are stolen. More fundamentally, however, basic scientific information about how nuclear fission or fusion occurs, like any other basic information about the physical world, can not really be "secret." If someone discovers a certain scientific principle or phenomenon, he can not truly keep it secret because others remain free to discover the very same principle or phenomenon.
>
> In all but a few highly exceptional cases ... *rediscovery of basic scientific and technological advances can be expected either simultaneously or in a very short period.* This is so because virtually all science and technology is an extension of discoveries previously made and because the general principles underlying any particular development are likely to be widely known. ... In most cases, therefore, the most that can be gained from keeping a scientific discovery "secret" is a small time advantage over a nation's competitors.[84]

This problem might be addressed, in part, by trying to restrict only the most dangerous biological material, which might be used as a weapon, and so give the state time to guard against particular biological weapons. But here, again, the difficulties of trying to compartmentalize microbiology abound. Measures attempting to stimulate certain forms of research by providing for secrecy in others may also have negative economic effects by burdening other areas. For instance, owing to the extended patent terms offered by Senator Joseph Lieberman's latest attempt to woo the pharmaceutical industry, insurance companies and the health care system will bear the expense as it takes ever more time

---

* Despite the Department of Energy's efforts to prevent the H-Bomb article from being published in the Progressive, for example, Chuck Hansen's letter to Senator Charles Percy, discussing the article, circulated widely; and Edward Teller, one of the creators of the weapon, published a similar article in the *Encyclopedia Americana*. L.A. Powe, Jr., *The H-Bomb Injunction*, 61 U. Colo. L. Rev. 55, 70 (1990).

to get less expensive, generic versions of medicine to market. Similarly, the increased mortality rates arising from stinted research in microbiology with dual-use applications – that is, use also in responding to naturally occurring disease – may increase mortality rates across society.

Initiatives restricting speech may also negate other efforts to improve national security. For instance, the continued high number of patent secrecy orders in the United States works against other patent incentives to develop new counterterrorist technologies. Although the crash of TWA 800 in 1996 did not result from a terrorist attack, the new Patent and Trademark Office provision created in response to the event instituted a fast-track application for inventions aimed to improve US counterterrorism efforts. The special category – like those created for HIV, AIDS, cancer, superconductivity, recombinant DNA research, and nuclear energy – jumps applicants to the front of an otherwise 18-month queue.[85] Technologies useful for counterterrorism include "systems for detecting/identifying explosives, aircraft sensors/security systems, and vehicular barricades/disabling systems."[86] In this category, between 1996 and October 2001, inventors submitted fewer than 100 applications, whose substance ranged from communications technologies and identification systems to weapons and blast-resistant construction materials. Although the number of applications denied under secrecy orders remains shielded from public scrutiny, organizations afraid of having to deal with research strictures may be less likely to accelerate their work to gain swift patent approval and thus contribute to increased national security.

The careful consideration of costs such as these, however, depends upon examining the particular threat posed by biological weapons. The issues are not obvious when tools used in the nuclear area are simply transferred over to this unique threat.

Resisting the Alteration of Judicial Rules and Executive Expansion

The alteration of judicial rules and the executive branch's tendency to take over judicial functions both fall within the legislature's domain because the authority for both derives from statute. Yet the judiciary, as I have remarked throughout this book, is already in a relatively weak position. Efforts to weaken it further raise concern. Here, the United Kingdom proves particularly instructive.

As I discussed in Chapter 2, relaxed standards of evidence and extended detention periods in Northern Ireland shifted law enforcement's emphasis to confessions. Together with a failure to ensure witness protection, coercive interrogation increased. Simultaneously, the state allowed adverse inferences to be drawn from silence. By weakening the standards of proof for membership in a proscribed organization, the state put the security forces into a judicial role. The inclusion of nonterrorist-related crimes meant that those accused of even ordinary crime found themselves without important protections – and thus struck at the heart of the principle that one is innocent until proven guilty. Together, these measures led to miscarriages of justice and undermined the rule of law. Some of them, moreover, brought the United Kingdom into conflict with its international obligations – agreements to which it had acquiesced in part, presumably, to bind other countries to similar standards. Many of the judicial changes stemmed from the state's wish to have enough solid evidence and unintimidated witnesses to be able successfully to prosecute those responsible for violence. There are ways, however, to address these factors without eroding public confidence in the judiciary.

Perhaps the most obvious solution in the British context is to allow the interception of communications to be used as evidence at trial. Although this is a popular proposal and has the support of law enforcement personnel, academicians, the judiciary, and others, the British government has solid reasons for resisting it. Yet there are ways to protect against the state's primary concerns – that the admission of wiretap evidence would implicate specific agents, give away state secrets, or undermine Britain's relationship with other countries' intelligence agencies. Such issues could be legislated around – and, in the meantime, the state would, where appropriate, amass stronger evidence on which to convict terrorists.

A second way in which to address the problem is to focus on strengthening the United Kingdom's witness protection program. Witness intimidation did not end with the peace process. If anything, as paramilitaries moved into organized crime, intimidation increased.[87] Labour reported, for instance, that between 2002 and 2003, the government recorded 58 instances of witness intimidation – twice the number of the previous year. Between 2003 and 2004, attacks on prison officers and their families and members of the police forces continued. A survey found that 68 percent of the young offenders being held at Hydebank Wood prison had been "subject to paramilitary threats, banned from a particular area, beaten or . . . shot."[88] One-third considered themselves still at risk.[89]* In 2002 alone, 13 children under the age of 17 had been shot by loyalists, and another 12 by republicans – and threats of shootings, beatings, mutilation, and exile continued.[90]

This intimidation took place in a broad context of continued violence. In 1998, more than 120 bombing incidents and 180 shootings occurred. In 2001, the number of bombing incidents topped 300, with more than 350 shootings.[91] According to Lord Carlile, the independent reviewer of counterterrorist powers in Part VII of the Terrorism Act 2000, by 2004 paramilitaries still exercised social and economic influence over communities.[92] Carlile continued, "On both sides of the sectarian divide there continues a clear danger of intimidation within living and working neighbourhoods. Armed robberies remain at a high level,

---

* Another member of Parliament discussed the case of Harry McCartan, a youth who had been convicted of joy riding. The Ulster Defense Association "used six-inch nails to impale his hands to a wooden fence and beat him mercilessly with nail-studded baseball bats about the head, arms, hands and legs. When received at the Royal Victoria Hospital late that day, he was so badly bloodied that his father could only identify him by a tattoo." Jane Kennedy, Minister of State, Northern Ireland Office, col. 5; First Standing Committee on Delegated Legislation, HC Debs, Feb. 5, 2004, col. 322.

and the raising of money for paramilitaries by various intimidatory methods remains part of the picture."[93]

Adrian Bailey explained in Parliament, "We are now witnessing the transformation of groups with a political ideology who carried on the sustained intimidation of local communities into groups that are specifically focused on common-or-garden criminality using techniques that they have honed to perfection over the years."[94] Bailey went on, "There is a huge body of evidence to demonstrate that many cases that could be won in court are lost because the original complainant or plaintiff decides not to give evidence. We all know that that happens because of threats to potential witnesses' personal safety."[95] Nigel Dodds from North Belfast added that terrorist organizations "impose their authority on vulnerable people who feel intimidated and are often unable to speak out against such a reign of terror."[96] Roy Beggs from East Antrim noted that the peace process had had little affect: "One only has to read the newspapers to see that paramilitary activities remain rife within both traditions: murders, threats, beatings and enforced exiles are reported almost daily."[97]

Calls for a more robust witness protection program, however, have been slow to yield results.[98] Public inquiries and inquests in Northern Ireland regularly grant anonymity, but the same does not exist in relation to the trial itself.[99] Nor is there any calibration or supervision of the inducements offered to informers, making it impossible to predict the eventual outcome with any certainty.[100] And paltry resources are made available to witnesses after proceedings conclude. Assistant Chief Constable Stephen White explained: witnesses were moved to council estates and put on the dole. Businessmen received no additional funds to reestablish themselves and were required to sell their businesses at their own expense. Their homes would be taken under the emergency provisions, giving the witness "the bare minimum for what that house is worth."[101] Those forced to go on the run also lost their social support, with precious little to replace it.[102] The Criminal Evidence (NI) Order 1999 made some provision for witnesses in the courtroom proceedings, but failed to address the witness protection issues.* In 2003, the Home Office made proposals to address this issue – as did a task force on racketeering. The Northern Ireland Office also commissioned a study by Professor Ron Goldstock to look at how prosecution witnesses believe they have been treated, particularly during the trial proceedings. The results of these studies have yet to yield effective implementation.[103]

---

* One British government report concluded that the programs in the United States and Italy were superior: "We find the picture of support for potential witnesses presented to us by the PSNI [Police Service Northern Ireland] very disappointing. The level of personal sacrifice required of the individual, as it was described to us, is unreasonable; it makes the individual and potentially his or her family victims twice over. It is not surprising that so few are currently willing to make a stand. We believe that the Government, in conjunction with the Executive where appropriate, must look again at the type and level of resources it makes available to support potential witnesses before, during and after cases which go to trial." Select Committee on Northern Ireland Affairs, Fourth Report, June 26, 2002.

Although the admission of wiretap evidence and increased witness protection would go some way toward addressing the gap in evidence available, juryless courts create their own problems. The suspension of juries went against cultural expectations and further distanced the minority community from the state. It also hurt the United Kingdom's relationship with the Republic of Ireland. The peace process helped move the political realm forward; the time is right now to reconsider the issue of juryless courts.*

Return to jury trial is not without its difficulties – such as the tendency to read prejudice into an individual's refusal to answer. One commentator has suggested that the judge provide a firmly worded direction to the jury – a course that has problems of its own: for instance, how far into fact-finding does the judge go when a jury is present? On the other hand, what kind of effect exactly would it have on juries (if any)?[104] Another solution might be to let the jury pause to deliberate occasionally through a trial. The risk here is prejudgment, but it might clarify possible misunderstandings in the course of the trial.[105] Nevertheless, in some situations a charge to the jury may not be sufficient to offset bias – in these cases, judges may be able to discharge entire juries or individual jurors.[106] The lesson of history, however, is that while benefits were gained, the decision to suspend jury trials, in concert with procedural changes designed to obtain more convictions, distanced the minority community in Northern Ireland.

As for executive expansion into the judicial domain, I recommend that legislators be acutely aware of this danger and resist it, especially when it takes the form of detention, internment, and control orders. In the United Kingdom, the admission of a police officer's testimony as evidence, together with that officer's public interest immunity – which prevented cross-examination – put law enforcement in the position of determining guilt. As with judicial alteration, at the center of such provisions is not just the balance of power among the three branches of government, but the rule of law.

In the United States, too, the rule of law has eroded, resulting – in light of the stated aim of the government to build liberal, democratic regimes – in a double deficit: not only has the state lost both its stature internationally and the ability to pursue its foreign policy and human rights agenda, but its actions have reduced the attractiveness of liberal democracy in the eyes of states it is trying to woo. The decision to act outside of the Geneva Conventions, and to reject the

---

* The government has resisted calls for a three-judge tribunal, citing potential costs to the taxpayer, delays in the criminal justice system, and lack of increased confidence in the judicial system. HC Debs on the Terrorism (Northern Ireland) Bill, Standing Committee, 9 Nov. 2005, cols. 21–29. Note in relation to claims of cost: a written answer to the Ulster Unionist Lord Laird noted in December 2005 that the costs in personal security for those under "substantial or severe terrorist threat" ran to £45 million over the past 5 years, with some current year £7.5 million estimated for 2005. The number was expected to drop to £3.8 million for 2006. Brian Walker, *New Post-Diplock Court System on Way: Rooker*, BELFAST TELEGRAPH, Dec. 21, 2005. Presumably, unless the time to trial or in trial increased significantly, movement to a three judge tribunal would affect these costs.

applicability of domestic criminal law, undermined the state's counterterrorist efforts and further harmed its ability to pursue its foreign policy interests.

Similarly, the current "black list" regime, in which the executive unilaterally decided culpability, has had severe political and humanitarian costs. To some extent, the US reliance on black lists stems from an overburdening of the regulatory regime. As one prominent lawyer noted, the process lacks a certain scientific accuracy.[107] Indeed, often the wrong people – or, at least, ones for whom the state has produced no evidence of culpability – become caught. As individuals increasingly challenge in court their terrorist designations, belief in the justness of antiterrorist seizures erodes and undermines both domestic and international support for the regime itself. The United States' refusal to allow any independent arbitration to accompany the creation of lists weakened the United Nations' attempt to build a dossier of dangerous individuals. Simultaneously, it opened the door to abuse: other states, particularly those in parts of the world where al Qaeda may have a particularly strong hold, may attempt to use any existing regime to target political opponents. Here US policy may be contradictory: although a significant aim of the global war on terror may be to establish democratic regimes (with the assumption that their presence will strengthen US national security), black lists themselves may become a tool with which other regimes silence voices demanding democratic change. And there will be little or no recourse without any independent arbitration about placing individuals on these lists.

The policy may even more directly increase the threat to national security. As states such as Egypt, Syria, Sudan, and Pakistan detain, torture, and confiscate the assets of "militants," local communities may become enraged, thus strengthening the hand of Islamists and likely having dangerous long-term consequences. In other words, as the rule of law erodes, so too may nonmilitant political space.

The United States defends its position by claiming that revealing the sources on which its list is based would compromise the state's intelligence-gathering abilities, as well as operatives in the field. In some cases, this defense is most certainly valid; in others, it may be just a way to conceal the lack of any real information beyond speculation. But even legitimate intelligence concerns should not deter the United States from seeking to establish mechanisms that could verify its underlying data. If anything, such an independent process would bolster the US claim that particular individuals contributed to terrorist movements, and allow the United States to freeze the assets of those it considers a real threat (assuming that freezing the assets is, indeed, the appropriate step to take – as opposed to following the money to determine who is responsible for violence), to interrupt operations, and to bring the perpetrators to justice.

Because counterterrorism is in many ways a propaganda battle, the nature of the process for constructing black lists matters. Whom the United States includes in its lists becomes as important as whom it excludes. In this connection, there are entities and individuals missing from the US lists that counterterrorist experts would expect to see, and whose absence tends to underscore the unique geopolitical ties of certain states and entities – notably Saudi Arabia and those connected to the ruling Saudi élite. By not including them on the lists, however, the United States undermines its claim to be acting in an even-handed manner. The inclusion, instead, of individuals either unconnected to terrorism or connected only in a minor capacity breeds a cynicism that undermines US counterterrorist efforts.

A crucial point here is international law and its role. The US Department of Defense has openly claimed that international law and judicial processes are weapons of the weak, that they are wielded against the state.[108] This view of international law as seriously diminishing the country's ability to answer terrorist challenge underlay the Bush administration's decision not to apply the Geneva Conventions – with disastrous consequences, as I discussed in Chapter 2. This is, to my mind, a mistaken assumption: legislators can use international law – and judicial processes – to strengthen their hand against terrorism. In answering a challenge to the political legitimacy of the state, the clear commitment to remain within the bounds of legitimate action gives the state the moral and political high ground – and, as I have discussed in detail, the ability to call on other states to join in fighting the terrorist challenge, which is increasingly global.

The message sent by the government matters. Perhaps one of the most important innovations in the development of British antiterrorist measures lies in the importance the state finally granted to the role of public communications. The Select Committee on Northern Ireland Affairs recognized that "publicity campaigns can be more effective than law enforcement in certain situations," and urged "the Government to give serious consideration to the role which such campaigns might play in the future strategy for dealing with specific facets of organized crime such as fuel laundering and tobacco smuggling."[109]

This effort required that the right information be accumulated. Prior to the creation of the Organized Crime Task Force, the United Kingdom's lack of even a definition of organized crime made it difficult for the Police Service of Northern Ireland to collect data on operational successes in this sphere. Once the state adopted the appropriate metrics, its public outreach mechanisms could take the information generated and move the battle to the next level: "We recommend that the Government ensure that the judiciary in Northern Ireland are fully apprised of the strong links which have now been established between paramilitary organisations, serious and organized crime and the range of offences which provide these groups and individuals with their income."[110]

The public proved an equally important target.[111] In discussing antiterrorist finance and paramilitary movement into organized crime, Members of Parliament lamented the situation in Northern Ireland, where it was acceptable to "pull one over" on the government. Indeed, much of the emphasis in the recent reports of the organized crime task force centers on the idea that paramilitary activities are not victimless crimes. This theme is repeated on the task force's

Web site, launched in 2002. In many ways, this is an extremely effective strategy: instead of falling into the early 1980s trap of calling paramilitaries criminals, the state is emphasizing the criminality of certain types of behavior in which paramilitaries engage. While this effort is limited to illicit sources of funding, it is nonetheless an effective way to address the criminal methods many terrorist organizations use to raise funds. It may be possible to pursue a similar route in the United States.*

BEYOND THE DICHOTOMY

Fifty-five years ago, President Harry S. Truman tried to preempt a national strike by seizing control of US steel mills: any lull in production – in the midst of the Korean War – threatened national security. Justice Felix Frankfurter, concurring with the Court in granting the steel companies injunctive relief, observed that dangerous executive power does not accumulate in a day. It builds up over time, as the executive reaches beyond the structures that previously restricted it.[112] Such concerns are not unique to America: Lord Lloyd of Berwick, a Lord of Appeal in Ordinary, warned in January 2006 that national security claims do not undermine civil liberties overnight, but will over time if left unchecked.

The accretion of dangerous executive power is indeed the hallmark of counterterrorist law. And time and again, such incremental progressions are justified under the security or freedom rubric. But, as I have expounded in the foregoing chapters, this dichotomy overlooks many grave and complex problems. The key to addressing many of these issues head on lies with the legislature. I hope that the guiding principles I have laid out – drawing attention to procedural norms, instituting inquiries, resisting sunset provisions, creating reporting requirements, emphasizing transparency and accountability, and sharply distinguishing between different areas of the law – will provide a starting point for the conversation that follows – a conversation that must follow if we are to take full account of the actual price we are paying for counterterrorist law. The stakes have never been higher.

We stand now on the threshold of a nuclear and biological age that may see the use of weapons far more destructive than what we have hitherto seen, and where a single man or woman could pose a threat to the very existence of the United Kingdom or the United States. What steps will these leading liberal, democratic states take to protect themselves from potential harm? If we are

---

* One intriguing approach is the creation of "white lists," which would confer rewards on regions, states, or entities that prove particularly helpful in tracing terrorist assets. *See* Jonathan Winer, *How to Clean up Dirty Money*, FIN. TIMES (London), Mar. 23, 2002, at 1. Apparently the US government has tried something similar: in October 2002, the United States agreed that the Financial Action Task Force would suspend its "name and shame" program to allow the International Monetary Fund to offer technical assistance to states that introduce more stringent anti-terrorist finance measures. Edward Alden, *The Money Trail: How a Crackdown on Suspect Charities is Failing to Stem the Flow of Funds to al Qaeda*, FIN. TIMES (London), Oct. 18, 2002, at 19.

to judge by the patterns I have identified in this book, their responses may fundamentally change the structure of each country.

We may, in the end, want the state structure to change. But if we do, that is the conversation we need to have. Backing into it, by asking what we need, in the short term, to counter a specific threat, is the wrong way to proceed. Yet that is the approach we currently are taking, blinded to the broader and more profound costs of our counterterrorist regime.

Notes

1. The Perilous Dichotomy

The following are the sources of the epigraphs: RICHARD POSNER, NOT A SUICIDE PACT: THE CONSTITUTION IN A TIME OF NATIONAL EMERGENCY (2006), p. 9; Tony Blair, HC Debs, Sept. 14, 2001, Vol. 372 Col. 606; ROY JENKINS, A LIFE AT THE CENTER (1991), p. 397.

1. Author interview with Rep. James Sensenbrenner, Palo Alto, California (Spring 2002). *See also* STEVEN BRILL, AFTER (2003), p. 73–76.
2. *See* Beryl A. Howell, *Seven Weeks: The Making of the USA PATRIOT Act*, 72 GEO. WASH. L. REV. 1145 (2004).
3. Jim Dempsey, Ctr. for Democracy and Tech., D.C., Guest Lecture at Stanford University Law School (Jan. 24, 2005).
4. BRILL, *supra* note 1, at 175.
5. Interview with Rep. James Sensenbrenner, *supra* note 1.
6. Dempsey Lecture, *supra* note 3.
7. *Department of Justice Oversight: Preserving our Freedoms While Defending Against Terrorism; Hearings before the Committee on the Judiciary, U.S. Senate,* 107th Cong. (Dec. 6, 2001) (statement of John Ashcroft, Attn'y Gen. of the United States).
8. USA PATRIOT Act, Pub. L. No. 107–56, § 218, 115 Stat. 272 (codified as amended at 50 U.S.C. §§ 1804(a)(7)(B), 1823(a)(7)(B) (2000 & Supp. 2001).
9. *House Approves Renewal of Patriot Act: Critics Voice Concern over Civil Liberties,* CNN.COM, July 22, 2005, *available at* www.cnn.com/2005/POLITICS/07/21/patriot.act/.
10. *See* USA PATRIOT Improvement and Reauthorization Act of 2005, Pub. L. No. 109–177, tit. I §§ 102–03120 Stat. 192, at § 115 (judicial review of national security letters), § 119 (audit of use of national security letters); Combat Methamphetamine Epidemic Act of 2005, Pub. L. No. 109–177, tit. VII, 120 Stat. 192 (codified as amended in scattered sections of 18 U.S.C.).
11. *See, e.g.,* HOME OFFICE, COUNTERING INTERNATIONAL TERRORISM: THE UNITED KINGDOM'S STRATEGY, July 2006, Cmd 6888, at 68 (stating, "the police and the security and intelligence agencies have disrupted many attacks against the UK since November 2000, including four since last July alone.")

12. RICHARD POSNER, NOT A SUICIDE PACT: THE CONSTITUTION IN A TIME OF NATIONAL EMERGENCY (2006), p. 9.

13. *See, e.g.*, POSNER, *supra* note 12, at 31; and Richard Posner, *Torture, Interrogation, and Terrorism*, in TORTURE: A COLLECTION 291(Sanford Levinson ed., 2004).

14. Adrian Vermeule & Eric Posner, *Emergencies and Democratic Failure*, 92 VA. L. REV. 1091, 1098 (2006).

15. *Id. See also* HOWARD BALL, THE USA PATRIOT ACT OF 2001: BALANCING CIVIL LIBERTIES AND NATIONAL SECURITY: A REFERENCE HANDBOOK (2004) (writing, e.g., "All . . . have different views about how far a society can balance civil liberties with national security. Those differences lie at the heart of this war against terror." (p. xv); and "National security matters do demand a degree of confidentiality and secrecy. However, there needs to be some balance so that the public is informed about the actions of government at appropriate times – without jeopardizing the ongoing war against terrorists," pp. 129–130); Alan Brinkley, *A Familiar Story: Lessons from Past Assaults on Freedoms*, in WAR ON OUR FREEDOMS, CIVIL LIBER-TIES IN AN AGE OF TERRORISM, 23 (Richard C. Leone, ed., 2003), (asserting, "The United States faces grave dangers in the aftermath of the attacks of September 2001, and the aggressive efforts of the government to seize new powers and to curb tra-ditional liberties cannot be dismissed as cynical or frivolous. Some alteration in our understanding of rights is appropriate and necessary in dangerous times, as even the most ardent civil libertarians tend to admit," p. 45); AMITAI ETZIONI, HOW PATRIOTIC IS THE PATRIOT ACT? FREEDOM VERSUS SECURITY IN THE AGE OF TERROR-ISM (2004), p. 43, (writing, "As I have made clear from the outset, I take it for granted that both individual rights and public safety must be protected, and given that on many occasions advancing one requires some curtailment of the other. The key question is: what is the proper balance between these two cardinal values?"); MARK SIDEL, MORE SECURE, LESS FREE?: ANTITERRORISM POLICY AND CIVIL LIBERTIES AFTER SEPTEMBER 11 (2004); Ruth Wedgwood, *The Rule of Law and the War on Terror*, N.Y. TIMES, Dec. 23, 2003, at A27 (stating: "In the ongoing war with Al Qaeda, America's civic ideals should not frustrate an effective defense.")

16. Prepared Remarks of Attorney General Alberto R. Gonzales at the US Attorney's National Security Conference, Jan. 11, 2007.

17. *See, e.g.*, *9/11 Commission's Recommendations: Balancing Civil Liberties and Security: Hearing Before the Subcommittee on National Security, Emerging Threats, and International Relations of the Committee on Government Reform*, House of Representatives, 109th Cong., 2nd sess. (June 6, 2006).

18. David Cole, *Enemy Aliens*, 54 STAN. L. REV. 953 (2002). *See also* David Cole & James X. Dempsey, TERRORISM AND THE CONSTITUTION: SACRIFICING CIVIL LIBER-TIES IN THE NAME OF NATIONAL SECURITY, (2002), p. 1 (writing that the 9/11 attacks "sparked a fundamental debate about the tension between liberty and security in the United States, and in particular about the capability of our government to keep us secure within the confines of due process, respect for freedoms of speech and association, and a system of government powers subject to checks and balances"); Mortin Halperin, Center for National Security Studies, *National Security and Civil Liberties: A Benchmark Report, Feb. 1981, CNSS Report No. 107*, at 37 (writ-ing, "Recall that the principles required a balancing of national security claims against the liberty of individuals rather than an uncritical acceptance of national security requirements"); Lawyers Committee for Human Rights, *Assessing the New Normal: Liberty and Security for the Post-September 11 United States* (2003) (stating, *e.g*, "Yet too many of the policies that have led to this new normal not

only fail to enhance U.S. security, as each of the following chapters discusses, but also exact an unnecessarily high price in liberty," p. v); Susan Herman, *The USA PATRIOT Act and the U.S. Department of Justice: Losing Our Balance?*, JURIST, Dec. 3, 2001 (writing, "Some of the more vocal members of Congress have been congratulating themselves for having struck an appropriate balance between our need for security and our need for civil liberties.... [H]ow will we ever be able to evaluate whether or not the powers now wielded by the Executive Branch are, as the legislation asserts, "required" to combat terrorism?...I don't know whether we have lost our balance, but I do know that power is careening in one direction."), available at http://jurist.law.pitt.edu/forum/.

19. Prime Minister's interview with CNN, *We Are at War with Terrorism*, Sept. 16, 2001, available at www.number10.gov.uk.

20. Lord Goldsmith, *Speech to the Royal Services Institute*, May 10, 2006, available at http://news.bbc.co.uk.

21. *Id.*

22. William Whitelaw, HC Debs, Mar. 18, 1981, Vol. 1, col. 341.

23. Ian Paisley, HC Debs, Dec. 8, 1977, Vol. 940, col. 1737.

24. A. V. DICEY, INTRODUCTION TO THE STUDY OF THE LAW OF THE CONSTITUTION 3 (Macmillan) (1915). *See also* WILLIAM BLACKSTONE, COMMENTARIES ON THE LAWS OF ENGLAND vol. iv, 160–161 (University of Chicago Press 1979) (1769).

25. A. W. BRADLEY AND KEITH EWING, CONSTITUTIONAL AND ADMINISTRATIVE LAW (2003).

26. *See* Clive Walker and R. Weaver, *The United Kingdom Bill of Rights* (2000) 33 UNIV. MICH. J. L. REFORM 497; and *R. v. McCormick* [1977] N.I. 105 (interpreting provisions in the Northern Ireland (Emergency Provisions) Act 1973, relating to the admissibility of statements from detainees, article 3 being the operative standard).

27. *See* M. Beloff & H. Mountfield, *Unconventional Behaviour? Judicial Uses of the European Convention on Human Rights in England and Wales*, EUR. HUM. RTS. L. REV. 467 (1996); M. HUNT, USING HUMAN RIGHTS LAW IN ENGLISH COURTS (1997); and *Waddington v. Miah* [1974] 1 W.L.R. 683.

28. *See R. v. Secretary of State for the Home Department, ex p. Brind* [1990] 1 All E.R. 469; *R. v. General Medical Council, ex p. Colman* [1990] 1 All E.R. 489; *R. v. Sec of State for Defence ex p Smith* [1996] 2 W.L.R. 305.

29. *See R. v. Chief Immigration Officer, Heathrow Airport, ex p. Salamat Bibi* [1976] 1 Wash. L. Rev. 979; *Fernandes v. Home Secretary* [1981] Immigration Appeal Reports 1; *R. v. Home Secretary, ex p. Kirkwood* [1984] 2 All E.R. 390.

30. *See, e.g., A.G. v. BBC* [1981] A.C. 303. For discussion of the citation of the European Convention in English cases, see M. J. Beloff & H. H. Mountfield, *supra* note 27; Hunt, *supra* note 27; R. SINGH, THE FUTURE OF HUMAN RIGHTS IN THE UNITED Kingdom (1997). *But see Rantzen v. Mirror Group Newspapers* [1994] QB 670; *Derbyshire County Council v. Times Newspapers* [1993] 2 Wash. L. Rev. 449.

31. European Communities Act 1972, § 2 & 3.

32. *Firma J. Nold K.G. v. E.C. Commission* [1974] 2 Comm. Mkt. L. Rev. 338. But note that in 1996 the Court of Justice held that the European Communities were not competent to accede directly to the Convention. *See Opinion 2/94: Accession by the Community to the Convention for the Protection of Human Rights and Fundamental Freedoms* [1996] ECR-I 1759; S. O'Leary, *Accession by the European Communities to the ECHR*, EUR. HUM. RTS. L. REV. 362 (1996); A. G. Toth, *The European Union and Human Rights*, 34 COMM. MKT. L. REV. 491 (1977).

33. *See Wauchauf v. F.R.G.* [1989] E.C.R. 2609; *E.R.T. v. Dimotiki Etairia Pliroforissis* [1991] E.C.R. 2925.

34. This is also true of the Amsterdam Treaty. *See* L. BATTEN & N. GRIEF, EUROPEAN UNION LAW AND HUMAN RIGHTS (1999); T. C. Hartley, *Constitutional and Institutional Aspects of the Maastricht Agreement*, 42 INT'L & COMP. L. Q. 213 (1993); M. Colvin & P. Noorlander, *Human Rights and Accountability After the Treaty of Amsterdam*, 191 EUR. HUM. RTS. L. REV. 191 (1998).

35. Human Rights Act, 1998, c. 42, §3(1).

36. *See* Beloff et al., *supra* note 27, and Hunt, *supra* note 27.

37. Additionally, unlike previous practice, the HRA imposes a legal duty on public authorities to act in a manner consistent with the ECHR Human Rights Act, 1998, c. 42, §6.

38. *See, e.g.*, POSNER, *supra* note 12, at 11, 72–73 (arguing it is *sui generis*). *See also* Eric Posner, *Fear and the Regulatory Model of Counterterrorism*, 25 HARV. J. L. & PUB. POL'Y 681 (2002).

39. Prime Minister Tony Blair, *Statement in Response to Terrorist Attacks in the United States*, Sept. 11, 2001, available at www. number10.gov.uk.

40. *Id.*

41. Prime Minister Tony Blair, *Briefing to the Press en Route to New York* (2001), available at www. number10.gov.uk.

42. President George Bush, *Address to a Joint Session of Congress and the American People*, Washington, D.C., Sept. 20, 2001.

43. *Id.*

44. *See* Sir Winston Churchill, "Sinews of Peace" address in Missouri, 1946 (saying, "Neither the sure prevention of war, nor the continuous rise of world organisation will be gained without what I have called the fraternal association of the English-speaking peoples ... a special relationship between the British Commonwealth and Empire and the United States.")

45. Bush, *supra* note 42.

46. *September 11 Attacks: Prime Minister's Statement Including Question and Answer Session*, available at www. number10.gov.uk.

47. Prime Minister's interview, *supra* note 19.

48. For report on Operation Veritas in Afghanistan see *Ministry of Defence Performance Report 2001/2002*, available at http://www.archive2.official-documents.co.uk/.

49. Prime Minister's interview, *supra* note 19.

50. Authorization for Use of Military Force, Sept. 18, 2001, Pub. Law 107-40, S.J. Res. 23, 107th Congress, available at http://news.findlaw.com.

51. *See also National Defense Strategy of the United States of America*, March 2005, p. 5, available at www.globalsecurity.org/military/.

52. U.S. Government Accountability Office, *Information Security: Department of Homeland Security Faces Challenges in Fulfilling Statutory Requirements*, Statement of Gregory C. Wilshusen, Director, Information Security Issues, Apr. 14, 2005, p. 8, available at http://www.gao.gov.

53. *See, e.g.*, referring to the "struggle" against terrorism: *Tony Blair, PM Praises 'High Point' in Pakistani Relations*, Nov. 19, 2006, available at www.pm.gov.uk; Tony Blair, *Prime Minister's Speech at Canary Wharf*, Mar. 21, 2006, available at www.pm.gov.uk; Tony Blair, *Press Conference with the Spanish Prime Minister*, July 27, 2005, available at www.pm.gov.uk. *See, e.g.*, referring to the "fight" against

terrorism: *Transcript of Door Step Interview: Prime Minister Tony Blair and President Chirac*, Sept. 20, 2001, available at www.number10.gov.uk; *Look Back at the PM's Week*, available at www.pm.gov.uk; *Remarks of the Prime Minister's Official Spokesman*, Sept. 26, 2001 and Nov. 9, 2005, available at www.pm.gov.uk; *Opening Statement of Prime Minister Tony Blair in Joint Press Conference with Shaukat Aziz*, Mar. 6, 2006, available at www.pm.gov.uk.

54. Lucy Bannerman, *There Is No War on Terror in Britain, says DPP*, THE TIMES (LONDON), Jan. 24, 2007.

55. *See, e.g.*, NEIL C. LIVINGSTONE, THE WAR AGAINST TERRORISM (1982); FIGHTING BACK: WINNING THE WAR AGAINST TERRORISM (Neil C. Livingstone & Terrell E. Arnold eds., 1986); NEIL C. LIVINGSTONE, INSIDE THE PLO: COVERT UNITS, SECRET FUNDS, AND THE WAR AGAINST ISRAEL AND THE UNITED STATES (1990).

56. *See, e.g.*, Mike Allen & Barton Gellman, *Going Backwards: Preemptive Strikes Part of U.S. Strategic Doctrine: 'All Options' Open for Countering Unconventional Arms*, WASH. POST, Dec. 11, 2002.

57. TERRORISM (Steven Anzovin ed., 1986); Eric Posner describes the state's operational intent: "The government does not so much punish the terrorists as disrupt their networks, harass their supporters, and defeat them on the field of battle. Authorities may use propaganda and censorship, and may abrogate civil liberties to a limited extent." Eric Posner, *Fear and the Regulatory Model of Counterterrorism*, 25 HARV. J. L. & PUB. POL'Y 681 (2002).

58. John Bellinger, *Armed Conflict with Al Qaida?*, OPINIO JURIS, Feb. 28, 2007, available at www.opiniojuris.org.

59. Online NewsHour, *Interview of Sandy Berger by Jim Lehrer*, President Clinton's National Security Adviser discusses the US missile strike against targets in Sudan and Afghanistan and future actions against the terrorist organization headed by Saudi millionaire Osama bin Laden, available at http://www.pbs.org/newshour.

60. M. MULHOLLAND, THE LONGEST WAR: NORTHERN IRELAND'S TROUBLED HISTORY (2002), p. 92; and P. BEW AND G. BILLESPIE, NORTHERN IRELAND: A CHRONOLOGY OF THE TROUBLES, 1968–1999 (1999), p. 36.

61. *Where are British Troops and Why?*, BBC News, Mar. 25, 2007, available at http://news.bbc.co.uk; and Ministry of Defence Performance Report 2001/2002, available at http://www.archive2.official-documents.co.uk/doc.

62. *See* Barrett, *in* INTERNATIONAL TERRORISM, CHALLENGE AND RESPONSE: PROCEEDINGS OF THE JERUSALEM CONFERENCE ON INTERNATIONAL TERRORISM (Benjamin Netanyahu ed., 1981), at 125.

63. For discussion of the hybrid war/crime model adopted by the United States post-9/11, *see* David Luban, *The War on Terrorism and the End of Human Rights*, 22(3) PHIL. & PUB. POL'Y Q. 9 (2002), available at http://www.publicpolicy.umd.edu.

64. Prime Minister's Official Spokesman, *Press Briefing*, Apr. 16, 2007, available at www.pm.gov.uk.

65. I agree here with Judge Richard Posner, who suggests that focus on this question rather misses the important issues. *See* POSNER, *supra* note 12, at 72.

66. ALEXANDER CHARNS. CLOAK AND GAVEL, FBI WIRETAPS, BUGS, INFORMERS, AND THE SUPREME COURT (1992), p. 25.

67. *Supplementary Detailed Staff Reports on Intelligence Activities and the Rights of Americans, Book III, Final report of the Select Committee to Study Governmental Operations with Respect to Intelligence Activities*, U. S. Senate, Apr. 23, 1976, p. 1, available at www.icdc.com.

68. *See United States v. Ehrlichman*, 376 F. Supp. 29 (D.D.C. 1974).

69. NICK KOTZ, JUDGMENT DAYS: LYNDON BAINES JOHNSON, MARTIN LUTHER KING, JR., AND THE LAWS THAT CHANGED AMERICA(2005), p. 96, 191, 196, 351; WILLIAM HENRY CHAFE, PRIVATE LIVES/PUBLIC CONSEQUENCES: PERSONALITY AND POLITICS IN MODERN AMERICA (2005), p. 225.

70. Hugh Davies, *Clinton Aide Faces Congress over Tax Files on Opponents*, TELEGRAPH (London), available at http://192.80.61.73/WebVAX/ETnew/.

71. Antiterrorism, Crime and Security Act, 2001, c. 24.

72. Civil Authorities (Special Powers) Act (Northern Ireland), 1922, 12 & 13 Geo. 5, c. 5, §1(1).

73. Adam Clymer, *How Sept. 11 Changed Goals of Justice Department*, N.Y. TIMES, Feb. 28, 2002, p. A1. *See also* 9/11 Commission Report, p. 210, citing Interview with Thomas Pickard, Acting Director of the Federal Bureau of Investigation, Jan. 21, 2004, available at http://www.9–11commission.gov/report/.

74. Prevention of Terrorism (Temporary Provisions) Act, 1974, c. 56.

75. Bush, *supra* note 42. *See also* Attorney *General John Ashcroft Testimony before the Senate Committee on the Judiciary*, Sept. 25, 2001, available at www.usdoj.gov. archive (stating "Every day that passes with outdated statutes and the old rules of engagement is a day that terrorists have a competitive advantage.")

76. BRILL, *supra* note 1, at 174.

77. *See* HC Debs 28 Nov. 1974, vol. 882, cols. 634–943; HL Debs 28 Nov. 1974 vol. 354, cols. 1500–1570; and C. P. Walker, THE PREVENTION OF TERRORISM IN BRITISH LAW (1992).

78. *See The Federal Raid on Ruby Ridge, ID: Hearings Before the Subcommittee on Terrorism, Technology, and Government Information of the Committee on the Judiciary*, United States Senate, 104th Cong., first session . . . September 6, 7, 8, 12, 14, 15, 19, 20, 21, 22, 26; and October 13, 18, and 19, 1995; *Continuation of Oversight of the Wen Ho Lee Case: Hearings Before the Subcommittee on Administrative Oversight and the Courts of the Committee on the Judiciary*, United States Senate, 106th Cong., second session, September 27 and October 3, 2000; and DAVID WISE, SPY: THE INSIDE STORY OF HOW THE FBI'S ROBERT HANSSEN BETRAYED AMERICA (2002).

79. Richard Posner, *The Reorganized U.S. Intelligence System After One Year*, NATIONAL SECURITY OUTLOOK AEI Online, Apr. 11, 2006, available at www.aei.org/publications/.

80. *See* LAURA K. DONOHUE, COUNTER-TERRORIST LAW AND EMERGENCY POWERS IN THE UNITED KINGDOM 1922–2000, pp. 1–206, 259–304.

81. *But see* POSNER, *supra* note 12, at 44 (writing, "Every time civil liberties have been curtailed in response to a national emergency, whether real or imagined, they have been fully restored when the emergency passed – and in fact before it passed, often long before."); ERIC A. POSNER & ADRIAN VERMEULE, TERROR IN THE BALANCE: SECURITY, LIBERTY, AND THE COURTS (2007), p. 131–32 (stating, "The ratchet theory lacks a mechanism that permits governmental powers to expand and prevents them from contracting, and it makes implausible assumptions about the rationality of officials and voters who consent to legal changes during emergencies."); Colm Campbell, *Wars on Terror and Vicarious Hegemons: The UK, International Law, and the Northern Ireland Conflict*, 54 INT'L & COMP. L. QUARTERLY 321 (2005) (arguing that the draconian nature of legislation runs in cycles depending on how close states feel to the triggering emergency).

82. Flags and Emblems (Display) Act (Northern Ireland), 1954, 2 & 3 Eliz. 2, c. 10; Repealed Under Direct Rule by Public Order (Northern Ireland) Order, 1987, S.I. 1987 No. 463 (N.I. 7).

83. Eric Lichtblau, *U.S. Uses Terror Law to Pursue Crimes from Drugs to Swindling*, N.Y. TIMES, Sept. 28, 2003, at A1.

84. *See The Attorney General's Guidelines on General Crimes, Racketeering Enterprise and Terrorism Enterprise Investigations*, May 30, 2002, available at www.usdoj.gov.olp; *The Attorney General's Guidelines Regarding the Use of Confidential Informants*, May 30, 2002, available at www.usdoj.gov.olp; and *Memorandum for the Heads and Inspectors General of Executive Departments and Agencies, From the Attorney General, May 30, 2002, Regarding Procedures for Lawful, Warrantless Monitoring of Verbal Communications*, available at www.usdoj.gov.olp.

85. *FBI Abused PATRIOT Act Powers, Audit Finds*, GUARDIAN, Mar. 9, 2007, available at http://www.guardian.co.uk/.

86. Privy Counsellor Review Committee, *Antiterrorism, Crime and Security Act 2001 Review: Report*. Presented to Parliament pursuant to §122(5) of the Anti-terrorism, Crime and Security Act 2002, Dec. 18, 2003, HC 100, p. 25.

87. THE HOUSE OF LORDS: ITS PARLIAMENTARY AND JUDICIAL ROLES (Paul Carmichael & Brice Dickson eds., 1999), Table 7.1, at 132.

88. JAMES MADISON, FEDERALIST NO. 51 (1788), reprinted in THE FEDERALIST PAPERS (Isaac Kramnick ed., 1987), p. 319.

89. For discussion of the rise of party politics in the United States *see* E.E. SCHATTSCHNEIDER, PARTY GOVERNMENT (1942); RICHARD HOFSTADTER, THE IDEA OF A PARTY SYSTEM: THE RISE OF A LEGITIMATE OPPOSITION IN THE UNITED STATES, 1780–1840 (1970); JOHN H. ALDRICH, WHY PARTIES?: THE ORIGIN AND TRANSFORMATION OF POLITICAL PARTIES IN AMERICA (1995).

90. *See* Daryl J. Levinson & Richard H. Pildes, *Separation of Parties, Not Powers*, 119 HARV. L. REV. 2314–5 (2006) (writing that "neither the Supreme Court nor any other federal court has ever quoted this critical insight, nor has it received much notice by legal scholars.")

91. *Youngstown Sheet & Tube Co. v. Sawyer*, 343 U.S. 579 (1952), at 654 (Jackson, J., concurring).

92. Levinson & Pildes, *supra* note 90, at 2341, citing DAVID EPSTEIN & SHARYN O'HALLORAN, DELEGATING POWERS, 121–62 (1999).

93. Id., at 2312.

94. *Executive Order Establishing the President's Board on Safeguarding Americans' Civil Liberties*, Aug. 24, 2004, available at www.whitehouse.gov/news/.

95. *Hamdan v. Rumsfeld*, 126 S.Ct. 2749 (2006).

96. 126 S. Ct. at 2799 (Breyer, J.)

97. A and others v. Secretary of State for the Home Department [2004] UKHL 56, 16 December 2004, available at www. publications.parliament.uk/pa.

98. A and others v. Secretary of State for the Home Department [2004] UKHL 56, para. 44, Lord Bingham of Cornhill.

99. *Kruse v. Johnson* [1898] 2 Q.B. 91; and *Papworth v. Coventry* [1967] 2 All E.R. 41.

100. *See, e.g., Brutus v. Cozens*, [1972] 3 WASH. L. REV. 521; *Kruse v. Johnson*, [1898] 2 Q.B. 91; and *Papworth v. Coventry*, [1967] 2 All E.R. 41; cited in Barnum, at 17–18.

101. Lord Donaldson of Lymington M.R., cited by Professor Graham J. Zellick, in ch. 10: Spies, Subversives, Terrorists and the British Government: Free Speech and other Casualties, in FREE SPEECH AND NATIONAL SECURITY, p. 95.

102. Charles Babington & Jonathan Weisman, *Senate Approves Detainee Bill Backed by Bush; Constitutional Challenges Predicted*, WASH. POST, Sept. 29, 2006, A01. *See also* R. Jeffrey Smith, *Specter's Rose in Passage of Detainee Bill Disputed*, WASH. POST, Oct. 16, 2006, at A19 (discussing Specter's efforts prior to the Bill's passage to amend it to restore *habeas*).

103. Babington & Weisman, *supra* note 101.

104. *Careless Congress; Lawmakers passed a detainee law of doubtful constitutionality*, L.A. TIMES, Nov. 3, 2006, A28.

105. Id., Babington & Weisman, *supra* note 101. *See also* Andrew Putz, *The Full Specter*, PHILADELPHIA MAG., Nov. 2006; Warren Richey, *Will the Supreme Court Shackle New Tribunal Law?*, CHRISTIAN SCIENCE MONITOR, Oct. 17, 2006; *The Two Arlen Specters*, LOWELL SUN, Oct. 19, 2006.

106. Careless Congress, *supra* note 103.

107. *Lakhdar Boumediene et al. v. George W. Bush*; and *Khaled A. F. al Odah, v. United States*, Nos. 06–1195 and 06–1196; 549 U.S. (2007), Apr. 2, 2007. *See also* Lyle Denniston, *Analysis: Court Denies Detainees' Habeas Cases*, Apr. 2, 2007, available at www.scotusblog.com.

108. *Liverppool S. S. Co. v. Commissioners of Emigration*, 113 U.S. 33, 39 (1885).

109. *Aetna Life Ins. Co. v. Haworth*, 300 U.S. 227, 240–1 (1937).

110. *Lujan v. Defenders of Wildlife*, 504 U.S. 555 (1992) (striking down a "citizen suit" provision in an environmental statute, but holding open the possibility that Congress could, in the future, articulate chains of causation to confer standing) (Kennedy, J.)

111. ROBERT L. STERN, EUGENE GRESSMAN, STEPHEN M. SHAPIRO, & KENNETH S. GELLER, SUPREME COURT PRACTICE, 8TH ED. (2002), at 812.

112. *See* PDF of H.R. 3162, available at http://frwebgate.access.gpo.gov/.

113. *But see New York Times Co. v. United States*, 403 U.S. 713; and 1866 *Ex Parte Milligan*, stating that if the civil courts are open for business, the writ cannot be suspended. During the American Civil War, President Lincoln suspended the writ of habeas corpus and subsequently detained twenty to thirty thousand people. In *Ex parte Merryman*, Chief Justice Taney, sitting as a circuit judge, did say such actions were unconstitutional; but the executive simply ignored the holding.

114. Espionage Act of June 15, 1917, ch. 30, title I, §3, 40 Stat. 219, amended by Act of May 16, 1918, ch. 75, 40 Stat. 553–54, reenacted by Act of Mar. 3, 1921, ch. 136, 41 Stat. 1359, current version codified at 18 U.S.C. §2388.

115. *See, e.g., Schenck v. United States*, 249 U.S. 47, 39 S. Ct. 247, U.S. 1919, Mar. 3, 1919; *Debs v. United States*, 249 U.S. 211, 39 S. Ct. 252, Mar. 10, 1919; *Abrams v. United States*, 250 U.S. 616, 40 S. Ct. 17, Nov. 10, 1919.

116. *Hirabayashi v. United States*, 320 U.S. 81 (1943), at 93 (Stone, C. J. citations omitted) and *Korematsu v. US*, 321 U.S. 760 (1944).

117. 320 U.S. at 93.

118. *Id.*

119. *Id.*

120. Lord Nicholls of Birkenhead, A (FC) and others (FC) v. Secretary of State for the Home Department; X (FC) and another (FC) v. Secretary of State for the Home

Department, Dec. 16, 2004 [2004] UKHL 56, at 79. *See also* Lord Walker of Gestingthorpe [2004] UKHL 56, at 192.

121. Lord Rodger of Earlsferry, [2004] UKHL 56, at 166.

122. *US* v. *Curtiss-Wright Export Corp.*, 299 U.S. 304 (1936), at 319.

123. *See, e.g., Korematsu* v. *US*, 323 U.S. 214 (1944); *Hirabayashi* v. *US*, 320 U.S. 81 (1943); *Zemel* v. *Rusk*, 381 U.S. I (1965); *Haig* v. *Agee*, 453 U.S. 280 (1981); *US* v. *Snepp*, 444 U.S. 507 (1980).

124. Posner, *supra* note 11, at 35–6.

125. *Id.*, at 36.

126. *Id.*, at 37 (emphasis in original).

127. *See, e.g., Greer* v. *Spock*, 424 U.S. 828 (1976) and *US* v. *Albertini*, 472 U.S. 675 (1985). *See also* POSNER, *supra* note 12; and ERIC POSNER & ADRIAN VERMEULE, TERROR IN THE BALANCE: SECURITY, LIBERTY AND THE COURTS (2007) (both suggesting that the judiciary is not functionally/institutionally suited to delve into the national security realm).

128. *See, e.g., Snepp* v. *United States*, 444 U.S. 507 (1980), at 510; *United States* v. *Marchetti*, 466 F.2d 1309.

129. One notable exception to this is the case of *Donovan* v. *FBI*, 806 F. 2d 55 (2d Cir. 1986).

130. 5 U.S.C. Sec. 552 (b)(3); *CIA* v. *Sims*, 471 U.S. 159 (1985) (holding that information collected by the CIA was exempt from review of classification assignation)

131. *Id.*, 471 U.S. at 175.

132. Posner et al., *supra* note 126.

133. *Id.*

134. CATHERINE MCNICOL STOCK, RURAL RADICALS: RIGHTEOUS RAGE IN THE AMERICAN GRAIN (1996), p. 18.

135. Author Interview with Mark Potok, Director, Intelligence Project, Southern Poverty Law Center, May 23, 2007, by telephone from Stanford, California; Mark Potok, *The American Radical Right: The 1990s and Beyond*, in WESTERN DEMOCRACIES AND THE NEW EXTREME RIGHT CHALLENGE (Roger Eatwell ed., 2003). *See also* www.splcenter.org.

136. *Id.*

137. *Fighting Terrorism: Leading FBI Official Discusses Domestic Terrorism*, INTELLIGENCE REPORT, Southern Poverty Law Center, 1998, Issue 92, p. 8.

138. Mark Potok, *supra* note 134.

139. GEORGE ORWELL, ANIMAL FARM (originally published 1946), (1996), p. 133.

140. BBC News, *Q&C: Terror Laws Explained*, Jan. 25, 2005, available at http://news.bbc.co.uk/.

141. *See* Metropolitan Police Authority, REPORT OF THE MPA SCRUTINY ON MPs STOP AND SEARCH PRACTICE, May 2004, p. 25; National Statistics Online, available at www.statistics.gov.uk/.

142. *Taking Liberties*, THE INDEPENDENT (London), Mar. 3, 2005, p. 1.

143. Catherine MacLeod, *MPs Back Terror Bill as Clark Gives in on Judges*, THE HERALD (Glasgow), Mar. 10, 2005, p. 1 (quoting Prime Minister Tony Blair).

144. David Charter, *Labour MPs Return to the Fold After Clarke's Charm Offensive*, THE TIMES (London), Mar. 10, 2005, p. 6.

145. *See, e.g.*, statement of Jeremy Corbyn, Labour MP for Islington North, in *Police shot Brazilian Eight Times*, BBC News, July 25, 2005, *available at* http://news.bbc.co.uk/.

146. Jeremy Corbyn, *Feature – On a Dangerous Path*, Morning Star (Plymouth, England), Aug. 10, 2005.
147. Posner, *supra* note 79.
148. *See, e.g.*, Mariano-Florentino Cuéllar, *Running Aground: The Hidden Environmental and Regulatory Implications of Homeland Security*, ACS Issue Brief, May 2007, available at www.acslaw.org/node/4919; and Charles Perrow, The Next Catastrophe: Reducing Our Vulnerabilities to Natural, Industrial, and Terrorist Disasters, (2007).
149. *See generally* World Tourism Organization, available at www.world-tourism.org. 2006 edition annexes available at www.unwto.orghttp://www.unwto.org/facts/eng/pdf/indicators/new/ITR05_americas_US$.pdf [Data collected as of November 2006].
150. World Health Report 2004, Statistical Annex, pp. 120–1.
151. Christopher F. Chyba, *Biotechnology and the Challenge to Arms Control*, Arms Control Today, Oct. 2006, available at http://www.armscontrol.org.
152. Justice Felix Frankfurter, *Youngstown Sheet & Tube Co. et al. v. Sawyer*, 343 U.S. 559, 889 (1952).
153. Lord Lloyd of Berwick, HL Debs, Feb. 1, 2006, Vol. 678, Col. 235.

2. Indefinite Detention and Coercive Interrogation

The following are the sources of the epigraphs: u.s. Army Field Manual, [FM 34–52], May 8, 1987; Convention Against Torture, Article 2(2), February 4, 1985, signed by the United Kingdom March 15, 1985; Memorandum from John Yoo, Deputy Assistant Attorney General, and Robert J. Delahunty, Special Counsel, US Department of Justice Office of Legal Counsel, to William J. Haynes II (Jan. 9, 2002); Captain Ian Fishback, 82nd Airborne, Letter to Senator John McCain, (Sept. 16, 2005); Tom Parker quoted in Jane Mayer, *Outsourcing Torture: The Secret History of America's "Extraordinary Rendition" Program*, The New Yorker, Feb. 7, 2005, available at www.newyorker.com.
1. Lord Rodger of Earlsferry, [2004] UKHL 56, at 166; *Ceremonies Mark Fifth Anniversary of 9/11 Attacks*, PBS Online NewsHour, Sept. 11, 2006, available at www.pbs.org/newshour/.
2. 1215 Magna Carta, cl. 39, available at www.cs.indiana.edu/statecraft/.
3. *Id.*, cl. 40.
4. *Id.*, cl. 20.
5. William Blackstone, Commentaries 3:129–37, 1768. [Blackstone, William. Commentaries on the Laws of England: A Facsimile of the First Edition of 1765 – 1769. Chicago: University of Chicago Press, 1979.]
6. *Id.*, at 4
7. 1628 Petition of Right, 3 Car. I, at III. available at http://britannia.com/history/.
8. 1679 Habeas Corpus Act, 31 Car. II. c. 2. *See also* 16 Car. I. c. 10. §. 8
9. Blackstone, *supra* note 5 at 4.
10. *Id.*
11. *Id.*
12. Lord Falconer of Thoroton, HL Debs, 26 Mar 2003, cols 851–4.
13. *Id.*
14. *Id.*

15. *Id.*
16. Winston Churchill, HC Debs, Feb. 16, 1922 (Second Reading of the Irish Free State Bill).
17. *Id.*
18. HC Debs, Dec. 11, 1972, Vol. 848, col. 80.
19. *Id.*
20. Humphrey Atkins, HC Debs, Jul. 2, 1979, Vol. 969, col. 928.
21. *Id.*
22. Tom Litterick, HC Debs, Dec. 8, 1977, Vol. 940, col. 1710.
23. Roy Jenkins, A Life at the Centre (1991), p. 377.
24. 1922 Civil Authorities (Special Powers) Act (Northern Ireland) 1922, 1. Each regulation was to be laid before the Northern Ireland Parliament, which had 14 days to annul it. *Id.* at 1(4).
25. Civil Authorities (Special Powers) Act (Northern Ireland) 1922, Regulation 23. *See also* Regulations 11, 12, and 13 (S.R.O. 191/1956, Dec. 15, 1956). For discussion of the regulations introduced under the 1922 Act *see* Laura K. Donohue, Counter-terrorist Law and Emergency Powers in the United Kingdom 1922–2000 (2000).
26. S.R.O. 34/1922, 20.5.22. *See also* Regulations 23A, 23B, 23C, and 23D.
27. Civil Authorities Special Powers Act (Northern Ireland), Regulation 23A; S.R.O. 36/1922, 1.6.1922, Belfast Gazette 30.6.1922.
28. *Id. See also* Donohue, *supra* note 25, at 45.
29. Civil Authorities (Special Powers) Act (Northern Ireland) 1922, 12 Geo. 5, c. 5; Civil Authorities (Special Powers) Act (Northern Ireland) 1928 (18 & 19 Geo. 5, c. 15); Civil Authorities (Special Powers) Act (Northern Ireland) 1933 (23 & 24 Geo. 5, c. 12). *See also* Civil Authorities (Special Powers) Act (Northern Ireland 1943, (6&7 Geo. 6, c. 2).
30. *See* Donohue, *supra* note 25, at 44–63.
31. Civil Authorities (Special Powers) Act (Northern Ireland) 1922, substituted by Regulation 10 of the Civil Authorities (Special Powers) Acts (Amending) (No. 6) Regulation (Northern Ireland) (S. R. & O. 1957, No. 132)]. Civil Authorities (Special Powers) Act (Amending) Regulations (Northern Ireland) 1956, Regulation 11(1).
32. *See Ireland v. United Kingdom* (1978) 2 EHRR 25, ¶ 35. (Giorgio Balladore Pallieri, President).
33. *In re Keenan and another* [1971] 3 W.L.R., at 537 (Lord Denning, M. R.) (The Order read, "I, R. E. G. Shillington, chief constable of the Royal Ulster Constabulary, hereby authorise you, for the preservation of peace and the maintenance of order, to arrest without warrant those named in the attached schedule and to detain them for a period of not more than 48 hours for the purpose of interrogation at a suitable police office.")
34. HC Debs, Vol. 831, col. 598 (Feb. 17, 1972).
35. Patrick Bishop & Eamonn Mallie, The Provisional IRA (1987), at 186.
36. *Id.*
37. HC Debs, Vol. 823, col. 10 (Sept. 22, 1971).
38. Donohue, *supra* note 25, at 59–60.
39. Charles Carlton, *Judging Without Consensus: The Diplock Courts in Northern Ireland*, 3 Law & Pol'y Quarterly, 225–42. (1981), citing the Sunday Times, 1972: 269.
40. Donohue, *supra* note 25, at 118.

41. Michael McKeown, Two seven six three: an analysis of fatalities attributable to civil disturbances in Northern Ireland in the twenty years between July 13, 1969 and July 12, 1989 (1989).

42. *In re Keenan and another* [1971] 3 W.L.R., at 537 (Lord Denning, M. R.)

43. *In re McElduff*, [1972] N.I. 1 1972 WL 37585.

44. *Id.*, and *In re Keenan, supra* note 42 at 537–8.

45. *In re Keenan and another, supra* note 42, at 844.

46. *Id.*

47. Sir William Blackstone, Commentaries on the Laws of England, 11th ed (1791), vol. 3, p. 131.

48. 1862 Habeas Corpus Act, 25 & 26 Vict., c. 20.

49. *In re Keenan and another, supra* note 42, at 542 (Lord Denning, M. R.)

50. *Id. See also* Stephenson, L. J. at 543 (writing, "I accept the Attorney-General's submission that since 1783 the judicature of Ireland has been completely independent, that its courts have had exclusive rights over all proceedings in them, and that, although the power of the English courts to send writs of habeas corpus to Ireland has not been expressly abrogated, no writs of habeas corpus have in fact been sent to any part of Ireland since that date for the good reason that the power of these courts to send them there has been impliedly abrogated by the three statutes of the 1780's.")

51. *In re McElduff, supra* note 43, p. 11, lines 11–14

52. *Id.*, p. 11, lines 22–36. (McGonigal, J.)

53. *Id.*, p. 11, lines 37–39 & p. 12, lines 1–5. (McGonigal, J.)

54. *Id.*, p. 23, lines 22–28. (McGonigal, J.)

55. *Id.*, pp. 12–13. (McGonigal, J.), quoting *Alderson v. Booth* [1969] 2 Q.B. 216 at p. 220 (Lord Parker).

56. *Id.*, p. 14, lines 32–40. (McGonigal, J.)

57. Brian Cashinella, *Ulster Consternation over Detainee Case*, The Times, Feb. 21, 1972, at 2.

58. *Id.*

59. *Kelly v. Faulkner and Others*, [1973] N.I. 31, p. 34, lines 18–26. (Gibson, J.)

60. *Kelly v. Faulkner and Others*, [1973] N.I. 31, p. 36, lines 11–19. (Gibson, J.) (writing, "It is true, say the defendants, that in ordinary circumstances the law is most solicitous for the protection of those arrested without a warrant to ensure that they know the reason for the arrest, but these personal considerations ought to be subordinated to the more vital necessities of guarding the public welfare even at the risk of some loss of personal protection where the regulations indicate that there may be an arrest without the suspicion of any offence having been committed or even without the suspicion of any conduct detrimental to the public safety.")

61. *Kelly v. Faulkner and Others*, [1973] N.I. 31, p. 36, lines 23–26. (Gibson, J.).

62. *Kelly v. Faulkner and Others*, [1973] N.I. 31, p. 44, lines 5–17. (Gibson, J.).

63. S.R.O. 71/1957, 16.4.57.

64. Donohue, *supra* note 25, at 121–123.

65. H. C. Debs, Feb. 23, 1972, Vol. 821, cols 1368–1499.

66. Northern Ireland Act, 1972, Eliz. II, c. 10.

67. S.I. 1972/1632 (N.I. 15).

68. Lowry, *Internment: Detention Without Trial in Northern Ireland* (1976), 5 Hum. Rights 261, 286–290.

69. The Detention of Terrorists (Northern Ireland) Order (1972 NO. 1632 (N.I. 15)).

70. Northern Ireland (Emergency Provisions) Act 1973 (c. 53), Sched. 1, ¶. 11(3).

71. *See, e.g.*, HC Debs Vol. 843, col. 380 (Oct. 26, 1972); Vol. 845 col. 226 (Nov. 4, 1972); Vol. 853, col. 250 (Mar. 20, 1973).

72. *See* H. C. Debs, Vol. 848, col. 47 (Dec. 11, 1972).

73. *Ireland v. United Kingdom, supra* note 32, ¶. 48. (Giorgio Balladore Pallieri, President).

74. HC Debs, Vol. 832, col. 242 (Mar. 28, 1972).

75. HC Debs, Vol. 837, col. 1639 (May 25, 1972).

76. Internment and Detention without Trial in Northern Ireland 1971–1975: Ministerial Policy and Practice, author interview with Viscount Whitelaw at the Privy Council on November 23, [19]84, MODERN L. REV., Vol. 49, Nov. 1986, p. 717.

77. Michael Zander, *Diplock, the Non-jury Judge*, GUARDIAN (London), Oct. 15, 1985.

78. *Obituary of Lord Diplock*, TIMES (London), Oct. 16, 1985.

79. *Id.*

80. TOM HADDEN & PADDY HILLYARD, JUSTICE IN NORTHERN IRELAND: A STUDY IN SOCIAL CONFIDENCE (1973).

81. *Id.* A study by Tom Hadden and Paddy Hillyard in 1973, for instance, found that in political cases, the court denied bail to 79% of the Catholics who came before it, but only 54% of the Protestants. TOM HADDEN & PADDY HILLYARD, JUSTICE IN NORTHERN IRELAND; A STUDY IN SOCIAL CONFIDENCE (1973).

82. Carlton, *supra* note 39. *See also* Joe Joyce & Paul Johnson, *Irish Minister Deplores Diplock Changes*, GUARDIAN (London), Jan. 6, 1986.

83. Text of Father Faul's Dungannon Lecture, IRISH TIMES, Dec. 2, 1969, at 8.

84. REPORT OF THE COMMISSION TO CONSIDER LEGAL PROCEDURES TO DEAL WITH TERRORIST ACTIVITIES IN NORTHERN IRELAND. Dec. 1972, Cmnd. 5185 [hereinafter Diplock Report].

85. DONOHUE, *supra* note 25, at 126.

86. Diplock Report, *supra* note 84. *See also* John D. Jackson & Sean Doran, *Conventional Trials in Unconventional Times: The Diplock Court Experience*, 4 CRIM. L. F. 503.

87. HC Debs, 17 April 1973, Vol. 855, col. 305.

88. *Id.*

89. Carlton, *supra* note 39, at 225–42.

90. *Id.*

91. HC Debs, 855, 277; Apr. 17, 1973.

92. *Id.*

93. For further discussion of these points see Laura K. Donohue, *Terrorism and Trial by Jury: The Vices and Virtues of British and American Criminal Law*, 59 STAN. L. REV. 1321, (2007).

94. Carlton, *supra* note 39, at 233.

95. *Id.*, at 234.

96. KEVIN BOYLE, TOM HADDEN, & PADDY HIHLLYARD, LAW AND STATE: THE CASE OF NORTHERN IRELAND (1975), pp. 144–50.

97. JOHN JACKSON & SEAN DORAN, JUDGE WITHOUT JURY 276–79 (1995)]; *see also* Carol Daugherty Rasnic, *Northern Ireland's Criminal Trials Without Jury: The Diplock Experiment*, 5 ANN. SURV. IN'L & COMP. L. 239, 253 (1999).

98. John D. Jackson, *The Restoration of Jury Trial in Northern Ireland; Can We Learn from the Professional Alternative?* ST. LOUIS-WARSAW TRANS'L 15 (2000).

99. *See* Criminal Evidence (Northern Ireland) Order, 1988, art. 3; Criminal Justice (Terrorism and Conspiracy) Act, 1998, c. 40. At the time of the act, a number of Parliamentarians objected to the inclusion of the provision, arguing that it would never be used. Indeed, as of July 2007, the state had yet to make use of the new provisions regarding the inference from silence. Author discussion with Lord Lloyd of Berwick, former Lord of Appeal in Ordinary, July 17, 2007, in London.

100. *See, e.g.*, Hugh Carnegy, *Irish Plea on Diplock Courts Refused*, FIN. TIMES (London), Nov. 6, 1986, at 9; Sarah Spencer & Fran Russell, *Agenda: Breaking the Diplock – A Three-Judge System*, GUARDIAN (London), Aug. 17, 1987; *Rebuff for Irish on Diplock*, TIMES (London), Nov. 6, 1986; *King Issues Warning to Dublin on Extradition Bill*, FIN. TIMES (London), Oct. 22, 1987.

101. NORTHERN IRELAND OFFICE, REPLACEMENT ARRANGEMENTS FOR THE DIPLOCK COURT SYSTEM: A CONSULTATION PAPER ¶ 2.2 (2006), available at http://www.nio.gov.uk/.

102. *Id.*, at ¶ 2.5 (noting also that approximately 60 cases returned for trial without jury, as opposed to 329 in 1986).

103. U.K. HOME OFFICE, JURIES IN SERIOUS FRAUD TRIALS ¶ 3.18 (1998), available at http://www.nationalarchives.gov.uk/.

104. Criminal Justice Act 2003, c. 44, § 43(2) and (5). The Lord Chief Justice, or a judge nominated by him, has to agree. Criminal Justice Act, 2003, c. 44, § 43(4). In the latter instance, the prosecution applies to a judge of the Crown Court, which must be satisfied "that there is evidence of a real and present danger that jury tampering would take place" and that "notwithstanding any steps (including the provision of police protection) which might reasonably be taken to prevent jury tampering, the likelihood that it would take place would be so substantial as to make it necessary in the interests of justice for the trial to be conducted without a jury." Criminal Justice Act, 2003, c. 44, § 44(4),(5).

105. *Id.*, at 780.

106. *Id.*, at 782.

107. Criminal Justice Act, 2003, c. 44, § 330(5)(b).

108. Fraud (Trials Without a Jury) Bill, 16th Nov. 2006 [Bill 6].

109. Report of a Committee to consider, in the context of civil liberties and human rights, measures to deal with terrorism in Northern Ireland, Chairman: Lord Gardiner, January 1975, Cmnd. 5847, ¶¶ 148–49, available at http://cain.ulst.ac.uk/.

110. A. Lawrence Lowell, *The Judicial Use of Torture: Part II The Treatment of Criminals in England* (1897) 11 HARV. L. REV. 220 at 291 *See also* JAMES HEATH, TORTURE AND ENGLISH LAW: AN ADMINISTRATIVE AND LEGAL HISTORY FROM THE PLANTAGENETS TO THE STUARTS (1982), 49 (stating, "[I]n the matter of torture, English judicial procedure is given a clean bill. Instead of reliance upon legal proofs, proofs classified and graded by learned doctrine, with torture woven into the system, the English at Common Law continued to rely upon the trial jury.")

111. HEATH, *supra* note 110, at 46, 49.

112. Lowell, *supra* note 110, at 292.

113. HEATH, *supra* note 110, at 46.

114. SIR JOHN FORTESCUE, DE LAUDIBUS LEGUM ANGLIAE, c. 1460–1470, trans. Francis Gregor, chap 22, pp. 47–53 (condemning torture while recognizing that civil law does have recourse to torture).

115. *See, e.g.*, Bracton: De Legibus Et Consuetudinibus Angliæ (Bracton on the Laws and Customs of England attributed to Henry of Bratton, c. 1210–1268), vol. II, p. 298, available at http://hlsl5.law.harvard.edu/; Sir Edward Coke, Third Instit. 35 "there is no law to warrant tortures in this land, nor can they be justified by any

prescription, being so lately brought in." In the Second and Third Institutes Coke asserted that the use of torture violated c. 39 of the Magna Carta of 1215 and c. 29 of the document of 1225.

116. HEATH, *supra* note 110, at 45.

117. *Id.*, at 45.

118. *Id.*, at 46.

119. FORTESCUE, *supra* note 114, at 72.

120. *Id.*, at 73.

121. SIR THOMAS SMITH, DE REPUBLICA ANGLORUM (1583), c. 24.

122. HEATH, *supra* note 110, at 140–41 (quoting Thomas Norton, imprisoned in the Tower of London).

123. *Id.*, at 141.

124. *Id.*, at 145.

125. SIR DAVID LINDSAY KEIR, THE CONSTITUTIONAL HISTORY OF MODERN BRITAIN 1485–1951, 5th Ed., Rev. (London: Adam and Charles Black, 1955, initially published in 1938), at 20 (noting that the Council " . . . evaded the Common Law rule against the use of torture."); SIR WILLIAM SEARE HOLDSWORTH, HISTORY OF ENGLISH LAW, VOL. IV, THE COMMON LAW AND ITS RIVALS, (Boston: Little, Brown & Co., 1924), p. 274 (stating, "torture was used to discover facts whenever the Council deemed it necessary. . . . "); Star Chamber, available at http://en.wikipedia.org/wiki/.

126. SIR WILLIAM BLACKSTONE, COMMENTARIES ON THE LAWS OF ENGLAND (1791) vol. IV, chap. 25, pp. 326. For discussion of civil law in contrast see SIR WILLIAM HOLDSWORTH, A HISTORY OF ENGLISH LAW, (1924), Vol. 5, 170–75.

127. *Id.*

128. *See, e.g.,* SUSAN L. CARRUTHERS, WINNING HEARTS AND MINDS: BRITISH GOVERNMENTS, THE MEDIA AND COLONIAL COUNTER-INSURGENCY 1944–1960 (1995), pp. 171, 173, 238; CAROLINE ELKINS, IMPERIAL RECKONING: THE UNTOLD STORY OF BRITAIN'S GULAG IN KENYA (2006); SPENCER MAWBY, BRITISH POLICY IN ADEN AND THE PROTECTORATES 1955–67: LAST OUTPOST OF A MIDDLE EAST EMPIRE (2005), at 167; David Percox, BRITAIN, KENYA AND THE COLD WAR: IMPERIAL DEFENCE, COLONIAL SECURITY AND DECOLONISATION (2004), p. 52; and JONATHAN WALKER, ADEN INSURGENCY: THE SAVAGE WAR IN SOUTH ARABIA 1962–1967 (2005), pp. 145, 186, 187, 188.

129. Kevin McNamara, HC Debs, Feb. 19, 1996, vol. 272, col. 61.

130. The Compton Report, the Gardiner Report, and other documents discuss these techniques.

131. Report of the Committee of Privy Counsellors appointed to consider authorized procedures for the interrogation of persons suspected of terrorism; Chairman: Lord Parker of Waddington, Mar. 1972, Cmd 4901, ¶ 10, available at http://cain.ulst.ac.uk/ [hereinafter Parker Committee Report]. *See also Ireland* v. *United Kingdom, supra* note 32; and Report of the enquiry into allegations against the Security Forces of physical brutality in Northern Ireland arising out of events on the 9th August, 1971, Chairman: Sir Edmund Compton, Nov. 1971, Cmd. 4823, available at http://cain.ulst.ac.uk/.

132. Author interviews with former detainees, in Londonderry, Northern Ireland, 1993.

133. Monsignor Denis Faul, *Obituary*, Timesonline, June 22, 2006, available at www.timesonline.co.uk/.

134. John McGuffin, THE GUINEAPIGS (1974, 1981), chapter 9. Author note on source: this book, written by an East Belfast Protestant-turned anarchist/republican, who was interned in the early 1970s, was initially published by Penguin. The publisher

sold out of the first run of 20,000 copies. A week into the first edition, Reginald Maudling, Home Secretary, banned the book, which was later reprinted in the United States by Minuteman Press. *See* http://cain.ulst.ac.uk/; and www.irishresistancebooks.com.

135. From Aug. 9, 1971 to Dec. 5, 1975, 1,981 people were detained; 1,874 were Catholic/republican, whereas 107 were Protestant/loyalist. See http://cain.ulst.ac.uk/.

136. REPORT OF THE INQUIRY INTO ALLEGATIONS AGAINST THE SECURITY FORCES OF PHYSICAL BRUTALITY IN NORTHERN IRELAND ARISING OUT OF EVENTS ON THE 9 AUGUST 1971, Session 1971/72 Cmnd. 4823, para. 23.

137. Parker Committee Report, *supra* note 131, ¶ 4.

138. *Id.,* ¶ 5.

139. *Id.,* ¶ 8.

140. *Id.,* ¶ 9.

141. *Id.*

142. *Id.,* ¶ 12.

143. *Id.,* ¶ 18.

144. *Id.,* ¶ 21.

145. *Id.,* ¶ 24.

146. *Id.,* ¶ 31.

147. *Id.,* ¶ 35.

148. *Id.,* ¶ 37.

149. *Id.,* ¶ 37.

150. *Id.,* ¶ 39.

151. *Id.,* ¶¶ 40, 41.

152. *Id.,* ¶ 42.

153. Gardiner Minority Report, published in the Parker Committee Report, *supra* note 131, ¶ 6.

154. *Id.,* ¶ 8.

155. *Id.,* ¶ 10.

156. *Id.,* ¶ 12.

157. *Id.,* ¶ 13(b)(i).

158. *Id.,* ¶ 13(b)(iii).

159. Geneva Convention III, Article 17.

160. *Id.,* ¶ 14(c)(ii)

161. *Id.,* ¶ 19(5).

162. *Id.,* ¶ 21.

163. HC Debs, Mar. 2, 1972.

164. *Ireland v. United Kingdom, supra* note 32, ¶ 135. (Giorgio Balladore Pallieri, President). *See also* special instructions issued to the army and RUC. Cited in *Id.*

165. *Ireland v. United Kingdom, supra* note 32, Judge Zekia, Separate Opinion, Parts A & C.

166. ECHR, Article 3.

167. *Ireland v. United Kingdom, supra* note 32, ¶ 170. (Giorgio Balladore Pallieri, President)

168. *Id.,* ¶ 167. (Giorgio Balladore Pallieri, President)

169. *Id.*

170. *Id.,* ¶, 198.

171. *Id.*

172. *Id.*
173. *Id.,* ¶ 223.
174. *Id.,* ¶ 214.
175. *Id.*
176. *Id.,* ¶¶ 214 & 224.
177. *Ireland* v. *United Kingdom, supra* note 32, ¶ 140. (Giorgio Balladore Pallieri, President)
178. GERARD HOGAN & CLIVE WALKER, POLITICAL VIOLENCE AND THE LAW IN IRELAND (1989), p. 101
179. CAJ Submission to the United Nations Committee Against Torture, Comments on the Third Periodic Report by the United Kingdom to the Committee Against Torture, Sept. 1998.
180. John Jackson & Sean Doran, *Juries and Judges: A View from Across the Atlantic,* CRIM. JUST, Winter 1997, at 15, 17 (1997). *See also* Howard J. Russell, *New Death Breathes Life into Old Fears,* 28 GA. J. INT'L & COMP. L. 199; *R.* v. *Harper,* 1990, N. Ir. 28, 30; *R.* v. *Dillon and Another,* 1984 N. Ir. 292, 292; and Denis Campbell, *18 Jailed Irishmen 'May Be Innocent,* IRISH TIMES, July 17, 1992, at 4.
181. KEVIN BOYLE, TOM HADDEN, & PADDY HILLYARD, TEN YEARS ON IN NORTHERN IRELAND (1980).
182. *In Belfast, Confession Is Good for the Crown,* N. J. LAW J., Apr. 12, 1993, at 17. *See also* United Kingdom/Northern Ireland Human Rights, US Department of State, Jan. 31, 1994
183. *See, e.g.,* David Sharrock, *Call to Halt Ulster Murder Trials,* GUARDIAN (London), June 9, 1992.
184. David Sharrock, *Justice "Going Through Motions,"* GUARDIAN (London), June 9, 1992, at 4.
185. Brian Michael Jenkins, *International Terrorism: A New Mode of Conflict, in* INTERNATIONAL TERRORISM AND WORLD SECURITY (David Carlton and Carlo Schaerf eds., 1975), p. 15. Westminster's Privy Counsellor Review Committee wrote that 9/11 "highlighted the existence of a formidable international terrorist threat, raising the prospect of further attacks on civilians on a previously inconceivable scale." Privy Counsellor Review Committee, Anti-Terrorism, Crime and Security Act 2001 Review: Report. Presented to Parliament pursuant to §122(5) of the Anti-Terrorism, Crime and Security Act 2002, Dec. 18, 2003, HC 100, p. 4.
186. Remarks by Robert C. Bonner, Royal Institute of International Affairs, Chatham House London, England, Sept. 20, 2004, available at www.cbp.gov/.
187. Article 3 of the European Convention of Human Rights, which prohibits torture, is used as a way to prevent extradition or deportation – even where regular judicial procedures in the recipient country sanction capital punishment. *See, e.g., Soering* v. *United Kingdom,* App. No. 14038/88, 11 EUR. HUM. RTS. REP. 439, 464, 467–69, 478 (1989) (where extradition to Virginia would violate Article 3).
188. Anti-Terrorism, Crime and Security Act 2001, c. 24, Part IV(21)(1).
189. ATCSA, 21(2).
190. ATCSA, sec. 22 & 23.
191. ATCSA, sec. 25. SIAC drew its authority from the 1997 Special Immigration Appeals Commission Act, which had sought to address national security concerns and procedural fairness for aliens deemed to be a danger to the state. The statute created a special commission that acted as a superior court of record, which would operate according to rules it set itself and were approved by Parliament. [Special

Immigration Appeals Commission Act 1997, c. 68, sec. 1, 5. *See also* ATCSA, sec. 35.

192. ATCSA, sec. 30. Article 5 of the European Convention of Human Rights states that individuals shall not be deprived of their freedom, save in a set of narrowly defined circumstances: following conviction by a competent court, in the wake of noncompliance with a court order, or in anticipation of bringing the individual before a competent legal authority on the basis of reasonable suspicion of having committed an offense – or "when it is reasonably considered necessary to prevent his committing an offence or fleeing after having done so." ECHR, Article 5(1)(c). The instrument also makes it possible to detain individuals for a limited number of other reasons, such as quarantine, drug addiction, and, for minors, educational supervision. Article 5(1)(d) & (e). *See also* ICCPR, Article 15(1). An individual can also be detained where lawful arrest is given effect to prevent the individual from entering the country without authorization or where deportation or extradition proceedings will be undertaken. ECHR, Article 5(1)(f). Any individual arrested must immediately be informed of the reasons for the arrest and the charge against him, and brought to trial within a reasonable time – or released, pending trial, ECHR, Articles 5(2) and 5(3). Article 15 of the Convention allows for abrogation of the entitlements in the provision, "In time of war or other public emergency threatening the life of the nation any High Contracting Party."

193. Total calculated from reports in David Barrett, *Why Clarke Was Forced to Act on Detainees*, PRESS ASSOCIATION, Feb. 22, 2005; Brian Barder, G2: Law; and Joshua Rozenberg, *National Security Safe as Houses*. Confirmed by Philip Johnson, *Your Questions on the New Legislation Answered*, DAILY TELEGRAPH (London), Feb. 23, 2005, 7. In addition to those cited above, following particularly the attacks on London in July 2005, the state subjected more individuals to control orders. *See, e.g., Bail for Five Terrorism Suspects*, DAILY POST (Liverpool), Dec. 17, 2005, p. 4 (discussing bail set for X, Y, AA, CC, and P).

194. *End this Internment Now*, GUARDIAN, Dec. 13, 2003, at www.guardian.co.uk/.

195. *See, e.g.*, Joint Committee on Human Rights, Second Report of Session 2001–2002 (paras 38–39), Fifth Report of Session 2002–3 (24 Feb. 2003, HL 38, HC 381, para 35), Eighteenth Report of Session 2003–04 (21 July 2004, HL 158, HC 713, paras 42–44).

196. *See* Committee of Ministers of the Council of Europe, 11 July 2002 (referring specifically to the ATCSA); European Commission Against Racism and Intolerance, 8 June 2004, General Policy Recommendation No 8 (referring more broadly to legislation passed by European states and calling on countries to review measures to ensure that they "do not discriminate directly or indirectly against persons or groups of persons . . . and to abrogate any such discriminatory legislation."); and UN Committee Against Torture, consideration of Fourth UK Periodic Report, 33rd session, 25 Nov. 2004, CAT/C/CR/33/3 (referring specifically to the ATCSA).

197. Parliamentary Assembly of the Council of Europe, Resolution 1271, Jan. 24, 2002.

198. Privy Counsellor Review Committee, Anti-Terrorism, Crime and Security Act 2001 Review: Report. Presented to Parliament pursuant to §122(5) of the Anti-Terrorism, Crime and Security Act 2002, Dec. 18, 2003, HC 100, p. 5.

199. *Id.*, at 8.

200. *Id.*

201. *Id.*, at 13.

202. *Id.*

203. *Id.*

204. Human Right Commission Opposes Detention without Trial for Terrorist suspects, NI HRC, Oct. 4, 2004, Press Release, available at www.nihrc.org/.

205. *A and others v. Secretary of State for the Home Department* [2004] UKHL 56, 16 December 2004, available at www.publications.parliament.uk/. SIAC itself determined in July 2002 that the detentions discriminated against foreign nationals, contradicting the 1998 Human Rights Act. *Terror Detainees Win Lords Appeal: Detaining Foreign Terrorist Suspects Without Trial Breaks Human Rights Laws, the UK's Highest Court Has Ruled*, BBC NEWS, Dec. 16, 2004, available at www. news.bbc.co.uk/. *See also* David Barrett, *Why Clarke Was Forced to Act on Detainees*, Press Association, Feb. 22, 2005; A, X and Y, 2002 Q.B. at 359, 382; and Sir David Williams, *The United Kingdom's Response to International Terrorism*, 13 IND. INT'L & COMP. L. REV. 683, 695–96 (addressing A, X, Y decision).

206. ECHR, Article 14.

207. *Terror Detainees Win Lords Appeal, supra* note 205.

208. *Lawless v. Ireland* (No 3) (1961) 1 EHRR 15.

209. Quoted in [2004] UKHL 56, para. 17, Lord Bingham of Cornhill.

210. Quoted in [2004] UKHL 56, para. 18 (Lord Bingham), citing Greek Case (1969) 12 YB 1, para 153.

211. *Id.*, at para. 29. (Lord Bingham)

212. *Id.*, at para 32. (Lord Bingham)

213. *Id.*, at para 33. (Lord Bingham)

214. *Id.*, at para 33. (Lord Bingham)

215. *Id.*, at para 31(4). (Lord Bingham)

216. *Id.*, at para 33. (Lord Bingham)

217. *Id.*, at 42. (Lord Bingham)

218. *Id.*

219. *Id. See also* Jowell, "Judicial Deference: Servility, Civility or Institutional Capacity?" [2003] PL 592, 597.

220. Bingham also cited articles 1 and 2 of the 1948 Universal Declaration of Human Rights, Article 26 of the ICCPR, and previous SIAC holdings. *Id.*, at 58–63. (Lord Bingham)

221. *Id.*, at 74. (Lord Nicholls of Birkenhead)

222. *Id.*, at 78. (Lord Nicholls of Birkenhead)

223. *Id.*, at 80–81. (Lord Nicholls of Birkenhead)

224. *A et al. v. Secretary of State for the Home Department*, [2004] UKHL 56, at 86. (Lord Hoffman)

225. *Id.*, at 86. (Lord Hoffman)

226. *Id.*, at 97. (Lord Hoffman)

227. *Id.*, at 166. (Lord Rodger of Earlsferry)

228. *Id.*

229. *Id.*, at 175. (Lord Rodger of Earlsferry)

230. Matthew Davies and Doron Blum, *Immigration and Asylum Update*, NEW L. J., Feb. 4, 2005, NLJ 155.7162(171).

231. Human Rights Act 1998 (Designated Derogation) Order 2001 SI No. 3644.

232. David Pannick, THE TIMES (London), Mar. 8, 2005, p. 3.

233. Matthew Davies & Doron Blum, *Immigration and Asylum Update*, NEW L.J., Feb. 4, 2005, NLJ 155.7162(171).

234. In 1966 the UK signed the European Convention of Human Rights. The 1998 Human Rights Act brought this provision directly into domestic legal considerations. The 1984 Police and Criminal Evidence Act gave effect to the United Nations'

Convention Against Torture and Other Cruel, Inhuman or Degrading Treatment or Punishment, which came into force in June 1987. UN Convention Against Torture and Other Cruel, Inhuman or Degrading Treatment or Punishment 1984 (1990) (Cm 1775). *See Jones* v. *Ministry of Interior Al-Mamlaka Al-Arabiya AS Saudiya (the Kingdom of Saudi Arabia) and others*, [2006] UKHL 26, at 15 (Lord Bingham of Cornhill).

235. For the lower court decisions see *A and others* v. *Secretary of State for the Home Department*, [2005] UKHL 71 at 9. (Lord Bingham of Cornhill); [2004] EWCA Civ 1123, [2005] 1 WLR 414. (Pill and Laws LJJ, Neuberger LJ in part dissenting).

236. *A and others* v. *Secretary of State for the Home Department*, [2005] UKHL 71 at 13. (Lord Bingham of Cornhill)

237. Originally part of the common law, the 1984 Police and Criminal Evidence Act had brought it into the statutory realm. For common law cases *see Ibrahim* v. *The King* [1914] AC 599, 609–610, *R* v. *Harz and Power* [1967] AC 760, 817, and *Lam Chi-ming* v. *The Queen* [1991] 2 AC 212, 220. Police and Criminal Evidence Act 1984, sec. 76. Cited in *A and others* v. *Secretary of State for the Home Department*, [2005] UKHL 71 at 14. (Lord Bingham of Cornhill)

238. *A and others* v. *Secretary of State for the Home Department*, [2005] UKHL 71 at 17. (Lord Bingham of Cornhill) (citing *Lam Chi-ming* v. *The Queen* [1991] 2 AC 212, 220 (Lord Griffiths); and *R* v. *Mushtaq* [2005] UKHL 25, [2005] 1 WLR 1513, paras 1, 7, 27, 45–46, 71.

239. *A and others* v. *Secretary of State for the Home Department*, [2005] UKHL 71 at 17. (Lord Bingham of Cornhill) (quoting *Rochin* v. *California*, 342 US 165 (1952), pp. 169–173 (Frankfurter, J.)

240. *A and others* v. *Secretary of State for the Home Department*, [2005] UKHL 71 at 17. (Lord Bingham of Cornhill) (quoting *Rochin* v. *California*, 342 US 165 (1952), p. 169 (Frankfurter, J.)

241. *Id.*, at 82. (Lord Hoffman)

242. *Id.*, at 113. (Lord Hope of Craighead)

243. *Id.*, at 113. (Lord Hope of Craighead)

244. *Id.*, at 30. (Lord Bingham of Cornhill)

245. *Id.*, at 33. (Lord Bingham of Cornhill) *See also* Lord Nicholls of Birkenhead, para 67; Lord Hoffman at para 84.

246. *Id.*, at 34. (Lord Bingham of Cornhill)

247. *Id.*

248. *Id.*, at 41. (Lord Bingham of Cornhill)

249. *Id.*, at 51. (Lord Bingham of Cornhill)

250. *Id.*

251. *Id.*, at 158. (Lord Carswell); para 166. (Lord Brown of Eaton-under-Heywood) paras. 142–5 (Lord Rodger of Earlsferry).

252. *Id.*, at 172. (Lord Brown of Eaton-under-Heywood, quoting test). Lord Hope of Craighead proposed a different test, paras. 119–21. For media commentary on the ruling *see* Geoffrey Bindman, *Should Britain Be Relying on Evidence Obtained by Torture?* THE TIMES (London), Oct. 18, 2005, p. 4.; Alan Travis & Duncan Campbell, *Torture Ruling: Crucial Decisions for Detention Judges*; THE GUARDIAN (London), Dec. 9, 2005, p. 4

253. Bob Glanville, *Wriggling on the Hook*, MORNING STAR, Jan. 27, 2005, 1. (Clarke speaking)

254. Alan Travis & Clare Dyer, *Terror Suspects Face House Arrest*, THE GUARDIAN (London), Jan. 27, 2005, p. 1. *See also* Lizette Alvarez, *Britain Moving to Raise*

Guard Against Terrorists, Int'l Herald Tribune, Jan. 28, 2005, p. 6; David Barrett, *Terrorist Laws Get Tougher,* Daily Post (Liverpool, UK), Jan. 27, 2005, p. 16; Frank Millaer, *Blair Government Seeks Sweeping New Powers,* Irish Times, Jan. 27, 2005, p. 12.

255. *Lawyers Condemn Clarke Plan,* Western Mail (UK), Jan. 27, 2005, p. 9.

256. Robert Verkaik & Nigel Morris, *MPs Condemn House Arrest and Tagging Plan for Terror Suspects,* The Independent (UK), Jan. 27, 2005.

257. Chris Moncrieff, Sian Clare & Jane Kirby, *Control Orders Plan for Terror Suspects,* Press Association, Jan. 26, 2005.

258. *Id.*

259. *See, e.g.,* Brian Barder, *Better than Belmarsh – Just,* The Guardian (UK), Jan. 28, 2005, p. 27; Verkaik et al., *supra* note 256.

260. Moncrieff et al., *supra* note 257.

261. *Terror Substitute,* Press Association News, Feb. 25, 2005.

262. Nigel Morris, *Cabinet Puts Pressure on Clarke to Dilute Terror Bill,* The Independent, Feb. 3, 2005.

263. Louise Nousratpour, *Clarke Tears up the Law,* Feb. 26, 2005, p. 1. For restriction orders in Northern Ireland *see* Donohue, *supra* note 25, at 44–64.

264. *See, e.g.,* Clare Dyer, *Terror Suspects: Lawyers Criticize House Arrest Plan,* The Guardian (London), Jan. 27, 2005, p. 4.

265. Moncrieff et al., *supra* note 257.

266. Frank Millar, *Tories, Liberals Attack Labour Detention Plans,* Irish Times, Feb. 3, 2005, p. 11. *See also* David Barrett, *Tories Voice 'Serious Misgivings' over House Arrest Plans,* Feb. 2, 2005, Press Association News Ltd., 10:51:00; Trevor Mason & Joe Churcher, *House Arrest for Terror Suspects "Unacceptable,"* Press Association, Feb. 8, 2005.

267. *Id.*

268. *See, e.g., An Affront to Justice; House Arrest Proposal Smacks of Political Repression,* The Herald (Glasgow), Jan 27, 2005.

269. Clare Dyer, *An Assault on Our Liberties,* The Guardian (London), Feb. 28, 2005, p. 18.

270. *Detention,* Press Association News Ltd, Feb. 8, 2005; 18:11:00.

271. *See, e.g., Think Again on Terror Cases,* Evening Standard (London), Feb. 22, 2005, p. 13; Editorial, *Anti-Terror Laws: Wider Still and Wider,* Guardian (UK), Jan. 27, 2005, p. 27; Editorial, *An Affront to Justice,* Herald (Glasgow), Jan.27, 2005, p. 21; Philip Johnston, *UK Terror Suspects Can Be Confined at Home,* Daily Telegraph (London), Jan. 27, 2005, p. 1; Simon Jenkins, *It Was You Who Wrote Magna Carta, My Lords. And Now You Must Defend It,* The Times (London), Feb. 23, 2005, p. 19; Mason et al., *supra* note 266; *Freedom Is What We Are Fighting For,* Daily Post (Liverpool), Feb. 14, 2005, p. 14. *But See We Can't Go Soft On Terrorists,* Daily Post (Liverpool), Feb. 19, 2005, p. 6.

272. Editorial, *An Affront to Justice House Arrest Proposal Smacks of Political Repression,* Herald (Glasgow), Jan.27, 2005, p. 21. *See also* Philip Johnston, *UK Terror Suspects Can Be Confined at Home,* Daily Telegraph (London), Jan. 27, 2005, p. 1.

273. Jenkins, *supra* note 271; Mason et al., *supra* note 266; *Freedom Is What We Are Fighting For, supra* note 271.

274. *Freedom Is What We Are Fighting For, supra* note 271.

275. Clare Dyer, *An Assault on Our Liberties,* The Guardian (London), Feb. 28, 2005, p. 18.

276. *See, e.g., Blair Fails to Win Political Pact on Terrorism Laws*, TURKISH DAILY NEWS, Feb. 19, 2005.

277. Moncrieff et al., *supra* note 257.

278. *Id.*

279. John Deane, *Blair-Howard Summit on House Arrest Plans*, WESTERN MORNING NEWS (Plymouth), Feb. 3, 2005, p. 22.

280. *Clarke "to Ditch House Arrest Plan"*, BELFAST NEWS LETTER (Northern Ireland), Feb. 14, 2005, p. 17; James Lyons, *Clarke's Terror U-Turn?*, BIRMINGHAM POST, Feb. 14, 2005, p. 8; *Plan for Terrorist House Arrests Ditched*, DAILY POST (Liverpool), Feb. 14, 2005, p. 7; David Charter, *Clarke Retreats from Home Arrest for Terror Suspects*, THE TIMES (London), Feb. 14, 2005, p. 4; *Terror and Liberty*, EVENING STANDARD (London), Feb. 23, 2005, p. 13.

281. FIN. TIMES INFORMATION, Feb. 3, 2005.

282. Deane, *supra* note 279. *See also Blair Meets Opposition over 'House Arrest' Plans*, EVENING STANDARD (London), Feb. 18, 2005, p. 2.

283. Philip Webster & Greg Hurst, *Tories and Lib Dems set to Block House Arrest Law*, THE TIMES (London), Feb. 3, 2005, p. 29.

284. Christopher Adams & Jimmy Burns, *Tories and LibDems Team Up Against Terror Laws*, FIN. TIMES, Feb. 23, 2005, p. 4.

285. Andrew Woodcock, *LibDems oppose Clarke over House-arrest Terror Law*, PRESS ASSOCIATION, Feb. 22, 2005.

286. Jamie Lyons, *"Keep Illegal Terror Measure Till Proper Solution" – Tories*, PRESS ASSOCIATION, Feb. 19, 2005. *See also* John Deane, *Blair and Howard's Terror Move Talks*, BIRMINGHAM POST, Feb. 3, 2005, p. 9.

287. Nick Pearce, *Spooks in court*, PROSPECT, Feb. 17, 2005. *See also* Nick Allen, *PA Chief Reported, "UK 'out of step' Not Allowing Phone Tap Evidence,"* Press ASSOCIATION NEWS LTD, Mar. 13, 2006.

288. Allen, *supra* note 287.

289. *See, e.g., Politicians Alone Must Not Decide Who Is a Terrorist*, INDEPENDENT ON SUNDAY (UK), Feb. 20, 2005, p. 26; *Editorial, Closing doors, Ministers Need to Show Greater Regard for Due Process*, TIMES (UK), Feb. 26, 2005, p. 23.

290. Allen, *supra* note 287.

291. Vivienne Morgan, *Terror Powers Need Judicial Role – Lib Dems*, PRESS ASSOCIATION, Feb. 18, 2005.

292. Mason et al., *supra* note 266.

293. James Blitz, *Clarke Firm on House Arrests*, FIN. TIMES (London, England), Feb. 14, 2005, p. 4.

294. Pearce, *supra* note 287.

295. *Id.*

296. Philip Johnston, *House Arrest Without Trial to Be Rushed Through in Days*, DAILY TELEGRAPH (London), Feb. 22, 2005, p. 1.

297. *Id.* Twelve individuals were still in custody as of Jan. 26, 2005. The state subsequently and unexpectedly freed detainee "C" and granted bail to Abu Rideh on January 31, 2005. Moncrieff et al., *supra* note 257; David Barrett, *Why Clarke Was Forced to Act on Detainees*, PRESS ASSOCIATION, Feb. 22, 2005.

298. Nigel Morris, *Anger over Two-Day Terror Bill Debate*, THE INDEPENDENT (London), Feb. 22, 2005.

299. *Id.*

300. *See, e.g.,* John Twomey, *Terror Suspects to Be Freed as Clarke Gets Commons Mauling*, THE EXPRESS, Feb. 23, 2005, p. 2.

301. Christopher Adams & Jimmy Burns, *Tories and Lib Dems Team Up Against Terror Laws*, Fin. Times (London), Feb. 23, 2005, p. 4.

302. Brian Walker, *Rebels Tackle PM on Terror*, Belfast Telegraph, Feb. 24, 2005.

303. *Id.*

304. Michael White & Richard Norton-Taylor, *Terror bill Climbdown by Labour*, The Guardian (London), Mar. 1, 2005, p. 1. *See also Blair Defends Terror Law Changes*, BBC News, Feb. 28, 2005, available at www.news.bbc.co.uk/; George Kerevan, *Let's See Action, Mr. Blair, Not More New Laws*, Scotsman (Edinburgh), Feb. 16, 2006; *The Great Deception: How Tony Blair Misled Us over the War on Terror*, Belfast Telegraph, Feb. 15, 2006; Peter Oborne, *The Use and Abuse of Terror*, Centre for Policy Studies.

305. The Great Deception, *supra* note 304; Oborne, *supra* note 304.

306. James Kirkup & Karen McVeigh, *No Deal over Terrorism Bill Amid Claim of 200 Al-Qaeda*, Scotsman, Mar. 7, 2005, p. 6.

307. *Id.*

308. Neville Dean, *Terror Law Needed to Combat 'Grave Threat' – Met Chief*, Press Association, Mar. 10, 2005. *See also* James Lyons, *Time to be Strong over Terror, says Blair*, Press Association News Ltd., Mar. 10, 2005; *Terror Scares, Deadlines and Election Fever Make for the Worst Kind of Law-making*, Independent (London), Mar. 10, 2005, p. 30. *But see* Philip Johnston, *Terror Law Defeat Will Not Mean Freedom for Suspects*, Daily Telegraph (London), Mar. 9, 2005, p. 8.

309. Lyons, *supra* note 308.

310. Lindsay McGarview, *Labour in Dundee: Blair: G8 Wreckers Risk House Arrest, Detention Without Trial "Cannot Be Ruled Out,"* Sunday Mail, Mar. 6, 2005, p. 2.

311. Andre Sparrow, *Angry MPs Offered Concession on Terror Bill*, Daily Telegraph (London), Feb. 24, 2005, p. 12.

312. Glen Own, *Stars Declare War on Blair's 'Nightmare' House Arrest Laws*, Mail on Sunday (London), Feb. 27, 2005, p. 7

313. *Id.*

314. *See, e.g., Editorial, Bill Warrants a Full Debate*, Sentinel (Stoke, UK), March 8, 2005, p. 8.

315. *UK Tabloids Say New Anti-terror Bill Puts Country 'at Greater Risk'*, World News Connection, Mar. 12, 2005.

316. Alan Travis, *No Current Need for House Arrest, Clarke Admits*, Guardian (London), Feb. 23, 2005. p. 13; Richard Ford, *Draconian Bill Seeks to Keep Threat Under Control*, Times (London), Feb. 23, 2005, p. 6.

317. George Jones, *Clarke is Forced to Retreat on House Arrest*, Daily Telegraph (London), Feb. 28, 2005, 1.

318. *Terror Substitute*, Press Association News, Feb. 28, 2005.

319. Andre Sparrow, *Angry MPs Offered Concession on Terror Bill*, Daily Telegraph (London), Feb. 24, 2005, p. 12. (Simon Hughes, LibDem)

320. Philip Johnston, *Terror Law Defeat Will Not Mean Freedom for Suspects*, Daily Telegraph (London), Mar. 9, 2005, p. 8; and *Terror Suspects Deal on Table*, Times (London), Feb. 25, 2005.

321. Philip Webster, *Concessions on House Arrest Do Not Win over an Angry Commons*, Times (London), Mar. 1, 2005, p. 9.

322. *Id.*

323. *Id.*

324. *Id.*

325. *Id.*
326. Michael White & Richard Norton-Taylor, *Terror Bill Climbdown by Labour*, THE GUARDIAN (London), Mar. 1, 2005, p. 1.
327. *This Week at Westminster*, PRESS ASSOCIATION NEWS, Mar. 4, 2005.
328. Lord Donaldson of Lymington, HL Debs, Mar. 1, 2005, Vol. 670, Col. 176.
329. Lord Lloyd of Berwick, HL Debs, Mar. 1, 2005, Vol. 670, Col. 163.
330. *Id.*
331. *MPs Let Us Down.*
332. *This Week at Westminster*, PRESS ASSOCIATION NEWS, Mar. 4, 2005.
333. "We are seeing the standard of proof being lowered and the presumption of innocence being chipped away. We are seeing it seeping into other areas of law too. We are told in the first instance that it is about terrorism but we are seeing it creeping into other aspects of our legal system. It is a trend and I warn noble Lords of it. We are told that it is in our interests. It is the paternalism of government saying, 'We are doing this for you.' When we hear civil liberties being turned into a term of abuse, we know that we are in trouble." Baroness Kennedy of the Shaws, HL DEBS, Mar. 4, 2005, Vol. 670, Col. 194.
334. Jamie Lyons, *Government to Make Fresh Terror Plan Concessions*, PRESS ASSOCIATION, Mar. 9, 2005.
335. Sophie Goodchild, Andy McSmith, Raymond Whitaker & Steve Bloomfield, *How Chaos in the Commons Descended into a Dangerous Farce: Inside Story*, INDEPENDENT ON SUNDAY (London), Mar. 13, 2005
336. Quoted in Ben Russell, *Peers line up to condemn 'terrifying' house arrest plan*, the INDEPENDENT, Mar. 2, 2005, available at http://news.independent.co.uk/uk/legal/article4292.ece.
337. *Proposed Anti-terror Laws Draw Ire*, TURKISH DAILY NEWS, Mar. 4, 2005.
338. *Id.*
339. *The House of Lords: A-leaping, with a Vengeance*, ECONOMIST, Feb. 11, 2006, p. 24.
340. *Id.*
341. *Id.*
342. *Id.*
343. *Id.*, Goodchild et al., *supra* note 335; *Law Lords Consider 'Torture' Appeal*, GUARDIAN, Oct. 17, 2005.
344. *Terror Scares, Deadlines and Election Fever Make for the Worst Kind of Lawmaking*, INDEPENDENT (London), Mar. 10, 2005, p. 30.
345. *Id.*
346. *Terror and Error*, THE TIMES (London), Mar. 9, 2005, p. 17; Jamie Lyons, *Government to Make Fresh Terror Plan Concessions*, PRESS ASSOCIATION, Mar. 9, 2005. Peers insisted on a higher standard of proof for low-level control orders, a 12-month time limit on the same, a Privy Counsellor review, allowance for the Lord Chief Justice to set the rules, and a requirement that the rules be consistent with the 1998 HRA. David Charter, *Labour MPs Return to the Fold After Clarke's Charm Offensive*, TIMES (London), Mar. 10, 2005, p. 6.
347. *Terror and Error*, THE TIMES (London), Mar. 9, 2005, p. 17.
348. *This Week at Westminster*, PRESS ASSOCIATION NEWS, Mar. 4, 2005.
349. *Id.*
350. *Terror and Error*, THE TIMES (London), Mar. 9, 2005, p. 17; *On This Day – March 7*, PRESS ASSOCIATION NEWS LTD., Mar. 7, 2006 (citing voting numbers).

351. Alan Cowell, *Blair Insists on Strict Terrorism Laws*, Int'l Herald Tribune, Mar. 11, 2005, p. 5; Joe Murphy, *Clarke Offers More Terror Concessions*, Evening Standard (London), Mar. 9, 2005, p. 2.

352. *Respect Our Liberty and Rights*, Evening Standard (London), Mar. 8, 2005, p. 13.

353. *Id.*

354. Goodchild et al., *supra* note 335. (The day continues until the Speaker declares it ended)

355. David Charter, *Labour MPs Return to the Fold After Clarke's Charm Offensive*, Times (London), Mar. 10, 2005, p. 6.

356. Alan Travis, Patrick Wintour & Vikram Dodd, *Judge to Free Detainees as Lords Are Forced into Dawn Terror Vote*, The Guardian (London), Mar. 11, 2005, p. 1.

357. Goodchild et al., *supra* note 335.

358. Catherine MacLeod, *MPs Back Terror Bill as Clarke Gives in on Judges*, Herald (Glasgow), Mar. 10, 2005, p. 1.

359. Andrew Sparrow & George Jones, *MPs Knock Terror Law Back into the Lords' Court*, Daily Telegraph (London), Mar. 10, 2005, p. 8.

360. Declaration of National Emergency by Reason of Certain Terrorist Attacks, Sept. 14, 2001, available at www.whitehouse.gov/.

361. Authorization for Use of Military Force, Pub. Law 107–40, 115 Stat. 224 (2001). [S.J. Res. 23], 107th Cong., Sept. 18, 2001, Sec. 2, available at www.news.findlaw.com/wp/.

362. Memorandum from John Yoo, Deputy Assistant Attorney General, Office of Legal Counsel, to Timothy E. Flanigan, the Deputy Council to the President (Sept. 25, 2001), reprinted in The Torture Papers: The Road to Abu Ghraib, 4 (Karen J. Greenberg & Joshua L. Dratel eds., 2005) [hereinafter Yoo Memo]; War Powers Resolution, Pub. L. No. 93–148, 87 Stat. 555 (1973), codified at 50 U.S.C. §§1541–1548.

363. Presidential Address to the Nation, Oct. 7, 2001, available at www.whitehouse.gov/news/releases/. *See also Bush Announced Opening Attacks*, CNN.com, Oct. 7, 2001, *available at* www.cnn.com/2001/.

364. *Id.*

365. Detention, Treatment, and Trial of Certain Non-Citizens in the War against Terrorism, Military Order of Nov. 13, 2001, Executive Orders, Federal Register: Nov. 16, 2001, Vol. 66, No. 2, Presidential Documents, page 57831–57836.

366. Bob Dart, *Afghan Prisoners Will Be Held at U.S. Base in Cuba*, Austin American-Statesman (Texas), Dec. 28, 2001, at A9.

367. *Id.*

368. Steve Vogel, *Afghan Prisoners Going to Gray Area*, Wash. Post, Jan. 9, 2002, at A1.

369. *Id.*

370. Rowan Scarborough, *Rumsfeld Offers Four Options for Taliban Fighters*, Wash. Times, Jan. 18, 2002, at A1.

371. Vogel, *supra* note 368.

372. Dart, *supra* note 366.

373. Memorandum from Patrick F. Philbin, Deputy Assistant Attorney General and John C. Yoo, Deputy Assistant Attorney General, to William J. Haynes, II, General Counsel, Department of Defense, (Dec. 28, 2001), reprinted in The Torture Papers: The Road to Abu Ghraib, 29 (Karen J. Greenberg & Joshua L. Dratel eds., 2005).

374. *Id.*, and Dart, *supra* note 366.
375. *Six Al Qaeda Britons heading for Cuba*, Birmingham Post, Jan. 14, 2002, at 9.
376. *Id.*
377. Anthony Shadid & Colin Nickerson, *Fighting Terror/The Prisoners/Imprisoned Fighters*, Boston Globe, Jan. 12, 2002, at A13.
378. Vogel, *supra* note 368.
379. Paul Gallagher, *Hoon Defends U.S. on Prisoners' Treatment*, Scotsman, Jan. 15, 2002, at 10. *See also More Taliban, Al Qaeda Detainees Flown to Cuba*, The Bulletin's Frontrunner, Jan. 14, 2002; Shadid et al., *supra* note 377.
380. *More Taliban, supra* note 379. *See also A Nation Challenged; A Second Group of Detainees Arrives at Base*, N.Y. Times, Jan. 14, 2002, at 8A.
381. Gallagher, *supra* note 379.
382. Shadid et al., *supra* note 377.
383. *Id.*
384. *Id.*
385. *Id.*
386. *Id.*
387. Larry Luxner, *Camp Delta at "Gitmo," Afghanistan Worlds Apart*, Wash. Times, Apr. 29, 2003, at A12.
388. David Johnston & Thom Shanker, *Pentagon Approved Intense Interrogation Techniques for Sept. 11 Suspect at Guantánamo*, N.Y. Times, May 21, 2004, at 9. *See also Time Report Fuels Guantánamo Criticism*, CNN.com, June 13, 2005.
389. John Mintz, *From Veil of Secrecy, Portraits of Prisoners Emerge*, Wash. Post, Mar. 15, 2002, at A3.
390. *Id.*
391. *Id.*
392. *Id.*
393. *Id.*
394. Stephanie Gaskell, *Some Guantanamo Detainees May be Only Footsoldiers*, San Mateo County Times, Mar. 30, 2002, at 1.
395. Greg Miller, *Many Held at Guantanamo Not Likely Terrorists*, Los Angeles Times, Dec. 22, 2002, at 1.
396. *Id.*
397. *Id.*
398. *Id.*
399. *"Mickey Mouse" Captives in U.S. Prison*, Scotsman, Dec. 23, 2002, at 8. *See also* Greg Miller, *Dozens Detained in Guantanamo May be Innocent*, Toronto Star, Dec. 22, 2002, at A4.
400. *"Mickey Mouse" Captives in U.S. Prison, supra* note 399.
401. *Id.*
402. Charlie Savage, *Guantánamo's 'Child Soldiers' in Limbo*, Boston Globe, Nov. 16, 2003, at A1.
403. *"Mickey Mouse" Captives in U.S. Prison, supra* note 399.
404. *Id.*
405. Elliot Blair Smith, *U.S. Set to Release Pakistani Detainees, Report Says*, USA Today, Sept. 6, 2002, at 8A.
406. *Id.*
407. *Id.*
408. Warren Hoge, *Investigators for U.N. Urge U.S. to Close Guantanamo*, N.Y. Times, Feb. 17, 2006, p. 6. *See also Inside*, N. Y. Times, Feb. 17, 2006, p. 1.

409. Alex Belida, *Secret Detainees*, VOICE OF AMERICA NEWS, May 14, 2003, Correspondent report 2–303210. *See also* Memorandum from Jack I. Goldsmith III, Assistant Attorney General, US Department of Justice Office of Legal Counsel, to Alberto R. Gonzales, Counsel to the President (Mar. 19, 2004), reprinted in THE TORTURE PAPERS: THE ROAD TO ABU GHRAIB, 367–80 (Karen J. Greenberg & Joshua L. Dratel eds., 2005); Duncan Campbell, *U.S. Interrogators Turn to 'Torture Lite'*, GUARDIAN (London), Jan. 25, 2003, at 17; and *U.S. Maintains Elaborate System of Detention Centers*, FRONTRUNNER, May 11, 2004, citing Stephens Priest, WASH. POST, May 11, 2004, at A1.

410. *Id.*

411. James Risen & Thom Shanker, *The Struggle for Iraq: Terror Captives*, N.Y. TIMES, Dec. 18, 2003, at 1.

412. *Id.*

413. Drew Brown, *Rumsfeld: U.S. Won't Move Suspect to Use Torture Tactics*, KNIGHT RIDDER WASH. BUREAU, Apr. 4, 2002; Risen et al., *supra* note 411; Belida, *supra* note 409.

414. Gaskell, *supra* note 394.

415. Scarborough, *supra* note 370.

416. Shadid et al., *supra* note 377.

417. Geneva Conventions of 1949, signed Aug. 12, 1949, Common Articles 3 and 3(d) (emphasis added), available at www.genevaconventions.org/.

418. Memorandum from John Yoo, Deputy Assistant Attorney General, and Robert J. Delahunty, Special Counsel, US Department of Justice Office of Legal Counsel, to William J. Haynes II, General Counsel, Department of Defense (Jan. 9, 2002), reprinted in THE TORTURE PAPERS: THE ROAD TO ABU GHRAIB, 38–79 (Karen J. Greenberg & Joshua L. Dratel eds., 2005). [hereinafter Yoo/Delahunty Memo] 18 U.S.C. 2441(a) and (b), War Crimes.

419. Yoo/Delahunty Memo, *supra* note 418, at 44.

420. *Id.* at 44–45.

421. *Id.* at 47.

422. Geneva Convention III, Article 4.

423. Yoo/Delahunty Memo, *supra* note 418, at 50.

424. *See* Fionnuala Ni Aolain, *The European Convention on Human Rights and Its Prohibition on Torture*, in TORTURE 213, 214–218 (S. Levinson ed. 2004).

425. Derek Jinks, *September 11 and the Laws of War*, 28 YALE J INT'L L. 1 (2003). (arguing that the real controversy during the drafting of the Geneva Conventions in 1949 was whether international standards ought to apply to armed conflict even if hostilities are confined to the territory of one state).

426. Mintz, *supra* note 389.

427. Yoo/Delahunty Memo, *supra* note 418, at 64.

428. Vienna Convention on Treaties Art. 60(2)(b).

429. Vienna Convention on Treaties, Art. 60(5).

430. Geneva Conventions, Common Article 1.

431. Memorandum from Alberto R. Gonzales, Counsel to the President, to the President (Jan. 25, 2002) reprinted in THE TORTURE PAPERS: THE ROAD TO ABU GHRAIB, 118–21 (Karen J. Greenberg & Joshua L. Dratel eds., 2005), at 118. [hereinafter Gonzales Memo]

432. Classified Memorandum from Donald Rumsfeld, Secretary of Defense, to the Chairman of the Joint Chiefs of Staff (Jan. 19, 2002), reprinted in THE TORTURE

PAPERS: THE ROAD TO ABU GHRAIB, 80 (Karen J. Greenberg & Joshua L. Dratel eds., 2005). Emphasis added.

433. COLIN POWELL & JOSEPH PERSICO, MY AMERICAN JOURNEY (1995).

434. Gonzales Memo, *supra* note 431, at 118.

435. *Id.*

436. *See, e.g.*, Memorandum from Jay S. Bybee, Assistant Attorney General, US Department of Justice Office of Legal Counsel, to Alberto R. Gonzales, Counsel to the President, and William J. Haynes II, General Counsel of the Department of Defense (Jan. 22, 2002), reprinted in THE TORTURE PAPERS: THE ROAD TO ABU GHRAIB, 105 (Karen J. Greenberg & Joshua L. Dratel eds., 2005). [hereinafter Bybee Memo I]

437. *Id.*, at 119.

438. *Id.*, at 120.

439. *Id.*

440. *Id.*

441. *Id.*

442. *Id.*, at 121.

443. *Id.*

444. *Id.*

445. *Id.*

446. Memorandum from Colin L. Powell, Secretary of State, to Counsel to the President, Assistant to the President for National Security Affairs, Re: Draft Decision Memorandum for the President on the Applicability of the Geneva Convention to the Conflict in Afghanistan, reprinted in THE TORTURE PAPERS: THE ROAD TO ABU GHRAIB, 122–25 (Karen J. Greenberg & Joshua L. Dratel eds., 2005).

447. *Id.*, at 122.

448. *Id.*, at 123.

449. *See, e.g.*, INDEPENDENT PANEL TO REVIEW DEPARTMENT OF DEFENSE DETENTION OPERATIONS, FINAL REPORT, Aug. 2004, at 7 [hereinafter Schlesinger Report].

450. *Rumsfeld Visits Camp X-Ray*, CNN.COM, Jan. 27, 2002, available at www.cnn.com/TRANSCRIPTS/.

451. *Id.*

452. *Id.*

453. Letter from John Ashcroft, Attorney General, to President George Bush (Feb. 1, 2002) reprinted in THE TORTURE PAPERS: THE ROAD TO ABU GHRAIB, 126–7 (Karen J. Greenberg & Joshua L. Dratel eds., 2005).

454. Memorandum from President George Bush, to the Vice President, the Secretary of State, the Secretary of Defense, the Attorney General, chief of Staff to the President, Director of Central Intelligence, Assistant to the President for National Security Affairs, Chairman of the Joint Chiefs of Staff, (Feb. 7, 2002), reprinted in THE TORTURE PAPERS: THE ROAD TO ABU GHRAIB, 134–5 (Karen J. Greenberg & Joshua L. Dratel eds., 2005) [hereinafter Bush Memo].

455. *Id.*, 2(b) at 134.

456. *Id.*, 2(a) at 134.

457. *Id.*, 2(c) at 134–5.

458. *Id.*, 2(d) at 135. *See also* Memorandum from Jay Bybee, Office of Legal Counsel, to Alberto R. Gonzales, Counsel to the President, (Feb. 7, 2002), reprinted in THE TORTURE PAPERS: THE ROAD TO ABU GHRAIB, 136 (Karen J. Greenberg & Joshua L. Dratel eds., 2005). [hereinafter Bybee Memo II]

459. Bush Memo, *supra* note 454, at 135 (emphasis added).

460. Pat Lancaster, *Charity Begins at Home*; MIDDLE EAST, Mar. 1, 2003.

461. *Rasul v. Bush*, 542 U.S. 466, 124 S.Ct. 2686, June 28, 2004.

462. *Hamdi v. Rumsfeld*, 542 U.S. 507, 124 S.Ct. 2633, June 28, 2004.

463. *Johnson v. Eisentrager*, 339 U.S. 763, 70 S.Ct. 936, June 05, 1950.

464. *Rasul v. Bush*, 542 U.S. 466, 124 S.Ct. 2686, June 28, 2004, at 476–479.

465. *Rasul v. Bush*, 542 U.S. 466, 124 S.Ct. 2686, June 28, 2004, at 475–476.

466. *Rasul v. Bush*, 542 U.S. 466, 124 S.Ct. 2686, June 28, 2004, at 476.

467. *Hamdi v. Rumsfeld*, 542 U.S. 507, 124 S.Ct. 2633, June 28, 2004, at 509.

468. 542 U.S. 507, at 537.

469. 542 U.S. 507 at 532.

470. 542 U.S. 507, at 536. Justice Souter concurred in part, dissented in part, concurred in judgment, and filed opinion in which Justice Ginsburg joined. 542 U.S. 507, at 539–554. Justice Scalia dissented and filed opinion in which Justice Stevens joined. 542 U.S. 507, at 554–579. Justice Thomas dissented and filed opinion. 542 U.S. 507, at 579–599.

471. Tony Mauro, *High Court: Detainees Should Get Due Process*, LEGAL INTELLI-GENCER, June 29, 2004, p. 4.

472. *Id.*

473. RADM McGarrah, Guantanamo Bay Panel, March 8, 2006, Stanford University Law School, Mar. 3, 2006.

474. *Id.*

475. *Id.*

476. *Id.*

477. DTA, § 1005(e), 119 Stat. 2741–2742.

478. *Id.*, para 2 of subsection (e).

479. § 1005(e)(3)(D), ibid.

480. App. To Pet. For Cert. 65a, cited in opinion at 2759. *Hamdan v. Rumsfeld*, 126 S. Ct. 2749, U.S. 2006, June 29, 2006.

481. 126 S. Ct. 2749, at 2773 (Stevens, J., citing U.S. CONST, Art. II, § 2, cl. 1; Art. I, § 8, cl. 11, 12, 10, and 14.)

482. 126 S. Ct. 2749, at 2773–2774 (Stevens, J.).

483. 126 S. Ct. 2749, at 2773–2774 (Stevens, J.).

484. 126 S. Ct. 2749, at 2795.

485. 126 S. Ct. 2749, at 2796.

486. 126 S. Ct. 2749, at 2796.

487. 126 S. Ct. 2749, at 2798.

488. 126 S. Ct. 2749, at 2798.

489. P.L. 109–366, sec. 7(e)(1), codified at 28 USCA § 2241.

490. P.L. 109–366, sec. 7(e)(2), codified at 28 USCA § 2241.

491. P.L. 109–366, sec. 7.

492. *Hamdan v. Rumsfeld*, 464 F.Supp.2d 9, D. D. C., Dec. 13, 2006 (NO. CIV. A. 04–1519 (JR)), at 12.

493. *Hamdan v. Rumsfeld*, 464 F.Supp.2d, at 16.

494. *Hamdan v. Rumsfeld*, 464 F.Supp.2d, at 18.

495. *Camp X-Ray Faces Hunger Strike*, MORNING STAR, Mar. 1, 2002, at 1; *Detainees Come from Varied Sources, Could be Rich Source of Intelligence*, BULLETIN'S FRONTRUNNER, Mar. 15, 2002.

496. Lynne Sladky, *Questioning Is Called Legal*, DESERET NEWS (Salt Lake City), Feb. 3, 2002, at A4.

497. Edward Epstein, *U.S. Accused of Mistreating al Qaeda, Taliban Detainees*, SAN FRANCISCO CHRON., Jan. 22, 2002, at A1; Gallagher, *supra* note 379.

498. *Id.*
499. Scarborough, *supra* note 370.
500. *Id.*
501. Gallagher, *supra* note 379.
502. Daniel McGrory & Frances Gibb, *Families Challenge Blair over Terror Suspects Held by U.S.*, TIMES (London), Feb. 26, 2002.
503. *Guantanamo Bay: Quality of Judgment*, GUARDIAN (London), Nov. 27, 2003, at 27.
504. *Id.*
505. Epstein, *supra* note 497.
506. Severin Carrell, *Britons Admit to Al-Qa'ida Link in Plea Bargain Deal*, INDEPENDENT (London), Aug. 17, 2003, at 2.
507. *Id.*
508. *Id.*
509. Vikram Dodd & Michael White, *Britons Freed: No Rights, No Charges, No Lawyers . . . Life in the Cuban Camp Beyond The Law*, GUARDIAN (London), Feb. 20, 2004, at 4.
510. *Id.*
511. *Id.*
512. *Id.*
513. *Detainees Could Return to Britain*, HOUSTON CHRON., Feb. 24, 2002, at A30.
514. Dodd et al., *supra* note 509.
515. Carrell, *supra* note 506.
516. *Id.*
517. *Powell: More Detainees to Be Freed*, CNN.COM, Apr. 29, 2004. *See also* Wikram Dodd, *Guantanamo Briton Fears Control Order*, GUARDIAN (London), Mar. 15, 2005, 9.
518. Tania Branigan, *Briton Accuses American Captors*, GUARDIAN (London), Mar. 13, 2004, at 6. *See also* Alison Hardie, *Tight Security as RAF Fly the Five Released Men into Britain*, SCOTSMAN, Mar. 10, 2004, at 1; and Alison Hardie, *Freedom After Two Years in Camp X-Ray*, SCOTSMAN, Feb. 20, 2004, at 3.
519. *Id.*
520. "Our interrogations in Guantanamo . . . were conducted with us chained to the floor for hours on end in circumstances so prolonged that it was practice to have plastic chairs for the interrogators that could be easily hosed off because prisoners would be forced to urinate during the course of them. . . . One practice that was introduced . . . was 'short shackling' where we were forced to squat without a chair with our hands chained between our legs and chained to the floor. If we fell over, the chains would cut into our hands. We would be left in this position for hours before an interrogation, during the interrogations (which could last as long as 12 hours) and sometimes for hours while the interrogators left the room. The air conditioning was turned up so high that within minutes we would be freezing. There was strobe lighting and loud music played that was itself a form of torture. Sometimes dogs were brought in to frighten us. We were not fed all the time that we were there, and when we were returned to our cells, we would not be fed that day. . . . We ourselves witnessed a number of brutal assaults upon prisoners. One, in April 2002, was of Jummah Al-Dousari from Bahrain, a man who had become psychiatrically disturbed, who was lying on the floor of his cage immediately near to us when a group of eight or nine guards . . . entered his cage. We saw them severely assault him. They stamped on his neck, kicked him in the stomach even

though he had metal rods there as a result of an operation, and they picked up his head and smashed his face into the floor. . . . Another detainee, from Yemen, was beaten up so badly that we understand he is still in hospital eighteen months later." *Letter from Shafiq Rasul & Asif Iqbal, Britons Released Without Charge After 2 Years in Guantánamo Bay, to the U.S. Senate Armed Services Committee, May 13, 2004. See also* John Mintz, *Britons Allege Guantanamo Abuse in Letter to Bush*, Wash. Post, May 14, 2004, at A16.

521. Branigan, *supra* note 518.

522. *Id.*

523. *Guananamo Bay Hellish to UK Detainees*, China Daily, Aug. 5, 2004.

524. *Id.*

525. *Guantanamo Detainees Describe Life at Prison Camp*, Guelph Mercury, Mar. 21, 2006, at B11.

526. *Id.*

527. Epstein, *supra* note 497.

528. Tony Winton, *100 Saudis Detained in Cuba, U.S. is Told*, Deseret News (Salt Lake City), Jan. 29, 2002, at A5; *Yemeni Investigators Head to Guantanamo*, Sun-Sentinel (Fort Lauderdale, FL), Feb. 5, 2002, at 8A; *Foreign Intelligence Agents Question Guantanamo Prisoners*, Bulletin's Frontrunner, June 25, 2002 (citing N.Y. Times June 25, 2002, article by Becker); Pakistan, Western Mail, May 7, 2002, p. 4.

529. Alison Hardie, *Freedom After Two Years in Camp X-Ray*, Scotsman, Feb. 20, 2004, at 3.

530. Luxner, *supra* note 387.

531. Epstein, *supra* note 497.

532. Parliamentary Assembly of the Council of Europe, Resolution 1271, Jan. 24, 2002. See also Committee of Ministers of the Council of Europe, July 11, 2002, Guidelines on Human Rights and the Fight Against Terrorism.

533. Epstein, *supra* note 497.

534. Dan McDougall, *Anger as U.S. Holds Children as POWs*, Scotsman, Apr. 24, 2003, at 2. *See also* Savage, *supra* note 402.

535. *Id.*

536. Laura E. Chatfield, *Child Prisoners Held by U.S. Military*, United Press International, Apr. 24, 2003.

537. *See, e.g., Camp Under the X-ray*, Weekend Australian, Jan. 29, 2005, at 23; Tamara McLean, *Interrogators told Habib They'd Killed His Family*, Australian Associated Press Pty. Ltd., Jan. 26, 2005; *Australian Held by U.S. Says He Was Tortured in Egypt*, Orlando Sentinel (Florida), Jan. 7, 2005, p. A9.

538. Sladky, *supra* note 496.

539. Phil Reeves, *Old Afghans Speak of Their Ordeal as Inmates of Guantanamo*, Independent (London), Oct. 30, 2002, at 13.

540. U.S. Army Intelligence Interrogation Field Manual, FM 34–52, c. 1, "Intelligence," "Prohibition against the Use of Force," Headquarters, Department of the Army, May 8, 1987, available at www.globalsecurity.org/. [hereinafter Army Field Manual]

541. *Id.*

542. *Id.*

543. *Id.*

544. US Department of State Initial Report to the UN Committee Against Torture (Oct. 15, 1999), available at www.state.gov/.

545. *Id.*

546. *Id.*, at II. Implementation of Specific Articles, Articles 1 and 2 – Definition and Prevention.

547. *See* Memorandum from Jay. S. Bybee, Assistant Attorney General, US Department of Justice Office of Legal Counsel, to William J. Haynes, II, General Counsel, Department of Defense (Feb. 26, 2002), reprinted in THE TORTURE PAPERS: THE ROAD TO ABU GHRAIB, 144–71 (Karen J. Greenberg & Joshua L. Dratel eds., 2005) [hereinafter Bybee Memo III]. *Miranda* v. *Arizona*, 384 U.S. 436 (1966).

548. Schlesinger Report, *supra* note 449, at 7.

549. Convention Against Torture and Other Cruel, Inhuman or Degrading Treatment or Punishment, G.A. res. 39/46, [annex, 39 U.N. GAOR Supp. (No. 51) at 197, UN Doc. A/39/51 (1984)], entered into force June 26, 1987, Article 1; Ratifications and Reservations, Office of the United Nations High Commissioner for Human Rights, available at www.ohchr.org/.

550. *Id.*, Article 2(1).

551. *Id.*, Article 2(2) (emphasis added). Similarly, claiming an order from a superior officer is not sufficient to justify the practice. *Id.*, Article 2(3).

552. *Id.*, Article 10.

553. *Id.*, Article 16.

554. *Id.*, Article 12.

555. *Id.*, Article 4.

556. United States of America, Reservation I(1), available at www.ohchr.org/english/.

557. David Luban, *Torture, American-Style: This Debate Comes Down to Words vs. Deeds*, WASH. POST, Nov. 27, 2005, at B1.

558. United States of America, Reservation II(1)(a).

559. *Id.*, Reservation II(1)(b).

560. *Id.*, Reservation II(1)(d).

561. 18 U.S.C. § 2340 ("Definitions").

562. 18 U.S.C. § 2340A.

563. *Id.*

564. *Id.*

565. Memorandum for Alberto R. Gonzales, Counsel to the President, from Jay Bybee, US Department of Justice Office for Legal Counsel, Aug. 1, 2002, Re: Standards of Conduct for Interrogation under 18 U.S.C. §§2340–2340A, reprinted in THE TORTURE PAPERS: THE ROAD TO ABU GHRAIB, 172 (Karen J. Greenberg & Joshua L. Dratel eds., 2005). [hereinafter Bybee Memo IV] *See also Id.*, at 185–91.

566. *Id.*, at 174.

567. *Id.*, at 175.

568. *Id.*, at 172. *See also* 176.

569. *Id.*, at 172. *See also* 177–79.

570. *Id.*, at 172. *See also* 179–83.

571. Memorandum from Diane Beaver, LTC, USA Staff Judge Advocate, Department of Defense Joint Task Force 170, to Commander, Joint Task Force 170, (Oct. 11, 2002), reprinted in THE TORTURE PAPERS: THE ROAD TO ABU GHRAIB, 229–35 (Karen J. Greenberg & Joshua L. Dratel eds., 2005), at 304 [hereinafter Beaver Memo].

572. *Id.*

573. Beaver Memo, *supra* note 571, and Dana Priest and Bradley Graham, *U.S. Struggled Over How Far to Push Tactics; Documents Show Back-and-Forth on Interrogation Policy*, WASH POST, June 24, 2004, p. A1.

574. Memorandum from James T. Hill, Commander, US Southern Command, to Chairman of the Joint Chiefs of Staff (Oct. 25, 2002), *reprinted in Id.* at 223.

575. DoD's General Counsel recommended to Rumsfeld that interrogators use only Categories I and II and "mild, non-injurious physical conduct" from Category III. Letter from William J. Haynes II, General Counsel, to Donald Rumsfeld, Secretary of Defense (Nov. 27, 2002), reprinted in THE TORTURE PAPERS: THE ROAD TO ABU GHRAIB, 237 (Karen J. Greenberg & Joshua L. Dratel eds., 2005).

576. *See, e.g.*, Alison Hardie, *Freedom After Two Years in Camp X-Ray*, SCOTSMAN, Feb. 20, 2004, at 3.

577. *Out of Mind*, HARPER'S MAG., May 1, 2004, at 22.

578. *Id.*

579. *Id. See also* Transcript, BBC Panorama, available at www.torito.nl/news/.

580. *Id.*

581. *Id.*

582. *Id.*

583. *Id.*

584. *Id.*

585. Adam Zagorin, *Exclusive: '20th Hijacker' Claims That Torture Made Him Lie*, TIME, Mar. 3, 2006, available at www.time.com.

586. Army Regulation 15–6: Final Report; Investigation into FBI Allegations of Detainee Abuse at Guantanamo Bay, Cuba Detention Facility, Apr. 1, 2005 (amended June 9, 2005), available at www.defenselink.mil/news/. [hereinafter Schmidt Report] (in this report, al Kahtani is Special Detainee #1), at 13.

587. *Id.*, at 20.

588. *Id.*, at 17–18.

589. *Id.*, at 18.

590. *Id.*, at 14.

591. *Id.*, at 16.

592. *Id.*, at 17.

593. *Id.*, at 19.

594. *Id.*

595. *Id.*

596. *Id.*

597. *Id.*, at 20. *See also* Jane Mayer, *The Memo: How an Internal Effort to Ban the Abuse and Torture Of Detainees Was Thwarted*, NEW YORKER, Feb. 27, 2006.

598. *See* US Department of Defense Office of the Assistant Secretary of Defense (Public Affairs), News Release: Guantanamo Provides Valuable Intelligence information, No. 592–05, June 12, 2005, available at www.defenselink.mil/

599. Zagorin, *supra* note 585.

600. Memorandum from Donald Rumsfeld, Secretary of Defense, to Commander USSOUTHCOM (Jan. 15, 2003), reprinted in THE TORTURE PAPERS: THE ROAD TO ABU GHRAIB, 239 (Karen J. Greenberg & Joshua L. Dratel eds., 2005).

601. *Id.*

602. Memorandum from Donald Rumsfeld, Secretary of Defense, to the General Counsel of the Department of Defense (Jan. 15, 2003), reprinted in THE TORTURE PAPERS: THE ROAD TO ABU GHRAIB, 238 (Karen J. Greenberg & Joshua L. Dratel eds., 2005).

603. Dana Priest & Bradley Graham, *U.S. Struggled Over How Far to Push Tactics; Documents Show Back-and-Forth on Interrogation Policy*, WASH. POST, June 24, 2004, p. A1.

604. *Id.*

605. Working Group Report on Detainee Interrogations in the Global War on Terrorism: Assessment of Legal, Historical, Policy, and Operational Considerations, Mar. 6, 2003, *reprinted in* The Torture Papers: The Road to Abu Ghraib, 241–85, 259 (Karen J. Greenberg & Joshua L. Dratel eds., 2005). at 275. [hereinafter Working Group Report I]. A 9th circuit case, *Cooper* v. *Dupnik* addressed techniques eerily similar to those employed in Guantánamo Bay: in Cooper, the techniques were "designed to instill stress, hopelessness, and fear, and to break [the suspect's] resistance." *Cooper* v. *Dupnik*, 963 F.2d 1220 (9th Cir. 1992) (en banc), at 1229, cited in The Torture Papers: The Road to Abu Ghraib, 275 (Karen J. Greenberg & Joshua L. Dratel eds., 2005).

606. *Id.*, at 277–82.

607. Presidential Address to the Nation, Mar. 19, 2003, available at www.whitehouse.gov/.

608. Working Group Report on Detainee Interrogations in the Global War on Terrorism: Assessment of Legal, Historical, Policy, and Operational Considerations, Apr. 4, 2002, reprinted in The Torture Papers: The Road to Abu Ghraib, 286–359 (Karen J. Greenberg & Joshua L. Dratel eds., 2005) [hereinafter Working Group Report II]. Emphasis added.

609. *Id.*, at 287.

610. *Id.*, at 343.

611. *Id.*, at 344.

612. *Id.*, at 353–54.

613. Memorandum from Donald Rumsfeld, Secretary of Defense, to the Commander, US Southern Command, Apr. 16, 2003, reprinted in The Torture Papers: The Road to Abu Ghraib, 260 (Karen J. Greenberg & Joshua L. Dratel eds., 2005).

614. *Id. See also* Stephen Grey, Ghost Plane: The True Story of the CIA Torture Program (2006).

615. Investigation of Intelligence Activities at Abu Ghraib [including Investigation of the Abu Ghraib Prison and 205th Military Intelligence Brigade LTG Anthony R. Jones, Investigation of the Abu Ghraib Detention Facility and 205th Military Intelligence Brigade MG George R. Fay], (2004), reprinted in The Torture Papers: The Road to Abu Ghraib, 987–1131, 1036–7 (Karen J. Greenberg & Joshua L. Dratel eds., 2005) [hereinafter Fay-Jones Report].

616. *Editorial, The Policy of Abuse*, Wash. Post, May 16, 2004, at B6.

617. *Id.*

618. Risen et al., *supra* note 411.

619. Branigan, *supra* note 518.

620. *The Policy of Abuse, supra* note 616.

621. *Id.*

622. *See, e.g.*, Mark Mazzetti, Julian E. Barnes, Edward T. Pund, David E. Kaplan, & Linda Robinson, *Inside the Iraq Prison Scandal*, U.S. News & World Rep., May 24, 2004, at 18.

623. Bryan Bender & Charlie Savage, *Memos Detail Debate on Prisoners: Rumsfeld Reversed OK of Severe Interrogations*, Boston Globe, June 23, 2004, at A1.

624. Pamela Hess, *Torture Memos Affect Military Reputation*, United Press Int'l, June 16, 2004.

625. *Id.*

626. Bender et al., *supra* note 623.

627. *Id.*

628. See THE TAGUBA REPORT, ARTICLE 15–6 INVESTIGATION OF THE 800TH MILITARY POLICE BRIGADE, Mar. 2004, reprinted in THE TORTURE PAPERS: THE ROAD TO ABU GHRAIB, 405–465 (Karen J. Greenberg & Joshua L. Dratel eds., 2005) [hereinafter Taguba Report]; THE MIKOLASHEK REPORT, DEPARTMENT OF THE ARMY, THE INSPECTOR GENERAL, DETAINEE OPERATIONS INSPECTION, July 21, 2004, reprinted in THE TORTURE PAPERS: THE ROAD TO ABU GHRAIB, 630–907 (Karen J. Greenberg & Joshua L. Dratel eds., 2005); Schlesinger Report, *supra* note 449. *See also* Eric Schmitt & Kate Zernike, *Australian to Be Charged: Prison interrogators Ordered Use of Dogs*, INT'L HERALD TRIB., June 12, 2004, at 3.

629. Mazzetti et al., *supra* note 622.

630. *Id.*

631. ASSESSMENT OF DOD COUNTER-TERRORISM INTERROGATION AND DETENTION OPERATIONS IN IRAQ (MG Miller's Assessment), referenced in Taguba Report, *supra* note 628, at 409.

632. Taguba Report, *supra* note 628, at 409–10.

633. *Id.*, at 416.

634. *Id.*

635. *Id. See also* Fay-Jones Report, *supra* note 615, at 1079.

636. Taguba Report, *supra* note 628, at 416. *See also* Fay-Jones Report, *supra* note 615, at 1079.

637. *Id.*

638. *Id.*, at 417. *See also* Fay-Jones Report, *supra* note 615, at 1076.

639. Taguba Report, *supra* note 628, at 417.

640. *Id.*

641. *Id.*

642. Fay-Jones Report, *supra* note 615, at 988.

643. *Id.*, at 989.

644. *Id.*

645. *Id.*

646. *Id.* Emphasis added.

647. *Id.*, at 1004–05.

648. *Id.*, at 393 *See also* Josh White, *Guantanamo Desperation Seen in Suicide Attempts*, WASH. POST, Nov. 1, 2005, at A1.

649. REPORT OF THE INTERNATIONAL COMMITTEE OF THE RED CROSS (ICRC) ON THE TREATMENT BY THE COALITION FORCES OF PRISONERS OF WAR AND OTHER PROTECTED PERSONS BY THE GENEVA CONVENTIONS IN IRAQ DURING ARREST, INTERNMENT AND INTERROGATION, Feb. 2004, *reprinted in* THE TORTURE PAPERS: THE ROAD TO ABU GHRAIB, 383–404, 384 (Karen J. Greenberg & Joshua L. Dratel eds., 2005), at 393

650. *Id.*

651. *Dossier: an Ounce of Detention*, AM. PROSPECT, Nov. 2005, p. 7. *See also US Maintains Elaborate System of Detention Centers*, THE FRONTRUNNER, May 11, 2004.

652. Army Maj. Gen Antonio M. Taguba said the practice was "deceptive, contrary to Army doctrine and in violation of international law." Dana Priest & Bradley Graham, *U.S. Struggled Over How Far to Push Tactics*, WASH. POST, June 24, 2004, p. A1.

653. Testimony on the Investigation of the 205th Military Intelligence Brigade at Abu Ghraib Prison, Iraq, Sept. 9, 2004, Senate Committee on Armed Services, General Paul J. Kern, USA Commanding General, US Army Materiel Command, 2d Session,

108th Cong. See also Bradley Graham and Josh White, *General Cites Hidden Detainees: Senators Told CIA May Have Avoided Registering Up to 100*, WASH. POST, Sept. 10, 2004, at A24.

654. Joint Investigation into September 11th: 5th Public Hearing, 26 September 2002, Joint House/Senate Intelligence Committee Hearing, available at www.fas.org/irp/congress/.

655. Richard Esposito, *CIA's Harsh Interrogation Techniques Described*, ABC NEWS, Nov. 18, 2005, available at http://abcnews.go.com/. A classified report issued by the CIA's Inspector General, John Helgerwon, in 2004, said that these techniques "appeared to constitute cruel, and degrading treatment under the (Geneva) convention." Douglas Jehl, *Report Warned C.I.A. on Tactics in Interrogation*, N.Y. TIMES, Nov. 9, 2005, available at www.nytimes.com/2005/.

656. *CIA Holds Terror Suspects in Secret Prisons*, WASH. POST; EU/US: *CIA Terrorist Prisons Scandal Refuses to Die Down*, EUR. REP., Jan. 7, 2006; Jane Mayer, *Outsourcing Torture: The Secret History of America's "Extraordinary Rendition" Program*, NEW YORKER, Feb. 7, 2005, available at www.newyorker.com; Yossi Melman, *CIA Holding al-Qaida Suspects in Secret Jordanian Lockup*, HAARETZ, Oct. 13, 2004, available at www.informationclearinghouse.info/.

657. *Dossier: An Ounce of Detention*, AMERICAN PROSPECT, Nov. 2005, p. 7. *See also CIA Runs Detention Center in Afghanistan*, ZINHUA GENERAL NEWS SERVICE, Jan. 22, 2006.

658. *US Maintains Elaborate System of Detention Centers*, *supra* note 651.

659. *Id.*

660. N.Y. TIMES, May 13, 2004.

661. *US Maintains Elaborate System of Detention Centers*, *supra* note 651.

662. Faye Bowers, *Interrogation Tactics Draw Fire*, CHRISTIAN SCIENCE MONITOR (Boston, MA), Mar. 20, 2005, p. 2.

663. DeNeen L. Brown & Dana Priest, *Deported Terror Suspect Details Torture in Syria: Canadian's Case Called Typical of CIA*, WASH. POST, Nov. 5, 2003, at A01. *See also* Bowers, *supra* note 662.

664. PDD 39, June 21, 1995, available at www.fas.org/irp/.

665. Formulation and Conduct of US Counterterrorism Policy: Hearing Before the National Commission on Terrorist Attacks Upon the United States (Interim Report) Mar. 23, 2004), available at www.9-11commission.gov.

666. Counterterrorism Policy: Hearing Before the National Commission on Terrorist Attacks Upon the United States (Mar. 24, 2004) (statement by George Tenet, former Director of Central Intelligence), available at www.9-11commission.gov (visited February 26, 2007).

667. Committee on International Human Rights of the Association of the Bar of the City of New York and The Center for Human Rights and Global Justice, New York University School of Law, Torture by Proxy: International and Domestic Law Applicable to 'Extraordinary Renditions', 2004, p. 4, available at www.chrgj.org/docs/ [hereinafter NYU Report]. It is important to recognize that there is a considerable amount of confusion between rendition and extraordinary rendition – officials often do not distinguish between them, and the lines are frequently blurred. Officials, moreover, will only speak off the record about the renditions.

668. David Crawshaw, *Bush Gave CIA Expansive Interrogation Power: Report*, AUSTRALIAN ASSOCIATED PRESS PTY. LTD., Mar. 6, 2005.

669. NYU Report, *supra* note 667, at 15.

670. Duncan Campbell, *September 11: Six Months On*, GUARDIAN (London), Mar. 12, 2002, at 4.

671. Dana Priest & Barton Gellman, *U.S. Decries Abuse but Defends Interrogations*, WASH. POST, Dec. 26, 2002, at A1; Ken Coates, *A Season of Cruelty*, MORNING STAR, Mar. 10,. 2003, at 7.

672. John Barry, Michael Hirsh, & Michael Isikoff, *The Roots of Torture*, NEWSWEEK, May 24, 2004, at 26.

673. Mayer, *supra* note 656.

674. *EU Endorses Damning Report on CIA*, BBC NEWS, Feb. 14, 2007, available at www.news.bbc.co.uk/.

675. Committee on International Human Rights of the Association of the Bar of the City of New York and The Center for Human Rights and Global Justice, New York University School of Law, Torture by Proxy: International and Domestic Law Applicable to 'Extraordinary Renditions', 2004, p. 5, available at www.test. extrajudicialexecutions.org/.

676. Foreign Affairs Reform and Restructuring Act of 1998 (FARRA), Pub. L. No. 105–277, div. G, Title XXII, Sec. 2242.

677. Mayer, *supra* note 656. *See also* US Dep't of State Country Reports on Human Rights Practices (2001), (2002), (2003), (2004).

678. Tamara McLean, *Interrogators Told Habib They'd Killed His Family: Lawyer*, AUSTRALIAN ASSOCIATED PRESS, Jan. 26, 2005. *See also Australian Held by U.S. Says He Was Tortured in Egypt*, ORLANDO SENTINEL (Florida), Jan. 7, 2005, p. A9.

679. Bowers, *supra* note 662. *See also* Paul Osborne, *Interrogators in Egypt Used ASIO Info: Habib*, AUSTRALIAN ASSOCIATED PRESS, Mar. 9, 2005; David Crawshaw, *Bush Gave CIA Expansive Interrogation Power: Report*, AUSTRALIAN ASSOCIATED PRESS, Mar. 6, 2005.

680. The German authorities say that his account is consistent with their information. Bowers, *supra* note 662. *See also* Hannah K. Strange, *UN Orders Guantanamo Abuse Inquiry*, UPI, Nov. 18, 2005.

681. NYU Report, *supra* note 667, at 31 ff.

682. Dana Priest & Joe Stephens, *Secret World of U.S. Interrogation: Long History of Tactics in Overseas Prisons is Coming to Light*, WASH. POST, May 11, 2004, at A01.

683. Josh White & John Mintz, *Red Cross Cites 'Inhumane' Treatment at Guantanamo*, WASH. POST, Dec. 1, 2004, p. A10. *See also* Eric Boehlert, *More Coldblooded than Abu Ghraib*, SALON.COM, Dec. 2, 2004.

684. *See, e.g.*, International Headline News, Central News Agency – Taiwan, Nov. 30, 2004; International Red Cross Finds 'Form of Torture' at Guantanamo, ONASA News Agency (Europe Intelligence Wire), Nov. 30, 2004.

685. Warren Hoge, *Investigators for U.N. Urge U.S. to Close Guantanamo*, N.Y. TIMES, Feb. 17, 2006, p. 6. *See also Inside*, N.Y. TIMES, Feb. 17, 2006, p. 1

686. Craig Whitlock, *New Swedish Documents Illuminate CIA Action*, WASH. POST, May 21, 2005, p. A01.

687. Paul Ames, *EU May Suspend Nations With Secret Prisons*, ABC News, November 28, 2005.

688. Condoleeza Rice, Remarks at Andrews Air Force Base, Dec. 5, 2005, US Administration View, FPA, p. 64, League of Women Voters, available at www. greatdecisions.org.

689. *Id*. Emphasis added.

690. *See* White et al., *supra* note 683; War Crimes Complaint against Rumsfeld et al., Center for Constitutional Rights, located at http://www.ccr-ny.org/v2/.

691. *Italy Indicts 31 Linked to CIA Rendition Case*, INTERNATIONAL HERALD TRIBUNE, Feb. 15, 2007.

692. *Portugal: Renditions: Judicial Investigation into CIA Flights Begins*, STATEWATCH NEWS ONLINE, February 5–6, 2007, available at www.statewatch.org/news/. See also *Portugal/CIA.- La Fiscalía General abre una investigación sobre los supuestos vuelos ilegales de la CIA en Portugal*, EUROPA PRESS, February 5, 2007, available at www.europapress.es/.

693. Lord Peter Goldsmith, QC, HM Attorney General, Keynote Address, Stanford Constitutional Law Center and Stanford Law Review, Symposium on Global Constitutionalism, Feb. 16, 2007.

694. Paul Reynolds, *Pressure Grows on Guantanamo Bay*, BBC NEWS, June 12, 2006, available at www.news.bbc.co.uk/.

695. Author interview with Sir David Omand, in person, February 2007, Palo Alto, California.

696. Author interview with Lord Lloyd of Berwick, in person, February 2007, Palo Alto, California.

697. *PACE Calls for Oversight of Foreign Intelligence Agencies Operating in Europe*, Press release – 379 (June 27, 2006), available at https://wcd.coe.int

698. *EU Endorses Damning Report on CIA*. BBC, available at www.news.bbc.co.uk/. *See also* EU Rendition Report: Key Excerpts, Feb. 14, 2007, available at www. news.bbc.co.uk/; and Dan Bilefsky, *European Inquiry Says C.I.A. flew 1,000 Flights in Secret*, N.Y. TIMES, Apr. 26, 2006, available at www.nytimes.com/ 2006/04/27/world/europe/27cia.html?ex=1303790400&en=f28193a7c7a919c0 &ei=5090&partner=rssuserland&emc=rss.

699. Arar Commission, located at http://www.ararcommission.ca/eng/index.htm.

700. *Arar v. Ashcroft* et al., 414 F. Supp.2d 250, E.D.N.Y., 2006, Feb. 16, 2006, at 253. Complaint, located at http://www.ccr-ny.org/v2/; Mayer, *supra* note 656.

701. Mayer, *supra* note 656.

702. *Arar v. Ashcroft*, 414 F. Supp.2d 250, E.D.N.Y., 2006, Feb. 16, 2006, at 254–55. *See also* Jane Lampman, *US Stand Against Torture: Firm Enough?* CHRISTIAN SCIENCE MONITOR, Boston, MA, Jan. 19, 2005, p. 11; Irwin M. Cohen, *State Torture in the Contemporary World*, INT'L J. COMP. SOCIOL., Feb. 1, 2005, No. 1–2, Vol. 46, p. 103; Michelle Shephard, *Abuses Cast Shadow over Terror Trials*, TORONTO STAR, Feb. 12, 2005, p. A18; and *Arar v. Ashcroft* Complaint.

703. Mayer, *supra* note 656.

704. Press Release, Arar Commission Releases its Findings on the Handling of the Maher Arar Case, Ottawa, Sept. 18, 2006, available at http://www.ararcommission.ca/.

705. *Id.*

706. Glenn Kessler, *State Dept. Study Cites Torture of Prisoners*, WASH POST, Mar. 1, 2005, p. A10.

707. Rice, *supra* note 688.

708. Strange, *supra* note 680.

709. *The World*, AUGUSTA CHRON. (Georgia), Apr. 27, 2005, at A02. See also *Rights Group Blasts U.S. 'Torture' at Base*, CHICAGO TRIB., Apr. 27, 2005, at 11; and *World Digest*, ST. LOUIS POST-DISPATCH (Missouri), Apr. 27, 2005, at A12.

710. Denis Staunton, *Amnesty Report Calls for Closure of Guantanamo*, IRISH TIMES, Feb. 6, 2006, at 10.

711. Judge Michel Picard, Pres., Human Rights Chamber; Bosnia-Herzegovina; BBC PANORAMA, Oct. 5, 2003

712. *Editorial & Opinion: Tony Blair and the Loss of Civilized Values*, INDEPENDENT, Feb. 24, 2006.

713. *Justice Not Being Served*, CANBERRA TIMES (Australia), Feb. 23, 2004, at 10.

714. *Editorial, Rules of the System*, WASH. POST, May 11, 2004, at A18.

715. *Editorial, Belated Reform*, WASH. POST, July 9, 2004, at A18.

716. *Editorial, Fueling the Hatred: Mishandling of Detainees Is Counterproductive to U.S. War on Terrorists*, COLUMBUS DISPATCH (Ohio), at 8A.

717. Mark Landler, *Germany: Delay in Extradition Ruling*, N.Y. TIMES, Jul. 26, 2003, at A2.

718. *Id.*

719. Pamela Hess, *Torture Memos Affect Military Reputation*, UNITED PRESS INT'L, June 16, 2004.

720. Cruel, Inhuman or Degrading Treatment (CID), Responses of Alberto R. Gonzales, Nominee to be Attorney-General of the United States to Written Questions of Senator Richard J. Durbin, Torture Policy, on file with author.

721. Letter from William E. Moschella, Assistant Attorney General, Department of Justice, to Senator Patrick J. Leahy, Ranking Minority Member, committee on the Judiciary, US Senate, Apr. 4, 2005, on file with author.

722. *See, e.g., Editorial, A Partial Disclosure*, WASH. POST, June 24, 2005, at A24.

723. President Bush's Signing Statement, Dec. 30, 2005, located in David Luban, forthcoming textbook (2006) (emphasis added).

724. Torture Victim Protection Act of 1991, 106 Stat. 73 (1992); *Arar Launches Lawsuit Against U.S. Government*, CBC NEWS, Jan. 22, 2004, available at www.cbc.ca/news/.

725. *Arar v. Ashcroft*, 414 F. Supp.2d 250, E.D.N.Y., 2006, Feb. 16, 2006; *U.S. Claims Maher Arar 'Extraordinary Rendition' Lawsuit Jeopardizes National Security*, Fan. 28, 2005, available at http://www.democracynow.org.

726. *Arar v. Ashcroft*, 414 F. Supp.2d 250, E.D.N.Y., 2006, Feb. 16, 2006, at 281.

727. *Khaled El-Masri v. George Tenet et al.*, 437 F.Supp.2d 530, E.D. Va., 2006, May 12, 2006, at 537.

728. Habeas Corpus Restoration Act of 2007, S. 185, Jan. 4, 2007.

729. *Boumediene v. Bush*, 127 S.Ct. 1478 (Mem.), 167 L.Ed.2d 578, 75 USLW 3528, U.S. Dist.Col., April 02, 2007 (NO. 06-1195, 06-1196). *See also Boumediene v. Bush*, 127 S.Ct. 1725, 167 L.Ed.2d 757, 75 USLW 3585, U.S., April 26, 2007 (NO. 06-1195, 06-1196).

730. *Khaled El-Masri v. United States*, 128 S.Ct. 373 (Mem), 75 USLW 3663, 76 USLW 3021, 76 USLW 3186, U. S., October 09, 2007 (NO. 06-1613).

731. *See, e.g.,* Michelle Shephard, *Abuses Cast Shadow over Terror Trials*, TORONTO STAR, Feb. 12, 2005, p. A18.

732. Rumsfeld explained, "What we think about is keeping them off the battlefield so they can't go out and kill more people, immediately interrogating them so we can find out what they know that can prevent future acts of terror against our country...and only last is the issue of a crime and some sort of a process that would make a judgment about that crime." Dana Priest and Bradley Graham, *U.S. Struggled Over How Far to Push Tactics*, WASH. POST, June 24, 2004, p. A1.

733. Convention Against Torture, Article 15.

734. Dodd et al., *supra* note 509. *But see* subsequent Law Lords decision allowing information obtained from torture as long as UK not complicit. *A (FC) and Others (FC) (Appellants) v. Secretary of State for the Home Department (Respondent)* (2004), [2005] UKHL 71; 8 Dec. 2005; on appeal from: [2004] EWCA Civ 1123.HL (Finding that the Special Immigration Appeals Commission can receive evidence that may have been procured by torture inflicted by officials of a foreign state without the complicity of the British authorities).

735. Beth Gorham, *Guantanamo Detainees Describe Life at the Prison Camp for the First Time in U.S.*, Canadian Press NewsWire, Mar. 20, 2006.

736. Partial list of detainees at Gitmo, compiled from transcripts released to AP under court order by DoD, approx. 5,000 pages.

737. Toni Locy, *Fates Unsure at U.S. Base in Cuba*, USA Today, Sept. 22, 2003, at 9A.

738. Partial list of detainees at Gitmo, compiled from transcripts released to AP under court order by DoD, approx. 5,000 pages.

739. *Id.*

740. Geoff Meade, Government's Human Rights Record Challenged, Press Association, Ltd., June 9, 2005.

741. *A and others v. Secretary of State for the Home Department*, [2005] UKHL 71 at 8 (Lord Bingham of Cornhill) See also Clare Dyer & Alan Travis, *Terror Suspect Awaits Bail Ruling: Decision Expected as Falconer Defends House Arrest*, Guardian (London), Jan. 31, 2005, p. 9. *See also* Robert Verkaik, *Belmarsh Detainees May Choose Jail over House Arrest*, Independent (London), Feb. 1, 2005.

742. Robert Verkaik, *Terror Suspect Overdoses after Release*, Independent (London), Mar. 23, 2005, 6; *Terror Suspect in Overdose Bid*, Western Morning News (Plymouth), Mar. 23, 2005, 26; *Detainee Speaks of Control Order Chaos*, UPI news, Mar. 24, 2005.

743. *Id.*

744. *Id.*

745. *Terror Suspect in Overdose Bid*, Western Morning News (Plymouth), Mar. 23, 2005, 26. *See also* Sarah Lyall, *U.K. Bars Return of Radical Preacher: 20 Year Resident Is Known for Strident Anti-West Sermons*, Int'l Herald Tribune, Aug. 13, 2005, 1.

746. *Britain Approves Three More 'Control Orders' on Security Suspects*, Agence France Presse, English Wire, Mar. 13, 2006.

747. Partial list of detainees at Gitmo, compiled from transcripts released to AP under court order by DoD, approx. 5,000 pages.

748. *Attempted Suicides Increase for Guantanamo Detainees*, Orlando Sentinel (Florida), Feb. 7, 2003, at A15 (reporting Jan. 16 attempt); *Guantanamo Detainee Treated after "Serious" Suicide Attempt*, Orlando Sentinel (Florida), Feb. 3, 2003, at A23 (reporting Jan. 16 attempt, man in his 20s).

749. Locy, *supra* note 737;. *In Brief*, Houston Chronicle, Mar. 7, 2003, p. A27.

750. *About 25 More Suspects Arrive at Guantanamo Bay*, Chicago Trib., Feb. 9, 2003, at 6 (noting at least five attempts in past three weeks; 15 since Guantanamo Bay opened); Manuel Roig-Franzia, *Guantanamo Was Prepared for Suicide Attempts; Risk That Detainees will Harm Themselves Is Heightened by Conditions at Prison, Say Psychologists*, Wash. Post, Mar. 2, 2003, at A7. (reporting that in one week in mid-Feb. 2003, three detainees tried to kill themselves, raising the total to 19 attempts – 9 since mid-Jan.; 16 different detainees).

751. *In Brief*, HOUSTON CHRONICLE, Mar. 7, 2003, p. A27. General Miller estimated at the time that at least 75 detainees were mentally ill. Luxner, *supra* note 387.

752. *Prisoner Suicide Attempts in Cuba Dismay the Pentagon*, L.A. TIMES, May 29, 2003, at 24. *See also Threats and Responses: Briefly Noted*, N.Y. TIMES, May 29, 2003, at A13 (noting 2 new attempts, total reached 27); *End the Legal Limbo for Guantanamo Detainees*, NEWSDAY (N.Y.), June 3, 2003, at A28 (giving 27 as total number); *Another Suicide Attempt at Guantanamo Prison*, L.A. TIMES, Aug. 15, 2003, at 20.

753. Charlie Savage, *Detainees Attempted to Hang Selves; Scrutiny Widens at Guantanamo*, BOSTON GLOBE, Jan. 25, 2005, at A1 (citing attempts Aug. 18–26). *See also* David Teather, *Suicide Protest at Camp Delta*, GUARDIAN (London), Jan. 25, 2005, at 2; Robert Varkaik and Terri Judd, *Mass Suicide Bid at Camp X-ray*, INDEPENDENT (London), Jan. 25, 2005, at 2.

754. Savage, *supra* note 753.

755. Locy, *supra* note 737.

756. Roig-Franzia, *supra* note 750.

757. Andrew Buncombe & Matthew Beard, *Red Cross Breaks Silence on Guantanamo Prisoners to Lambast US Approach*, INDEPENDENT (London), Oct. 11, 2003, at 2; Dodd et al., *supra* note 509.

758. Richard Woods & David Leppard, *How Liberal Britain Let Hate Flourish*; SUNDAY TIMES (UK), Feb. 12, 2006, 12.

759. *Id.*

760. *Id.*, at 16.

761. *See* Alan Travis, *Free Foreign Suspects on Control Orders, Says Terror Watchdog*, GUARDIAN (London), Feb. 3, 2006; David Barrett, *Three Britons Subject to Terror Control Orders*, PRESS ASSOCIATION NEWS LTD., Mar. 13, 2006; *Britain Approves Three More 'Control Orders' on Security Suspects*, AGENCE FRANCE PRESSE, English Wire, Mar. 13, 2006.

762. Colin Burke, *Letter: Stand by for the Big Round-up of Terrorists*, INDEPENDENT, Mar. 9, 2005.

763. *See* Tim Shipman, *Group 4 to Guard Terror Suspects*, SUNDAY EXPRESS, Mar. 13, 2005, pp. 4–5.

764. *Id.* The problem of the stigma that attaches to individuals is common in the American setting as well. Rustam Akhmiarov, for instance, a 26-year-old Russian, was held in Pakistan and Afghanistan before being transferred to Guantánamo Bay. He was studying Arabic at an Islamic university in Karachi when he was picked up by the Pakistani police and imprisoned with no explanation. After three weeks, Pakistanis gave him to the United States in return for $5,000. When he was finally released, he said, "At the moment I feel my life is in suspense, because I"ll be branded forever as an international terrorist, so I don't know how I can lead a normal life with that brand. Also my family, my relatives, they will be the family and relatives of an international terrorist. It can't be erased, it will stay with me forever." Strange, *supra* note 680.

765. Lord Condon, HL Debs, 13 Dec. 2005, col. 1175.

766. Lord Condon, HL Debs, 13 Dec. 2005, col. 1174.

767. *Anti-Terrorism Laws in Trouble*, ECONOMIST, U.S. Edition, Feb. 19, 2005.

768. *Commons Terror, Parliamentary News*, PRESS ASSOCIATION, Oct. 26, 2005; *Terror Laws Undermine Human Rights, Says Amnesty*, GUARDIAN (London), Feb. 23, 2006.

769. Madeleine Brindley, *Radical Preacher and Terror Suspect to be Deported from UK*, WESTERN MAIL, Aug. 12, 2005, 9.

770. Oborne, *supra* note 304.

771. *Id.*

772. Author interview with Editor of the Arab-American News, the largest Arab newspaper in the United States, Autumn 2004.

773. Louise Cainkar, Assessing the Need: Addressing the Problem, The Faith Communities and Urban Families Project, November 2003; sponsored by the Annie E. Casey Foundation. *See also* Nancy Dunne, *US Muslims See Their American Dreams Die: Since September 11 the Community Has Felt Threatened*, FIN. TIMES (London), Mar. 28, 2002, p. 10.

774. *Editorial, Gitmo Gone Wrong*, UNIVERSITY WIRE, Jan. 31, 2005.

775. *Sacrilegious Act Taken up with U.S.*, BUSINESS RECORDER, May 11, 2005.

776. *U.S. Assures Full Probe into Holy Quran Desecration*, THE NATION (Pakistan), May 10, 2005. *See also Answer to a Question taken at May 10 State Department Press Briefing*, available at STATES NEWS SERVICE, Pakistan Voices; *Concerns over alleged Misconduct at Guantanamo; alleged desecration of Quran under investigation, State Department Says*, STATES NEWS SERVICE, May 11, 2005.

777. Katharine Q. Seelye & Neil A. Lewis, *Newsweek Says it Is Retracting Koran Report*, N.Y. TIMES, May 17, 2005, at 1; Saman Zia-zarifi & John Sifton, *A Genuine Inquiry into Abuses*, INT'L HERALD TRIB., May 21, 2005, at 7.

778. Luther Keith, *Quran Story Rage Rooted in Religion*, DETROIT NEWS (Michigan), May, 19, 2005, at 2A; Zia-zarifi et al., *supra* note 777. *See also* Howard Kurtz, *Newsweek Retracts Guantanamo Story*, WASH. POST, May 17, 2005, at A03.

779. Keith, *supra* note 778.

780. Seelye et al., *supra* note 777.

781. *Id.*

782. Pak Prez, *PM Express Dismay over Alleged Desecration of Quran*, PRESS TRUST OF INDIA, May 14, 2005.

783. *Id.*

784. *Id.*

785. *U.S. Image Abroad Took a Beating Due to Quran Story*, PRESS TRUST OF INDIA, May 18, 2005.

786. Seelye et al., *supra* note 777.

787. *Id. See also* Richard A. Serrano, *Gitmo "Lifetime," Interrupted*, LA TIMES, Apr. 14, 2005, at A16.

788. *See, e.g., Rumours persist of Koran Smear*, HAMILTON SPECTATOR (Ontario, Canada), May 18, 2005, at A15; Zia-zarifi et al., *supra* note 777; Farhan Bokhari, *Looking Beyond the Desecration of the Quran*, GULF NEWS, May 26, 2005; Howard Kurtz, *Newsweek Apologizes: Inaccurate Report on Koran Led to Riots*, WASH. POST, May 16, 2005, at A1.

789. Richard B. Schmitt, *Detainees Told FBI of Koran Desecration*, LA TIMES, May 26, 2005, at A18.

790. *Id.*

791. Interview with Michael Isikoff, author of the Koran article, *Newsweek Reporter Michael Isikoff Discusses His coverage of Koran Desecration at Gauntanamo*, DEMOCRACY NOW, July 6, 2005, transcript available at www.democracynow.org [hereinafter Isikoff Interview].

792. Zia-zarifi et al., *supra* note 777.

793. *Id.*

794. *Id.*
795. Bokhari, *supra* note 788. Adnan Rehmat, running a media training program in Pakistan financed by the United States, suggested that the issue exploded not just because of the sacrilegious nature of the allegations, but because it demonstrated yet another horror assailing detainees in Guantánamo Bay. Seelye et al., *supra* note 777.
796. Warren P. Strobel, *Independent Investigation of Detainee Abuse Unnecessary, Rice says*, Knight Ridder Wash. Bureau, May 28, 2005.
797. *Id.*
798. Brian Knowlton, *Cheney Backs Handling of Detainees at Cuba Base*, N.Y. Times, May 31, 2005, at 15.
799. Kurtz, *supra* note 788.
800. *Id.*
801. Isikoff Interview, *supra* note 791.
802. Kurtz, *supra* note 788.
803. *Id.*
804. Isikoff Interview, *supra* note 791.
805. *U.S. Admits to Quran Desecration at Guantanamo*, Press Trust of India, June 4, 2005.
806. Bob Herbert, *America A Symbol Of...*, N.Y. Times, May 30, 2005, at A15.
807. *Id.*
808. *Editorial, Beyond Guantanamo*, Wash. Post, June 12, 2005, at B8.
809. *Editorial: Fueling the Hatred*, *supra* note 716.
810. *Id.*
811. Strange, *supra* note 680.
812. David Rose, *They Tied me up like a Beast and Began Kicking Me*, Observer (London), May 17, 2004.
813. *Id.*

3. Financial Counterterrorism

The following are the sources of the epigraphs: *People's Mojahedin Organization of Iran v. U.S. Department of State*, 1999. 182 F.3d 17 (4th Cir. 1999); Justice Sandra Day O'Connor, *Hamdi v. Rumsfeld*, 2004, 542 U.S. 507 at 532 (2004). Richard Wolffe, *"Wake-up Call" Warns Banks to Co-operate Freezing Assets*, Fin. Times (London), Sept. 25, 2001, at 3.

  1. *See* Owen Bowcott & Ted Oliver, *£20m Stolen in UK's Biggest Bank Robbery*, Guardian (London), Dec. 22, 2004, at 3; Alan Erwin, *Millions Stolen in Belfast Bank Raid*, Indep. E-Mail Newsl., Dec. 21, 2004; Simon Hunter, *IRA Issues Bank Robbery Denial*, Belfast News Letter, Jan. 19, 2005, at 5; Jonathan McCambridge, *We Didn't Botch our Job, Insists Detective; Police at Scene 5 Minutes After Alert*, Belfast Telegraph, Dec. 24, 2004; *Morning View: Lessons to be Learnt from this Huge Robbery*, Belfast News Letter, Dec. 22, 2004, at 8.
  2. *See* Derec Henderson, *Police Chief Blames IRA for £26m Bank Heist*, Indep. E-Mail Newsl., Jan. 7, 2005; Jonathan McCambridge, *Rubbish Searched in Bank Heist Hunt; Police Sift Through Refuse at Council Site*, Belfast Telegraph, Dec. 31, 2004; Jonathan McCambridge & Maureen Colemann, *Bank Heist Swoop; Police Raid Home of Leading Republican*, Belfast Telegraph, Dec. 24, 2004; David McKittrick, *Blow to Peace Process as IRA Blamed for Bank Heist*, Independent (London), Jan. 7, 2005, at 14; *Police Say IRA Behind Bank Raid*,

BBC News, Jan. 7, 2005, available at www/newsvote.bbc.co.uk; *Robbery Probe Chief to Quit*, BELFAST NEWS Letter, Mar. 17, 2005, at 7; Jonathan McCambridge, *West Belfast Target in Bank Heist Probe; More Premises Are Searched*, BELFAST TELEGRAPH, Dec. 30, 2004.

3. Ian Graham, *Bank Raid Cash "Planted by IRA*,*"* BELFAST NEWS LETTER, Feb. 21, 2005, at 6.

4. *See* Andrew Anthony, *The Price of Peace*, OBSERVER (London), Mar. 6, 2005, at 20.

5. Angelique Chrisafis, *IRA "Laundering Stolen Cash in UK Housing Market*,*"* GUARDIAN (London), Mar. 30, 2005, at 7.

6. *Suspicion over Ulster Notes at Race Meeting*, BELFAST NEWS LETTER, Mar. 28, 2005, at 4.

7. Hunter, *supra* note 1, at 5. *See also Don't Fall for Pinnochio O'Neill Lies, Says Wilson*, BELFAST NEWS LETTER, Jan. 20, 2005, at 9.

8. For the connection drawn by the government to Sinn Féin, see David Charter, *No. 10 Urged to Cancel its Invitation to Sinn Féin*, THE TIMES (London), Jan. 21, 2005, at 31; Stephen Dempster, *IMC Must be Given Bite to Match its Bark*, BELFAST NEWS LETTER, Feb. 15, 2005, at 8; *Minister Names MPs as Members of IRA Ruling Army Council*, BELFAST NEWS LETTER, Mar. 28, 2005, at 4; *Sinn Féin Leaders "Backed Raids*,*"* BBC NEWS, Feb. 10, 2005, available at www.news.bbc.co.uk; Ann Treneman, *Murphy He May Be, But He's Hardly Stout*, THE TIMES (London), Feb. 23, 2005, at 24.

9. Anthony, *supra* note 4.

10. *See, e.g.*, 106 Parl. Deb., H.C. (6th ser.) (1986) 423. *See also* James Glover, Defence Intelligence Staff, Northern Ireland: Future Terrorist Trends (1978); JAMES ADAMS, THE FINANCING OF TERROR 131 (1986).

11. Gary Anderson, *Two Arrested After Bank Notes Found*, BELFAST NEWS LETTER, Jan. 11, 2005, at 6; Jonathan McCambridge, *'Heist' notes obsolete*, BELFAST TELEGRAPH, Apr. 8, 2005.

12. Jonathan McCambridge, *The Northern Job: What We Need to Know*, BELFAST TELEGRAPH, Dec. 23, 2004; Andrew Anthony, *The Price of Peace*, OBSERVER, Mar. 6, 2005.

13. *See, e.g., Morning View: Lessons to be Learnt from this Huge Robbery*, *supra* note 1, at 8 (reporting, "This was a very highly organised robbery in a league well above anything that has gone before in Northern Ireland."); Alan Murray, *Query on Everyone's Lips: Why Wasn't an Alarm Triggered?*, BELFAST TELEGRAPH, Dec. 22, 2004 (leading off, "A heist on the scale of the Northern Bank robbery is the stuff of Hollywood movies.")

14. Angelique Chrisafis, *Sinn Féin and Dublin in Grudge Match*, GUARDIAN (London), Feb. 4, 2005, at 6.

15. *See, e.g., Id.*; Email exchange between Danny Morrison & Charles Moore, *printed in* Charles Moore & Danny Morrison, *Bite My Bullet: Take Two: Are Irish Republicans Really Committed to Peace, Charles Moore and Danny Morrison Thrash it Out*, OBSERVER (London), Mar. 5, 2005, at 21.

16. *See, e.g.*, Sixth Standing Committee on Delegated Legislation, House of Commons, Session 2004–2005, Column No. 16-23 (2005). *See also* Anthony, *supra* note 4; David McKittrick, *supra* note 2, at 2.

17. *See, e.g.*, Secretary of State for Northern Ireland, Official Report 2005, H.C. Vol. 429, Column No. 429; Henry McDonald, *Man Questioned over Bar Killing*, OBSERVER (London), Feb. 27, 2005, at 3; *Sinn Féin Has to Renounce Crime: Party Financing Must be Above Board*, OBSERVER (London), Feb. 20, 2005, at 28.

18. Sixth Standing Committee on Delegated Legislation, *supra* note 16, at Column No. 23.

19. *Id.* Column No. 8; *Public "Must Not Pay Cost of Raid,"* BELFAST NEWS LETTER, Jan. 10, 2005, at 5. *But see* Angelique Chrisafis, *Election 2005: Sinn Féin Likely to Tighten Grip in SDLP Heartlands*, OBSERVER (London), Apr. 20, 2005, at 7.

20. Henry McDonald, *IRA "Untouchables" Still Out of Reach: Witnesses Remain Silent on the Murder of Robert McCartney as His Sisters Carry on their Fight for Justice*, OBSERVER (London), Mar. 13, 2005, at 6.

21. Ian Graham, *Irish Police Officers to Cross the Border*, BELFAST NEWS LETTER, Feb. 21, 2005, at 5.

22. *See Northern Raid Raised in Euro Cash Debate*, BELFAST NEWS LETTER, Jan. 11, 2005, at 9.

23. *See Crack Down*, THE TIMES (London), Mar. 3, 2005; *Sinn Féin's Challenge*, THE TIMES (London), Mar. 16, 2005, at 19.

24. *See, e.g., House of Commons*, THE TIMES (London), June 3, 1921, at 6; *Irish Bank Robbers Sentenced*, THE TIMES (London), June 22, 1926, at 7; *Bank Messenger Robbed, Thieves' Escape with £2,000*, THE TIMES (London), June 24, 1936, at 18; *The Free State Election: Sectional Interests*, THE TIMES (London), Aug. 11, 1923, at 10.

25. *See, e.g., DeValera's Telegram: Sinn Féin Defence*, THE TIMES (London), Oct. 27, 1927, at 10.

26. *See, e.g., Irish Deportees: Hearing of Further Claims*, THE TIMES (London), Jan. 15, 1924, at 8.

27. *Mr. Eamon DeValera: The Embodiment of Irish Nationalism*, THE TIMES (London), Aug. 30, 1975, at 14. *See also O'Brien's Defence*, THE TIMES (London), July 3, 1923, at 16.

28. Northern Ireland Affairs Committee, The Financing of Terrorism in Northern Ireland, 2001-2, H.C. 978-I, at 5.

29. *See* Christopher Walker, *Provisional IRA Man Dies in Parkhurst After Hunger Strike*, THE TIMES (London), June 4, 1974, at 1; Christopher Walker, *Three IRA Men at Albany Begin Hunger Strike*, THE TIMES (London), Apr. 11, 1974, at 2.

30. *See* Laura K. Donohue, *Anti-Terrorist Finance in the United Kingdom and United States*, MICH. J. INT'L L., Vol. 27, No. 2, Winter 2006, 303–435.

31. *See* Criminal Damage (Compensation) (Northern Ireland) Order, 1977, S.I. 1247 (N.Ir 14), art. 11. *See also* Kennedy Lindsay, The British Intelligence Services in Action 158 (1980).

32. Northern Ireland Organized Crime Task Force, Counterfeit Currency, www.octf.gov.uk [hereinafter OCTF Report]; Stephen Dempster & Dan McGinn, *Sinn Fein Told: Support the Law*, BELFAST NEWS LETTER, Jul. 6, 2006, at 6.

33. OCTF 2004 Report *supra* note 32, at 51. Available at www.octf.gov.uk.

34. *New Violence in Ulster May be Linked to Reforms – Mr. Maudling*, THE TIMES (London), Feb. 16, 1971, at 9.

35. Robert Fisk, *Three Civilians Killed in Belfast Battle Between Troops, Protestants and Catholics*, THE TIMES (London), Jun. 12, 1972, at 1; Paul Martin, *The Cost of Libya's Revolutionary Largesse*, THE TIMES (London), Aug. 17, 1972, at 12.

36. GERARD HOGAN & CLIVE WALKER, POLITICAL VIOLENCE AND THE LAW IN IRELAND 161-2 (1989).

37. Author interviews with members of the Ulster Defense Association, Londonderry, Northern Ireland (circa 1994).

38. *New York Irish March Supports IRA Violence*, THE TIMES (London), Mar. 10, 1983, at 1; *New York Honour for IRA Man*, THE TIMES (London), Feb. 16, 1984, at 8; Philip Webster, *Thatcher Rejects Inquiry on Noraid Incident*, THE TIMES (London), Aug. 21, 1984, at 1.

39. Adams, *supra* note 10, at 154.

40. *Id.* at 136.

41. *U.S.-Ireland Extradition Deal Signed*, THE TIMES (London), July 15, 1983, at 7.

42. *Att'y Gen. of the United States v. Irish N. Aid Comm.*, 668 F.2d 159 (1982); *Att'y Gen. of the United States v. The Irish People, Inc.*, 796 F.2d 520 (1986); *The IRA; Luck of the Irish*, ECONOMIST (U.K. Edition), Nov. 13, 1982, at 50.

43. *Id.*, at 136.

44. Jimmy Burns, *Battle Over Ulster Fraud Stepped Up: Renewed Fears on Racketeering*, FIN. TIMES, Dec. 9, 1994, at 8.

45. *Police Service Northern Ireland*, reprinted in *Select Committee on Northern Ireland Affairs: The Financing of Terrorism in Northern Ireland, Fourth Report, HC 978-I, Northern Ireland Affairs committee Report, Session 2001–2002*. Bill Tupman, *The IRA as a Profit-Making Concern*, J. MONEY LAUNDERING CONTROL, Vol. 1 No. 4 (April 1998) pp. 303–311.

46. SEAN O'CALLAGHAN, THE INFORMER (1998), at 168.

47. *See, e.g., Sinn Féin March in London To-Day: The Dead Lord Mayor Prisoners' Tribute*, THE TIMES (London), Oct. 28, 1920, at 12; *Irish Plots in Britain: Rebel Campaign of Outrage*, THE TIMES (London), Mar. 16, 1923, at 12.

48. *See, e.g., The Past Two Weeks*, FORTNIGHT, Feb. 19, 1971, at 16 (reporting women residents of New Lodge Road in Belfast parading outside the Army Barracks in protest); *The Past Two Weeks*, FORTNIGHT, May 28, 1971, at 17 (reporting a meeting of over 1,000 people to protest the same).

49. Editorial, *A Special Powers Act?*, THE TIMES (London), Mar. 1, 1972, at 15.

50. *Id.*

51. Northern Ireland (Emergency Provisions) Act, 1973, 21 & 22, ch. 53, § 11(3) (taken directly from reg. 23 of 1922 Special Powers Act) [hereinafter 1973 EPA and 1922 SPA].

52. *Id.*, § 17 (taken directly from reg. 2 of the Restoration of Order in Ireland Regulations, reg. 8 of the 1922 SPA).

53. *See* 1973 EPA, *supra* note 51, § 25 (taken directly from reg. 11 of the 1922 SPA).

54. *See* 1973 EPA, *supra* note 51, schedule 1(12) for inclusion of contributions as a scheduled offense and the remainder of statute for special Diplock proceedings.

55. The state added the Irish National Liberation Army to the list of illegal organizations in 1984. Prevention of Terrorism (Temporary Provisions) Act, 1984, ch. 8, § 1.

56. Prevention of Terrorism (Temporary Provisions) Act, 1976, ch. 8, § 10.

57. *Id.*

58. *Id.*, § 10(4).

59. Richard Evans, *Tough Powers in Bill to Tackle Drug Traffickers*, THE TIMES (London), July 30, 1985, at 1.

60. *Id.* This article is the first time the words "money laundering" ever appeared in the newspaper.

61. *See* Drug Trafficking Offences Act, 1986.

62. *See* Prevention of Terrorism (Temporary Provisions) Act, 1989, §§ 9–13.

63. Prevention of Terrorism (Temporary Provisions) Act, 1989, § 10.

64. *Id.*, § 11.

65. *Id.*, § 12.
66. *Id.*, § 18A.
67. *Id.*, § 13.
68. Northern Ireland (Emergency Provisions) Act 1991, c. 24, § 53.
69. *Id.*, § 54.
70. *Id.*, §§ 47–52.
71. *Id.*, § 9, schedule 4.
72. *Id.*, § 57, schedule 5, §§ 2–3.
73. Northern Ireland (Emergency Provisions) Act, 1996, c. 22, § 24.
74. *MPs to Raise Secret Ulster Memo in Commons*, THE TIMES (London), Jan. 22, 1977, at 2.
75. *See* Betting, Gaming, Lotteries and Amusements (N.I.) Order 1985 S.I. No. 1204 (N.I. 11); Registration of Clubs (N.I.) Order 1987 S.I. No. 1278.
76. Adams, *supra* note 10, at 178–82.
77. *See* P. Norman, *The Terrorist Finance Unit and the Joint Action Group on Organised Crime: New Organisational Models and Investigative Strategies to Counter 'Organized Crime' in the UK*, (1998), HOWARD J. CRIM. JUSTICE, Vol. 37, No. 4, pp. 375–392.
78. Northern Ireland (Emergency Provisions) Act, 1987, c. 30, §§ 17–20.
79. *See generally* Organized Crime Task Force, Extortion, www.octf.gov.uk.
80. Criminal Justice Act, 1993, ch. 36, § 7.
81. *Id.*, § 8.
82. *Id.*, § 9.
83. *Id.*, § 16.
84. *Id.*, § 18.
85. *Id.*, §§ 35.
86. *Id.*, § 27.
87. *Id.*, § 36.
88. *Id.*, § 36(4).
89. *Id.*, § 39.
90. *Id.*, §§ 48, 51.
91. Drug Trafficking Act, 1994, ch. 37, § 2.
92. *Id.*, § 4.
93. *Id.*, § 8.
94. *Id.*, § 44.
95. Author interview with senior civil servant in Northern Ireland, Nov. 2006.
96. Drug Trafficking Act, 1994, ch. 37, § 52.
97. Tony Blair, 317 Parl. Deb., H.C. (6th ser.) (2 Sept 1998) 705.
98. Jack Straw, 317 Parl. Deb., H.C. (6th ser.) (2 Sept 1998) 747.
99. *Id.*
100. Kevin McNamara, 317 Parl. Deb., H.C. (6th ser.) (2 Sept 1998) 782.
101. *See* Terrorism Act 2000, ch. 11, §§ 15-19, & § 63.
102. *Id.*, § 23.
103. *Id.*, §§ 29.
104. *Id.*, § 5, schedule 6.
105. OCTF 2004 Report *supra* note 32; Mervyn Wilson & Brian French, Northern Ireland Office, Statistics and Research Branch, *Views on Organised Crime in Northern Ireland: Findings from the Apr. 2004 Northern Ireland Omnibus Survey*, RES. & STAT. BULL. 4 (2004). Available at www.nio.gov.uk.

106. *See* NIO 2004 Report, *supra* note 105, at 1.
107. *See* OCTF 2004 Report, *supra* note 32, at 9 & 54.
108. *See* Financial Investigations (Northern Ireland); Northern Ireland Grand Committee, Mar. 22, 2001, Westminster, Financial Investigations (N.I.) Order, Session 2000–01 (Statement of Adam Ingram, Minister of State, Northern Ireland Office), available at www.publications.parliament.uk (last visited Mar. 9, 2006).
109. *Id.* (requesting that the committee consider a proposal for draft Financial Investigations (N.I.) Order 2001).
110. 2001 Financial Investigations (N.I.) Order, art. 4.
111. *Id.*, art. 5.
112. *Id.*, art. 3.
113. *Id.*, art. 6.
114. Financial Investigations (N.I.), Northern Ireland Grand Committee, Mar. 22, 2001, Westminster, Financial Investigations (N.I.) Order, Session 2000–01, available at www.publications.parliament.uk.
115. *Id.*
116. *Id.*
117. 2001 Financial Investigations (N.I.) Order.
118. Anti-Terrorism, Crime and Security Act, 2001, ch. 24, Part I. The new provisions replaced § 24 with § 31 of the Terrorism Act 2000.
119. *Id.*, ch. 24, Part II.
120. *Id.*, schedule 3.
121. Anti-Terrorism, Crime and Security Act, 2001, ch. 24, schedule 1.
122. *Id.*, Part III.
123. *Id.*, schedule 3A, Part 1(1), § 21.
124. For a discussion of the previous efforts by the state to get this measure through see Anthony Kennedy, *Winning the Information Wars: Collecting, Sharing and Analysing Information in Asset Recovery Investigations*, (2007) 14 J. Fin. Crime 4.
125. In June 2000 the Performance and Innovation Unit issued a report, *Recovering the Proceeds of Crime*, available at www.cabinetoffice.gov.uk (last visited May 9, 2006).
126. *But see* Anthony Kennedy, *Justifying the Civil Recovery of Criminal Proceeds*, J. Fin. Crime, Aug 2004. Vol. 12, Iss. 1; p. 8; Anthony Kennedy, *Civil Recovery of Criminal Proceeds: A Troubling Loss of Faith in the Criminal Law?*, The Company Lawyer, 2007.
127. Edward Rees & Richard Fisher, 4 Blackstone's Guide to The Proceeds of Crime Act 2002 (2005). *See also* Proceeds of Crime Act, 2002, c. 29, Part IV, §§ 189–191, 199.
128. Proceeds of Crime Act, *supra* note 127, Part V, §§ 281–9.
129. Rees & Fisher, *supra* note 127, at 2.
130. *Id.*
131. Proceeds of Crime Act, *supra* note 127, Part IV, § 160.
132. *Id.*, § 182.
133. Jane Kennedy, After Dinner Speech to the Ulster Society of Chartered Accountants and Law Society for Northern Ireland, Sept. 25, 2002, available at www.octf.gov.uk. *See also Identification Rules are Over the Top, Say IFAs*, Investment Adviser, Apr. 21, 2003.
134. Proceeds of Crime Act, *supra* note 127, Part I.

135. Northern Ireland Grand Committee, Draft Budget (Northern Ireland) Order 2005, House of Commons, Mar. 8, 2005, Column Nos. 10–11 (2005).

136. *Id.*

137. Gavin Hinks, *Numbers Game*, ACCOUNTANCY AGE, July 17, 2002, at 3.

138. *See* press releases available at www.assetsrecovery.gov.uk; *see also IRA "Laundering Stolen Cash in UK Housing Market,"* GUARDIAN (London), Mar. 30, 2005, at 7.

139. For discussion of the "global trend to use stand-alone civil proceedings as a means of recovering the proceeds of crime in the hope that they will be more effective than proceedings which are ancillary to, and dependent on, a criminal prosecution," see Anthony Kennedy, *Justifying the Civil Recovery of Criminal Proceeds*, J. FIN. CRIME, Aug 2004. Vol. 12, Iss. 1; p. 8.

140. Statutory Instrument 2003 No. 3075: The Money Laundering Regulations 2003, reg. 4 (sets 15,000 euro as the threshold after which identification procedures are required); reg. 6 (requires that records be retained for five years after the relationship or one-off transaction ends; requires the business to retain a copy of identification records or information as to where they can be obtained); reg. 7 (details internal reporting measures); reg. 3 (requires businesses to train employees on how to recognize and deal with transactions that may be related to money laundering; also requires that employees are familiar with the 2002 POCA and the 2000 Terrorism Act §§ 18, 21A. Failure to do so carries a criminal penalty.).

141. Statutory Instrument 2003 No. 3075: The Money Laundering Regulations 2003, regs. 9, 14, 20.

142. National Commission on Terrorist Attacks Against the United States, Monograph on Terrorist Financing: Staff Report to the commission, Aug. 21, 2004, available at www.9-11commission.gov [hereinafter Staff Report], at 33.

143. *Id.*, at 20, 34.

144. *Id.*

145. 50 U.S.C.S. appendix § 3. Prior to that time, however, the executive could exercise its foreign affairs power to exert control of non-US persons. *See United States v. Curtiss-Wright Export Corporation*, 299 U.S. 304 (1936) (finding a joint congressional resolution authorizing the president to ban sale of weapons to states enmeshed in conflict in Bolivia constitutional under the president's foreign affairs power).

146. Trading with the Enemy Act, 50 U.S.C. § 1702(a)(1) (1977). In times of war, the Trading with the Enemy Act remains in force.

147. 50 U.S.C. § 1702(a)(1)(B) (2001).

148. Exec. Order No. 12,947, 60 Fed. Reg. 5,079 (Jan. 23, 1995), *reprinted as amended in* 50 U.S.C.A. § 1701 (2003).

149. Exec. Order No. 13,099, 63 Fed. Reg. 45,167 (Aug. 20, 1998).

150. Rudolph Lehrer, *Unbalancing the Terrorists' Checkbook: Analysis of U.S. Policy in its Economic War on International Terrorism*, 10 TUL. J. INT'L & COMP. L. 333, 345 (2002).

151. *Dames & Moore v. Regan, Sec'y of the Treas., et al.*, 453 U.S. 654, 660 (1981).

152. *Regan, Sec'y of the Treas., et al. v. Wald, et al.*, 468 U.S. 222, 232 (1984).

153. *INS v. Chadha*, 462 U.S. 919 (1983).

154. Lehrer, *supra* note 150, at 341–44; *see also Havana Club Holding, S.A. v. Galleon S.A.*, 961 F. Supp.498, 500 (S.D.N.Y. 1997); *Milena Ship Mgmt. Co. v. Newcomb*, 995 F.2d 620, 625 (5th Cir. 1993).

155. Antiterrorism and Effective Death Penalty Act § 302(a), *codified in* 18 U.S.C. § 2339B.

156. 18 U.S.C § 2339A(b).

157. *Charangeet Singh-Kaur* v. *Ashcroft*, 385 F.3d 293 (3d Cir. 2004).

158. *State Department Releases Facts on Foreign Terrorist Organizations*, 79 Interpreter Releases 1240 (2002).

159. *People's Mojahedin Organization of Iran* v. *United States Department of State*, 182 F.3d 17 (4th Cir. 1999). The court looked to *United States* v. *Verdugo-Urquidez*, 494 U.S. 259, 271 (1990) for precedent. It found that INA § 219 did not deprive the organization of due process (thus distinguishing the case from *Joint Anti-Fascist Refugee Committee* v. *McGrath*).

160. *People's Mojahedin Organization of Iran* v. *United States Department of State*, 182 F.3d 17 (4th Cir. 1999), at 25. Emphasis added.

161. *Id.*

162. *Id.*, at 25. Emphasis added and internal citations omitted.

163. *National Council of Resistance of Iran* v. *State* 251 F.3d 192 (D.C. Cir. 2001).

164. *Id.*, at 208-09 (Sentelle, J.).

165. *But see Fuentes* v. *Shevin*, 407 U.S. 67, 92 (1972) (explaining that it may be necessary to postpone notice or a hearing "to meet the needs of a national war effort"). *See also United States* v. *Rahmani*, 209 F. Supp.2d 1045 (C.D. Cal. 2002) (holding that the statutory scheme for FTO designation deprived supporters of their right to due process and any meaningful opportunity to be heard); *Due Process: Constitutional Violation in Terrorism Designation Process*, 16 Crim. Prac. Rep. 13, July 24, 2002.

166. *See, e.g., United States* v. *Mohamad Youssef Hammoud*, 381 F.3d 316 (4th Cir. 2004); 65 Fed. R. Evid. Serv. 338.

167. *Humanitarian Law Project* v. *Reno*, 205 F.3d 1130 (9th Cir. 2000), *cert. denied*, 532 U.S. 904 (2001).

168. *Humanitarian Law Project* v. *U.S. Dep't. of Justice*, 352 F.3d 382 (9th Cir. 2003).

169. *Scales* v. *United States*, 367 U.S. 203 (1961).

170. *Id.*, at 224–25.

171. *Id.*, at 403 (emphasis added).

172. Money Laundering and Financial Crimes Strategy Act of 1998, Pub. L. 105–310, 112 Stat. 2941.

173. Bank Secrecy Act of 1970, Pub. L. No. 91-508, 84 Stat. 1114 (1970) (codified as amended in parts of 12 U.S.C., 15 U.S.C., 18 U.S.C., and 31 U.S.C.). *See also Cal. Bankers Ass'n* v. *Shultz*, 416 U.S. 21, 47–49, 61 (1974) (upholding record keeping as a way to detect criminal activity); *United States* v. *Miller*, 425 U.S. 435 (1976) (focusing on the justifications for the record-keeping requirements).

174. Staff Report, *supra* note 142, at 54–56.

175. *United States* v. *Miller*, 425 U.S. 435 (1976).

176. Financial Institutions and Interest Rate Control Act of 1978, Pub. L. No. 95-630, 92 Stat. 3641, 3697–3710 (1978) (*codified as amended at* 12 U.S.C. §§ 3401–3422); *See also* H.R. Rep. No. 95-1383, at 34 (1978), *reprinted in* 1978 U.S.C.C.A.N. 9273, 9306.

177. Money Laundering Control Act of 1986, Pub. L. No. 99-570, 100 Stat. 3207 (1986) (codified as amended at 18 U.S.C. §§ 1956-1957); *see also* Anti-Drug Abuse Act of 1988, Pub. L. No. 100-690, 102 Stat. 4181 (1988) (*codified as amended in different parts of the United States Code*).

178. 31 U.S.C. § 5317(c) (2003).

179. Housing and Community Development Act of 1992, Pub. L. No. 102-550, 106 Stat. 3672 (1992). Title XV is also known as the Annunzio-Wylie Anti-Money Laundering Act.

180. Since 1985, regulatory authorities had required SARs for the Federal Reserve Board and Office of the Comptroller of the Currency. *See* U.S. Dep't of the Treas., Annual Money Laundering Strategy 85 n. 21 (2000).

181. Bruce Zagaris, *The Merging of the Anti-money Laundering and Counter-terrorism Financial Enforcement Regimes After Sept. 11, 2001*, 22 BERKELEY J. INT'L L. 123 (2003). *See also* Bruce Zagaris, *The Merging of the Counter-terrorism and Anti-Money Laundering Regimes*, 34 LAW & POL'Y INT'L BUS. 45 (2002).

182. Mariano-Florentino Cuéllar, *The Tenuous Relationship Between the Fight Against Money Laundering and the Disruption of Criminal Finance*, 93 J. CRIM. L. & CRIMINOLOGY 311-465, 351 (2003).

183. Stephen Fidler & Haig Simonian, *IMF Chief Urges United Response to Slowdown*, FIN. TIMES (London), Oct. 6, 2001, at 4.

184. *See* Know Your Customer, 64 Fed. Reg. 14845 (withdrawn Mar. 29, 1999); Robert O'Harrow, Jr., *Disputed Bank Plan Dropped*, Staff Report, *supra* note 142.

185. WASH. POST, Mar. 24, 1999, at E1.

186. Staff Report, *supra* note 142, at 3, 131.

187. *See, e.g., President's Fiscal Year 2000 Budget: Hearing Before the Subcomm. for the Departments of Commerce, Justice, and State, the Judiciary, and Related Agencies, of the Sen. Comm. on Appropriations*, 106th Cong. (1999) (statement of Louis J. Freeh, Director, Federal Bureau of Investigation), available at www.fbi.gov; Staff Report, *supra* note 142, at 144; JAMES ADAMS, THE FINANCING OF TERROR 165 (1986); Sean O'Callaghan, THE INFORMER 159-60 (1998); Mathew A Levitt, *War on Terrorism Scorecard*, MIDDLE E.Q., Summer 2002, at 39; The Al Qaeda Manual, UK/BM-3, [E] 19/220, eng. trans., at UK/BM-22, available at www.usdoj.gov (last visited Feb. 26, 2005) [hereinafter Al Qaeda Manual].

188. Staff Report, *supra* note 142.

189. *Id.*, at 6. *See also* COUNCIL ON FOREIGN RELATIONS, TERRORIST FINANCING 5 (2002) [hereinafter Terrorist Financing].

190. *See* Robert Clow, Andrew Edgecliffe-Johnson, Adrian Michaels & Richard Wolffe, *Team Set Up to Block Terrorist Funds; Asset Breakers New Group of Intelligence Agents and Law Enforcement Officials to be Headed by U.S. Treasury*, FIN. TIMES (London), Sept. 17, 2001, at 6.

191. Staff Report, *supra* note 142, at 20, 34. For the previous assumption, *see, e.g.,* Financial Action Task Force on Money Laundering, Guidance for Financial Institutions in Detecting Terrorist Financing 4 (Apr. 24, 2002); Financial Action Task Force on Money Laundering, Report on Money Laundering Typologies, 2001-2002 2 (Feb. 1, 2003).

192. *Id.*

193. Mark Huband, Gwen Robinson & John Willman, *US Urges Allies to Step up Efforts to Track Down Terrorist Cell Assets*, FIN. TIMES (London), Nov. 28, 2001, at 1. *But see* Michael Mann & Richard Wolffe, *US Accuses Africa Banks of Failing to Assist Search*, FIN. TIMES (London), Oct. 3, 2001, at 4.

194. Staff Report, *supra* note 142.

195. David E. Kaplan, Monica Ekman & Aamir Latif, *The Saudi Connection: How Billions in Oil Money Spawned a Global Terror Network*, U.S. NEWS & WORLD REPORT, Dec. 15, 2003, available at www.usnews.com/usnews.

196. *Id.*

197. *Id.*
198. *Id.*
199. *Id.*
200. *Id.*
201. *Id.*
202. Terrorist Financing, *supra* note 189, at 8.
203. Kaplan et al., *supra* note 195. *See also* Staff Report, *supra* note 142, at 39.
204. Kaplan et al., *supra* note 195.
205. *Id.*
206. Staff Report, *supra* note 142, at 34.
207. Kaplan et al., *supra* note 195; Staff Report, *supra* note 142, at 34.
208. Kaplan et al., *supra* note 195.
209. Staff Report, *supra* note 142, at 21.
210. Robert Clow, Andrew Edgecliffe-Johnson, Adrian Michaels & Richard Wolffe, *Team Set Up to Block Terrorist Funds*, Fin. Times (London), Sept. 17, 2001, at 6.
211. Staff Report, *supra* note 142, at 21.
212. *See id*; *see also* Madeline Gruen, *White Ethno-Nationalist & Political Islamist Methods of Fundraising and Propaganda on the Internet*, *in* Terrorism and Counterterrorism 289 (Russell D. Howard & Reid L.Sawyer eds., 2003).
213. *See, e.g.*, U.S. Dep't of the Treas. & U.S. Dep't of Justice, 2002 National Money Laundering Strategy, at 36.
214. 2003 Financial Action Task Force Report, *supra* note 191, at 4.
215. Robert Looney, *Hawala: The Terrorist's Informal Financial Mechanism*, 10 Middle E. Pol'y 164 (2003).
216. Sec'y of the U.S. Dep't of Treas., A Report to Congress in Accordance with Section 359 of the Uniting and Strengthening America by Providing Appropriate Tools Required to Intercept and Obstruct Terrorism Act of 2001 5 (2002).
217. Estimates from Pakistani officials suggest that more than $5 billion goes into Pakistan alone, each year, through the hawaladars. This makes the system the largest source of hard currency. Interpol suggests that hawala provides approximately 40% of India's gross domestic product. Roughly $680 billion passed through the state in this manner in 1998. *Id.*
218. *Small World*, Economist (U.S. Edition), Oct. 18, 2002.
219. 2003 Financial Action Task Force Report, *supra* note 191, at 4–8.
220. Alan Beattie, *Informal Foreign Cash Transfers Cheaper, Says Study*, Fin. Times (London), Apr. 1, 2005, at 5.
221. These include the National Security Strategy of the United States of America, available at www.whitehouse.gov (focuses on interdicting and disrupting material support for terrorists); and the National Strategy for Homeland Security, available at www.whitehouse.gov/homeland (which includes eliminating terrorist financing). In the classified realm, the National Military Strategic Plan for the War on Terrorism goes into detail on how the US military should confront state sponsors of terrorism, disrupt and destroy terrorist organizations, and create a global environment hostile to terrorism.
222. U.S. Dep't of the Treas., Annual Money Laundering Strategy, reports for 2001–2003, available at www.treas.gov.
223. Staff Report, *supra* note 142, at 41.
224. 2002 Money Laundering Strategy, *supra* note 214, p. 20 n.22.

225. Press Release, U.S. Dep't of the Treas., U.S. Treasury Department Announces New Executive Office for Terrorist Financing and Financial Crimes (Mar. 3, 2003), available at www.ustreas.gov.

226. *See Hearing on the Administration's National Money Laundering Strategy for 2001 Before the Senate Banking Committee*, at 10, 107th Cong. (2001) (testimony of Hon. Jimmy Gurule, Undersecretary for Enforcement, U.S. Dep't. of the Treas.); Jason Peckenpaugh, *Building a Behemoth: The Challenge of Constructing a Homeland Security Department May Make the Epic Struggle to Create the Defense Department Look Easy*, Government Executive, Sept. 1, 2002, at 34; Zagaris, *supra* note 181, at 6.

227. Peter Spiegel, *U.S. Team Created to Target al Qaeda Finances*, FIN. TIMES, Oct. 26, 2001, at 5.

228. Michael Isikoff & Mark Hosenball, *Terror Watch: Whose War on Terror?* NEWSWEEK, Apr. 9, 2003.

229. Memorandum of Agreement and Collaborative Procedures Concerning Terrorist Financing Investigations, *reprinted in* Richard M. Stana, Director, Homeland Security and Justice Issues, Letter to the Hon. Thad Cochran, Chair and the Hon. Robert C. Byrd, Ranking Minority Member, Subcommittee on Homeland Security Committee on Appropriations, United States Senate; Subject: Investigations of Terrorist Financing, Money Laundering, and Other Financial Crimes, General Accounting Office, GAO-04-464R, Financial Crimes Investigations, Feb. 20, 2004, Enclosure II, at 14-18, ¶ 2 [hereinafter Memorandum of Understanding]. Available at www.gao.gov.

230. *Id.*, ¶ 4.

231. U.S. Dep't of the Treas. & U.S. Dep't of Justice, 2003 National Money Laundering Strategy, at 22.

232. Bureau of International Information Programs, U.S. Dep't of State, U.S. Boosts Money Laundering Investigation Capabilities, Secretary Ridge Announces New Financial Investigations Initiatives, July 8, 2003, www/usinfo.state.gov.

233. Senate Report 108-86 (July 2003), Title I of Senate Appropriations Committee report on the DHS Appropriations Bill for 2004, available at www.frwebgate. access.gpo.gov.

234. Memorandum of Understanding, *supra* note 268, at 9.

235. *Id.*, at 5.

236. Fidler & Simonian, *supra* note 183.

237. Kaplan et al., *supra* note 195 at 18.

238. PATRIOT Act Title III: The International Money Laundering Abatement and Financial Anti-Terrorism Act of 2001.

239. Zagaris, *supra* note 181.

240. Bruce Zagaris, *The Money Laundering Provisions of the USA PATRIOT Act of 2001*, 323 PLI/Est 417 (2003).

241. *See* Uniting and Strengthening America by Providing Appropriate Tools Required to Intercept and Obstruct Terrorism (USA PATRIOT Act) Act of 2001 215, *codified in* 50 U.S.C. 1861 [hereinafter USA PATRIOT Act]; *Id.*, § 314 (semi-annual report on suspicious activity); *Id.* § 324 (general report on Title III); *Id.*, § 326(b) (ways to improve the ability of financial institutions to identify foreign nationals); *Id.*, § 356(c) (joint Treasury, Federal Reserve, and SEC report on how to apply bank secrecy act requirements to investment companies); *Id.*, § 357 (role of IRS in administration of Bank Secrecy Act); *Id.*, § 359 (additional measures for alternative

remittance systems); *Id.*, § 361 (how to improve compliance with the regulatory requirements in the USA PATRIOT Act); *Id.*, § 366 (exemptions to currency transaction reports).

242. *Id.*, § 106.

243. *Id.*

244. *Id.*, § 318 (expanding the definition of financial institution to include those operating outside the United States).

245. *Id.*, § 326. On May 9, 2003, Treasury issued the final regulations governing this section. *See* 2003 National Money Laundering Strategy, *supra* note 232, appendix G, at 50.

246. USA PATRIOT Act *supra* note 242, § 352.

247. *Id.*

248. Jay Stanley, *The Surveillance-Industrial Complex: How the American Government is Conscripting Businesses and Individuals in Construction of a Surveillance Society*, AMERICAN CIVIL LIBERTIES UNION, Aug. 2004, at 17.

249. USA PATRIOT Act, *supra* note 242, 2, § 365. Interim final rule issued Dec. 31, 2001; 2003 National Money Laundering Strategy, *supra* note 232, appendix G, at 52.

250. USA PATRIOT Act, *supra* note 242, 2, § 373.

251. *Id.*, § 314(b).

252. *Id.*, § 312; 2003 National Money Laundering Strategy, *supra* note 232, appendix G, at 49.

253. USA PATRIOT Act, *supra* note 242, 2, § 311.

254. 2003 National Money Laundering Strategy, *supra* note 232, at 13.

255. USA PATRIOT Act, *supra* note 242, 2, § 313. The United States issued interim guidance almost immediately following passage of the USA PATRIOT Act on Nov. 27, 2001, proposed a rule on Dec. 27, 2001, and issued a final rule on Sept. 18, 2002. 2003 National Money Laundering Strategy, *supra* note 232, appendix G, at 49. Soon after passage of the USA PATRIOT Act, Treasury listed al-Taqwa, "fear of god" in Arabic, to demonstrate that terrorists use shell banks. Zagaris, *supra* note 181, at 133; Michael Isikoff & Mark Hosenball, *Terror Watch: Preaching Violence*, NEWSWEEK, Sept. 29, 2004.

256. USA PATRIOT Act, *supra* note 242, 2, § 314.

257. Staff Report, *supra* note 142, at 60.

258. Zagaris, *supra* note 241.

259. Proposed rule issued Mar. 4, 2002; final rule issued Sept. 18, 2002. 2003 National Money Laundering Strategy, *supra* note 232, appendix G, at 49.

260. Zagaris, *supra* note 181, at 135 (citing *Counter-terror Initiatives in the Terror Finance Program: Hearing Before the Senate Committee on Banking, Housing, and Urban Affairs*, 108th Cong. 5 (2003) (statement of David D. Aufhauser, General Counsel, U.S. Dep't of the Treas.).

261. Special Information Sharing Procedures to Deter Money Laundering and Terrorist Activity: Final Rule, 67 Fed. Reg. 60,579 (Sept. 26, 2002) (Final Rule); 67 Fed. Reg. 9874 (Mar. 2002) (Interim Rule and Proposed Rule). *See also* Michael Isikoff, *Show Me the Money: Patriot Act Helps the Feds in Cases with No Tie to Terror*, NEWSWEEK, Dec. 1, 2003, available at www.msnbc.com.

262. USA PATRIOT Act, *supra* note 242, § 315.

263. *Id.*, § 320.

264. Zagaris, *supra* note 241.

265. USA PATRIOT Act *supra* note 242, § 373.

266. *Id.*, § 371.

267. *Id.*, § 317.

268. *Id.*, § 319. Interim guidance issued Nov. 27, 2001; proposed rule issued Dec. 27, 2001; final rule issued Sept. 18, 2002. 2003 National Money Laundering Strategy, *supra* note 232, appendix G, at 50.

269. Kennedy, *Information Wars, supra* note 124.

270. Eric Lichtblau & James Risen, *Bank Data Sifted in Secret by U.S. to Block Terror*, N.Y. TIMES, June 23, 2006, at A1.

271. *Id.*

272. Sheryl Gay Stolberg & Eric Lichtblau, *Cheney Assails Press on Report on Bank Data*, N.Y. TIMES, June 24, 2006, A1.

273. Edmund L. Andrews, *Republicans Criticize Lack of Briefings on Bank Data*, N.Y. TIMES, July 12, 2006, A1.

274. *Id.*

275. Lichtblau et al., *supra* note 271.

276. *Id.*

277. Frontline, February 20, 2007, part 9 of Media Wars, 04:20-05:00, available at www.pbs.org.

278. Stolberg et al., *supra* note 273.

279. Lichtblau et al., *supra* note 271.

280. John W. Snow, *Bank Data Report: Treasury Dept.'s View*, N.Y. TIMES, June 28, 2006.

281. Edmund L. Andres, *Republicans Criticize Lack of Briefings on Bank Data*, N.Y. TIMES, July 12, 2006, p. A1.

282. Stuart Levey, under secretary at Treasury Department, in Lichtblau et al., *supra* note 271.

283. *Id.*

284. *Id.*

285. Brian Groom, John Willman & Richard Wolffe, *Bush Targets Terrorist Funds*, FIN. TIMES (London), Sept. 25, 2001, at 1.

286. Exec. Order No. 13,224, 3 C.F.R. 786, 790 (2001), *reprinted as amended in* 50 U.S.C.A. § 1701 (2002). The order also issued under the authority of the National Emergencies Act (50 U.S.C. § 1601 (2001)), the United Nations Participation Act of 1945 (§ 5, 22 U.S.C. § 287(c) (1945) (amended 2001)), and 3 U.S.C. § 301 (1951) (amended 2005). In addition, Bush cited S.C. Res. 1214, U.N. Doc. S/RES/1214 (Dec. 8, 1998), S.C. Res. 1267, U.N. Doc. S/RES/1267 (Oct. 15, 1999), S.C. Res. 1333, U.N. Doc. S/RES/1333 (Dec. 19, 2000), and S.C. Res. 1363, U.N. Doc. S/RES/1363 (July 30, 2001).

287. Staff Report, *supra* note 142, at 45.

288. Exec. Order No. 12,947, 31 C.F.R. 595 (2001), *reprinted as amended in* 50 U.S.C.A. § 1701 (2003); Foreign Terrorist Organizations Sanctions Regulations, 31 C.F.R. § 597 (2001), *reprinted as amended in* 50 U.S.C.A. § 1701 (2003); Staff Report, *supra* note 142, at 78-80; Zagaris, *supra* note 181, at 130.

289. White House Press Releases, News Archive, President Freezes Terrorists' Assets, Sept. 24, 2001, www.whitehouse.gov/.

290. *Id.*

291. *Id.*

292. Such strong, presentational remarks continued. *See, e.g.*, U.S. Dep't of the Treas., Contributions by the Department of the Treasury to the Financial War on Terrorism: Fact Sheet 6 (Sept. 2002) ("The war on terrorism is only beginning, and it is certain to demand constant vigilance. In the year since that terrible day, we have hit them hard. Our goal is to bankrupt their institutions and beggar their bombers.") *See also* Matthew Levitt, *Policy Watch #585: Navigating the U.S. Government's Terrorist Lists*, The Washington Institute for Near East Policy: Police Watch/Peace Watch, Nov. 30, 2001, available at www.washingtoninstitute.org.

293. U.S. Dep't of the Treas., Office of Public Affairs, U.S.-EU Designation of Terrorist Financiers Fact Sheet (PO-3070) (May 3, 2002), available at www.treas.gov/press/releases/po3070.htm.

294. U.S Dep't of the Treas., Treasury Designates Individual Financially Fueling Iraqi Insurgency, al Qaida (JS-2206) (Jan. 25, 2005), available at http://www.ustreas.gov. The complete lists are available from OFAC online. *See also* Mike Allen & Steven Mufson, *U.S. Seizes Assets of Three Islamic Groups*, WASH. POST, Dec. 5, 2001, at A1.

295. *U.S. Investigates Scams for Terrorist Ties*, 104 BUSINESS CREDIT, Sept. 1, 2002, at 1.

296. Staff Report, *supra* note 142, at 48–49.

297. 2003 National Money Laundering Strategy, *supra* note 232, at 14.

298. *Schaumburg* v. *Citizens for a Better Env't*, 444 U.S. 620 (1980).

299. Author interview with editor of the ARAB-AMERICAN NEWS (Autumn 2004).

300. Louise Cainkar, Strategies for what matters most: Assessing the Need: Addressing the Problem, The Faith Communities and Urban Families Project 27 (Nov. 2003) (sponsored by the Annie E. Casey Foundation). *See also* Nancy Dunne, *U.S. Muslims See Their American Dreams Die: Since September 11 the Community Has Felt Threatened*, FIN. TIMES (London), Mar. 28, 2002, at 10 (discussing the disappointment of the Muslim community in the Bush administration stemming from government raids).

301. U.S. Dep't of the Treas., Office of Foreign Assets Control. The total number includes aliases and different spellings of names cited elsewhere on the list.

302. Author interviews with large firm investment bankers, New York City, New York (June 27, 2005).

303. Author participation in Global Security and Cooperation program of the Social Science Research Council on the impact of post-September 11 measures on the Islamic community in the United States.

304. *The Needle in the Haystack*, ECONOMIST, Dec. 14, 2002, at 81.

305. Rob Garver, *Will USA Patriot Act Prove A Recipe for Trouble? Government Access to Banking Information vs. Right to Privacy*, AMERICAN BANKER, Apr. 23, 2002, at 10 [hereinafter *Recipe for Trouble?*]. *See also* Rob Garver, *Launder Rules Will Apply Across Financial Services*, AMERICAN BANKER, Apr. 23, 2002, at 1 [hereinafter *Launder Rules*].

306. *Recipe for Trouble?*, *supra* note 306; *Launder Rules*, *supra* note 306.

307. Bridger Insight, https://secure.bridgerinsight.com (last visited Dec. 2, 2005).

308. Press Release, Bridger Insight, Bridger Systems Announces Release of Bridger Tracker™ Online 5.5.0.0 (Sept. 4, 2003), www.bridgerinsight.choicepoint.com.

309. Trustco Bank, N.A., in Glenville, New York became the first bank cited for violations of the USA PATRIOT Act. *See* T.J. Grasmick & Robert M. McNamara Jr.,

Bank Secrecy Act Can Affect Expansion, Charter Value and Stock Price, COMMU-NITY BANKER, Dec. 2002, at 50.

310. *See, e.g., The Needle in the Haystack, supra* note 305.

311. The Privacy Protection Study Comm'n, Personal Privacy in an Information Society: The Report of the Privacy Protection Study Comm'n ch. 9, at 3 (1977), available at www.epic.org [hereinafter Privacy Comm'n Report].

312. *Global Relief Found., Inc. v. O'Neill*, 207 F. Supp. 2d 779, 802 (N.D. Ill. 2002), *aff'd* 315 F.3d 748 (7th Cir. 2002) ("Many courts have recognized that a temporary blocking of assets does not constitute a taking because it is a temporary action and not a vesting of property in the United States.").

313. *The PATRIOT Act: Investigating Patterns of Terrorist Financing: Hearing Before the Subcomm. on Oversight and Instigations of the H. Comm. On Fin. Serv.*, 107th Cong. 10 (2002) (statement of Juan C. Zarate, Dep. Ass't Secretary for Terrorism & Violent Crime), available at www/financialservices.house.gov [hereinafter Zarate]. *See also* Michael Isikoff & Mark Hosenball, *Terror Watch: Preaching Violence*, NEWSWEEK, Sept. 29, 2004.

314. Zarate, *supra* note 314. Federal agents raided offices in Minnesota, Ohio, Massachusetts, and Washington. *Id.* at 6. Bush announced that the networks provided al Qaeda with fundraising, financial, communications, weapons-procurement, and shipping assistance. Matthew Levitt, *Policy Watch #585: Navigating the U.S. Government's Terrorist Lists*, The Washington Institute for Near East Policy: Police Watch/Peace Watch, Nov. 30, 2001, available at www.washingtoninstitute.org.

315. *See* Donald G. McNeill, Jr., *Italian Arab is Perplexed by Swiss Raid*, N.Y. TIMES, Nov. 8, 2001, at B8.

316. *Arab Bank Says It Didn't Know of Payments to Bombers' Families*, Bloomberg, Feb. 10, 2005, available at www.bloomberg.com.

317. President George W. Bush, Remarks to Troops and Families at Fort Campbell (Nov. 21, 2001), available at www.whitehouse.gov.

318. President George W. Bush, Remarks at the Dinner of Senatorial Candidate Norm Coleman and Congressional Candidate John Kline in Minneapolis (July 15, 2002), *in* 38 Weekly Compilation of Presidential Documents 1177, 1181.

319. Mark Kantor, *The War on Terrorism and the End of Banking Neutrality*, 118 BANKING L.J. 891, 892 (2002) (citing press briefing by White House Press Secretary Ari Fleischer on September 24, 2001).

320. 50 U.S.C. § 1825(g).

321. Joan M. O'Sullivan-Butler, *Combating Money Laundering and International Terrorism: Does the USA PATRIOT Act Require the Judicial System to Abandon Fundamental Due Process in the Name of Homeland Security?*, 16 ST. THOMAS L. REV. 395 (2004).

322. *Chew v. Colding*, 344 U.S. 590, 596 (1953); *Zadvydas v. Davis*, 533 U.S. 678, 693 (2001).

323. *Greene v. McElroy*, 360 U.S. 474, 496 (1959).

324. Defs.' Mem. in Supp. of Their Mot. to Submit Evidence *in Camera* and *ex Parte, Benevolence Int'l Found., Inc. v. John Ashcroft*, 200 F. Supp. 2d 935 (N.D. Ill. 2002) (No. 02 C 763); *see also U.S. v. Ott*, 827 F.2d 473, 476 (9th Cir. 1987) (holding that secret proceedings do not violate due process).

325. *Global Relief Foundation, Inc. v. O'Neill*, 207 F Supp 2d 779, 791 (ND Ill 2002).

326. *See Abourezk v. Reagan*, 785 F.2d 1043 (D.C. Cir. 1986), *aff'd*, 484 U.S. 1 (1987); *Global Relief Found., Inc. v. O'Neill*, 207 F. Supp. 2d 779, 802 (N.D. Ill. 2002).

327. In *Benevolence International*, the plaintiff's lawyers argued against this, saying "The government cannot . . . be permitted to seize an American corporation's assets indefinitely, never bring criminal or civil charges, and obtain dismissal of the corporation's suit for return of its property by using 'evidence' that the corporation cannot see or respond to." Pl.'s Mem. in Opp'n to Defs.' Mot. to Submit Evidence *in Camera* and *ex Parte* at 15, *Benevolence Int'l Found., Inc.* v. *John Ashcroft*, 200 F. Supp. 2d 935 (N.D. Ill. 2002) (No. 02 C 763). In addition, the lawyers argued that this violated due process rights guaranteed under *Matthews* v. *Eldridge. Id.*

328. Hany Kiareldeen, Testimony before the House Judiciary Committee on the Use of Secret Evidence, May 23, 2000, available at www.fas.org. *See also* Ronald Smothers, Cold War Secrecy, Reheated by Terror, N.Y. TIMES, Oct. 27, 1999, at 1.

329. *Id.*, at 17.

330. 31 C.F.R. §§ 535.311–312, 595.310.

331. 50 U.S.C. §§ 1821–29.

332. Global Relief Found., Inc., 207 F. Supp. 2d at 787.

333. Global Relief Found., Inc., 207 F. Supp. 2d at 792.

334. Staff Report, *supra* note 142, at 11 n.4.

335. *Id.*, at 11.

336. Global Relief Found., Inc., 207 F. Supp. 2d at 803–04.

337. Corrected Mem. in Supp. of Pl.'s Mot. for Prelim. Inj., at 38, *Benevolence Int'l Found., Inc.* v. *John Ashcroft*, 200 F. Supp. 2d 935 (N.D. Ill. 2002) (No. 02 C 763).

338. 18 U.S.C. § 1957 does not prevent the state from freezing criminal funds that could be used for legal defense. *See* D. Randall Johnson, *The Criminally Derived Property Statue: Constitutional and Interpretive Issues Raised by 18 U.S.C. § 1957*, 34 WM. & MARY L. REV. 1291 (1993).

339. *See* Benjamin Wallace-Wells, *Private Jihad: How Rita Katz got into the spying business*, NEW YORKER, May 29, 2006, available at www.newyorker.com.

340. *Moving Targets*, ECONOMIST, Sept. 14, 2002, at 80. *See also* John Sugg, *Terrorist Chicken Laundering*, AlterNet, June 12, 2003, available at www.bintjbeil.com.

341. *See, e.g., Global Relief Found., Inc.* v. *New York Times Co.*, 390 F.3d 973 (7th Cir. 2004).

342. Renesselaer Lee, Congressional Research Service, Terrorist Financing: The US and International Response 12, 27 (Dec. 6, 2002), at 1, available at www.boozman. house.gov.

343. Staff Report, *supra* note 142, at 48.

344. Fidler and Simonian, *supra* note 183, at 1.

345. Cilina Nasser, *Closure of U.S. Terror-designated Charity Shatters Many Lives*, DAILY STAR (Lebanon), Aug. 27, 2004.

346. Palestinians Relief and Development Fund, paras. 10, 11 (The Charity Commission, Sept. 24, 2003), available at www.epolitix.com (results of the Charity Commission's inquiry into the affairs of the Palestinians Relief and Development fund, known as INTERPAL).

347. P.K. Abdul Ghafour, *Aqeel Sues U.S. Officials*, Arabnews.com, May 14, 2005, www.arabnews.com/search (search "Aqeel Sues US Officials"; then follow hyperlink to article).

348. Staff Report, *supra* note 142, at 84.

349. For the current UN list, see U.N. Security Council, 1267 Comm., *The New Consolidated List of Individuals and Entities Belonging to or Associated with the Taliban*

and al-Qaida Organization as Established and Maintained by the 1267 Committee, available at www.un.org/Docs.

350. Press Release, 1267 Committee Approves Deletion of Three Individuals and Three Entities From its List, U.N. Doc. SC/7490 (Aug. 27, 2002), available at www.un. org/News/.

351. Staff Report, *supra* note 142, at 79. Emphasis added.

352. *Id.*

353. David Crawford, *The Black Hole of a UN Blacklist*, WALL STREET J. Oct. 2, 2006.

354. *Id.*

355. *See* Edward Alden, Mark Huband & Mark Turner, *Al Qaeda "Financiers" Active in Europe: A UN Report Reveals a Lack of Action Over Youssef Nada and Ahmed Idris Nasreddin*, FIN. TIMES (London), Nov. 14, 2003, at 11; Michael Isikoff & Mark Hosenball, *Terror Watch: Dubious Link between Atta and Saddam*, NEWSWEEK, Dec. 17, 2003 (Web exclusive).

356. Alden et al., *supra* note 356.

357. For example, Yasin al Qadi (aka Yasin Kadi), the former director of Blessed Relief (Muwafaq Foundation), sued in the European Court of Justice to have his name removed from the list. Constant Brand, *EU Court Hears Terror Blacklist Case*, GUARDIAN (London), Oct. 14, 2003, available at www.guardian.co.uk.

358. Looney, *supra* note 216.

359. *See* Nigel Dudley, *Islamic Banking – Structure is a Necessary Target – A New Institution Aims to Set Industry-wide Standard for Islamic Banking*, THE BANKER, May 1, 2003; James Drummond, *Islamic Banks Stung by Claims They Fund Violent Extremists*, FIN. TIMES (London), Oct. 8, 2001, at 6.

360. Richard Wolffe, *"Wake-up Call" Warns Banks to Co-operate Freezing Assets*, FIN. TIMES (London), Sept. 25, 2001, at 3.

361. Katrin Bennhold, *Parliament Tells Europeans to Explain What they Knew About U.S. Tracking of Bank Data*, N.Y. TIMES, July 7, 2006, at A1.

362. *Id.*

363. *Id.*

364. *Id.*

365. Robert Marquand, In Europe, Pushback Against US 'War on Terror,' CHRISTIAN SCIENCE MONITOR, Feb. 5, 2007, at www.csmonitor.com.

366. Katrin Bennhold, *Parliament Tells Europeans to Explain What they Knew About U.S. Tracking of Bank Data*, N.Y. TIMES, July 7, 2006, at A1.

367. Eric Lichtblau, *Europe Panel Faults Sifting of Bank Data*, N.Y. TIMES, Sept. 26, 2006, A1.

368. Staff Report, *supra* note 142 summary. *See also* Lee, *supra* note 343, at 1.

369. Nasser, *supra* note 346.

370. Complaint, *Benevolence Int'l Found., Inc. v. John Ashcroft*, 200 F. Supp. 2d 935 (N.D. Ill. 2002) (No. 02 C 763); Pl.'s Mem. in Opp'n to Defs.' Mot. to Submit Evidence *in Camera* and *ex Parte*, *Benevolence Int'l Found., Inc. v. John Ashcroft*, 200 F. Supp. 2d 935 (N.D. Ill. 2002) (No. 02 C 763); *see also* Enaam M. Arnaout, *Muslim Official Indicted or Aiding Terrorists; Benevolence International Foundation*, 199 CHRISTIAN CENTURY, Oct. 23, 2002, at 15.

371. Edward Alden, Robert Shrimsley & Mark Turner, *Closing Down Bank "Will Hit Somalis,"* FIN. TIMES (London), Nov. 9, 2001, at 8.

372. Hale E. Shappard, *U.S. Actions to Freeze Assets of Terrorism: Manifest and Latent Implications for Latin America*, 17 AM. U. INT'L L. REV.625, 628 (2002).

373. "Although the blocking powers enumerated in the Order are broad, my Administration is committed to exercising them responsibly, with due regard for the culpability of the persons and entities potentially covered by the order." *See Text of Bush's Message to Congress on Freezing Assets Available to Terrorists*, Wash. Post Online, Sept. 23, 2001, www.washingtonpost.com.
374. Zagaris, *supra* note 241, at 13.
375. Shappard, *supra* note 373.
376. Marc Frank & Richard Lapper, *U.S. Squeeze Angers Cubans: Bush Clampdown is Seen as Blow to Family Ties*, Fin. Times (London), May 10, 2004, at 4.

4. Privacy and Surveillance

The following are the sources of the epigraphs: Judge Luzius Wildhaber, *Rotaru v. Romania*, 2000, App. No. 28,341/95, 2000 Eur. Ct. H.R. 192; U.S. National Strategy for Homeland Security, 2002, p. 55; Justice William O. Douglas, *Laird v. Tatum, 1972* [408 U.S. 1, 92 S.Ct. 2318, June 26, 1972 at 24]; Memorandum from Robert Noonan, Deputy Chief of Staff for Intelligence, Department of the Army, November 5, 2001; Scott McNealey, CEO Sun Microsystems, 1999, quoted in Wired News, Jan. 26, 1999.

1. George Orwell, 1984 (1949).
2. Vance Packard, The Naked Society (1964).
3. Alan Westin, Privacy and Freedom (1967).
4. *Privacy and 1984: Public Opinions on Privacy Issues*, Hearing before a Subcommittee of the Committee on Government Operations, House of Representatives, 98th Congress, First Session, Apr. 4, 1984, p. 2 (Opening Statement of Chairman English).
5. *Id.*, at 3, 7 (Statement of Louis Harris, Chairman, Louis Harris & Associates, Inc.) 4, 7.
6. For a thoughtful discussion of the social rigidity that shapes the British constitution and contributes to an unspoken understanding on matters such as state security, *see* Peter Hennessy, The Hidden Wiring: Unearthing the British Constitution (1995).
7. Interception Commissioners Report, 2005–2006, Feb. 19, 2007, p. 17.
8. Robert O'Harrow, Jr., *U.S. Hopes to Check Computers Globally*, Wash. Post, Nov 12, 2002, at A4; John Markoff, *Pentagon Plans A Computer System that Would Peek at Personal Data of Americans*, N.Y. Times, Nov. 9, 2002, at A12; *see also* Info. Awareness Office, Def. Advanced Research Project Agency, Report to Congress Regarding the Terrorism Information Awareness Program: Detailed Information 1 (2003), available at www.globalsecurity.org/security [hereinafter TIA Report]. For a good discussion of the privacy issues raised by TIA and subsequent data mining efforts, *see* James X. Dempsey & Lara M. Flint, *Commercial Data and Nat'l Sec.*, 72 Geo. Wash. L. Rev. 1459 (2004).
9. Stewart Hoover et al., The Pew Internet & Am. Life Project, Faith Online: 64% of Wired Americans Have Used the Internet for Spiritual Or Religious Purposes (2004), p. 2 available at www.pewinternet.org/pdfs/PIP_Faith_Online_2004.pdf.
10. Amanda Lenhart et al., The Pew Internet & Am. Life Project, Content Creation Online: 44% of U.S. Internet Users Have Contributed Their Thoughts and Their Files to the Online World (2004), available at http://www.pewinternet.org.

11. See Susannah Fox & Deborah Fallows, The Pew Internet & Am. Life Project, Internet Health Resources: Health Searches and Email Have Become More Commonplace, But There Is Room for Improvement in Searches And Overall Internet Access (2003), available at www.pewinternet.org; Susannah Fox, The Pew Internet & Am. Life Project, Trust and Privacy Online: Why Americans Want to Rewrite The Rules 4 (2000), available at www.pewinternet.org; Lee Rainie & John Horrigan, The Pew Internet & Am. Life Project, Holidays Online – 2002: Email Grows as a Seasonal Fixture and E-shopping Advances (2003), available at www.pewinternet.org.

12. Press Release, Cisco Sys., CRS-1 Heralds New Era for Modern Communications (May 24, 2004), www.newsroom.cisco.com.

13. *See* Susan Landau, *National Security on the Line*, J. Telecomm. High Tech. L., Vol. 4, Issue 2 (2006), pp. 409–47.

14. Number of mobile phone users worldwide to increase to 2 billion by 2007, Aug. 8, 2003, available at www.geekzone.co.nz.

15. Daniel J. Solove, The Digital Person: Technology and Privacy in the Information Age 3–4 (2004).

16. *Id.*

17. *The Privacy Commission: A Complete Examination of Privacy Protection: Hearing Before the Subcomm. on Gov't Mgmt., Info., and Tech. of the H. Comm. on Gov't Reform*, 106th Cong. 28–42 (2nd Sess. 2000).

18. *See* Glenn R. Simpson, *Big Brother-in-Law: If the FBI Hopes to Get the Goods on You, It May Ask ChoicePoint*, Wall St. J., Apr. 13, 2001 at A1; Jay Stanley, Am. Civil Liberties Union, The Surveillance-Industrial Complex: How the American Government Is Conscripting Businesses and Individuals in Construction of a Surveillance Society, at 26 n.107 (2004) (citing William Matthews, *Commercial Database Use Flagged*, Fed. Computer Week.com, Jan. 16, 2002, www.fcw.com/fcw/; Electronic Privacy Information Center, EPIC ChoicePoint Page, www.epic.org/privacy/choicepoint/default.html (last visited Mar. 3, 2006).

19. *See* Report of the Committee of Privy Counsellors Appointed to Inquire into the Interception of Communications (1957), available at www.fipr.org/rip/Birkett.htm [hereafter Birkett Report].

20. *Id.*

21. *Id.*, ¶ 15.

22. *Id.*, ¶ 32.

23. Post Office Act 1953, 1 & 2 Eliz. II, c. 36, §87(1) (Eng.).

24. Birkett Report, *supra* note 19, at ¶ 39.

25. *Id.*, ¶ 40.

26. *Id.*

27. *Id.*, ¶ 41.

28. *Id.*, ¶ 56.

29. *Id.*, ¶ 57.

30. *Id.*, ¶ 58–59.

31. *Id.*, ¶ 63.

32. *Id.*, ¶ 64.

33. *Id.*, ¶ 64–67.

34. Directive to the Director General of the Security Services, issued by Home Secretary Sir David Maxwell Fife, 24 Sept. 1952, *reprinted in* Lord Denning's Report, [Profumo Affair], 962–63, Cmnd. 2152, at 80.

35. *Id.*, ¶ 68.

36. *Id.*, ¶ 69.

37. *Id.*, ¶ 70.

38. *Id.*, ¶ 71.

39. *Id.*, ¶ 90.

40. BIRKETT REPORT, *supra* note 19, ch. 5 ¶ 131.

41. *Malone* v. *Metropolitan Police commissioner* (No. 2) [Chancery Division] Ch D, The Vice-Chancellor (Sir Robert Megarry), Jan. 22, 23, 24, 25, 26, 29, 31, Feb. 28, 1979.

42. European Convention on Human Rights, art. 8(1) and 8(2), Nov. 4, 1950, 213 U.N.T.S. 221 (emphasis added), available at www.hri.org/docs/ECHR50.html.

43. *Id.*, at art. 13

44. *Malone* v. *Comm'r for the Metro. Police* (no. 2), (1979) 2 All E.R. 620 (Ch.) (Sir Robert Megarry); and Criminal Law Act, 1967, c. 58, § 13 (Eng.).

45. *Klass* v. *Fed. Republic of Germany*, 2 Eur. H.R. Rep. 214 (Ser. A, no. 28) (1979).

46. *Malone*, 2 All E.R. 620 [1974 Ch. 344]

47. *Malone* v. *United Kingdom*, 7 Eur. Ct. H.R. 14 (1985).

48. *Malone* v. *United Kingdom*, App. No. 8691/79 (Pettiti, J., concurring) (judgment of Aug. 2 1984) (translated).

49. Malone, 7 Eur. Ct. H.R. 14.

50. Interception of Communications Act, 1985, c. 56, § 1.

51. *See id*; COMMISSIONER, REPORT, 1988, Cm. 652, ¶ 8. *See also* HOME OFFICE, INTERCEPTION OF COMMUNICATIONS IN THE UNITED KINGDOM, 1985, Cmnd. 9438 at annex 2.

52. *About Harriet*, available at www.harrietharman.org.

53. National Council for Civil Liberties (Liberty) (1934-to date), available at www.hull.ac.uk/arc. *Id.*, at 15.

54. *Hewitt & Harman* v. *United Kingdom*, 14 E.H.R.R. 657 (1992).

55. Ms. Massiter's affidavit, cited in Hewitt et al., at para. 15.

56. DENNING'S REPORT, *supra* note 34, c. XVII.

57. BIRKETT REPORT, *supra* note 19.

58. *Hewitt & Harman* v. *United Kingdom*, 14 Eur. Ct. H.R. 657 (1992).

59. *Id.*, paras 25–55.

60. *See Attorney-Gen.* v. *Newspapers Publishing Plc.* [1987] 3 W.L.R. 942, 946 (Ch. D); *A–G* v. *Guardian Newspapers Ltd.* (No. 2) [1988] 2 W.L.R. 805, 815 (Ch. D); *Attorney-Gen.* v. *Observer, Ltd.* (C.A. July 25, 1986).

61. *Newspapers Publishing*, 3 W.L.R. at 946; and *Attorney General* v. *The Observer Ltd & Others; Attorney General* v. *Guardian Newspapers Ltd & Others*; Court of Appeal (Civil Division); 136 NLJ 799, TIMES July 25, 26, 1986; and *Attorney General* v. *The Observer Ltd & Others; Attorney General* v. *Guardian Newspapers Ltd & Others*; Court of Appeal (Civil Division); 136 NLJ 799, TIMES, July 26, 1986.

62. *Observer and Guardian* v. *the United Kingdom* (13585/88) [1991] ECHR 49 (26 Nov. 1991), paras. 39–44. *See also A-G* v. *South China Morning Post Ltd.*, No. 114 (Civil) Sept. 8, 1987; and *A–G* v. *South China Morning Post Ltd.*, No. 4644 (HC) Aug. 24, 1987.

63. Security Service Act, 1989, c. 5, §1(2); and Security Service Act, 1996, c. 35, §4.

64. Security Services Act, 1989, c. 5, §3.

65. Security Services Act, 1989, c. 5 §3(2)(a). *See also* The Rt. Hon. Lord Justice Stuart-Smith, Security Service Act 1989, Chapter 5: Report of the Commissioner for 1999, Mar. 31, 2000, Cm. 47, ¶ 7–8, available at www.archive.official-documents.co.uk.

66. Security Service Act 1989, c. 5, §§ 3(4)-(5).
67. *Entick v. Carrington*, (1765) 19 St. Tr. 1030 (K.B.); and Police and Criminal Evidence Act, 1984, § 8, ¶ 1 (U.K.), available at www.opsi.gov.uk.
68. Police Act 1997, c. 50, §93.
69. Annual Report of the Security Service Commissioner for 1999, *supra* note 65, at ¶ 22.
70. Police Act 1997, c. 50, § 93(2).
71. *Id.* §93(4).
72. *Alison Halford: Former Top Cop & Ex Labour AM Who Joined The Tories*; BBC/Wales North East, available at http://www.bbc.co.uk/wales/northeast.
73. *Halford v. United Kingdom*, 24 Eur. Ct. H.R. 523 (1997), ¶10.
74. *Id.*, ¶ 16–18.
75. *Id.*, ¶ 53–58.
76. *Id.*, ¶56.
77. The court thus found that the practice violated Article 13. *Id*, ¶63–65.
78. Regulation of Investigatory Powers Act, 2000, c. 23 [hereinafter RIPA]. While *Halford* helped stimulate this piece of legislation, other factors also played a role. *See* Yaman Akdeniz et al., *Bigbrother.gov.uk: State Surveillance in the Age of Information and Rights*, Feb. 2001 CRIM. L. REV. 73.
79. Regulation of Investigatory Powers Bill, 2000, H.C. Bill [64], available at www.publications.parliament.uk.
80. The Rt. Hon. Sir Swinton Thomas, Report of the Interception of Communications Commissioner for 2001, (Oct. 31, 2002), H.C. 1243, at 9, ¶50, available at www.ipt-uk.com/docs/.
81. *See* Peter J. Young, Note, *The Case Against Carnivore: Preventing Law Enforcement from Devouring Privacy*, 35 IND. L. REV. 303, 313 (2001).
82. *Your Privacy Ends Here*, OBSERVER, June 4, 2000, available at www.observer.guardian.co.uk.
83. RIPA, *supra* note 78, at §59(1).
84. The Rt. Hon. Sir Swinton Thomas, Report of the Interception Communications Commissioner for 2002 (Sept. 9, 2003), H.C. 1047, at 7, available at http://www.archive2.official-documents.co.uk.
85. Lord Brown of Eaton-Under-Haywood, Report of the Intelligence Services Commissioner, Report, 2004 (Nov. 3, 2005), H.C. 548, ¶ 31, available at www.official-documents.co.uk.
86. The Rt. Hon. Lord Justice Simon Brown, Report of the Intelligence Services Commissioner 2002, (Sept. 9, 2003), H.C. 1048 at 8, available at http://www.archive2.official-documents.co.uk; *see also* Lord Brown of Eaton-Under-Haywood, Report of the Intelligence Services Commissioner 2003 (Jul. 22, 2004), H.C. 884 at 8, available at www.archive2.official-documents.co.uk.
87. RIPA, *supra* note 78, at §§ 57–61.
88. BIRKETT REPORT, *supra* note 19, ¶ 121.
89. Annual Report of the Security Service Commissioner for 1999, *supra* note 65, at ¶ 37.
90. *Id.*, ¶ 36 (citing 1997 report: "It will be noted that in all cases neither the Tribunal nor myself had found in the favour of the complainant") and ¶39 (stating for the 1999 figures, "No determination has been made in favour of a complainant").
91. *See, e.g.*, The Rt. Hon. Lord Nolan, Interception of Communications Act 1985, c. 56, Report of the Commissioner for 1999 (Jul. 2000), ¶ 32, available at http://www.archive.official-documents.co.uk; and The Rt. Hon. Sir Swinton Thomas, Report

of the Interception of Communications Commissioner for 2001, (Oct. 31, 2002), H.C. 1243, at 4.

92. Lord Brown of Eaton-Under-Heywood, Report of the Intelligence Services Commissioner for 2005–2006, (Feb. 19, 2007), HC 314, at 8, ¶38, available at http://www.official-documents.gov.uk.

93. Lord Brown of Eaton-Under-Heywood, Report of the Intelligence Services Commissioner for 2005–2006, (Feb. 19, 2007), HC 314, at 7, ¶36, available at http://www.official-documents.gov.uk.

94. RIPA, *supra* note 78, at § 1; *see* Interception of Communications Act 1985, c. 56, §§ 1(1), 1(2)(s), 2(2).

95. Author interview with former intelligence official, February 2007.

96. RIPA, *supra* note 78, at § 6.

97. *Id.*, § 15.

98. *Id.*, §17.

99. *Id.*, § 19.

100. *See, e.g.*, HC Debs, Mar. 3, 2003, Vol. 400, Col. 588 (David Blunkett, Home Secretary, stating, "Anything that prevents the security services from being able to undertake the kind of work that leads them to preemptive action, and not just prosecution – or undermines that work – is deeply unfortunate. If people were to withdraw from their normal practice, or if they thought that by engaging in normal communications they would be subject to court action and therefore seized – and that puts us at greater risk – we would have gained nothing and lost much.").

101. *See, e.g.*, Privy Counsellor Review Committee, Report: Anti-terrorism, Crime and Security Act Review, 2005, H.C. 100, at 6, available at www.statewatch.org/news/; Home Affairs Select Committee, Minutes of Evidence (2003) (testimony of Lord Carlile of Berriew QC on Mar. 11, 2003, answering question 16), available at www.publications.parliament.uk.htm. *See also* HL Debs (June 19, 2000), Vol. 614, Col. 111 (Lord Bach); and Lord Lloyd, Inquiry into Legislation against Terrorism, 1996, Cm. 3420, c. 7.

102. *R v. Khan* (Sultan), [1997] A.C. 558 (1996) (appeal taken from Eng. A.C.).

103. Intelligence Services Act 1994, c. 13, § 5(2), available at www.opsi.gov.uk.

104. *R v. Khan (Sultan)*, 2 CHRLD 125 (1996).

105. *Id.*

106. *Khan v. United Kingdom*, 31 Eur. H.R. Rep. 45 (2001); *see also Hewitson v. United Kingdom*, 37 Eur. Ct. H.R. 31 (2003).

107. *See* Police and Criminal Evidence Act, 1984, § 78.

108. Regulation of Investigatory Powers (Directed Surveillance and Covert Human Intelligence Sources) Order, 2003, S.I. 2003/3171, art. 2 ¶ 7 (U.K.), available at www.opsi.gov.uk/si/si2005/20053171.htm.

109. Police Act 1997, c. 50, *available at* http://www.opsi.gov.uk; Chief Surveillance Commissioner, Report to the Prime Minister and to Scottish Ministers, 2002–2003, H.C. 1062, at 4, available at http://www.archive2.official-documents.co.uk [Annual Report of the Chief Surveillance Commissioner].

110. 2002–03 Annual Report of the Chief Surveillance Commissioner, *supra* note 109. *See also* Chief Surveillance Commissioner, Annual Report to the Prime Minister and to Scottish Ministers, 2003–2004, H.C. 668, at 11, available at www.surveillancecommissioners.gov.uk [hereinafter 2003–04 Annual Report of the Chief Surveillance Commissioner].

111. RIPA, *supra* note 78, at §38–9, available at www.opsi.gov.uk.

112. 2003–4 ANNUAL REPORT OF THE CHIEF SURVEILLANCE COMMISSIONER, *supra* note 110 at 11.

113. RIPA, *supra* note 78, at § 49.

114. *Id.*, § 54.

115. *Id.*, § 55.

116. 2003–04 ANNUAL REPORT OF THE CHIEF SURVEILLANCE COMMISSIONER, *supra* note 110, at 3 (statement by the Rt. Hon. Sir Andrew Leggatt), available at www.spy. org.uk.

117. *See, e.g.*, Horace E. Anderson, Jr., *The Privacy Gambit: Toward a Game Theoretic Approach to International Data Protection*, 9 VAND. J. ENT. & TECH. L. 1, Fall 2006; Carl Felsenfeld, *Unnecessary Privacy*, 25 SUFFOLK TRANSN'L L. REV., Symposium 265 (2002); Michael L. Rustad & Thomas H. Koenig, *Harmonizing Cybertort Law for Europe and America*, 5 J. HIGH TECH. L. 13, 40 (2005); James Q. Whitman, *The Two Western Cultures of Privacy: Dignity Versus Liberty*, 113 YALE L. J. 1151, 1156–58 (2004).

118. Whitman, *supra* note 117, at 1160.

119. *See generally Id.*

120. Alexander Zinser, *The Safe Harbor Solution: Is It an Effective Mechanism for International Data Transfers Between the United States and the European Union?*, 1 OKLA. J. L. TECH 11 (2004), available at www.okjolt.org/articles/; Felsenfeld *supra* note 117, at 370.

121. Rustad et al., *supra* note 117.

122. Treaty of Rome, (1957) art. 2., available at www.hri.org/docs/rome57 (last visited May 29, 2005).

123. Rustad et al., *supra* note 117, at 24.

124. *See Id.*

125. Anderson, *supra* note 117, at 20.

126. Council Directive 95/46/EC, 1995 O. J. (L 281) 31.

127. *Id.*, Article 2(a). *See also* Felsenfeld, *supra* note 117, at 370.

128. *Id.*, Article 2(b).

129. Felsenfeld, *supra* note 117, at 371. *But see Id.* at 373–74, arguing that as a *de facto* matter, the EU has not followed a strict opt-in standard.

130. Council Directive 95/46/EC, 1995 O. J. (L 281) 31, Article 12.

131. *See also* Anderson, *supra* note 117, at 20–22.

132. *See* Whitman, *supra* note 117.

133. Anderson, *supra* note 117, at 18, citing also Federal Trade Commission, Self-Regulation and Privacy Online: A Report to Congress (1999), available at www.ftc.gov/os/; Chris J. Hoofnagle, Privacy *Self Regulation: A Decade of Disappointment* (Electronic Privacy Information Center, Wash., D.C.), Mar. 4, 2005, www.epic.org/reports/.

134. *See, e.g.*, Clinton Administration's framework for global electronic commerce, available at www.technology.gov/digeconomy/framewrk.htm.

135. For comments on the fragmented nature of US federal privacy law *see* Felsenfeld, *supra* note 117 at 367–8; Gregory Shaffer, *Reconciling Trade and Regulatory Goals: The Prospects and Limits of New Approaches to Transatlantic Governance Through Mutual Recognition and Safe Harbor Agreements*, 9 COLUM. J. EUR. L. 29, 61 (2002); Stephen J. Davidson & Daniel M. Bryant, *The Right of Privacy: International Discord and the Interface with Intellectual Property Law*, COMPUTER & INTERNET L., Nov. 2001, at 1; Rustad et al., *supra* note 117. *See also* Fair Credit

Reporting Act of 1970, 15 U.S.C. § 1681 (2001); Electronic Fund Transfer Act of 1978, 15 U.S.C. § 1693 (2001); Fair Debt Collection Practices Act, 15 U.S.C. § 1692 (2001); Fair Credit Billing Act, 15 U.S.C. § 1666 (2001); Telephone Consumer Protection Act of 1991, 47 U.S.C. § 609 (2001); Telemarketing and Consumer Fraud and Abuse Prevention Act of 1991, 15 U.S.C. §§ 41–58 (2001); Right to Financial Privacy Act of 1978, 12 U.S.C. § 3401–3422 (2001); Electronic Communication Privacy Act of 1986, 18 U.S.C. § 2521–3127 (2001); Cable Communications Policy Act of 1884, 47 U.S.C. § 521–559 (2001); Comprehensive Crime Control Act of 1984, 18 U.S.C. § 3141–3742 (2001).

136. *See, e.g.,* the Draft Personal Data Privacy and Protection Security Act of 2005, S. 1789, 109th Cong. (2005); the draft Online Privacy Protection Act of 2005, H.R. 84, 109th Cong. (2005); and the draft Consumer Privacy Protection Act of 2005, H.R. 1263, 109th Cong. (2005); Felsenfeld, *supra* note 117, at 375.

137. Felsenfeld, *supra* note 117, at 375.

138. *See, e.g.,* The Gramm-Leach-Bliley Act of 1999, [Pub. L. No. 106–102, 113 Stat. 1338 (codified at 12 U.S.C. § 1811 (2001)].

139. Felsenfeld, *supra* note 117, at 371.

140. Council Directive 95/46/EC, 1995 O. J. (L 281) 31, Article 25.

141. Felsenfeld, *supra* note 117, at 370–71.

142. Anderson, *supra* note 117, at 23.

143. *Id.,* at 23.

144. *See Id.,* at 23–24.

145. *See* Rustad et al., *supra* note 117; Whitman, *supra* note 117, at 1156; *Symposium, Data Protection Law and the European Union's Directive: The Challenge for the United States,* 80 Iowa L. Rev. 431 (1995). For documents on the Safe Harbor Agreement, *see* Daniel J. Solove & Marc Rotenberg, Information Privacy Law 743–54 (2003). For the Safe Harbor Privacy Principles themselves, see Issuance of Safe Harbor Principles and Transmission to European Commission, 65 Fed. Reg. 45,666 (July 24, 2000).

146. See Anderson, *supra* note 117, at 25–28.

147. *See* Rustad et al., *supra* note 117.

148. Anderson, *supra* note 117, at 28. For discussion of the adoption of the principles and the interaction between the US Department of Commerce and the European Commission *see* Felsenfeld, *supra* note 117, at 378–79. *See also* Steven R. Salbu, *The European Union Data Privacy Directive and International Relations,* 35 Vand. J. Transnat'l L. 655, 684 (2002); David Scheer, *Europe's New High-Tech Role: Playing Privacy Cop to the World,* Wall St. J., Oct. 10, 2003, at A1.

149. Felsenfeld, *supra* note 117, at 372.

150. *See* Anderson, *supra* note 117, at 43–44.

151. RIPA, *supra* note 78, §22(2).

152. Clive Walker, Blackstone's Guide to The Anti-Terrorism Legislation (2002), p. 157 (citing Home Office, Home Office Regulatory Impact Assessment: Retention of Communications Data (2001), ¶6).

153. Clive Walker & Yaman Akdeniz, *Anti-terrorism Laws and Data Retention: War is Over?,* 54 N. Ireland Legal Q. 159, 162 n.21 (2003) (citing Roger Gaspar, NCIS Submission to the Home Office; Looking to the Future: Clarity on Communications Data Retention Law 9 (2000), available at www.cryptome.org).

154. Walker & Akdeniz, *supra* note 153, at 163.

155. While Lord Rooker formally denied this language in the House of Lords, similar claims proliferate. *See* HL Debs, Dec. 4, 2001, Vol. 629, Col. 770.

156. Anti-Terrorism Crime and Security Act, 2001, c. 24, §§ 102–04 (Eng.), available at www.opsi.gov.uk. *See also* S. A. Mathieson, *The Net's Eyes are Watching*, GUARDIAN ONLINE, Nov. 15, 2001, *available at* www.guardian.co.uk/internetnews/.

157. Walker & Akdeniz, *supra* note 153, at 170.

158. *Id.*, at 166.

159. *Id.*; HL Debs, Dec. 4, 2001, Vol. 629, col. 774, (Lord Rooker); HL Debs, Dec. 6, 2001, vol. 629, col. 981 (listing those opposed to amendment); HL Debs, Dec. 13, 2001, Vol. 629, cols. 1478–79 (Baroness Buscombe arguing for Lords Amendments Numbers 40 and 44, Lord Rooker opposing them, saying "As I said before, quite extravagant language is being used which is designed to frighten people into believing that they will be subjected to mass surveillance. They will not be." (col. 1478); Amendment agreed to by a vote of 196 to 145). *See also* Author interview with Casper Bowden, Director of the Foundation for Information Policy Research, in person in Montreal, Canada, May 1, 2007.

160. Anti-Terrorism, Crime and Security Act 2001: Retention and Disclosure of Communications Data Summary of Counsels' Advice, ¶ 13, available at www. privacyinternational.org.

161. *See* Council Directive 2002/58/EC, 2002 O.J. (L 201) 37–47 (EC), available at http://europa.eu.int/eur-lex/ (concerning the processing of personal data and the protection of privacy in the electronic communications sector) (Directive on privacy and electronic communications).

162. Welcome to Guardster, www.guardster.com (last visited May 2, 2006). *See also* WALKER, *supra* note 152, at 160.

163. *See* Anonymity 4 Proxy (A4Proxy) – Web Anonymizing Software for Surfing with Privacy, www.inetprivacy.com/a4proxy/ (last visited Mar. 6, 2006).

164. Anti-Terrorism, Crime and Security Act 2001: Retention and Disclosure of Communications Data Summary of Counsels' Advice, *supra* note 160, ¶ 15.

165. *Rotaru v. Romania*, App. No. 28,341/95, 2000 Eur. Ct. H.R. 192 (Wildhaber, J., concurring). *See also* Walker & Akdeniz, *supra* note 153, at 174.

166. WALKER, *supra* note 152, at 161–62, citing Information Commissioner news release, Information Commissioner contributes to scrutiny of antiterrorism bill, www. cyber-rights.org.

167. *Id.*, at 159.

168. *See* 1971 Immigration Act, c. 77, amended by Immigration Act 1988 (c.14), s. 7(3); and 1974 Prevention of Terrorism (Temporary Provisions) Act; 1989 Prevention of Terrorism (Temporary Provisions) Act, section 16 and schedule 5. For discussion of port controls *see* CLIVE WALKER, THE PREVENTION OF TERRORISM IN BRITISH LAW, (1992), ch. 8.

169. Lord Lloyd, *supra* note 101, at ¶ 10.57.

170. Terrorism Act 2000, c. 11, Part V, § 53 [hereinafter Terrorism Act 2000].

171. HL Debs, vol. 613 cols 736–737, May 23, 2000 (Lord Bassam).

172. WALKER, *supra* note 152, at 150; Terrorism Act 2000 (Carding) Order 2001 (SI 2001 No. 426).

173. Terrorism Act 2000, *supra* note 170, Schedule 7(1).

174. *Id.*, Schedule 7(2), (4).

175. *Id.*, Schedule 7(5).

176. Walker, *supra* note 152, at 151.

177. Terrorism Act 2000, *supra* note 170, Schedule 7(7) & (8).

178. *Id.*, Schedule 7(11).

179. Anti-Terrorism, Crime and Security Act 2001, c. 24, §§118, 119 (amending Terrorism Act 2000, Schedule 7(12).

180. Terrorism Act 2000, *supra* note 170, Schedule 7(17).

181. *Id.*, Schedule 14(4).

182. Terrorism Act 2000 (Code of Practice for Examining Officers) Order 2001 (SI 2001, No. 427), para. 10. Text of Code reprinted in WALKER, *supra* note 152, at 154.

183. Text of guidance note reprinted in WALKER, *supra* note 152, at 154–55 (emphasis in WALKER omitted).

184. The cameras were first introduced into the United Kingdom in 1956. Quentin Burrows, *Scowl Because You're on Candid Camera: Privacy and Video Surveillance*, 31 VAL. U. L. REV. 1079, 1080 (1997). For further discussion of CCTV in the United Kingdom *see* Clive NORRIS & GARY ARMSTRONG, THE MAXIMUM SURVEILLANCE SOCIETY: THE RISE OF CCTV (1999); CLIVE NORRIS, JADE MORAN, & GARY ARMSTRONG SURVEILLANCE, CLOSED CIRCUIT TELEVISION AND SOCIAL CONTROL (1999).

185. MICHAEL COUSENS, SURVEILLANCE LAW (2004), at 59–60.

186. *Id.*, at 60 (citing THE TIMES (London), Nov. 8, 2003).

187. David Shenk, *Watching You*, NAT'L GEOGRAPHIC MAG. Nov. 2003, at 16.

188. *Privacy vs. Security: Electronic Surveillance in the Nation's Capital: Hearing Before the Subcomm. on the D.C of the Comm. on Government Reform*, 107th Cong. 2 (2002) [hereinafter *Privacy vs. Security Hearing*] (statement of Rep. Constance A. Morella, Chairman), available at www.dcwatch.com/issues/).

189. For the Hayes/Taylor trial *see* Matt Seaton, *Charge of the New Red Brigade*, INDEPENDENT ON SUNDAY, Jan. 1995, available at www.redaction.org/media/independent.html.

190. Joyce W. Luk, Note, *Identifying Terrorists: Privacy Rights in the United States and United Kingdom*, 25 HASTINGS INT'L & COMP. L. REV. 223, 229 n.33 (2002) (citing Alastair Dalton, *Controls Urged on Big Brother's All-Seeing Eyes*, SCOTSMAN, July 23, 1998, at 9).

191. *See* Luk, *supra* note 190, at 228 (citing Burrows, *supra* note 184, at 1099).

192. *See* Luk, *supra* note 190, at 228 (citing John Deane, *CCTV Boost Follows Crime-Fighting Success*, PRESS ASS'N NEWSFILE, Oct. 13, 1995).

193. Data Protection Act 1998, c. 29, § 1 (U.K.), available at www.opsi.gov.uk.

194. 2003–04 ANNUAL REPORT OF THE CHIEF SURVEILLANCE COMMISSIONER, *supra* note 110 (statement by the Rt. Hon. Sir Andrew Leggatt).

195. *Peck v. United Kingdom* (44647/98), 36 Eur. Ct. H.R. (2003); *see also R v. Brentwood BC* [1998] EMLR. 697 (U.K.).

196. *Privacy vs. Security Hearing*, *supra* note 188, 1 (statement of Rep. Constance A. Morella, Chairman).

197. *Id.*, at 1–2.

198. *Id.*, at 21 (statement of Chief of Police Charles Ramsey).

199. *Id.*, at 48.

200. Stephen Kinzer, *Chicago Moving to 'Smart' Surveillance Cameras*, N.Y. TIMES, Sept. 21, 2004, at A18.

201. *Id.*

202. *Id.*

203. *Id.*

204. *Id.*

205. *Id.*

206. Luk, *supra* note 190, at 227 (citing Mark Boal, *SpyCam City*, VILLAGE VOICE, Oct. 6, 1998, at 38).

207. *See* Luk, *supra* note 190, at 227 (citing Mark Hansen, *No Place to Hide*, 83 A.B.A. J. 44, 44–45 (1997)).

208. Pelco News Release, Oct. 26, 2001, available at www.pelco.com.

209. *Privacy vs. Security Hearing, supra* note 188, at 107 (statement of Richard Chace, Executive Dir., Security Industry Association (SIA), who represents more than 400 electronic security manufacturers, distributors, and service providers).

210. *History of the FBI: Origins 1908–1910*, www.fbi.gov/libref/ (last visited Mar. 3, 2006).

211. ROBERT K. MURRAY, RED SCARE: A STUDY IN NATIONAL HYSTERIA, 1919–1920, (1955) (reprinted in 1980), at 213; GEOFFREY STONE, PERILOUS TIMES: FREE SPEECH IN WARTIME FROM THE SEDITION ACT OF 1798 TO THE WAR ON TERRORISM (2004), p. 223.

212. NATIONAL COUNTERINTELLIGENCE CENTER, *Chapter 4, Counterintelligence Between the Wars, in* AMERICAN REVOLUTION TO WORLD WAR II, ED. BY FRANK J. RAFALKO, available at www.fas.org/irp/, citing Memorandum from Harlan Fiske Stone, Attorney Gen., Dep't of Justice, to J. Edgar Hoover, Dir., Fed. Bureau of Investigation (May 13, 1924).

213. *Socialist Workers Party v. Attorney Gen.*, 642 F. Supp. 1357, 1390 (1986).

214. *Socialist Workers Party*, 642 F. Supp. at 1375–76 (citing Memorandum by J. Edgar Hoover, Dir., Fed. Bureau of Investigation, (Aug. 24, 1936); CHRISTOPHER M. ANDREW, FOR THE PRESIDENT'S EYES ONLY: SECRET INTELLIGENCE AND THE AMERICAN PRESIDENCY FROM WASHINGTON, (1996), p. 88.

215. *Id.*

216. NATIONAL COUNTERINTELLIGENCE CENTER., *supra* note 212, (citing Memorandum from J. Edgar Hoover, Dir., Fed. Bureau of Investigation, to all FBI field offices, (Sept. 5, 1936)).

217. *Id.*, at 161 (citing Memorandum from J. Edgar Hoover, Dir., Fed. Bureau of Investigation, enclosed with letter from Cummings to the President, (Oct. 20, 1938)).

218. *Id.*, at 179 (citing Memorandum from J. Edgar Hoover, Dir., Fed. Bureau of Investigation, to all field offices (Dec. 6, 1939)).

219. *See generally Id.*, at 180–81.

220. WESTIN, *supra* note 3, at 177.

221. *Irvine v. California*, 347 U.S. 128, 132 (1954).

222. *Socialist Workers Party v. Attorney Gen.*, 642 F. Supp. 1357, 1391 (1986).

223. WESTIN, *supra* note 3, at 181.

224. *Id.*, at 182.

225. *Id.*, at 199–200.

226. Presidential memorandum, issued June 30, 1965, authorized wiretaps "in connection with investigations related to national security." *Socialist Workers Party*, 642 F. Supp. at 1391.

227. *Katz v. United States*, 389 U.S. 347 (1967). (Charles Katz, a small-time gambler, used a public phone down the street from his boarding house to place bets. The FBI attached an electronic bug to the outside of the phone booth and recorded his calls to bookies in Miami and Boston.)

228. *Katz v. United States*, 389 U.S. 347, 351 (1967) (citation omitted).

229. *Id.*

230. *Id.*, at 353. Emphasis added.
231. *Id.*, at 358, 363–64 (White, J., concurring).
232. *Id.*, at 359 (Douglas, J., concurring).
233. *Id.*, at 359–60 (Douglas, J., concurring).
234. *Id.*, at 360 (Douglas, J., concurring).
235. President Lyndon Johnson, State of the Union Address (Jan. 10, 1967), available at www.infoplease.com. Emphasis added.
236. Omnibus Crime Control and Safe Streets Act of 1968, Pub. L. No. 90–351, tit. III § 802, 82 Stat. 212 (codified as amended at 18 U.S.C. §§ 2510–20 (2000)).
237. *Id.*, *See also* Wayne R. LaFave et al., Criminal Procedure (4th ed. 2004) p. 333.
238. Omnibus Crime Control Act, § 802 (codified as amended at 18 U.S.C. § 2511(3)). *See also* PHILIPPA STRUM, PRIVACY: THE DEBATE IN THE US SINCE 1945 (1998), pp. 141–44.
239. *United States v. United States Dist. Court*, 407 U.S. 297, 308 (1972).
240. *Id.*, at 314–15.
241. *Id.*, at 316–17.
242. *Id.*, at 317 (internal citation removed).
243. *Id.*
244. *Id.*, at 320.
245. *Id.*
246. *Id.*
247. *See Hearings Before the Select Committee to Study Governmental Operations with Respect to Intelligence Agencies*, 94th Cong. Vol. 5 (1975) [hereinafter *Church Committee* Vol. 5], available at www.aarclibrary.org/publib/.
248. An Act for the Protection of Government Records, ch. 57, 48 Stat. 122 (1933), *transferred to* 18 U.S.C. § 815 (current version at 18 U.S.C. § 952 (2000)).
249. 18 U.S.C. § 798, ch. 655, § 24(a)(a)(3), 65 Stat. 719 (1951).
250. *Church Committee* Vol. 5, *supra* note 247, at 150 (Charter for Sensitive SIGINT Operation Minaret (C)).
251. *Id.*
252. *Id.*, at 12.
253. *Id.*, at 151 (Memorandum from the Bureau of Narcotics and Dangerous Drugs to Dir., Nat'l Sec. Agency Fort George G. Meade, Md., Request for COMINT of Interest to Bureau of Narcotics and Dangerous Drugs (BNDD)).
254. *Id.*, at 14.
255. *Id.*, at 156 (Memorandum from Nat'l Security Agency to Sec'y of Defense and Attorney Gen. from Noel Gayler, Vice Admiral, U.S. Navy, Director NSA (Oct. 1, 1973)).
256. *Id.*, at 22–25.
257. *Id.*, at 12–13. *See also James* Bamford, THE PUZZLE PALACE (1983), pp. 111–12 (first to testify to Congress).
258. *Id.*
259. For how this approach played out in the Iraq context, see DANIEL BENJAMIN & STEVEN SIMON, THE NEXT ATTACK (2005).
260. *See Hearings Before the Select Committee to Study Governmental Operations with Respect to Intelligence Agencies*, 94th Cong. (1975); *Supplementary Detailed Staff Reports of the Intelligence Activities and the Rights of Americans: Book III, Final Report of the Select Committee to Study Governmental Operations with Respect to Intelligence Activities*, 94th Cong. (1976) [hereinafter *Final Report*]. *See also*

COINTELPRO: THE FBI'S SECRET WAR ON POLITICAL FREEDOM (Cathy Perkus ed., 1975).

261. *Socialist Workers Party v. Attorney Gen.*, 642 F. Supp. 1357, 1376, 1384, 1396 (S.D.N.Y. 1986); at 1384–85.

262. *Id.*, at 1385–88.

263. *Id.*, at 1388.

264. STONE, *supra* note 211, at 490 (internal footnotes omitted).

265. *Socialist Workers Party*, 642 F. Supp. at 1389.

266. STONE, *supra* note 211, at 488.

267. *Socialist Workers Party*, 642 F. Supp. at 1389, at 1369.

268. *Id.*, at 1369–70.

269. *Id.*, at 1373.

270. *Id.*, at 1375.

271. *Id.*, at 1394.

272. *Id.*, at 1393.

273. *Id.*, at 1389.

274. *Id.*, at 1394.

275. *Id.*, at 1395. The Bureau also maintained a "JUNE mail" system, where documents were placed in a "Special File Room." *See* Athan G. Theoharis, *FBI Surveillance: Past and Present*, 69 CORNELL L. REV. 883, 888 (1984).

276. *Socialist Workers Party v. Attorney Gen.*, 100 S.Ct. 217, 444 U.S. 903, 903 (1979) (White, J., dissenting); and *Socialist Workers Party*, 642 F. Supp. at 1382.

277. *Id.*, at 1379.

278. *Id.*, at 1382.

279. *Id.*, at 1380.

280. STONE, *supra* note 211, at 494–5.

281. *Id.* at 491–4. *See also* Theoharis, *supra* note 275, at 884–85; *Final Report, supra* note 260; *Socialist Workers Party*, 642 F. Supp. at 1395; and discussion in Laura K. Donohue, *Anglo-American Privacy and Surveillance*, 96 CRIM. L. & CRIMINOLOGY 1059 (2006).

282. For example, in 1967 Project MERRIMAC, aimed at protecting CIA employees and facilities against antiwar protestors, infiltrated and monitored a number of antiwar organizations, such as SDS and the Women's Strike for Peace. The same year Project RESISTANCE began to compile information on radical organizations in the United States, bringing more than 12,000 students under surveillance. STONE, *supra* note 211, at 491.

283. *Church Committee* Vol. 5, *supra* note 247; *see also* STONE, *supra* note 211, at 491.

284. THE ROCKEFELLER COMM'N, REPORT TO THE PRESIDENT BY THE COMMISSION ON CIA ACTIVITIES WITHIN THE UNITED STATES (1975).

285. STONE, *supra* note 211, at 491.

286. The government claimed, e.g., that "any President who takes seriously his oath to 'preserve and protect' and defend the constitution will no doubt determine that it is not unreasonable to utilize electronic surveillance to gather intelligence information concerning those organizations which are committed to the use of illegal methods to bring about changes in our form of government and which may be seeking to foment violent disorders." JASON EPSTEIN, THE GREAT CONSPIRACY TRIAL: AN ESSAY ON LAW, LIBERTY, AND THE CONSTITUTION (1970), pp. 111–12.

287. *See, e.g., Halkin v. Helms*, 690 F.2d 977 (D.C. Cir. 1982).

288. *See Laird v. Tatum*, 408 U.S. 1 (1972); STONE, *supra* note 211, at 492.

289. STONE, *supra* note 211, at 492; *see also* ATHAN THEOHARIS, SPYING ON AMERICANS: POLITICAL SURVEILLANCE FROM HOOVER TO THE HUSTON PLAN (1978).

290. *See id.* at 1–40.

291. *Id.* at 11.

292. *Laird v. Tatum*, 408 U.S. 1, 92 S.Ct. 2318, June 26, 1972 at 24 (Douglas, J., dissenting).

293. *Id.*, at 28.

294. *Id.*

295. *Id.*

296. STONE, *supra* note 211, at 493.

297. *Id.*

298. OFFICE FOR INTELLECTUAL FREEDOM, AM. LIBRARY ASS'N, INTELLECTUAL FREEDOM MANUAL 154–55 (5th ed. 1996) [hereinafter ALA MANUAL]; *see* also HERBERT FOERSTAL, SURVEILLANCE IN THE STACKS: THE FBI's LIBRARY AWARENESS PROGRAM (1991). American Library Association, Position Statement on the Confidentiality of Library Records, available at www.ala.org/ala/ (last visited Apr. 8, 2006). Anne Klinefelter, *The Role of Librarians in Challenges to the USA PATRIOT Act*, 5 N.C. J.L. & TECH. 219, 223 (2004); STRUM, *supra* note 238, at 151.

299. *Id.*, at 150–51.

300. *Church Committee* Vol. 5, *supra* note 247, at 64.

301. *Id.*, at 65.

302. *Final Report*, *supra* note 260, at 5–6.

303. STONE, *supra* note 211, at 496.

304. James Q. Wilson, *The Case for Greater Vigilance*, TIME, May 1, 1995, at 73; *see* also STONE, *supra* note 211, at 496–7.

305. STRUM, *supra* note 238, at 152–56.

306. Privacy Act of 1974, 5 U.S.C. § 552a (2000).

307. GINA MARIE STEVENS, AM. LAW DIV., PRIVACY: TOTAL INFORMATION AWARENESS PROGRAMS AND RELATED INFORMATION ACCESS, COLLECTION, AND PROTECTION LAWS 6 (2003).

308. *Id.*, at 6.

309. *Id.*, at 6.

310. 5 U.S.C. § 552552 a(b); *see also* Stevens, *supra* note 307, at 7.

311. STRUM, *supra* note 238, at 153.

312. PERSONAL PRIVACY IN AN INFORMATION SOCIETY: THE REPORT OF THE PRIVACY PROTECTION STUDY COMMISSION, available at www.epic.org/privacy/ (last visited Mar. 6, 2006) (transmitted to President Jimmy Carter on July 12, 1977), Chapter 13.

313. *Id.*, at 4.

314. *Id.*

315. STRUM, *supra* note 238, at 153–54.

316. *See* OVERVIEW OF THE PRIVACY ACT OF 1974 (2004), available at www.usdoj.gov/04foia/; *see also* STRUM, *supra* note 238, at 154–56.

317. Foreign Intelligence Surveillance Act of 1978, Pub. L. No. 95–511, tit. 1, § 102, 92 Stat. 1786 (1978) (codified as amended at 50 U.S.C. § 1801–11 (2000)).

318. 50 U.S.C. § 1801(a)(4) (2000).

319. *Id.*, § 1801(b).

320. *Id.*, § 1801(f)(1); *see also id.* § 1801(f)(4); DANIEL BLINKA, ELECTRONIC SURVEILLANCE: COMMENTARIES AND STATUTES (2004).

321. 50 U.S.C. § 1801 (f)(1)-(4).

322. 50 U.S.C. § 1804(a)(1), (3).

323. *Id.*, § 1804(a)(4).
324. *Id.*, § 1805(b).
325. *Id.*, § 1804(a)(6).
326. *Id.*, § 1804(a)(7).
327. *Id.*, § 1804(a)(8).
328. *Id.*, § 1804(a)(9).
329. *Id.*, § 1804(a)(10).
330. *Id.*, § 1804(a)(11).
331. *Id.*, § 1804(d).
332. *Id.*, § 1821(a)(1)(A)(i).
333. *Id.*, § 1822(a)(1)(A).
334. *Id.*, § 1823.
335. *Id.*, § 1826.
336. *Id.*, § 1842(a)(1).
337. *Id.*, § 1842(a)-(b). As with the application for electronic surveillance, the applicant must include the name of the official seeking surveillance, as well as certification that "the information likely to be obtained is relevant to an ongoing foreign intelligence or international terrorism investigation." *Id.*, § 1842(c)(1)-(2).
338. *Id.*, § 1842(c)(A).
339. *Id.*, § 1842(e).
340. *Id.*, § 1843(a).
341. *Id.*, § 1843(a)(2).
342. *Id.*, § 1845(c).
343. *See generally* Foreign Intelligence Surveillance Act, www.fas.org/irp/. Statistics compiled by author.
344. Interview with Department of Justice officials, in S.F., Cal. (2003); in San Jose, Cal. (2004); in N.Y., N.Y. (2005).
345. For discussion of the 1986 Electronic Communications Privacy Act, the 1994 Communications Assistance for Law Enforcement Act *see* Donohue, *supra* note 281.
346. USA PATRIOT Improvement and Reauthorization Act of 2005, Pub. L. No. 109–177, tit. I §§ 102–03120 Stat. 192, at § 115 (judicial review of national security letters), § 119 (audit of use of National Security Letters).
347. USA PATRIOT Act, Pub. L. No. 107–56, § 218, 115 Stat. 272 (codified as amended at 50 U.S.C. §§ 1804(a)(7)(B), 1823(a)(7)(B) (2000 & Supp. 2001)); *see also id.* §§ 201 (codified as amended at 18 U.S.C. § 2516 (2000 & Supp. 2001)), 207 (codified as amended at 50 U.S.C. § 1805(e)(1) (2000 & Supp. 2001)), 805 (codified as amended at 18 U.S.C. § 2339A (2000 & Supp. 1)).
348. Memorandum from Attorney Gen. John Ashcroft, to the Dir. of the Fed. Bureau of Investigation, the Assistant Attorney Gen., the Criminal Div. Counsel for Intelligence Policy, and United States Attorneys (Mar. 6, 2002), available at www.fas.org/irp/ ("[The USA PATRIOT Act] allows FISA to be used *primarily* for a law enforcement purpose, as long as a significant foreign intelligence purpose remains.").
349. *In re* All Matters Submitted to Foreign Intelligence Surveillance Court., 218 F. Supp. 2d 611, 621 (Foreign Intel. Surv. Ct. 2002).
350. *Id.*, at 620.
351. *Id.*, at 623.
352. *Id.*, at 624.
353. *Id.*, at 625.

354. *In re* Sealed Case No's 02–001, 02–002, 310 F.3d 717, 722 (Foreign Intel. Surv. Ct. Rev. 2002).

355. *Id.*

356. *In re* All Matters, 218 F. Supp. 2d at 746.

357. *In re* Sealed Case, 310 F.3d at 727–39.

358. *Id.*, at 735.

359. *Id.*

360. *United States* v. *Troung*, 629 F.2d 908 (4th Cir. 1980).

361. *In re Sealed Case*, 310 F.3d at 744.

362. *Id.*, at 745.

363. Michael P. O'Connor & Celia Rumann, *Going, Going, Gone: Sealing the Fate of the Fourth Amendment*, 26 FORDHAM INT'L L.J. 1234, 1244 (2002).

364. *See* O'Connor, *supra* note 363, at 1249 *See also* Peter Swire, *The System of Foreign Intelligence Surveillance Law*, 72 GEO. WASH. L. REV. 1306 (2004).

365. U.S. CONST. amend. IV.

366. O'Connor, *supra* note 363, at 1260 *See In re* All Matters Submitted to Foreign Intelligence Surveillance Court., 218 F. Supp. 2d 611, 625 (Foreign Intel. Surv. Ct. 2002).

367. Replies by Peter P. Swire, Patriot Debates: A Sourceblog for the USA PATRIOT Debate, www.patriotdebates.com (last visited May 2, 2006). Just two months before the Oklahoma City attack, President William J. Clinton issued Executive Order 12,949, which expanded the use of FISA for physical searches. *See* Exec. Order 12,949, 60 Fed. Reg. 8169 (Feb. 13, 1995).

368. USA PATRIOT Act, Pub. L. No. 107–56, § 501, 115 Stat. 272 (codified as amended at 50 U.S.C. § 1861 (Supp. 2001).

369. *Id.*

370. The statute added an insignificant stipulation drawn from the original FISA: that such an order could only follow if the "investigation of a United States person is not conducted solely upon the basis of activities protected by the first amendment to the Constitution." This left open the possibility of an investigation based "substantially" or "largely" upon protected activities. USA PATRIOT Act, § 501(a); *see also* Swire, *supra* note 364, at 1335.

371. Dan Eggan & Robert O'Harrow, Jr., *U.S. Steps Up Secret Surveillance: FBI, Justice Dept. Increase Use of Wiretaps, Records Searches*, WASH. POST, Mar. 24, 2003, at A1, available at www.washingtonpost.com/ac2/; *see also* James Bovard, *Surveillance State: Since September 11, A Flood of Federal Legislation Has Reduced American Freedom Without Increasing Our Safety*, AM. CONSERVATIVE, May 19, 2003, at 1, available at www.amconmag.com.

372. Roving wiretaps are authorized in the USA PATRIOT Act § 206 (codified as amended at 50 U.S.C. § 1805(c)(2)(B) (2000 & Supp. 2001).

373. *America After 9/11: Freedom Preserved or Freedom Lost? Hearing Before the S. Comm. on the Judiciary*, 108th Cong. (2003) (statement of James X. Dempsey, Executive Dir., Ctr. for Democracy & Tech.) available at www.cdt.org/testimony/ (referencing a Department of Justice letter of Oct. 24, 2003 to Senator Stevens detailing the use of § 213 for nonterrorism-related purposes).

374. Letter from the Honorable F. James Sensenbrenner to the Chairman of the Comm. on the Judiciary (July 12, 2005), available at www.house.gov/judiciary_democrats/.

375. USA PATRIOT Improvement and Reauthorization Act, Pub. L. No. 109–177, §114, 120 Stat. 192.

376. *Id.*

377. USA PATRIOT Act § 210 (codified as amended at 18 U.S.C. § 2703(c)(2) (2000 & Supp. 2001)).

378. 18 U.S.C. § 2709(b)(1)(B).

379. Swire, *supra* note 364, at 1333 nn. 185–86 (citing Eric Lichtblau & James Risen, *Broad Domestic Role Asked for CIA and the Pentagon*, N.Y. TIMES, May 2, 2003, at A21).

380. *In re* Doubleclick Inc., 154 F. Supp. 2d 497, 511 n.20 (S.D.N.Y. 2001).

381. Brief for Electronic Frontier Foundation et al. as Amicus Curiae in Support of Plaintiffs John Doe and American Civil Liberties Union, Doe v. Ashcroft, 334 F. Supp. 2d 471 (S.D.N.Y. 2004) (No. 04 Civ. 2614).

382. LEIGH S. ESTABROOK, LIBRARY RESEARCH CTR., PUBLIC LIBRARIES AND CIVIL LIBERTIES (2003), available at www.lrc.lis.uiuc.edu (last visited Apr. 8, 2006). For a discussion of the impact of the USA PATRIOT Act on libraries in particular, *see* Klinefelter, *supra* note 298; Susan Nevelow Mart, *Protecting the Lady from Toledo: Post-USA PATRIOT Act Electronic Surveillance at the Library*, 96 LAW LIBR. J. 449 (2004).

383. The authorization for these NSLs came from the Intelligence Authorization Act for 2004. *See* discussion *infra*.

384. JAY STANLEY, *supra* note 18, at 13 n.51 (2004) (citing Editorial, *Surveillance City*, LAS VEGAS REV. J., Jan. 11, 2004, available at www.reviewjournal.com).

385. *Id.*; *see* Rod Smith, *Sources: FBI Gathered Visitor Information Only in Las Vegas*, LAS VEGAS REV. J., Jan. 7, 2004, available at www.reviewjournal.com.

386. *Net Effect: Antiterror Eavesdropping: Privacy Advocates Worry Civil Rights May Be Trampled*, ASSOCIATED PRESS, May 27, 2002, available at www.tinyurl.com/xmai [hereinafter *Net Effect*].

387. *Net Effect*, *supra* note 386.

388. *FBI Abused PATRIOT Act powers, audit finds*, GUARDIAN, Mar. 9, 2007, available at www.guardian.co.uk.

389. Barton Gellman, *The FBI's Secret Scrutiny: In Hunt for Terrorists, Bureau Examines Records of Ordinary Americans*, WASH. POST, Nov. 6, 2005, at A1.

390. *Id.*

391. *Id.*

392. *Doe v. Ashcroft*, 334 F. Supp. 2d 471, 479 (S.D.N.Y. 2004) (citing 18 U.S.C. § 2709(c) (2000)).

393. USA PATRIOT Improvement and Reauthorization Act, Pub. L. No. 109–177, § 116(a), 120 Stat. 192.

394. *Doe*, 334 F. Supp. 2d at 478.

395. *Id.* at 479. Emphasis added.

396. *Id.*

397. *Id.*

398. "[R]eady availability of judicial process to pursue such a challenge is necessary to vindicate important rights guaranteed by the Constitution or by statute." *Id.* at 475. The court also held that, as applied, the demand that ISPs produce customer records potentially infringed citizens' First Amendment rights of anonymous speech and association. *Id.*, at 506.

399. *Id.*, at 502. Note, however, that the citation used by the court in the case is inaccurate: footnote 145 refers to a letter from July 26, 2002.

400. *Id.*, at 504.

401. *Id.*, at 511.

402. *Id.*, at 516; see also *id.*, at 511–16 for the court's discussion.

403. *Id.*, at 519.

404. *Id.*, at 520.

405. *Id.*

406. Barton Gellman, *The FBI's Secret Scrutiny: In Hunt for Terrorists, Bureau Exam-ines Records of Ordinary Americans,* WASH. POST, Nov. 6, 2005, at A1; and *Doe v. Gonzales,* 386 F. Supp. 2d 66, 70 (D. Conn. 2005).

407. Gellman, *supra* note 406.

408. *Doe v. Gonzales,* 126 S. Ct. 1, 23 (2005).

409. *Id.*, at 3.

410. *Id.*, at 2.

411. *Id.*

412. *Id.* (quoting Emergency Application to Vacate Stay at 22–23).

413. *Doe v. Gonzales,* 126 S. Ct. 1, 3 (2005) (quoting Emergency at 23).

414. *Id.*, at 1.

415. *See Id.*

416. *Id.*, at 4–5.

417. Section by section analysis of Draft Domestic Security Enhancement Act of 2003, (Jan. 9, 2003), available at www.publicintegrity.org, available at www.publicintegrity.org).

418. *Anti-Terrorism Intelligence Tools Improvement Act of 2003: Hearing on HR 3179 Before the Subcomm. on Crime, Terrorism, and Homeland Security of the H. Comm. on the Judiciary,* 108th Cong. (2004), available at www.thomas.loc.gov/cgi-bin/ (last visited Apr. 8, 2006).

419. H.R. 3179 Bill Status, www.govtrack.us/congress/bill; and USA PATRIOT Improvement and Reauthorization Act of 2005, Pub. L. No. 109–177, § 117, 120 Stat. 192 (2006).

420. FBI Memorandum from Gen. Counsel, Nat'l Security Law Unit, Fed. Bureau of Investigation, to All Field Offices National Security Letter Matters, Ref: 66F-HQ-A1255972 Serial 15 (Nov. 28, 2001), at 2, available at www.sccounty01.co.santa-cruz.ca.us.

421. *Id.*

422. *Id.*, at 5.

423. *Id.*

424. Intelligence Authorization Act for Fiscal Year 2004, Pub. L. No. 108–177, § 374, 117 Stat. 2599 (2003) (codified as amended at 12 U.S.C. § 3414 (2000)) [hereinafter Intelligence Authorization Act]; *see also* Kim Zetter, *Bush Grabs New Power for FBI,* WIRED NEWS, Jan. 6, 2004, available at www.wired.com.

425. *See* Intelligence Authorization Act, *supra* note 424, § 374(d).

426. *See* 35 U.S.C. § 5312 (2000).

427. *House Approves Renewal of Patriot Act: Critics Voice Concern over Civil Liberties,* CNN.COM, July 22, 2005, www.cnn.com/2005/.

428. Author discussion with Sen. Ron Wyden, at Stanford Law School, in Palo Alto, Cal. (Feb. 17, 2006).

429. USA Patriot Improvement and Reauthorization Act of 2005, Pub. L. No. 109–177, § 118, 120 Stat. 192 (2006).

430. *Id.*, § 119.

431. *Id.*

432. *Id.*, §§ 119–20.

433. *Id.*, at § 120.

434. John Solomon & Barton Gellman, *Frequent Errors in FBI's Secret Records Requests: Audit Finds Possible Rule Violations,* WASH. POST, Mar. 9, 2007, at A01.

435. *Id.*

436. *Id.*

437. *Id.*

438. Press Release, Response to DOJ Inspector General's Report on FBI's Use of National Security Letters, Mar. 9, 2007, available at www.fbi.gov/pressrel/.

439. Telephone interview with Senator Diane Feinstein's office, Mar. 20, 2007, from Sunnyvale, California.

440. James Kuhnhenn, *Patriot Act Renewal Clears Hurdle in Senate*, MERCURY NEWS.COM, Feb. 16, 2006, www.mercurynews.com.

441. USA Patriot Improvement and Reauthorization Act § 115.

442. *How investigators Have Used the Patriot Act*, L. A. TIMES, Jul. 31, 2005, M3.

443. *Id.*

444. National Security Agency/Central Security Service, Transition 2001, Dec. 2000, marked "Secret," available at www.gwu.edu/ñsarchiv/.

445. James Risen & Eric Lichtblau, *Bush Lets U.S. Spy on Callers Without Courts*, N.Y. TIMES, Dec. 16, 2005, available at www.nytimes.com/2005/.

446. *Id.*

447. *Id.*

448. *Id.*

449. *American Civil Liberties Union v. National Sec. Agency*, 438 F.Supp.2d 754, E.D.Mich., 2006, Aug. 17, 2006.

450. Memorandum from Paul Wolfowitz, Deputy Sec'y of Def., to the Secretaries of the Military Dep'ts, Chairman of the Joint Chiefs of Staff, Under Sec'ys of Def., Assistant Sec'ys of Def., Gen. Counsel of the Dep't of Def., Inspector Gen. of the Dep't of Def., Assistants to the Sec'y of Def., Dirs. of the Def. Agencies, and Dirs. of the Dep't of Def. Field Activities, Collection, Reporting, and Analysis of Terrorist Threats to DoD within the United States (May 2, 2003), available at www.blogs.washingtonpost.com/earlywarning/ [hereinafter Wolfowitz Memo].

451. Michael Isikoff, *The Other Big Brother*, NEWSWEEK, Jan. 30, 2006, available at www.msnbc.msn.com.

452. *Id.*

453. *Id.*

454. Wolfowitz Memo, *supra* note 450, at 1.

455. *Id.*

456. *Id.*, at 2.

457. *Id.*, at 3.

458. *Id.*

459. *Id.*

460. Talon Report 902–03–02–05–071_full_text, Feb. 3, 2005; and Talon Report 902–21–04–05–358_full_text.txt, Apr. 21, 2005, available at www.sldn.org/binary-data/.

461. Talon Report 902–03–02–05–071_full_text, Feb. 3, 2005, available at www.sldn.org/binary-data/.

462. *Id.*, at 2.

463. *Id. See also* Talon Report 902–22–04–05–358_full_text.txt, Apr. 20, 2005, at 2, available at www.sldn.org/binary-data/.

464. Walter Pincus, *Pentagon Will Review Database on U.S. Citizens: Protests Among Acts Labeled 'Suspicious.'* WASH. POST, Dec. 15, 2005, at A1 [hereinafter Pincus, *Review*].

465. Robert Block & Jay Solomon, *Neighborhood Watch; Pentagon Steps Up Intelligence Efforts Inside U.S. Borders*, WALL STREET J., Apr. 27, 2006, at A1, available at www.nps.edu; Walter Pincus, *Pentagon Expanding its Domestic Surveillance Activity: Fears of Post-9/11 Terrorism Spur Proposals for New Powers*, WASH. POST, Nov. 27, 2005, at A6 [hereinafter Pincus, *Pentagon*].

466. Pincus, *Pentagon, supra* note 465.

467. *Id.*

468. Memo from Robert W. Noonan, Jr., Lieutenant General, GS, Deputy Chief of Staff for Intelligence, Department of the Army, RE: Collecting Information on U.S. Persons, Nov. 5, 2001, DAMI-CDC (25–30q), available at www.fas.org/irp/.

469. *Id.*

470. *Id.*

471. Block & Solomon, *supra* note 465.

472. *Id.*

473. Mark Hosenball, *America's Secret Police? Intelligence Experts Warn That a Proposal to Merge Two Pentagon Units Could Create an Ominous New Agency*, NEWSWEEK.COM, Apr. 14, 2006, www.msnbc.msn.com.

474. Walter Pincus, *Counterintelligence Officials Resign*, WASH. POST, Aug. 10, 2006, A01 [hereinafter Pincus, *Resign*]. *See also* Pincus, *Pentagon, supra* note 465; and Walter Pincus, *Defense Facilities Pass Along Reports of Suspicious Activity*, WASH. POST, Dec. 11, 2005, at A12 (discussing CIFA's expanded remit) [hereinafter Pincus, *Defense*].

475. Pincus, *Resign, supra* note 474.

476. Pincus, *Pentagon, supra* note 465 (quoting CIFA brochure).

477. *Id.*

478. Isikoff, *supra* note 451.

479. Isikoff, *supra* note 451.

480. Pincus, *Review, supra* note 464.

481. Isikoff, *supra* note 451.

482. *Id.*

483. *Id.*

484. Pincus, *Pentagon, supra* note 465.

485. *Id.*

486. *Id.*

487. *Id.*

488. *Id.*

489. Hosenball, *supra* note 473.

490. Eric Lichtblau & Mark Mazzetti, *Military Expands Intelligence Role in U.S.*, N.Y. TIMES, Jan. 14, 2007.

491. William M. Arkin, *Mission Creep Hits Home*, LA TIMES, Nov. 23, 2003.

492. Carroll Publishing, *Who's New in National Intelligence Organizations?*, available at www.carrollpub.com.

493. Pincus, *Review, supra* note 464. For hearings on the NSA program see, e.g., *An Examination of the Call to Censure the President: Hearing Before the S. Judiciary Comm.*, 109th Cong. (2006); *NSA III:; Wartime Executive Power and the NSA's Surveillance Authority II: Hearing Before the S. Judiciary Comm.*, 109th Cong. (2006); *Wartime Executive Power and the NSA's Surveillance Authority: Hearing Before the S. Judiciary Comm.*, 109th Cong. (2006).

494. Pincus, *Review, supra* note 464.

495. Pincus, *Defense, supra* note 474.

496. *See* Donohue, *supra* note 281.

497. Office of Legal Policy, U.S. Dep't of Justice, The Attorney General's Guidelines on General Crimes, Racketeering Enterprise and Terrorism Enterprise Investigations 6 (2002), available at www.usdoj.gov/olp/ [hereinafter AG Terrorism Guidelines].

498. Swire, *supra* note 364, at 1335.

499. *Id.*

500. AG Terrorism Guidelines, *supra* note 497, at 2.

501. *Id.*, at 17.

502. *Id.*, at 21.

503. *Id.*, at 21–22.

504. Eric Lichtblau, *FBI Scrutinizes Antiwar Rallies; Officials Say Effort Aims at 'Extremist Elements,'* N.Y. Times, Nov 23, 2003, §1, at 1.

505. Editorial, *FBI Files Are Chilling*, Contra Costa Times, July 22, 2005.

506. Neil King, Jr., *FBI's Wiretaps to Scan E-Mail Spark Concern*, Wall St. J., July 11, 2000, at A3.

507. Stephen P. Smith et al., Ill. Inst. of Tech., Chiicago-Kent College of Law, Independent Technical Review of the Carnivore System: Final Report viii (2000) (marked DOJ Sensitive; obtained by EPIC in 2004 FOIA request).

508. Graham B. Smith, Notes and Comments, *A Constitutional Critique of Carnivore, Federal Law Enforcement's Newest Electronic Surveillance Strategy*, 21 Loy. L.A. Ent. L. Rev. 481, 492 (2001). Full content communications collected under 18 U.S.C. §§ 2510–22 (2000) and 50 U.S.C. §§ 1801–29 (2000); address information taken under 18 U.S.C. §§ 3121–27 and 50 U.S.C. §§ 1841–46.

509. Robert Graham, Carnivore FAQ, available at www.corz.org/public/docs/.

510. Federal Bureau of Investigation, Carnivore/DCS-1000 Report to Congress 1 (2003) [hereinafter FBI Carnivore Report] (submitted to Judiciary Committees of the United States House of Representatives and United States Senate on Feb. 24, 2003 and Dec. 18, 2003). Both reports are available at www.epic.org/privacy/.

511. *See Fourth Amendment Issues Raised by the FBI's 'Carnivore' Program: Hearing Before the Subcomm. on the Constitution of the H. Comm. on the Judiciary*, 106th Cong. (2000), available at www.commdocs.house.gov/committee/; *Digital Privacy and the FBI's Carnivore Internet Surveillance Program: Hearing Before the S. Comm. on the Judiciary*, 106th Cong. (2000).

512. Smith, *supra* note 508, at 495.

513. *Id.*, Smith et al., *supra* note 507.

514. Smith, *supra* note 508, at 496.

515. *See* FBI Carnivore Report, *supra* note 510, at 1. There were five instances of use in FY 2002 and eight in FY 2003.

516. *See* Kevin Poulsen, *FBI Retires Its Carnivore*, Security Focus, Jan. 14, 2005, available at www.securityfocus.com/news/.

517. *See* Daniel J. Solove & Marc Rotenberg, Information Privacy Law (2006). (2003).

518. Peter J. Young, Note, *The Case Against Carnivore: Preventing Law Enforcement from Devouring Privacy*, 35 Ind. L. Rev. 303, 306 (2001).

519. *See* Elinor M. Abreu, *FBI Confirms Magic Lantern Exists*, Reuters, Dec. 12, 2001, *originally published at* www.msnbc.com/news/, currently available at www.commondreams.org (last visited Apr. 8, 2006); Alex Salkever, *A Dark*

Side to the FBI's Magic Lantern, BUSINESS WEEK ONLINE, Nov. 27, 2001, www.businessweek.com; Bob Sullivan, *FBI Software Cracks Encryption Wall*, MSNBC, Nov. 20, 2001, www.seclists.org/isn/; Robert Vamosi, *Commentary, Warning: the FBI Knows What You're Typing*, ZDNET, Dec. 4, 2001, www.zdnet. com.com.; *see also* Christopher Woo & Miranda So, Note, *The Case for Magic Lantern: September 11 Highlights the Need for Increased Surveillance*, 15 HARV. J.L. & TECH. 521, 521 (2002).

520. *See* Sullivan, *supra* note 519.

521. Woo & So, *supra* note 519, at 524 (citing Carrie Kirby, *Network Associates Mired in Security Debate*, S.F. CHRON., Nov. 28, 2001, at B1).

522. *United States v. Scarfo*, 180 F. Supp. 2d 572, 578 (D.N.J. 2001).

523. *Id.*, at 583.

524. STANLEY, *supra* note 18,, at 3.

525. Ritt Goldstein, *U.S. Planning to Recruit One in 24 Americans as Citizen Spies*, SYDNEY MORNING HERALD, July 15, 2002, at 2, available at www.smh.com.au/.

526. *Id.*

527. Editorial, *Ashcroft vs. Americans*, BOSTON GLOBE, July 17, 2002, at 22, available at www.commondreams.org; *see also* Editorial, *What is Operation TIPS?*, WASH. POST, July 14, 2002, at B6; Ellen Sorokin, *Planned Volunteer-Informant Corps Elicits '1984' Fears; Accessing Private Homes is Objective of 'Operation TIPS,'* WASH. TIMES, July 16, 2002, at A3, available at www.commondreams.org.

528. Adam Clymer, *Ashcroft Defends Plan for National Hotline on Terrorism*, N.Y. TIMES, July 25, 2002, available at www.nytimes.com.

529. *See, e.g.*, William Matthews, *Ashcroft: No Central Database for Citizen Tips*, FCW.COM, July 29, 2002, www.fcw.com/fcw/articles/.

530. *See* H.R. REP. 108–2555, §880 (2003) (Conf. Rep.) available at www.ala.org.

531. STANLEY, *supra* note 38518, at 5.

532. Press Release, The White House, President Promotes Citizen Corps for Safer Communities (Apr. 8, 2002), www.whitehouse.gov/news/.

533. Highway Watch Fact Sheet, www.highwaywatch.com (last visited April 2005). *See also* www.tmta.com/Resources/News/.

534. Highway Watch, Transportation Security Administration and the American Trucking Associations Team up to Prevent and Respond to Possible Terrorist Threats, www.highwaywatch.com/announcements/tsa.html (last visited Mar. 5, 2006).

535. STANLEY, *supra* note 18, at 5 n.11.

536. *See, e.g.*, Neighborhood Crime Watch, Anchorage Police Dep't, www.muni. org/apd2/ (extolling the virtues of the Anchorage neighborhood watch program) (last visited Apr. 8, 2006); Neighborhood Watch, City of San Diego, www.sandiego.gov (underscoring the value of the San Diego neighborhood watch program) (last visited Apr. 8, 2006); Neighborhood Watch, Lane County, Or., www.co.lane.or.us (referring to Neighborhood Watch as "a proven crime-reduction program.") (last visited Apr. 8, 2006).

537. U.S. Air Force Eagle Eyes, available at www.osi.andrews.af.mil.

538. U.S. Air Force Office of Special Investigations, Eagle Eyes Program, www.public. afosi.amc.af.mil/ (last visited Mar. 5, 2006).

539. *See, e.g.*, STEVEN GREER, SUPERGRASSES: A STUDY IN ANTI-TERRORIST LAW ENFORCEMENT IN NORTHERN IRELAND (1995).

540. STANLEY, *supra* note 18, at 8.

541. *Id.*

542. *Id.*, at 8–9.

543. *Id.*, at 4.

544. Nat'l Crime Prevention Council, United for a Stronger America: Citizens' Preparedness Guide 12 (2002), available at www.ojp.usdoj.gov/ojpcorp/.

545. *Id.*, at 18.

546. *Id.*, at 6.

547. *Id.*, at 15.

548. *Church Committee Vol. 5, supra* note 247.

549. *Id.*, at 30–33.

550. U.S. Gen. Accounting Office, Information Technology: Terrorist Watch Lists Should Be Consolidated to Promote Better Integration and Sharing 12 (2003), available at www.gao.gov/new.items; *see also Progress in Consolidating Terrorist Watchlists – The Terrorist Screening Center (TSC): Joint Hearing Before the Subcomm. on Crime, Terrorism, and Homeland Security of the H. Comm. on the Judiciary and the Subcomm. on Intelligence and Counterterrorism of the H. Select Comm. on Homeland Security*, 108th Cong. 8–13 (2004) (statement of Donna A. Bucella, Dir., Terrorist Screening Ctr., Fed. Bureau of Investigation) (discussing Terrorist Screening Center watch list derived from Terrorist Threat Integration Center's main database); *Review: 'No-fly list' Lacks Rules, Procedures: Watch List Meant to Stop Terrorists from Flying Is Under Scrutiny*, CNN.com, Oct. 10, 2004, www.cnn.com.

551. Eric Lichtblau, *Inquiry Finds a Weakness in Terror Watch List*, N.Y. Times, June 14, 2005, A12.

552. *Morning Edition*, "Problems Plague 'No-Fly' List, TSA Considers Changes." (Nat'l Pub. Radio radio broadcast, Apr. 26, 2005).

553. Telephone interview with Thomas R. Burke, Partner, Davis Wright Tremaine LLP, in Palo Alto, Cal. (May 5, 2005).

554. Bob Cuddy & Angilee Shah, *Jan Adams & Rebecca Gordon, in* Am. Civil Liberties Union of N. Cal., Caught in the Backlash: Stories from Northern California (2002), available at www.aclunc.org/issues (last visited Apr. 15, 2006); Sara Kehaulani Goo, *Sen. Kennedy Flagged by No-Fly List*, Wash. Post, Aug. 20, 2004, at A01; Interview with David Cole, Professor of Law, Georgetown Univ. Law Ctr., in Palo Alto, Cal. (Sept. 17, 2005).

555. James Bovard, *The Surveillance State*, Am. Conservative, May 19, 2003, at 10; interview with Cole, *supra* note 554.

556. *See Review: 'No-fly list' Lacks Rules, Procedures, supra* note 550.

557. ACLU of Northern Calif., No-Fly Lawsuit Client Biography: David C. Nelson, www.aclunc.org/911/ (last visited Mar. 5, 2006).

558. Robert O'Harrow, Jr., *Intricate Screening of Fliers in Works*, Wash. Post, Feb. 1, 2002, at A1.

559. *Id.*

560. *See Id.*

561. *Id.* Emphasis added.

562. Cynthia L. Webb, *Uncle Sam Mothballs Screening Program*, Wash. Post.com, July 16, 2004, www.washingtonpost.com.

563. *Compare* Secure Flight Program: Test Phase: Privacy Impact Assessment, 69 Fed. Reg. 57,352 (Sept. 24, 2004), *with* Privacy Act of 1974: System of Records; Secure Flight Test Records, 69 Fed. Reg. 57,345 (Sept. 24, 2004).

564. Mark Clayton, *U.S. Plans Massive Data Sweep*, Christian Science Monitor, Feb. 9, 2006, available at www.csmonitor.com.

565. *Homeland Security Team to Focus on American Terrorists*, USA TODAY, May 14, 2007, at 6A. *See also* Carroll Publishing, Who's New in National Intelligence Organizations?, available at www.carrollpub.com.

566. Hall, *supra* note 565.

567. U.S. GEN. ACCOUNTING OFFICE, REPORT TO THE RANKING MINORITY MEMBER, SUB-COMMITTEE ON FINANCIAL MANAGEMENT, THE BUDGET, AND INTERNATIONAL SECU-RITY, COMMITTEE ON GOVERNMENTAL AFFAIRS, U.S. SENATE: DATA MINING: FED-ERAL EFFORTS COVER A WIDE RANGE OF USES 2 (2004) [HEREINAFTER DATA MINING REPORT].

568. *Id.*

569. For discussion of quantum leap, *e.g.*, *see* Bill Powell, *How George Tenet Brought the CIA Back From the Dead*, FORTUNE, Sept. 29, 2003, at 129, 134; Michael J. Sniffen, *Controversial Terror Research Lives On*, WASH. POST., Feb. 23, 2004, available at www.washingtonpost.com.

570. DATA MINING REPORT, *supra* note 567, at 11.

571. DATA MINING REPORT, *supra* note 567, at 12.

572. Robert O'Harrow, Jr., *U.S. Hopes to Check Computers Globally*, WASH. POST, Nov 12, 2002, at A4; John Markoff, *Pentagon Plans A Computer System that Would Peek at Personal Data of Americans*, N.Y. TIMES, Nov. 9, 2002, at A12; *see also* TIA REPORT, *supra* note 8, at 1. INFO. AWARENESS OFFICE, DEF. ADVANCED RESEARCH PROJECT AGENCY, REPORT TO CONGRESS REGARDING THE TERRORISM INFORMATION AWARENESS PROGRAM: DETAILED INFORMATION 1 (May 20, 2003), available at www.globalsecurity.org [hereinafter TIA REPORT]. For a thoughtful discussion of the privacy issues raised by TIA and subsequent data-mining efforts, *see* James X. Dempsey & Lara M. Flint, *Commercial Data and Nat'l Sec.*, 72 GEO. WASH. L. REV. 1459 (2004).

573. *See* THE INTENSIFICATION OF SURVEILLANCE: CRIME, TERRORISM AND WARFARE IN THE INFORMATION AGE 3 (Kirstie Ball & Frank Webster, eds., 2003).

574. *See, e.g.*, Warblogging.com, Who is John Poindexter?, www.warblogging.com (last visited Apr. 15, 2006); Peter Barnes, *Tracking John Poindexter*, TECH LIVE WASHINGTON, D.C., Dec. 20, 2002, available at www.g4tv.com.

575. Department of Defense Appropriations Act, Pub. L. No. 108–87, 117 Stat. 1054 (2004).

576. Sniffen, *supra* note 569.

577. Shane Harris, *TIA Lives On*, NATIONAL JOURNAL, Feb. 23, 2006, available at www.nationaljournal.com.

578. *Id.*

579. *Id.*

580. *Id.*

581. *Id.*

582. *Id.*

583. *Id.*

584. *Id.*

585. *Id.*

586. *Id.* Shane Harris, *TIA Lives On*, NATIONAL JOURNAL, Feb. 23, 2006, available at www.nationaljournal.com.

587. DEP'T OF DEF., TECHNOLOGY AND PRIVACY ADVISORY COMMITTEE CHARTER (2003), available at www.faca.disa.mil/.

588. TECH. & PRIVACY ADVISORY COMM., SAFEGUARDING PRIVACY IN THE FIGHT AGAINST TERRORISM: REPORT OF THE TECHNOLOGY AND PRIVACY ADVISORY COMMITTEE viii

(2004), available at www.cdt.org/security [hereinafter TAPAC 2004 REPORT]. *See also* Ryan Singel & Noah Shachtman, *Army Admits Using JetBlue Data*, WIRED NEWS, Sept. 23, 2003, http://www.wired.com/news/privacy/0,1848,60540,00. html; Ryan Singel, *JetBlue Shared Passenger Data*, WIRED NEWS, Sept. 18, 2003, www.wired.com/news/; Sara K. Goo, *Northwest Gave U.S. Data on Passengers*, WASH. POST, Jan. 18, 2004, at A1; John Schwartz et al., *Airlines Gave F.B.I. Millions of Records on Travelers After 9/11*, N.Y. TIMES, May 1, 2004, at A10; Electronic Privacy Information Center, Northwest Airlines' Disclosure of Passenger Data to Federal Agencies, www.epic.org/privacy/ (last visited Mar. 6, 2006); *American Released Passenger Data*, ASSOCIATED PRESS, Apr 10, 2004, www.wired.com/news/.

589. TAPAC 2004 Report, *supra* note 588, at viii. The report recognized that although data mining may be a "vital tool in the fight against terrorism...when used in connection with personal data concerning U.S. persons, data mining can present significant privacy issues." *Id.*

590. Homeland Security Act of 2002, Pub. L. No. 107–296, § 201(d)(1), 116 Stat. 2135, 2146 (codified as amended at 6 U.S.C. § 121 (Supp. 2002)).

591. GINA M. STEVENS, PRIVACY: TOTAL INFORMATION AWARENESS PROGRAMS AND RELATED INFORMATION ACCESS, COLLECTION, AND PROTECTION LAWS, RL 31730, at 20 (2003) (citing Homeland Security Act, § 201(d)(14), 116 Stat. at 2147 (codified as amended at 6 U.S.C. § 121 (Supp. 2002)).

592. Clayton, *supra* note 564; *see Hearing Before H. Comm. on Science*, 109th Cong. (2005) (statement of Dr. Charles McQueary, Under Sec'y for Sci. and Tech., Dep't of Homeland Sec.) (referencing ADVISE knowledge-generating architecture and highlighting plans to use it to "Create a National Homeland Security Support System (NH3S)"), available at www.house.gov/science/.

593. SANDIA NAT'L LABS. & LAWRENCE LIVERMORE NAT'L LAB., DATA SCIENCES TECHNOLOGY FOR HOMELAND SECURITY INFORMATION MANAGEMENT AND KNOWLEDGE DISCOVERY 6, 7 (2004), available at www.csmr.ca.sandia.gov.

594. Clayton, *supra* note 564.

595. DATA SCIENCES, *supra* note 593, at 6–11.

596. Clayton, *supra* note 564.

597. *Id.*

598. *Id.* In addition to the federal efforts that continue apace, many states have initiatives that mirror TIA aims. *See, e.g.*, Line56.com, E-Business Company Profiles, www.line56.com/directory/ (last visited Mar. 4, 2006); SEISINT INC., SEISINT'S FACTS FOR THE MATRIX PROJECT 8 (2003), available at www.aclu.org/FilesPDFs/.; STANLEY, *supra* note 38518, at 26 n.108 (citing INST. FOR INTERGOVERNMENTAL RESEARCH, APPLICATION FOR FEDERAL ASSISTANCE TO THE OFFICE OF JUSTICE PROGRAMS BUREAU OF JUSTICE ASSISTANCE (2002)); Brian Robinson, *Reenter the Matrix*, FED. COMP. WEEK.COM, Aug. 30, 2004, www.fcw.com; Press Release, LexisNexis Completes Acquisition of Seisint, Inc.: Acquisition Enhances Ability to Provide Customers with Powerful, Fast and Easy-to-Use Risk Management Products and Services (Sept. 1, 2004), available at www.accurint.com/news/ (last visited Apr. 7, 2006). Anita Ramasastry, *Why We Should Fear the Matrix*, FIND LAW, Nov. 5, 2003, available at www.writ.news.findlaw.com; Briefing by Seisent, Inc., Matrix Michigan Briefing, slide "Seisint's Core Capabilities" (May 8, 2003), available at www.aclu.org/privacy/ (last visited Apr. 7, 2006); Multistate Anti-Terrorism Information Exchange, www.matrix-at.org (last visited Apr. 8, 2006; and Donohue, *supra* note 281.

599. Office of Homeland Sec., National Strategy for Homeland Security 55 (2002) available at www.whitehouse.gov.

600. *Id.*, at 56.

601. *Homeland Security Team to focus on American Terrorists, supra* note 465.

602. *Id.*

603. *See* Big Brother 101, Popular Science, Aug. 2006, pp. 70–71.

604. Anne Joseph O'Connell, *The Architecture of Smart Intelligence: Structuring and Overseeing Agencies in the Post-9/11 World,* 94 Cal. L. Rev. 1655 (2006), citing Bert Chapman, Researching National Security and Intelligence Policy 234–43 (2004). On the House side, the Appropriations, Armed Services, Budget, Energy and Commerce, Government Reform, Homeland Security, International Relations, and Judiciary Standing Committees, as well as the House Permanent Select Committee on Intelligence oversee some part of the intelligence community. On the Senate side, Appropriations, Armed Services, Budget, Energy and Natural Resources, Foreign Relations, Homeland Security and Governmental Affairs, and Judiciary Standing Committees and the Senate Select Committee on Intelligence have some jurisdiction. O'Connell, at 1662–63.

605. O'Connell, *supra* note 604, at 1663.

606. Numbers calculated from data provided by the Washington University and Pennsylvania State University joint project, available at www.policyagendas.org.

607. *Id.*

608. *Id.*

609. For a concise statement of the conservative claim, see Robert F. Turner, *FISA vs. the Constitution, Opinion,* Wall St. J., Dec. 28, 2005, at A14.

610. Eric Lichtblau, *Despite a Year of Ire and Angst, Little Has Changed on Wiretaps,* N. Y. Times, Nov. 25, 2006, A1.

611. Rules of the House of Representatives, 108th Cong., prepared by Jeff Trandahl, Clerk of the House of Representatives, Jan. 7, 2003, Rules X, XI, available at http://www.rules.house.gov/ruleprec/108rules.pdf.

612. Author interview with Senator Ron Wyden, at Stanford University, spring 2006.

613. Author interview with former Stanford University President Gerhard Casper, relaying comments made by Rep. Waxman to Stanford University program in Washington, D.C., at Stanford University, March 16, 2007.

614. U.S. General Accounting Office, Central Intelligence Agency: Observations on GAO Access to Information on CIA Programs and Activities; Statement of Henry L. Hinton, Jr., Managing Director Defense Capabilities and Management, July 18, 2001, at 1.

615. The Commission on the Intelligence Capabilities of the United States Regarding Weapons of Mass Destruction, Report to the President of the United States, Mar. 31, 2005, at 20, available at www.wmd.gov (writing, "Either the Intelligence Community is inherently resistant to outside recommendations, or it lacks the institutional capacity to implement them. In either case, sustained external oversight is necessary."); and The 9/11 Commission Report: Final Report of the National Commission on Terrorist Attacks upon the United States, Executive Summary (stating, "The United States needs a strong, stable, and capable congressional committee structure to give America's national intelligence agencies oversight, support, and leadership."); the 9/11 Commission Report, (2004), § 13.4 Unity of Effort in the Congress: Strengthen Congressional Oversight of Intelligence and Homeland Security, available at www.9–11commission.gov.

616. Intelligence Reform Act, 118 Stat. at 3649, 3673.

617. H Res 35: To enhance intelligence oversight authority. 110th Cong., Jan. 5, 2007.

618. Although the Senate made some motions toward addressing the issue of committee oversight, as of April 2007 it has adopted no permanent changes. See S. Res. 445, 108th Cong (2004), *Unfinished Intelligence Work*, N.Y. Times, Oct. 11, 2004, and O'Connell, *supra* note 604, at 1671.

619. RIPA, *supra* note 78, §8.

620. RIPA, *supra* note 78, § 8(4).

621. Author interview with former Director of GCHQ Mar. 16, 2007, by telephone, Stanford, California.

622. Report of the Senate Select Committee on Intelligence to Accompany 3237, at section 408, 433.

623. Exec. Order 12863, and President's Foreign Intelligence Advisory Board, available at www.whitehouse.gov/pfiab/.

624. Executive Order 12863, President's Foreign Intelligence Advisory Board, Sept. 13, 1993, available at www.fas.org/irp/.

625. President's Foreign Intelligence Advisory Board, available at www.whitehouse. gov/pfiab/.

626. Exec. Order 12,863. *See also* Executive Order No. 10656 of February 6, 1956; Executive Order No. 10938 of May 4, 1961; Executive Order No. 12334 of December 4, 1981, and Executive Order No. 12537 of October 28, 1985.

627. RIPA, *supra* note 78, §5 (2).

628. *Arizona v. Evans*, 514 U.S. 1 (1995).

629. *Id.*, at 22 (Stevens, J., dissenting).

630. *Id.*, at 25 (Ginsburg, J., dissenting) (quoting *State v. Evans*, 177 Ariz. 201, 204 (Ariz. 1994)).

631. STRUM, *supra* note 238, at 133.

632. PRIVY COUNSELLOR REVIEW COMM., *supra* note 101, at 25–26.

633. *See also* Roger Clarke, *Information Technology and Dataveillance*, *in* CONTROVERSIES IN COMPUTING 10 (C. Dunlop & R. Kling eds., 1991), available at www. anu.edu.au/.

634. *Toyosaburo Korematsu v. United States*, 323 U.S. 214, 65 S. Ct. 193 (1944).

635. STRUM, *supra* note 238, at 134.

636. American Civil Liberties Union, List of Communities That Have Passed Resolutions, www.aclu.org (last visited Apr. 16, 2006).

637. *See, e.g.*, Jeff Johnson, *Congressional Opponents Lash Out at PATRIOT Act, Ashcroft*, CNSNEWS.COM, Sept. 25, 2003, www.cnsnews.com; *Learning Activity*, CNN STUDENTNEWS, Sept. 8, 2003, www.cnn.com/2003.

638. United States Department of Justice, Preserving Life and Liberty, www. lifeandliberty.gov (last visited Mar. 6, 2006).

639. *Church Committee Vol. 5*, *supra* note 247, at 390. The Army undertook extensive LSD testing toward the same ends.

640. *Id.*, at 393.

641. *Id.*, at 394.

642. Jay Stanley & Barry Steinhardt, Am. Civil Liberties Union, *Bigger Monster, Weaker Chains: The Growth of an American Surveillance Society*, 8 (2003), at 14, available at www.aclu.org.

643. WESTIN, *supra* note 3, at 323.

644. WHITFIELD DIFFIE & SUSAN LANDAU, PRIVACY ON THE LINE: THE POLITICS OF WIRE-TAPPING AND ENCRYPTION (1998), at 42.

645. *Id.*

646. *See* Duncan Campbell, IPTV Ltd., Interception Capabilities 2000 (1999) available at www.cyber-rights.org; Steve Wright, Omega Found., European Parliament, An Appraisal of Technologies of Political Control (Dick Holdsworth ed. 1998), available at www.statewatch.org.

647. *Encryption: Individual Right to Privacy vs. National Security: Hearing Before the Subcommittee on International Economic Policy and Trade of the Committee on International Relations,* 105th Cong. (1997).

648. *Id.,* at 9.

5. Terrorist Speech and Free Expression

The following are the sources of the epigraphs: US Constitution, 1st Amendment; Al Qaeda Manual, UK/BM-3; European Convention on Human Rights, Nov. 4, 1950, Article 10; Douglas Hurd, UK Home Secretary, October 20, 1988, quoted in the INTERNATIONAL HERALD TRIBUNE, Oct. 20, 1988, at 2; UK Public Order Act 1986, c. 64, §4A.

1. Dennis Pluchinsky, *They Heard it All Here, and That's the Trouble,* WASH. POST, June 16, 2002, at B03.

2. AL QAEDA MANUAL, UK/BM-80–81, www.usdoj.gov (last visited July 21, 2005); *see also* Steve Mckenzie, *War on Terrorism: Laden's Blueprint to Destroy West; Trainees Told to Slaughter US Like Lambs,* SUNDAY MAIL, Jan. 6, 2002, at 9.

3. AL QAEDA MANUAL, *supra* note 2, at UK/BM-3.

4. *Id.*

5. Robert D. McFadden, *Times and The Washington Post Grant Mail Bomber's Demand,* N.Y. TIMES, SEPT. 19, 1995, at A1.

6. *Brandenburg v. Ohio,* 395 U.S. 444 (1969).

7. Alien Act, ch. 58, 1 Stat. 570 (1798); Sedition Act, ch. 74, § 2, 1 Stat. 596, 596–97 (1798).

8. *See* GEOFFREY STONE, PERILOUS TIMES (2005) at 67.

9. For discussion of the political fallout that ensued see MICHAEL KENT CURTIS, FREE SPEECH, "THE PEOPLE'S DARLING PRIVILEGE": STRUGGLES FOR FREEDOM OF EXPRESSION IN AMERICAN HISTORY 52–116 (2000), STONE, *supra* 8, at 44–73; Gregg Costa, *John Marshall, the Sedition Act, and Free Speech in the Early Republic.* 77 TEX. L. REV. 1011, 1030–31 (1999).

10. STONE, *supra* note 8, at 73 (citation omitted).

11. *Id.*

12. An Act Relating to Habeas Corpus, and Regulating Judicial Proceedings in Certain Cases, March 3, 1863, ch. 81, § 2, 12 Stat. 755, 756 (1863); *see also* US CONST. art. I, § 9.

13. James Parker Hall, *Free Speech in War Time,* 21 COLUM. L. REV. 526 (1921), at 527.

14. *Id.,* at 528.

15. *Id.,* at 527.

16. STONE, *supra* note 8, at 137 (citation omitted).

17. Espionage Act of June 15, 1917, ch. 30, tit. I, § 3, 40 Stat. 217, 219.

18. *Id.*

19. STONE, *supra* note 8, at 150.

20. STONE, *supra* note 8, at 156–58.
21. *Id.,* at 171 (quoting *Shaffer v. United States,* 255 F. 886 (9th Cir 1919)).
22. *Id.,* at 173.
23. *Masses Publishing Co. v. Patten,* 244 F. 535 (S.D.N.Y 1917), *rev'd.,* 246 F. 24 (2d Cir. 1917).
24. *Id.,* at 540–41.
25. STONE, *supra* note 8, at 186.
26. Sedition Act, ch. 75, § 3, 40 Stat. 553 (1918).
27. *Schenck v. United States,* 249 U.S. 47, 51 (1919).
28. *Id.,* at 52.
29. 249 U.S. 204 (1919).
30. *Frohwerk v. United States,* 249 U.S. 204, 208–09 (1919).
31. *Debs v. United States,* 249 U.S. 211, 214 (1919).
32. 250 US 616 (1919). For the text of the circular see Zechariah Chafee Jr., *A Contemporary State Trial – the United States versus Jacob Abrams et al.* 33 HARV. L. REV. 747, 748 n.2 (1920).
33. 249 U.S. 182 (1919).
34. *Abrams,* 250 U.S. at 628 (Holmes, J., dissenting).
35. *Id.*
36. *See, e.g.,* John H. Wigmore, *Abrams v. U.S.: Freedom of Speech and Freedom of Thuggery in War Time and Peace-Time,* 14 ILL. L. REV. 539 (1920).
37. STONE, *supra* note 8, at 220–22.
38. *Id.,* at 221.
39. *Id.,* at 223.
40. *Id.*
41. *Id.,* at 224.
42. *Gitlow v. New York,* 268 U.S. 652 (1925).
43. *Gitlow,* 268 U.S. at 668–70.
44. *Gitlow,* 268 U.S. at 668–70, 672–73 (Holmes, J., dissenting).
45. *Whitney v. California,* 274 U.S. 357 (1927).
46. *See Herndon v. Lowry,* 301 U.S. 242 (1937); *De Jonge v. Oregon,* 299 U.S. 353 (1937); *Fiske v. Kansas,* 274 U.S. 380 (1927).
47. *Bridges v. California,* 314 U.S. 252, 263 (1941).
48. Smith Act of 1940, ch. 439, 54 Stat. 670 (1940).
49. Smith Act of 1940, ch. 439, 54 Stat. 670 (1940).
50. Subversive Activities Control Act of 1950, ch. 1024, tit. I, 64 Stat. 987.
51. Communist Control Act of 1954, ch. 886, 68 Stat 775 (1954).
52. 100 CONG. REC. S15121 (1954).
53. *Dennis v. United States,* 341 U.S. 494 (1951).
54. *Dennis,* 341 U.S. at 510. Although Chief Justice Vinson, who authored *Dennis,* claimed to be using Holmes's clear and present danger test, he cited Hand's opinion in *Gitlow. Gitlow v. New York,* 268 U.S. 652 (1925).
55. *Dennis,* 341 U.S at 519 (Frankfurter, J., concurring).
56. STONE, *supra* note 8, at 330.
57. *Dennis,* 341 U.S. at 564, 570 (Jackson, J., concurring).
58. STONE, *supra* note 8, at 348–52.
59. *Id.,* at 352.
60. *Brandenburg,* 395 U.S. 444.
61. *Brandenburg,* 395 U.S. at 447.
62. *Hess v. Indiana,* 414 U.S. 105 (1973).

63. STONE, *supra* note 8, at 13, 73–76, 528–30.

64. *Watts v. United States*, 394 U.S. 705 (1969).

65. 2 FREDERICK POLLOCK & FREDERIC WILLIAM MAITLAND, THE HISTORY OF ENGLISH LAW BEFORE THE TIME OF EDWARD I503 n.2 (2d ed. 1968) (citing Glanville, i. 2); *see also* J. G. BELLAMY, THE LAW OF TREASON IN ENGLAND IN THE LATER MIDDLE AGES (1970); MICHAEL SUPPERSTONE, BROWNLIE'S LAW OF PUBLIC ORDER AND NATIONAL SECURITY 230–45 (Butterworths 2d ed. 1981).

66. 2 SIR JAMES FITZJAMES STEPHEN, A HISTORY OF THE CRIMINAL LAW OF ENGLAND 299–300 (London, MacMillan 1883), at 62.

67. 4 JUDGE STEPHEN, MR. SERJEANT STEPHEN'S NEW COMMENTARIES ON THE LAWS OF ENGLAND 138 (Butterworth & Co. 16th ed. 1914).

68. Treason Act, 1351, 25 Edw. 3, c. 2.

69. 2 STEPHEN, *supra* note 66, at 241–242, 263.

70. 2 POLLOCK & MAITLAND, *supra* note 65, at 500.

71. 4 WILLIAM BLACKSTONE, COMMENTARIES ON THE LAWS OF ENGLAND 160–61 (University of Chicago Press, photo. reprint 1979) (1769), at 92.

72. *See* BELLAMY, *supra* note 65; RANULF DE GLANVILLE, THE TREATISE ON THE LAWS AND CUSTOMS OF THE REALM OF ENGLAND (G.D.G. Hall, ed., Nelson 1965); MATTHEW HALE, THE HISTORY AND ANALYSIS OF THE COMMON LAW OF ENGLAND (Lawbook Exchange 2000) (London 1713); 2 STEPHEN, *supra* note 66, at 241–84.

73. Treason Act, 1795, 36 Geo. 3, c. 7.

74. Treason Felony Act, 1848, 11 & 12 Vic., c. 12. This included printing, writing, or engaging in any act to convince anyone to "compel [the monarch] to change his methods or counsels, or, in order to put force or constraint upon, or to intimidate or overawe, either House of parliament." JUDGE STEPHEN, *supra* note 67, at 147.

75. Crime and Disorder Act, 1998, c. 37, § 36.

76. *R. (on the application of Rusbridger) v. Attorney Gen.*, [2002] EWCA (Civ) 397, [1].

77. *Id.* (formatting omitted).

78. *Id.*, at [4].

79. *Id.*, at [16].

80. *Id.*, at [21].

81. *Id.*, at [23].

82. *Id.*, at [24].

83. A.V. DICEY, INTRODUCTION TO THE STUDY OF THE LAW OF THE CONSTITUTION, (8th ed. 1915); at 269 (citations omitted).

84. *Beatty v. Gillbanks*, (1882) 9 Q.B.D. 308.

85. *Id.*, at 314 (Field, J.)

86. *Reg. v. Justices of Londonderry* (1891) 28 L.R. Ir. 440, 450 (O'Brien, J.).

87. DICEY, *supra* note,83, at 273.

88. *Id.*, at 175; *see also O'Kelly v. Harvey*, (1883) 14 L.R. Ir. 105.

89. Civil Authorities (Special Powers) Act, 1922, 12 & 13 Geo. 5, c. 5, (N. I.) [hereinafter SPA].

90. SPA, § 2, ¶ 4.

91. Memo. at the Ministry of Home Affairs, PRONI HA/32/1/465.

92. Public Order Act, 1951, 14 & 15 Geo. 6, c. 19 (N. Ir.).

93. *Id.*, § 3.

94. S.R.O. 173/196626.7.1966.

95. S.R.O. 312/1969, B.G. 28.11.1969.

96. S.R.O. 198/1970, 23.7.1970.

97. *See* Laura K. Donohue, Counter-terrorist Law and Emergency Powers in the United Kingdom 1922–2000 (2000).

98. Letter from The Coleraine Drumming Club to the Ministry of Home Affairs, Northern Ireland, Public Records Office Northern Ireland.

99. Letter from The Falls Road Methodists to the Ministry of Home Affairs, Northern Ireland, Public Records Office Northern Ireland. *See also* Letter from Brown's Dental Depot to Minister of Home Affairs, 6 March 1926, PRONI HA/32/1/295.

100. Letter from D.G. Evans to the Minister of Home Affairs, 4 March 1948, PRONI HA/32/1/475.

101. Northern Ireland (Emergency Provisions) Act, 1973, c. 53, § 21.

102. *Id.*, § 22.

103. Defence of the Realm Consolidation Act, 1914, 5 Geo. 5, c. 8.

104. Emergency Powers Act, 1920, 10 & 11 Geo. 5, c. 55.

105. K.D. Ewing & C.A. Gearty, The Struggle for Civil Liberties, Political Freedom and the Rule of Law in Britain, 1914–45 (2000), pp. 94 et seq.

106. Public Order Act, 1936, Edw. 1, c. 8 & Geo. 6, c. 62, § 5.

107. *Id.*

108. K.D. Ewing & C.A. Gearty, Freedom under Thatcher: Civil Liberties in Modern Britain (1990), at 87.

109. Public Order Act, 1936, Section 5, amended in 1965. *See Id.*

110. Ewing & Gearty, *supra* note 108, at 90 (citing R. v. Howell, [1982] Q.B. 416).

111. *See, e.g., Thomas v. Sawkins*, [1935] 2 K.B. 249; *Duncan v. Jones*, [1936] 1 K.B. 218; *Piddington v. Bates*, [1960] 3 All ER 660 (Q.B.D.).

112. Public Order Act, 1986, c. 64, §§ 1, 2.

113. *Id.*, §§ 12, 14.

114. Ewing & Gearty, *supra* note 108, at 119.

115. Public Order Act, 1986, c. 64, § 5(1) (emphasis added).

116. *Masterson v. Holden*, [1986] 1 W.L.R. 1017.

117. Ewing & Gearty, *supra* note 108, at 123 (quoting *Letter from the Irish Freedom Movement*, Independent, Sept. 12, 1988).

118. *Id. Chaplinsky v. New Hampshire*, 315 U.S. 568 (1942).

119. *But see Terminiello v. Chicago*, 337 U.S. 1 (1949); *R.A.V. v. City of St. Paul*, 505 U.S. 377 (1992); *Virginia v. Black*, 538 U.S. 343 (2003). For a lower court decision granting similar deference to hate speech on constitutional grounds see *Village of Skokie v. National Socialist Party of America*, 373 N.E.2d 21 (Ill. 1978).

120. Race Relations Act, 1965, c. 73, § 6(1).

121. Public Order Act, 1986, c. 64, §§ 5, 6; Protection From Harassment Act, 1997, c. 40, § 7.

122. *Jersild v. Denmark*, App. No. 15890/89, 19 Eur. H.R. Rep. 1 (1994).

123. *Percy v. Director of Public Prosecutions* [2001] EWHC (Q.B.) 1125; *see also* C.A. Gearty, Principles of Human Rights Adjudication 55 (2004).

124. *Westminster City Council v. Haw*, [2002] All ER 59 (Gray J.); *see also* Gearty, *supra* note 123, at 55.

125. European Convention for the Protection of Human Rights & Fundamental Freedoms, art. 10(2), Nov. 4, 1950, available at www.echr.coe.int/.

126. David Feldman, Civil Liberties and Human Rights in England and Wales (2d ed. 2002), at 34–112, 756–757.

127. JUDGE STEPHEN, *supra* note 67, at 149–50.

128. *Id.*, at 150.

129. *Id.*

130. 5 WILLIAM BLACKSTONE, COMMENTARIES 151–52 (St. George Tucker ed., William Young Birch & Abraham Small, 1803).

131. *Id.*, at 152.

132. 2 STEPHEN, *supra* note 66, at 355–59.

133. Michael Lobban, *From Seditious Libel to Unlawful Assembly: Peterloo and the Changing Face of Political Crime c. 1770–1820*, 10 OXFORD J. LEGAL STUD. 307–52 (1990).

134. 2 STEPHEN, *supra* note 66, at 379.

135. *Id.*, at 380.

136. *Id.*, at 386.

137. *See, e.g.*, *Hector v. Attorney-General of Antigua and Barbuda* (1990) 2 AC 312; EWING & GEARTY, *supra* note 108, at 136–144.

138. Regulation 26(1) and 26(2), S.R.O. 137/1943, Dec. 13, 1943.

139. S.R.O. 40/1971, Jan. 29, 1971.

140. *Id.*

141. DONOHUE, *supra* note 97, at 88–90.

142. S.R.O. 58/1930, Feb. 5, 1930.

143. Memorandum at the Ministry of Home Affairs, PRONI HA/32/1/627 (27 May 1930).

144. Memorandum from E.W. Shewell at the Ministry of Home Affairs, PRONI HA/32/1/569 (27 May 1930).

145. List of Films banned by the Home Office, PRONI HA/32/1/569.

146. DONOHUE, *supra* note 97, at 94.

147. Prevention of Terrorism (Temporary Provisions) Act, 1984, c.8.

148. *Id.*, § 11.

149. EWING & GEARTY, *supra* note 108, at 241–2.

150. Margaret Thatcher, HC Debs, Vol. 130, Col. 194, 22 Mar. 1988.

151. INT'L HERALD TRIB., Oct. 20, 1988, at 2.

152. *The British Broadcasting Ban: An Update*, CENSORSHIP NEWS, October 1991, available at www.article19.org (last visited December 1, 2004).

153. *See* 139 PARL. DEB., H.C. (6th ser.) (1988) 1082.

154. *Id.*, at 1128.

155. Annette Gartland, *Terrorist Ban Hits Pop Song*, THE OBSERVER, Nov. 20, 1988, at 4.

156. *1991: Birmingham Six Freed After 16 Years*, BBC NEWS, Mar. 14, 1991, www.news.bbc.co.uk.

157. The British Broadcasting Ban, *supra* note 152.

158. SF Political Report, Feb 1–3, 1991 Party Conference, at 29.

159. *Brind v. Secretary of State for the Home Department*, [1991] 1 AC 696.

160. *Brind v. United Kingdom*, 18 Eur. H.R. Rep. C.D. 76 (1994). *See also* *Purcell v. Ireland*, 70 Eur. Comm'n H.R. Dec. & Rep. 262 (1991).

161. Peter Oborne, *The Use and Abuse of Terror*, Centre for Policy Studies (2006), at 4, available at www.channel4.com/news/.

162. James Slack, *Terror Plan Faces New Setback as 17 Suspects Could Be Freed*, DAILY MAIL, Mar. 14, 2006, p. 13; Paul Waugh, *100 More Hamzas Still in Britain*, EVENING STANDARD (London), Feb. 8, 2006, 1.

163. Beth Gardiner, *Britain's House of Commons Votes to Outlaw the 'Glorification' of Terrorism*, CANADIAN PRESS, Feb. 15, 2006.

164. Amardeep Bassey, *Fanatic May Stand Trial*, SUNDAY MERCURY (Birmingham, UK), Feb. 12, 2006, 16. *Butt claims that he has since become disillusioned with al Qaeda and left the network. See Bob Simon interview with Hassan Butt, 60 Minutes*, The Network, Hassan Butt Tells Bob Simon Killing in the Name of Islam Is a "Cancer." available at www.cbsnews.com.

165. *Id.*

166. Interview with Newsnight on BBC2, August 2005, cited in Paul Waugh, Martin Bentham, *100 More Hamzas still in Britain*, EVENING STANDARD (London), Feb. 8, 2006, 1.

167. Waugh, *supra* note 162.

168. *Id.*

169. *Id.*

170. *Labour Finally Moves to Deport Extremists*, DAILY TELEGRAPH (London), Aug. 12, 2005, p. 25.

171. Paul Waugh, *First Move to Deport "Al Qaeda Hate Cleric,"* EVENING STANDARD (London), Aug. 11, 2005, p. 6.

172. *See* Brian Whitaker & agencies, *Muslims Angry at New Danish Cartoons Scandal*, GUARDIAN, Oct. 10, 2006, available at www.guardian.co.uk.

173. Richard Woods & David Leppard, *How Liberal Britain Let Hate Flourish*, SUNDAY TIMES (UK), Feb. 12, 2006, 12.

174. BEN RUSSELL AND NIGEL MORRIS, *Blair victorious in battle over 'glorification' of terrorism*, INDEPENDENT (LONDON), FEB. 16, 2006, available at www.news.independent.co.uk. *See also MPs Back Ban on Glorifying Terror*, BBC News, FEB. 15, 2006, available at www.newsbbc.co.uk.

175. Ronald J. Jackson et al., *Expression of a Mouse Interleukin-4 by a Recombinant Ectromelia Virus Suppresses Cytolytic Lymphocyte Responses and Overcomes Genetic Resistance to Mousepox*, 75 J. VIROLOGY 1205 (2001). *See also* Christopher F. Chyba & Alex L. Greninger, *Biotechnology and Bioterrorism: An Unprecedented World*, SURVIVAL, Summer 2004, at 143.

176. *See, e.g.*, William J. Broad, *Australians Create a Deadly Mouse Virus*, N.Y. TIMES, Jan. 23, 2001, at A6; Tim Radford, *Lab Creates Killer Virus by Accident*, GUARDIAN, Jan. 11, 2001, at 13; Clive Cookson, *International Economy: Scientists Convert Virus Into Killer: Biowarfare Fear*, FIN. TIMES, Jan. 12, 2001, at 15; Thomas Barlow, *The Perpetrators of Biological Warfare*, FIN. TIMES, July 28, 2001, at 2.

177. *Secrets and Lives*, ECONOMIST, Mar. 9, 2002.

178. Telephone Interview with Samuel Kaplan, Chair, Publishing Board, American Society of Microbiology, in Palo Alto, Cal. (Oct. 26, 2004).

179. ASM Code of Ethics, www.asm.org (last visited Sept. 4, 2005).

180. 147 Cong. Rec S12378 (statement of Sen. Joseph Lieberman regarding S. 1764).

181. *Id.*

182. Richard Preston, *The Specter of a New and Deadlier Smallpox*, N.Y. TIMES, Oct. 14, 2002, at A19.

183. *Id.*

184. Daniel J. Kevles, *Biotech's Big Chill*, TECH. REV. July-Aug., 2003, at 41.

185. Kevles, *supra* note 184, at 46.

186. *Id.*

187. Voluntary Tender Act, ch. 95, 40 Stat. 394 (1917) (repealed by Invention Secrecy Act of 1951, ch. 4, 66 Stat. 3).

188. Act of July 1, 1940, ch. 501, 54 Stat. 710, (1940).

189. Act of Aug. 21, 1941, ch. 393, 55 Stat. 657 (1941).

190. Act of June 16, 1942, ch. 415, 56 Stat. 370 (1942).

191. H.R. Rep No. 96–1540, at 47 (1980).

192. *Patent Disclosure: Hearings on H.R. 4687 Before Subcomm. No. 3, Comm. on the Judiciary of the House of Representatives*, 82d Cong., 25, 26 (1951).

193. H.R. Rep No. 96–1540, at 47 (1980).

194. Proclamation No. 2974, 3 C.F.R. 158 (1949–1953), *reprinted in* 50 U.S.C. app., note prec. 1, *and in* 66 Stat. c. 31 (1952).

195. H.R. Rep No. 96–1540, at 47 (1980).

196. Invention Secrecy Act of 1951, ch. 4, § 1, 66 Stat 3.

197. *Id.*, §§ 2–4, 66 Stat. 4–5.

198. Proclamation No. 2914, 15 Fed. Reg. 9029 (Dec. 19, 1950).

199. National Emergencies Act, Pub. L. No. 94–412, 90 Stat. 1255 (1976) (terminating "existing declared emergencies" two years after enactment of the Act).

200. *Halpern* v. *United States*, 258 F.2d 36 (2d Cir. 1958); *see also* Exec. Order No. 10,457, 18 Fed. Reg. 3,083 (May 28, 1953); Exec. Order No. 13,286, 6 U.S.C.A. § 111 (Feb. 28, 2003).

201. H.R. Rep No. 96–1540, at 1–2 (1980).

202. National Emergencies Act, Pub. L. No. 94–412, 90 Stat. 1255 (1976).

203. Gary L. Hausken, *The Value of a Secret: Compensation for Imposition of Secrecy Orders Under the Invention Secrecy Act*, 119 MIL. L. REV. 201–02 (1988).

204. *Id.*, at 202 n.10; Secrecy Order Statistics from the USPTO (2004), www.fas.org (last visited July 24, 2005).

205. *See, e.g.*, Edmund L. Andrews, *Patents: Cold War Secrecy Still Shrouds Inventions*, N.Y. TIMES, May 23, 1992, at A35.

206. Statistics for 1979–1986, Hausken, *supra* note 203, at 202 n.10. Statistics for 1988–2003, Secrecy Order Statistics from the USPTO (2004), www.fas.org (last visited July 24, 2005).

207. Lee Ann Gilbert, *Patent Secrecy Orders: The Unconstitutionality of Interference in Civilian Cryptography Under Present Procedures*, 22 SANTA CLARA L. REV.325, 325 n.1 (1982) (citing Sanders, *Data Privacy: What Washington Doesn't Want You to Know*, REASON, Jan. 1981, at 25, 35).

208. John/Jane Doe Secrecy Orders Issued by Year: 1997 (23), 1998 (99); 1999(18); 2000(24); 2001 (44); 2002 (37); 2003 (51). Secrecy Order Statistics, *supra* note 206.

209. Andrews, *supra* note 205 (cold fusion); Sabra Chartrand, Patents; *Speeding the Way for Processing Patents of Antiterrorism Devices, at Times Cloaked in Secrecy*, N.Y. TIMES, Oct. 8, 2001, at C1 (space technology); Teresa Riordan, *Patents*, N.Y. TIMES, Sept. 20, 1993, at D2 (radar missile systems); Evans Witt, N.Y. TIMES, Sept. 2, 1978, at 66 (voice scramblers).

210. *Secrets and Lives, supra* note 177. *But see Sealectro Corp.* v. *L.V.C. Indus., Inc.*, 271 F. Supp. 835 (E.D.N.Y.1967) (holding that a semiconductor receptacle that eliminates the need for solder does *not* fall within a clear national security interest).

211. John Markoff, *Paper on Codes Is Sent Despite U.S. Objections*, N.Y. TIMES, Aug. 9, 1989, at A16.

212. One of the first two recipients of NSA funding, Professor Martin E. Hellman of Stanford University, said, "One of the fears is that they are trying to buy people. If they support you, then they own you, and you really are going against them if they ask you not to publish something and you do." David Burnham, *The Silent Power of the NSA*, N.Y. TIMES, Mar. 27, 1983, at 6.

213. Christina Ramirez, *The Balance of Interests Between National Security Controls and First Amendment Interests in Academic Freedom* 13 J. C. & U.L. 179, 182 (1986).

214. Burnham, *supra* note 210, at 6–7.

215. *Id.*

216. Atomic Energy Act of 1954, ch. 1073, 68 Stat. 919 (1954).

217. *Org. for a Better Austin v. Keefe*, 402 U.S. 415, 419 (1971); *see also Carroll v. President & Comm'rs of Princess Anne*, 393 U.S. 175, 181 (1968); *Bantam Books, Inc. v. Sullivan*, 372 U.S. 58, 70 (1963).

218. Atomic Energy Act of 1954, ch. 1073, § 11(r), 68 Stat. 919, 924 (1954).

219. *Id.*, § 142(a), 68 Stat. 941. *See also* Harold Green, *The Atomic Energy Information Access Permit Program*, 25 GEO. WASH. L. REV. 548, 549 (1957).

220. *See, e.g.*, Mary M. Cheh, *The* Progressive *Case and the Atomic Energy Act: Walking to the Dangers of Government Information Controls*, 48 GEO. WASH. L. REV. 163, 168 n.26 (1980) (citing *Hearings on H.R. 4280 Before the House Comm. on Military Affairs*, 79th Cong., 80–82, 97–100, 118 (1945)).

221. *Id.*, at 179.

222. *United States v. Progressive, Inc.*, 467 F. Supp. 990 (W.D. Wis. 1979).

223. Cheh, *supra* note 220, at 176–77.

224. Cheh, *supra* note 220, at 165 n.10.

225. *Progressive*, 467 F. Supp. at 994.

226. *Id.*, at 995.

227. *Mayhem Manuals and the Internet: Hearings Before the Subcommittee on Terrorism, Technology and Government Information of the Senate Committee on the Judiciary*, 104th Cong., (1995) (statement of Robert S. Litt, Deputy Assistant Attorney General, Criminal Division, Department of Justice).

228. S. 735. 104th Cong. § 901(a); 141 CONG. REC. S7682 (daily ed. June 5, 1995) (statement of Sen. Feinstein).

229. S. 735. 104th Cong. § 901(a).

230. Antiterrorism and Effective Death Penalty Act of 1996, Pub. L. No. 104–132, § 709, 110 Stat. 1214, 1297.

231. *Id.*, § 709(a); *see also* 142 CONG. REC. S7271–74 (daily ed. June 28, 1996) (Amend. No. 4428 and statement of Sen. Feinstein); 142 CONG. REC. H9303 (daily ed. July 30, 1996).

232. U.S. Dep't of Justice, *Report on the Availability of Bombmaking Information, the Extent to Which Its Dissemination is Controlled by Federal Law, and the Extent to Which Such Dissemination May Be Subject to Regulation Consistent with the First Amendment to the United States Constitution*, (1997), http://cryptome.org/abi.htm [hereinafter *Bombmaking Report*].

233. *Bombmaking Report*, *supra* note 232, at 1–2.

234. *Id.*, at 7.

235. *Id.*

236. *Id.*, at 10.

237. *Id.*

238. *Id.*, at 12.

239. *Id.*, at 11.

240. *Id.*

241. *Id.*

242. 18 U.S.C. § 844(h), (m), (n) (2004).

243. *Bombmaking Report, supra* note 232, at 15.

244. *Id.*

245. 18 U.S.C. § 373(a) (2000).

246. *Bombmaking Report,supra* note 232, at 16–17, 29–30.

247. *Central Bank of Denver N.A.* v. *First Interstate Bank of Denver N.A.*, 511 U.S. 164, 181 (1994) (citing *Nye & Nissen* v. *United States*, 336 U.S. 613, 619 (1949)).

248. Antiterrorism and Effective Death Penalty Act, Pub. L. No. 104–132, § 323, 110 Stat. 1214, 1255 (1996).

249. *Bombmaking Report, supra* note 232, at 20.

250. *Id.*, at 21.

251. *See Id.*, at 30.

252. *Herceg* v. *Hustler Magazine, Inc.*, 814 F.2d 1017, 1019 (5th Cir. 1987).

253. *See Yakubowicz* v. *Paramount Pictures Corp.*, 536 N.E. 2d 1067 (Mass. 1989); and *Rice* v. *Paladin Enter., Inc.*, 128 F.3d 233 (4th Cir. 1997).

254. *Bombmaking Report, supra* note 232, at 30 (citing *The Florida Star* v. *B.J.F.*, 491 U.S. 524, 541 (1989)).

255. *Smith* v. *Daily Mail Pub. Co.*, 443 U.S. 97, 103 (1979); *see also Bombmaking Report, supra* note 232, at 30–31 (quoting *United States* v. *Aguilar*, 515 U.S. 593, 605 (1995) and citing *Butterworth* v. *Smith*, 494 U.S. 624, 632 (1990)).

256. *Daily Mail*, 443 U.S. at 106 (Rehnquist, J., concurring).

257. *Bombmaking Report, supra* note 232, at 31.

258. *Brandenburg* v. *Ohio*, 395 U.S. 444, 456 (1969) (Douglas, J., concurring).

259. *Id.*, at 447–48.

260. *Id.*, at 448; *see also Scales* v. *United States*, 367 U.S. 203 (1961).

261. *Dennis* v. *United States*, 341 U.S. 494, 581 (Douglas, J., dissenting).

262. *Bombmaking Report, supra* note 232, at 2.

263. *Id.*, at 41.

264. *Id.*

265. *Id.*, at 42 (citing *Haig* v. *Agee*, 453 U.S. 280 (1981)).

266. *Rice* v. *Paladin Enter., Inc.* 940 F. Supp. 836 (D. Md. 1996).

267. *Bombmaking Report, supra* note 232, at 43 (emphasis added).

268. *Id.*, at 43–44.

269. *Id.*, at 49.

270. S.606, 106th Cong. (1999).

271. *Id.*

272. Act of Aug. 17, 1999, Pub. L. No. 106–54. § 2, 113 Stat. 398, 398–99.

273. *Activist Gets Year in Jail for Hosting, Link to Bomb Info, Electronic Frontier Found*, at www.eff.org \ (Aug. 7, 2003). *See also* www.cryptome.org.

274. www.forbiddenspeech.org (last visited Sept. 23, 2005).

275. *Id.*

276. www.forbiddenspeech.org (last visited Sept. 23, 2005).

277. *Id.*

278. *Molotov Cocktails*, www.forbiddenspeech.org (last visited July 16, 2005).

279. *See, e.g., Pipe bombs: Low-tech, Lethal Tools of Terror*, CNN, at www.cnn.com (July 27, 1996); *Molotov Cocktail*, WIKIPEDIA, at http://en.wikipedia.org/wiki/ (last visited July 16, 2005); *How Nuclear Bombs Work*, at www.science. howstuffworks.com (last visited July 16, 2005).

280. *See* David S. Touretzky, *What the FBI Doesn't Want You to See at* RaisetheFist.com, at www-2.cs.cmu.edu (last modified July 12, 2005).

281. *Id.*

282. *House of Commons Third Report from the Defence Committee, Session 1979–80.* HC 773, Aug. 6, 1980, at v [hereinafter Defence Committee Report].

283. Radcliffe Committee on Security Procedures in the Public Service, Cmnd 1681, 1962.

284. Minutes of Evidence at 3.

285. *See Introduction and Standing DA-Notices*, DEFENCE, PRESS AND BROADCAST-ING ADVISORY COMMITTEE, *at* http://www.dnotice.org.uk/notices.htm#notices (last updated June 29, 2005).

286. *See How the System Works*, DEFENCE, PRESS AND BROADCASTING ADVISORY COM-MITTEE, at www.dnotice.org.uk (last updated Apr. 6, 2005).

287. Official Secrets Act, 1989, c. 6.

288. *See infra* Part II.B.I.

289. D. Fairley, *D Notices, Official Secrets and the Law*, 10 OXFORD J. LEGAL STUD. 430, 435 (1990).

290. *Id.*

291. *Id.*

292. *Id.*, at 436.

293. *Id.*

294. *See infra* Part II.B.2.

295. Fairley, *supra* note 289, at 439.

296. *Id.*, at 438.

297. HOUSE OF COMMONS, SCIENCE AND TECHNOLOGY COMMITTEE, THE SCIENTIFIC RESPONSE TO TERRORISM, 2002–3, H.C. 415-I, at 62, available at www. publications.parliament.uk.

298. *Id.*

299. *Id.*

300. Clive Walker, *Biological Attack, Terrorism and the Law*, 16 TERRORISM & POL. VIOLENCE 175, 187 (2005).

301. FOREIGN AFFAIRS COMMITTEE, THE BIOLOGICAL WEAPONS GREEN PAPER, 2002–3, H.C. 150, at para. 31.

302. Bruce Alberts & Robert M. May, *Scientist Support for Biological Weapons Controls*, 298 SCIENCE 1135 (2002).

303. www.royalsoc.ac.uk (last visited Dec. 1, 2004).

304. THE SCIENTIFIC RESPONSE TO TERRORISM, *supra* note 297, at 5.

305. Telephone Interview with Dr. Ronald Fraser, Executive Secretary, Society for General Microbiology, in Palo Alto, Cal. (Oct. 29, 2004).

306. Society for General Microbiology, Policy on Scientific Publication, Security and Censorship available at www.sgm.ac.uk (last visited September 11, 2005).

307. *Id.*

308. *Id.*

309. Interview with Dr. Ronald Fraser, *supra* note 305.

310. Anti-Terrorism, Crime and Security Act, 2001, c. 24, § 50.

311. *Id.*, at §§ 57–61.

312. THE SCIENTIFIC RESPONSE TO TERRORISM, *supra* note 297, at 58–61.

313. *Report of the Enquiry into the Export of Defence Equipment and Dual-Use Goods to Iraq and Related Prosecutions* (The Scott Report) (HC 115). HMSO Feb. 1996.

314. Export Control Act, 2002, c. 28, § 8.

315. Export Control Bill, 2002, H.L. Bill [75]; *see also* 632 PARL. DEB., H.L. (5th ser.) (2002) 16–19.

316. Export Control Act, 2002, c. 28, § 8.

317. THE GOVERNMENT REPLY TO THE EIGHTH REPORT FROM THE HOUSE OF COMMONS SCIENCE AND TECHNOLOGY SELECT COMMITTEE, SESSION 2002–2003 HC 415-I, at 31 (2004), available at www.homeoffice.gov.uk.

318. *Secrets and Lives*, *supra* note 177.

319. David Cole, *The D.C. Gang That Couldn't Shoot Straight*, L.A. TIMES, Sept. 19, 2004, 5.

320. *Id.*

321. Interview with Helal Omeira, Council on American Islamic Relations, in San Francisco, Calif. (Sept. 2004). Zip code information was obtained by a Freedom of Information Act request and is available at www.eff.org.

322. *Scales v. United States*, 367 U.S. 203 (1961).

323. Pub. L. No. 104-132, 110 Stat. 1214 (1996).

324. U.S. DEPARTMENT OF STATE, OFFICE OF THE COORDINATOR FOR COUNTERTERRORISM, COUNTRY REPORTS ON TERRORISM 2004, at 92 (2005), available at www.state.gov.

325. 182 F.3d 17 (D.C. Cir. 1999).

326. *Am.-Arab Anti-Discrimination Comm. v. Reno*, 119 F.3d 1367, 1376 (1997), *vacated*, 525 U.S. 471 (1999).

327. Seditious Meetings and Assemblies Act, 1817, 57 Geo. 3, c. 19; Corresponding Societies Act, 1799, 39 Geo. 3, c. 79.

328. Corresponding Societies Act,1799; 39 Geo. 3, c. 79.

329. *Id.*

330. Sedititous Meetings and Assemblies Act, 1817, 57 Geo. 3, c. 19.

331. 1920 ROIA: S.R.O. 1530/1920, 13 Aug. 1920; 1922 SPA: S.R.O. 33/1922, 18 May 1922, B.G. 26 May 1922.

332. Regulation 24A, S.R.O. 25/1922, 22 May 1922.

333. S.R.O. 11/1933, Jan. 14, 1933, B.G. 20.1.1933.

334. *See* DONOHUE, *supra* note 97, at 103.

335. Cynthia L. Irvin, *Terrorists' Perspectives: Interviews, in* TERRORISM AND THE MEDIA 62, 70 (David L. Paletz & Alex P. Schmid eds., 1992) (citing 1986 internal Sinn Féin document).

336. *See, e.g.*, Report of a Committee to Consider, in the Context of Civil Liberties and Human Rights, Measures to Deal with Terrorism in Northern Ireland. Chairman: Lord Gardiner, Jan. 1975. Session 1974/75 Cmnd. 5847.

337. Baker Report, ¶ 412. [Review of the Northern Ireland (Emergency Provisions) Act 1978, 1984, Cmnd. 9222, para. 414 (conducted by the Rt. Hon. Sir George Baker, OBE) [hereinafter Baker Report].]

338. *Id.*, ¶ 414.

339. 882 PARL. DEB., H.C. (5th ser.) (1974) 636 (emphasis added).

340. *Id.*, at 746.

341. Criminal Justice (Terrorism and Conspiracy) Act, 1998, c. 40. Recall Article 11 of the European Convention on Human Rights: "Everyone has the right to freedom of peaceful assembly and to freedom of association with others." European Convention for the Protection of Human Rights & Fundamental Freedoms, art. 11, Nov. 4, 1950, available at www.echr.coe.int. This measure limits the restrictions that can be placed on the exercise of these rights, "other than such as are prescribed by law and are necessary in a democratic society in the interests of national security or public safety, for the prevention of disorder or crime, for the protection of health or morals or for the protection of the rights and freedoms of others." *Id.* art. 11(2). Despite the national security exception, this provision may dampen proscription measures in the United Kingdom. In 1998, for instance, Strasbourg considered Turkey's dissolution of the Communist Party, and the transfer of the party's assets to the state treasury, to be a violation of Articles 10 and 11 of the ECHR. *United Communist Party of Turkey* v. *Turkey*, 26 Eur. Ct. H.R. 121 (1998); *see also Socialist Party* v. *Turkey*, 27 Eur. Ct. H.R. 51 (1998). The court suggested that the right to vote in Article 3 of the ECHR would be meaningless without the free formation and participation of political parties. "[O]nly convincing and compelling reasons" would justify inroads into Article 11. *Socialist Party* v. *Turkey*, 27 Eur. Ct. H.R. at 86. While authorities could challenge associations that jeopardized the state institutions, a pattern of subversive action would be necessary. GEARTY, *supra* note 123, at 46–47. The organizations currently proscribed by the United Kingdom, however, include militant groups, in regard to which the standard for limits on freedom of association would likely be met.
342. Racketeer Influenced and Corrupt Organizations Act (RICO), Pub. L. No. 91–452, tit. IX, §§ 1961–68, 84 Stat. 941 (1970).
343. MODEL PENAL CODE § 5.03(1) (1962).
344. RICO, § 1962(a), 84 Stat. 942.
345. *Id.*, § 1962(b)-(c), 84 Stat. 942–43.
346. *United States* v. *Indelicato*, 865 F.2d 1370 (2d Cir.1989) (en banc).
347. Robert P. Faulkner, *Evidence of First Amendment Activity at Trial: The Articulation of a Higher Evidentiary Standard*, 42 UCLA L. REV. 1, 4–5 (1994).
348. EUGENE VOLOKH, THE FIRST AMENDMENT: PROBLEMS, CASES AND POLICY ARGUMENTS 340 (2001).
349. Faulkner, *supra* note 347, at 9; *see also* FED. R. EVID. 401–02.
350. Faulkner, *supra* note 347, at 11.
351. *See, e.g.*, *Haupt* v. *United States*, 330 U.S. 631, 67 S. Ct. 974, Mar. 31, 1947 (1947) (speech as evidence in trial for treason); *Wisconsin* v. *Mitchell*, 508 U.S. 476, 113 S.Ct. 2194, Jun. 11, 1993 (1993) (beliefs and associations as evidence of racist motivations during sentencing phase of trial for aggravated battery and theft).
352. *Speiser* v. *Randall*, 357 U.S. 513, 523–24 (1958); Peter E. Quint, *Toward First Amendment Limitations on the Introduction of Evidence: the Problem of United States* v. *Rosenberg*, 86 YALE L.J. 1622, 1651 (1977) (citing *Gertz* v. *Robert Welch, Inc.*, 418 U.S. 323, 342 (1974)).
353. *See, e.g.*, Faulkner, *supra* note 347; Quint, *supra* note 352.
354. Faulkner, *supra* note 347, at 6.
355. Quint, *supra* note 352, at 1662.
356. Criminal Justice (Terrorism and Conspiracy) Act, 1998, c. 40.
357. *Keyishian* v. *Board of Regents*, 385 U.S. 589, 606 (1967); *see also Wieman* v. *Updegraff*, 344 US 183 (1952).

358. See *United States* v. *Robel*, 389 US 258 (1967).
359. *Baird* v. *State Bar of Arizona*, 401 US 1, 9 (1971) (Stewart, J., concurring).
360. See *Pickering* v. *Board of Educ.*, 391 U.S. 563 (1968).
361. *Id.*, at 568.
362. See *Board of County Comm'rs* v. *Umbehr*, 518 U.S. 668 (1996).
363. See *Connick* v. *Myers*, 461 U.S. 138 (1983).
364. George Lardner Jr., *CIA Defends Its Selective Censorship of Ex-Agents' Writings*, WASH. POST, Apr. 6, 1980, at A10.
365. *Id.*
366. See *United States* v. *Marchetti*, 466 F.2d 1309, 1311, 1312 n.1 (4th Cir. 1972).
367. Lardner, *supra* note 364.
368. *Snepp* v. *United States*, 444 U.S. 507, 510 (1980).
369. ERWIN CHEMERINSKY, CONSTITUTIONAL LAW: PRINCIPLES AND POLICIES 929 (2d ed. 2002).
370. L.A. Powe, Jr., *The H-Bomb Injunction*, 61 U. COLO. L. REV. 55, 62 (1990); *see also* Marchetti, 466 F.2d at 1313.
371. *Id.*, at 62–63.
372. *Id.*, at 63.
373. Exec. Order No. 12,065, 3 C.F.R. § 190 (1978): § 6–102, 3 C.F.R. § 204.
374. *Id.*, § 1–602.
375. Floyd Abrams, *The New Effort to Control Information*, N.Y. TIMES, Sept. 25, 1983, at 21, 26.
376. Exec. Order No. 12,356, 47 Fed. Reg. 14874, § 1.1(a)(3) (Apr. 2, 1982).
377. Ramirez, *supra* note 213, at 210–11.
378. *Id.*
379. Press Release, Computerworld, *White House Orders All Federal Offices to Review Content of Their Web Sites for Sensitive – but Not Classified – Materials* (Mar. 25, 2002), available at www.fact.trib.com.
380. Steven Aftergood, *Torture and Secrecy*, IN THESE TIMES, June 2, 2004, www.inthesetimes.com.
381. Exec. Order No. 13,292, 68 Fed. Reg. 15,315, § 1.7(a) (Mar. 25, 2003).
382. *Id.*
383. See Powe, *supra* note 370, at 58.
384. *New York Times Co.* v. *United States*, 403 U.S. 713, 714 (1971).
385. *Id.*, at 714 (quoting *Organization for a Better Austin* v. *Keefe*, 402 U.S. 415, 419 (1971)).
386. *Near* v. *Minnesota ex rel.* Olson, 283 U.S. 697 (1931).
387. *New York Times*, 403 U.S. at 730 (Stewart, J., concurring); *Id.* at 726–27 (Brennan, J., concurring).
388. See, e.g., *United States* v. *Morison*, 604 F. Supp. 655 (D. Md. 1985).
389. 18 U.S.C. § 641 (2000); *see also United States* v. *Boyce*, 594 F.2d 1246, 1249 (9th Cir. 1979).
390. *Morison*, 604 F. Supp. at 660–61.
391. *See, e.g.*, DAVID VINCENT, THE CULTURE OF SECRECY: BRITAIN, 1832–1998 (1998).
392. *Memorandum of Guidance for Officials Appearing Before Select Committees*, May 16, 1980, General Notice GEN80/38.
393. *Cabinet Office, Departmental Evidence and Response to Select Committees. But see* 292 PARL. DEB. H.C. (6th ser.) (1997) 1046–47; 579 PARL. DEB. H.L. (5th ser.) (1997) 1057.

394. *See Attorney-Gen.* v. *Newspapers Publishing Plc.* [1987] 3 W.L.R. 942, 946 (Ch. D); *A-G* v. *Guardian Newspapers Ltd.* (No. 2) [1988] 2 W.L.R. 805, 815 (Ch. D); *Attorney-Gen.* v. *Observer, Ltd.* (C.A. July 25, 1986) (LEXIS, Enggen library, Cases file); *Attorney-Gen. (UK)* v. *Heinemann Publishers Austl. Ltd* [1987] 8 N.S.W.L.R. 341; *A-G* v. *South China Morning Post Ltd.*, [1988] 1 H.K.L.R. 143 (C.A.); *A-G* v. *South China Morning Post Ltd.*, No. 4644 (HC) Aug. 24, 1987; *see also* The Guardian, Aug. 5, 1987, at 1, col. 8.

395. *Guardian Newspapers*, 2 W.L.R. 805, *supra* note 394, at 815; and *Attorney General* v. *Guardian Newspapers* [1990] AC 109, [1988] 3 All ER 545, [1989] 3 WLR 776 (Judgment 1: Lord Keith of Kinkel).

396. Philomena M. Dane, Case Comment, *The Spycatcher Cases*, 50 Ohio St. L.J. 405, 406 (1989).

397. *Newspapers Publishing*, 3 W.L.R. at 946; and *Attorney General v The Observer Ltd & Others*; *Attorney General v Guardian Newspapers Ltd & Others*; Court of Appeal (Civil Division); 136 NLJ 799, The Times 26 July 1986.

398. For discussion of the previous public claims echoed in Wright's allegations see *Attorney General v Guardian Newspapers*, Chancery Division [1990] AC 109, [1988] 3 All ER 545, Nov. 23, 24, 25, 26, 27, and 30, 1987, and Dec. 1, 2, 3, 4, 7, and 21, 1987, 21 (Scott, J.), at 3 and 5, on Dec. 21, 1987.

399. *Attorney General v The Observer Ltd & Others*; *Attorney General v Guardian Newspapers Ltd & Others*; Ct of Appeal (Civil Div), [1986] 136 NLJ 799, The Times 26 July 1986.

400. *Guardian Newspapers*, 2 W.L.R. 805, *supra* note 394, at 816.

401. *Attorney General v Guardian Newspapers Ltd and others*; and related appeals, CHANCERY DIVISION, Ct of Appeal (Civil Div) [1987] 3 All ER 316, [1987] 1 WLR 1248, Jul. 20, 21, 22, 23, 24, 1987, HL July 27–30, Aug. 13, 1987, (Judgment 1: Sir Nicolas Browne-Wilkinson V-C)

402. *Attorney General v Guardian Newspapers*, HL, [1990] AC 109, [1988] 3 All ER 545, [1989] 3 WLR 776, June 14, 15, 16, 20, 22, 23; Oct. 13, 1988.

403. *Guardian Newspapers*, 2 W.L.R. 805, *supra* note 394, at 816–17.

404. *Id.*, at 816.

405. *Id.*, at 817.

406. *See The Sunday Times (No. 2)* v. *The United Kingdom*, Ap. 13166/87, Oct. 12, 1990, summary available at: the Netherlands Institute of Human Rights, www/sim.law.uu.nl.

407. *Guardian Newspapers*, 2 W.L.R. 805, *supra* note 394, at 409.

408. Appellate Committee of the House of Lords, 30 July 1987; see particularly decisions rendered by Lord Brandon of Oakbrook, Lord Templeman, and Lord Ackner.

409. *Observer & Guardian v. the United Kingdom* (13585/88) [1991] ECHR 49 (26 Nov. 1991), paras. 39–44. *See also A-G* v. *South China Morning Post Ltd.*, No. 114 (Civil) Sept. 8, 1987; and *A-G* v. *South China Morning Post Ltd.*, No. 4644 (HC) Aug. 24, 1987.

410. *Id.*, at 410.

411. *Saltman Eng'g Co., Ltd.* v. *Campbell Eng'g Co., Ltd.*, [1963] 3 All E.R. 413, Lord Greene at 414.

412. Dane, *supra* note 396, at 411.

413. *See, e.g., Franchi* v. *Franchi* [1967] R.P.C. 149; *Exchange Tel. Co., Ltd.* v. *Central News Ltd.* [1897] 2 Ch. 48; Dane, *supra* note 407, at 378 n.65 (citing Francis Gurry, Breach of Confidence 3 (1984)).

414. *See generally* Dane, *supra* note 396, at 411–12.
415. *Id.*, at 412 n.69 (citing *Seager v. Copydex Ltd.*, [1967] 1 W.L.R. 923, 931 (C.A.)).
416. *Id.*, at 413 n.84 (citing *Lion Lab., Ltd. v. Evans*, [1985] 1 Q.B. 526, 536 (C.A.)).
417. *Id.*, at 435.
418. *Id.* (citing *Attorney-Gen. v. Guardian Newspapers, Ltd.* (No. 2), [1988] 2 W.L.R. 805, *supra* note 394, at 822–31 (Ch. D)).
419. Dane, *supra* note 396, at 431.
420. Public Records Act, 1967, c. 44; Public Records Act, 1958, 6 & 7 Eliz. 2, c. 51; *see also* STANLEY A. DE SMITH, CONSTITUTIONAL AND ADMINISTRATIVE LAW 489–90 (Rodney Brazier ed., 6th ed. 1989).
421. Official Secrets Act of 1911, c. 28, § 1.
422. *See, e.g., Chandler v. DPP*, [1964] A.C. 763, [1962] 3 All ER 142, (H.L.).
423. *See* EWING & GEARTY, *supra* note 108, at 138.
424. *Id.*, at 138–139.
425. *Id.*, at 139.
426. *Sec'y of State v. Guardian Newspapers, Ltd.*, [1983] T.L.R., No. 765 (Ch. Dec. 16, 1983), *aff'd on other grounds*, [1984] 1 Ch. 156 (C.A. 1983), *aff'd*, [1985] A.C. 339 (1984).
427. *Troubled History of Official Secrets Act*, BBC NEWS, Nov. 18, 1998, www/news.bbc.co.uk; *see also* Contempt of Court Act, 1981, c. 49, §10.
428. *Secretary of State v. Guardian Newspapers, Ltd.*, [1985] A.C. at 357 (Lord Fraser).
429. Para. 6 of government affidavit, *reprinted in* EWING & GEARTY, *supra* note 108, at 142.
430. *R. v. Ponting* [1985] CRIM. L. REV. 318.
431. EWING & GEARTY, *supra* note 108, at 144.
432. *Id.*, at 144–145.
433. Feldman, *supra* note 126, at 894–95.
434. The following account is drawn from *The Times* (London), between January and April 1987. *See also* EWING & GEARTY, *supra* note 108, at 147–52.
435. EWING AND GEARTY, *supra* note 108, at 149.
436. 74 PARL. DEB., H.C. (5th ser.) (1985) 128–30.
437. EWING & GEARTY, *supra* note 108, at 207 (quoting Lord Jenkins of Hillhead). Emphasis in original.
438. Official Secrets Act, 1989, c. 6.
439. FELDMAN, *supra* note 126, at 795–97.
440. *Id.*, at 890.
441. *Id.*, at 871.
442. Select Committee on Public Administration, Minutes of Evidence, HC Question 220 (29 June 29, 1999) (evidence given by Lord Lester of Herne Hill, QC), available at www.publications.parliament.uk.
443. *R. v. Shayler* [2002] UKHL 11, [2003] 1 A.C. 247 (quoting David Michael Shayler's statement at the Charing Cross Police Station in response to the charge on August 21, 2000).
444. *Shayler*, [2002] UKHL 11 at para. 23.
445. *Id.*, at para. 26.
446. *Id.*, at para. 67 (citation omitted).
447. *Attorney-Gen v. Guardian Newspapers Ltd.* (No 2) [1990] 1 A.C. 109, 221.
448. Fairley, *supra* note 290, at 438 (*citing* Lord Diplock in *CCSU v. Minister for the Civil Service* [1985] A.C. 374, 412).

449. *Id.*, at 437.

450. *See* Laura K. Donohue, *Censoring Science Won't Make Us Any Safer*, WASH. POST, June 26, 2005, at B5.

451. 147 CONG. REC. S12379 (daily ed. Dec. 4, 2001) (statement of Sen. Lieberman).

452. *Secrets & Lives, supra* note 177.

453. A partial list includes: clostridium botulinum toxin, botulism; francisella tularensis, tularaemia; Ebola hemorrhagic fever, Marburg hemorrhagic fever, Lassa fever, Julin, Argentine hemorrhagic fever; Coxiella burnetti, Q fever; brucella species, brucellosis; burkholderia mallei, glanders; Venezuelan encephalomyelitis, eastern and western equine encephalomyelitis, epsilon toxin of clostridium perfringens, staphylococcus entretoxin B, salmonella species, shigella dysenteriae, escherichia coli 0157: H7, vibrio cholerae, cryptosporidium parvum, nipah virus, hantaviruses, tickborne hemorrhagic fever viruses, tickborne encephalitis virus, and yellow fever. FN 147 CONG. REC. S12379 (daily ed. Dec. 4, 2001) (statement of Sen. Lieberman).

454. PANEL ON SCIENTIFIC COMMUNICATION AND NAT'L SEC. & COMM. ON SCIENCE, ENGINEERING, AND PUB. POLICY, SCIENTIFIC COMMUNICATION AND NATIONAL SECURITY2 (1982), available at www.nap.edu/openbook [hereinafter SCIENTIFIC COMMUNICATION AND NATIONAL SECURITY].

455. William J. Broad, *Bioterror Researchers Build a More Lethal Mousepox*, N.Y. TIMES, Nov. 1, 2003, at A8.

456. Debora MacKenzie, *US Develops Lethal New Viruses*, NEW SCIENTIST, Oct. 29, 2003, available at www.newscientist.com.

457. SCIENTIFIC COMMUNICATION AND NATIONAL SECURITY, *supra* note 454, at 4.

6. Auxiliary Precautions

The following are the sources of the epigraphs: James Madison, Federalist No. 51, 1788, in JAMES MADISON, ALEXANDER HAMILTON AND JOHN JAY: THE FEDERALIST PAPERS, ed. by Isaac Kramnick, pp. 319–20.

1. Rosie Cowan, *Most Senior al Qaeda Terrorist Yet Captured in Britain Gets 40 Years for Plotting Carnage*, GUARDIAN, Nov. 8, 2006, available at www.guardian.co.uk; and United States District Court Southern District of New York, Sealed Indictment, *U.S. of America* v. *Dhiren Barot*, available at \ www.washingtonpost.com.

2. Cowan, *supra* note 1.

3. *Id.*

4. *Id. See also Prosecution Case Against al-Qaeda Briton*, BBC NEWS, Nov. 6, 2006, available at www.news.bbc.co.uk; *Dhiren Barot: India-born Kihadi in 9/11 Net*, THE TIMES OF INDIA, Aug. 18, 2004, available at www.timesofindia.indiatimes.com; United States District Court Southern District of New York, Sealed Indictment, *U.S. of America* v. *Dhiren Barot*, available at www.www.washingtonpost.com.

5. *Al-Qaeda Plotter Jailed for Life*, BBC NEWS, Nov. 7, 2006, available at www.news.bbc.co.uk.

6. *Id.*

7. *British Terror Plotter Gets Life in Prison*, CBS NEWS, Nov. 7, 2006, available at www.cbsnews.com.

8. Author interview with OMB officials, by telephone, from Stanford University, Palo Alto, California, April 5, 2007. *See also* Performance Assessment Rating Tools at www.results.gov.

9. *Brandenburg* v. *Ohio*, 395 U.S. 444 (1969).

10. *Hamdan* v. *Rumsfeld*, 126 S.Ct. 2749 (2006),

11. *A and others* v. *Secretary of State for the Home Department* [2004] UKHL 56, 16 December 2004, available at www.publications.parliament.uk.

12. Christopher F. Chyba, *Biotechnology and the Challenge to Arms Control*, ARMS CONTROL TODAY, Oct. 2006, available at www.armscontrol.org.

13. INTELLIGENCE AND SECURITY COMMITTEE REPORT INTO THE LONDON TERRORIST ATTACKS ON 7 JULY 2005, Chaired by the Rt. Hon. Paul Murphy, May 2006, Cm 6785, at 3.

14. *Id.*, at 4.

15. *Id.*, at 3. *See also* www.london.gov.uk.

16. *Id.*

17. Lord Hailsham of St. Marylebone, HL Debs, 28 Nov. 1974, Vol. 354, col. 1509.

18. Review of the Operation of the Prevention of Terrorism (Temporary Provisions) Act 1976., by the Rt. Hon. Earl Jellicoe, DSO, MC. Feb. 1983. Session 1982/83, Cmnd 8803, para. 207.

19. Review of the Northern Ireland (Emergency Provisions) Act 1978, by the Rt. Hon. Sir George Baker OBE. April 1984. Session 1983/84 Cmnd. 9222, para 414.

20. Ian Paisley, HC Debs, Feb. 19, 1996, Vol. 272, col. 104.

21. Nick Hawkins, HC Debs, Jan. 9, 1996, Vol. 269, col. 43.

22. National Security Act of 1947, §501–503, 50 USC §413–413(b).

23. 50 USC ch. 15, §413b. *See also* Congressional Research Service, Statutory Procedures Under Which Congress is to Be Informed of US Intelligence Activities, Including Covert Actions, Jan. 18, 2006, available at www.fl1.findlaw.com/news.

24. Pub. L. No. 89–487, 80 Stat. 250 (1966). In 1974, 1976, 1986, and 1996 Congress amended FOIA. Pub. L. No. 93–502, §§ 1–3, 88 Stat. 1561, 1563, 1564 (1974); Pub. L. No. 94–409, § 5(b), 90 Stat. 1241 (1976); Pub. L. No. 99–570, tit. I(N), §§ 1802, 1803, 100 Stat. 3207–48, 3207–49 (1986); *Pub. L. No. 104–231*, §§ 3–11, 110 Stat. 3048 (1996).

25. Memorandum from Attorney General Janet Reno to the Heads of All Individual Components of the Department of Justice on the Subject of Freedom of Information Act Backlog Reduction Within the Department, available at www.usdoj.gov/oip/foia_updates/Vol_XIV_3/page3.htm; and Memorandum from Attorney General Janet Reno to Heads of Departments and Agencies on the Subject of the Freedom of Information Act (Oct. 4, 1993), available at www. usdoj.gov/oip.

26. Memorandum from Attorney General John Ashcroft to the Heads of All Federal Departments and Agencies on the Subject of The Freedom of Information Act (Oct. 12, 2001), available at www. usdoj.gov/oip.

27. Memorandum from Attorney General Janet Reno to the Heads of All Individual Components of the Department of Justice on the Subject of Freedom of Information Act Backlog Reduction Within the Department, available at www. usdoj.gov/oip (last visited Sept. 11, 2005); and Ashcroft Memorandum, *supra* note 26.

28. Memorandum from Chief of Staff Andrew Card to the Heads of Executive Departments and Agencies on the Subject of Action to Safeguard Information Regarding Weapons of Mass Destruction and Other Sensitive Documents Related to Homeland Security, (Mar. 19, 2002), available at www. usdoj.gov/oip.

29. Memorandum from Laura Kimberly, Acting Director of the Information Security Oversight Office, Richard Huff & Daniel Metcalfe, Co-Directors of the Office of Information and Privacy, Department of Justice to Departments and Agencies on the

Subject of Safeguarding Information Regarding Weapons of Mass Destruction and Other Sensitive Records Related to Homeland Security, (Mar. 19, 2002), available at www. usdoj.gov/oip.

30. U.S. GEN. ACCOUNTING OFFICE, FREEDOM OF INFORMATION ACT: AGENCY VIEWS ON CHANGES RESULTING FROM NEW ADMINISTRATION POLICY 2 (2003), available at www.gao.gov.

31. Homeland Security Act of 2002, Pub. L. No. 107–296, 116 Stat. 2135.

32. Sarah Lesher, *Senators Attempt to Close 'Secrecy' Hole: Watchdog Groups Worry Too Much Can be Made Secret*, THE HILL, July 8, 2003, available at www.foi.missouri.edu.

33. *Id.*

34. *See, e.g., Id.* (quoting Tim Edgar, legislative counsel to ACLU and Mark Tapscott, director of media services of the Heritage Foundation); and Comment, *What's in the Water?: New Rules Make it Harder for Reporters (Or Anyone Else) to Find Out*, COLUM. JOURNALISM REV.,Mar.-Apr. (2003), available at www.cjr.org.

35. National Defense Authorization Act for Fiscal Year 2004, Pub. L. No. 108–136, 117 Stat. 1392 (2003).

36. Ariel Sabar, *Bill Would Tighten Cloak of NSA Secrecy, Critics Say: Spy Agency Says Proposal Would be Labor-Saver on Requests Routinely Denied*, BALTIMORE SUN, May 16, 2003, at 3A.

37. Press Release, The National Security Archive, Spy Agencies Abuse Freedom of Information Exemptions but Congress May Grant New One to Intercepts Agency (June 11, 2003), www.gwu.edu.

38. Sabar, *supra* note 36.

39. *Hearings Before the Select Committee to Study Governmental Operations with Respect to Intelligence Activities*, 94th Congress, Vol. 5: The National Security Agency and 4th Amendment Rights, 1976; Senate Resolution 21, *Hearings Before the Select Committee to Study Government Operations with Respect to Intelligence Activities of the US Senate*, 94th Cong., Volume 6: Federal Bureau of Investigations, (1976); Supplementary Detailed Staff Reports of the Intelligence Activities and the Rights of Americans: Book, III, Final report of the Select Committee to Study Governmental Operations with Respect to Intelligence Activities, US Senate, 94th Cong., 2d Sess (Apr. 23, 1976).

40. DAVID FELDMAN, CIVIL LIBERTIES AND HUMAN RIGHTS IN ENGLAND AND WALES (2002), at 782.

41. Parliamentary Ombudsman, Access to Official Information: Monitoring of the Non-Statutory Codes of Practice 1994–2005, www.ombudsman.org.uk (last updated May 27, 2005). For the 1997 version of the code, see CODE OF PRACTICE ON ACCESS TO GOVERNMENT INFORMATION (1997), available at www.cfoi.org.uk.

42. *See* Patrick Birkinshaw & Alan Parkin, *Freedom of Information*, in CONSTITUTIONAL REFORM: THE LABOUR GOVERNMENT'S CONSTITUTIONAL REFORM AGENDA 173–201 (Robert Blackburn & Raymond Plant eds., 1999); R. Austin, *Freedom of Information: The Constitutional Impact*, in THE CHANGING CONSTITUTION 319–71 (Jeffrey Jowell & Dawn Oliver eds., 4th ed. 2000).

43. FELDMAN, *supra* note 40, at 782.

44. *Id.*, at 783.

45. *Id.*, at 783–85.

46. Freedom of Information Act, 2000, c. 36, §§ 23, 24, 25 (Eng.).

47. *Id.*, § 26.
48. *Id.*, § 41.
49. *Id.*, § 47.
50. *Id.*, § 53.
51. *Id.*, § 57.
52. Daryl J. Levinson & Richard Pildes, *Separation of Parties, Not Powers*, 119 HARV. L. REV., 2343 (2006).
53. For discussion of the money laundering cycle wherein dirty money is made clean, *see* Bruce Zagaris, *A Brave New World: Recent Developments in Anti-Money Laundering and Related Litigation Traps for the Unwary in International Trust Matters*, 32 VAND. J. TRANSNAT'L L. 1023 (Oct. 1999).
54. National Commission on Terrorist Attacks Against the United States, Monograph on Terrorist Financing: Staff Report to the commission, Aug. 21, 2004, at 56, available at http://www.9-11commission.gov.
55. Financial Action Task Force on Money Laundering, Guidance for Financial Institutions in Detecting Terrorist Financing (Apr. 24, 2002), at 4, ¶ 10. *See also* Financial Action Task Force on Money Laundering, Report on Money Laundering Typologies: 2001–02 (2002).
56. Financial Crimes Enforcement Network, U.S. Dep't of Treas, SAR BULL., Jan. 2002.
57. *See, e.g.*, Mariano-Florentino Cuéllar, *The Tenuous Relationship Between the Fight Against Money Laundering and the Disruption of Criminal Finance*, J. CRIM. L. & CRIMINOLOGY 311, 437 (2003); Gavin Hinks, *On the Trail of the Terrorists*, ACCOUNTANCY AGE, Oct. 31, 2002, at 7; Lucy Warwick-Ching, *Drive Against "Dirty Money" Is Attacked: Money Laundering Crackdown*, FIN. TIMES (LONDON), July 12, 2003, at 28.
58. USA PATRIOT Act, Pub. L. No. 107–56, Title III, § 302(a)(1).
59. *Compare* U.S. Dep't of the Treas., Annual Money Laundering Strategy (2001) (emphasizing the importance of asset forfeiture as the most direct way of preventing criminals from benefiting from money and describing its centrality to anti-money laundering efforts), and US Department of the Treasury and US Department of Justice, United States 2003 NATIONAL MONEY LAUNDERING STRATEGY, at 2, available at www.ustreas.gov. *See also* GLOBAL FINANCIAL CRIME: TERRORISM, MONEY LAUNDERING AND OFF SHORE CENTRES (Donato Masciandaro ed., 2004).
60. *See Underground Finance Mechanisms: Hearing Before the Subcomm. on Banking, Housing and Urban Affairs, Subcomm. on Int'l Trade and Fin. of the S. Comm. On Banking, Housing and Urban Affairs.* 107th Cong. 1 (2001). *See also Moving Target*, ECONOMIST (U.S. Edition), Sept. 14, 2002.
61. Stephen Fidler & Haig Simonian, *IMF Chief Urges United Response to Slowdown*, FIN. TIMES (London), Oct. 6, 2001, p. 1 (citing UN report in 2004).
62. *See Still Flush*, ECONOMIST, Sept. 7, 2002. *See also Moving Target, supra* note 41.
63. *See, e.g.*, *U.S. Says al Qaeda Hurting for Funds*, REUTERS, May 18, 2005.
64. Because statistical data for SAR report filings are continually updated as previous filings are processed and new reports are received, there may be some discrepancy between different sources. The numbers are from the Bank Secrecy Act Advisory Group, SAR Activity Review: By the Numbers, Issue 7, (2006), available at www.fincen.gov.
65. *Money Laundering: Coming Clean*, ECONOMIST, Oct. 16, 2004, p. 37.
66. Jimmy Burns, *Rise in Reports of Dubious Financial Transactions*, FIN. TIMES (London), Nov. 23, 2001, at 2.

67. Gavin Hinks & Paul Grant, *Analysis; Pressure on to Beat Laundering*, Accountancy Age, June 19, 2003, at 5.

68. Privy Counsellor Review Committee, Anti-Terrorism, Crime and Security Act 2001 Review: Report Presented to Parliament Pursuant to § 122(5) of the Anti-Terrorism, Crime and Security Act 2002, Dec. 18, 2003, HC 100.

69. *Compare* Jimmy Burns, *UK Rethinks Its Strategy on Fighting Money Launderers*, Fin. Times (U.S. Edition), July 2, 2003, at 4, *with* the December 2002 report of the US Treasury Office of the Inspector General (stating that many of the half-million SARs filed between April 1996 and December 2000 had incomplete or wrong information and multiple duplications), cited in Bruce Zagaris, *The Money Laundering Provisions of the USA PATRIOT Act of 2001*, 323 PLI/Est 417 (2003), at 451.

70. Bank Secrecy Act Advisory Group, The SAR Activity Review: Trends, Tips, and Issues, Issue 5, (2003), at 22.

71. Bank Secrecy Act Advisory Group, The SAR Activity Review: Trends, Tips, and Issues, Issue 8 (2005).

72. *Id.*, at 10.

73. Bank Secrecy Act Advisory Group, Issue 5, *supra* note 69, at 22–23. This trend continued. *See* Bank Secrecy Act Advisory Group, Issue 8, *supra* note 70, at 15.

74. Bank Secrecy Act Advisory Group, Issue 8, *supra* note 70, at 10, 13.

75. Bank Secrecy Act Advisory Group, Issue 5, *supra* note 69, at 13.

76. *See Cotton v. Private Bank*, 235 F. Supp. 2d 809 (N.D. Ill. 2002). The Bank Secrecy Act is the source of this authority, although FinCEN regulations and federal bank regulators' regulations establish absolute privilege. *See* Bank Secrecy Act Advisory Group, Issue 5, *supra* note 69.

77. Zagaris, *supra* note 68.

78. Bank Secrecy Act Advisory Group, Issue 8, supra note 70, at 38.

79. Money Transmitter Regulators Association, *News – Streamline Suspicious Activity Reports*, www.mtraweb.org (last visited Apr. 19, 2006).

80. T.J. Grasmick & Robert M. McNamara Jr., *Bank Secrecy Act Can Affect Expansion, Charter Value and Stock Price*, Community Banker, Dec. 2002, at 50.

81. *See, e.g.*, 1999 ME SB 675; 1999 CA SB 570; 1999 DE HB 323; 1999 DE S.C.R. 12; 1999 GA SB 71; 1999 NY AB 7876; 1999 ny AB 9038; 1999 WV SB 202.

82. *See, e.g.*, 1999 CA SB 69; 1999 CT SB 916; 1999 PA HB 1238; 1999 TX HB 726; 1999 OH HB 277.

83. Pub. L. No. 107–56, 115 Stat. 272 (2001); *see, e.g.* David Malakoff, *Bioterrorism: Student Charged With Possessing Anthrax*, 297 Science Magazine 751, 751–52 (2002) (discussing the case of Thomas Foral, 26, a graduate student who moved anthrax from one freezer to another); Charles Piller, *A Trying Time for Science: Bioterrorism-Related Charges Are Sending a Noted Researcher onto Court for His Handling of Plague Vials. In U.S. Labs, the Case Elicits an Outcry*, L.A. Times, Oct. 28, 2003, at A1 (addressing the case of Thomas Butler, Chief of Infectious Diseases at Texas Tech, who was prosecuted for failing to report that he destroyed his samples of bubonic plague).

84. Mary M. Cheh, *The Progressive Case and the Atomic Energy Act: Waking to the Dangers of Government Information Controls*, 48 Geo. Wash. L. Rev. 163, 204, n.268 (1980). Emphasis added.

85. Sabra Chartrand, *Patents: Speeding the Way for Processing Patents of Antiterrorism Devices, at Times Cloaked in Secrecy*, N.Y. Times, Oct. 8, 2001, at C1.

86. *Id.* (quoting the *Manual of Patent Examining Procedure*, section 708.02, XI).

87. *See, e.g.,* Select Committee on Northern Ireland Affairs, Fourth Report, June 26, 2002, at para 130 (noting that 46% of the victims in extortion cases request no police action to be taken for fear of reprisal; another 39% later withdrew their complaint and said they had not been contacted by extortionists – although the assessment suggested that in such cases "it is strongly suspected that the victim has, in fact, acceded to the extortionists' demands").

88. Jane Kennedy, Minister of State, Northern Ireland Office, col. 5; First Standing Committee on Delegated Legislation, HC Debs, Feb. 5, 2004, cols 3–12.

89. *Id.,* at col. 317 (Jane Kennedy).

90. *Id.,* at col. 322 WH (Barnes).

91. PSNI statistics, cited in The Terrorism (Northern Ireland) Bill, Bill 52 of 2005–6, Research paper 05/70, House of Commons Library, Miriam Peck, Home Affairs Section, Oonagh Gay, Parliament and Constitution Centre, Gavin Berman, Social and General Statistics, Oct. 27, 2005.

92. Report on the Operation in 2004 of Part VII of the Terrorism Act 2000, by Lord Carlile of Berriew, Q.C., para 2.11, available at www.statewatch.org.

93. *Id.*

94. Terrorism Financing (Northern Ireland); discussion of Financing of Terrorism in Northern Ireland – Fourth Report from the Northern Ireland Affairs Committee, Session 2001–02, HC 978-I and the Government's response thereto, Sixth Special Report, Session 2001–02, HC 1347; Westminster Hall, Jul. 10, 2003, cols. 311 WH–348 WH, at col. 311 WH.

95. Westminster Hall, Jul. 10, 2003, at col. 315 WH.

96. *Id.,* at col. 327 WH.

97. *Id.,* at col. 316 WH.

98. *See, e.g., Id.,* at col. 329WH (Nigel Dodds, Belfast).

99. Response of the Northern Ireland Human Rights Commission to the Home Office Discussion Paper on Counter-terrorism Measures: Reconciling Security and Liberty in an Open Society, NIHRC, Aug. 2004, p. 8.

100. *Id.*

101. Select Committee on Northern Ireland Affairs, Fourth Report, *supra* note 86, at para. 131, quoting ACC White.

102. *Id.*

103. Jane Kennedy, Terrorism Financing (Northern Ireland); discussion of Financing of Terrorism in Northern Ireland – Fourth Report from the Northern Ireland Affairs Committee, Session 2001–02, HC 978-I and the Government's response thereto, Sixth Special Report, Session 2001–02, HC 1347; Westminster Hall, Jul. 10, 2003, cols 341WH-342WH.

104. John D. Jackson, *The Restoration of Jury Trial in Northern Ireland; Can We Learn from the Professional Alternative?* 2001 ST. LOUIS-WARSAW TRANS'L 15, at 24.

105. *Id.,* at 26–27.

106. *Id.*

107. Laura Rozen, *Strange Bedfellows,* THE NATION, Nov. 10, 2003, at 6 (quoting David Cole).

108. US Department of Defense, National Defense Strategy of the United States of America, March 2005, p. 5.

109. Select Committee on Northern Ireland Affairs, Fourth Report, *supra* note 86, at List of Conclusions and Recommendations, ¶ (k).

110. *Id.*, ¶ (u).

111. *Id.*, ¶ 101.

112. *Youngstown Sheet & Tube Co. et al.* v *Sawyer*, 343 U.S. 559, 889 (1952) (Frankfurter, J.).

Index

JAN 2 9 2009